the CREEDS AND PLATFORMS of CONGREGATIONALISM

the CREEDS AND PLATFORMS of CONGRE-GATIONALISM

WILLISTON WALKER

Introduction by
Elizabeth C. Nordbeck

United Church Press
Cleveland, Ohio

United Church Press, Cleveland, Ohio 44115
Introduction to this Edition Copyright © 1991 by
The Pilgrim Press

All rights reserved. Except for brief quotations used in critical articles or reviews, no part of this book may be reproduced, stored in a retrieval system, or transmitted by any means without the prior written permission of the publisher.

Library of Congress Cataloging-in-Publication Data

The Creeds and platforms of Congregationalism / [compiled by]
Williston Walker ; introduction by Elizabeth C. Nordbeck.
p. cm.
Reprint, with new introd. Originally published: 1893.
Includes bibliographical references and index.
ISBN 0-8298-0854-X (alk. paper)
1. Congregational churches—Creeds. 2. Congregational churches—Doctrines. I. Walker, Williston, 1860–1922.
BX7236.C74 1991
238′.58—dc20 91-12049
CIP

This book is printed on acid-free paper.

Printed in the United States of America.

TO MY FATHER

GEORGE LEON WALKER

WHOSE INTEREST

IN CONGREGATIONAL HISTORY FIRST AWAKENED MY DESIRE

TO KNOW SOMETHING OF

Congregational Creeds and Platforms

AND WHOSE SYMPATHY

HAS ENCOURAGED ME THROUGHOUT THESE STUDIES

THIS VOLUME

IS AFFECTIONATELY DEDICATED

CONTENTS

INTRODUCTION TO THE 1991 EDITION

Some books not only interpret history, they become part of it. So it is with Williston Walker's *The Creeds and Platforms of Congregationalism*, originally published in 1893. With its companion volume, *A History of the Congregational Churches in the United States*, issued just a year later, *Creeds and Platforms* was the capstone of an era of unprecedented scholarly activity among American Congregationalists. For a century the book has been unrivaled, not only as a basic text for students of Congregationalism but also as an indispensable sourcebook in the vast and sophisticated field of American Puritan studies.

Reprinted in 1923 and again in 1960, Walker's *Creeds and Platforms* has, astonishingly, never been altered or revised. Indeed, in his introduction to the 1960 edition, Douglas Horton wrote that the book "could not be added to without impairing its present usefulness." In one sense, Horton is correct, since (with the few exceptions noted) it is needless to correct Williston Walker's painstaking scholarship and pointless to alter the timeless, nonpartisan tone of the whole. This new edition, however, does offer three addenda to the original text—which is here reprinted, once again, in unchanged form—in the firm conviction that these will be useful to the present-day student of historic Congregationalism.

First, the Constitution of 1913, which includes the Kansas City Statement of Faith, is included in an appendix, preceded by a brief interpretive text that is intended to be consonant with Walker's own. The Kansas City Statement, along with the Burial Hill Declaration of 1865, the Oberlin Declaration on the Unity of the Church (1871), and the "Commission" Creed of 1883, represents a culmination of the gradual movement in American Congregationalism away from the orthodox Calvinism of its origins and toward a broader, more unified and catholic self-understanding. The constitution, drafted by members of the famous Commission of Nineteen, on which Williston Walker himself served, moved Congregationalism decisively toward a more centralized, structured system of governance. Indeed, without these important documents the story of modern Congregationalism is necessarily truncated.

Second, Douglas Horton's interpretive introduction is also reprinted as an appendix. That essay, written by one who was a prime mover in the Congregational Christian and Evangelical and Reformed merger that created the United Church of Christ in 1957, reflects some of the biases of that heady ecumenical moment.[1] But it also offers a helpful understanding of *Creeds and Platforms* as a work concerned primarily with the "idea" of Congregationalism, rather than with Congregationalism as a set of institutions or a group of persons in history.

Third, the new introductory essay of this 1991 edition places Walker's documentary history, albeit very briefly, in its own broad historical context, with some commentary on the ways in which a present-day perspective on the "idea of Congregationalism" may differ somewhat from Walker's—or even Horton's—own.

The period of scholarly activity to which Walker's book was a kind of grand coda was occasioned, in part, by the need of American Congregationalists to discover and articulate their distinctive identity in an era of increasing denominational competition. This was no easy task. As the name indicates, of course, "Congregationalism" describes neither a system of doctrine nor a spiritual founder but, in Puritan John Cotton's words, a "way" and a "walk"—or to use Horton's phrase, an *idea* of church organization that insists on the autonomy and authority of locally gathered churches. Although cooperation and fellowship among the Congregational churches were always assumed, nevertheless the principle of local autonomy was, and remains, definitive of the movement itself. A disinclination toward binding creeds and confessions underscored that principle. As a consequence, early Congregationalism did not have a particularly strong sense of its communal nature (or as Horton suggests, of *diakonia*) in the way that Lutheranism or even Presbyterianism did. Congregationalism was a movement of church*es*: it was not a "church."

In America the principle of autonomy has always been a kind of two-edged sword for Congregational believers. It provided, at first, what the Pilgrim and Puritan founders insisted was a sound scriptural basis for their common order: but that same order early encouraged troublesome differences and rapid change among the churches of the faithful. In the preface to his son Cotton's *Magnalia Christi Americana,* Increase Mather admitted in 1719 that "for certain Modalities, there has been a Variety of Practice, in these Churches." But, he added hastily, "in Essentials, both of Doctrine and of Discipline, they agree."[2] Almost from the beginning, Congregationalism included a range of diversity unimaginable in more connectional or hierarchic systems of the time. Recent studies, in fact, have indicated that Congregationalism was considerably more than the lengthened shadow of Plymouth or Massachusetts Bay; not only in Connecticut but also in western Massachusetts, New Hampshire, and what is now Maine, the Congregational churches differed among themselves significantly in both theology and practice.

In the seventeenth and early eighteenth centuries, of course, this nascent diversity was limited—and homogeneity was fostered—by geography and a common recent history of protest and migration. Congregational churches were contained entirely within the boundaries of New England. Demographically, they were comprised primarily of the British immigrants and their progeny who made up the bulk of New England's population. Theologically, they were heirs of Calvin, their beliefs reshaped somewhat by the New England experience but recognizable in their characteristic emphasis on sin and grace, God's power and human powerlessness.

For nearly two hundred years these safeguards held in tenuous check the potential for dissent and divisiveness always latent within the Congregational fold. But by the beginning of the nineteenth century, with clergy and laity now spread out along the theological spectrum from orthodox Calvinism to Arminianism, these differences finally erupted into overt theological warfare with the election of the liberal Henry Ware to Harvard's prestigious Hollis Professorship of Divinity. The ensuing "Unitarian Controversy" produced Congregationalism's first schism, hastening the departure of numerous New England congregations into what became, in 1825, the American Unitarian Association.

The early decades of the nineteenth century offered challenges from without as well as from within the fellowship. The historian Sidney E. Mead has described the period from roughly 1787 to 1850 as the "formative period" for American denominations.[3] Not surprisingly, Congregationalists were slow starters in this emerging, competitive arena, because for nearly two hundred years competition had been virtually unnecessary. As the "established" churches of New England, they had enjoyed a tax-supported preeminence among a growing population of religious bodies. But by 1800, with schism imminent and increasingly vocal protests from groups such as the Baptists and Methodists, their position was no longer tenable. These factors, coupled with a growing conviction among Congregationalists themselves that government support of sectarian religion was scripturally unsound, led to formal disestablishment. With the acquiescence of Massachusetts in 1833, this formerly dominant body of churches found itself, ironically, competing in a busy theological marketplace in which it was ill-equipped to assert anything like a distinctive identity.

Change, however, was occurring not only in the Northeast. While New England's Congregationalists were debating Christology and the role of humankind in the process of salvation, their transplanted relations in the West were embarking on an innovative ecumenical venture with Presbyterians. Designed to promote an orderly and efficient process of evangelism and church planting on the opening frontier, the 1801 Plan of Union attempted to subordinate "denominational preferences to the interests of Christian progress." From the start, however, the more structured, connectional Presbyterian system tended to encourage new churches to relate formally to that denomination. By 1852, both groups had shelved the plan, a corporate decision that was an historic "first" for Congregationalists. In all, the experience revealed both the growing gap between East and West, and even more important, the need for a denominational identity and structures that could promote united action on the mission field and elsewhere.

These several critical developments gradually forced Congregationalists more aggressively to define and articulate the nature of the life and faith they shared. To this end, denominational leaders formed new ministerial associations, began their own domestic missionary enterprises, and, eventually, organized a trio of national meetings that helped to defuse longstanding fears of centralization. Three new doctrinal statements, produced between 1865 and 1883, identified the commonly held faith of Congregationalists as broadly orthodox, centered in "the unity of the spirit in the bond of peace" despite inevitable theological differences among them. What fired all these responses with genuine evangelical zeal, however, was a developing sense of the unique ideological role of historic Congregationalism itself in American democratic society—the conviction that, as one journalist wrote in 1852,

> God may see that in coming crises, a full and powerful development of the principles of Congregationalism may be essential to the perpetuation, defense, and perfection of our civil institutions. It is not impossible that God may need Congregationalism as a means of introducing the highest and most perfect state of human society.[4]

From about 1850 on, therefore, denominational leaders waged a kind of holy war of words to counter what they believed was massive public ignorance about the true faith of the founders and its formative role in public life. Pastor-scholars such as Joseph S. Clark, Henry Martyn Dexter, and A. Hastings Ross produced dozens of articles and books that reexamined the Congregational heritage, and new periodicals such as the *Congregationalist* and *Congregational Quarterly* were begun; a denominational library in Boston made all these materials accessible to the people. And at the close of the century, Williston Walker's two history books offered summation and synthesis, affirming the place of American Congregationalism, both as idea and as institution, squarely in the center of America's cherished values of liberty and democracy.

Thus from the longstanding "liabilities" of their order: autonomy, diversity, individualism, change—the same tendencies that had hindered them from forming a cohesive identity in the first place—Congregationalists had now identified a positive principle. Here was the "unity in diversity" at which Increase Mather had hinted years before, but with a new and potent twist: the unity lay not, as formerly, in a shared confessional position that was external to Congregational polity and dependent for its stability upon a homogeneous mix of culture and community. Rather, it lay, precisely, in faithful allegiance to the very diversity encouraged and embraced by the polity itself.

In this new climate of assurance and optimism, *The Creeds and Platforms of Congregationalism* looked back on three centuries of what its author characterized as "unity and growth" within the fellowship. But it also looked forward to a century in which a new statement of faith, as well as new structures, ecumenical ventures, and mergers, would alter the churches of the Pilgrims and Puritans even more radically. Williston Walker, who lived to participate in the formulation of the Kansas City Statement but not the Congregational Christian merger of 1931, may well have foreseen the likelihood of some of these developments. Indeed the last paragraphs of *Creeds and Platforms* hint at a future that would almost certainly embrace change: "The Congregational body of to-day is no mere residuum of sixteenth century discussions," wrote Walker. It "can no more rest in its present status than in that of the Cambridge Platform."

At the opening of the twentieth century there was little likelihood of "rest" in this active fellowship with its renewed sense of mission and identity. Congregationalists of the time shared with American Protestants in general an optimistic view of human progress: exponents of the new Social Gospel, such as the New York pastor Washington Gladden, articulated for many of them the vision of a church called to work actively for justice, to fight public as well as private sin and evil. Perhaps even more important for the future of Congregationalism was a longstanding commitment to ecumenical cooperation and exploration, framed by the Oberlin Declaration of Unity and formalized structurally during the 1880s by the Committee on Inter-denominational Comity. This commitment found nonbinding but significant common creedal expression in the new Kansas City Statement of 1913, itself a product and symbol of the growing social awareness and theological openness of the time. In a closing section on "The Wider Fellowship," the statement reaffirmed the liberty of the Congregational churches but expressed a "hearty" intent to unite with other branches of the church catholic in response to Jesus' prayer "that they all may be one."

Where does one chapter in the long history of Congregationalism end and another begin? Perhaps an early inclination toward fraternal relations with other church bodies may be discerned in the Puritans' "nonseparating" relationship with the Anglican Church, in Connecticut consociationism, and the 1801 Plan of Union with the Presbyterians. In any case, by the late nineteenth century that inclination had been formalized in overtures to the Freewill Baptists, the Congregational Methodists, the Disciples of Christ, and others. During the 1890s, discussion with churches of the "Christian Connection" produced a first abortive attempt at merger—a failure that resulted, in part, from the hesitancy among some Christians to unite with a "sectarian" group such as the Congregationalists. Abandoned for two decades, the possibility of union was again broached in 1923, this time with stronger commitments on both sides.

The origins of these two groups, on the face of it, were startlingly different. Unlike the transplanted Congregationalists, the

Christians were an indigenous, rural, and revivalistic movement of religious populism that had emerged simultaneously in New England, Virginia, and Kentucky in the late eighteenth and early nineteenth centuries: their leadership included defectors from the Presbyterian, Methodist, and Baptist communions. Held loosely together by a network of correspondence in their innovative periodical *The Herald of Gospel Liberty*, they shared informal allegiance to a familiar slogan: "No creed but Christ, no authority but the Bible, no name but Christian." Nevertheless, with Congregationalists they affirmed a strong belief in individual, personal freedom of conscience, an insistence on the autonomy and fellowship of local congregations, and above all a thoroughgoing commitment to Christian unity. In 1931, after two years of careful negotiations, a constitution for the proposed united fellowship was adopted, and a new body, the General Council of the Congregational and Christian Churches, came into being. Twenty-six years later this merged group would unite again, this time with the Evangelical and Reformed Church of German heritage, to form today's United Church of Christ.

The values, ideals, and spirit of Congregationalism, of course, did not disappear with either of these denominational shifts, but the line of succession was significantly complicated. Today at least three fellowships claim the mantle of the historic faith.

The smallest of these groups is the Conservative Congregational Christian Conference (the "Four C's"), organized in 1948 by some who were convinced that the Congregational Christian merger was a departure from the beliefs and practices of historic Congregationalism. Evangelical theologically, the loosely structured conference is active in missions, intentional about the study of Congregational history, and adamant about maintaining the complete autonomy of its local churches. In a similar fashion, the Congregational Christian Churches (National Association) was formed by a majority of those churches that voted not to participate in the merger of 1957. More liberal theologically than the "Four C's," the CCCNA preserves the autonomy of local churches but encourages their fellowship in local associations. Its ongoing commitment simply to "be the people of God" reveals the traditional Congregational openness to theological diversity. By far the largest and theologically the most liberal of the "inheriting" bodies, the United Church of Christ represents Congregationalism in what many would call a diluted or attenuated form. Yet despite the connectional tendencies borrowed from the Evangelical and Reformed wing, the constitution of the church preserves the autonomy of the local congregation: the denominational Statement of Faith remains a "test, not a testimony" of belief; and the ecumenical, activist spirit of nineteenth-century Congregationalism informs the whole.

This phenomenon of "inheriting groups" reveals a significant perceptual change among those concerned today with the history and nature of Congregationalism—a change that has accelerated even since the most recent edition of *Creeds and Platforms* in 1960. Williston Walker and his generation took for granted that there is *one* Congregationalism, a unified and unifying impulse or principle that is traceable across time and history. Of course, Walker understood that Congregationalism in its institutional forms had developed and changed from what it was in the seventeenth century. For example, in his commentary, in this volume, on a report from the Committee on Polity of the Boston Council of 1865, he noted that, while much of the committee's description of Congregational polity would have agreed with the Cambridge Platform, "a Mather or a Cotton would have looked with astonishment on [its] statement that the duly established ministry implies 'no power of government.' " Nevertheless, for Walker this evolutionary development was all of a piece: Congregationalism, he explained, "has carried its polity to its logical outcome in pure democracy." Confronted with his generation's need for the recovery of a distinctive Congregational identity, Walker was concerned to present source documents for the shared "idea" of the historic faith and to discover therein its pure and unbroken stream of development.

The fragmenting experience of the twentieth century, however, offers a somewhat different perspective. It is still possible, of course, to identify the elements of the idea of Congregationalism—in particular, the twin principles of autonomy and fellowship—and to trace their development over the centuries. But few today understand these apart from the particular groups or institutions in which they are (or have been) embodied: and fewer still are inclined, like Walker, to interpret their development as part of God's providential design for America.

An ongoing debate over the nature of "true" or "pure" Congregationalism—in part the result of the mergers of this century—is symptomatic of this perceptual difference. Often focusing on the relative weight given by different groups to the twin principles of "autonomy" on the one hand, and "fellowship" on the other, this debate seeks to identify the "real" contemporary heirs of the historic faith. Thus for some, true Congregationalism is the Congregationalism typified by the Pilgrims at Plymouth: simple and separatistic, untainted by either the kingdom-building vision of Massachusetts Bay or the consociationism of Connecticut. For others, true Congregationalism is more nearly that of the Puritans, characterized by shared theology, culture, and piety. Understood in either of these ways, Congregationalism itself is a relatively stable set of beliefs and practices. Deviation from it may be understood, at worst, as heresy and, at best, as something that is simply other than Congregationalism. For still others, true Congregationalism is the faith of both these groups, as well as of groups that have followed them. Characterized equally by the principles of fellowship and autonomy, it is defined by neither but rather by its ability to adjust and change to meet the challenges of culture. Understood in this way, Congregationalism is essentially fluid; it is a *way of being* more than it is a constellation of particular principles and practices frozen in time. From this perspective, indeed, it is possible to identify not one, but several "varieties of Congregationalism," each with its own distinctive structures and practices.

In all this, it is evident that the clarity about their history and identity, which Williston Walker and his coreligionists discovered at the end of the last century, seems more elusive at the close of the present age. For this reason, we have elected in this new edition of *Creeds and Platforms* to add only the material produced by the National Council of 1913. This, arguably, brings to a close one chapter in the long history of American Congregationalism. Significant documents produced after 1913—those dealing, for example, with the events of 1931, or with the establishment of new associations of Congregationalists—belong logically in a new and different volume, one that deals with the complicated twentieth-century experience of merger, fragmentation, and redefinition. Moreover, such a volume will need, as Douglas Horton suggested thirty years ago, to locate these American developments in the larger context of global Congregationalism. in the meantime, it is to be hoped, Williston Walker's magnificent work may serve as a reminder of the vitality, resilience, and vision of this historic—and still contemporary—faith.

ELIZABETH C. NORDBECK

Notes

1. Not too surprisingly, Horton tends to assume in his comments that the sole inheritor of the mantle of Congregationalism is the United Church of Christ—an assumption that is reflected, for example, in his stress on the present-day importance of *koinonia*. While a statement about the autonomy of local churches, such as "the parts are not themselves except as they belong to the whole," certainly reflects one strand of evolved Congregational thought, it does not describe that thought in its full range of diversity.

2. Cotton Mather, *Ratio Disciplinae Fratrum Nov-Anglorum. A Faithful Account of the Discipline Professed and Practiced: in the Churches of New-England* (New York: Arno, 1972), i–iv.

3. Sidney E. Mead, *The Lively Experiment: The Shaping of Christianity in America* (New York: Harper & Row, 1963).

4. "The Convention at Albany," *The Congregationalist*, 1 Oct. 1852, 157.

PREFACE

CONGREGATIONALISM has always accorded large liberty to local churches in their interpretation of doctrine and polity. Its creeds are not exclusively binding, and its platforms have always been held to be open to revision. They have been witnesses to the faith and practice of the churches rather than tests for subscription. But by reason of this liberty a collection of Congregational creeds and platforms illustrates the history of the body whose expressions they are better than if those symbols were less readily amended. The points wherein they agree may therefore confidently be believed to set forth that which is abiding in the faith and practice of the churches, while the features of change and the traces of discussion of more temporary importance which these creeds and platforms exhibit illustrate as clearly that which is mutable in our ecclesiastical life. It is because the writer deems such a collection of prime value in illuminating the history of Congregationalism that this compilation has been made.

This volume has grown out of the experiences of the classroom. In his endeavors to teach the story of Congregationalism the writer has been hindered at all points by the inaccessibility of much of the material which must be before the student or the minister if a knowledge of denominational history is to be more than second hand. He has therefore collected the most important Congregational creeds and platforms, and has illustrated them as far as he is able by such historic notes and comments as may serve to make the circumstances of their composition and their meaning plain. He has had in mind the necessities of the general reader whose knowledge of the sources of our denominational history is rudimentary, and has endeavored to point out with the utmost plainness the basis of every important statement, and to indicate the literature of each symbol, hoping that by this fullness of annotation the student may find his way comparatively readily should he desire to make a minute study of Congregational beliefs and usages.

In reproducing these symbols the writer has reprinted the text of the earliest editions known to him to be extant. He has endeavored faithfully to reproduce the spelling and punctuation, and even the misprints, deeming that the dress in which these documents were presented to the world, sometimes by persecuted congregations and with the scantiest resources, is of value in forming our estimate of the impression which they were calculated to produce on their time. That the writer has wholly avoided misprints of his own in this reproduction he hardly dares to hope,—he has used great pains so to do;—but he trusts that before the reader condemns an illprinted passage it may be compared with the original to see if the fault was not that of the earliest printer.

The writer is under obligation to many scholars for suggestions, but he would especially acknowledge his indebtedness to the librarians of the American Antiquarian Society at Worcester, the Public Library at Boston, the Connecticut Historical Society and Watkinson Library at Hartford, the Massachusetts Historical Society at Boston, and of Yale University, for the access which they have afforded him to the treasures in their custody.

This volume is sent forth with the hope that it may serve to make easier the pathway to a knowledge of Congregational history, and may illustrate the essential unity as well as the healthful growth which has marked the development of creed and practice from the founders of Congregationalism to our own day.

WILLISTON WALKER
Hartford, Conn., July 15, 1893

I

ROBERT BROWNE'S STATEMENT OF CONGREGATIONAL PRINCIPLES, 1582

TEXT

I. *A Booke | which Sheweth the | life and manners of all true Christians, | and howe vnlike they are vnto Turkes and Papistes, | and Heathen folke. | Also the pointes and partes of all diui- | nitie, that is of the reuealed will and worde of God, are | declared by their seuerall Definitions, | and Diuisions in order as | followeth. | Robert Brovvne. | Middelbvrgh, | Imprinted by Richarde Painter. | 1582.* 4°, pp. 111.

II. A few of the sections, extracted from Browne's work, are given in Hanbury, *Historical Memorials Relating to the Independents*, etc., London 1839, I: 20–22; in Fletcher, *History . . . of Independency*, London 1862, II: 114–117; and in Punchard, *History of Congregationalism*, Boston [1867], III: 14–17.

LITERATURE

The works of Hanbury, Fletcher, and Punchard, above cited; [Waddington], *Historical Papers*, London 1861, pp. 33–48; Waddington, *Congregational History, 1567–1700*, London 1874, p. 16; Bacon, *Genesis of the New England Churches*, New York 1874, pp. 81–90; Browne, *History of Congregationalism . . . in Norfolk and Suffolk*, London 1877, chs. I–III; Dexter, *The Congregationalism of the last three hundred years, as seen in its Literature*, New York 1880, pp. 61–128.

MODERN Congregationalism is a legitimate outcome of a consistent application to church polity of the principles of the Reformation. The fundamental religious thought of that movement was the rejection of all authority save that of the Word of God. But, while this cardinal principle was recognized by all the reformers, there was great variety in the extent to which they carried its application. All of them agreed that the will of God had prescribed in the Bible the sufficient test of Christian doctrine, but none of the reformers of the first rank felt the necessity of a complete conformity of their systems of church polity to the same standard. The paramount importance of doctrinal reform, the necessity for the orderly control of the church in the trying period of transition from its ancient form, and especially the disorders which the advent of ecclesiastical freedom excited among the lower classes, induced Luther and Zwingli, neither of whom were organizers by nature, to put aside their early inclinations toward the substantially Congregational system[1] which they recognized in the New Testament example, in favor of a would-be temporary dependence on the civil rulers of the lands in which they lived for the organization of their new churches. Calvin was an organizer, and though he sought scripture warrant for the system which he established, he seems to have been led to its adoption largely by the necessities of his position in the foremost outpost of Protestantism at Geneva; and he admitted, on one occasion at least, that his eldership was primarily a device of expediency.[2] And if these men did not fully recognize that the legitimate outcome of the principles of the Reformation was the test of church government as well as Christian doctrine by the standard of the Bible, this truth was even less clearly perceived in England, where the state Establishment which was the outcome of the Reformation was designedly a compromise, in which a large portion of the ancient government and ceremonial was retained, and in which the fountain of ecclesiastical authority was the sovereign.

But if the leaders of the Reformation thus fell short of a full application of their principles, there were those from almost the beginning of the movement who sought to go further. These men, nicknamed usually by their opponents the "Anabaptists,"[3] first came to notice about 1523–4[4] in the portions of Switzerland which had felt the reforming touch of Zwingli. Persecuted at once by Protestants and Catholics, they were dispersed with great rapidity all over Germany and the Netherlands and came even to England.[5] They were drawn chiefly from the lower orders of the population, and were often characterized by extreme fanaticism.[6]

---

[1] See *inter alia*, Gieseler, *Church History*, ed. New York 1876, IV: 518; Fisher, Reformation, pp. 488–495; Dexter, *Cong. as seen*, p. 51; Schaff, *Hist. of the Christian Church*, VI: 538.

[2] For valuable quotations illustrative of this point see Dexter, *Ibid.*, pp. 52, 53.

[3] I. e., "Re-baptizers," because they held infant baptism no baptism.

[4] See the valuable paper of Rev. Dr. Burrage, *Anabaptists of the Sixteenth Century*, *Papers of the Am. Soc. Church Hist.*, III: 145–164. Keller in his suggestive *Die Reformation und die älteren Reformparteien*, Leipzig 1885, holds, as many others have done, the Anabaptists to be successors of mediaeval sects, but his thesis is not fully proven.

[5] As early as 1535 fourteen were burned in one year in England. Executions continued under English Protestant sovereigns, e. g. under Elizabeth in 1575, and James in 1612.

[6] The most conspicuous illustration is of course the Münster anarchy, 1532–5.

But the fanatics were only a fraction of the Anabaptists, and under the lead of men like Menno Simons,[1] in Holland especially, they settled down into orderly and valuable citizens.[2] They were everywhere marked by a desire to carry the principles of the Reformation to their logical outcome, and hence they tried to test not only doctrine but polity and Christian life by the same rule. The natural tendency of men to put differing constructions on the same facts of revelation, increased in their case by the ignorance of a great part of the body and an inclination to lay stress on the direct illumination of the believers by the Holy Spirit, led to diversities of belief among them, so that we can lay down no rigid creed for the Anabaptists as a whole; but there were certain features in their beliefs which appear also in the views of the Baptists, the Quakers, and the Congregationalists.[3]

The Protestant bodies founded by the great reformers of the sixteenth century were all at one in recognizing every baptized person, residing within the territories where they were established and not formally excommunicate, as a church member. Church and state were practically co-extensive. Even the Puritans of England, who labored under Elizabeth for the purification and full Protestantizing of the Establishment, and from whom the majority of early Congregationalists were to come, held to the church-membership of all non-excommunicate Englishmen, and looked upon the true method of reform as a vigorous purging from within by the rigid enforcement of discipline, the appointment of the officers whom they believed to be designated in the Scripture model, and the aid of civil magistrates, rather than a separation from the national church.[4] The Anabaptists, on the other hand, maintained that a church was a company of Christian believers, gathered out of the world,[5] to which men were admitted by con-

---

[1] 1492–1559.

[2] See the articles by Prof. de Hoop Scheffer on Menno and the Mennonites in the Herzog *Real-Encyclopädie für protestantische Theologie*, Leipzig, 1881 (briefly abridged in the Schaff-Herzog, *Encyclopædia*, New York [1882]).

[3] This relation has been positively, perhaps too positively, insisted upon by Campbell, *Puritan in Holland, England, and America*, New York, 1892, II: 177–209.

[4] Compare Dexter, *Cong. as seen*, pp. 54–58. Briggs, *American Presbyterianism*, New York, 1885, p. 43.

[5] For the doctrines of the Anabaptists, especially the Mennonite branch, which had the

fession and baptism; that each congregation of believers should be independent of all external control, civil or ecclesiastical, and that the civil magistrate had no authority over the church; that no believer should bear the sword, take oath, or hold the office of a magistrate; that each congregation should be kept pure by discipline, and should be led by elders chosen by itself, who should serve it without compensation. So they held the New Testament pattern of a Christian church to require.

Like the modern Baptists, the Anabaptists had no creeds of general binding force. Some confessions were issued by individuals and congregations, and some as formulæ of union between various branches of the much divided body, but each congregation accepted or rejected what it chose. In general, however, the agreement regarding all the more essential features of doctrine and polity was close. A few extracts from the popular confession prepared by the Mennonite ministers Hans de Ries and Lubbert Gerrits for the benefit of the one time Congregationalist John Smyth and his company in 1609 at Amsterdam,—a confession based on and representative of the writings of the older Mennonite Anabaptists and widely used by the Mennonite churches of Holland,—may serve to set forth some of these beliefs more clearly:[1]

"22. Such faithful, righteous people, scattered in several parts of the world, being the true congregations of God, or the church of Christ, whom he saved, and for whom he gave himself, that he might sanctify them, ye [yea] whom he hath cleansed by the washing of water in the word of life: of all such is Jesus the Head, the Shepherd, the Leader, the Lord, the King, and Master. Now although among these there may be mingled a company of seeming holy ones, or hypocrites; yet, nevertheless, they are and remain only the righteous, true members of the body of

---

most influence in Holland, see beside the articles of Prof. de Hoop Scheffer, before cited; Barclay, *Inner Life of the Religious Societies of the Commonwealth*, London, 3d ed., 1879, pp. 75–92; Dr. Burrage, *Papers Am. Soc. Ch. Hist.*, III: 157; Prof. Schaff, in *Baptist Quarterly Review*, July 1889. Much further and minuter information is contained in the works of the Mennonite historian, Hermann Schyn, *Historia Christianorum Qui in Belgio Fœderato inter Protestantes Mennonitæ appellantur*, Amsterdam, 1723, and *Historiæ Mennonitarum Plenior Deductio*, ibid, 1729.

[1] Regarding the circumstances of the appeal of Smyth and his brethren for admission to the Amsterdam Mennonite church of which Gerrits was minister, and the preparation of this Confession, see Evans, *Early English Baptists*, London, 1862, I. 201–224; Barclay, *Inner Life*, etc., pp. 68–73; De Hoop Scheffer, *De Brownisten te Amsterdam*, etc. (Memoir before the Royal Academy), published Amsterdam, 1881; Dexter, *True Story of John Smyth, the Se-Baptist*, etc., Boston, 1881. The Confession as originally prepared consisted of 38 articles, drawn up by Hans de Ries at the request of Smyth's company. Translated into English, it was signed by Smyth and his friends and laid before the Mennonite congregation. It was enlarged by its author and put forth

Christ,[1] according to the spirit and the truth, the heirs of the promises, truly saved from the hypocrites and dissemblers.

"23. In this holy church hath God ordained the ministers of the Gospel, the doctrines of the holy Word, the use of the holy sacraments, the oversight of the poor, and the ministers of the same offices; furthermore, the exercise of brotherly admonition and correction, and, finally, the separating of the impenitent; which holy ordinances, contained in the Word of God, are to be administered according to the contents thereof.

"24. And like as a body consisteth of divers parts, and every part hath its own proper work, seeing every part is not a hand, eye, or foot; so it is also in the church of God; for although every believer is a member of the body of Christ, yet is not every one therefore a teacher, elder, or deacon, but only such who are orderly appointed to such offices. Therefore, also, the administration of the said offices or duties pertaineth only to those that are ordained thereto, and not to every particular common person.

"25. The vocation or election of the said officers is performed by the church, with fasting, and prayer to God; for God knoweth the heart; he is amongst the faithful who are gathered together in his name; and by his Holy Spirit doth so govern the minds and hearts of his people, that he by them bringeth to light and propoundeth whom he knoweth to be profitable to his church.

"26. And although the election and vocation to the said offices is performed by the foresaid means, yet, nevertheless, the investing into the said service is accomplished by the elders of the church[2] through the laying on of hands. . . .

"29. The Holy Baptism is given unto these in the name of the Father, the Son, and the Holy Ghost, which hear, believe, and with penitent heart receive the doctrines of the Holy Gospel. For such hath the Lord Jesus commanded to be baptized, and no unspeaking children. . . .

"33. The church discipline, or external censures, is also an outward handling[3] among the believers, whereby the impenitent sinner, after Christian admonition and reproof, is severed, by reason of his sins, from the communion of the saints for his future good; and the wrath of God is denounced against him until the time of his contrition and reformation. . . .

"35. Worldly authority or magistracy is a necessary ordinance of God, appointed and established for the preservation of the common estate, and of a good, natural, politic life, for the reward of the good and the punishing of the evil: we acknowledge ourselves obnoxious, and bound by the Word of God to fear, honour, and show obedience to the magistrates in all causes not contrary to the Word of

---

for the use of the Dutch probably in 1610, apparently with the approval of Gerrits. Though in no sense binding upon the Mennonite body, it has been their most venerated expression of faith. A full Latin version of the enlarged form is given by Schyn, *Historia*, etc., Amsterdam, 1723, pp. 172–220, who remarks: "Ecce . . . *Confessionem*, non solum fere per sesqui sæculum apud plurimas & maximas illorum Ecclesias, in Belgio pro *formula* Consensus inter *Waterlandos* sic dictos habitam," etc. On the great doctrinal controversy which agitated Holland at the time of its composition the Confession is Arminian, but that which here concerns us is its view of church polity, in which it is representative of all Mennonite teaching and the theories doubtless which were current among the Anabaptists who found settlement during the previous half-century in England. The extracts are from the English version signed by Smyth and his associates in 1609, and printed by Evans, *Ibid.*, I: 245–252. It is substantially and almost verbally identical with the revised form given by Schyn.

[1] I. e., the righteous are the only true members, etc.

[2] Schyn, "a Senioribus populi coram Ecclesia."

[3] *Ibid.*, "actio."

the Lord. We are obliged to pray God Almighty for them, and to thank the Lord for good reasonable magistrates, and to yield unto them, without murmuring, beseeming tribute, toll, and tax. This office of the worldly authority the Lord Jesus hath not ordained in his spiritual kingdom, the church of the New Testament, nor adjoined to the offices of his church. Neither hath he called his disciples or followers to be worldly kings, princes, potentates, or magistrates; neither hath he burdened or charged them to assume such offices, or to govern the world in such a worldly manner; much less hath he given a law to the members of his church which is agreeable to such office or government. . . .

"36. Christ, the King and Lawgiver of the New Testament, hath prohibited Christians the swearing of oaths; therefore it is not permitted that the faithful of the New Testament should swear at all."

It is clear, therefore, that there were prevalent in the domain of Protestantism, during the latter half of the sixteenth century, two radically differing theories of the church,— the one supported by the leading reformers and their successors and upheld by the civil authorities, but representing nevertheless a partial rather than a complete application of the principles of the Reformation; the other maintained with many vagaries, and much that was positively fanatical, by men of little education or social position, subject to almost universal persecution,[1] but representing, however mistakenly, an attempt to apply the principles of the Word of God not merely to doctrine but to every feature of polity and life.

Though the Anabaptists flourished in Holland, they made few direct disciples during the sixteenth century on English soil. Yet they were present in the island and cannot have been without some influence. After the religious and political tyranny of Philip II. had begun its reign of terror in the Netherlands, the Dutch and Walloons, who had always found in the eastern counties of England a favorite field for immigration, flocked across the North Sea in almost astounding numbers. By 1562 these exiles on English soil numbered 30,000.[2] Six years later they embraced some 5,225 of the population of London, while in the cities of the eastern coast they were yet more largely represented, forming a majority of the people of Norwich in 1587, and making a con-

[1] The one exception was the protection of the Dutch Anabaptists by William of Orange. Campbell, *Puritan*, I: 247, 248.

[2] These figures are from Campbell, *Ibid.*, 488.

spicuous element in the population of Dover, Sandwich, and other important towns. Of course these thousands of Hollanders were not to any large extent Anabaptists; but there were Anabaptists among them,[1] and probably many more than openly appeared, for to own the sentiments of the hated sect under the reign of Elizabeth was to be liable to death at the stake. It seems not unreasonable to suppose that their views, modified and partially presented, may have, more or less unconsciously, become part of the thinking of the more zealous of the English seekers after a fuller reformation with whom they were brought in contact. But while it is certainly within the bounds of probability to admit such a degree of influence on the part of the Dutch Anabaptists on English religious thought in the eastern counties during the last quarter of the sixteenth century, it should not be forgotten that the New Testament was before the English reader as well as in the hands of the Dutch Anabaptist, and that its pages might convey the same lesson independently to the English student. Certainly the early English Congregationalists had no consciousness that their views were derived from any other source than the New Testament; and while there is much in their history, and especially in the geography of their origin, to make it probable that some considerable infiltration of Anabaptist thought aided in shaping their interpretations of the Scripture; they were more than mere successors or offshoots of the Anabaptists of the Continent.[2]

Some attempt to realize a further reformation in directions looking toward later Congregationalism may have been made by Richard Fitz and his associates at London in 1567, but the first Englishman[3] to proclaim Congregational principles in writing was

[1] On the occasion when the two whose burning in 1575 has already been noticed were arrested in London, twenty-five others were taken into custody.

[2] Mr. Douglas Campbell, in his suggestive work, *The Puritan in Holland, England, and America*, II: 180, holds strongly that Browne received his ideas directly from the Anabaptists. This matter will be further considered later in this chapter.

[3] The origin of Congregationalism as an organized polity has been frequently attributed, and notably by Waddington (*Congregational History, 1200–1567*, London, 1869, pp. 742–745), to a company broken up by the government at Plumbers' Hall, June 19, 1567. But though the evidence of their opposition to the existing state of the Church of England is ample, and it seems certain that they had adopted Separatist principles and chosen their own ministry, their Congregationalism was yet very rudimentary. See Punchard, *Hist. of Cong.*, Boston [1865], II: 454–459; Dexter, *Cong. as seen*, pp. 114, 115, 631–4; Scott, *Pilgrim Fathers neither Puritans nor Persecutors*, London,

Robert Browne,[1] a man of sincere purpose, at least in early life; but one whose erratic disposition and final reconciliation with the English Establishment have cost him the personal repute which would otherwise have been his. Possessed of only ordinary ability, he nevertheless saw some truths clearly which had been ignored by the ecclesiastical teachers of his age.

Browne was born about the middle of the sixteenth century, of a family related to that of Elizabeth's great statesman, Lord Burghley. His education was at Corpus Christi College, Cambridge, an institution which he entered in 1570. The university was already strongly Puritan, and under the vigorous teaching of the greatest of the early Puritans, Thomas Cartwright,[2] was filled with the idea that a further reformation of the English Church was needful,—a reform to be brought about, in his estimation,

---

1891: C. R. Palmer, *Historical Address*, before New Haven Cong. Club, Oct., 1892, New Haven, 1893; MacKennal, *Story of the Eng. Separatists*, London, 1893; Adeney, *Ch. in the Prisons*, in *Early Independents*, London, 1893.

[1] The discoveries and investigations of the late Dr. Dexter have so re-made the portrait of Browne that all previous literature regarding him is of secondary value. The student will do well, therefore, to consult Dexter, *Congregationalism as seen*, etc., pp. 61–128. The article on Browne by Aug. Jessopp in the *Dictionary of National Biography*, VII: 57–61, is also of value. The main facts of his life, so far as not related in the text, are as follows:—He was born, probably in 1550, at Tolethorpe, Rutlandshire. After his student life in Cambridge, and chaplaincy to the Duke of Norfolk, he taught school till 1578: then followed his second period of Cambridge study, his preaching and silencing by the bishop, and his full adoption of Congregational principles and settlement in Norwich about 1580. Late in 1581, probably, he went to Holland, and in 1582 published the books with which we have to do. Quarrels distressed his church in Middelburg, and as a result Browne and a few followers went from Holland to Scotland in 1583. At Edinburgh he was received with much disfavor by the Presbyterian authorities. By the summer of 1584 he was apparently back in London, having failed to found a permanent congregation either in Norwich, Holland, or Scotland. Here in London he was imprisoned, as he had been repeatedly before; but here, as elsewhere, he was saved from the most serious consequences of his opposition to the English ecclesiastical system by his relationship to Lord Burghley. Released from prison, he seems to have gone to Northampton in 1586, and was then excommunicated by the Bishop of Peterborough. He was now, it would appear, utterly discouraged. Dr. Dexter held, with much show of reason, that his mind had become affected by his long disappointments and imprisonments. At all events, he became reconciled to the Establishment late in 1586, and was appointed master of a grammar school in Southwark, a position which he held till September, 1591, when, having been restored to the ministry of the Church of England, he received from his ever kindly relative, Lord Burghley, the living of Achurch cum Thorpe. Here he ministered till near his death, an event which occurred in Northampton jail (when he was a prisoner probably in consequence of a debt) sometime between June, 1631, and November, 1633. His later life was wholly insignificant and comports well with the view that he was a broken-down man.

[2] Cartwright was about forty years old when Browne entered the university and was at the height of his fame and influence. He had been identified with Cambridge as student, fellow, and teacher since 1547. In 1569 he had been made professor of divinity; but his Puritan views were at once attacked by the Anglicans, led by Whitgift, the later archbishop, and he was compelled to relinquish his professorship in December, 1570, and his fellowship in September, 1571. This discussion must have stirred Browne profoundly.

however, from within and not by separation from its fold. Browne soon combined the duties of a student's life with the occupation of a chaplain in the family of the Duke of Norfolk; but here he showed opinions at variance with those of the ecclesiastical authorities, the exact nature of which it is impossible to affirm, but which were probably Puritan rather than fully Congregational. The duke, at all events, sympathized with him sufficiently to plead in his behalf that a chaplaincy was a privileged office beyond the reach of the ordinary processes of ecclesiastical law. Whether his patron's intervention was sufficient to check further proceedings in Browne's case or not does not appear; but for about three years thereafter he taught school, apparently at Southwark, preaching also to such as he could gather in illegal meetings in a gravel-pit at Islington. But desire for further study drew him back to Cambridge, and, as was natural for an earnest young Puritan minister, he entered the household theological school of Rev. Richard Greenham, an eminent Puritan of Dry Drayton, not far from the university town. Here he was encouraged to preach in pulpits of the Church of England where the hearers were of Puritan sympathies, and such was the favor with which he was regarded that he took charge of a church in Cambridge itself. Here it was, apparently, that he underwent the spiritual struggle which led him to Congregational views.[1] The church to which he had preached for about six months desired him to remain, but Browne's Puritan scruples regarding bishops had made him feel that an appointment dependent upon one of their order was no proper ministry. The conviction now came to him that the all-inclusive membership of the Church of England was well-nigh fatal to real piety. The only course for those who would seek a full Christian life was to separate from it and unite among themselves. He felt that "the kingdom off God Was not to be begun by whole parishes, but

[1] Dr. Dexter, whose admirable account of Browne is the source of the facts of his biography above given, was the discoverer of an undated little work by Browne himself, *A Trve and Short Declaration, both of the Gathering and Ioyning Together of Certaine Persons: and also of the Lamentable Breach and Division which fell Amongst Them*, which is really a "spiritual autobiography." A manuscript copy is in the Dexter Collection, now in the possession of Yale University, and a reprint has been issued, without date or place, [by Dr. Dale?]

rather off the worthiest, Were they never so fewe."[1] Naturally such views were offensive to his ecclesiastical superiors, and the result was that Browne was silenced.

Thus far Browne's primary desire seems to have been the development of a more earnest spiritual life. He had followed the Puritan path and he had gone far beyond Puritanism into a belief in the necessity of actual separation from the Establishment. But he had not yet fully thought out the constitution of the purified church for which he longed. It is interesting to observe that in this transition period, after he had been silenced by the bishop, he learned that in the neighboring county of Norfolk, a county in which Dutch artisans were present in large numbers and presumably Dutch Anabaptists among them, were persons who were eager for religious reform in the direction toward which his own thoughts turned, and he resolved to go to them. Before this determination was put into practice, however, an acquaintance, Robert Harrison,[2] who was also to be a fellow-laborer with Browne, came to Cambridge from Norwich, the principal town of Norfolk. With him, probably in 1580, Browne removed to Norwich, and here in conversation with Harrison, in study of the Scripture, and it may be also through contact with Anabaptist views (though on this point proof is lacking), Browne fully thought out his system of church-government. Here, too, at some uncertain time in 1580 or 1581,[3] he formed with others whom he gathered about him the first Congregational Church of the long series which has continued since that day.

So conspicuous action in defiance of constituted ecclesiastical authorities could not escape notice, the more so that Browne extended his field of preaching as far as Bury Saint Edmunds.[4] By

---

[1] *Trve and Short Declaration*, p. 6; Dexter, *Cong. as seen*, p. 67.

[2] Robert Harrison had entered Cambridge university in 1564, he had graduated B. A. at Corpus Christi in 1567, and M. A. in 1572. After the latter graduation, at some uncertain date, he was made master of a Norwich hospital. At Norwich, Browne lived in his house. Harrison accompanied Browne to Middelburg and remained there, probably as pastor, after Browne's departure. He did not long survive, dying about 1585. See Cooper, *Athenæ Cantabrigienses*, II: 177; and *Dict. National Biography*, XXV: 38.

[3] Dexter, *Cong. as seen*, p. 70.

[4] Bishop Freake of Norwich declared that, apparently at Bury Saint Edmunds, "the vulgar sort of people . . . greatly depended on him, assembling themselves together to the number of an hundred at a time in private houses and conventicles to hear him." See quotations in Dexter, p. 70.

April, 1581, the bishop of Norwich had taken official cognizance of his doings. But the relationship of the young Congregationalist to Lord Burghley, and the help extended by that powerful kinsman,[1] prevented any more serious consequences to Browne than a six-months of great personal annoyance. These experiences, however, convinced the infant church that it had nothing to hope for in England, and therefore after much deliberation, Browne, Harrison, and a part of the Norwich company emigrated to the city of Middelburg in the Dutch province of Zeland,[2] probably in the autumn of 1581. It would appear that some of the Norwich flock remained behind and continued a Congregational organization, for a time at least, on English soil.[3]

It was soon after his arrival in Holland that Browne put forth, with the pecuniary aid of Harrison, some time in 1582, three tracts[4] designed primarily to further his views in England, and from one of which our statement of his principles is drawn. These little works were sent to England, and in spite of a proclamation in the name of Queen Elizabeth forbidding their circulation,[5] they were scattered abroad; at Bury Saint Edmunds they were distributed through the agency of two of Browne's followers, John Coppin and Elias Thacker, who were at the time in not very strict imprisonment for their religious opinions, but who for their connection with these tracts were condemned and hanged in the summer of 1583.[6]

With Browne's further fortunes we have little to do. His own impulsive temperament, and the value placed on church discipline by the early Separatists, led to quarrel in his Middelburg flock, a quarrel which resulted in his leaving Harrison and the majority of his congregation on Dutch soil, and going with a few followers to

---

1 Burghley had no sympathy with Browne's views on church-government.

2 Dexter, *Cong. as seen*, p. 72.

3 Dexter, pp. 73, 74, shows that a Congregational church existed at Norwich as late as 1603, which was regarded as an "elder sister" by the church formed at London in 1592.

4 Beside the *Booke which sheweth*, etc., from which our selections are taken, these tracts were *A Treatise vpon the 23. of Matthewe*, and *A Treatise of Reformation vvithout Tarying for anie*.

5 Given June 30, 1583. In full, Dexter, p. 75. The tracts were described as "sundry seditious, scismaticall, and erronious printed Bookes and libelles, tending to the deprauing of the Ecclesiastical gouernment established within this Realme."

6 See Dexter, pp. 208–210; Campbell *Puritan*, II: 182, 183.

Scotland late in 1583. Here he found the opposition of the Presbyterian authorities as fatal to his peace as that of the bishops of England had been; and, after some time vainly spent in various Scotch towns, he returned to England, once more to meet defeat, with the added pain of imprisonment. Broken down in body and mind at last, it would appear, he made his peace with the Church of England in 1586, and through the kindness of Lord Burghley, he obtained, in 1591, the rectorship of Achurch cum Thorpe, in which office he passed the forty remaining years of his now uneventful life.

The system which Browne laid down in the three treatises of 1582, is imperfectly worked out in detail, but it nevertheless presents with great clearness the essential features of modern Congregationalism. As Dr. Dexter has shown,[1] the starting point in Browne's thinking was not a desire to establish a novel polity, but to foster the spiritual development of the believer by his separation from communion with the non-faithful whom all the State churches allowed a place in the church. He broke with the Church of England primarily, because its bishops and other authorities approved its general, and, as Browne thought, anti-Christian, inclusion of all non-excommunicate baptized persons, an inclusiveness, which, to his way of thinking, made the real elevation of the Establishment in spiritual tone impossible. He broke with the Puritans, for, though they desired a spiritual reformation as sincerely as he, they would wait for it from the hand of the civil magistrate;[2] and Browne, first of English writers, set forth the Anabaptist doctrine that the civil ruler has no control over the spiritual affairs of the church, that church and state are separate realms. His views on this important question were expressed in the clearest fashion:[3]

"Yet may they [magistrates] doo nothing concerning the Church, but onelie ciu-

[1] *Cong. as seen*, pp. 96–104.

[2] See his work of 1582, *A Treatise of Reformation vvithout Tarying for anie* [i. e., without waiting for the civil authorities to act, as the Puritans wished], *and of the wickednesse of those Preachers which will not reforme till the Magistrate commaunde or compell them.*

[3] I have given this quotation at length because the point is not so clearly shown in the selections on a later page. It is from the *Treatise of Reformation*, p. 12. See also Dexter, pp. 101, 102.

ilie, and as ciuile Magistrates; that is, they haue not that authoritie ouer the church, as to be Prophetes or Priestes, or spiritual Kings, as they are Magistrates ouer the same: but onelie to rule the common wealth in all outwarde Iustice, to maintaine the right welfare and honor therof with outward power, bodily punishment, & ciuil forcing of mē. And therfore also because the church is in a common wealth, it is of their charge: that is concerning the outward prouision & outward iustice, they are to looke to it; but to cōpell religion, to plant churches by power, and to force a submission to Ecclesiastical gouernement by lawes & penalties, belongeth not to them."[1]

If, then, a full spiritual life in a community was impossible under the existing government of the Church of England, and if it was not only useless but wrong to wait for the reform of that Establishment, as the Puritans were waiting, at the hand of the civil authorities, how were the Christians, who must thus of necessity separate themselves from their old churchly connections, to be organized into new societies? The model for their organization Browne found in the New Testament.[2] The believers should be united to God and one to another by a covenant, entered into, not by compulsion, but willingly.[3] Such a body, so united, and recognizing their obligations to God the Father and to Christ as their law-giver and ruler, are a church. Of this church Christ is the head,[4] and his powers and graces are for the use of every member[5] There are officers of divine appointment, some of temporary use to aid all churches, apostles, prophets, and evangelists, who belong to the past rather than the present;[6] and others designated as the abiding officers of individual churches, the pastor, teacher, elders, deacons, and widows, who "haue their seuerall charge in one Churche onely."[7] Yet these officers do not stand between Christ and the ordinary believer, they "haue the grace & office of teaching and guiding;" but "euerie one of the church is made a Kinge, a Priest, and a Prophet vnder Christ, to vpholde and further the kingdom of God."[8] The offices of Christ are for the use of each member of the church, as well as for those who "teach and guide" it.[9] It is this immediateness of relationship between

[1] It is interesting to notice that Harrison did not share Browne's view on this point, Dexter, p. 85.

[2] Compare extracts from the *Booke which Sheweth* at the close of this chapter, Answer 35.

[3] *Ibid.*, Ans. 36–38. [4] *Ibid.*, Ans. 44. [5] *Ibid.*, Ans. 55.

[6] *Ibid.*, 52. [7] *Ibid.*, 53, 54. [8] *Ibid.*, 50, 55. [9] *Ibid.*, 56–58.

Christ, the head of the church and each member, that, as Dr. Dexter has pointed out,[1] makes Browne's polity essentially though unintentionally democratic, and that gives it a closer resemblance in some features to the purely democratic Congregationalism of the present century than to the more aristocratic, one might almost say semi-Presbyterianized, Congregationalism of Barrowe and the founders of New England.

Church officers are to be chosen by the congregations which they serve, and ordination is to be at the hands of the "elders," an expression which Browne uses as signifying in this connection the "forwardest" or most worthy of a congregation, rather than a particular order of church officers.[2] Unlike the teachers of the prelatical churches, Browne held that the essence of a minister's claim to office lay not in the imposition of hands in ordination, but in his inward calling by divine providence and his choice by the people of his charge.[3] Among the duties of a church officer, discipline had a large place,[4] but the ordinary member was in no way relieved from responsibility regarding his brethren, he, too, must "watch" and "trie out all wickednes."[5] In fact, the whole conception entertained by Browne of the position of a church officer was, that he should be a leader and example to his brethren rather than a master and judge.

Browne saw that not only individuals within a local church, but the local churches as separate bodies had duties one to another. His theory on this point was not elaborated in detail, but he recognized clearly the propriety of "synodes," or councils,—the "meetings of sundrie churches: which are when the weaker churches seeke helpe of the stronger, for deciding or redressing of matters or else the stronger looke to them for redresse."[6]

It is interesting to note that Browne perceived that his theory of the relation of an officer to a church was applicable, in large measure, to civil society. Though he recognized that the claims of some to civil office were based, as one element, on "parentage and birth," he held that all in rightful authority were so by the

---

1 *Cong. as seen*, pp. 106, 107.
2 *Booke which Sheweth*, *Ans.* 117, 119, also 51.
3 *Ibid.*, 119.
4 *Ibid.*, 126.
5 *Ibid.*, 56.
6 *Ibid.*, 51.

command of God and "agreement of men." His picture of the covenant-relation of men in the church, under the immediate sovereignty of God, he extended to the state; and it led him as directly, and probably as unintentionally, to democracy in the one field as in the other. His theory implied that all governors should rule by the will of the governed, and made the basis of the state on its human side essentially a compact.[1]

Whence were these views of Browne derived? Clearly from the New Testament, in whose pages he thought he saw delineated the pattern of the church which God designed. But whether he was brought to this system of polity by unaided study of the Scriptures and thought upon the state of the Church of England; or whether his theories and interpretations were assisted by some knowledge of the beliefs of the Dutch Anabaptists, is a question not so easy to answer. The late Dr. Dexter held strongly to the position that Browne owed nothing to Anabaptist influences and that he was a disciple of no one.[2] Mr. Douglas Campbell maintains, on the other hand, that Browne derived one of his most important doctrines,—that of the separation of Church and State,—from the Anabaptists;[3] and the inference is that his debt to these Dutch exiles was extensive. Much may be said in defense of either of these views. Browne held, as we have seen, that it was the duty of Christians to separate from communions where non-Christians were tolerated. This was a position held by the Anabaptists.[4] He would not wait for reformation at the hand of the civil magistrate with the Puritans, for he believed that the magistrate had no right to coerce men's consciences; and this was the view also of the Anabaptists.[5] And when we look at more particular features of Browne's system we find that his theories of the independence of the local congregation, its right to choose its own officers, and the fundamental necessity of a vigorous exercise of discipline, were all exemplified among the Anabaptists. Then it will be remembered that when Browne had first determined on

---

[1] *Ibid.*, 114–118. [2] *Cong. as seen*, p. 103. [3] *Puritan in Holland*, etc., II: 179, 180, 200.

[4] See *ante*, p. 3.

[5] See Schyn, *Historiæ Mennonitarum Plenior Deductio*, Amsterdam, 1729, pp. 147, 221, 275, etc.

separation, he heard that some far advanced in religious reformation were in Norfolk, and planned to join them;[1] and he worked out his system in conversation with a friend, Robert Harrison, who had been sometime a resident of Norwich, and put it into practice at Norwich and probably at Bury Saint Edmunds also. These were places filled with Dutch refugees, and in both he found a considerable following among the lower classes.[2] There Anabaptist ideas must have been considerably disseminated. These considerations lend weight to the views of Mr. Campbell.

But, on the other hand, Browne utterly rejected the great Anabaptist tenet of believers' baptism.[3] Furthermore, unlike the Anabaptists, he held that oaths were sometimes not only lawful but a "speciall furtheraunce of the kingdome of God."[4] He evidently saw nothing unbecoming to a Christian in the tenure of civil office;[5] and, moreover, he would not have hesitated to bear arms.[6] He expressly repudiated the charge that his doctrine regarding the power of magistrates deserved the name of Anabaptist.[7] And though a strong geographical argument may be drawn in support of probable contact with these Christians of the Dutch dispersion, Browne's candid spiritual autobiography[8] gives no hint of any such indebtedness, and he mentions no Dutch names among his supporters.[9] It is safe to affirm that he had no conscious indebtedness to the Anabaptists.

Yet if a balance is to be struck between the views of Dr. Dexter and Mr. Campbell, I venture with some diffidence to hold that the truth lies between. It is clear that Browne belonged in large measure to that great radical party which felt that the early reformers of prominence had not carried their principles to their logical or Scriptural result. Of this party the chief representatives were the Anabaptists; and however Browne may have reached his theories, it is with the radical reformers that he must be classed. It

---

[1] *Ante*, p. 10. [2] *Ante*, p. 10.

[3] See the selections from the *Booke which Sheweth*, on later page, Ans. 40.

[4] *Ibid.*, 110. [5] *Ibid.*, 112–118. [6] *Booke which Sheweth*, p. 100.

[7] "They charge vs as Anabaptistes & denying Magistrates, because we set not vp them, nor the Magistrates, aboue Christ Iesus and his glorious kingdome."—*Treatise of Reformation*, p. 13. See Dexter, p. 103.

[8] The *Trve and Short Declaration*. [9] Compare Dexter, p. 73.

is plain also that many of Browne's most characteristic views had been already advanced by the Anabaptists. But it is no less evident that Browne differed from the Anabaptists on points of great importance, and had no conscious connection with them. Yet certain of their views may have circulated much more widely in the manufacturing cities of eastern England than their acknowledged disciples penetrated; and Browne may have unconsciously absorbed much from this atmosphere, taking into his own thinking such truths as were acceptable to his own study and speculation. It may well be thus that Browne was really indebted to the Anabaptists for some features of his system, though honestly believing it to be the product of his own study of the Word of God.

But while we may admit thus much regarding the possible indebtedness of Browne to older thinkers of the radical school, we must recognize that he made the polity which he elaborated wholly his own. Its details were not yet fully developed, but its great outlines were there, and the system of Browne can be mistaken for no other of the polities of the Christian church. It had a definiteness and a logical consistency which the Anabaptists had not attained. It based the local church on a definite covenant, entered into by the believers with God and with one another, more clearly than they, thus affording a logical and Scriptural foundation for the existence and obligations of the local fellowship. It showed, at least in principle, that the local independence of the individual congregation is consistent with a real and efficient unity with other churches. It steered a safe course between the sacrifice of the self-government of the local church for the sake of a strong central authority which is the evil feature of all systems from Romanism to Presbyterianism, and the abandonment of real mutual accountability between churches which had been the vulnerable point of the polity of the Anabaptists. Though he proved unfaithful himself to the beliefs which he preached and for which he suffered, Robert Browne must be accounted the father of modern Congregationalism.

Extracts from Browne's "Booke which Sheweth the life and manners of all true Christians," etc.,[1] Middelburg, 1582.

[2] *The state of Christians.*	*The state of Heathen.*
Christians. Their knowledge. The Godhead.	Heathen. Their ignorance. False Gods.
[1] WHerefore are we called the people of God and Christians?	[1] *WHerefore are the Heathen forsaken of God, and be the cursed people of the worlde?*
Because that by a willing Couenaunt made with our God, we are vnder the gouernement of God and Christe, and thereby do leade a godly and Christian life.	Because they forsake or refuse the Lords couenaunt and gouernement: and therefore they leade an vngodly and worldly life.

[1] Browne's *Booke* embraces 185 Questions, each with answer, counter-question, definition, and division as above given. Each series extends over parts of two opposite pages. This first question, with its train of subdivisions, may serve as an example of the whole book, but so little additional is contained in the repetitious matter that from this point onward I give only the questions and answers, omitting counter-questions, definitions, and divisions. I have also changed the type from here onward from Old English to Roman.

[Questions 2 to 34 relate to the knowledge of God by men, His nature, attributes, providence, the fall of man and salvation by Christ. These doctrines are treated in the usual Calvinistic sense, and present nothing peculiar to Browne.]

[20[1]] 35 What is our calling and leading vnto this happines?[2]

In the new Testament our calling is in plainer maner: as by the first planting and gathering of the church vnder one kinde of gouernement.

Also by a further plãting of the church according to that gouernement.

But in the olde Testament, our calling was by shadowes and ceremonies, as among the Iewes.

36 Howe must the churche be first planted and gathered vnder one kinde of gouernement?

[1] The bracketed numbers indicate the pages of Browne's work.

[2] I. e., the happiness purchased by Christ.

Definitions.		*Diuisions.*		[3]
Christians.	*Their knovvledge.*	*The Godhead.*		
[1] Christians are a companie or number of beleeuers, which by a willing couenaunt made with their God, are vnder the gouernement of God and Christ, and keepe his Lawes in one holie communion: Because they are redeemed by Christe vnto holines & happines for euer, from whiche they were fallen by the sinne of Adam.		*Christians whiche should leade a godlie life*	*By knowing God and the dueties of godlinesse.*	
			By keeping those dueties.	

First by a couenant and condicion, made on Gods behalfe.

Secondlie by a couenant and condicion made on our behalfe.

Thirdlie by vsing the sacrament of Baptisme to seale those condicions, and couenantes.

37 What is the couenant, or condicion on Gods behalfe?

His promise to be our God and sauiour, if we forsake not his gouernement by disobedience.

Also his promise to be the God of our seede, while we are his people.

Also the gifte of his spirit to his children as an inwarde calling and furtheraunce of godlines.

[22] 38 What is the couenant or condicion on our behalfe?

We must offer and geue vp our selues to be of the church and people of God.

We must likewise offer and geue vp our children and others,

being vnder age, if they be of our householde and we haue full power ouer them.

We must make profession, that we are his people, by submitting our selues to his lawes and gouernement.

39 How must Baptisme be vsed, as a seale of this couenaunt?

They must be duelie presented, and offered to God and the church, which are to be Baptised.

They must be duelie receiued vnto grace and fellowship.

40 How must they be presented and offered?

The children of the faithfull, though they be infantes are to be offered to God and the church, that they may be Baptised.

Also those infantes or children which are of the householde of the faithfull, and vnder their full power.

Also all of discretion which are not baptised, if they holde the Christian profession, and shewe forth the same.

[*24*] *41 How must they be receaued vnto grace and felloshippe?*

The worde must be duely preached in an holie assemblie.

The signe or Sacrament must be applied thereto.

42 How must the word be preached?

The preacher being called and meete thereto, must shewe the redemption of christians by Christ, and the promises receaued by faith as before.

Also they must shewe the right vse of that redemption, in suffering with Christ to dye vnto sinne by repētance.

Also the raising and quickning again vpon repentance.

43 Howe must the signe be applied thereto?

The bodies of the parties baptised, must be washed w^t^ water, or sprinckled or dipped, in the name of the Father, and of ye Sonne, and of the holy Ghost, vnto the forgeuenes of sinnes, and dying thereto in one death and burial with Christ.

The preacher must pronounce thē to be baptised into ye bodie and gouernement of Christ, to be taught & to professe his lawes, that by his mediatiō & victorie, they might rise againe with him vnto holines & happines for euer. The church must geue thankes for the partie baptised, and praye for his further instruction, and traininge vnto saluation.

[*26*] *44 How must it* [*the church*] *be further builded, accordinge vnto churche gouernement?*

First by communion of the graces & offices in the head of ye church, which is Christ.

Secondlly, by communion of the graces and offices in the bodie, which is the church of Christ.

Thirdly, by vsing the Sacrament of the Lords supper, as a seale of this communion.

45 Howe hath the churche the communion of those graces & offices, which are in Christ?

It hath the vse of his priesthoode: because he is the high Priest thereof.

Also of his prophecie: because he is the Prophet thereof.

Also of his kingdome and gouernement: because he is the kynge and Lord thereof.

46 What vse hath the churche of his priesthoode?

Thereby he is our mediatour, and we present and offer vppe our praiers in his name, because by his intreatie, our sinnes are forgeuen.

Also he is our iustification, because by his attonement we are iustified.

Also he is our sanctification, because he partaketh vnto vs his holines and spirituall graces.

[28] 47 What vse hath the church of his prophecie?

He him selfe hath taught vs, and geuen vs his lawes.

He preacheth vnto vs by his worde & message in the mouthes of his messengers.

He appoynteth to euerie one their callinges and dueties.

48 What vse hath the churche of his kinglie office?

By that he executeth his lawes: First, by ouerseeing and trying out wickednes.

Also by priuate or open rebuke, of priuate or open offenders.

Also by separation of the wilfull, or more greeuous offenders.

[30] 49 What vse hath the churche of the graces and offices vnder Christ?

It hath those which haue office of teaching and guiding.

Also those which haue office of cherishing and releeuing the afflicted & poore.

Also it hath the graces of all the brethren and people to doo good withall.

50 Who haue the grace & office of teaching and guiding?

Some haue this charge and office together, which can not be sundred.

Some haue their seueral charge ouer manie churches.

Some haue charge but in one church onlie.

51 How haue some their charge and office together?

There be Synodes or meetings of sundrie churches: which are when the weaker churches seeke helpe of the stronger, for deciding or redressing of matters: or else the stronger looke to them for redresse.

There is also prophecie, or meetings for the vse of euerie mans gift, in talk or reasoning, or exhortation and doctrine.

There is the Eldershippe, or meetings of the most forwarde and wise, for lookinge to matters.

[*32*] *52 Who haue their seueral charge ouer many churches?*

Apostles had charge ouer many churches.

Likewise Prophetes, which had their reuelations or visions.

Likewise helpers vnto these, as Euāgelistes, and companions of their iourneis.

53 Who haue their seuerall charge in one Churche onely, to teache and guide the same?

The Pastour, or he which hath the guift of exhorting, and applying especiallie.

The Teacher, or he whiche hath the guift of teaching especially: and lesse guift of exhorting and applying.

They whiche helpe vnto them both in ouerseeing and counsailinge, as the most forward or Elders.

54 Who haue office of cherishing and releeuing the afflicted and poore?

The Releeuers or Deacons, which are to gather and bestowe the church liberalitie.

The Widowes, which are to praye for the church, with attendaunce to the sicke and afflicted thereof.

[*34*] *55 How hath the church the vse of those graces, which al yͤ brethrē & people haue to do good withal?*

Because euerie one of the church is made a Kinge, a Priest, and a Prophet vnder Christ, to vpholde and further the kingdom of God, & to breake and destroie the kingdome of Antichrist, and Satan.

56 Howe are we made Kinges?

We must all watch one an other, and trie out all wickednes.

We must priuatlie and openlie rebuke, the priuat and open offendours. We must also separate the wilful and more greeuous offenders, and withdraw our selues frō them, and gather the righteous togither.

57 How are all Christians made Priestes vnder Christ?

They present and offer vp praiers vnto God, for them selues & for others.

They turne others from iniquitie, so that attonement is made in Christ unto iustification.

In them also and for them others are sanctified, by partaking the graces of Christ vnto them.

58 How are all Christians made prophetes vnder Christ?

They teach the lawes of Christ, and talke and reason for the maintenaũce of them.

They exhorte, moue, and stirre vp to the keeping of his lawes. They appoint, counsel, and tell one another their dueties.

[*36*] *59 How must we vse the Sacrament of the Lords supper, as a seale of this communion?*

There must be a due preparation to receaue the Lords supper. And a due ministration thereof.

60 What preparation must there be to receaue the Lords supper?

There must be a separation frō those which are none of the church, or be vnmeete to receaue, that the worthie may be onely receaued.

All open offences and faultings must be redressed.

All must proue and examine them selues, that their conscience be cleare by faith and repentance, before they receaue.

61 How is the supper rightlie ministred?

The worde must be duelie preached.

And the signe or sacrament must be rightlie applied thereto.

[*38*] *62 How must the worde be dulie preached?*

The death and tormentes of Christ, by breaking his bodie and sheading his bloud for our sinnes, must be shewed by the lawfull preacher.

Also he must shewe the spirtuall vse of the bodie & bloud of Christ Jesus, by a spirituall feeding thereon, and growinge into it, by one holie communion.

Also our thankefulnes, and further profiting in godlines vnto life euerlasting.

[*40*] *63 How must the signe be applied thereto?*

The preacher must take breade and blesse and geue thankes, and thē must he breake it and pronounce it to be the body of Christ, which was broken for thē, that by fayth they might feede thereon spirituallie & growe into one spiritual bodie of Christ, and so he eating thereof him selfe, must bidd them take and eate it among them, & feede on Christ in their consciences.

Likewise also must he take the cuppe and blesse and geue thankes, and so pronounce it to be the bloud of Christ in the newe Testament, which was shedd for remission of sinnes, that by fayth we might drinke it spirtuallie, and so be nourished in one spirituall bodie of Christ, all sinne being clensed away, and then he drinking thereof himselfe must bydd them drinke there of likewise and diuide it amōg them, and feede on Christe in their consciences.

Then muste they all geue thankes praying for their further profiting in godlines & vowing their obedience.

[Questions 64 to 81 relate to the Jewish dispensation; and Questions 82 to 111 to Christian graces and duties. Two of the latter are of interest.]

[68] *110 What speciall furtheraunce of the kingdome of God is ther?*

In talke to edifie one an other by praising God, and declaring his will by rebuke or exhortation.

In doubt and controuersie to sweare by his name on iust occasions, and to vse lottes.

Also to keepe the meetinges of the church, and with our especiall friends for spirituall exercises.

111. What special duties be ther for the Sabbathe?

All the generall duties of religion & holines towards God, and all the speciall dueties of worshipping God, & furthering his kingdome, must on the Sabbath be performed, with ceasing from our callinges & labour in worldlye thinges. Yet such busines as can not be putt of tyll the daie after, nor done the daie before, may then be done.

[Questions 112 to 185,—the remainder of the book,—relate to the duties of man to man.]

[70] *112 Whiche bee the dueties of righteousnes concerning man?*

They be eyther more bounden, as the generall dueties in gouernement betwene gouernours and inferiours:

Or they be more free, as the generall dueties of freedome.

Or else they be more speciall duties for eche others name, and for auoyding couetousnes.

113 What be the dueties of Gouernours?

They consist in the entraunce of that calling.

And in the due execution thereof by ruling well.

114 How must Superiours enter and take their calling?

By assuraunce of their guift.

By speciall charge.and commaundemente from God to put it in practise.

By agreement of men.

115 What gift must they haue?

All Gouernours must haue forwardnes before others, in knowledge and godlines, as able to guide.

And some must haue age and eldershippe.

Also some must haue pareintage and birth.

[72] *116 What charge or commaundement of God must they haue to vse their guift?*

They haue first the speciall commaundement of furthering his kingdome, by edifyinge and helping of others, where there is occasion and persones be worthie.

Also some speciall prophecie and foretelling of their calling, or some generall commaundement for the same.

Also particular warninges from God vnknowne to the world, as in oulde time by vision, dreame, and reuelation, and now by a speciall working of Gods spirite in our consciences.

117 what agreement must there be of men?

For Church gouernours there must be an agreement of the church.

For ciuil Magistrates, there must be an agreement of the people or Common welth.

For Houshoulders, there must be an agreement of the houshouldes. As Husbandes, Parents, Maisters, Teachers, or Scholemaisters, &c.

[74] *118 What agreement must there be of the church, for the calling of church gouernours?*

They must trie their guiftes and godlines.

They must receyue them by obedience as their guides and teachers, where they plante or establish the church.

They must receyue them by choyse where the church is planted.[1]

The agreement also for the calling of ciuill magistrates should be like vnto this, excepting their Pompe and outward power, and orders established meete for the people.

119 What choyse should there be?

The praiers and humbling of all, with fasting and exhortation, that God may be chiefe in the choise.

The consent of the people must be gathered by the Elders or guides, and testifyed by voyce, presenting, or naming of some, or other tokens, that they approue them as meete for that calling.

---

[1] The meaning of this blind passage is, I take it, that where the minister gathers a church and it originates through his labors, he is to be received by it "by obedience"; but where an already established church calls a minister, he is to be received "by choyse."

The Elders or forwardest must ordeine, and pronounce them, with prayer and imposition of handes, as called and authorised of God, and receyued of their charg to that calling.

Yet imposition of handes is no essentiall pointe of their calling, but it ought to be left, when it is turned into pompe or superstition.

[*76*] *120 What agreement must ther be in the householdes, for the gouernement of them?*

There must be an agrement of Husband and Wife, of Parentes & Children: Also of Maister and Seruant, and likewise of Teachers & Schollers, &c.

This agreement betweene parentes and children is of naturall desert and duetie betweene them:

But in the other there must be triall and iudgment of ech others meetnes for their likinge and callinge, as is shewed before.

Also there must be a due couenaunt betweene them.

[*78*] *121 How must Superiours execute their callinge by ruling their inferiours?*

They must esteeme right and due.

They must vphould the same:

By appointing to others their dueties.

They must take accountes.

122 How must they esteeme right and due?

They must be zealouse for equitie and innocencie.

They must loue those and reioyse ouer them, which doe their dueties.

They must hate all vanite and wickednes and be angrie and greeued therat.

[*80*] *123 How must they appoint vnto others their worke and duetie?*

They must teach them.

They must direct them by their guiding and helpe.

They must giue them good example.

124 How must they teach them?

They must teach them the groundes of religion, and the meaning of the Scriptures.

They must exhort and dehort particularly for reformation of their liues.

They must require thinges againe which are taught, by particular applying and trying their guift.

[*82*] *125 How must they direct them by their guiding and helpe?*

They must guide thē in the worshipp of God, as in the Worde, Praier, Thanksgiuing, &c.

They must gather their Voices, Doubtes and Questions, and determine Controuersies.

They must particularlie commaunde and tell them their dueties.

126 How must they take accountes?

They must continually watch them by visiting and looking to them them selues, and by others helping vnto them.

They must trie out and search their state and behauiour by accusations and chardgings with witnesses.

They must reforme or recompense by rebuke or separation the wicked and vnruly.

[*84*] *127 what say you of the dueties of submission to Superiours?*

They consist in esteeming them.

In honoring them.

In seruing them.

[The remaining Questions and Answers contain so little that is peculiar to Browne that I have omitted them.]

II

THE LONDON CONFESSION OF 1589

EDITIONS AND REPRINTS

I. *A Trve Description ovt | of the Word of God, | of the visible Church.* Without title page. Dated 1589 at the end. Printed at Dort. 4° pp. 8.

II. The same in form and with the same date, the only variation from the first edition being a rearrangement of the order of the paragraphs treating of excommunication. Printed at Amsterdam before 1602.[1]

III. With the substitution of *Congregation* for *Church* in the title and other passages; and a few minor verbal changes. Printed at [?] 1641. 4° pp. 8.[2]

IV. The text of the first edition was reprinted and criticised paragraph by paragraph by R. Alison, *A Plaine Confutation of a Treatise of Brownisme, Published by some of that Faction, Entituled A Description*, etc., London, 1590.

V. The text of the second edition was reprinted in Lawne, *Brownisme Tvrned the In-side Out-ward*, etc., London, 1613. Also, VI. in Wall, *More Work for the Dean*, London, 1681, pp. 20–28. Also, VII. in Hanbury, *Historical Memorials Relating to the Independents*, etc., London, 1839–44, I: 28–34.

LITERATURE

Beside the controversial pamphlets already cited, the Creed is treated briefly in Hanbury, *Memorials*, I: 25–27. By far the most satisfactory and complete discussion of this interesting document is, however, to be found in Dexter, *The Congregationalism of the last three hundred years*, pp. 258–262.

THE abandonment by Browne of the work which he had undertaken and the rupture of his exiled flock at Middelburg did not bring the Congregational movement to an end. As has been seen, a portion of Browne's congregation appear to have maintained their organization at Norwich, though nothing is

[1] I am indebted to the late Rev. Dr. H. M. Dexter for the following facts regarding these editions: — The place of publication of the first edition and the circumstances of the issuance of the second are made clear by a passage in Henoch Clapham, *Errour on the Right Hand*, etc., London, 1608, p. 11, in which he declared that this *Trve Description* was originally printed at D[ort], where Barrowe's other writings were printed; but that a second edition, bearing the original date, was brought out, "some yeares after his [Barrowes] death," at A[msterdam] at the expense of Arthur Billet or Bellot. In this second edition, Clapham affirms, the paragraph beginning: "All this notwithstanding," was transferred from its original place "after the excommunication" (apparently after the paragraph commencing: "Further, they are to warne"), and inserted after the paragraph: "If the fault be private;" the intention being, it is charged, to make excommunication a severer matter than Barrowe intended — he believing it to be "a power to edification not to destruction." Arthur Billet died in Febr., 1602.

[2] See Hanbury, *Memorials*, I: 28.

known regarding their state and fortunes.[1] But Congregational believers carried the doctrine to other cities, though their movements are now impossible to trace.[2] We are first certainly aware of the existence of a Separatist congregation in London in 1587 or 1588, though it may have been formed a year or two earlier.[3] But so hunted was it by the officers of the law that a large proportion of its membership were imprisoned, and though certain church acts, such as the admission of members and the excommunication of the unworthy, were performed, the severity of the persecution prevented the election of appropriate church officers till September, 1592, when Francis Johnson was chosen pastor, John Greenwood teacher, and two elders and two deacons associated with them.[4]

Yet three years before its full organization this struggling London church, in the persons of its two leading members, put forth the creed which is the subject of present discussion. The principles enunciated by Browne, which have just been considered, though doubtless those in accordance with which his congregation was gathered, were published by him and his friend Harrison as a missionary tractate rather than a church creed. The publication, and probably the composition, of this London symbol has been traced conclusively[5] to Henry Barrowe[6] and John Green-

---

[1] See *ante*, p. 11.

[2] The Preface to the Confession of 1596, given in the next chapter, speaks of sufferers for Congregationalism in London, Norwich, Gloucester, Bury St. Edmunds, and "manye other places of the land."

[3] Dexter, *Cong. as seen*, pp. 255, 634. If Greenwood's arrest was in 1586, the congregation must certainly have been formed even earlier than 1587.

[4] *Ibid.*, pp. 232, 264, 265.

[5] *Ibid.*, pp. 234, 258–262.

[6] Henry Barrowe, one of the most noted and deserving of the proclaimers of modern Congregationalism, was of a good Norfolk family, and from 1566 to his graduation as Bachelor in 1569–70 he was a student at Clare Hall, in the Puritanically inclined University of Cambridge. But whatever may have been the influences with which he was then surrounded, he left the University an irreligious man. Turning his attention to the study of law, he was admitted a member of Gray's Inn in 1576; and, through what means we know not, he became personally acquainted with Queen Elizabeth, to whose court and presence he had access. A chance sermon was the means of his conversion, and his conversion was followed by the adoption of the strictest Puritan principles. Acquaintance with Greenwood, it would appear, led him, some time possibly before 1586, to embrace Congregational views. His visit to his friend Greenwood, in the place of the latter's imprisonment, was the occasion of his own arrest in Nov., 1586. From that time onward to his execution, April 6, 1593, he was a prisoner, at first in the Clink, and then in the Fleet in London. His unwearied literary activity, under the most discouraging circumstances, made this long period of imprisonment the most productive portion of his life. Beside his elaborate exposi-

wood,[1] then prisoners for their faith, shut up in the Fleet prison in London, and four years later to give their lives as martyrs to the truths here set forth. Though the statement nowhere appears in the document itself, the circumstances of the publication of the first and second editions, as far as they can now be ascertained, certainly justify the conclusion that we have here not only the expression of the individual beliefs of Barrowe and Greenwood, but a statement which the partially formed church in London looked upon as expressive of the views of the whole brotherhood. It is, therefore, essentially a church creed.

The *Trve Description* is substantially an ideal sketch. It could not well be otherwise. Shut up in prison for the advocacy of the opinions here presented, the framers of this creed could look nowhere upon earth for full exemplification of the polity in which they believed. The church-order which they longed for was, they were confident, of the divinely appointed pattern. They read its outlines in the New Testament. But they had had no experience with its practical workings, and hence they pictured a greater degree of spiritual unity and brotherliness than even

tion of Congregational principles in his *Brief Discouerie of the false Church*, 1590, and the *Plaine Refutation of M. Giffards Booke*, etc., 1591, which was to be the means of Francis Johnson's conversion to Congregationalism, Barrowe had a share in three controversial pamphlets. The pathetic story of Barrowe's imprisonment and death, with some account of his writings, may be found in the work of Dr. Dexter, already cited, pp. 211–245. Other sources of information are Brook, *Lives of the Puritans*, London, 1813, II: 23–44; Cooper, *Athenæ Cantabrigienses*, Cambridge [England], 1861, II: 151–153; Bacon, *Genesis of the New England Churches*, New York, 1874, pp. 91–154, *passim;* A. B. Grosart, in the *Dictionary of National Biography*, III: 297, 298 (London and New York, 1885). Additional references may be found appended to the articles of Cooper and Grosart.

[1] John Greenwood, the associate of Barrowe in his imprisonment and death, and his fellow-worker in the production of most of the writings mentioned in the previous note, was of less conspicuous social station than Barrowe, and somewhat younger in age. His education was obtained at Corpus Christi College, Cambridge, where he was a sizar or pecuniarily assisted student; and upon graduating in 1580–1 he had entered the established ministry, and been duly ordained to the diaconate and priesthood. His Puritan views led him for a time to serve as chaplain in the family of the Puritan Lord Rich of Rockford, Essex; but his progress toward Congregationalism was decided, and by 1586 he was preaching, as opportunity would permit, in London. His friendship with Barrowe has already been mentioned. Cast into prison in the autumn of 1586, he was released, apparently on bail, for a short time in 1592, and in September of that year was elected teacher by the London church, then for the first time choosing officers. His recommittal to prison speedily followed, and on April 6, 1593, he was hanged. Though a man of considerable ability, his part in the writings issued in conjunction with Barrowe was evidently secondary. Compare Dexter, *Congregationalism as seen*, pp. 211–245; Brook, *Lives of the Puritans*, II: 23–44; Bacon, *Genesis of the N. E. Churches*, pp. 93–154, *passim;* Cooper, *Athenæ Cantabrigienses*, II: 153, 154; *Dictionary of National Biography*, XXIII: 84, 85. Further bibliographical references may be found in connection with the two articles last cited.

Christian men and women have usually shown themselves capable of, and they made little provision for the avoidance of the friction inevitable at times in conducting the most harmonious societies composed of still imperfect men. But the essential features of early Congregationalism are here. It is first of all a "Description ovt of the Word of God." The Bible is made the ultimate standard in all matters of church government, as well as points of doctrine. Its delineations of church polity and administration are looked upon as furnishing an ample and authoritative rule for the church in all ages. This true church is not the whole body of the baptized inhabitants of a kingdom, but a company of men who can lay claim to personal Christian experience, and who are united to one another and to Christ in mutual fellowship. The nature of the officers of this church, their number, duties, and character, are all held to be ascertainable from the same God-given Word. They are not the bishops, priests, and deacons of the Anglican hierarchy, but are pastor and teacher, elders, deacons, and widows; and they hold their office not by royal appointment or the nomination of a patron, but "by the holy & free election of the Lordes holie and free people." The whole administration of the church is the concern of all the brethren, and the laws governing this administration are all derivable from the Scriptures. But on this very question of administration, while the *Trve Description* is not as clear as we could wish, it is plain that the creed is far removed from the practical democracy of Robert Browne or the usage of modern Congregationalism. The elders are indeed chosen by the whole church, but once having chosen them, the people are to be "most humble, meek, obedient, faithfull, and loving." The elders are to see that the other officers do their duties aright, and the people obey. But who shall see that the elders do their duty, or who shall seriously limit them in their action? That is not made clear. It is evident that the *Trve Description* would place the elders apart from and above the brethren as a ruling class, having the initiative in business, being themselves the church in all matters of excommunication, and leaving to the brethren only the power of election, approval of the elders' actions, and an undefined right to reprove the elders if their conduct should not be in accord with the New Testament standard. This conception of the elders as a ruling oligarchy in the church is, in fact, the view elaborated by Barrowe in his other writings, and is the theory which Dr. Dexter happily termed Barrowism, in distinction from the unintentional but thoroughgoing democracy of Robert Browne.[1] It is a theory which colors the creeds of more than a century of early Congregationalism.

The almost complete absence of distinctly doctrinal statement in this creed is accounted for by the fact that these London Separatists were in full doctrinal sympathy with the then predominantly Calvinistic views of the English Established Church from which they had come out, and did not feel the necessity of demonstrating their doctrinal soundness, as they were shortly after impelled to do, when settled among strangers in a foreign land.

---

[1] See Dexter, *Cong. as seen*, pp. 106, 107, 235–239, 351.

A TRVE DESCRIPTION OVT

OF THE WORD OF GOD,

of the visible Church.[1]

AS there is but * one God and Father of all, one Lord over all, and one Spirit: So is there but ‡ one truth, one Faith, one Salvation, one Church, called in one hope, ioyned in one profession, guided by one † rule, even the Word of the most high. * *Genes. 1. 1. Exod. 20. 3.* ‡ *1 Tim. 2. 4. Phil. 1 27. Ephe. 2. 18. Ioh. 8 41.* † *Deut. 6. 25. Rom. 10. 8. 2 Tim. 3. 15. Ioh. 8, 51 1 Ioh 2. 3, 4. &c.*

This Church as it is vniversallie vnderstood, conteyneth in it all the ♣ Elect of God that have bin, are, or shalbe: But being considered more particularlie, as it is seen in this present world, it consisteth of a companie and fellowship of * faithful and holie people ‡ gathered in the name of Christ Iesus, their only † King, ' Priest, and ♣ Prophet,* worshipping him aright, being ‡ peaceablie and quietlie governed by his Officers and lawes,† keping the vnitie of faith in the bond of peace & love 'vnfained. ♣ Genes. 17. chap. 1 Pet. 1 2. Revel. 7. 9. *1 Cor. 10. 3. Ioh. 17, 10. 20.* * *Psal. 111. 1. & 149. 1. Isa. 62. 12. Ephes. 1, 1. 1 Cor. 1. 2. Deut. 14. 2.* ‡ *Deut. 12, 5. Ioh. 6, 37 & 3. 14. & 12. 32. Luke 17. 37.* † *Gen. 44. 10. Psal. 45 6. Zach 9. 9. Heb. 1, 8.* ' *Rom. 8. 34. Ioh 17. chap. Heb. 5. 9. & 8, 1. & 4. 14.* ♣ *Deut. 18, 15. Mat. 17. 5. Heb. 1, 2. Gen. 14. 18.* * *Exo 20. 4. 5. 6. 7. 8 Lev. 10. 5. Ioh 4. 23.* ‡ *Mat. 11. 29. 1 Cor. 11, 16. Mar. 13, 34. Rev. 22. 9.* † *Ephe. 4. 3. 1 Cor. 1. 13. Mar. 9. 50.* ' *Ioh. 13. 34. 1 Cor. 13. 4. 1 Pet. 1. 22. 1 Ioh 3. 18.*

Most * ioyful, excellent, and glorious things are everie where in the Scriptures spoken of this Church. It is called the ‡ Citie, † House ♣ Temple, & 'mountaine of the eternal God: the * chosen generation. the holie nation. the peculiar people, the ‡ Vineyard, the † garden enclosed, the spring shut vp, the sealed fountaine, the

[1] From the 2d edition, now in the Dexter Collection of Yale University.

orchyard of pomgranates, with sweet fruites, the ♣ heritage, the ″kingdome of Christ: [2] yea his * sister, his love, his spouse, his ‡ Queene, & his † bodie, the ioye of the whole earth. To this societie is the ♣ covenant and all the promises made of * peace, of love, and ‡ of salvation, of the † presence of God, of his graces, of his power, and of his * protection. * Psal. 87. 3. ‡ *Ibid.* † *1 Tim. 3, 15. Heb. 3, 6.* ♣ *1 Cor. 3, 17. 'Isaiah 2, 2. Micha, 4, 1. Zach. 8, 3.* * *1 Pet. 2. 9.* ‡ *Isaiah. 5, 1. & 27, 2.* † *Song. 4, 12. Isa. 51, 3.* ♣ *Isa. 19, 25.* ″ *Micha. 5, 2. Mat. 3. 2. Ioh. 3, 5.* * *Song. 5. 2.* ‡ *Psal. 45. 9.* † *1 Cor. 12. 27. Ephes. 1. 23.* ♣ *Gil. 4, 28. Rō. 9. 4.* * *Psalm. 147. 14. 2 Thes. 3. 16.* ‡ *Isay. 46, 13. Zach. 14, 17.* † *Isa. 60. ch. Ezech. 47. ch. Zach. 4, 12.* * *Ezech. 48, 35. Mat. 28, 20. Isai. 62. chap.*

And surely if this Church be considered in her partes, it shal appeare most beautifull, yea most wonderfull, and even ‡ ravishing the senses to conceive, much more to behold, what then to enioy so blessed a communion. For behold, her † King and Lord is the King of peace, & Lord himself of all glorie. She enioyeth most holie and heavenlie * lawes, most faithfull and vigilant ♣ Pastours, most syncere & pure ″ Teachers, most careful and vpright ‡ Governours, most diligent and trustie † Deacons, most loving and sober * Releevers, and a most * humble, meek, obedient, faithfull, and loving people, everie ‡ stone living elect and precious, everie stone hath his beautie, his † burden, and his * order. All bound to ‡ edifie one another, exhort, reprove, & comfort one another † lovingly as to their owne members, * faithfully as in the eyes of God. ‡ Song. 6. 4. 9. † Isai. 62. 11. Ioh. 12. 15. Heb. 2. 7. 8. * *Mat. 11, 30. 1 Ioh. 5, 3.* ♣ *Eph. 4. 11. Act. 20. ch.* ″ *Rō. 12 7.* ‡ *1 Cor. 12. 28. Rom. 12. 8.* † *Actes. 6. ch.* * *Rom. 12, 8.* ♣ *Mat. 5, 5. Ezec. 36. 38. Isa. 60, 8. Deut. 18. 9–13.* ‡ *1 Pet. 2, 5. 1 King. 7, 9. Zac. 14, 21.* † *Gal. 6, 2.* * *1 Cor. 12 ch. Rom. 12, 3. &c.* ‡ *Heb. 10. 24.* † *Lev. 19, 17. 1 Thes. 4, 9.* * *Col. 3, 23. 1 Ioh. 3. 20.*

No ‡ Office here is ambitiously affected, no † law wrongfully wrested or * wilfully neglected, no ✠ trueth hid or perverted, ″ everie one here hath fredome and power (not disturbing the peaceable order of the Church) to vtter his complaintes and griefes, & freely to reprove the transgression and errours of any without exception of persons. ‡ *2 Cor. 2, 17. 3 Ioh. 9.* † *1 Tim. 4, 2. 3. & 5. 21. & 6. 14. Gal. 6, 12.* * *1 Cor. 5.* ✠ *Ier. 23, 28. 1 Tim. 3, 15.* ″ *1 Cor. 6. & 14, 30. Col. 4, 17.*

[3] Here is no *intrusion or climing vp an other way into the sheepefolde, then ‡ by the holy & free election of the Lordes holie and free people, and that according to the Lordes ordinance, humbling themselves by fasting and prayer before the Lord, craving the direction of his holy Spirit, for the triall and approving of giftes, &c. ‡ Ioh *10, 1.* † *Actes. 1, 23. & 6, 3. & 14. 23.*

Thus they orderly proceed to ordination by fasting and prayer, in which *action the Apostles vsed laying on of handes. Thus hath everie one of the people interest in the election and ordination of their officers, as also in the administration of their offices, vpon ‡ transgression, offence, abuse, &c. having an especiall care vnto the inviolable order of the Church, as is aforesaid. * 1 Tim. 4. 14. & 5. 22. ‡ Luk. *17, 3. Rom. 16, 17. Col. 4, 17.*

Likewise in this Church they have holy † lawes, as limits & bondes, which, it is lawfull at no hand to transgresse. They have lawes to direct them in the choise of everie officer, what kind of men the Lord will have. Their Pastour must be apt to *teach, no yong Scholer, ‡ able to divide the worde aright, † holding fast that faithful word, according to doctrine, that he may be able also to exhort, rebuke, improve, with wholesome doctrine, & to convince them that say against it: He must be *a man that loveth goodnes: he must be wise, righteous, holy, temperate: he must be of life vnreproveable, as Gods Steward: hee must be generally well reported of, & one that ruleth his owne houshold vnder obedience with al honestie: he must be modest, humble, meek, gentle, & loving: hee must be a man of great ‡ patience, compassion, labour and diligence: hee must alwaies be carefull and watchfull over the flock whereof the Lord hath made him overseer, with al willingnes & chearefulnes, not holding his office in respect of persons, but doing his duetie to everie soule, as he will aunswer before the chief Shepheard, &c. † Mat. 5. 19. 1 Tim. 1. 18. * Deut. 33. 10. *Mal. 2. 7. 1 Tim. 3, 1. &c.* ‡ *2 Tim. 2, 15.* † *Tit. 1, 9. 2 Tim. 4, 2.* * *Tit. 1, 7, 8.* ‡ *Num. 12, 3. 7. Isay. 50, 4. 5. 6. Iere 3, 15. Ezec. 34, 18. Act. 20 ch. 1 Pet. 5, 1, 2, 3, 4. 1 Tim. 5, 21.*

Their Doctor or Teacher must be a man apt to teach, able to diuide the word of God aright, and to diliver sound and wholesom doctrine from the same, still building vpon that sound groundwork, he must be mightie in the Scriptures, able to convince the gainsayers, & carefull to deliver his doctrine pure, sound & plaine, not with curiositie or affectation, but so that it may edifie the most simple, approving it to every mans conscience: he must be of life vnreproveable, one that can [4] governe his owne houshold, he must be of manners sober, temperate, modest, gentle and loving, &c. *1 Tim. 3. chap. Titus. 1. ch. 2 Tim. 2, 15. 1 Cor. 1. 17. & 2, 4.*

Their Elders must be of wisedome and iudgement endued with the Spirit of God, able to discerne between cause & cause, between plea & plea, & accordingly to prevent & redres evilles, alwayes vigilant & intending to see the statutes, ordinances, and lawes of God kept in the Church, and that not onelie by the people in obedience, but to see the Officers do their dueties. These men must bee of life likewise vnreproveable, governing their owne families orderly, they must be also of maners sober, gentle, modest, loving, temperate, &c. Numb. 11. 24, 25. *2 Chro. 19. 8. Actes. 15. ch. 1 Tim. 3. & 5. chap.*

Their Deacons must be men of honest report, having the mysterie of the faith in a pure conscience, endued with the holy Ghost: they must be grave, temperate, not given to excesse, nor to filthie lucre. *Actes. 6, 3. 1 Tim. 3, 8. 9.*

Their Relievers or Widowes must be women of 60. yeares of age at the least, for avoyding of inconveniences: they must be well reported of for good works, such as have nourished their children, such as have bin harberous to straungers: diligēr & serviceable to the Saints, cōpassionate & helpful to them in adversitie, given to everie good worke, continuing in supplications and prayers night and day. *1 Tim. 5. 9. 10.*

These Officers muste first be duely proved, then if they be found blameles, administer, &c. *1 Tim. 3 10.*

Nowe as the persons, giftes, conditions, manners, life, and proofe of these officers, is set downe by the holie Ghost: So are their offices limited, severed, and divers: *1 Cor. 12. 12. 18. 28.*

The Pastours office is, to feed the sheep of Christ in green and wholesome pastures of his word, and lead them to the still waters, even to the pure fountaine and river of life. Hee must guyde and keep those sheep by that heauenly sheephook & pastorall staffe of the word, thereby drawing them to him, thereby looking into their soules, even into their most secret thoughtes: Thereby discerning their diseases, and thereby curing them: applying to every disease a fit and cōuenient medicine, & according to the qualitie & danger of the disease, give warning to the Church, that they may orderly proceed to excommunication.

Further, he must, by this his sheepehook watch over and defend his flock from rauenous beastes and the Wolfe, and take the litle foxes. &c. *Psa. 23. Lev. 10, 10, 11. Nū. 18. 1. Ezek. 44. 23. & 33, & 34. Ioh. 21. 15. Act. 20. 28. 1 Pet. 5. 1.–4. Zach. 11. 7. Rev. 22. 2. Luk. 12. 42. 2 Cor. 10. 4. 5. Heb. 4, 12. Ioh. 10, 11, 12. Song. 2. 15.*

[5] The Doctours office is alreadie sett downe in his description: His speciall care must bee. to build vpon the onely true groundwork, golde, silver, and pretious stones, that his work may endure the triall of the fire. and by the light of the same fire, reveale the Tymber, Hay, and Stubble of false Teachers: hee must take diligent heed to keep the Church from errours. And further hee must deliver his doctrine so plavnlie simplie, and purelie, that the church may increase with the increasing of God, & growe vp vnto him which is the head, Christ Iesus. *1 Cor. 3 11. 12. Levit. 10. 10. Ezech. 33 1. 2, &c. and 44. 24 Mal. 2, 6 1 Cor. 3, 11. 1 Cor. 1 17. 1 Tim. 4, 16. & 6. 20. Ephe 2, 20 Heb. 6, 1. 1 Pet 2, 2.*

The office of the Auncientes is expressed in their description: Their especiall care must bee, to see the ordinaunces of God truely taught and and practized, aswel by the officers in dooing their duetie vprightlie, as to see that the people obey willinglie and readily. It is their duetie to see the Congregation holily and quietly ordered, and no way disturbed, by the contentious and disobedient froward and obstinate: not taking away the libertie of the least, but vpholding the right of all, wiselie iudging of times and circumstances. They must bee readie assistauntes to the Pastour and Teachers, helping to beare their burden, but not intruding into their office. Num. 11. 16. Deut. 1. 13 & 16. 18. 2 Chro. *19, 8 Exo 39, 42. 1 Tim. 3, 15. 2 Tim. 1, 13. 1 Cor. 11, 16. and 14 33. Gal. 2, 4. 5, 14 Col 4, 16, 17. Act. 20. 1 Pet. 5, 1. Rom. 12, 8.*

The Deacons office is, faithfully to gather & collect by the ordinance of the Church, the goods and benevolence of the faithfull, and by the same direction, diligentlie and trustilie to distribute them according to the necessitie of the Saincts. Further they must enquire & consider of the proportion of the wantes both of the Officers and other poore, and accordinglie relate vnto the Church, that provision may be made. *Actes 6. Rom 12, 8.*

The Relievers & Widowes office is, to minister to the sicke, lame, wearie, & diseased, such helpefull comforts as they need, by watching, tending and helping them: Further, they must shew good example to the yonger Women, in sober, modest, & godly conversation, avoyding idlenes, vaine talke, & light behaviour. *Rom. 12, 8. 1 Tim. 5, 9. &c.*

These Officers, though they be divers and severall, yet are they not severed, least there should be a division in the body, but they are as members of the bodie, having the same case [care] one of another, ioyntlie doing their severall dueties to the service of the Sainctes, and to the edification of the Bodie of Christ, till wee all meet together in the perfect measure of the fulnes of Christ, by whom all the bodie being in the meane whyle thus coupled and knit togither by everie ioynt for the [6] furniture thereof, according to the effectuall power which is in the measure of everie part, receiveth increase of the bodie, vnto the edifying of it self in love: neither can any of these Offices be wanting, without grievous lamenes, & apparant deformitie of the bodie, yea violent injurie to the Head Christ Iesus. Luk. 9. 46. 47. 48. Ioh. 13. *12.–17. 1 Cor. 12, 12. 25. 28. Ephes 4, 11, 12, 13. 16.*

Thus this holie armie of saintes, is marshalled here in earth by these Officers, vnder the conduct of their glorious Emperour CHRIST, that victorious Michaell. Thus it marcheth in this most heavenlie order, & gratious araye, against all Enimies both bodilie and ghostlie: peaceable in it self as Ierusalem, terrible to the enemy as an Armie with baners, triumphing over their tyrannie with patience, their crueltie with mekenes, and over Death it self with dying. Thus through the blood of that spotles Lambe, and that Word of their testimonie, they are more then Conquerours, brusing the head of the Serpent: yea through the power of his Word, they have power to cast down Sathan like lightning: to tread vpon Serpents aud Scorpions: to cast downe strong holds, and everie thing that exalteth it self against GoD. The gates of Hell and all the Principalities and powers of the world, shall not prevayle against it. Rom. 12. ch. 1 Cor. 12. Rev. 14. 1. 2. Song. 6. 3. *Rev. 12. 11. Luk. 10, 18, 19.* 2 *Cor. 10. 5. Mat. 16, 18. Rō. 8, 38, 39.*

Further, he hath given them the keyes of the Kingdome of Heaven, that whatsoever they bynd in earth by his word, shalbe bound in heaven: and whatsoever they loose on earth, shalbe loosed in heaven. *Mat. 16, 19. Iohn. 20, 23. Mat. 18, 18.*

Now this power which Christ hath given vnto his Church, and to every member of his Church, to keep it in order, hee hath not left it to their discretions and lustes to be vsed or neglected as they will, but in his last Will and Testament, he hath sett downe both an order of proceeding, and an end to which it is vsed. Mat. 16. 16. 19 & 18. 15. *16. 17, 18. & 28. 20. Deut. 12, 31. 32. Rev. 22, 18. 19.*

If the fault be private, holy and loving admonition & reproof is to be vsed, with an inward desire & earnest care to winne their brother: But if hee wil not heare, yet to take two or three other brethren with him, whom he knoweth most meet for that purpose, that by the mouth of two or three witnesses, every word may be confirmed: And if he refuse to heare them, then to declare the matter to the Church, which ought severelie and sharpelie to reprehend, gravelie to admonish, and lovinglie to perswade the partie offending: shewing him the heynousnes of his offence, & the daunger of his obstinacie, & the fearefull judgements of the Lord. Lev. 19. 17. 18. Mat. 18. 15. Deut. *19, 15. Mat, 18, 16.*

[7] All this notwithstanding the Church is not to hold him as an enimie, but to admonish him and praye for him as a Brother, prooving if at any time the Lord will give him repentaunce. For this power is not given them to the destruction of any, but to the edification of all. *2 Thes. 3, 15. 2 Cor. 10, 8. and 13, 10.*[1]

If this prevaile not to draw him to repentance, then are they in the Name aud power of the Lord IESVS with the whole Congregation, reverently in prayer to proceed to excommunication, that is vnto the casting him out of their congregation & fellowship, covenaunt & protectiō of the Lord, for his disobedience & obstinacie, & committing him to Sathan for the destructiō of the flesh, that the Spirit may be saved in the day of the Lord Iesus, if such bee his good wil and pleasure. Mat. 18. *17. 1 Cor 5 11.*

Further, they are to warne the whole Congregation and all other faithfull, to hold him as a Heathen and Publicane, & to absteine themselves from his societie, as not to eat or drink with him, &c. vnles it bee such as of necessitie must needes, as his Wife, his Children, and Familie: yet these (if they be members of the Church) are not to joyne to him in any spirituall exercise. Mat. 18. 17. 1 Cor. 5. 11.

If the offence bee publike, the partie is publiquely to bee reproved, and admonished: if hee then repent not, to proceed to

[1] The difference between the first and second editions of this creed lies in the position of this paragraph. In the first edition it was placed "after the excommunication," *i. e.*, apparently after the paragraph beginning, "Further, they are to warne." (See note to page 28 as to the alleged reasons for this change.)

excommunication, as aforesaid. 1 Tim. 5. 20. Gal. 2. 14. Ios. 7. 19. 2 Cor. 7. 9.

The repentance of the partie must bee proportionable to the offence, viz. If the offence bee publique, publique: If private, private: humbled, submissive, sorrowfull, vnfained, giving glorie to the Lord. *Lev. 19, 17. 18. Pro. 10, 12. Rom. 12, 19. & 13, 10. and 14. 1.*

There must great care bee had of admonitions, that they bee not captious or curious finding fault when none is; neyther yet in bitternes or reproch: for that were to destroye and not to save our brother: but they must bee carefullie done, with prayer going before, they must dee seazoned with trueth, grauitie, love & peace. Mat. 18. 15. & 26. 8. Gal. 6. 1. 2. *2 Tim. 2. 24. Mark. 9, 50. Ephes.* 4, *29. Iam. 5, 15, 19, 20.*

Moreover in this Church is an especiall care had by every member thereof, of offences: The Strong ought not to offend the Weak, nor the weake to iudge the stronge: but all graces here are given to the service and edification of each other in love and long suffering. *Luke. 17, 1. Pro. 10, 12. Rom. 14, 13, 19. Gal. 6, 2.*

In this Church is the Truth purelie taught, and surelie kept: heer is the Covenaunt, the Sacramentes, and promisses, the graces, the glorie, the presence, the worship of God, &c. Gen. 17. ch. Lev. 26. 11. 12. *Isa. 44. 3. Gal. 4, 28 & 6, 16. Isay, 60, 15. Deut. 4, 12. 13. Isay, 56, 7. 1 Tim. 3, 15. Isay. 52. 8.*

[8] Into this Temple entreth no vncleane thing, neither whatsoever worketh abhominatiōs or lyes, but they which are writē in the Lambes Book of life. *Isay. 52. 1. Ezek. 44 9. Isay. 35. 8. Zach. 14. 21. Rev. 21, 27.*

But without this CHVRCH shalbe dogs and Enchaunters, & Whoremongers, & Murderers, and Idolatours, and whosover loveth & maketh lyes. *Rom. 2. 9. Rev. 22. 15.*

1589.

III

THE SECOND CONFESSION OF THE LONDON-AMSTERDAM CHURCH, 1596

EDITIONS AND REPRINTS

I. *A Trve Confession*, etc.[1] 1596. No place of publication given, but almost certainly printed at Amsterdam.

II. *Confessio Fidei Anglorvm Qvorvndam in Belgia Exvlantivm: Vna cum Præfatione ad Lectorem: Quam ab omnibus legi et animadverti cupimus*, etc., 1598. Probably printed at Amsterdam. A Latin translation of I. with a new preface and some slight modification of a few articles.

III. *The Confession of faith of certayne English people living in exile in the Low Countreys*, etc., 1598. Apparently an English edition of II.

IV. A Dutch translation, before 1600.[2]

V. Printed also in English in *Certayne Letters*,[3] *translated into English*, etc.; 1602.

VI. In English also in Johnson and Ainsworth's, *Apologie or Defence of svch Trve Christians as are commonly (but vniustly) called Brovvnists:* etc., 1604. pp. 4–29. (Reprint of III.).

VII. In Latin, *Confessio Fidei Anglorum quorundam in Inferiori Germania exulantium*, etc., 1607. 16° pp. ii, 56.

VIII. In English, same title as No. III., with the addition of the Points of Difference from the Church of England, given in the next chapter, 1607.

IX. In Dutch, in a translation of No. VI., 1614.

X. In Dutch, in a new translation of No. VI., Amsterdam, 1670.

LITERATURE

Hanbury, *Historical Memorials*, I: 91–98, with extracts from the preface and articles; Punchard, *History of Congregationalism*, 2d ed., Boston [1867], III: 223–226; Dexter, *Cong. as seen*, pp. 270, 271, 278–282, 299–301, 316; Fletcher, *History . . . of Independency*, 2d ed., London, 1862, II: 215–222.

THE organization of the London Church, perfected in September, 1592, by the choice of Francis Johnson[4] as pastor and John Greenwood as teacher, was followed by Greenwood's speedy

---

[1] Full title in connection with the reprint at the close of this chapter.

[2] Mentioned by Francis Johnson in *An Answer to Maister H. Iacob*, etc., p. 134. I owe this information to the late Dr. Dexter.

[3] The letters here referred to were between Francis Junius, professor of Theology at Leyden, and the exiled church. See Dexter, *Cong. as seen*, p. 301.

[4] Francis Johnson was born in 1562, of a Yorkshire family of some prominence. While a student at Cambridge, and still more as a fellow of Christ's College at that University, he became imbued with Presbyterian principles. His public proclamation of his views in 1589 was fol-

arrest and execution. Johnson shared also in his colleague's committal and detention,[1] though his life was spared; and in the spring of 1593 no less than fifty-six of the little flock followed their pastor and teacher into confinement in the London prisons.[2] These multiplied arrests, embracing many of humble position and little political importance, led the government to look upon emigration as the best method of ridding London of the Separatists; and therefore, though Johnson and other of the leaders were kept in prison, the way was made easy, from the summer of 1593 onward, for them to slip over to Holland.[3] After being scattered for a time, it would appear, in villages in the neighborhood of Amsterdam, the bulk of the congregation found their home in that city itself. This regathering of the scattered church in Amsterdam, which took place as early as 1595,[4] was accompanied or followed by the election[5] of

---

lowed by his imprisonment. After considerable influence had been brought to bear on the authorities by his friends, he was allowed to leave England, and became pastor of the Puritanically inclined church of English merchants at Middelburg in the Dutch province of Zeland. It was while here, in 1591, that Barrowe and Greenwood's *Plaine Refvtation of M. Giffards Booke*, etc., came to his knowledge, as it was passing through the press at Dort. Having notified the English ambassador, Johnson was commissioned to destroy the forth-coming edition. This he did, saving two of the volumes for himself and a friend. But in reading the work he was convinced of the truth of the principles it set forth. He therefore gave up his pleasant position at Middelburg, and going to London sought out Barrowe and Greenwood in prison. From that time onward he was associated with the fortunes of the London church. Elected its pastor in 1592, he was imprisoned in London from 1593 to 1597, and was then released on condition of going to a newly projected colony in the Gulf of St. Lawrence. The loss of one of the vessels on the Nova Scotian coast compelled the return of the expedition to England. Once back in London Johnson contrived to escape to Holland in the autumn of 1597. The London church was thus completely transferred to Amsterdam. Johnson's pastorate here was stormy. In 1610 the church was divided between him and Ainsworth, in a quarrel in which Ainsworth seems to have been in the right. But whatever his faults may have been, he was a man of sincerity, earnestness, and ability. He died in January, 1618, at Amsterdam. His controversial works were numerous and vigorous. Dexter, *Cong. as seen*, Bibliog. enumerates nine titles. Compare for Johnson's biography Brook, *Lives of the Puritans*, II: 89–106. Hanbury, *Memorials*, I, Ch. V, and following: Dexter, as cited, pp. 263, 264, 272–278, 283–310; Gordon in *Dictionary of National Biography*, XXX: 9–11. The account of his conversion is given by Gov. William Bradford of Plymouth, in a *Dialogue*. written in 1648, and is distinctly stated to be based on Johnson's own statement, Young, *Chronicles of the Pilgrims*, pp. 424, 425. Boston, 1844. A few facts may be found in Neal, *History of the Puritans*, Toulmin's ed. Bath, 1793, I: 468; II: 43–49.

[1] Both were arrested Dec. 5, 1592. Dexter, *Cong. as seen*, p. 266. [2] *Ibid.*

[3] *Ibid*, pp. 266–268. Their departure was expedited by a law passed by Parliament in 1593, entitled "An Act to retain the Queen's Majesty's subjects in due obedience," providing that any above 16 years of age who should refuse to go to church for a month, or attend any religious conventicle, should be imprisoned without bail until he publicly submit and conform. If he refuse this, on conviction he is to "abjure this realm of England, and all other the Queen's dominions for ever." If he return he is guilty of "felony, without benefit of clergy." *i. e.*, worthy of death. 35 Eliz., 1, 2, 3, 5. T. W. Davids, *Annals of Evangelical Nonconformity in the County of Essex*, London, 1863, pp. 86, 87. See also Neal, *History of the Puritans*, I: 465–467. Perry, *History of the English Church* (Student's Series, 1881), p. 336.

[4] *Ibid.*, p. 268. [5] The date is entirely uncertain.

Henry Ainsworth[1] to the vacant post of teacher, the pastor, Francis Johnson, still remaining in his London prison. Conscious once more of a distinct, though divided, corporate existence, and domiciled in a foreign city, the church desired to define its doctrinal position, lest it should fall under the charge of heresy; and to make clear its views on polity, lest its separation from the English Establishment should seem unjustifiable schism or rebellion against civil authority. With this two-fold object in view, therefore, the London-Amsterdam church put forth a new creed sometime in 1596.

Though some consultation was probably held between the exiles at Amsterdam and those of the flock who were still in confinement in London,[2] the Preface of the Confession clearly indicates it was chiefly the work of the former.[3] Who of the church were instrumental in its preparation cannot be surely affirmed, but the conjecture is natural that a large share of the labor fell to Ainsworth. Probably the Preface was not entirely from his hand. Its tone is

[1] Henry Ainsworth, the most learned of the founders of modern Congregationalism and one of its saintliest ministers, was born, according to his own testimony, in 1570 or '71; but all the details of his early life are tantalizingly obscure. It is probable that he never enjoyed a university education, but, however acquired, his learning was from our first acquaintance with him far beyond that which was usual even among professedly learned men. He wrote a Latin style of considerable felicity, while his knowledge of Hebrew, quickened and increased by opportunities for intercourse with Jews which Amsterdam afforded, was such that Bradford was able to record the opinion of competent scholars at the university of Leyden that "he had not his better for the Hebrew tongue in the university, nor scarce in Europe." Even better testimony to the extent and modernness of his knowledge of Hebrew is the fact that his *Annotations* on the Pentateuch and Psalms are held in esteem to this day as a still valuable aid to the study of the Scriptures. The same obscurity which veils Ainsworth's early life and education hides from us all certain knowledge as to the circumstances which led to his adoption of Congregational views or his first association with the Separatists. His abilities, when once known, would readily account for his election to the teachership of the exiled church. A man of peace, Ainsworth's service in the Amsterdam Church was vexed by the strifes which rent that distracted body, and which finally, in 1610, led to a separation between him and Johnson. He remained in his ministry at Amsterdam till his death in 1622 or 1623, an event which Neal and Brook attributed to poison, and Dexter in his *Cong. as seen*, suggests may have been due to pulmonary complaints. The true cause was, however, later discovered by Dr. Dexter, and the full proofs will doubtless soon be published. I may perhaps be permitted to say that the disease was the stone, and that poison had no share in Ainsworth's death. Ainsworth's works were very numerous. Some 23 are enumerated by Dr. Dexter in *Cong. as seen*, p. 346, and further particulars may be found in the *Dictionary of National Biography*, I: 192, 193.

For Ainsworth's biography see Bradford, *Dialogue*, in Young's *Chronicles of the Pilgrims*, pp. 448, 449. Neal, *History of the Puritans*, Toulmin's ed., II: 43–45. Stuart in preface to reprint of *Two Treatises*, *i. e.*, Ainsworth's *Communion of Saincts* and *Arrow against Idolatry*, Edinboro, 1789. Brook, *Lives of the Puritans*, II: 299–303. Hanbury, *Memorials*, I: Chs. V–XXIV *passim*. Dexter, *Cong. as seen*, pp. 269, 270, 299–346. W. E. A. Axon in *Dict. National Biography*, I: 191–194.

[2] Dexter, *Cong. as seen*, p. 270.

[3] See *Preface*, opening paragraph.

one of sense of personal wrong, somewhat in contrast to the introduction to the Latin translation which is almost certainly the work of his pen. But whether many or few of the London-Amsterdam church shared in its preparation, the *Confession* was put forth as the symbol of the whole body, and its value in witnessing to their doctrine, polity, and attitude toward the English Establishment from which they had come out is correspondingly great.

The Preface breathes a spirit of hostility to the supporters of the National Church natural in men who had suffered so much at the hands of the prelates. But it is a hostility based clearly on principle. Whatever added touch of bitterness the arraignment may have derived from the recollection of prisons and death, the real motive of its composition was not enmity to persons, but a profound conviction that the English Church, when tried by the Scripture standards, was un-Christian. As such it was, in these men's thinking, a positive peril to the soul to be of its membership. And if the premises of their argument are correct, if their principle, which was but a logical application of the fundamental thought of the Reformation, is right in asserting that nothing should be practiced in the government of the church or the worship of God which is not fully patterned in the Bible, the cogency of the arguments of the Preface is undeniable. With far more readableness of style than is usual in controversial writings of the period, the writers of this introduction put questions to their opponents regarding the divine warrant of the liturgy, rites, ministry, and membership of the Church of England which must have been exceedingly difficult for the Puritan wing of the Establishment to answer. And at the same time they gave biographical facts regarding the martyrs of their own body which are not elsewhere to be found. No other single document of so brief compass so well sets forth the sufferings and the motives of these much-tried Separatists.

The creed itself consists of forty-five articles, treating some of doctrine, others of polity. In matters of belief they are in substantial harmony with the positions of the Calvinistic churches of the Continent, and with the Puritan wing of the Church of England.

On these heads their creed is but little more than a re-affirmation of the current beliefs of a vast majority of the Protestant churches at that day. In polity it lays down the propositions already presented in the *Trve Description*, but with much greater fullness of elaboration. It is no longer an ideal sketch. Questions of actual administration have evidently led to minuter definition in regard to certain problems. An instance or two may illustrate. In the *Trve Description* no provision was made for the reception of the members of one church into another, or for the relations of church to church. Now it is hard to see, perhaps, how these questions could have become very pressing to the London-Amsterdam church. But the divided condition of that body, if nothing else, had caused them to be thought of; and therefore the creed of 1596 enunciates the truly Congregational, because truly Scriptural, doctrine that members coming from one church to another should bring certificates of their character and standing.[1] It declares further that while the individual independence of each church is to be recognized, churches owe counsel and help to one another in matters of more than usual concern.[2] The *Trve Description*, in similar manner, made no provision for the removal of such church officers as might prove unworthy of their trust, save what might be implied in the very general remarks as to the right of a church to excommunicate any offending member. The creed before us, on the contrary, declares that a church may depose a minister unfit for his post, and counsels procedure to excommunication only when continued evil conduct demands a further step.[3] These examples, which the student can readily multiply for himself, show plainly that the creed of 1596 is not merely greater in verbal extent than that of 1589, but marks a growth in appreciation and application of Congregational principles.

The document is more than a general statement of faith and polity. It is evidently the answer of its writers also to the question which must frequently have been put to them as to the method of procedure by which they would reform the Church of England if they could have their way. The thirty-second to the

[1] Article 37. [2] Article 38. [3] Article 23.

thirty-ninth articles are a program for action. They would have all who are convinced of the truth of the charges here formulated against the Establishment lay down any offices which they may have held within it and at once renounce its communion. No one, holding the rightful view of what Christ intended a church to be, is to contribute longer to the financial support of the legal church, even though such a refusal make him obnoxious to the law.[1] These religious men, who have come forth from the Church of England, are next to join in local congregations, united by a covenant and a common confession of faith.[2] In these congregations any who are able, and have the approval of their associates, are to teach and preach ; but the sacraments are not to be administered until some of these preachers, whose qualifications have appeared eminent, are chosen and ordained to the divinely appointed offices of pastor, teacher, elder, and deacon, or as many of these offices as the church finds men fitted to fill. Then baptism is to be administered to the children and wards of the members of the local church, and its members of mature years are to unite in the Lord's supper.[3] But baptism does not admit its recipient to the full privileges of the church. While all who will are to be urged to be present at the preaching of God's word, and while the duty of professing faith in Christ is to be pressed upon them, the church is to be increased only by the admission of those who make a profession of personal belief and who publicly unite in the covenant fellowship.[4] Thus the Christian people of any given town in England, so the makers of this creed thought, might be released from the Establishment and organized into true churches. But what should be done with the Establishment and with those who refused to come out of it? The answer is characteristic of the times, and illustrative of the partial vision to which these men had attained. The old system was to be uprooted and the buildings and revenues which it enjoyed were to be confiscated by civil authority. The magistrate was to enforce upon the reluctant the commands of God.[5] There is something ludicrous as well as pathetic in the

[1] Article 32.
[2] Article 33.
[3] Article 34, 35.
[4] Article 37.
[5] Article 39.

readiness with which these exiles of Amsterdam and prisoners of London call upon the power from which they had themselves suffered so much to enforce on others that which they had had to bear. But in this matter the nineteenth century is apt to judge the sixteenth hardly. Such a thought as that of honest difference of opinion in regard to the main, and even the minor truths of Christianity was foreign to the great mass of men for more than two centuries after the Reformation. Dissent from their own convictions men believed to be due to defect in moral character, such failure to see the truth could be owing only to willfulness, or to a divine withholding of light which was in itself high evidence of the sinfulness of those thus deprived. There could be but one right view. These Separatists held it. They had called on their opponents to show its falsity, and to their thinking their opponents had failed. And since it is the duty of a magistrate, they thought, to support the truth, the magistrates of England should overthrow an Establishment, which civil government had so often altered during the last fifty years, and which the Separatists believed they had demonstrated to be utterly unworthy. We may well regret that these early Congregationalists and the founders of New England also did not share the truer view of Browne,[1] and of the Anabaptists regarding the limits of civil authority, but there is little reason for surprise that they did not.

This is, after all, a minor matter. England was not to be reformed on the lines here laid down. But as a statement of Congregationalism this creed marks a decided gain in clearness. As a setting forth of the essential and permanent features of the system in definite form, it was fitted to stand for many years, as the frequent reprints show it did stand, as an adequate and valued exposition of Congregational doctrine and polity.

As has already been seen, the creed, as it was issued in 1596, was preceded by an introduction breathing the spirit of strong indignation against the oppressors from whose hands the church had so recently escaped, and who still held some of the brethren in bondage. The very warmth of this feeling, justifiable as it was,

[1] See *ante*, p. 12.

rendered this preface less likely to be favorably received by those unfamiliar with English ecclesiastical affairs. And as the church at last gathered together all its scattered membership at Amsterdam (1597), and came to be more and more a recognized, though humble, element in the religious life of the city, the desire to set themselves right in the eyes of Protestant Christendom, which had prompted the original draft of the creed, impelled the brethren to make a translation of their profession into the only tongue which learned Europe could understand, and preface it with an account of the government and rites of the legally established church of their native country designed to make clear to the non-English reader the reasons for their separation. The new preface is milder in tone than the old, though it retains passages from the latter. But it cannot be said to have gained in strength or cogency. The translation of the old creed, thus introduced, appeared late in 1598;[1] and was, doubtless, the work of the scholarly Henry Ainsworth. Its typographical dress indicated the improved outward estate of the exiled company, as surely as the mute witness of the wretched printing and the scanty font of type revealed the dire poverty of these exiles for what they believed to be the truth of God at their first coming into Holland.

---

[1] Dexter, *Cong. as seen*, p. 299. The following articles were slightly revised, not for content, but for clearness of statement, in the edition of 1598; xvii, xxviii, xxx, xliii, and xliv.

A TRVE CONFESSI- | ON OF THE FAITH, AND HVM- | BLE ACKNOVVLEDGMENT OE THE ALE- | geance, vvhich vvee hir Maiesties Subjects, falsely called Brovvnists, | doo hould tovvards God, and yeild to hir Majestie and all other that | are ouer vs in the Lord. Set dovvn in Articles or Positions, for the | better & more easie vnderstanding of those that shall read yt: And | published for the cleering of our selues from those vnchristian slan- | ders of heresie, schisme, pryde, obstinacie, disloyaltie, | sedicion, &c. vvhich by our adversaries are | in all places given out against vs. | *wee beleeue therfore haue we spoken.* 2 *Cor.* 4, 13. | *But,* | *who hath beleeued our report, and vnto whom is the* | *arme of the Lord reueuled?* *Isai.* 53, 1. | M.D. XCVI.

[ii Blank.]

[iii]. To all that desire to feare, to loue, & to obey our Lord Iesus Christ, grace, wisdom and vnderstanding.

Thou[1] canst not lightly bee ignorant (gentle Reader) what evills and afflictions, for our profession and faith towards God wee haue susteined at the hands of our owne Nation: How bytterly wee haue been, an yet are, accused, reproched and persecuted wich [with] such mortall hatred, as yf wee were the most notorious obstinate hereticks, and disloyall subiects to our gracious Queen Elizabeth, that are this day to bee found in all the Land. And therfore, besides the dayly ignominie wee susteine at the hands of the Preachers and Prophets of our tyme, who have given theyr tongnes the reins to speacke despightfully of vs, wee haue been further miserably entreated by the Prelats and cheef of the Clergie: some of vs cast into most vile and noysome prisons and dungeons,*°[2] laden with yrons, and there, withont all pitie, deteyned manie yeeres, no man remembring our affliction: vntill our God released some of vs out of theyr cruell bands by death, as the Cities of Londō, Norwich, Glocester, Bury,[3] and manye other places of the land can testifie. Yet heere the malice of Satan stayed not it self, but raysed vp against vs a more greevous persecution, even vnto the violent death of some,†° and lamentable exile of vs all; causing heavie decrees to come forth against vs, that wee should forsweare our own Contrey

*° They shut op our lyves in the Dnngeon, they cast a stone upon vs. Lam. 3. 53.

†° Anno 1593. April. 10.[4]

[1] From this point onward the preface is in Old English black letter. I have tried to give it *literatim*, even to the misprints.

[2] This and the subsequent notes are on the margin of the pages, often with no mark indicating their exact reference to the text. When not so indicated I have added a o.

[3] Bury St. Edmunds.

[4] The martyrdom of Barrowe and Greenwood is probably meant, though that was Apl. 6.

& depart, or els bee slayne therein. This have onr adversaries vsed, as their last and best argument against vs, (when all other fayled) followinge the stepps of theyr bloody Prodecessors, the popish Priests and Prelats. Now therfore that the true cause of this their hostilitie & hard vsage of vs may appeere vnto all men; wee haue at lengh amyds our manie troubles, through Gods favonr, obteyned to publish vnto the view of the world, a confession of our fayth & hope in Christ, and loyal harts, towards our Prince, the rather to stop the mouths of impious and vnreasonable men, who have not ceased some of them, both openly in their Sermons & printed pamphlets, notoriously to accuse and defame vs, as alsoo by all indirect meanes secretly to suggest the malice of their owne evill harts, therby invegling our soveraign Prince and Rulers against vs: that when the true state of the controversie between them and vs shalbe manifested, the christian (or but indiffirent) Reader may iuge whether our adversaries have not followed the way of Cain and *a* Balaam, to kill and curse vs Gods sernants without cause. For if in this onr Confession appeere no matter worthie such mortal inmitie and persecution, then we protest (good Reader) that, to our knowledge, they neyther haue cause nor colour of cause so to entreat vs, the mayne and entire difference betwixt their Synagogs and vs, beeing in these Articles fully & wholly comprised.

An other motive inducing vs to the publication of this our testimonie, is, the rufull estate of our poore Contrymen, who remayne yet fast locked in Egipt, that hous of servants, in slavish subjection to strange LLs[1] & lawes, enforced to beare the burdens and iutollerable yoke of their popish canons & decrees, beeing subiect every day they rise to * 38 antichristian ecclesiasticall offices, and manie moe Romish statutes and traditions, almost without number: besides their high trangression dayly in their vaine will-worship of God, by reading over a few prescribed prayers and collects, which they haue translated verbatim out of the Mass-book, and which are yet taynted with manie popish hereticall errors and superstions, instead of true spirituall invocation vpon the name of the Lord.

[iv] These and manie other greevous enormities are amongst them, not suffred only but with a high hand mainteyned, and Gods servants, which by the powre of his Word and Spirit witnes against & condemne such abhominations, are both they & their testimonie, reiected, persecuted & plasphemed. What a wofull plight then are such people in, how great is their iniquitie, how fearfull indgments doo abide them: wee have therfore, for their sakes, manifested this onr Confession of and vowed obedience vnto that Fayth which was once gyven vnto the *a* Saincts, wherby they may bee drawne (God shewing mercy vnto them) vnto the same faith and obedience with vs, that they perish not in their sinnes. For how could wee behould so manie soules of our dear Contrymen to dye before our eyes & wee hould our peace: And wheras they have been heertofore greatly abused by their tyme-serving Priests, beeing givē to vnderstād that wee were a dangerous people, holding manie errors, renting our selves

[1] Lords?

* Arch Bbs. L.[ord] Bbs. Suffragans, Chancellors, Deanes, Arch-Deacōs, Commissaries, Officials, Doctors, Proctors, Registers, scribes, Purcevants, Summoners, Subdeans, chaplaines, Prebēdaries, Cannons, Peti-Canons, Gospellers, pistellers Chanters, Sub-chanters, Vergiers, organ-players, Queristers, Parsons, Vicars, Curats, Stipendaries, Vagrant-Preachers, Priests, Deacons or half Priests, Churchwardens, Sidemē Collectors, Clerks, Sextins.

a Gen. 4. Num. 12. *a* Jude 3.

from the tue Church, because of some infirmities in men, some falts in their worship, Ministerie, Church-gouvernment, etc. that wee were Donatists, Anabaptists, Brownists, Schismaticks, &c. these few leaves (wee trust) shal now cleer vs of these and such like criminations, and satisfie anie godly hart, yea every reasonable man, that will but with an indifferent ear heare our cause. For wee have always protested, and doo by these presents testifie vnto all mē, that wee neyther our selves doo, neyther accompt it lawfull for others to seprrate frō anie true church of Crist, for infirmities falts or errors whatsoever except their iniquitie bee come to such an heith, that for obstinatie they cease to be a true visible Church, aud bee refused and forsaken of God. And for this their renowmed Church of England, wee *a* have both by word and writing, proved it vnto them to bee false and counterfeit, deceyving hir children with vaine titles of the word, Sacraments, Ministerie, &c. having indeed none of these in the ordinance and powre of Christ emongst them. They have been shewed, that the people in Their Parish-assemblies, neyther were nor are meet stones for Gods house, meet members for Christs glorious body, vntill they *b* bee begotten by the seed of his word vnto fayth, and renewed by repentance. Their generall irreligious profannes ignorance, Atheisme and Machevelisme on the one side, & publique Idolitrie, vsuall blasphemie, swearing, lying, kylling, stealing, whoring, and all maner of imptetie [impiety] on the other side, *c* vtterly disableth them from beeing Citizens in the new Hierusalem, sonnes of God & heires with Christ and his Saints, vntill they become new creatures. Their slavish bondage vnto the antichristiaen tyrannous Prelats, whom they celibrate and honour as their Lords & reverend Fathers spiritnall, accepting their popish Canons and Iniunctions for laws in their Church, their marcked Priests, Preachers, Parsons, and Vicars &c. in lewe of Christs true Pastors and Teachers, running to their Courts and Consistories at every summons &c. doo manifest *d* whose servants they are, & to whom they yeeld their obedience. Their learned Ministerie even from the highest Arch-prelat to the lowest Vicare & half-Priest, thath [hath] been, by the powre of our Lord Jesus Christ, cast down into the smoky fornace of that pyt of bottomles diepth *e* from whence they arose, revealed by the light of his word, to bee strange, false, popish & antichristian, the very same, and no other, then were hatched and advanced in their Metropolitane Sinagoge of Rome, from whence they have feched the very patterne nnd mould of their Church, Ministerie, Service & Regiment, even the very expresse Character and image of that first wild beast of Italy, as all in whom anie spark of true light is, may easely discerne. With these and manie other lyke weightie arguments have wee pleaded against that our whorish mother, hir Priests and Prelats, which as a heavie mylstone presseth hir down to hell: for the vyalls of Gods wrathfull iudgments are powred vpon them, which maketh

a Conferences betwixt certeine Preachers and prysoners Marc, 1590[1]. Discoverey of the false Church 1590.[2] Refutation of Mr. Giffard prynted. 1591.[3]

b I Peter 1, 23. John 3, 3.

c Revel. 21, 27. 2 Cor. 5, 17. Ezech. 44, 9. Act 8, 37.

d Rom. 6, 16. Mat. 6, 24. Reue. 13, 16, & 14, 9. 10. &c.

e See Revel. 9, 3. with their owne annotatation, vpon that place. 2 King. 16, 10. 11. &c. Reu. 13, 14. Hos. 2, 2. Rev. 16, 10, 11.

[1] [Barrowe & Greenwood], *A collection of certaine Letters and Conferences, lately passed Betwixt Certaine Preachers, & Two Prisoners in the Fleet* [Dort], 1590.

[2] Barrowe, *A Brief Discouerie of the false Church*, etc. [Dort], 1590.

[3] Barrowe & Greenwood, *A Plaine Refvtation of M. Giffards Booke, intituled, A short treatise gainst the Donatistes of England*, etc. [Dort], 1591.

them so to [v] storme rage and curse, gnawing their tongues for sorrow & payne of these wounds, and not yet finding grace to repent of and turne from their sinnes. For when wee have proclamed this our testimonie against them, how have they behaved themselves, but as savage beasts renting and tearing vs with their teeth, never daring to come vnto the triall of the word of God, eyther by free wryting or conference, but greedily hunting after Christs poore lambes, and so manie as they could get into their pawes, misvsing their bodyes with all exqvisite tyrannie in long and lamentable emprisonment, bedsies [besides] despight and reproches without mesure. So that through their barbarous crueltie* 24. soules have perished in their prisons, with in the Cittie of London only, (besides other places of the Land) & that of late yeeres. Manie also have they, by their immanitie, caused to blaspheme and forsake the faith of our glorious Lord Jesus Christ, and many mo they terrifie and keep from the same. For all this, yet were not these savage men satisfied, though blood in abonndance ran out of their wyde mouths, but they procured certeine of vs (after manie yeeres emprisonment) to be indighted, arrayned, condemned and hanged as felons (how uniustly, thou Lord iust and true knowest) Henry Barrow, John Greenwood, and John Penry, whose perticular examinations araignments and maner of execution, with the circumstances about them, if thou didst truly vnderstand (gentle Reader) it would make thy hart to bleed, considering their vnchristian and vnnaturall vsage. About the same tyme they executed also one William Denis,[1] at Thetford in Northfolke, and long before they kylled two men, at Bury in Suffolk, Coppyn and Elias,[2] for the like testimonie. Others they deteyne in their prysons to this day, who looke for the like measure at their mercelesse hands, yf God in mercye release them not before. Our God (wee trust) will one day rayse vp an other John Fox, to gather and compile the Actes and Monuments of his later Martyrs, for the vew of posteritie, tho yet they seem to bee buryed in oblivion, and sleep in the dust. Then will this last infernall Clergie alsoo appeere in their proper colours, and be found nothing inferiour to their bloody predecessours in poysoned malice and and tyrannie, but rather even to exceed them, in regard of the tyme. Alas for our poore Countreye, that it should bee so againe defiled with the blood of the seints, which cryeth lowde from vnder the Altar, and speaketh no beter things for it, then did the blood of *a* Habel. Needs

* In Newgate Mr. Crane a man about 60 yeers of age Richard Jacson, Thomas Stevens, William Howton, Thomas Drewet, John Gwalter, Roger Ryppon, Robert Awoburne, Scipio Bellot, Robert Bowle, John Barnes beeing sic vnto death, was caryed forth & departed this lyfe shortly after. Mothor Maner of 60. yeers, Mother Roe of 60. yeers, Anna Tailour, Judeth Myller, Margaret Farrer beeing sick vnto death was caried forth, and ended hir lyfe within a day or two after. John Purdy in Brydwel, Mr. Denford in the Gate-house about 60. yeers of age. Father Debnham in the white-lyon about 70. yeers, George Bryty in Counter wood street, Henry Thomsō in the clynk, John Chandler in the Connt. Poultry, beeing sick vuto death was carryed forth & dyed within few dayes. Waltar Lane in the Fleet, Thomas Hewet in Counter Woodstreet.[3]

a Gen. 4, 10.

[1] Of him nothing is known beyond the fact above given. Even Bradford knew no details, Young, *Chronicles of the Pilgrim Fathers*, Boston, 1844, p. 427.

[2] John Coppin and Elias Thacker of Bury St. Edmunds. Executed for circulating Browne's books on June 4 and 5, 1583. See Dexter, *Cong. as seen*, p. 208–210.

[3] Unfortunately we know nothing of most of these men and women. Regarding Roger Rippon see Dexter, *Cong. as seen*, p. 207.

must the righteons Lord reserue a fearfull vengeance for such a Land, and make it an example to all Natons, yf speedely they purge not thewselnes [themselves] by notable repentance. But oh how far are they from this, which harden their harts against vs, as did the Egiptians, and cease not to add vnto their formor iniquities, still pursuing vs with their accustomed hatred, who seeke the welfare of their soules, & Offer them the things which concerne their peace, which they refuse. Thy peace o England hath wrought thy woe, and thy long prosperitie, thy ruin, thou hast been fat, thou has waxed grosse, thy hart is covered, thow hast forsaken the God that made thee, and despised the rock of thy salvation, thy sinnes have reached vp to Heaven, & God hath remembred thine iniquities to gyue vnto thee according to thy worcks. Behold, the tempest of the Lord is gon forth with wrath, the wirlewinde that hangeth over shall light vpon the heads of the wicked, the indignation of the Lords wrath shall not returne vntill hee hane [have] doon, and vntil hee hane performed the intents of his hart: In the later dayes thow shalt vnderstand it.* Our God shew mercy to them that are his in thee, and hastely draw them out ot the fire, that they perish not in thy sinnes. And most of all wee are sorie for our dread sovereigne Queen, whom wee haue alwayes loued, reverenced and obeyed in the Lord, that shee should so bee drawn by the subtle suggestion of the Prelats to smyte hir faithfullest subjects ha[vi]ving hir finger so deep in the blood of Gods children, wherby shee hath not only defiled hir precious soule in the eyes of hir God, but also brought an evill name vpon hir meek and peaceable Government heere on Earth, in all Nations rownd aboul hir who doo with greef behold that Land to persecute and waste true Christians now, which was erewhiles an harbour and refuge for Christians persecuted in other places. But as wee are verily perswaded that hir Matis. clemencie hath been much abused by the wretched vnconcionable false reports and instigations of the Priests, so will wee not cease (though wee bee exiled hir Dominions) with fervent harts to desier hir Highnesse prosperitie, & pray that hir sinnes may bee forgiven hir, lamenting that Gods benefits, and great delyverances, should so soone of hir bee forgotton, & so ill requited, by this hard vsage of his poore servants for his sake. And if shee proceed in this course, alas how shall shee ever bee able to behold the face of hir God with comfort; wherfore our soules shall weep in secret for hir, and wee will not cease to pray the Lord to shew hir mercy, and open hir eyes before shee dye. And lykewyse for those honorable Peeres hir grave Councellors, who also have consented to this our hard measure, although our innocencie hath been sufficiētly manifested vnto the cō-sciēces of some of the cheefest of thē, our humble reqnest is, that they in the feare of God may weigh their proceedings against vs, & rcmēber [remember] their accompt that they shall shortly make vnto the Judge of heavē and earth,†° where Christ will reckon vnto them al the tribulations of his poore despised members on earth, as if they had been inflicted vpon his own glorious person, and will render reward accordingly. The Lord giue them true wisdome, that they may learne, at last, to kisse the Soone before hee bee angry, and they prrish in the way.‡° As for the Priests and Preachers of the land, they, of all other men, haue bewrayed their notable hypocrisie, that standing erewhile against the English Romish hierachie, and their popish abhominations, haue now so redely submytted themselves to the Beast, and are not only content to yeeld their canonicall obedience vnto him, and receiue his mark, but in most hostile

* Och that they were wise, then would they vnderstand this, they would consider their later end. Deut. 32 29.

†° Mat. 10. 40. 41. & 25. 44. 45. ‡° Psal. 2. 10.

maner oppose and set themselues against vs, not ceasing to add vnto our aflictions, scorning and reviling vs, and alienating the mynds of manie simple harted people, whoe are (wee doubt not) inclinable enough vnto the truth, were it not that these their lying Prophets did strengthen their hands, that they may not returne from their wicked wayes, by promising them lyfe and peace, where no peace is. These haue long busied themselues in seeking out new shifts and cavills to turne away the truth, which presseth them so sore, and haue at last been dryven to palpaple & grosse absurdities, seeking to dawbe vp that ruinous autichristan muddy wall, which themselves did once craftily vndermine. And heerin wee report vs to the learned discourses of Dr. Robert Some,[1] and Mr. Giffard,[2] who haue so referced their wrytings with reproches, slanderous vntruths, and false collections on the one side, and manifest digressions, shiftings & turnings from the state of the question in hand, on the other side, as wee think the lyke presidents can hardly be shewed in anie wrytings of controversie in these times, and specially Mr. Giffards last answere[3] which (it seemeth) hee did in haste: whcrin besides his boyes-play, in skipping over many whol leaves of his adversaries booke, (leaving thē both vnanswered & vntouched) hee hath so wisely caryed himself in those things which hee professeth to answere, as a man afrayd once to come neere the battel and mayne coutroversie in hand, running out into vaine and frutlesse excursories, never approving by the word of God the places and offices of his Lords the Prelats, with their retinue, Courts, Cānons, &c. neither the publick worship, ministerie, or people of this their Church of England. No hee knew well his adversaries were fast locked & wached in pry[vii]son from wryting anie more, and their books intercepted, so that few men could come to the view of them: Hee might therfore deale as hee lysted himself for his own best advantage, and beare the people in hand that hee had confuted the Brownists and Donatists, for the prynt was as free for him, as the close pryson for them. But God (wee trust) will give meanes one day, that some things, which as yet are hid, shall come to light. In the meane tyme, thow for thy satisfying (Christian Reader) examin the mans wrytings, and see how hee hath answered vnto these criminations, or purged his Church of them. Look what scriptures hee hath brought for defence of his spirituall Lords, their places and procedings, their Courts, Cannons, Dignities, &c. what warrant in Christs Testament hee hath found for his service-booke and all the abhominable rites therin, for his Angelles, Saincts and Lady-days, popish Fastes, Lent, Embers and Eves: How hee hath approved their English missall Prayers, Letanie, Collects aud Trentalls, their maryng, burying, churching of women, wretched abuse of both Sac-

---

[1] R. Some, *A Godly Treatise containing and deciding certaine questions, mooued of late in London and other places touching the Ministerie, Sacraments, and Church.* London, 1588; Ibid, *A Defence of svch points in R. Somes last treatise as M. Penry hath dealt against*, etc., London, 1588; Ibid, *A Godly Treatise wherein are examined & confvted many execrable fancies giuen out & holden, partly by Hen. Barrowe and Iohn Greenwood: partly by other of the Anabaptisticall order*, etc., London, 1589.

Some was rector of Girton and master of Peterhouse Coll., Cambridge, a man somewhat inclined to Puritanism. For his biography see Cooper *Athenæ Cantabrigienses*, ii: 510–3.

[2] G. Gifford, *A Short Treatise against the Donatists of England, whome we call Brownists*, etc., London, 1590; Ibid, *A Plaine Declaration that our Brownists be full Donatists*, etc., London, 1590; Ibid, *A short Reply vnto the last printed books of Henry Barrow and Iohn Greenwood*, etc., London, 1591.

Gifford was a prominent and learned Puritan, vicar of Maldon, Essex, and a sufferer for the Puritan cause. See Brook, *Lives of the Puritans*, London, 1813, ii: 273–8; Bradley in *Dict. National Biog.*, xxi: 300.

[3] See previous note.

raments, their Romish Gossipps, hollowed Font, Crosse, inchanted Collects, their processions, bishopping of children, and a thowsand such like trnmperies, which were all blamed vnto him. yea, come vnto their own Ministerie, & behold from whence hee hath fetched the genealogie of those Anakims and horned heads of the Beaste. Archbbs, Lordbbs, Deanes, Arch-Deacons, Chancellors, &c. or of their Mr. Parson, Vicar, Curat, and the rest of that rable: How hee approveth their offices, ellections, callings, entrāce, administrations, Bishopricks, Deanries, Prebends, benefices, &c. by the ordinance of our Lord Jesus in his newe Testament *f* left vnto his Church to the worlds end.

These are some of the innumerable abhominations, wherwith wee charged their Church, which they must eyther justifie by Gods word, or cleere their Church of them. Now hee that findeth not these things approved in his wrytings, may easely perceiue how hee hath uever [never] medled with the mayne coutroversie between vs. Wherfore eyther let him dischardge his Church of these accusations, or els must wee and all Gods children still by the powre of the word of God condenme them, and send home againe these Romish wares into the Land of Shinar*° from whence they came, and the Lord that condemneth them is a strong God.

On the other side wee desire thē that they wold shew vs by the Scriptures our errors wherwith they chardge vs, & for which they thus hate vs, what they reproue in our Doctrinc or practise. As for our selves, wee protest with simple harts in the presence of God, and his holy Angelles, vnto al men, that wee doo not wittingly & willingly mataine anie one error against the word of truth (though wee doubt not but as all other men wee arc liable to error, which our God wee trust will in mercy forgiue vnto vs,) but hold the grounds of Christian Religion with all Gods antient Churches in Iudea, Rome, Corinth, Ephesus, Galatia, Pontus, Cappadocia, Asia and Bythinia, and with all faythfull people at this day in Germanie, France, Scotland, the Lovv-Contries, Bohemia, and other Christian Churches rownd about vs, whose confessions published†° wee call heere to wytnes the sinceritie of our [f]aith, and our agreement and vnitie with them in the points of greatest moment and controversie between vs and our adversaries. And wheras our Preachers were wont to tell vs, that their Church holdeth the foundation and substantiall grounds of Rilligion, Faith in God and Justification by Christ alone, &c. and therfore, notwithstanding their wants and corruptions, they had the essence, lyfe and beeing of a true people of God: wee trust now they will let vs that make the lyke plea, find the lyke favour, & accompt of vs as a true Congregation of Christ, and blaspheme vs no longer by the names [viii] of Brownists, Donatists, Anabaptists, Schismaticks &c. for will they slay those that Christ gyveth lyfe vnto? shall profession of faith saue them, and shall yt not vs lykewise, that make the same profession? Or yf they take exception at ours, let them shew what one truth they hold, wherin wee agree not with thē, or what good thing they have in practice, that wee do not the samew. ee [same. We] worship the true

f Mat. 28. 20. Heb. 1. 2. Eph. 4. 11; 12. 13. Gal. 1. 9. 10.

*° Zach. 5. 11.

†° Harmanie of Confess.[1]

[1] The collection here referred to is the *Harmonia Confessionum Fidei Orthodoxarum, et Reformatarum Ecclesiarum, quae in præcipuis quibusque Europæ Regnis, Nationibus, et Provinciis, sacram Evangelii doctrinam pure profitentur: . . .* Geneva, 1581. An English translation was published at Cambridge in 1586. This was the chief general epitome of the doctrines of the Reformed (Calvinistic) Churches, with some Lutheran creeds added. See Schaff, *Creeds of Christendom*, New York, 1877, I: 354.

God in spirit and truth,*° having his word truly taught, his Sacraments rightly administred (at such tyme as our God vouchafeth vs the meanes for administration of thē at all:) That ministerie of Pastors, Teachers, Elders, Deacons, &c. which they somtymes stood for,[1] wee (through Gods great mercy) obteyned them before their faces, which they yet never did. That government of Christ by his own lawes, ordinances, & holy censures (which they call Discipline) wee faithfully obey and execute:*g* receiving into our societie all that with faith and repentance come vnto vs willingly:*h* casting out againe, and removing by the powre of our Lord Jesus Christ all notorious & obstinate sinners, hereticks, schismaticks, or wicked lyvers whosoever, without respect of persons. Only wee reiect the abominable Romish reliques which they yet retein and mainteine, to the high dishonour of God. And for the sinnes wherwith wee charge them, they are so apparant, as even our forest adversarie somtymes confessed and complayned of them, & that in great measure openly, muchmore secretly emongst themselves, as is well known. But let vs heare themselves speak, as they have published in prynt to the view of the world. Of their people, the members of their Church they gyve this commendation.[2]

i The greaeest multitude, by many partes doo not vnderstand the Lords prayer, the ten Commandements, or the articles of the faith, or the Doctrine and vse of the Sacraments, in anie competent measure. There bee thouvvsands, *w*hich bee men & vvoemen grovvne, vvhich if a man aske them bo*w* [how] they shalbee saued, they cannot tell. As for vvickednes†° in pryde, eu*v*ie, hatred, and all sinnes that can bee named almost, yt doth overflo*w*: & yet you are not ashmed to say, are they not C*h*ristians? Concerning their o*w*n ministerie and government, they haue lyke*w*ise *k* complayned hovv they lack both a rig*h*t Ministerie of God, and a rig*h*t go*v*ernment of *h*is C*h*urc*h*, according to the Sc*h*riptures. More perticularly *l* T*h*at t*h*at prop*h*ane iurisdiction of Lordly Lord Arc*h*. bb^s^. Bb^s^. Arc*h*-Deacous, C*h*ancellors, Officials, &c. are contrary to Gods go*v*ernment, and vv*h*olly *v*nderpropt by t*h*e Canon and popis*h* la*w*,

*° Thou Lord preparest a table before vs in sight of our adversaries. Psal. 23. 5.

g Act. 2. 41.

h Mat. 18. 8. 17, 1 Cor. 5. 4. 5, Tit. 3. 10. Rom. 16. 17.

i Dialogue of the strife of their Church, Page. 99.[3]

†° Are not these meet stones now for gods hous? 1 Pet. 2. 5. 9. Heb. 8. 11.

k Admonition to the Parl. in the Preface, defended by T. C.[4]

l Table of Articles propounded by the Divinitie Reader in Cambridg. T. C.[5]

[1] Reference is here made to the Puritan wing of the Church of England which desired many of these reforms but refused to separate from the Establishment. So also in the succeeding passages.

[2] These quotations are in Roman, mixed with Italics.

[3] *A Dialogue concerning the strife of our churche . . . with a briefe declaration of some such monstrous abuses, as our Byshops haue not bene ashamed to foster.* London? 1584.

[4] Cartwright is meant. The original work quoted was, I suppose, that by J. Field and T Wilcox of London, *An Admonition to Parliament.* London, 1571. This was answered by Whitgift and defended by Cartwright in a series of pamphlets.

[5] With the bibliographical means at my disposal I am unable fully to identify the work of Cartwright indicated.

and *with*all ioyned *with* *h*ypocrisie, vaineglorie, lordlines & tyrannie, euē for t*h*ese respects, if t*h*er *w*ere no more, are to bee *v*tterly rooted out of t*h*e C*h*urc*h*, except possible *w*ee meane by reconciliation to ma*k*e C*h*rist and antic*h*rist friends. Item *m* t*h*at t*h*at ougly & ylfauored *h*yerarc*h*ie or C*h*urc*h*-princelynes, *w*hich instituted at t*h*e first by Antic*h*rists de*v*ise, did after*w*ard *v*ilely serue t*h*e Pope of Rome to accomplis*h*e t*h*e mysterie of iniquitie, and to distroy t*h*e C*h*urc*h* of C*h*rist, and dot*h* yet still at t*h*is day serue *h*im, must bee so abolis*h*ed t*h*at no remnants, ne yet anie s*hew* t*h*erof remayne, yf so bee *w*ee *w*ill [ix] haue C*h*rist to reign ouer *v*s. Item *n* that the Lord Gouerners of their Church bee Peti-popes, & Peti-Antic*h*rists, and Bis*h*ops of t*h*e Deuill.

These[2] Testimonies have wee from their own wrytings,[3] and manie such lyke. For these impieties haue wee seperated our selues from those cages of vncleane byrds, following the *o* counsell of the Holy-Gost, lest wee should communicate with their sinnes, and bee partakers of their plagues. With what equitie now can these Priests so blaspheme and persecute vs for reiecting the heavie yoke of their tyrānous Prelats, whom they themselues call antichristian & Bishops of the Devill; for forsaking their Priesthood, which they haue complayned is not the right Ministerie. With what conscience could Mayster Giffard (of all other men)*p* so vehemently charge vs with intollerable pryde, presumption, and intrusion into Gods iudgment seate, to judg and condemn wholl assembles which professe the Faith of Christ sincerely &c. in most savage and desperate maner to rend and teare vp the weake plants &c. The Lord rebuke Sathan, and iudge betwixt vs. Our enimies cheefest arguments against vs hitherto, haue been reproch and cursed speaking, with violence and oppression. But let them know and vnderstand, that for all these things God wil bring them vnto iudgment, whē they shall receiue such recompence of their error and wickednes as is meet.

The last and great scandall which offendeth manie and turneth them out of the way, is the seed of discord which Sathan hath sought to sowe emongst our selues, setting variance emong brethren, prevayling mightely in the children of perdition, whom hee hath eyther turned back into apostacie, or dryven into heresie or schisme. Heerby hee hath caused the truth of God to bee much evill spoken of, and to suffer great reproch at our aduersaries hands, whoe haue long wayted for our halting. Such things (good Reader) are neyther new nor strange vnto vs,[4] (though much to bee lamented,)

---

m In the same Table.

n Martin Marprelat.[1]

o Gen. 19, 14. Isa. 52, 11. Jir. 51. 9. Act. 2, 40. 2 Cor. 6. 17. Rev. 18, 4.

p Answere to the Brownists, pag. 4. & 50.[5]

1 Regarding the tracts published under this pseudonym see, *inter alia*, Dexter, *Cong. as seen*, pp. 131–202.

2 Black Letter again.

3 *I. e.* Those of the Puritans.

4 Some of the quarrels in this church, always a discordant body, are described by Dexter, *Cong. as seen*, pp. 271–351.

5 The reference fits Gifford's *Plaine Declaration that our Brownists be full Donatists*, London, 1590, better than his *Short Reply vnto the last printed books of Henry Barrow and Iohn Greenwood*, London, 1591.

yt beeing the lot of Christs Church *° to haue such trobles within yt self, and as incident to the same as is the crosse of outward tribulation. Neyther can anie that knoweth the state of Gods people, or the word of God aright, looke for other things in this world, where wee are but strangers & pylgrims, warring against manie and mightie adversaries, even the Prince of darknes, with his band of spirituall wickednesses. wee are taught of God *a* that ther must bee discentiōs & heresies emōgst our selves, that they which are approved may bee knowne, *b* that greevous wolves should enter in emongst vs, and of our selves men arise, speaking perverse things to draw away disciples after them. By such suborned guests of satan doth our *c* Lord sift & trye vs, whither wee love him with our wholl harts or no. wherfore though *d* never so many forsake vs, & oure own *e* frends dele vnfaithfully with vs, *f* yet wee know assuredly it shalbe well with Israell, even to the pure in hart. when wee call to mynde, *g* the murder of Cain, *h* the deviding of Cham, *i* the flowting of Ismael, *k* the hatred of Esau, *l* the envie of the Patriarks, *m* the rebellion of Corah, *n* the conspiracie of Absalon, *o* the treason of Judas, *p* the hypocrisie of Ananias and Saphira, *q* the Apostacie of Demas, *r* the heresie of Nicholas, and manie suchlike mischevous practises in old tyme, with in the housholds of the Saincts, and Churches of God, wee mervell not though in these last & evill dayes some childrē of Belial, that were of old ordeyned vnto this condemnation, rise vp in the Church and work the vnrest and sorrow of the same. The tyme is come that iudgment must begin at the house of God, the Lord will proue vs to the vtmost, and suffer Sathan to wynnow vs as wheat, but Peters Faith is prayed for that it fayle not, and hee that shall contynue to the end, hee shalbee saued. This is our comfort, that God will heerby purge his vine, and disclose [x] the disguysed hypocrits which come vnto vs in sheeps garments, but his own portion hee will bring thorow the fire, and fine them as the Silver is fined, and will trye them as the Gold is tryed, to the prase & glory of his own great name.*° These things are stumbling blocks vnto the blynde and hard harted worldlings, who haue no loue vnto the truth, nor wilbee brought vnto the obedience of the same. It is iust with God to let them bee offended by such things. But hee knoweth to delyuer the godly out of temptation. Let him therfore that readeth consider, & the Lord gyue him vnderstanding in all.†° Weigh all things vprightly in the ballance of the Sanctuarie, and iudg righteous iudgment. Bee not offended at the sunplicitie [simplicity] of the Gospell, neyther hold the Faith of our glorious Lord Jesus Christ in respect of mens persons. Gods cause shall stand when al that handle yt amisse shall fall before yt.‡° Wee offer heere our Fayth to the view and tryall of all men. Try all things and keep that which is good: and yf thou shalt reape anie frute by these our labors (gentel Reader) gyue God the glory.

Though Babel should mount vp to heauen, and though she should defend hir strengh on high, Yet from me shall hir destroyers come saith the Lord. Ierem. 51. 53.

Saue vs o Lord our God and gather vs from among the nations, for to celebrate thy holy name, For to glory in thy prayse. Psal. 106. 47.

---

*° Dan. 11, 34. *a* 1 Cor. 11, 15. *b* Act. 20, 29, 30.
c Deut. 13. 3. *d* Joh. 6, 5,6. *e* Lam. 1, 2.
f Psal. 73, 1. *g* Gen. 4. *h* Gen. 9.
i Gen. 2. *k* Gen. 27. *l* Gen. 37.
m Num. 16. *n* 2 Sam. 15. *o* Mat. 26.
p Act. 5. *q* 2 Tim. 4. *r* Revel. 2.
*° 2 Thes. 2, 10. 11. 12. †° 2 Pet. 2. 9. ‡° Mat. 11. 5. 6.

[xi] A[1] TRVE CONFESSION OF THE FAITH, AND HVMBLE ACKNOVVLEDGMENT OE THE ALEgeance, vvhich vve hir Maiesties Subjects, falsely called Brovvnists, doo hould tovvards God, and yeild to hir Majestie and all other that are ouer vs in the Lord. Set dovvn in Articles or Positions, for the better & more easie vnderstanding of those that shall read yt: And published for the cleering of our selues from those vnchristian slanders of heresie, schisme, pryde, obstinacie, disloyaltie, sedicion, &c. vvhich by our adversaries are in all places given out against vs.

Wee beleeue with our hearts & confes with our mouths.

THat ther is but[a] one God, one Christ, one Spirit, one Church, one truth, one Faith,[b] one Rule of obedience to all Christians, in all places.

a Deut. 6, 4. Hos. 13, 4. Mark. 12, 29, 32. Eph. 4, 4. 5. 6. 1 Cor. 12, 13. b Rom. 16, 26. 1 Cor. 4, 17. & 16. 1. Gal. 1, 8. 9.

2 That God is a [c]Spirit, whose[d] beeing is of himself, and[e] giveth beeing, moving, and preservation to all other things beeing himself[f] eternall, most holy, every way infinit, in greatnes, vvisdome, povvre, goodnes, justice, truth, &c. And that in this Godhead there bee three[g] distinct persons [h]coeternall, coequall, & [k]coessentiall, beeing every one of thē one & the same God, & therfore not divided but distinguished one frō another by their severall & peculiar propertie: The [l]Father of none, the Sonne[m] begotten of the Father from everlasting, the holy [n]Gost proceding from the Father and the Sonne before all beginnings.

c John. 4, 24. d Exod. 3, 14. Esa. 43, 10, 11. e Rom. 11, 36. Act 17, 28. Gen. 1. f 1 tim. 1, 17. Reu. 4, 18. Esa. 6, 3. and 66. 1. 2. Psal. 145, 3. 8. 9. 17. & 147. 5. Rom. 1, 20. g 1. Joh. 5, 7. Mat. 28, 19. Hag. 2, 5. 6. Heb. 9, 14. h Pro. 8, 22. Joh. 1. 1. Heb. 9, 14. i Phil. 2, 6. Joh. 5, 18. Eph. 4, 4. 5. 6. k Joh. 10, 30. 38. 1 Corint. 2, 11. 12. Heb. 1, 3. l Joh. 5, 26. 1 Cor. 8, 6. m Joh. 1, 14. 18. & 3. 16. Mica. 5, 2. Psal. 2, 7. n Joh. 14, 26. & 1. 16. Gal. 4, 16.

3 That God[o] hath decreed in himself from everlasting touching all things, and the very least circumstances of every thing, effectually to vvork and dispose thē according to the counsell of his ovvn vvill, to the prayse and glorie of his great name. And touching his cheefest Creatures that God hath in[p] Christ[q] before the foundation of the world,[r] according to the good pleasure of his vvill,[s] ordeyned som men and Angells, to eternall lyfe to

[1] The Confession is printed in Roman, with the texts on the margin of the page. I have put the texts after each section for convenience, following in this the Latin edition of 1598.

bee[t] accomplished through Iesus Christ, to the [v]prayse of the glorie of his grace. And on thother hand hath li*k*evvise [w]before of old accor*a*ing[x] to his iust purpose[y] ordein*e*d other both Angels and men, toe ternall condemna-[xii]tion, to bee[z] accomplished through their o*w*n corruption to the[a] prayse of his iustice.

o Esa. 46, 10. Rō. 11, 34. 35. 36. Act. 15, 18. & 2, 22. Gen. 45, 5. 6. 7. 8. Mat. 10, 29, 30. and 20. 15. Eph. 1, 11. p Eph. 1, 3. 4. 11. q ibid & mat. 25, 34. r Eph. 1, 5. Rom. 9, 11, 12, 13. Mal. 1, 2. 2, Tim. 1, 9. s Act. 13, 48. Eph. 1, 4. 5. 1. Tim. 5, 21. Mat. 25, 31. 34. t Ephes. 1, 5. 7. 10. Col. 1, 14. 17. 18. 19. & 2. 10. Rom. 8. 19. 30. Rev. 19. 10. v eph. 1, 6 to 9, 11. w Jud. ver. 4. x Rom. 9, 11. 12. 15. 17. 18. with Mal. 1, 3. Exod. 9. 16. y Jud. ver. 4, & 6. ro 9, 22. Mat. 25, 41. z 2. Pet. 2, 12. 2. Cor. 4, 3. 4. 1 pet. 2, 8. joh. 3. 19. & Pro. 16, 4. rom. 2, 5. and 9. 22.

4 T*h*at in the [c]beginning God made all t*h*ings of not*h*ing *v*ery good: and [d]created man after his o*w*n image and lykenes in rig*h*teousnes and *h*olines of trut*h*. That[e] streig*h*t *w*ays after by the subtiltie of the Serpent *w*hich Sathan vsed as his instrument[f] himself *w*it*h* *h*is Angells *h*aving sinned before and not kept t*h*eir first estate, but left their own *h*abitation; first [g]E*v*a, t*h*en Adam by *h*ir meanes, did *w*ittingly & *w*illingly fall into disobedience & transgression of t*h*e commādement of God. For t*h*e w*h*ic*h* deat*h*[h] reigned over all: yea e*v*en[i] ouer infants also, *w*hic*h* *h*ave not sinned, after the lyke maner of the transgression of Adam, t*h*at is, actually: Yet are[k] all since t*h*e fall of Adam begotten in his o*w*n likenes after *h*is image, beeing conceyued and borne in iniquitie, and soo by nature the chi*l*dren of *w*rath and servants of sinne, and subiect to deat*h*, and all ot*h*er calamities due vnto sinne in this world and for euer.

c Gen. 1. Col. 1, 16. Esa. 45, 12. Heb. 11, 3. Revel. 4, 11. d Gen. 1, 26. 27. Eph. 4, 24. Eccles. 7, 31. e Gen. 3, 1. 4. 5. 2. Cor. 11, 3. Joh. 8, 44. f 2. Pet. 2, 4. Joh 8, 44. Jud. 6. g Genes. 3, 1. 2. 3. 6 1. Tim. 2, 14. Eccles. 7, 31. Gal. 3, 22. h Rom. 5, 12. 18. 19. and 6. 23. with Gen. 2, 17. i Rom. 5. 14. and 9, 11. k Gen. 5, 3. Psal. 51, 5. Eph. 2, 3.

5 *Th*at all man*k*inde beeing t*h*us fallen and become altoget*h*er dead in sinne, & subiect to t*h*e eternall v*v*rat*h* of God both by origina*l* and actuall corruption: T*h*e [l]elect are redeemed, quickned, raysed *v*p and saued againe, not of t*h*emselues, neit*h*er by v*v*orks, lest ani*e* man s*h*ould bost *h*imself; but vv*h*olly and only by God of *h*is free grace and mercy through faith in Christ Iesus,[m] vvho of God is made vnto vs vvisdome, & righteousnes, & sanctificatiō, & redemption, that according as it is vvritten, Hee that reioyceth let him reioyce in the Lord.

l Gen. 3, 15. Eph. 2, 4. 5. Gen. 15. 6. with Rom. 4, 2. 3. 4. 5. and 3. 24. 25. 26. Joh. 3, 16. m 1. Cor. 1, 30. 31. Phil. 3, 8. 9. 10. 11. Jir. 23. 5. 6. and 9. 23. 24.

6 That this therfore only is lyfe[n] eternall to *k*novv the only true God, & vvhom hee hath sent into the vvorld Iesus Crist. And that on the contrarie the [o]Lord vvill rēder vengeance in flaming fire vnto them that knovv not God, & vvhich obey not the Gospell of our Lord Iesus Christ.

n Joh. 17, 3. and 3 36. Jir. 31, 33. 34. o 2. Thes. 1, 8. Eph. 1, 6. joh. 3, 36.

7 That the rule of this *k*novvledge faith & obedience, concerning the [p]vvorship & service of God & [q]all other christiā dutyes, is not the [r]opinions, devises, lavves, or constitutions of mē, but the vvritten vvord of the everlyving God, conteyned in the canonicall bookes of the old and nevv Testament.

p Exod. 10, 4. 5. 6. Deu. 4, 2. 5. 6. Gen. 6, 22. Exod. 39, 42. 43. 1. Chron. 28. 19. q Psal. 119. 105. r Esa. 29, 13. Mat. 15, 9. Joh. 5, 39. 2. Pet. 16, 19. 2. tim. 3, 16. 17.

8 That in this vvord[s] Iesus Christ hath reveled vvatsoever his father thought needfull for vs to knovv, beleeue & obey as touching his[t] person & Offices, in[v] v*v*hom all the promises of God are yea, & in v*v*hom they are Amen to the prayse of God through vs.

s Deut. 18, 18. Joh. 1, 18. & 15, 15. & 4. 25. Act. 3. 22. t the whol Epistle to the Hebr. throughout, & 2. Cor. 1, 28.

[xiii] 9 That touching his person, the Lord Iesus, of vvhō[x] Moses & the Prophets vvrote, & vvhō the Apostles preached, is the [y]everlasting *S*onne of *G*od, by eternall generation, the brightnes of his Fathers glorie, & the engrauen forme of his Person; coessentiall, coequall, & coeternall, god vvith him & vvith the holy Gost, by vvhō hee hath made the vvorlds, by vvhom hee vphouldeth and governeth all the works hee hath made; vvho also *vv*hen the[z] fulnes of tyme vvas come, *vv*as made man of a vvoman, of [a]the Tribe of *I*udah, of the [b]seed of Dauid & Abraham, to vvyt of Mary that blessed Virgin, by the holy Ghost comming vpon hir, & the povvre of the most high ouershadovving hir; & vvas also[c] in all things lyke *v*nto *v*s, sinne only excepted.

x Luk. 24, 44. Joh. 5, 46. Act. 10, 41. 43. y Pro. 8, 22. mica. 5, 2. Joh. 1, 1. 2. 3. Heb. 1. Collos. 1, 15. 16. 17. z Gal. 4, 4. Gen. 3, 15. a Heb. 7. 14. Revel. 5, 5. b Rom. 1, 3. Gen. 22, 18. Mat. 1. 1. etc. Luk. 3, 23 etc. Esa. 7, 14. Luk. 1. 26. 27. etc. Hebr. 2, 16. c Heb. 4. 15. Esa. 53, 3. 4. 9. Phil. 2, 7. 8.

10 That touching his Office, hee[d] only is made the Mediator of the nevv Testament, *e*ven of the euerlasting Couenant of grace betvveen God & man, to bee perfectly & fully the [e]*P*rophet, Priest & Kin*g* of the Church of *G*od for euermore.

d 1. Tim. 2, 5. Heb 9. 15. & 13. 20. Dan. 9 24. 25. e Deut. 18, 15. 18. Psal. 110. 4. Psal. 45, Esa. 9, 6. 7. Act. 5. 31. Esa. 55. 4. Heb. 7, 24. Luk. 1, 32, 33.

11 *T*hat hee[f] *v*vas frō euerlasting, by the iust & sufficient authoritie of the father, & in respect of his manhood frō the womb, called & seperated heervnto, & anoynted also most fully & aboundantly vvith all necessarie *g*ifts, as is [g] vvritten; God hath not measured out the Spirit vnto him.

f Pro. 8, 23. Esa. 42, 6. & 49. 1. 5. and 11, 2. 3. 4. 5. Act. 10. 38. g Joh. 3, 34.

12 That this[h] Office, to bee Mediator, that is, Prophet, Priest and King of the Church of God, is so proper to him, as neither in the *w*hol, nor in anie part therof, it cā be trāsferred frō him to anie ot*h*er.

h 1. Tim. 2, 5. Heb. 7. 24. Dan. 7. 14. Act. 4, 12. Esa. 43, 11. Luk. 1, 33.

13 *Th*at touching his[i] Prop*h*ecie, C*h*rist *h*at*h* perfectly re*v*ealed out of the bozome of his father, the vvholl vvord & vvill of God, that is needfull for his seruants, either ioyntly or seuerally to knovv, beleeue & obey : That hee hath spoken & doth speake to his Church in his ovvn[k] ordinance, by his ovvn ministers and instruments only, and not by anie false[l] ministrie at anie tyme.

i Deu. 18, 15. 18. Act. 3, 22. 23. 24. Mat. 3, 17. Joh. 1. 18. & 17. 8. Eph. 1. 8. 9. 2. Tim. 3. 15. 16, 17. k Pro. 9, 3. Joh. 13, 20. Luk. 10. 16. Mat. 10. 40. 41. Deu. 33, 8. 10. l Mat. 7, 15. 16. & 24. 23. 24. 2. Pet. 2. 2. Tim. 4. 3. 4. Rom. 10, 14. 15. ier. 23, 21. 2. ioh. 10.

14 That toching his[m] Priest*h*ood, beein consecrated, hee hath appeered once to put avvay sinne, by offring & sacrificing of himsell ; and to th*i*s end hath fully performed aud suffred all those things, by *w*hich God through the blood of that his crosse, in an acceptable sacrifice, might bee reconciled to his elect; & *h*aving[n] brokē *dovv*n *th*e partition *vv*all, & *th*er*vv*ith finished & remoued al those legal rites, shadovves, & ceremonies, is *now*[o] entred *vv*ithin the *v*ayle into t*he* holy of *H*olies to the *v*ery heauen, and prescnce of *G*od, *vv*here hee for euer lyueth, and sitteth at the right hand of Maiestie* appering before the face of his Father, to make intercession for [xiv] such as come vnto the Throne of grace

by that nevv & living vvay; And not that only, but maketh his people a[p] spirituall hovvse, an holy Priesthood, to offer up spirituall sacrifices, acceptable to God through him. Neither doth the Father accept, or Christ offer anie other sacrifice, vvorship, or vvorshippers.

m Joh. 17, 19. Heb. 5, 7. 8. 9. & 91 [9. 26] 1. Esa. 53, Ro. 5, 19. 1. Pet. 1, 2. Collos. 1, 20. Eph. 5, 2. n Eph. 2, 1. 4. 15. 16. Heb. 9, & 10. o Heb. 4, 14. 16. & 9. 24. and 10. 19. 20. * Rom. 3, 34. p 1. Pet. 2, 5. Rev. 1, 5. 6. and 8. 3. 4. Rom. 12, 1. Mar. 9, 49. 50. Mal. 1, 14. Joh. 4 23. 24. Mat. 7, 6. 7. 8. Esa. 1, 12. etc.

15 That touching his[q] *K*ingdom, beeing risen, ascended, entred into glory, set at the right hand of God, al povvre in Heaven and earth giuē vnto him; vvhich povvre hee[r] novv exerciseth ouer all Angells and men, good and dad [bad], to the preservation and saluation of the elect, to the overruling and destruction of the reprobate;[s] communicating and app*l*ying the benefits, virtue and ſrutes of his prophecy and Priesthood vnto his elect, namely to the remission, subduing, and takeing avvay of their sinnes, to their iustification, adoption-of-sonnes, regeneration, sanctification, preservation & strēgthning in all their spirituall conflicts against Sathan, the vvorld & the flesh &c. continually dvvelling in, governing & *k*eeping their hearts in his tue [true] faith and fear by his holy spirit, vvhich having[t] once givē yt, hee never taketh avvay from them, but by yt still begetteth and nourisheth in them repentance, faith, loue, obedience, comfort, peace, ioy, hope, and all christian vertues, vnto immortallitie, notvvithstanding that yt be sometymes through sinne and tentation, interrupted, smothered, and as yt vvere overvvhelmed for the tyme. Againe on the contrary,[v] ruling in the vvorld over his enimies, *S*athan, and all the vessels of vvrath; limiting, vsing, restrayning them by his mightie povvre, as seemeth good in diuiue vvisdome and iustice, to the e*x*ecution of his determinate counsell, to vvit to their seduction, hardning & condemnation, delyvering them vp to a reprobate mynde, to bee *k*ept in darcknes, sinne and sensuallitie vnto iudgment.

q 1. Cor. 15, 4. etc. 1. Pet. 3, 21. 22. Mat. 28, 18, 20. r Josh. 5, 14. Zech. 1, 8. etc. Mark 1, 27. Heb. 1. 14. s Eph. 5, 26, 27. Ro. 5, and 6. and 7. and 8. Chap. Rom. 14, 17. Gal. 5, 22. 23. 1. Joh. 4, 13. etc. t Psal. 51, 10. 11. 12. and 89. 30. 31. 32. 33. 34. Job. 33, 29. 30. Esa. 54, 8. 9. 10. Joh. 13, 1. and 16. 31. 32, with Luc. 22, 31. 32. 40. 2. Cor. 12, 7. 8. 9. Eph. 6, 10. 11. etc. Rom. 11, 29. Gal. 5, 17. 22. 23. v Job. 1, 6. and 2. Chap. 1. King. 22. 19. Esa. 10, 5. 15. Rom. 9, 17. 18. Rom. 1, 21. and 2. 4. 5. 6. Eph. 4, 17. 18. 19. 2. Pet. 3, 3. 1. Thess. 5, 3. 7. Esa. 57, 20. 21. 2. Pet. 2, the whol Chapter.

16 *T*hat this Kingdom shall bee then fully perfected vvhen hee shal the[x] second tyme come in glorie vvith his mightie Angells vnto iudgment, to abolish all rule, authoritie and povvre, to put all his enimies vnder his feet, to seperate and free all his chosen from them for ever, to punish the vvicked vvith e*v*erlasting perdition from his presence, to gather, ioyne, and c*a*rry the godly *w*ith himself into endlesse *g*lory, and then to dely*v*er, *v*p the Kingdome to God, e*v*en the Father, that so the *g*lorie of the father may bee full and perfect in the Sonne, the glorie of the Sonne in all his members, and God bee all in all.

x Dan. 12, 2. 3. Joh 5, 22. 28. 29. Mat. 25, 31. 1. Cor. 15. 24. Mat. 13, 41. 49. 2. Thes. 1, 9. 10. 1. Thes. 4, 17. Joh. 17, 22. 23. 1. Cor. 15, 28.

[xv] 17 That in the meane tyme, bisides his absolute rule in the *w*orld, Christ hath here in earth a[y] spirituall *K*ingdome and æ canonicall regiment in his Church ouer his ser*v*ants, which Church hee hath[z] purchased and redeemed to himself, as a peculiar inheritance (not*w*ithstanding[a] manie hypocrites do for the tyme lurk emongest thē) [b]calling and *w*inning them by the po*w*re of his *w*ord *v*nto the faith, [c]seperating them from emongst *v*nbelee*v*ers, from idolitrie, false *w*orship, superstition, *v*anitie, dissolute lyfe, & *w*orks of darknes, &c; making them a royall Priesthood, an holy Nation, a people set at libertie to she*w* foorth the *v*irtues of him that *h*ath called them out of darknes into his meruelous light, [d]gathering and *v*niting thē together as members of one body in his faith, loue and holy order, *v*nto all generall and mutuall dutyes,[e] in*st*ructing & *go*v*e*rning thē by such officers and lawes as hee hath prescribed in his *w*ord; by *w*hich Officers and la*w*es hee go*v*erneth his Church, and by[f] none other.

y Joh. 18. 36. Heb 3, 6. and 10. 21. 1. Tim. 3, 15. Zach. 4, 17. z Act. 20, 28. Tit. 2, 14. a Mat. 13, 47. and 22. 12. Luk. 13, 25. b Mar. 16, 15. 16. Col. 1, 21, 1. Cor. 6 11. Tit. 3, 3. 4. 5. c Esa. 52. 11, Ezr. 6, 21. Act. 2, 40. 2. Cor. 6, 14. Act. 17, 3. 4. and 19. 9. 1. Pet. 2, 4. 5. 9. 25. d Esa. 60, 4. 8. Psal. 110, 3. Act. 2 41. Eph. 4, 16. Col. 2, 5. 6. e Esa. 62, 6. Jer. 3, 15, Ezek. 34. Zech. 11, 8. Heb. 12, 28. 29. Mat. 28, 20. f Mat. 7, 15. and 24. 23. 24. 2. Tim. 4, 3. 4. Jer. 7, 30. 31. and 23. 21. Deu. 12, 32. Reu. 2, 2. & 22. 18. 19

18 That to this[g] Church hee hath made the promises, and giuen the seales of his Covenant, presence, loue, blessin*g* and protection:[h] Heere are the holy Oracles as in the side of the Arke, suerly kept & puerly tau*g*ht. Heere are[i] all the fountaynes and springs of his *g*race continually replenished and flo*w*ing forth. Heere is[k] hee lyfted *v*p to all Nations, hither hee[l] inuiteth all mē to

his supper, his mariage feast; hither ought[m] all men of all estates and degrees that acknowledg him their Prophet, Priest and King to repayre, to bee[n] enrolled emongst his houshold seruants, to bee vnder his heauenly conduct and government, to leade their lyues in his walled sheepfold, & watered orchard, to haue communion heere with the Saincts, that they may bee made meet to bee partakers of their inheritāce in the kingdome of God.

g Lev. 26, 11. 12. Mat. 28, 19. 20. Rom. 9, 4. Ezek. 48. 35, 2. Cor. 6. 18 h Esa. 8, 16. 1. tim. 3, 15. and 4. 16. & 6. 3. 5. 2. Tim. 1, 15. tit. 1, 9. Deu. 31. 26. i Psal. 46, 4. 5. Ezek. 47, 1. etc. Joh. 38, 39. k Isa. 11. 12. Joh. 3, 14. Isa. 49, 22. l Esa. 55. 1. Mat. 6, 33. & 22. 2. Pro. 9, 4. 5. Joh. 7, 37. m Deu. 12, 5. 11. Esa. 2, 2. 3. Zach. 14, 16. 17. 18. 19. n Esa. 44. 5. Psal. 87, 5. 6. Can. 4. 12. Gal. 6, 10. Col. 1, 12. 13. Eph. 2, 19.

19 That as[o] all his seruants and subiects are called hither, to present their bodyes and soules, and to bring the guyfts God hath given them; so beeing come, they are heer by himself bestowed in their severall order, peculiar place, due vse, beeing fitly compact and knit together by euery ioynt of help, according to the effectuall work in the measure of euery parte, vnto the edification of yt self in loue; whervnto whē hee[p] ascended vp on high hee gaue guifts vnto men, [xvi] that hee might fill all these things, and hath distributed these guifts, vnto seuerall functions in his Church, hauing instituted and ratified to[q] contynue vnto the worlds end, only this publick ordinarie Ministerie of Pastors, Teachers, Elders, Deacons, Helpers to the instruction, government, and seruice of his Church.

o See the 18. Article before, and Exod. 25. 2. and 35. 5. 1 Cor. 12, 4. 5. 6. 7. 12. 18. Rom. 12. 4. 5. 6. 1. Pet. 4. 10. Eph. 4, 16. Colos. 2, 5. p Eph. 4, 8. 10. 11. 12. 13. Rom. 12, 7. 8. & 16. 1. 1. Cor. 12. 4. 5. 6. 7, 8. 11. 14. 15. 16. 17. 18. 28. 1. Tim. 3, & 5. 3. 9. 17. 21. Act. 6, 2. 3. & 14. 23. and 20. 27. 28. Phil. 1, 1. q Rev. 22, 18. 19. Mat. 28, 20. 1. Tim. 6, 13, 14.

20 That this ministerie is exactly[r] described, distinguished, limited, concerning their office, their calling to their office, ther administration of their office, and their maintenance in their office, by most perfect and playne [s]lawes in Gods word, which lawes it is not lawfull for these Ministers, or for the wholl Church wittinly to neglect, transgresse, or violate in anie parte; nor yet to receiue anie other lawes brought into the Church by anie person whatsoever.

r Pro. 8, 8. 9. heb. 3. 2. 6. the first Epistle to Timothy wholly. Act. 6, 3. 5. 6. & 14. 23. & 20, 17. etc. 1. pet. 5, 2. 3. 1. Cor. 5, 4. 5. 11. 12. 13. etc. and 9. 7. 9. 14. s Heb. 2. 3. and 3. 3. and 12. 25. etc. 2. Tim 3, 14. 15. Gal. 1, 8. 9. 1 tim. 6, 13. 14. Deut. 12, 32. and 4. 2. Revel. 22, 18. 19.

21 That[t] none may vsurp or execute a ministerie but such as are rightly called by the Church whereof they stand ministers; and that such so called ought to gyve all diligence to[v] fulfill ther ministerie, to bee found faithfull and vnblamable in all things.

t Num. 16, 5. 40. & 18. 7. 2. Chron. 26. 18. Joh. 10. 1. 2 and 3. 27. Heb. 5. 4. Act. 6, 3. 5. 6. & 14. 23. Tit. 1, 5. v Act. 2. 28. 1. cor. 4, 1. 2. Col. 4, 17. 1. Tim. 1, 18. 19. & 4. 12. and 5 21 & 6. 11. 12. 13. 14. 2. Tim. 1, 13. 14. and 3. 14. and 4. 5, 1. Pet. 5, 1. 2. 3. 4.

22 That this ministerie is alyke given to euery Christian congregation, with like povvre and commission to haue and enioy the same, as God offereth fit men and meanes, the same rules given to all for the election and execution therof in all places.

Mat. 28, 20. 1. cor 14, 33. 36. 1. Cor. 12, 4. 5. 6. 7. and 4. 17. and 16. 1. eph. 4, 10. 11. 12. 13. 1. cor. 3, 21. 22. 23. Mat. 18. 17. see Article 20.

23 That as every christian Congregation[x] hath povvre and commandement to elect and ordeine their ovvn ministerie according to the rules prescribed, and[y] whilest they shal faithfully execute their office, to haue them in superaboundant loue for their vvorke sake, to provide for them, to honour them and reuerence them, according to the dignitie of the office they execute. So have they also[z] povvre and commandement when anie such defalt, either in their lyfe, Doctrine, or administration breaketh out, as by the rule of the word debarreth them from, or depriveth them of their ministerie, by due order to depose them from the ministerie they exercised; yea if the case so require, and they remayne obstinate and impenitent, orderly to cut them off by excommunication.

x Act. 6, 3. 5. 6. & 14. 23. 2. Cor. 8. 19. Act. 15. 2, 3. 22. 25. 1. Tim. 3, 10. and 4. 14, & 5. 22. Num. 8, 9. 10. y 1. Thes. 5, 12. 13. 1. Tim. 5, 3. 17. Heb. 13, 17. 1. cor. 9. Gal. 6. 6. z 1. Tim. 3, 10. and 5. 22. Rom. 16, 17. Phyl. 3, 2. 18. 19. 1. Tim. 6, 3. 5. Ezek. 44, 11. 13. Mat. 18, 17.

24 That[a] Christ hath given this povvre to receiue in or to cut off anie member, to the vvholl body together of euery Christian Congregation, and not to anie one member aparte, or to moe members sequestred from the vvholl, or to anie other Congregation to doo it for thē: yet that[b] ech Congregation ought to vse the best help they can heer vnto, and the most meet member they haue to pronounce the same in their publick assembly.

a Psal. 122. 3. Act. 1, 47. Rom. 16, 2. Lev. 20, 4. 5. & 24. 14. Num. 5, 3. Deu. 13, 9. Mat. 18, 17. 1. cor. 5, 4. 2. cor. 2, 6. 7. 8. b 1. Cor. 3, 21. 22. 23. Act. 15. 1. cor. 3, 4. 5. & 12. 20.

[xvii] 25 That euery member of ech Christian Congregation, hovv excellent, great, or learned soeu*er*, ought to be subiect to this censure & iudgment of Christ; Yet ought not the Church vvithout great care & due advise to procede against such publick persons.[1]

Lev. 4. Psal. 141, 5. and 2, 10. 11. 12. & 149. 8. 9. 1. Chro 26, 20. Act. 11, 2. 4. 1. Tim. 5, 19. 20. 21.

26 T*h*at for t*h*e [c]keeping of this C*h*urc*h* in *h*oly & orderly communion, as Christ *h*at*h* placed some speciall men o*v*er the Church, *w*ho by t*h*eir office are to governe, ouersee, visite, *w*atch, &c. So[d] lykev*v*ise for t*h*e better keeping therof in all places, by all t*h*e members, hee hath giuen aut*h*oritie & layd duty *v*pon thē all to *w*atch one ouer another.

c Cant. 3, 3. Esa. 62, 6. Eze. 33. 2. Mat. 14, 45. Luk. 12, 42. Act. 20, 28. Heb. 13, 17. b Mar. 13, 34, 37. Luk. 17, 3. 1. Thes. 5, 14. Gal. 6, 1. Jude. 3, 20. Hebr. 10, 24, 25. & 12. 15.

27 That *vvh*ilest the Ministers and people t*h*us remayne toget*h*er in this holy order and c*h*ristian communion, ech one endevoring to do the *w*ill of God in t*h*eir calling, & thus to vvalke in t*h*e obedience of fait*h* C*h*rist *h*at*h* promised to bee present *w*ith t*h*em, to blesse & defend them against all adverserie povvre, & that t*h*e gates of Hell s*h*all not prevayle against t*h*em.

Deu. 28, 1. etc. Mat. 28, 20. Luk. 12, 35. 36. 37. 38. Mat. 16. 18. Zach. 2, 5. & 12, 2. 3. 4. Psal. 125, 2. & 132. 12. 13. etc.

28 But *w*hen & vv*h*ere this holy order & diligent vvatch *w*as intermitted, neglected, violated. Antichrist that man of sinne corrupted & altered t*h*e holy ordinances, offices, & administratiōs of the c*h*urc*h* broug*h*t in & erected a strange ne*w* forged ministerie, leitourgie and government & the Nations *K*ingdoms & inhabitants of the eart*h*, *w*ere made drunken vvith t*h*is cup of fornications & abhominations, & all people enforced to receiue the Beasts marke and wors*h*ip his image & so brought into confusion & babilonish bondage.

Rev. 9. & 13. & 17. & 18. 1. Thes. 2, 3. 4. 9. 10. 11. 12. psal. 74. Esa. 14. 13. 14. Dan. 7. 25. and 8. 10. 11. 12. & 11. 31. 1. Tim. 4, 1. 2. 1. joh. 2, 18. 22. & 4. 3.

29 T*h*at the present ministerie reteyned & vsed in Englād of Arch. b[bb]. Lo[bb].[2] Deanes, Prebendaries, Canons, Peti-Canons, Arch-

[1] An answer to the frequent question what would they do with a sovereign worthy of excommunication.

[2] Lord bishops, the favorite Separatist designation for a diocesan bishop as distinguished from a New Testament bishop.

Deacons, Chancellors, Commissaries, Priests, Deacons, Parsons, Viccars Curats, Hireling rouing Preachers, Church-wardens, Parish-clerkes their Doctors, Proctors, & wholl rable of those Courts with all from & vnder them set ouer these Cathedrall & Parishionall Assemblies in this confusion, are a strange & Antichristian ministerie & offices; & are not that ministerie aboue named instituted in Christs Testament, or allovved in or ouer his Church.

Revel. 9, 3. etc. & 13. 15. 16. 17. & 18. 15. 17. compared with Rom. 12, 7. 8. Eph. 4, 11. 12. 1. Tim. 3. 15. & 5. 17. Compare this Art. with the 1. 7. 12. 13. 14. 19. 20. 21. 22. 23. 24. 28. Articles aforesaid.

30 That their [e]Offices, Entrance, Administration and maintenance, with their [f]names, titles, prvileges, & prerogatiues the povvre & rule they vsurp ouer and in these Ecclesiasticall assemblies ouer the wholl ministerie, wholl ministration and affaires therof, yea one ouer another by their making Priests, citing, suspending, silencing, deposing, absoluing, excommunicating, &c. Their confounding of Ecclesiasticall and Civile iurisdiction, causes & proceedings in ther persons, courts, [xviii] cōmissions, Visitations, the rest of lesse rule, taking their ministerie frō and exercising it vnder them by their [g]prescription and limitation, swearing Canonicall obedience vnto them, administring by their devised imposed, stinted popish Leiturgie, &c. are sufficient proofs of the former assertion, the perticulars therin beeing duly examined by and compared to the Rules of Christs Testament.

e Compare with Articles 1, 7. 12. 13. 14. 19. etc. Rev. 9. 3, etc. & 18. 15. 17. Joh. 10, 1. Dan. 7, 8. 25. and 8. 10. 11. 12. 2 Thes. 2. 3. 4. 8. 9. rev. 17, 4. 5. 16. f Luk. 22, 25. 26. Rev. 14. 11. & 17. 3. 4. 5. & 13. 15. 16. 17 1. Pet. 5, 3. with Joh. 3, 29. & with Rev. 2. 1. 1. King. 12. 27. zac. 11. 15. 16. g Rev. 13, 15. 16. 17. Esa. 29. 13. Mat. 7, 7. 8. Ga. 1, 10. etc. & 2, 4. 5. Col. 2, 20. 22. 23. Ezek. 8, 5. & 13. 9. 10. 11. 18. 19. Mica 2, 11. mal. 1, 8. 13. 14.

31 That these Ecclesiasticall Assemblies, remayning in confusion and bondage vnder this Antichristian Ministerie, Courts, Canons, worship, Ordinances. &c. without freedom or povvre to redresse anie enormitie, have not in this confusion and subiection, Christ their Prophet, Priest, and King, neither can bee in this estate, (whilest wee iudge them by the rules of Gods word) esteemed the true, orderly gathered, or cōstituted churches of Christ, wherof the faithfull ought to beecome or stand Members, or to haue[h] anie Spirituall communion vvith them in their publick vvorship and Administration.

Rev. 18, 2. 1. Cor. 14, 33. Jir. 15, 19. Mal. 1, 4. 6. 8. Hos. 4, 14. etc. Rom. 6, 16. 2. Pet 2, 19. compare with. Art. 1. 7. 11. 12. 13. 14. 15. 17. 18. 19. 20. 24. 28. 29. 30. aforesaid. h Levit. 17, Hos. 4, 15, 1. Cor. 10. 18. 19. 20. 2. Cor. 6, 14. 15, 16. Rev. 18, 4. Cant. 1, 6. 7.

32 That[i] by Gods Commandement all that *w*ill bee saued, must vvith speed come forth of this Antichristian estate,[k] leaving the suppression of it vnto the Magistrate to vvhom *i*t belongeth.[1] And that both all such as haue receyued or exercised anie of these false Offices or anie pretended function or Ministerie in or to th*i*s false and Antichristian constitution, are v*v*illingly in Gods feare, to giue ouer and leaue those vnlav*v*full Offices, and no longer to minister in this maner to these Assemblies in this estate And that[l] none also, of what sort or condition soever, doo giue anie part of their *G*oods, Lands, Money, or money v*v*orth to the maintenance of this false Ministerie and v*v*orship vpon anie Commandement, or vnder anie colour *v*vhatsoeuer.

i Reu. 18, 4. Esa. 48, 20. and 52. 11. Jir. 50, 8. & 51. 6. 45. Zech. 2, 6. k 2. Chro. 15, and 27. 6. 2. King. 23, 5 etc Rom. 13, 4. Mat. 22, 21. Rev. 17, 16. l Zech. 13, 2. 4. 5. 6. Jir. 51, 26. Psal. 119, 59. 60. 128. Prov. 5, 20. Esa. 8, 11. 12. and 35. 8. Zach. 14, 21. Prov. 3, 9. 10. compared with Exod. 20. 4, 5. Judg. 17. 3. 4. 5. Ezek. 16. 17. 18. 19. 1. Cor. 10. 19. 20. 21. 22. compared with Heb. 13, 10. & with 2. Cor. 8. 3. 4. 5. 1. Tim. 5, 17.

33 *T*hat beeing come forth of this antic*h*ristian estate *v*nto the freedom and true profession of Christ, besides the[m] instructing and [xix] *v*vell guyding of their ovvn Families, they are[n] vvillingly to ioyne together in c*h*ristian communion and orderly couenant, and by confession of Faith and obedience of Christ, to[o] *v*nite themselues into peculiar Congregatiōs; vvherin, as members of one body *v*vherof Christ is the only head, t*h*ey are to *v*vorship and serue God according to his v*v*ord, remembring[p] to keep holy the Lords day.

m Gen. 18. 19. Exod. 13, 8. 14. Pro. 31, 26. 27. Eph. 6, 4. Deut. 6, 7. Psal. 78, 3. 4 n Luk. 17, 37. Psal. 110, 3. Mat. 6, Esa. 44. 5. Act. 2, 41, 42. Jir. 50, 4. 5. Neh. 9, 38. Act. 2, 41. 42. o 1. Cor. 1, 2. and 12. 14. Rev. 1, 20 and 2. 1. 8. 12. 18. & 3. 1. 7. 14. Eph. 2, 19. Col. 2, 19. p Exod. 20, 8. Rev. 1, 10. Act. 20, 7. 1. Cor. 16, 2.

34 That such as[q] God hath giuen *g*uiftes to enterpret the Scriptures, tryed in the exercise of Prophecie, gi*v*ing attendance to studie and learn*i*ng, may and ought by the appointment of the Congregation, to teach publickly the vvord, *v*ntill the people bee meet for, and God manifest men *v*vith able guifts and fitnes to such Of-

[1] See *ante*, p. 46.

fice or Offices as Christ hath appointed to the publick ministerie of his church; but [r]no Sacraments to bee administred *v*ntill the Pastors or Teachers bee chosen and ordeyned into their Office.

q 1. Cor. 14, rom. 12. 6. 1. Cor. 12, 7. 1. Pet. 4, 10. Act. 13. 15. 1. Thes. 5, 20. r Num. 16, 10. 39. 40. Rom. 12. 7. Heb. 5, 4. Joh. 1, 23. 25.

35 That[s] v*v*heras ther shalbee a people fit, and men furnished *w*ith meet and necessarie *g*uifts, they doo not only still continue the exercise of Prophecie aforesayd, but doo also vpon due tryall, proceed vnto choyce and ordination of Officiers for the ministerie and ser*v*ise of the Church, according to the rule of *G*ods *vv*ord; And that soe they[t] hold on still to vvalke for*w*ard in the *w*ayes of Christ for their mutuall edification and comfort, as it shall please God to giue knowledge and grace thervnto. And perticularly, that[v] such as bee of the seed,[1] or vnder the go*v*ernment of anie of the Church, bee euen jn their infancie receiued to Baptisme, ond made perta*k*ers of the signe of Gods Couenant made with the faithfull and their seed thro*v*ghout all Generations. And that[x] all of the Church that *a*re of yeeres, and able to examine themselues, doo communicate also in the Lords Supper both men[y] and vvomen, and in[z] both kindes bread and vvyne in *w*hich[a] Elements, as also in the *v*vater of baptisme, euen after their are consecrate, there is neyt*h*er transubstantiation into, nor Consubstantiation with t*h*e bodye and bloode of *I*esus Christ; vvhome [b]the *H*eauens must conteyne; *v*ntill the tyme [xx] that al things bee restored. [c]But they are in the ordinance of God signes and seales of Gods euerlasting couenant, representing and offring to all the receiuers, but exhibiting only to the true beleevers the Lord Iesus Christ and all his benefits vnto righteousnes, sanctification and eternall lyfe, through faith in his name to the glorie and prayse of God.

s Lev. 8. Act. 6, 3. 5. 6. & 14. 21. 22. 23. Tit. 1, 5. etc. 1. Cor. 12, 7. 8. 14. 15. 1. Tim. 3. t Col. 2, 5. 6. 7. 2. Thes. 2. 15. Jud. 3, etc. Mat. 28, 20. v Act. 2, 38, 39. 1. Cor. 7, 14. Rom. 11, 16, Gen. 17, 7. 12. 27. 1. cor. 10, 2. Psal. 22, 30. Exod. 12, 48. 49. Act. 16, 15. 33. 1. Cor. 1, 16. Mar. 10, 13, 14. 15. 16. Gal. 3, 29. x Mat. 26, 26. 27. 1. Cor. 11. 28. and 10. 3. 4. 16. 17. act. 2, 42, & 20. 7. 8. y Gal. 3, 28. Act. 2. 42. with 1. 1 4. 1. Cor. 12, 13. z Mat. 26, 26. 27. 1. Cor. 10, 3. 4. 16. & 11. 23. 24. 25. 26. 27. 28. 29. a 1. Cor. 10, 16. 17. & 11. 23. 24. 25. 26. etc. Mat. 26, 26. 27. 29. & 15. 17. Joh. 12, 8. b Act. 3, 21. & 7. 56. c Gen. 17, 11. rom. 4, 11. Exod. 12, 13. with Heb. 13, 20. d 1. Cor. 11, 26. 27. 28. 29. & 10. 3. 4. 5. Rom. 2. 28. 29. Act. 15. 9. Rom. 5, & 6. 7. & 8. Chapt.

---

[1] *I. e.*, Children of those who are members of the local church, thus in covenant relation with God.

36 That thus[e] beeing righly gathered, established, and still proceeding in christian communion & obedience of the Gospell of Christ, none is to seperate for falts and corruptions which may and so long as the Church consisteth of mortall men, will fall out & arise emong them, even in a true constituted Church, but by due[f] order to seeke redresse therof.

e Lev. 4. 13. etc. 2. Chro. 15, 9. 17. and 30. 18. 19. rev. 2, and 3. 1. Cor. 1. 10. Phil. 2, 1. 2. 3. 4. 5. 6. and 3. 15. 16. heb. 10. 25. ind [Jude] 19. f 2. Cor. 13. 1. 2. rev. 2. and 3. 1. Thes. 5. 14. 2. Thes. 3, 6. 14. Mat. 18, 17. 1. Cor. 5, 4. 5. Act. 15. 1. 2.

37 That[g] such as yet see not the truth, may heare the publik doctrine and prayers of the church, and *w*ith al mee*k*nes are to bee sought by all meanes: Yet [h]none *w*ho are gro*w*ne in yeeres to bee recei*v*ed into their communion as members, but such as doo make confession of their faith, publickly desiring to bee receiued as members, and promising to *w*alke in the obedience of Christ. Neither anie[i] Infants, but such as are the seed of t*h*e faithfull by one of the parents, or *v*nder their education and gouernment. And further not anie[k] from one Congregation to bee receiued members in another, *w*ithout bringing certificate of their former e*st*ate and present purpose.

g 1. cor. 14, 24. 25. Psal. 18. 49. rom. 15, 9. 10. 1. Tim. 2, 4. 2. Tim. 2, 25. h 2. Cor. 6, 14. 15. 16. Ezra. 4, 3. Exod. 12, 43. Lev. 22. 25. Exod, 34. 12. Deu. 7, Esa. 44. 5. Act. 19, 18. i Exod. 20, 5. 6. 1. Cor. 7, 14. Gen. 17, 7. 12. 27. Exod. 12, 48. 49. Act. 16. 15, 33. k Act. 9, 26. 27. rom. 16, 1. 2. 2. Cor. 3, 23. Col. 4, 10.

38 That though Congregations bee thus distinct and se*v*erall bodyes, every one as a compact Citie in it self, yet are they all to *w*alke by one and the same rule, & by all meanes con*v*enient to haue the counsell and help one of another in all needfull affayres of the Church, as members of one body in the common Faith, vnder Christ their head.

Look Articles 1. 22. 23. Psal. 122 3. Cant. 8. 8. 9. 1. cor. 4, 17. and 16. 1.

39 That it is the Office and duty of Princes and Magestrates, [l]*w*ho by the ordinance of God are supreme Governers *v*nder him over all persons and causes *w*ithin their Realmes and Dominions, to[m] suppress and root out by their authoritie all false ministeries, *v*oluntarie Relligions and counterfeyt *w*orship of God, to abolish and destroy the Idoll Temples, Ima*g*es, Altares, Vestments, and all other monuments of *I*dolatrie and superstition and to take and con*v*ert to their o*w*n ci*v*ile vses not only the benefit of all such

idolitrous buyldings & monuments, but also the Revenues, Demeanes, Lordships, Possessions, Gleabes and maintenance of anie false ministeries and vnla*w*full Ecclesiasticall functions *w*hatsoever *w*ithin their Dominions. [xxi] And on the other hand[n] to establish & mayntein by their la*w*es e*v*ery part of Gods word his pure Relligion and true ministerie to cherish and protect all such as are carefull to *w*orship God according to his *w*ord, and to leade a godly lyfe in all peace and loyalltie; yea to enforce al their Subiects *w*hether Ecclesiasticall or civile, to do their dutyes to *God* and men, protecting & mainteyning the *g*ood, punishing and restreyning the evill according as God hath commanded, vvhose Lieuetenants they are *h*eer on earth.

l Rom. 13, 3. 4. 1. Pet. 2. 3, 14. 2. Chro. 19, 4. etc. and. 29. and 34. Chap. Judg. 17, 5. 6. Math. 22. 21. Tit. 3, 1. m 2. King. 23, 5, etc. Psal. 110. Deu. 12, 2. 3. with 17. 14. 18. 19. 20. 2 King. 10. 26. 27. 28. 2. Chro. 17, 6. Pro. 16, 12. and 25. 2. 3. 4. 5. Act. 19, 27. Rev. 17. 16. n Deut. 17. 14, 18. 19. 20. Josua. 1, 7. 8. 2 Chro. 17, 4. 7. 8. 9. & 19. 4. etc. & 29. & 30. Dan. 6, 25. 26. Psal. 2, 10. 11. 12. & 72. 1. etc. Esa. 49, 23. Rev. 21. 24. Ezra. 7. 26.

40 That therfore the[o] protection & commandement of the Princes and Magistrats maketh it much more peaceable, though[p] no *w*hit at all more la*vv*full, to *v*valke in the vvayes and ordinances of Iesus C*h*rist vvhich hee hath commanded his church to keep vvithout spot and vnrebukeable vntill *h*is appeering in the end of the vvorld. [q]And that in this behalf the brethren thus mynded and proceeding as is beforesaid, doo both contynually supplicate to God, and as t*h*ey may, to their Princes and Gouernours that thus and vnder them they may leade a quiet and peaceable lyfe in all *g*odlynes and honestie.

o Pro. 16, 15. Ezr. 5. aud 6. Act. 9, 31. 1. Tim. 2, 2. Dan. 6, 25. 26. Rev. 21, 24. p Act. 4, 18. 19. and 5. 28. 29. Dan. 6, 7. 8. 9. 10. 22. Luk. 21, 12. 13. Mat. 28, 20. 1. tim. 5, 21. and 6. 13. 14. q Psal. 72, 1. etc. 1. tim. 2, 2. 2 chro. 15, 1. 2. Hag. 1. 4. 14. and 2. 5.

41 That if God encline the Magistrates *h*earts to the allo*v*vance & protection of them therin they accompt it a happie blessing of God *wh*o granteth such nourcing Fathers and nourcing Mothers to his Church, & be carefull to *w*alke vvorthie so great a mercy of God in all thankfulnes and obedience.

Psal. 126, 1. etc. Esa. 49, 13. and 60 16. Psal. 72, 1. etc. Rom. 13, 3. 1. Tim. 2, 2. 3. 4.

42 *T*hat if God vvithold the Magistrates allovvance and furtherãce heerin, they[r] yet proceed together in christian coue-

nant & communion thus to vvalke in the obedience of Christ evē through the middest of all tryalls and aflictions, not accompting their goods, Lands VVyves, Children, Fathers, Mothers, brethren, Sisters, no nor their *ovv*n lyues dear vnto thē, so as they may finish t*h*eir course *w*ith ioy, remembring al*v*vayes that wee [s]ought to obey *G*od rather thē mā, & grounding[t] vpon the commande-ment, commission and prom*i*se of our Saviour Christ, vvho as hee hath all povvre in heauē & in earth, so hath also promised if they keep his commandements vvhich hee hath giuē *w*ithout limitatiō of tyme, place, Magistrates allovvance or disallo*w*ance, to bee *w*ith them *v*nto tbe end of the world and *vv*hen they haue finished their course and kept the fait*h*, to giue them t*h*e cro*vv*n of right-eousnes *v*vhich is layd vp for all them that loue his appeering.

r Act. 2, 40. 41. 42. and 4. 19. and 5. 28. 29. 41. and 16. 20. etc. and 17. 6. 7. and 20. 23. 24. 1. Thes. 3. 3. Phil. 1. 27. 28. 29. Dan. 3, 16. 17. 18. and 6. 7. 10. 22. 23. 24. Luk. 1 4, 26. 27. & 21. 12. 13, 14. 2. tim. 2, 12. and 3, 12. heb 10, 32. etc. 1. Pet. 4. Rev. 2, 10. 25. 26. and. 6. 9. and 12. 11 [s]Act. 5, 29. and 17. 6. 7. t Mat. 28. 18. 19. 20. 1. Tim. 6, 13. 14. 15. 16. 2. Tim. 4, 7. 8. Rev. 2, 10. and 14. 12. 13. and 22. 16. 17. 18. 19. 20.

43 That they doo also *v*villingly and orderly pay and per-forme all maner of la*vv*full and *a*ccustomed dutyes *v*nto all men, submitting [xxii] in the Lord themselues, their bodyes, Landes, *G*oods and lyves to the *M*agistrates pleasure. And t*h*at euery *vv*ay they ac*k*no*vv*ledge, reverence and obey them according to godlynes, not because of vvrath only but also for conscience sake.

Rom. 13, 1. 5. 6. 7. Mat. 22, 21. 2. chro 27, Ezr 7, 26. Tit. 3, 1. 1. Pet. 2, 13 etc.

44 And thus doo vvee the *S*ubiects of God and hir Ma[tie.] falsely called Brovvnists labour to giue vnto God that vvhich is Gods, & vnto *C*æsar that *vv*hich is Cæsars, endevoring our selues to haue alvvayes a cleere conscience tovvards God and tovvards men: And if anie ta*k*e this to be heresie, then doo vvee vvith the [v]Apostle freely confesse that after the vvay vvhic*h* they call heresie vve vvorship Cod the Father of our Lord *I*esus Christ; beleeving all things that are vvritt*e*n in the La*vv*, and in the Prophets & Apostostles: And vvhatsoeuer is according to this vvord of truth published by this *S*tate or holden by anie reformed churches abrode in the vvorld.

v Act. 24, 14.

45 Finally, vvheras vvee are much slandered, as if vve denyed or misliked t*h*at forme of prayer commonly called the

Lords Prayer vvee thought it needfull heere also concerning it to make knovvn that *vv*ee beleeue and ackno*vv*ledg it to bee a most absolute & most excellent forme of prayer sush [such] as no men or Angells can set do*w*ne the like And that it was taught & appointed by our Lord Iesus C*h*rist, not that vvee should bee tyed to the *v*se of those very *w*ords, but *t*hat vvee should according to that rule mak*e* all our requests & *t*hanksgyuing *v*nto God, forasmuch as i*t* is a perfect forme and patterne conteynin*g* in it playne & sufficient directions of prayer for all occasions and necessities that haue been, are, or shalbee to the church of God, or anie member therof to the end of the world.

Mat. 6, 9. etc. Luk. 11, 2. etc. compared with Mat. 14, 30. and 26. 39. 42. Act. 1. 24. 25. and 4. 24. etc. Rom. 8, 26. 27. Rev. 8, 3, 4. Eph. 6. 18, 19. Phyl. 4, 6. Heb. 11, 18. 19. 20. 21. Jude vers. 24, 25.

Now vnto him that is ahle [able] to keep vs that wee fall not, & to present us faltlesse before the presence of his glorie with joy; that is to God only wise our Sauiour, bee glory, & Majestie & dominion, & powre both now & for ever. Amen.

IV

THE POINTS OF DIFFERENCE BETWEEN CONGREGATIONALISM AND THE CHURCH OF ENGLAND, 1603

EDITIONS AND REPRINTS

I. In Johnson and Ainsworth's *Apologie or Defence of svch Trve Christians as are commonly (but vniustly) called Brovvnists:* etc., 1604, pp. 36–38.[1]

II. With the Confession of 1596–98 in *Confessio Fidei Anglorum quorundam in Inferiori Germania exulantium. Vnâ cum annotatione brevi præcipuarum rerum in quibus differimus ab Ecclesia Angliæ*, etc. 1607.[2]

III. Also with the Confession of 1596–98 in *The Confession of faith of certayn English people, living in exile, in the Low Countreyes. Together with a brief note of the special heads of those things wherin we differ frō the Church of Englād*, etc. 1607.[3]

IV. Dutch version of the *Apologie*, 1614,[4] (probably).

V. Dutch version of the *Apologie*, 1670.[5]

VI. Dexter, *Congregationalism, as seen in its Literature*, pp. 307, 308.

LITERATURE

Our chief source of information regarding these petitions and the circumstances under which they were presented is Johnson and Ainsworth's *Apologie*, already cited; Hanbury, *Memorials*, I: 112–117, with extracts from the enlarged form of the *Points of Difference;* Punchard, *History of Congregationalism*, III: 253–265, with an abstract of the *Points* and extracts from the petitions; Dexter, *Congregationalism as seen*, pp. 306–310.

WHEN death removed, in 1603, the great queen under whose reign the London-Amsterdam church had been driven into exile, the throne was taken by James I., — a man whose affiliations and promises had excited the hopes of all parties, from the Catholics to the Puritans, but who was to disappoint religious men of every shade of opinion except the supporters of the royal prerogative and the Church in the form established by Elizabeth. At first, however, the king's real sentiments were unknown, and it was with some confidence of a favorable hearing that about 750 ministers of the Establishment, of Puritan sympathies, laid before

---

[1] See *ante*, p. 41, VI. [2] *Ante*, p. 41, VII. [3] *Ante*, p. 41, VIII.
[4] *Ante*, p. 41, IX. [5] *Ante*, p. 41, X.

him the famous Millenary Petition,[1] praying for a reform of the English Church in the direction of a more thorough-going Protestantism. These hopes of the Puritans were shared by the little Separatist body at Amsterdam, and in like manner they prepared a petition and sent it to London with a copy of their perfected creed of 1598, to convince the new king at once of their loyalty and the correctness of their views. There seems little doubt that Johnson and Ainsworth were its bearers.[2] Not hearing from this petition, the representatives of the church sent to the king a second appeal, containing the brief summary of the fourteen points of difference between the petitioners and the Church of England, which is the document here republished. Whether the king, or his ministers, saw fit to make any inquiries or not, we do not know; but the Separatists now prepared a third petition, recapitulating the points already presented and supporting them elaborately by arguments and citations from the Scriptures. This document seems to have failed of a hearing altogether, and after a considerable waiting, a man of position or influence at court was persuaded to present in their behalf a brief little prayer[3] that the Amsterdam Separatists might be permitted to live in their native land on the same terms as the French and Dutch churches then enjoyed on English soil, and that their opponents might be required to answer their points and arguments, and the whole question be fairly laid before the king. The result was unsatisfactory enough. The Separatists received none of the things for which they sued. And by the close of January, 1604, the Hampton Court Conference must have made it plain to all men that no essential reforms of any sort were to be looked for from the new English ruler.

Doubtless the Convocation of the province of Canterbury, which considered and adopted 161 canons during May, June, and July, 1603, had little if any knowledge of the petitions which the obscure brethren from Amsterdam were pressing upon the attention of the

---

[1] The Petition may be found in full in Fuller, *Church History of Britain*, ed. London, 1842, III: 193–196; or in Perry, *History of the English Church* (Student's Series), London, 1881, pp. 372, 373 (from Fuller).

[2] Dexter, *Cong. as seen*, p. 306. All these Separatist petitions are in the *Apologie*.

[3] Johnson and Ainsworth, *Apologie*, p. 82; see also, Punchard, III: 264.

king.[1] But as one reads the rules for church government which that body prepared, under royal license, and which the king's letters-patent soon approved,[2] one sees clearly that Johnson and Ainsworth had nothing to hope from men so diametrically opposed to the theories of the church which the Separatists drew from the New Testament. Those canons declared that to deny the true and apostolic character of the Church of England, as then established; to hold that the forms of prayer or the rites of that Church were in any way repugnant to Scripture, or superstitious; to question the Christian character of such offices as archbishoprics, bishoprics, or deaneries; to doubt the lawfulness of the ordination and call of bishops, priests, and deacons, when tested by the Word of God; to separate from the Church of England, or to assert that any other bodies of English subjects than those assembling according to the forms established by law can constitute a true church; to do or declare any one of these things is *ipso facto* to incur the penalty of excommunication, in such severity that naught but a public recantation and the satisfaction of the archbishop as to the genuineness of his repentance can restore the offender to the Church. The Separatists might well feel that if Elizabeth had chastised them with whips, James bade fair to chastise them with scorpions. The best that they could hope to do was to remain beyond his reach in their Amsterdam exile.

THE POINTS OF DIFFERENCE.

"1. That Christ the Lord hath by his last Testament given to his Church, and set therein, sufficient ordinary Offices, with the maner of calling or Entrance, Works, and Maintenance, for the administration of his holy things, and for the sufficient ordinary instruction guydance and service of his Church, to the end of the world.[3]

---

[1] Perry, *History of the English Church*, pp. 367, 368. Neal, *History of the Puritans*, II: 27, 31-36, gives an epitome of the canons which concern dissent. See also Punchard, *Hist. of Cong.*, III: 273, 274.

[2] James ordered that these canons should be read in every church at least once a year.

[3] This was a point of difference from the old ecclesiasticism of the early Elizabethan divines rather than from the rising school of high churchmen which had its beginnings about the time of the publication of the *Trve Description*. As Perry has pointed out, the early Elizabethan church theories were Erastian, — that the sovereign preferred Episcopacy was the real warrant for its existence. Even Whitgift, the archbishop who was instrumental in the deaths of Barrowe and Green-

2. That every particular Church hath like and full interest and power to enioy and practise all the ordinances of Christ given by him to his Church to be observed therein perpetually.

3. That every true visible Church,[1] is a company of people called and separated from the world by the word of God, and joyned together by voluntarie profession of the faith of Christ, in the fellowship of the Gospell. And that therfore no knowne Atheist, vnbelever, Heretique, or wicked liver, be received or reteined a member in the Church of Christ, which is his body; God having in all ages appointed and made a separation of his people from the world, before the Law, vnder the Law, and now in the tyme of the Gospell.

4. That discreet, faithfull, and able men (though not yet in office of Ministerie) may be appointed to preach the gospell and whole truth of God, that men being first brought to knowledge, and converted to the Lord, may then be ioyned togeather in holy communion with Christ our head and one with another.

5. That being thus ioyned, every Church hath power in Christ to chuse and take vnto themselves meet and sufficient persons, into the Offices and functions of Pastors, Teachers, Elders, Dea-

---

wood, used language which at least implied that there might be other systems of church-government more warranted by Scripture example than Episcopacy. But with Bancroft's sermon at Paul's Cross, in 1589, the claim was set up (rather indistinctly and indirectly, it must be said) that Episcopacy is of divine warrant and apostolic example. This view was further developed by Thomas Bilson, bishop of Worcester 1596–7, and of Winchester from 1597 to his death in 1616, in his *Perpetval Governement of Christes Chvrch*, 1593, wherein not only is Episcopacy asserted to be the only Scriptural method of church government, but apostolic succession is affirmed to be essential to the very existence of the church. Even the moderate Richard Hooker, in his *Ecclesiasticall Politie*, 1594, while denying that Episcopacy is necessary to the existence of the church, or under all circumstances to be required, asserted it to be the form of government most agreeable to Scripture. Bancroft and Bilson's views gained constantly over the Erastian theories, and with Bancroft's appointment as archbishop, in 1604, mounted the throne of Canterbury. Yet the divergence of this article even from their view is considerable, for though the high churchmen would find in Episcopacy the only form of polity warranted by the Word of God, they hardly claimed that all the minutiæ of offices and rites were prescribed in the New Testament. See Perry, *History of the Church of England*, (Student's Series,) 342–349. Bancroft's sermon may be found in Hicks, *Bibliotheca Script. Eccles. Angl.*, London, 1709, pp. 247–315 (where the old style date of 1588 is assigned to it). His views are set forth with more elaboration in his *Svrvay of the Pretended Holy Discipline*, 1593. A new edition of Bilson's *Perpetval Governement* was brought out by Robert Eden, at Oxford, 1842.

[1] It may not be amiss to add, as an illustration of the conception of the form of a church here set forth, the definition given by Henry Jacob, Johnson's opponent in the extreme Separatism of the latter, but a Congregationalist of great desert, the friend of Robinson, who founded, in 1616, in Southwark, London, the first Congregational church to maintain a continuous existence on English soil. It is in his *Divine Beginning and Institution of Christs True Visible or Ministerial Church*, Leyden, 1610, p. [18]: "A true Visible & Ministeriall Church of Christ is a nomber of faithfull people joyned by their willing consent in a spirituall outward society or body politike, ordinarily comming togeather into one place, instituted by Christ in his New Testament, & having the power to exercise Ecclesiasticall government and all Gods other spirituall ordinances (the meanes of salvation) in & for it selfe immediatly from Christ."

cons and Helpers, as those which Christ hath appointed in his Testament, for the feeding, governing, serving, and building vp of his Church. And that no Antichristiā Hierarchie or Ministerie, of Popes, Arch-bishops, Lord-bishops, Suffraganes, Deanes, Arch-deacons, Chauncellors, Parsons, Vicars, Priests, Dumb-ministers, nor any such like be set over the Spouse and Church of Christ, nor reteined therein.

6. That the Ministers aforesaid being lawfully called by the Church where they are to administer, ought to continew in their functions according to Gods ordinance, and carefully to feed the flock of Christ committed vnto them, being not inioyned or suffered to beare Civill offices withall, neither burthened with the execution of Civill affaires, as the celebration of marriage, burying the dead &c. which things belong aswell to those without as within the Church.[1]

7. That the due maintenance of the Officers aforesaid, should be of the free and voluntarie contribution of the Church, that according to Christs ordinance, they which preach the Gospell may live of the Gospell: and not by Popish Lordships and Livings, or Iewish Tithes and Offerings. And that therefore the Lands and other like revenewes of the Prelats and Clergie yet remayning (being still also baits to allure the Iesuites and Seminaries[2] into the Land, and incitements vnto them to plott and prosecute their woonted evill courses, in hope to enioy them in tyme to come) may now by your Highnes be taken away, and converted to better vse, as those of the Abbeyes and Nunneries have been heertofore by your Maiestyes worthie predecessors, to the honor of God and great good of the Realme.

8. That all particular Churches ought to be so constituted, as having their owne peculiar Officers, the whole body of every Church may meet togeather in one place, and iointly performe their duties to God and one towards another. And that the censures of admonition and excommunication be in due maner executed, for sinne, convicted, and obstinatly stood in. This power

[1] This article, the last clauses of which are so foreign to modern Congregational sentiment, represents the view also of the founders of New England regarding marriages and funerals. As far as known, the first instance of prayer at a New England funeral was at Roxbury in 1685 (Palfrey, *Hist. N. E.*, III: 495). The next year, 1686, saw the first marriage by a minister in Mass. (*Proc. Mass. Hist. Soc.*, 1858–60, p. 283). Connecticut permitted ministers to join in marriage by a law of Oct. 1694 (*Conn. Records*, IV: 136).

[2] *I. e.*, the priests from the Seminary which Cardinal William Allen established in 1568 at Douai in the then Spanish Netherlands. These men, trained for work in England, from 1577 onward were looked upon as the most dangerous foes of English Protestantism.

also to be in the body of the Church wherof the partyes so offending and persisting are members.

9. That the Church be not governed by Popish Canons, Courts, Classes, Customes, or any humane inventions, but by the lawes and rules which Christ hath appointed in his Testament. That no Apocrypha writings, but only the Canonicall scriptures be vsed in the Church. And that the Lord be worshipped and called vpon in spirit and truth, according to that forme of praier given by the Lord Iesus, Math. 6. and after the Leitourgie of his owne Testament, not by any other framed or imposed by men, much lesse by one trāslated from the Popish leitourgie, as the Book of common praier &c.

10. That the Sacraments, being seales of Gods covenant, ought to be administred only to the faithfull, and Baptisme to their seed or those vnder their governement. And that according to the simplicitie of the Gospell, without any Popish or other abuses, in either Sacrament.

11. That the Church be not vrged to the observation of dayes and tymes, Iewish or Popish, save only to sanctify the Lords day: Neyther be laden in things indifferent, with rites and ceremonies, whatsoever invented by men; but that Christian libertie may be reteined: And what God hath left free, none to make bound.

12. That all monuments of Idolatry in garments or any other things, all Temples, Altars, Chappels, and other place, dedicated heertofore by the Heathens or Antichristians to their false worship, ought by lawfull aucthoritie to be rased and abolished, not suffered to remayne, for nourishing superstition, much lesse imploied to the true worship of God.

13. That Popish degrees in Theologie, inforcement to single life in Colledges, abuse of the study of prophane heathen Writers, with other like corruptions in Schooles and Academies, should be remooved and redressed, that so they may be the welsprings and nurseries of true learning and godlinesse.

14. Finally that all Churches and people (without exception) are bound in Religion only to receave aud submit vnto that constitution, Ministerie, Worship, and order, which Christ as Lord and King hath appointed vnto his Church: and not to any other devised by Man whatsoever.

V

THE SEVEN ARTICLES OF 1617 AND THE MAY-FLOWER COMPACT OF 1620

A. The Seven Articles, 1617

This important declaration long remained forgotten among the documents of the State Paper Office at Westminster. It was at last brought to light by the historian, George Bancroft, and communicated by him to

I. *Collections of the New York Historical Society*, Second Series, New York, 1857; III. Pt. I. pp. 301, 302. It was reprinted by

II. Punchard, *History of Congregationalism*, Boston, 1867. III: 454, 455;

III. Waddington, *Congregational History, 1567–1700*, London, 1874, 206, 207;

IV. Doyle, *The English in America, The Puritan Colonies*, London, 1887, I: 49, 50; and

V. Goodwin, *The Pilgrim Republic*, Boston, 1888, p. 41.

Beside some brief comments in the works of Doyle, Goodwin, and Punchard, and an important letter from Bancroft in communicating the document to the New York Society (*Collections*, as cited, 295–99), a few facts will be found in Bradford's *History of Plymouth Plantation*, pp. 30, 31 (ed. Boston, 1856), and a somewhat extended discussion in Bacon's *Genesis of the New England Churches*, New York, 1874, pp. 264–8.

B. The Brief Notes of Explanation, 1618

These supplementary definitions are preserved for us by Bradford, *Hist. Plym. Plantation*, pp. 34, 35. They were copied from Bradford's manuscript by Nathaniel Morton into the records of the Plymouth Church, and may be found in Hazard, *Historical Collections*, Philadelphia, 1792, 1794, I: 364,365; and in Young, *Chronicles of the Pilgrim Fathers*, pp. 64, 65, from that source. They are discussed by Bacon, *Genesis of the N. E. Chs.*, pp. 267–269, and are given by Waddington.

C. The Mayflower Compact, 1620

Texts and Reprints. — Since the original manuscript is not known to be extant, we are dependent upon copies for our knowledge of this important document. Of these there are three which may claim about equal rank as original sources and are in substantial harmony.

I. In G. Mourt's (*i. e.* George Morton's[1]) *A Relation or Iournall of the beginning and proceedings of the English Plantation settled at Plimoth*, etc., London, 1622, p. 3. Reprinted (among others) by Young, *Chronicles of the Pilgrim Fathers*, Boston, 1841–4, p. 121; Geo. B. Cheever in partial fac-simile, New York, 1848, pp. 30, 31: Dr. Dexter, with introduction and notes, and in fac-simile, Boston, 1865, pages 6, 7.

[1] Dexter's reprint, introduction, xviii–xxxi. This portion of the *Relation* was probably by Bradford.

II. In Gov. Bradford's *History of Plymouth Plantation*, long in manuscript. The compact was printed from this manuscript by Thomas Prince, *A Chronological History of New England*, etc., Boston, 1736, I: 84, 85. Gov. Hutchinson again printed it, either from the manuscript or from Prince, in *The History of the Province of Mass. Bay*, Boston, 1767, II. Appendix 455, 456.[1] It may now be found also in the careful edition of Bradford's whole work issued by the Mass. Hist. Society, *History of Plymouth Plantation*, etc., Boston, 1856, pp. 89, 90.

III. In Nathaniel Morton's (son of George) *New England's Memoriall*, etc., Cambridge, N. E., 1669, p. 15. (Fifth[2] edition, John Davis, Boston, 1826, pp. 37, 38; Sixth, Boston, 1855, pp. 24–26). It was reprinted from Morton by Neal, *History of New England*, etc., London, 1720, I: 81, 82;[3] and by Hazard, *Historical Collections*, etc., Philadelphia, 1792, 1794, I: 119. Morton, as keeper of the public records of the Colony from 1645 to 1685, may well have had access to the original document. He alone gives the list of signatures.

Reprints of one or other of these forms, in addition to those already pointed out, are numerous. The following may perhaps be cited:

1. J. Belknap, *American Biography*, Boston, 1794–8, II: 190.
2. Baylies, *Historical Memoir of the Colony of New Plymouth*, Drake's ed. Boston, 1866, p. 28.
3. Hanbury, *Memorials*, I: 398.
4. Elliott, *New England History*, New York, 1857, I: 102.
5. Uhden, *New England Theocracy*, Conant's translation, Boston, 1858, p. 57.
6. Palfrey, *History of New England*, Boston, 1859, I: 165.
7. Punchard, *History of Congregationalism*, III: 411.
8. Waddington, *Congregational History*, 1567–1700, p. 222.
9. Bancroft, *History of the United States*, ed. Boston, 1876, I: 243.
10. Windsor, *Narrative and Critical History of America*, Boston, 1884, III: 269.
11. Goodwin, *The Pilgrim Republic*, Boston, 1888, p. 63.
12. Thwaites, *The Colonies*, 1492–1750, New York, 1891, p. 118.
13. Fisher, *The Colonial Era*, New York, 1892, p. 93.

THE documents thus far considered have been the product of the London-Amsterdam church; the one now presented had for its source the Scrooby-Leyden-Plymouth company. Obscure as is the origin of the London church, the beginnings of the Scrooby congregation are yet more involved in darkness. But it seems certain that a Separatist congregation was gathered by the afterwards celebrated John Smyth, probably about 1602, at Gainsborough, a town some forty miles southeast of York and nearly half way between York and Boston. This church attracted members from the

[1] Carelessly—three misreadings.

[2] Possibly sixth, see Dexter, *Cong. as seen*, Bibl. 1986

[3] With one transposition in the dating clause.

adjacent parts of Nottinghamshire, Lincolnshire, and Yorkshire.[1] Hither came, not far from 1604, John Robinson, from his studies at Cambridge and several years of labor near Norwich, where his Congregational sentiments had attracted the unfavorable notice of his ecclesiastical superiors. But Gainsborough was distant from the residences of a number of the congregation, and, being a town of some size, the church was likely to bring down governmental censure, and, therefore, in 1605 or more probably 1606, a portion of the Gainsborough church organized separately and met statedly at the house of William Brewster, the postmaster at Scrooby, a station on the main road between London and Berwick, about ten miles from Gainsborough. In 1606 also the congregation remaining at Gainsborough removed, together with Smyth, to Amsterdam, where they united with and turmoiled the London-Amsterdam church for a time. Probably the Scrooby company now further perfected its organization, if it had not already done so, by the choice as officers of Richard Clyfton and John Robinson.[2] But this church, too, soon found England a hard place in which to worship God after the Congregational fashion, and through much difficulty they, therefore, made their way to Amsterdam in 1607 and 1608. Here the major part of the church soon came to look with concern on the havoc which the well-meaning but unstable Smyth had already wrought in the always contentious London-Amsterdam church; and so, fearing lest their own brotherhood be drawn into like confusion, they emigrated in 1609 to Leyden. Clyfton preferring to

---

[1] It seems not impossible that Bradford has given us the form, as well as the substance, of the covenant of this church. He tells us (*Hist. Plym. Plant.*, 9.) "They shooke of this yoake of antichristian bondage, and as ye Lords free people, joyned them selves (by a covenant of the Lord) into a church estate, in ye felowship of ye gospell, *to walke in all his wayes, made known, or to be made known unto them, according to their best endeaours, whatsoever it should cost them, the Lord assisting them.*" [The italics are mine.] It is true that Bradford wrote at least a quarter of a century after the events he here describes, and therefore absolute identity is hardly to be affirmed. But the tone and form of this sentence-long covenant is very like that which we shall see used at Salem in 1629 and Boston-Charlestown in 1630, and some others which will be cited in connection with them.

[2] Bacon, *Genesis of the N. E. Chs.*, pp. 207, 230, 231, says that Clyfton was pastor and Robinson teacher at Scrooby. The greater age and long pastoral experience of Clyfton would make his choice as pastor of the new church probable; but it seems to me that the records do not warrant us in asserting positively that he held this office rather than that of teacher. Bradford is obscure. See his *Hist. Plym. Plant.*, pp. 10, 16, 17.

remain at Amsterdam, Robinson[1] was now chosen to the pastorate, if not already in that office, and probably for want of a suitable candidate in the little company, the teachership was left vacant.[2] The post of elder was now worthily filled[3] by the selection of William Brewster.[4] Here at Leyden all the company were to remain

[1] John Robinson, the most celebrated member of the Leyden company, was born in 1575 or '76, probably in the neighborhood of Gainsborough, where we have seen Smyth gathering a Separatist church at a later period. In 1592 he entered Corpus Christi College in the great Puritan university of Cambridge, and here rose in 1598-9 to the dignity of Fellow. About 1600, it would appear, he went to the vicinity of Norwich, or to that city itself, and entered on religious work, probably as a curate. But here his Separatist views became so pronounced that, about 1604, he appears to have incurred censure from his bishop and to have left Norwich for the region of Gainsborough, where we have seen him joining himself to the Separatist church. His election as pastor of the Scrooby-Leyden body has already been noticed. At Leyden he made his home to the end of his days. Here, with others, he purchased a considerable property, more for the use of the church than his own comfort; and here he not only ministered to his flock, but enjoyed the privileges of the University and participated in the controversies aroused by the followers of Arminius, taking the Calvinistic side with much earnestness. Here, too, he ministered to those of his congregation who did not cross the ocean, till his death in March, 1625; and here he was buried in lowly fashion indicative of a considerable degree of poverty; but with evidence of public estimate of his real worth on the part of the Dutch community. His numerous works are written in a sweet-tempered spirit, but are far from presenting the inclination toward so-called progressive thought in doctrinal matters, which has often been attributed to him. In regard to the *polity* of the church he looked upon change as not impossible in consequence of further study of God's word. Among the many sources of information regarding his life and labors I may cite J. Belknap, *American Biography*, Boston, 1794-98, II: 151-178; Brook, *Lives of the Puritans*, II: 334-44: Hanbury, *Memorials*, I: 185-463, *passim* (with much reference to his writings); Hunter, *Collections Concerning the Church . . . formed at Scrooby*, London, 1854, pp. 90-99; Fletcher, *History . . . of Independency in England*, London, 1862, II: 249-III: 80, *passim;* Punchard, *History of Congregationalism*, III: 300-344 (a summary of his writings); Bacon, *Genesis of the N. E. Chs.*, *passim;* Dexter, *Cong. as seen*, 359-410. Dexter's Bibliography gives the titles of eleven separate writings of which Robinson is the author; ten of which may be found in R. Ashton's *Works of John Robinson*, etc., 3 vols., London, 1851. A somewhat extended memoir, by the editor, may be found in the *Works*, I: xi-lxxiv., and is reprinted in *4 Coll. Mass. Hist. Soc.*, I: 111-164.

[2] Bacon, *Genesis*, p. 232, makes this suggestion.

[3] That this event did not occur till the company reached Leyden is implied by Gov. Bradford, *History of Plymouth Plantation*, pp. 10, 17.

[4] William Brewster, in whose house at Scrooby the church had gathered after its separation from the Gainsborough body, was one of the most eminent of the company in station and influence. His birthplace is uncertain, but was not improbably in the vicinity of Scrooby, and his life began some time between 1560 and 1564. He studied Latin so as to have a ready use of the language, had some knowledge of Greek, and was for a brief and uncertain period at the University of Cambridge. We next find him in the service of the Puritan, William Davison, Ambassador and Secretary of State to Queen Elizabeth. With Davison, Brewster went on a mission to Holland in 1585, and doubtless may have cherished hopes of political advancement till the Queen dismissed Davison in disgrace, in 1587, as having been too zealous in procuring the execution of Mary, Queen of Scots. Thrown thus out of employment, Brewster went to Scrooby, and there succeeded his father as postmaster about the beginning of 1589. (His father, also named William Brewster, survived till the summer of 1590.) His office implied the furnishing of lodging and transport for government servants, as well as the forwarding of letters. In discharge of his duties he occupied a large "manor house," belonging to the Archbishop of York for centuries, and which, though in bad repair, gave ample room for the gathering of the Separatist church. He held office till Sept., 1607, just previous to his attempt to leave England for Holland in company with his brethren of the church. Settled at last in Leyden, he supported himself by teaching and printing. Here he was elected ruling elder, and when a portion of the church emigrated to Plymouth in 1620, he was the spiritual leader of the expedition. As the Plymouth company looked upon themselves as in a de-

for eleven years and many for the remainder of their earthly lives. But, though settled in one of the most attractive cities of Europe, their life was hard and their circumstances uncongenial. As Englishmen they longed to be under English law. They would gladly live on English soil could they find a spot where they might worship God and train up their children in the institutions of the Gospel. Probably their type of Separatism was not so uncompromising as that of the London-Amsterdam Church, and certainly we have much evidence that the opposition of their pastor, Robinson, as he advanced in years, was more against the ceremonies of the Church of England than the doctrine of royal supremacy.[1] They were anxious to go to America, and they were desirous of going as Englishmen and under an English charter. And so it happened that when they applied to the London-Virginia company, in 1617, for permission to settle somewhere on the wide stretch of American coast then known by the name of Virginia, the agents of the church, Deacon John Carver and Robert Cushman, carried with them to London the seven articles of belief which are here presented, designing them to serve as an assurance to the company or the king should doubt be cast upon their orthodoxy or loyalty. Of course, under such circumstances, the points of difference between them and the Church of England would be minimized. Yet that these differences

---

gree still part of the Leyden body and, while competent to act for themselves, as still under Robinson's pastorate, Brewster, though retaining the title of ruling elder, was practically the pastor of the Plymouth church in all save the administration of the sacraments for the ten years or thereabout which elapsed between the landing in 1620 and the beginning of the pastorate of Ralph Smith. Here he was noted as a vigorous and effective preacher and as possessed of much gift in prayer. He died in April, 1643 or 1644. His friend Bradford, and Morton in his *Memoriall*, give the former date; the Plymouth church records, from the hand of Morton, give the latter. His memory is that of a strong, earnest, spiritual-minded man. The facts of his life may be found in Bradford, *History of Plymouth Plantation*, *passim*, especially the biographical sketch on pp. 408–14. This memoir is also printed in Young's *Chronicles of the Pilgrim Fathers*, pp. 461–69, and in substance from the Plymouth Ch. records by Davis in his edition of Morton's *Memorial* (1826), 222–224. Belknap, *American Biography*, II: 252–266, has a sketch. Hunter, *Collections concerning the Ch. . . . formed at Scrooby*, etc., (1854,) 53–90, has many valuable facts. A life of Brewster was published by A. Steele, *Chief of the Pilgrims*, etc., Philadelphia, 1857. Bacon, *Genesis of the N. E. Chs.*, *passim*. T. F. Henderson in *Dict. National Biography*, (1886,) vi: 304, 305. Deane has published a letter of Stanhope to Davison, of Aug. 22, 1590, throwing light upon the time when Bradford became postmaster. *Proc. Mass. Hist. Soc.*, May 1871, 98–103.

[1] Dexter, *Cong. as seen*, pp. 392–397, notes and illustrates his gradual change from extreme Separatism to a position not far from that of the Puritans, a position which held that the English Church was unchristian in ceremonies and constitution, but not in a condition where reform was hopeless or Christian life within its fold impossible. This view seems to prevail in Robinson's, *Ivst and Necessarie Apologie*, 1625, *Works*, III: 5–79. See also Cotton's testimony, *Way of Cong. Churches Cleared*, London, 1648, Pt. I: pp. 8, 9.

should be ignored to such a degree, and that Robinson and Brewster should be willing to sign the document, seems little less than amazing. At the first glance it seems the surrender of much for which they witnessed and suffered; and further examination but confirms this opinion. But we shall do injustice to men in a very difficult position should we deem it a complete surrender. Robinson and Brewster were willing to accept a substantially Erastian theory of the relations of church and sovereign. They were willing to admit that there is no "apeale from his authority or judgment in any cause whatsoever, but y in all thinges obedience is dewe unto him," at least passive obedience, even when his commands are contrary to God's word. The[1] king's right to appoint bishops, or other officers, and endow them with civil authority to rule the churches "civilly according to ye Lawes of ye Land" was fully admitted. But they nowhere acknowledged or implied that the officers of the Church of England have any divine warrant or spiritual authority. They said, in effect, that the bishops and other clergy are magistrates, like the justices or sheriffs, whom the king as absolute civil ruler has a legal right to appoint, and to whom the laws give certain powers. The Separatists of Leyden were not rebels, and even if they disliked the system they would not oppose the undoubted royal right. Yet as to the spiritual character or powers of these persons they would maintain their own opinions. They wished peace with the king and the realm, and to secure it, while not willing to unite with the Established Church, they were willing to show respect to the constituted officers of that Church so far as they represent the royal authority.[2] That it was by no means regarded by the English authorities in church and state as a submission to the Church by law established is shown by the fact that though many of the Virginia company found the articles satisfactory, King James, and Abbot, the Archbishop of Canterbury, opposed the request for a charter.[3] In hope, therefore, that a

[1] This duty of obedience or at least passive submission to the will of the magistrate is further set forth by Robinson, *Ivst and Necessarie Apologie*, *Works*, III: 62, 63.

[2] As illustrative of this interpretation compare Robinson *Ivst and Necessary Apologie*, (1625,) *Works*, III: 69–71.

[3] Compare Bradford, *Hist. Plym. Plant*, pp. 29–41.

further explanation would accomplish the desired result, Robinson and Brewster sent, in January, 1618, two notes to Sir John Wolstenholme, a member of the Virginia company whom they had reason to think was favorably disposed toward their enterprise. These notes were designed to define the beliefs of the Leyden church more clearly, and were alternate forms to be laid before the Privy Council as Sir John should deem best.[1] As of value in showing the position of the Leyden church at this period, they will be found appended to the *Seven Articles*. In spite of all explanations, however, the utmost that the church could obtain was an unrecorded promise that if its members behaved themselves peaceably the king would overlook their doings, and a patent from the Virginia company granting to one of their friends in England (of course in intention as their representative) some lands supposed to lie not far from the Hudson river;[2] a document which, as the event proved, was never to be used.

But though the end of their preparation of creeds for submission to the English authorities had come, their difficulties in going to America were by no means over, and it was not till after further tedious negotiation, into the details of which it would be aside from our purpose to enter, that somewhat less than half the church, under the spiritual guidance of Brewster, got away at last from Leyden, in July, 1620, leaving the remainder under Robinson to keep a place for their return should the adventure fail, or follow them in case of success, as opportunity would permit. Never did an enterprise start more unpropitiously. It was only after numberless hindrances in England, and two unsuccessful attempts to sail from that island, that the more steadfast members of the little company were able to get off in their single ship from the English Plymouth, September 6, (O. S.) 1620. On November 9, they were in sight of Cape Cod, and on November 11, having been compelled to abandon the attempt to reach the neighborhood of the Hudson, they came to anchor in Provincetown Harbor. Here it was, on this eleventh of November, that the little

[1] Compare *Ibid.*, pp. 33–36.

[2] *Ibid.*, pp. 40–41. This charter, granted to a John Wincob, probably a Puritan minister in the service of the Countess of Lincoln, was early lost and its exact provisions are unknown.

company combined themselves into a civil body politic. They were in a region belonging nominally indeed to the English crown, but they were outside the limits of their patent, for though we do not know the terms of that document, we know that the London-Virginia company had no jurisdiction north of 41°.[1] Then, too, there were others beside the Leyden Separatists on the ship, whose loyalty to the purposes of the colony was dubious, and the organized force of the community might be needed to hold them in check. Gov. Bradford thus explains the circumstances:[2]

"I shall a litle returne backe and begine with a combination made by them before they came ashore, being ye first foundation of their govermente in this place; occasioned partly by ye discontented & mutinous speeches that some of the strangers amongst them had let fall from them in ye ship—That when they came a shore they would use their owne libertie; for none had power to comand them, the patente they had being for Virginia, and not for Newengland, which belonged to an other Goverment, with which ye Virginia Company had nothing to doe. And partly that shuch an acte by them done (this their condition considered) might be as firme as any patent, and in some respects more sure."

It is more than possible, also, that such a combination had been planned even before the expedition left Leyden. A letter of Robinson has been preserved, written to the company just after they had left Holland, in the summer of 1620, in which he warns them:

"Your intended course of ciuill communitie wil minister continuall occasion of offence, and will be as fuell for that fire, except you diligently quench it with brotherly forbearance."

And, a little later adds the exhortation:

"Lastly, whereas you are to become a body politik, vsing amongst your selues ciuill gouernment, and are not furnished with any persons of speciall eminencie aboue the rest, to be chosen by you into office of gouernment: Let your wisedome and godlinesse appeare, not onely in chusing such persons as do entirely loue, and will diligently promote the common good, but also in yeelding vnto them all due honour and obedience in their lawfull administrations.[3]

---

1 The forty-first degree of latitude falls a little north of New York city.

2 Bradford, *Hist. Plym. Plant*, p. 89.

3 I quote from Mourt's *Relation*, pp. x, xi (Dr. Dexter's edition xliv–xlvi). A note of Dr. Dexter puts this interpretation on the passages. The letter may also be found in Bradford, *Hist. Plym. Plant*, pp. 64–67; Morton's *Memoriall*, pp. 6–9 (Davis ed. pp. 25–29); Hazard's *Historical Collections*, I: 96–99; Hanbury, *Memorials*, I: 394–396. I am aware that Bradford omits the important word *to* in the clause beginning *Lastly, whereas;* and that Robinson may therefore be made to mean simply that they are now under the Virginia patent; but he seems to me to mean more than that, when both passages are considered.

The Mayflower Compact is in no sense a creed or a religious covenant; but it is none the less the direct fruit of the teachings of Congregationalism. That system recognized as the constitutive act of a church a covenant individually entered into between each member, his brethren, and his God, pledging him to submit himself to all due ordinances and officers and seek the good of all his associates. In like manner this compact bound its signers to promote the general good and to yield obedience to such laws as the community should frame. The Separatist Pilgrims on the Mayflower constituted a state by individual and mutual covenant, just as they had learned to constitute a church; and therefore the Mayflower Compact deserves a place among the creeds and covenants of Congregationalism.[1]

The Seven Articles[2]

Seven Artikes which ye Church of Leyden sent to ye Counsell of England to bee considered of in respeckt of their judgments occationed about theer going to Virginia Anno 1618.

1. To ye confession of fayth published in ye name of ye Church of England[3] & to every artikell theerof wee do wth ye reformed churches wheer wee live & also els where assent wholy.

2. As wee do acknolidg ye docktryne of fayth theer tawght so do wee ye fruites and effeckts of ye same docktryne to ye begetting of saving fayth in thousands in ye land (conformistes & reformistes) as ye ar called wth whom also as wth our bretheren wee do desyer

---

[1] The literature having to do with the history of the Scrooby-Leyden Plymouth church is very voluminous; but the following readily accessible works will either put the student in possession of about all the facts or show him where they may be obtained. SOURCES. Bradford, *History of Plymouth Plantation;* Mourt's *Relation;* Young's *Chronicles of the Pilgrim Fathers* (Boston, 1841–4); Morton's *Memoriall* (for these works see *ante* p. 81); Dexter, *English Exiles in Amsterdam*, in 2 *Proc. Mass. Hist. Soc.*, VI: 41 (June, 1890). LITERATURE. *a.* Formation of the church and sojourn in Holland. Geo. Sumner, *Memoirs of the Pilgrims at Leyden*, in *3 Coll. Mass. Hist. Soc.*, IX: 42–74; W. H. Bartlett, *The Pilgrim Fathers*, London, 1853 (especially valuable for its beautiful engravings of the scenes associated with the Pilgrims); Hunter, *Collections concerning the Church . . . formed at Scrooby*, London, 1854; Dexter, *Recent Discoveries concerning the Plymouth Pilgrims*, in *Cong. Quarterly*, IV: 58–66, (Jan. 1862); Ibid., *Letter*, in *1 Proc. Mass. Hist. Soc.*, XII: 184–186 (Jan. 1872); Ibid., *Cong. as seen*, 316, 317, 359–410; Ibid., *The Pilgrims of Leyden*, in the *New England Magazine*, I: 49–61 (Sept. 1889. This number is filled with interesting sketches of Scrooby and Plymouth). *b.* General accounts of the origin of the church and settlement of the colony. Palfrey, *Hist. New England*, I: 133–231; Punchard, *Hist. Congregationalism*, III: 277–434; Bacon, *Genesis of the N. E. Churches*, pp. 199 *et seqq*; Prof. F. B. Dexter, in Winsor's *Narrative and Crit. Hist.*, III: 257–294; Goodwin, *The Pilgrim Republic*, Boston, 1888 (a valuable treasure-house of facts regarding Plymouth colony).

[2] Text from Bancroft.

[3] i. e., the XXXIX Articles.

to keepe speritual communion in peace and will pracktis in our parts all lawfull thinges.

3. The King's Majesty wee acknolidg for Supreame Governer in his Dominion in all causes and over all parsons,[1] and y[2] none maye decklyne or apeale from his authority or judgment in any cause whatsoever, but y in all thinges obedience is dewe unto him, ether active, if ye thing commanded be not agaynst God's woord, or passive yf itt bee, except pardon can bee obtayned.[3]

4. Wee judg itt lawfull for his Majesty to apoynt bishops, civill overseers, or officers in awthoryty onder hime, in ye severall provinces, dioses, congregations or parrishes to oversee ye Churches[4] and governe them civilly according to ye Lawes of ye Land, untto whom y^e^[5] ar in all thinges to geve an account & by them to bee ordered according to Godlynes.

5. The authoryty of ye present bishops in ye Land wee do acknolidg so far forth as ye same is indeed derived from his Majesty untto them and as ye proseed in his name, whom wee will also theerein honor in all things and hime in them.[6]

6. Wee beleeve y^t^ no sinod, classes, convocation or assembly of Ecclesiasticall Officers hath any power or awthoryty att all but as ye same by ye Majestraet geven unto them.[7]

7. Lastly, wee desyer to geve untto all Superiors dew honnor to preserve ye unity of ye speritt wth all y feare God, to have peace wth all men what in us lyeth & wheerein wee err to bee instructed by any.

Subscribed by
JOHN ROBINSON,
and
WILLYAM BRUSTER.

THE NOTES OF EXPLANATION[8]

The first breefe note was this.

Touching ye Ecclesiasticall ministrie, namly of pastores for teaching, elders for ruling, & deacons for distributing ye churches

1 Persons. 2 *I. e., that*, and so elsewhere.

3 The article does not mean that the signers are willing to do all that the king commands. But they promise that if the action required is so contrary to the law of God that they cannot perform it, they will peacefully submit to the penalties for its omission, making no resistance to the ordinary course of the law other than a proper effort to obtain a pardon.

4 Observe the plural form. 5 *I. e.*, the churches.

6 Notice the care with which this article avoids ascribing any spiritual authority to the clergy of the Establishment.

7 This article is designed to be a denial of Presbyterianism.

8 Text from Bradford's *History Plym. Plant.*

contribution, as allso for ye too Sacrements, baptisme, and ye Lords supper, we doe wholy and in all points agree with ye French reformed churches, according to their publick confession[1] of faith.

The oath of Supremacie we shall willingly take if it be required of us, and that conveniente satisfaction be not given by our taking ye oath of Alleagence.[2]

JOHN ROB:
WILLIAM BREWSTER.

Y^e 2. was this.

Touching ye Ecclesiasticall ministrie, &c. as in ye former, we agree in all things with the French reformed churches, according to their publick confession of faith; though some small differences be to be found in our practises, not at all in ye substance of the things, but only in some accidentall circumstances.

1. As first, their ministers doe pray with their heads covered; ours uncovered.

2. We chose none for Governing Elders but such as are able to teach; which abilitie they doe not require.

3. Their elders & deacons are anūall, or at most for 2. or 3. years; ours perpetuall.

4. Our elders doe administer their office in admonitions & excommunications for publick scandals, publickly & before ye congregation; theirs more privately, & in their consistories.

5. We doe administer baptisme only to such infants as wherof ye one parente, at ye least, is of some church, which some of ther churches doe not observe; though in it our practice accords with their publick confession[3] and ye judgmente of ye most larned amongst them.

Other differences, worthy mentioning, we know none in these points. Then aboute ye oath, as in ye former.[4]

Subscribed,
JOHN R.
W. B.

---

[1] This confession may be found in Schaff's *Creeds of Christendom*, III: 356–382. See especially Articles XXIX–XXXVIII.

[2] The oath of Supremacy, imposed by Henry VIII. in 1531, was reëstablished in the first year of Elizabeth. The person taking it swore "that the queen's highness is the only supreme governor of this realm . . . as well in all spiritual and ecclesiastical things or causes as temporal." All allegiance to foreign powers or prelates is renounced. The oath of Allegiance was imposed in 1605 under James, and implied complete submission to the king as temporal sovereign. See Young, *Chron. of the Pilgrim Fathers*, p. 64, note. The text of the oath of Supremacy may be found in Hallam, *Constit. Hist. England*, Ch. III, note (ed. New York, 1882, p. 121).

[3] Article XXXV of French Confession. Schaff, *Creeds*, III: 379.

[4] This sentence and the opening clause of this note are doubtless simply Bradford's summary of the statements given in full in the preceding note.

The Mayflower Compact [1]

In the name of God, Amen. We whose names are vnderwritten, the loyall Subiects of our dread soveraigne Lord King Iames, by the grace of God of Great *Britaine*, *France*, and *Ireland* King, Defender of the Faith, &c.

Having vnder-taken for the glory of God, and advancement of the Christian Faith, and [2] honour of our King and Countrey, a Voyage to plant the first Colony in the Northerne parts of Virginia, doe by these presents solemnly & mutually in the presence of *God* and one of [3] another, covenant, and combine our selues together into a civill body politike, for our better ordering and preservation, and furtherance of the ends aforesaid ; and by vertue hereof to[4] enact, constitute, and frame such iust and equall Lawes, Ordinances, acts, constitutions,[5] offices[6] from time to time, as shall be thought most meet and convenient for the generall good of the Colony : vnto which we promise all due submission and obedience. In witnesse whereof we haue here-vnder[7] subscribed our names,[8] *Cape Cod*[9] 11. of *November* in the yeare of [10] the raigne of our soveraigne Lord King Iames, of *England*, *France*, and *Ireland* 18.[11] and of Scotland 54.[12] *Anno Domino* 1620.

---

1 Text from Mourt's *Relation*.

2 Morton, *Memoriall*, inserts *the* after *and*.

3 Morton, *Memoriall*, omits *of*.

4 Morton reads *do*.

5 Bradford and Morton insert *and*.

6 Morton reads *officers*.

7 Morton reads *hereunto*.

8 Bradford and Morton insert *at*.

9 Bradford and Morton insert *the*.

10 Morton omits *the yeare of*.

11 Bradford and Morton read *the eighteenth*.

12 Bradford and Morton read *the fiftie fourth*.

VI

THE DEVELOPMENT OF COVENANT AND CREED IN THE SALEM CHURCH, 1629–1665

TEXTS

No record appears to have been kept during the first six or seven years of the history of the church at Salem. About 1637 a church-book was started, but as it came to be in dilapidated condition and was filled with personal reflections of a somewhat censorious nature, it was sequestered in 1660;[1] and its more important portions copied in that year, or the year following, into a new book, which still exists,—a second and older copy will be described shortly. This record of 1637 began, it is well-nigh certain, with the covenant[2] as renewed at the settlement of Hugh Peter in 1636. The covenant of 1629 is nowhere separately preserved; it exists embedded in the renewal and enlargement of 1636. But, as already noted, even the original record of this renewal is lost. The renewed covenant of 1636 is preserved in the two copies, already mentioned, either of which may be considered as representative of the original text, and differing only in slight verbal points, as follows:

A. It is to be found in a book of excerpts from the original records of the Salem church, made by Rev. John Fiske,[3] between 1636 and 1641, while he was serving as an occasional assistant to Rev. Hugh Peter, then pastor of the church. This little book was apparently a private record of parochial affairs.[4] The covenant here contained is printed in the *Hist. Coll. Essex Institute*, Vol. I. No. 2, pp. 37, 38 (May, 1859).[5]

B. The other copy is in the revised church-book of 1660 or 1661, prepared soon after the settlement of John Higginson. This document is printed *verbatim* in the *Proceedings of Essex Institute*, I: 262–264 (1856); by White, *New England Congregationalism*, pp. 13, 14; by Webber and Nevins, *Old Naumkeag*, Salem, 1877, pp. 14–16; by Rev. Edmund B. Willson in the *History of Essex County, Mass.*, Philadelphia, 1888, p. 24; and in modern spelling, by Upham, *Address at the Re-Dedication of the Fourth Meeting-House of the First Church in Salem*, Salem, 1867, pp. 63–65.

---

[1] The record of these transactions is to be found in White, *New England Congregationalism*, Salem, 1861, pp. 47, 48. The first vote is Sept. 10, 1660.

[2] So to be inferred from the fact that it begins the church-book copy, *Ibid.*, 117.

[3] A life of Rev. John Fiske may be found in Mather, *Magnalia*, ed. 1853–5, I: 476–480; Brook, *Lives*, III: 468, 469; Sprague, *Annals of the Am. Pulpit*, New York, 1857, I: 106, 107. He came to New England in 1637, lived in Salem, but soon moved to Wenham, where he became pastor of the church gathered there in 1644. About 1656 he removed to Chelmsford, and there died in 1676, leaving records of great value for New England Church History.

[4] See some observations by J. A. Emmerton, in *Hist. Coll. Essex Ins.*, XV: 70–72 (1878).

[5] From the MS. note book, then in the possession of David Pulsifer, Esq., of Boston. Some account of the preservation of this book may be found in White, *N. E. Cong.*, p. 20.

OTHER PRINTED COPIES

Beside the carefully printed texts, already noticed, this renewal covenant of 1636 early found a place on the pages of writers on New England ecclesiastical affairs.

I. Rathband, *A Briefe Narration of some Church Courses held in Opinion and Practise in the Churches lately erected in New England*, London, 1644, pp. 17–19.[1] From Rathband it was copied into Hanbury, *Memorials*, II: 310. II. *A Copy of the Church Covenants which have been used in the Church of Salem*, Boston, 1680.[2] III. Mather, *Magnalia*, ed. 1702, Bk. I: Ch. IV. Ed. 1853–5, I: 71. IV. Neal, *History of New England*, London, 1720, I: 126–28 (from Mather). V. Rev. William Bentley, *A Description and History of Salem*, in *1 Coll. Mass. Hist. Soc.*, VI: 283–285. VI. Morton's *Memoriall*, Davis, ed. Boston, 1826, *Appendix*, 389–90. VII. Upham, *Second Century Lecture of the First Church*, Salem, 1829, pp. 67, 68. VIII. S. M. Worcester, *Discourse delivered on the First Centennial . . . of the Tabernacle Church*, Salem, 1835; Appendix U.[3] IX. Hanbury, *Memorials*, 1841, as cited under I. X. *N. E. Historical and Genealogical Register*, I: 224, 225 (1847). XI. Morton's *Memoriall*, ed. Boston, 1855, Appendix, pp. 462-464. XII. Uhden, *New England Theocracy*, Conant's translation, Boston, 1858, pp. 61, 62. XIII. Fletcher, *History . . . of Independency in England*, London, 1862, III: 131, 132. XIV. Waddington, *Congregational History, 1567-1700*, pp. 260, 261. XV. T. W. Higginson, *Life of Francis Higginson*, New York [1891], pp. 80, 81.

The ANTI-QUAKER CLAUSE *of 1660–1* is to be found in the new church record, made early in John Higginson's pastorate, and is printed *verbatim* at the close of the renewed covenant of 1636 in the *Proceedings of Essex Institute*, I: 264; in White, *New England Congregationalism*, p. 14; and in Webber and Nevins, *Old Naumkeag*, p. 16; and in Willson's article in the *History of Essex County*, p. 24.

The DIRECTION *of 1665* was printed in that year and does not appear in full on the church records, as it was not formally adopted by the church, though used by the pastor in certain admissions. This pamphlet was long lost to sight, but was discovered by Rev. Dr. J. B. Felt, the antiquary, and communicated by him to Rev. Dr. S. M. Worcester. It has since been printed in I. S. M. Worcester, *New England's Glory and Crown. A Discourse delivered at Plymouth, Dec. 22, 1848*, Boston, 1849, pp. 54, 55. II. *Ibid.*, in *Salem Gazette*, April 4, 1854.[4] III. Morton, *Memoriall*, ed. 1855, *Appendix*, pp. 459–462. IV. Felt, *Did the First Church of Salem originally have a Confession of Faith distinct from their Covenant?* Boston, 1856, *Appendix*, pp. 23–25. V. White, *New England Congregationalism*, Salem, 1861, 190–192 (from Worcester). VI. Felt, *Reply to the New England Congregationalism*, etc., Salem, 1861, *Appendix*. The *Confession of Faith* may also be found in the *Congregationalist*, Jan. 2, 1890.

---

[1] Rathband gives with it the covenant of the church of Rotterdam, Holland, "renewed when Mr. *H. P.* [Hugh Peter] was made their Pastour." More will be said of this later.

[2] This excessively rare pamphlet is mentioned by Thomas, *Hist. Printing in America*, Albany, 1874, II: 323. A MS. copy exists among the records of the Tabernacle Church, Salem.

[3] White, *N. E. Cong.*, p. 185. In the controversy between Worcester, White, and Felt, the document was several times printed in newspapers or pamphlets.

[4] White, *N. E. Cong.*, p. 206.

LITERATURE

The Salem *Covenant* and *Direction* have given rise to a considerable literature, much of it of a sharply controversial nature and not a little affected by doctrinal polemics. On the one hand, Rev. Dr. S. M. Worcester[1] and Rev. J. B. Felt, LL.D.,[2] insisted, in numerous publications,[3] that the Salem church had a creed as well as a covenant at its beginning and that the *Direction* of 1665 contains, to all intents and purposes, the form of creed adopted by the church in 1629; basing their arguments, for the most part, on a strict construction of the phrase employed by John Higginson in the title to the *Direction* itself;[4] and the expressions of Morton in writing of the formation of the Salem church.[5] They also held from the phraseology of its opening paragraph, the adaptation of its articles to 1636 rather than 1629, and possible hints in a pamphlet issued by the Salem church in 1680,[6] and in the *Magnalia*,[7] that the full covenant with nine articles (styled by me the "Covenant of 1636"), could not date from 1629. Dr. Worcester also shrewdly guessed, simply from the wording of the opening sentences of this fuller covenant, that it embedded the covenant of 1629 in a single sentence.[8] This latter view of Dr. Worcester's was adopted, though without any special advance in clearness of proof over his argument, by Hon. Charles W. Upham[9] and by Mr. George Punchard,[10] who do not, however, follow him in his claims for the *Direction*. On the other hand, Judge D. A. White[11] has shown[12] that the church

---

[1] S. M. Worcester was born in 1801, graduated at Harvard 1822, taught in Amherst College 1823–1835. In the latter year he became pastor of the Tabernacle Church, Salem, and so remained till 1860. He died in 1866. He was always a warm defender of Trinitarian Congregationalism. See Appleton's *Cyclopeaia Am. Biog.*, VI: 613.

[2] J. B. Felt was born 1789, graduated at Dartmouth in 1813. He was pastor at Sharon, Mass., 1821–1824, and at Hamilton, Mass., 1824–1833. Being compelled by ill-health to abandon the active work of the ministry, he obtained employment congenial to his antiquarian tastes, engaging from 1836 to 1846 in the arranging of the Mass. State Archives at Boston. In 1853 he became librarian of the Congregational Library, Boston. He died in 1869. In theology he sympathized with Dr. Worcester, See *N. E. Hist. and Genealogical Register*, XXIV: 1–5 (1870).

[3] The most important of these have been cited in the list of reprints of the various Salem documents, especially those under the title "Direction of 1665," in the preceding paragraphs of this chapter. I may add Felt, *Annals of Salem*, 2d ed., Salem, 1845, 1849, II: 567; and Felt, *Ecclesiastical Hist. N. E.*, Boston, 1855, I: 115, 116, 267. Some references to newspaper publications are gathered up by White in his *N. E. Congregationalism*.

[4] See text on page 119.

[5] Morton, *Memoriall*, 73–76; Davis ed., 145–147; Hubbard, *Gen. Hist. N. E.*, 118–120, follows Morton.

[6] Worcester, *Discourse delivered on the First Centennial . . . of the Tabernacle Ch.*, Salem, 1835, *Appendix U*. White, *N. E. Congregationalism*, 187, 188.

[7] Ed. 1853–5, I: 71, "Covenant . . . which was about seven years after solemnly *renewed*."

[8] Worcester, *Ibid*. White, *Ibid*.

[9] Upham, *Address at the Re-Dedication of the Fourth Meeting-House of the First Church in Salem*, Salem, 1867, 20–30. He is disposed to give weight to the fact that a later hand has underscored the sentence in question, as if to render it specially conspicuous, in the copy recorded in the church-book of 1660–1.

[10] *History of Congregationalism*, IV: 14. Punchard leaves the general controversy undecided. Webber and Nevins, in *Old Naumkeag*, 13, 14, take the same view as Upham, but without argument. They also hold that the introduction to the enlarged covenant dates from 1660, a theory which a glance at Rathband proves untenable.

[11] D. A. White, born in 1776, graduated at Harvard, 1797. After studying law, he was chosen to the Mass. legislature. He was made Probate Judge of Essex County in 1815 and held the office till 1853. From 1848 till his death he was president of the Essex Institute. He died in 1861. He was a Unitarian of the old school, a member of the First Church in Salem. See *Proc. Mass. Hist. Soc.*, VI: 262–330 (Sept. 1862); and *Hist. Coll. Essex Institute*, VI: 1–24, 49–71 (1864).

[12] In various writings, all of which are summed up in his *New England Congregationalism*, Salem, 1861.

records themselves amply account for the origin of the *Direction* in 1665. The use of any other standard than the Covenant at the formation of the church is to be denied because of the silence of those records as to any confession of faith adopted by the church, and the fact that the *Magnalia*, though preserving the Covenant, does not hint at the existence of any other document, while the words of the other historians[1] do not necessarily imply more than one formula, since, as he claims, the description "confession" and "covenant" is not an unnatural one to apply to the many-articled Covenant [of 1636]. But Judge White goes so far as to claim also that the whole of the enlarged Covenant, except the brief formula of renewal at its beginning, should be dated back to 1629.[2]

It is with considerable diffidence that the writer presumes to pass judgment upon the views of these learned contestants. But, it seems to him that material evidence has been overlooked on both sides. In his opinion Drs. Worcester and Felt were wholly wrong in claiming that the *Direction* of 1665 can be the creed of 1629, as they would have it. The arguments of Judge White against this view are conclusive. But, if any proof was wanting, the writer would find it in the fact, which a few moments' examination seems to him to demonstrate, that the "confession of faith" of the *Direction* is essentially an epitome of portions of the Westminster Catechism, from which much of its phraseology appears to be borrowed. It can therefore by no possibility be dated back to 1629. The utmost that can be claimed for the phrase employed by John Higginson in the title of the *Direction* is that, in his judgment, it represented the doctrinal position approved, in general, by the church from the beginning. But while Judge White was right on this point, he fell into error regarding the enlarged covenant, when he claimed that it dates back, in its entirety, to 1629. Dr. Worcester's surmise was correct; the main portion of this Covenant is, at the earliest, of 1636;[3] and the covenant of 1629 which has come down to us is a single brief sentence embedded in it. Evidence which Dr. Worcester seems to have overlooked enables us not only to bring fresh weight to the correctness of his surmise, but to assert with considerable confidence that the preamble and articles of the Covenant in its enlarged form are from the pen of Hugh Peter. William Rathband has preserved in a work published in London in 1644,[4] two covenants as illustrative of the practice of the Congregational churches. One is that adopted by the church in Rotterdam, Holland, when Peter became its pastor,[5] the other our enlarged Salem Covenant. So similar are they in phraseology that the conclusion is hard to avoid that they were written by the same person. The enlarged Covenant, with the exception of the single sentence which the preamble distinctly affirms to be the original Covenant, cannot therefore antedate Peter's coming to Salem.[6]

---

[1] *I. e.*, Morton and Hubbard, see *ante*, p. 95, note 5.

[2] White's arguments were summed up and reinforced by Dr. Dexter in an article in the *Congregationalist*, Jan. 28, 1875, p. 3. See note 6, below.

[3] Since Peter was not settled at Salem till December of that year.

[4] Rathband. *A Briefe Narration of some Church Courses held in Opinion and Practise in the Churches lately erected in New England*, pp. 17–19. This portion of Rathband's work is quoted by Hanbury, *Memorials*, II: 309, 310. White twice alludes to Hanbury's reprint of the Salem Covenant, *New England Cong.*, pp. 21, 258; but seems not to have compared it with the Rotterdam Covenant preserved in the same passage.

[5] In 1629.

[6] The strongest argument which can be brought against the view here presented is the statement of Morton (and Hubbard) that the Salem church adopted "a confession of faith and covenant" in 1629. This dual expression, which applies admirably to the nine articled and lengthy covenant of 1636, cannot be made to fit the single sentence of 1629. It should, however, be remembered that Morton was not a contemporary writer. His work was published in 1669. Let it be con-

THE Congregationalists whose standards have thus far been presented were Separatists, but the vast majority of those who were to come to the shores of New England were not Separatists but Puritans.[1] Doctrinally there was little difference between the two parties. Both were Calvinists of a pronounced type and both belived that in the Bible is to be found a sufficient rule for faith and church practice. But while the Separatist would withdraw from the English Establishment at once and forever, the Puritan remembered that the sixteenth century had seen the constitution, liturgy, and doctrinal standards of the English Church essentially altered at least four times by the united action of the sovereign and of Parliament.[2] He was not inclined, therefore, to look upon the State Church as by any means in a hopeless condition. At first, in the early days of Elizabeth, Puritan opposition had been directed chiefly against certain rites and vestments; as the movement went on, the Puritans began to question more and more the warrant for the whole church constitution in its episcopal form; but they constantly hoped that that which had been established by law would be changed by legislative act. Nor was there, at first, anything which seemed unlikely in this supposition. Throughout the reign of Elizabeth the Puritans were a growing party; they might soon, it was easy to believe, incline the sovereign and Parliament to enact the reforms for which they longed. But, as we have seen,[3] there grew

---

ceded, nevertheless, that he may have got his information from John Higginson, one of the members of the church in 1629 and a contemporary. Higginson was only 13 in 1629. He left Salem within a year or two and did not return till 1659. The church records were not kept from 1629 to 1636 or 1637; and the book of records which John Higginson found on his return bore on its opening pages the covenant as enlarged in 1636. (See *ante*, p. 93, note 2.) The opening paragraph of that enlarged covenant declares that *something* which follows is the "Church Covenant we find this Church bound unto at theire first beginning." It is not easy, from the document itself, to see *how much* of what follows that declaration implies. In the absence of any ready means of test, such as Rathband affords, Higginson, or Morton, made the mistake of applying it to *all* rather than to a single sentence. The error was easy and natural and once made was readily followed by Hubbard and Mather.

It is with satisfaction that I am able to record that the late Dr. Dexter, to whose judgment the conclusions thus outlined were submitted, expressed his concurrence, in a letter of Oct. 29, 1890, not only in this note but in the entire position here taken in regard to the merits of the discussion.

[1] The contrasts between the Separatist colony of Plymouth and the Puritan settlements of Massachusetts Bay have been sharply drawn by S. N. Tarbox, *Plymouth and the Bay*, in *Cong. Quarterly*, XVII: 238–252.

[2] The extent to which the Church of the Tudor period was the creature of the State is clearly shown in G. W. Childs' *Church and State under the Tudors*, London, 1890.

[3] See *ante*, p. 77, note.

up alongside of Puritanism, as the sixteenth century waned, the new *jure divino* Episcopacy of Bancroft and Bilson, a view which much increased the opposition between the Puritan and the High Anglican parties, while just in the degree in which it dominated those charged with the conduct of government it made vain the expectation of legislative change. Yet it was not till the elevation of Laud to the bishopric of London by Charles I., in 1628, put a man at the head of one of the most Puritanically inclined of English dioceses who was determined to enforce absolute conformity to his high church views and who at the same time heartily supported the growing absolutism and tyranny of the crown, that the great majority of the Puritan party began to despair of churchly reform at home. Laud's elevation to the see of Canterbury in 1633, as well as his influence over the king, placed all ecclesiastical England at his mercy; while the frustration by Charles of all attempts of Parliament to limit the exercise of royal authority made men doubtful as to the prospects of civil liberty. It was natural, therefore, that the descriptions of the experiences of the Plymouth settlers, such as Mourt's *Relation*, or Winslow's *Good News from New England*,[1] should attract attention among the Puritans and stimulate inquiry among the more adventurous as to the feasibility of planting colonies beyond the ocean out of the reach of Laud. It would be far from correct to say that it was any general longing for freedom of conscience or universal toleration that moved these men to think of America; it was an impulse of a much simpler and, considering the age in which they lived, of a far more natural character. They believed certain practices in the government and worship of the Church of England to be contrary to the Word of God. They did not desire to separate from that great body,[2] or brand it as in its entirety anti-Christian, as some

[1] Published in 1622 and 1624, respectively.

[2] See the views on separation reported by Mather (*Magnalia*, ed. 1853–5, I: 362) to have been uttered by Francis Higginson as he left England. But perhaps the kindly feeling of these emigrants toward the Church of England, in spite of its errors, is best seen in the *Hvmble Reqvest of . . . the Governour and the Company late gone for Nevv-England; To the rest of their Brethren, in and of the Church of England. For the obtaining of their Prayers*, etc. London, 1630 (also Hubbard, *Gen. Hist.*, pp. 126–128; Hutchinson, *Hist. Mass. Bay*, I: 487–489; Hazard,

of the extremer Separatists had done. They wanted to get out of the way of the ecclesiastical courts and the high church bishops to some place where they could discard such of the ceremonies of the church as seemed superstitious and practice such things as seemed to them directly enjoined by Scripture.

It was not long after the landing of the Plymouth founders that attempts looking toward further settlements on the coast of the present State of Massachusetts were made. Some of these attempts were by Church of England and royalist sympathizers, sent out by Sir Ferdinando Gorges and others, to take possession of the lands about Massachusetts Bay, to which he held claim. These settlements, begun in 1622, and permanently carried on after 1623, caused trouble enough to the Separatists of Plymouth and to the Puritans who afterward occupied the soil on which they were established.[1] But our concern here is with the endeavors of the Puritans to secure a home in the new world. These efforts had their remote beginnings in the fishing trade, which then, as now, could advantageously be carried on by vessels making those shores

---

Historical Collections, Philadelphia, 1792–4, I: 305–307; Young, *Chron. . . . Mass.*, 295–298. Palfrey, *Hist. N. E.*, I: 312, reports a rumor ascribing its composition to Rev. John White of Dorchester, Eng.). This document was signed by Winthrop, Dudley, Johnson, Phillips, and others. A single extract will suffice: "Wee desire you would be pleased to take Notice of the Principals, and Body of our Company, as those who esteeme it our honour to call the *Church* of *England*, from whence wee rise, our deare Mother. . . . Wee leave it not therefore, as loathing that milk wherewith we were nourished there, but blessing God for the Parentage and Education, as Members of the same Body, shall always rejoice in her good." Of course there were differences in degree of opposition against English ecclesiastical officers and institutions. When Winthrop and his brethren came to choose Wilson as teacher of the Boston-Charlestown church, August 27, 1630, they "used imposition of hands, but with this protestation by all, that it was only as a sign of election and confirmation, not of any intent that Mr. Wilson should renounce the ministry he received in England." Winthrop *Hist. N. E.* (or *Journal*), Savage's 2d ed., Boston, 1853, I: 38–39. But the same George Phillips, who signed the *Hvmble Reqvest* with Winthrop, and who had been a minister of the Church of England in Essex, told Doctor Fuller of Plymouth, in June, 1630, 16 days after landing, that "if they will have him stand minister, by that calling which he received from the prelates in England, he will leave them." Bradford's Letter Book, *1 Coll. Mass. Hist. Soc.*, III: 74; Dexter, *Cong. as seen*, p. 417. The Boston church was so well known to be Non-conformist rather than Separatist, that when Roger Williams was invited in 1631 to supply its pulpit during Wilson's absence, he refused because he "durst not officiate to an unseparated people, as, upon examination and conference, I [he] found them to be." Williams' Letter to Cotton the younger, in *1 Proc. Mass. Hist. Soc.*, III: 316, Mch. 1858. See also Dexter, *As to Roger Williams*, p. 4; and G. E. Ellis, *Puritan Age . . in . . Mass.*, Boston, 1888, p. 271. Many illustrations of the varying positions taken by the founders of New England on the validity of episcopal ordination are given by Dr. J. H. Trumbull in a note to his reprint of Lechford's *Plain Dealing*, Boston, 1867, pp. 16, 17.

[1] The best account of these anti-Puritan settlements, and of the doings of Thomas Morton and other leaders in them, is that of Charles Francis Adams, *Three Episodes of Massachusetts History*, Boston, 1892, I: 1–360.

a base of supply. Since more men could be employed in fishing than were needed to sail the vessels home, it occurred to some of those interested in the business that it would be well to have the unnecessary members of the crews remain in New England and form a permanent colony, from which supplies could be drawn. Such a plan was put into practice by the Dorchester (county of Dorset) Fishing Company, a stock partnership organized by the Puritan, Rev. John White, of that place; and in 1623 or 1624 men were actually sent out and settled on Cape Ann.[1] About a year after the beginning of this settlement Roger Conant, an earnest Puritan, who had been some time at Plymouth, but in disfavor, went thither to take its affairs in charge. The colony proved a poor venture, but Conant was minded to stay; and accordingly, since he did not think the rocky shores of Cape Ann favorable for a settlement, he removed, in 1626, to the spot then called Naumkeag, but better known by its later name of Salem.[2]

Thus far the work had been done without a special or certainly valid patent,[3] and had had trade as its principal aim. But White had conceived the idea of a Puritan colony beyond the sea, and set

---

[1] See J. W. Thornton's handsome monograph, *Landing at Cape Anne*, etc. Boston, 1854, pp. 39–60. The Plymouth colonists secured a grant from Lord Sheffeild (one of the Council for New England) dated Jan. 1, 1623 (O. S.), *i. e.* Jan. 11, 1624, of our reckoning, authorizing them to establish a fishing settlement and town where Gloucester now is. Thornton gives the full text of the patent (pp. 31–35) and a beautiful fac-simile. Capt. John Smith, in his *Generall Historie*, London, 1624, p. 247, records that the Dorchester company's colony sheltered itself under the Plymouth colonist's patent. But they cannot have much regarded it, indeed, it was really worthless (see *Memorial Hist. of Boston*, I: 60, 74, 92), and they were soon in open quarrel with Standish and others of Plymouth, and were holding the Cape-Ann territory by force. Compare also Prof. H. B. Adams, *Fisher-Plantation on Cape Anne*, in *Hist. Coll. Essex Inst.*, XIX: 81–90 (1882). See also Hubbard, 110, 111; and a note, by Deane, to Bradford, *Hist. Plym. Plant.*, ed. 1856, 168, 169. A good sketch of Conant is that by Felt, in *N. E. Hist. and Genealogical Register*, II: 233–239, 329–335 (1848). The whole matter of this colony and its enlargement into a Puritan settlement is set forth briefly in John White's most valuable *Planter's Plea*, London, 1630; reprinted in part in Young, *Chron. . . . Mass.*, pp. 3–16.

[2] Our chief source of information, aside from White, *Planter's Plea*, on all these matters is Hubbard, *General History of New England*, printed at Boston (2d ed.) 1848, pp. 101–120. See also Young, *Chronicles . . . of Massachusetts*, Boston, 1846, *passim;* and Phippen in *Hist. Coll. Essex Inst.*, I: 94, 145, 185. Palfrey, *History of N. E.*, I: 283–301, and Deane in Winsor's *Narrative and Critical Hist.* III: 295–312, have good accounts of these events. Prof. Adams's *Origin of Salem Plantation*, in *Hist. Coll. Essex Inst.* XIX: 153–166, has facts of value; and Haven's *The Mass. Company*, in Winsor's *Memorial Hist. of Boston*, Boston, 1882, I: 87–98, is worth consulting.

[3] See above, note 1. Conant was a Puritan, but, like White, a conformist enough to be attached to the Church of England and opposed to Separatism. With him came to minister to the wants of the little colony a John Lyford, a clergyman of the Church of England in sympathy with the Establishment, who had made much trouble at Plymouth when there with Conant, and who

out now to procure a patent and enlist Puritan sympathy. The body having nominal authority over New England was the "Council established at Plymouth, in the County of Devon, for the planting, ruling, ordering, and governing of New England in America," a corporation whose charter had been sealed on November 3, 1620;[1] and which, though possessing a title, in name at least, to all land between 40° and 48° from the Atlantic to the Pacific, was essentially a trading and fishing monopoly for Sir Ferdinando Gorges and his friends, and soon attracted the unfavorable notice of Parliament.[2] This Plymouth Council, being anxious to make such use of their property as they could, was persuaded to grant to a Puritan land company,[3] of which John Endicott was a member, that portion of the New World lying between lines drawn three miles north of the Merrimac and the same distance to the south of the Charles, by an instrument issued March 19, 1628. As the agent of this new company, Endicott came out with a few settlers, landing at Salem September 6 of the same year. Meanwhile White was zealously introducing the Puritanly inclined members of this new land company to like-minded men in England, with a view to building up large Puritan settlements in America. The result was that the land company was re-formed with many new members, and, on March 4, 1629, was provided with a royal charter[4] organizing it into the "Governor and Company of the Mattachusetts Bay in Newe England," and giving it power to admit freemen, elect officers, and make laws of local application to all its territories. This organization at once pushed on the work with vigor. A large band of colonists was got together, to be sent over to Salem in the spring of 1629. As the Company was strongly Puritan and the aim of the emigration chiefly religious, it is no wonder that we find them early negotiating for ministers to serve the spiritual

had left Plymouth for Nantasket in Conant's company. Lyford's character was none of the best. See Hubbard, pp. 106, 107. Bradford, *Hist. Plym. Plant.*, pp. 171, 173, 192–196. Young, *Chron. . . . Mass.*, p. 20. There was no church at Salem, in a Congregational sense, till after the coming of Endicott.

[1] The text of this patent may be found in Hazard, *Historical Collections*, Philadelphia, 1792–1794, I: 103–118.

[2] See C. F. Adams, *Three Episodes of Mass. History*, I: 127–129.

[3] Some quotations from this charter are preserved in the charter of 1629. See note 4.

[4] Text, *Records of . . . Mass. Bay*, Boston, 1853, I: 3–20.

wants of the new colony. Three were secured,[1] Francis Bright,[2] Francis Higginson,[3] and Samuel Skelton;[3] and another, Ralph Smith,[4] obtained passage in the Company's ships; but only Higginson and Skelton remained permanently with the Salem colonists.

On their arrival, late in June, 1629, the ministers found the ground fully prepared for the planting of religious institutions. As has been already pointed out, the Salem settlers, though Puritans, were not Separatists, and had most of them been inclined to look upon the men of Plymouth as dangerous innovators. But sickness had laid heavy hand on the little company under Endicott at Salem during the winter preceding the minister's arrival, and the governor had sent to Plymouth for the professional help of Dr. Samuel Fuller, a deacon of the Plymouth church. With him came more definite acquaintance with the Plymouth way and the removal of much prejudice; so much so that Endicott acknowledged, in a letter to Bradford, that he recognized that the outward

---

[1] See Young, *Chronicles . . . of Mass.*, pp. 65, 96, 99, 134, 135, 142–144, 207–212. Hubbard, pp. 112, 113. Felt, *Annals of Salem*, 2d ed., Salem, 1845, I: 510–513.

[2] Francis Bright, it would appear, quarrelled with the rest of the company before he had been long with them. He soon left Salem, and after a little time in Charlestown, returned to England in August, 1630. The exact cause of his disagreement we do not know; but we may conjecture that he was more of a conformist than either Higginson or Skelton, and failed to agree with them regarding church discipline. Hubbard, pp. 112, 113, asserts this to be a fact, and quotes with approbation a passage of much obscurity from Johnson's *Wonder-working Providence*, London, 1654, p. 20 (reprinted by W. F. Poole, Andover, 1867). But the Company state in a letter to Endicott, April 17, 1629, that the ministers had "declared themselves to us to be of one judgment, and to be fully agreed on the manner how to exercise their ministry." (Young, *Chron. . . . Mass.*, p. 160.)

[3] Francis Higginson, the teacher of the Salem church, was born in 1588, graduated at Cambridge, A.B. in 1609–10, and A.M. in 1613. He then became minister at Claybrooke, a parish of Leicester; but while there the influence of Thomas Hooker, afterwards of Hartford, and others, turned his Puritan inclinations into non-conformity. Like many other Puritans, he was silenced; but his friends employed him as a "lecturer." While still at Leicester he was engaged to go to Salem. Here he arrived June 29, 1629; and was ordained on July 20, following. He died August 6, 1630. His life is treated in Mather, *Magnalia*, ed. 1853–5, I: 354–366; Bentley, *Description and Hist. of Salem*, in *1 Coll. Mass. Hist. Soc.*, VI; Eliot, *Biog. Dict. . . . of the First Settlers . . . in N. E.*, Boston, 1809, pp. 248–253; Brook, *Lives of the Puritans*, II: 369–375; Young, *Chron. . . . Mass.*, p. 317; Felt, in *N. E. Hist. and Genealogical Register*, VI: 105–127 (1852); Sprague, *Annals of the Am. Pulpit*, New York, 1857, I: 6–10; White, *N. E. Congregationalism*, pp. 283, 284; Appleton's *Cyclop. Am. Biog.*, III: 198; T. W. Higginson, *Life of Francis Higginson*, New York, 1891.

Samuel Skelton, the pastor of the Salem church, is less well known than Higginson. He was graduated at Cambridge, A.B. in 1611, and A.M. in 1615. He then probably settled in Dorsetshire (though Mather, *Magnalia*, ed. 1855, I: 68, says Lincolnshire). Endicott had known him and profited by his ministry in England. He was ordained over the Salem church on the same day as Higginson. He died Aug. 2, 1634. See Brook's *Lives*, III: 520; Bentley, as cited in previous note; Young, *Chron. . . . Mass.*, pp. 142, 143; White, *N. E. Cong.*, pp. 284, 285.

[4] Young, *Ibid*, pp. 151, 152. His passage was granted before the Company understood his Separatist tendencies. He soon went from Salem to Nantasket, and thence to Plymouth, where he became pastor of the church, but not meeting with entire success in the work, he resigned in 1636. He died in Boston in 1662. See also Bradford, *Hist. Plym. Plant.*, pp. 263, 278, 351.

form of God's worship, as observed at Plymouth, and explained by Fuller, was the same that he had himself long believed to be the true method.[1] The miles of ocean between Salem and England made the separation from the English Establishment a practical fact, whatever the theory might be; and the exigencies of life in a new settlement, where so much had to be created anew, brought out the real unity of belief regarding Scriptural doctrine and polity which had always characterized Puritans and Separatists. So it came about that, not long after Higginson and Skelton had landed, Endicott appointed a day for the choice of pastor and teacher, and in spite of the fact that both were ministers of the Church of England, Skelton and Higginson were chosen and ordained to their new work. We are fortunately in possession of a graphic and absolutely contemporary account of these events, from the pen of one who was afterward a deacon in the Salem church, and written to Bradford at Plymouth:[2]

"S^{r}: I make bould to trouble you with a few lines, for to certifie you how it hath pleased God to deale with us, since you heard from us. How, notwithstanding all opposition that hath been hear, & els wher, it hath pleased God to lay a foundation, the which I hope is agreeable to his word in every thing. The 20. of July, it pleased ye Lord to move ye hart of our Govr to set it aparte for a solemne day of humilliation, for ye choyce of a pastor & teacher. The former parte of ye day being spente in praier & teaching, the later parte aboute ye election, which was after this maner. The persons thought on (who had been ministers in England) were demanded concerning their callings; they acknowledged ther was a towfould calling, the one an inward calling, when ye Lord moved ye harte of a man to take y^{t} calling upon him, and fitted him with guiftes for ye same; the second was an outward calling, which was from ye people, when a company of beleevers are joyned togither in covenante, to walke togither in all ye ways of God, and every member (being men) are to have a free voyce in ye choyce of their officers, &c. Now, we being perswaded that these 2. men were so quallified, as ye apostle speaks to Timothy, wher he saith, A bishop must be blamles, sober, apte to teach, &c., I thinke I may say, as ye eunuch said unto Philip, What should let from being baptised, seeing ther was water? and he beleeved. So these 2. servants of God, clearing all things by their answers, (and being thus fitted,) we saw noe reason but we might freely give our voyces for their election, after this triall. [Their choice was after this manner: every fit member wrote, in a note,[3] his name whom the Lord moved him to think

---

[1] Letter in Bradford, *Hist. Plym. Plant.*, pp. 264, 265. See also Dexter, *Cong. as seen*, pp. 414–420.

[2] Letter in Bradford, *Hist. Plym. Plant.*, pp. 265, 266, and Bradford's Letter-Book, *1 Coll. Mass. Hist. Soc.*, III: 67, 68. Gott had spent the winter of 1628–9 in Salem.

[3] On the possibly Dutch derivation of this system of voting,—the first use of the written ballot in America,—see Douglas Campbell, *The Puritan in England, Holland, and America*, New York, 1892, II: 438.

was fit for a pastor, and so likewise, whom they would have for teacher; so the most voice was for Mr. Skelton to be Pastor, and Mr. Higginson to be Teacher;[1]] So M^{r}. Skelton was chosen pastor and Mr. Higgison to be teacher;[2] and they accepting ye choyce, M^{r}. Higgison, with 3. or 4. of ye gravest members of ye church, laid their hands on M^{r}. Skelton, using prayer therwith. This being done, ther was imposission of hands on M^{r}. Higgison also. [Then there was proceeding in election of elders and deacons, but they were only named, and laying on of hands deferred, to see if it pleased God to send us more able men over;[3]] And since that time, Thursday (being, as I take it, ye 6.[4] of August) is appoynted for another day of humilliation, for y^{e}[5] choyce of elders & deacons, & ordaining of them.

And now, good S^{r}, I hope y^{t} you & ye rest of Gods people (who are aquainted with the ways of God) with you, will say that hear was a right foundation layed, and that these 2. blessed servants of ye Lord came in at ye dore, and not at ye window. Thus I have made bould to trouble you with these few lines, desiring you to remember us, &c. And so rest,

At your service in what I may,

Salem, July 30. 1629. CHARLES GOTT."

The transaction thus narrated seems to be plain. Higginson and Skelton were ministers duly engaged by the Company in England to assume the spiritual charge of the Salem settlement. Gov. Endicott, as representative of the Company, might properly have been expected to welcome them and aid them in beginning their work. But he, and the majority of those who had wintered with him at Salem, had come to the conclusion that the Plymouth method of ordering the church-estate was the right one; and hence the governor appointed a day for some at least of the colonists to vote for pastor, teacher, and other officers. But here a difficulty appears. The uniform representation of the later writers is that the church in Salem was not formed till August 6,[6] and that its covenant was prepared by Mr. Higginson at the request of some of the members about to be. Yet the absolutely contemporary letter of Gott speaks three times of "members" in a way which certainly seems to imply that a covenant had

[1] This statement is omitted in the letter as given in Bradford's *History*, but is contained in the copy in Bradford's Letter Book, *1 Coll. Mass. Hist. Soc.*, III: 67, 68.

[2] Letter Book copy omits this clause.

[3] In Letter Book, but not in History.

[4] Letter Book says 5. An error, for the 6 Aug., 1629, was Thursday.

[5] Letter Book inserts *full*. A number of minor variations between the two copies I have left unnoticed.

[6] This opinion is first put on record by John Higginson, himself present as a 13-year-old boy at the ordination of his father, on the title page of his brief *Direction* printed in 1665; Morton, *Memoriall*, 1669, pp. 73–76 (Davis ed., pp. 145, 146) gives an extended account. Hubbard (writing not far from 1680), pp. 116–120, gives many details chiefly drawn from Morton. Mather, *Magnalia*, ed. 1853–5, pp. 70–72, has a brief narrative.

been entered into at some time previous to July 20. The statement that the votes were cast by "every fit member" would seem to render untenable the natural supposition that the election on July 20 was by all the colonists, while the ordination of that day is expressly declared to have been by "3. or 4. of ye gravest members of ye church." And the letter which records these events was written, it will be remembered, a week before the supposed gathering of the church on August 6. Hence, in spite of the circumstantial accounts of later historians, the earliest of whom wrote nearly forty years after the events he describes, we are forced to the conclusion that there was some sort of covenanted church organization at Salem, previous to July 20, 1629, and that it was this church, and not the colonists as a whole,[1] that chose Higginson and Skelton on that day. At the same time much new material was brought into the religious life of the colony by the influx of emigrants in June and July of that year; and it may well have been that the existing covenant was submitted to Higginson for approval or revision, and that the 6th of August saw, in addition to the ordination of ruling elders and deacons, the acceptance of the covenant by a number of the recently arrived emigrants, who now became members of the church. It can hardly be doubted, too, that on August 6, the Plymouth church, in the persons of Gov. Bradford and other representatives, extended the hand of fellowship to their new brethren of Salem.[2] But that the church in Salem was first formed

[1] Hubbard, *General History*, p. 119; and Gov. Hutchinson, *Hist. Colony of Mass. Bay*, London, 1765, I: 10–12, represent the choice distinctly as the work of the colonists before the formation of the church. Palfrey, *Hist. N. E.*, I: 295, is more guarded, but implies the same thing. Webber and Nevins, *Old Naumkeag*, p. 11, speak of this assembly of July 20, as a "town meeting"; Bacon, *Genesis N. E. Chs.*, pp. 472–475, elaborates this view at length. On the other hand, Punchard, *Hist. Cong.*, IV: 12–31, is in substantial accord with the view taken by the writer; but I am not able to follow him in all particulars. The observations of Rev. Mr. Willson, *Hist. of Essex County*, pp. 22, 23, are also of value.

[2] The statement in Morton's *Memoriall*, p. 75, is too circumstantial to be without a substantial basis of truth: "Mr. *Bradford* . . . . and some others with him, coming by Sea, were hindered by cross winds that they could not be there at the beginning of the day, but they came into the Assembly afterward, and gave them the *right hand of fellowship*," though Bradford himself makes no mention of it in his *Hist. Plym. Plant.* Hubbard, p. 119, repeats the story. It seems hardly likely, in spite of the intimations of Morton and Hubbard, that the Salem church formally invited the Plymouth church to assist them. Had such been the case some allusion ought to be found in Gott's letter. It is more probable that, on receipt of Gott's letter, Bradford and others started on their own motion to welcome the new church.

on August 6, seems certainly an error. Yet, however originating, the fact is of prime importance that the first Puritan church on New England soil was formed on the Congregational model. The example thus set was one easy to follow.

The Salem covenant of 1629 was a single sentence, embracing a simple promise to walk in the ways of the Lord. In brevity and contents it resembles other covenants of the period which have come down to us.[1] From this brevity and simplicity it has been erroneously concluded that our New England churches, in their early state, applied no doctrinal tests as a condition of membership.[2] No opinion could be farther from the truth. The causes which led our ancestors to America related to church polity rather than to doctrinal views; and hence the public formulæ of our churches on this side of the water concern themselves at first with matters of organization rather than with points of faith.[3] This agreement with the Puritan-Calvinistic portion of the English establishment was so entire that their doctrinal position could be taken for granted, and was not therefore at first formulated. But if the doctrinal beliefs of the churches as a whole needed no general statement, the case was far different with the individual applicants for church-membership. They had to submit to a searching private examination by the elders of the church both as to "their *knowledge* in the principles of religion, & of their *experience in the wayes of grace*, and of

1 Some illustrations will be given in connection with the text of this covenant.

2 This matter has given rise to a considerable literature, much of it cast in a controversial mould. The following articles, on one side or the other, may be cited as likely to prove of value to the student: Cummings, *Dict. of Cong. Usages and Principles*, Boston, 1855, Art. *Creeds*, pp. 131–139; Bacon, *Ancient Waymarks*, New Haven, 1853; Gilman, *Confessions of Faith*, in *Cong. Quarterly*, IV: 179–191 (April, 1862); Mead, *A New Declaration of Faith: Is it Desirable*, etc., *Minutes of National Council Cong. Chs.*, 1880, pp. 144–173; Dexter, *A Serious Misconception*, in *Congregationalist* for Jan. 2, 1890; Calkins, *Creeds as Tests of Church Membership*, in *Andover Review*, XIII: 237–255 (Mch., 1890); Dexter, *Did the early Churches of New England Require assent to a Creed?* in *Magazine of Christian Literature*, II: 129–138 (June, 1890). Of less value are Thompson, *Formation of Creeds*, *New Englander*, IV: 265–274 (Apl. 1846); Shedd, *Congregationalism and Symbolism*, *Bibl. Sacra*, XV: 661–690 (July, 1858); Pond, *Church Creeds*, *Bibl. Sacra*, XXXIX: 538–546 (July, 1872).

3 Compare the opening paragraphs of the preface to the *Cambridge Platform*, and the preface to the *Confession* of 1680, both of which will be found on a later page. Even when nearly a century had elapsed since the foundation of our churches, Cotton Mather was able to declare (*Ratio Disciplinæ*, Boston, 1726, p. 5): "The *Doctrinal Articles* of the Church of *England*, also, are more universally held and preached in the Churches of *New-England*, than in any Nation . . . It is well known, that the Points peculiar to the Churches of *New-England*, are those of their *Church Discipline*."

their *godly conversation* amongst men."[1] And the evidence is ample that this "knowledge" implied familiarity with and assent to the main doctrines of the Scripture as expounded by the Calvinism of the period. Once accepted by the elders, the candidate had to render an account to the church, dwelling largely, of course, on experience, but not wholly omitting doctrine.[2] In case of men this relation was usually oral; the women frequently rendered it by means of a written statement, and men sometimes exercised the same privilege.[3] But so far were these tests from being matters of form, that even in the early days of the first generation of our New England settlers the decided majority of the colonists were unable to show sufficient evidence of faith and experience to enter into church relationship.[4]

But circumstances soon compelled our New England churches to bear a more public testimony to their corporate and collective faith. There were troubles at home, notably in the doctrinal dis-

---

[1] Cotton, *Way of the Churches*, London, 1645, p. 54. See Cotton's "Twelve Fundamental Articles of Christian Religion: the Denial whereof . . . makes a man an Heretick." Tract published in 1713. These articles are summed up by Dexter in *Magazine of Christ. Literature*, II: 135; and are given in more detail by Lechford, *Plain Dealing*, London, 1642, pp. 9, 10 (Trumbull's reprint, Boston, 1867, pp. 25–28). Lechford declares them to be from a sermon preached in Oct., 1640.

[2] Compare on these proceedings, Lechford, as cited, pp. 4–11 (Trumbull's reprint, 18–29); Cotton, as cited, 54–65; Weld, *Brief Narration of the Practices of the Chs. in N. E.*, London, 1645 (reprinted in *Cong. Quarterly*, XVII: 253–271, see pp. 255, 261, 262). The method employed at Boston is shown by the account of the admission of Rev. John Cotton, and his wife, in 1633, Winthrop, *Hist. N. E. (Journal)*, Savage's ed., 1853, I: 130–132. At the Hartford church, under Hooker, fitness for membership was shown by public question and answer, rather than by relation, Mather, *Magnalia*, ed. 1853–5, II: 68. The method of the Salem church in 1661 is given in its records, White, *N. E. Cong.*, p. 50.

[3] A considerable number of these relations have come down to our own day. Fifty, dating from the ministry of Thos. Shepard of Cambridge, and most of them previous to 1640, are still in existence. (See Paige, *History of Cambridge*, Boston, 1877, pp. 252, 253, where a specimen is given.) More than 20 exist in the records of the Wenham church under John Fiske, 1644–1656, and are of a strongly doctrinal character. (See Dexter, *Serious Misconception*, in *Congregationalist*, Jan. 2, 1890.) Other specimens, dating from a much later period when the severity of the test had been considerably relaxed, may be found in Hill, *Hist. of Old South Church*, Boston, 1890, I: 309 (of 1744); and in Gilman, *Ancient Confessions of Faith*, in *Cong. Quarterly*, XI: 516–527 (of 1752–58).

[4] Lechford, *Plain Dealing*, p. 73: "Againe, here is required such confessions, and professions, both in private and publique, both of men and women, before they be admitted, that three parts of the people of the Country remaine out of the Church." Dr. Trumbull has illustrated this statement with valuable notes (Reprint, p. 151). Cotton, *Way of the Congregational Churches Cleared*, London, 1648, pp. 71, 72, denied the accuracy of Lechford's statement; but in Richard Mather's reply to the first of the XXXII Questions propounded by English Puritans to New England divines, a reply written in 1639, and published at London in 1643 under the title *Church-Government and Church-Covenant Discvssed*, pp. 7, 8, it is said: "Whether is the greater number, those that are admitted hereunto [church-communion], or those that are not we cannot certainly tell? But . . . we may truely say, that for the heads of Families, those that are admitted are farre more in number then the other."

turbances engendered by Mrs. Hutchinson and afterwards by the Quakers; and there were doubts cast upon the orthodoxy of our churches by their enemies in England.[1] As similar criticisms had led the London-Amsterdam church to put forth its doctrinal statement in 1596 and 1598, so our New England churches at last felt constrained to make the doctrinal positions which they had held from the beginning more evident to the world. We therefore find traces of the use, soon after 1640, of what we would now call confessions of faith by a few churches;[2] and in 1648 we see the Westminster Assembly's Confession heartily endorsed by the representatives of all our churches as a substantially adequate doctrinal expression.[3] Of course when such standards were recognized as presenting the views of a church, or of the whole of the churches, it would be natural to ask the assent of the candidate thereto, in addition to his relation, or occasionally instead of his relation. But the adoption of such standards did not introduce the doctrinal test as a precedent to church-membership, that had existed from the beginning.

A good illustration of this general evolution of definite written creed statement is afforded by the Salem church, whose brief covenant of 1629 has just been considered. The years following its adoption were stormy seasons in that church's history. Higginson died in 1630, Skelton followed him in 1634; and for a brief time in 1631, and again from 1633 onward Skelton had been assisted by the famous and exceedingly erratic Roger Williams.[4] On

---

1 See preface to *Cambridge Platform*, later in this volume, regarding such criticisms.

2 John Fiske's church at Wenham records, among other similar entries, the following: "8 *Nov.* 1644: *Voted*, that a consent & assent should be required *to ye profession of faith of ye church;* and that ye Confession should be read distinctly to them [candidates] & time given them to returne yr answer." "28 *Sept.* 1645: Geo. Norton gave his assent to *Confess'n of faith*, & ye covt administred to him." Quoted by Dexter in *Magazine Chris. Lit.*, II: 137 (June, 1890). See also the strongly doctrinal creed-covenant of the Windsor, Conn., church, of 1647, which may be found on a later page of this volume.

3 See preface to *Cambridge Platform*, later in this volume.

4 The story of Roger Williams has been well told by Dexter, *As to Roger Williams*, Boston [1876],—an indispensable monograph for any who would know the truth regarding this much misrepresented man. The student will do well also to consult the chapter on Roger Williams in G. E. Ellis, *Puritan Age . . in . . Mass.*, Boston, 1888, pp. 267–299; and an article by the same writer in Winsor's *Memorial Hist. of Boston*, Boston, 1882, I: 171, 172; to which Dr. Winsor has added an extensive note on the bibliography of the subject, *Ibid.*, 172, 173. Williams was not at this time a Baptist, nor did he become so before his "banishment." It is possible, though not certain, that he was ordained at Salem in 1631. In that year he began ministerial work in Plymouth and remained there till 1633, when he went back to Salem. Dexter, as cited, pp. 5, 7, 26.

Skelton's death, the Salem people asked Williams to be their pastor, though he had already made himself obnoxious to the government of the Company by his denunciations of the patent as no valid title, and his attack on the character of the king and the churches of England.[1] Circumstances into which we need not enter here in further detail led to the cognizance of Williams's doings by the Court, and a considerably prolonged controversy, in which the government appears to have acted with a good degree of forbearance. While this controversy was in progress a petition relative to some lands claimed by the Salem people was presented to the Court, and by it laid on the table pending the adjustment of the disputes already existing between it and Williams, who had the support of his church at Salem. This act of the Court roused Williams's anger, and on his insistance the Salem church called on the other churches of the colony to discipline such of their members as had voted as magistrates in the General Court on the land question.[2] The time was most unwise for such an attack, even if far more justifiable than it was, as the enemies of the colony in England were actively at work and had already taken steps looking toward the immediate destruction of the legal existence of the Massachusetts Company.[3] In this crisis the government needed the help of all loyal men. And it is, therefore, not surprising that the Salem church, which had been persuaded by its young pastor to censure the officers of the imperilled Company, soon began to yield to the reasonable arguments of the other churches and feel a degree of shame for what they had done.[4] Seeing that he no longer had the support of his people, Williams, with his usual headstrongness, sent a letter to his flock, on August 16, 1635, announcing that he had cast off all communion with the churches of the Bay as false and unclean; and that he would have nothing more to do with the people of Salem unless they would join him in cutting loose from all the other churches of the colony.[5] The good sense of the church prevailed, and as a whole they did

---

[1] Dexter, *Ibid.*, 26–28.
[2] *Ibid.*, 38–40.
[3] *Ibid.*, 20–23.
[4] *Ibid.*, 43.
[5] *Ibid.*, 43–45.

not heed him; but, as is usual in such cases, it cost heart rnıngs and sore divisions, and some went off to the new service which Williams set up. But now the Court, before which his case had some time been pending, after a considerable hearing in which it was aided by the advice of the most prominent ministers then in New England, ordered him out of its jurisdiction, by a sentence passed October 9, 1635;[1] and based on his attacks on the authority of the magistrates, and his persistence in defaming them and the churches of which they were members, in spite of all warnings to desist.[2] His settlement of Providence, his adoption of Baptist views while there, and his after changes are aside from the purpose of the present narrative.

Enough has been said to show that when Williams left the Salem plantation, in January, 1636,[3] the church must have been in a divided and distracted state.[4] But it was at last provided with a pastor in the person of the able, versatile, and distinguished Hugh Peter,[5] who was settled at Salem December 21, 1636. Under

---

[1] *Ibid.*, 46–60. [2] *Ibid.*, 65 and following. [3] *Ibid.*, 61, 62.

[4] Compare also, as illustrative of the state of the church after Williams left, Winthrop, *Hist. of N. E. (Journal)*, 2d ed., Boston, 1853, I: 221.

[5] Hugh Peter was one of the most picturesque characters among the early ministry of New England. Born in 1599, in Cornwall, he studied at Cambridge, graduating A.M. in 1622. Contact with such eminent Puritans as Thomas Hooker and John Davenport led him to abandon his early profligacy and devote himself to the ministry. Admitted to Episcopal orders, he preached with much success at St. Sepulcre's, London; but his growing Puritanism led to his association with the leaders of the Massachusetts Company, of which he was one of the early members. Being silenced by Laud in London, he went to Rotterdam in 1629, and was settled over the church there, with Dr. William Ames as colleague. The tongue of slander has attacked his moral character while in London, but seemingly with no cause save enmity. Here in Holland he remained till the English authorities moved the Dutch to render his position insecure. He therefore came to New England, arriving Oct. 6, 1635; and was from the first a man of prominence. After visiting all the new towns of the infant colony, he settled at Salem. Here his work was universally beneficial. Under his ministry more were added to the church in five years than in eighteen under his successor. The wounds in the church were healed. But Peter had an aptitude for the practical side of life. He did much to develop the manufactures of Salem, such as salt, glass, ship-building, and hemp raising. He showed great success in promoting trade; so that at the earnest solicitation of the government, and with much reluctance on the part of his people, he was persuaded to go to England, Aug. 3, 1641, as one of the agents for the Colony. His connection with the Salem church was ended. Arrived in England just as the civil conflict was about to begin, his talents soon secured him prominence on the Puritan side. He almost immediately became secretary to Cromwell, and then a popular chaplain in the army. His fame was soon that of one of the most effective of the king's opponents. In April, 1646, he preached before the Houses of Parliament, a body which estimated his general services to the cause to be worthy of a pension. His work as army chaplain took him with Cromwell's expedition to Ireland in 1649. Parliament then, 1651, employed him on a commission to revise the laws. 1654 saw him one of the *tryers* of candidates for ministerial appointments. By 1658 Peter was chaplain to the garrison of Dunkirk. At the Restoration the hatred of the royalist party against Peter showed its intensity. Absurd rumors were circulated, such as that he was the actual executioner of Charles I.; he was charged with high treason for having had

him the church enjoyed a degree of growth, unity, and prosperity in marked contrast to its distraction under Williams. And as one of the earliest steps toward this desirable result, probably at Peter's ordination, the covenant of 1629 was renewed, and very much enlarged by the addition of nine specific articles of promise, several of which were more or less directly occasioned by the late disturbances. In view of what we have seen, it is no wonder that the members of the church felt it incumbent upon them to pledge themselves "to walke with our brethren and sisters . . . avoyding all jelousies, suspitions, backbyteings, censurings, provoakings, secrete risings of spirite against them."[1] Nor was it unnatural that their repentance for their opposition to the other churches and the magistrates of the colony should find expression in a promise to act "noe way sleighting our sister Churches, but useing theire Counsell as need shalbe";[2] and "to carrye our selves in all lawfull obedience, to those that are over us, in Church or Commonweale."[3] Truly it is the sense of contrition for disagreement and ill-feeling that finds expression in this enlarged and particularized pledge of fellowship.

But other changes brought addition also to the written symbols of the Salem church. Their pastor, Peter, ended his ministry in 1641; and was succeeded, in the full duties of ministerial office, by one who, since March, 1640, had been his colleague as teacher, Edward Norris.[4] It was while Norris was fulfilling a respected but not very eventful ministry that the new sect of the Quakers first made their appearance in Salem, in 1656.[5] At this time they

---

an active share in the king's death. On Oct. 16, 1660, he was executed with all the barbarous circumstances then attendant upon the punishment for treason. Among the many sources of information, or of defamation, the following may be cited: Harris, *Historical and Critical Account of the Lives . . . of James I. and Charles I.*, etc. New ed. London, 1814, I: ix–li; Bentley, *Descrip. Salem*, in *1 Coll. Mass. Hist. Soc.*, VI: 250–254; Eliot, *Biog. Dict. . . . of the First Settlers . . . in N. E.*, Boston, 1809, pp. 372–377; Brook, *Lives*, III: 350–369; Young, *Chron. . . . Mass.*, pp. 134, 135; Felt, *Memoir*, in *N. E. Hist. and Genealogical Register*, V: 9–20, 231–238, 275–294, 415–439 (with portrait), (1851 and separately same year); Felt, *Ecclesiastical Hist. N. E.*, Boston, 1855, I: 228, 229, 267, 426, 434–436; Sprague, *Annals Am. Pulpit*, I: 70–75; Palfrey, *Hist. N. E.*, I: 582–584, II: 426–428; White, *N. E. Cong.*, 287, 288; Appleton's *Cyclop. Am. Biog.*, IV: 741, 742.

[1] Art. 3. [2] Art. 6. [3] Art. 7.

[4] See White, *N. E. Congregationalism*, pp. 289, 290.

[5] Bentley, *1 Coll. Mass. Hist. Soc.*, VI: 255, says 1657; but Felt, *Annals of Salem*, 2d ed., Salem, 1849, II: 580, puts the beginnings of prosecution of Quakers in Salem in July, 1656.

were far from being the staid and law-abiding citizens who, in our own day, have made the name of Quaker synonymous with honesty, piety, and good order; and if we are sometimes tempted to think that the fathers dealt out hard measure to them, it is well to remember that the provocation was great and such as would attract the speedy notice of law in our own century.[1] It was while these new elements of disturbance were turmoiling the Salem community that Norris died, December 23, 1659. A few months earlier had seen the almost chance beginning of the work of his successor, John Higginson,[2] the son of the first teacher, and the connecting link between the founders of New England and the historians at the close of the seventeenth century.[3] Higginson's settlement followed more than a year of ministerial supply, August 29, 1660. The influence of the new ministry speedily showed itself in the toning up of the church's affairs. The Quaker disturbances continued,[4] and other questions, especially the great discussion regarding the proper subjects of baptism, occupied men's minds.[5] Higginson evidently saw the need of more careful doctrinal instruction, and therefore, less than a month after his ordination,[6] and probably

---

[1] Compare, among many sources of information regarding the New England Quakers, the following: Palfrey, *Hist. N. E.*, II: 452-485; Dexter, *As to Roger Williams*, pp. 124-141, with citations from Quaker documents and historians. Ellis, *The Puritan Age . . . in . . . Mass.*, Boston, 1888, pp. 408-491.

[2] John Higginson was born in August, 1616, in England, from which land his parents did not remove till 1629. He appears to have been an early member of the Salem church, uniting with it during the year of his arrival. His father dying in 1630, John was aided by the ministers and magistrates toward an education. By April, 1636, before he was 20, he was chaplain at the Fort at Saybrook, Conn.; a post which he occupied about four years. In 1637 he was one of the scribes at the Hutchinson Synod. By 1641 he was a teacher in Hartford and a student under Thomas Hooker. He thence removed to Guilford, Conn., in 1643, and was one of the prominent members of the church there and assistant to its pastor, Henry Whitfield. Here he remained, in sole pastoral service after 1651, till 1659, when he started for England. On his voyage the vessel was forced to put into Salem. Here he was asked to preach, and agreed to remain a year — March or April, 1659. In March, 1660, he was called to a permanent settlement, and was ordained August 29 of that year, by the hands of two deacons and a brother of the church's fellowship, though in the presence of the ministers and representatives of the neighbor-churches. Here he continued as minister till his death, Dec. 9, 1708, 92 years of age. His good sense, and his familiarity with the elder generation, gave him much weight throughout the colony. See Bentley, *Desc. of Salem*, *1 Coll. Mass. Hist. Soc.*, VI: 259-272; Felt, *Annals of Salem*, *passim*; Felt, *Eccles. Hist. New England*, I: 253, 312, 517, 519-521, II: 218, 224; Sprague, *Annals of the Am. Pulpit*, I: 91-93; White, *N. E. Cong.*, 45-96, 290-292.

[3] As illustrative, see his *Attestation* to the *Magnalia*, ed. 1853-5, I: 13-18.

[4] See Felt, *Annals of Salem*, 2d ed., II: 580-587, for instances between 1656 and 1669.

[5] See later in this volume, in connection with the Synod of 1662 (Chapter XI).

[6] Sept. 10, 1660. Church records in White, *N. E. Cong.*, p. 47.

at his motion, the church voted "that Mr. Cotton's Catechism[1] be used in their families in teaching their children in order to public catechising in the congregation."

Soon after the beginning of this teaching, the brethren were induced not only solemnly to renew their former covenant but to add to the nine articles, which had come down from Peter's day, a tenth, pledging the members "to take heed and beware of the leaven of the doctrine of the Quakers."[2] Thus, by degrees, and chiefly owing to the rise of errors in faith or practice in the church itself, the single sentence of 1629 became expanded into a fairly elaborate and particularized rule.

Mr. Higginson was evidently a believer in the value of written creeds, and desirous of having the customs of the church which had been handed down from the beginning put in documentary form. At the same time he was a warm advocate, in company with many of the best men in New England at that day, of what is known as the half-way covenant,—a system which to his mind, as to that of many others, was designed to give the church a larger hold upon its children and ultimately to bring a large portion of them into the enjoyment of full spiritual privilege.[3] But to accomplish these results Higginson clearly felt that improved instruction by parents at home, and a careful examination of all applicants for church membership by the elders, were needed.[4] All these considerations had increased force when the half-way principles, some of which the church had already adopted, were made part of the recognized ecclesiastical usage of the colony by the Synod of 1662,

---

[1] *I. e.*, Cotton's *Milk for Babes*, London, 1646, long a popular catechism in New England. A heliotype copy of the title-page may be found in Ellis, *Hist. First Ch. in Boston*, Boston, 1881, between pp. 36, 37.

[2] This occurred March 6, 1661. See page 118 of this chapter.

[3] That this view of the probable effects of the half-way covenant system, erroneous as it may seem to us, was held by Higginson, is clear from his record of the "propositions concerning the state of the children of members" agreed upon by the church Sept. 9, 1661; and his speech urging the adoption of the practices recommended by the Synod of 1662, delivered in July, 1665; see Church records, in White, *N. E. Cong.*, pp. 49, 50, 60, 61.

[4] The "propositions" of 1661 declare the belief of the Salem church in the membership of all baptized children in the covenant fellowship of the church, so as to be under the church's watch and care. They are silent on the other great question, as to whether these covenanted children of the church, who have not yet made profession of personal regeneration, can claim baptism for their children. That further principle was adopted July 18, 1665, and put in practice on the 30th. *Records*, *Ibid.*

and fully put into practice at Salem in 1665. With these aims in view, therefore, we find Higginson promising the church, at a meeting, November 6, 1664, when the recommendations of the Synod of 1662 were publicly read, that "he would communicate unto the brethren a short writing as a help for the practice of the Synod's propositions."[1] It was not till nearly a year later, however, October 5, 1665, that the pastor was able to announce to the church that his "writing" was printed and ready for distribution.[2] The document has fortunately come down to our day. The little pamphlet bears on its face the evidence of its purpose; it is expressly declared to be *A Direction for a publick Profession in the Church Assembly, after private examination by the Elders;* and it contains a creed and a covenant answering to the documents which modern Congregationalism would understand by those now somewhat technical terms. The phraseology of the confession of faith, modeled on that of the Westminster catechism, is of course Trinitarian and Calvinistic; and, while there is no ground for the assertion, which some have made, that this creed was adopted by the church in 1629,[3] there can certainly be no impropriety in concluding that the opinion which John Higginson expressed in the title of the *Direction*, thirty-six years after the formation of the church,—"Being the same for Substance which was propounded to, and agreed upon by the Church of *Salem* at their beginning. *the sixth of the sixth Moneth*, 1629,"—warrants us in holding the creed to be fairly representative of the type of theologic belief which the candidates for membership in the Salem church were expected to manifest to "the elders" from the beginning. As such, it may in a true sense be taken as representative of the kind of doctrinal test applied to members entering this first Puritan church in New England during the first half century of its existence. But while this affirmation is doubtless warranted, too much must not be claimed regarding this document of 1665 itself. A careful reading of the church records regarding it shows that, unlike the covenants of

---

[1] Church records, *Ibid.*, 59.
[2] *Ibid.*, 62.
[3] See *ante*, p. 95.

1629 and 1636, the *Direction* was not formally adopted by the church. It remained a recognized, but, in some sense, private, guide, and was designed primarily for the use of the candidates for church privileges under the half-way covenant, and for those who would pass from the baptized membership of the church to its full communion. For those not already of the church by baptism, who desired full membership, the older method of relation and personal profession was still employed.[1] The steps have thus been pointed out by which the Salem church passed from a brief and simple covenant to an elaborate compact; and to the use, if not the formal adoption, of a somewhat extended creed. The process was not one of change of doctrine, save perhaps on the question of baptism as applied to the offspring of the "children of the church." It was one of increasing written definition, a definition induced by the rise of errors and differences of belief in the church or community. In this matter the story of the Salem church is typical of New England ecclesiastical development as a whole.[2]

---

[1] White has pointed out, and the church records amply warrant him in the assertion, that "children of the covenant" since members of the church already by baptism, were admitted to full communion after examination by the pastor and a public confession and renewal of covenant before the church—*but without church vote*. It is for such confession and covenanting, after examination, that the *Direction* was designed. On the other hand "non-members" were voted into full communion on the old terms. An instance or two may illustrate. "1667. At a Church meeting, 4th of 5th month. John Gidney, Sam. Archer, jun., Jo. Peas, Martha Barten, Martha Foster, were presented before the Church, the Pastor expressed himself that after examination he approved of them as able to examine themselves, and discern the Lord's body, they professing their consent to the Confession of Faith and Covenant read unto them [*i. e.*, the *Direction* of 1665], they had their liberty to partake of the Lord's Supper, as other children of the Covenant formerly [*i. e.*, since the full adoption of the half-way principles in 1665, White, 67]. Goodie Guppa, Eliz. Clifford, Mary Merit, being non-members, having been propounded a month, and no exception against them, they made their confession and were on the Lord's day following received unto membership by vote of the Church, and by their own entering into Covenant." *Church records*, White, 71. How this confession was still made, in the admission of non-members, is shown by a further entry: "1678. At a Church Meeting, March 9, Sam. Eburn, [etc.] . . . these eight . . . making their profession of faith and repentance in their own way, some by speech, others by writing, which was read for them, they were admitted to membership in this Church, by consent of the brethren, they engaging themselves in the Covenant." *Ibid.*, 83.

[2] The adoption of new forms and covenants by the Salem church did not stop here. A new covenant "more accomodated to our times" was adopted, apparently in addition to the old covenant, April 15, 1680, in consequence of the exhortations of the "Reforming Synod" of 1679. *Church records*, White, pp. 84, 85. The text was printed at Boston in that year (Thomas, *Hist. Printing in America*, Albany, 1874, II: 323); and exists in a MS. copy, among the records of the Tabernacle Church, Salem. This text may be found in White, *N. E. Cong.*, pp. 186, 187, 207–209, in rather a disjointed form, from the *Tabernacle Ch. Centennial Discourse*, by Worcester, 1835, Appendix U; and the *Salem Gazette* of Apl. 6, 1854. As it is, however, largely devotional and penitential, and presents nothing that is new in doctrine or practice, I have thought best to omit it.

THE SALEM SYMBOLS

THE COVENANT OF 1629

We Covenant with the Lord and one with an other; and doe bynd our selves in the presence of God, to walke together in all his waies, according as he is pleased to reveale himself unto us in his Blessed word of truth.[1]

THE ENLARGED COVENANT OF 1636[2]

Gather my Saints together unto me[3] that have made a Covenant with me by sacrifyce. Psa. 50:5:[4]

Wee whose names are here under written, members of the present Church of Christ in Salem, having found by sad experi-

---

[1] This simplicity is characteristic of the early covenants. It seems probable that the essence of the covenant of the London-Amsterdam (Johnson's) church has been preserved for us in the examination of Daniel Buck, scrivener, in 1593, who being inquired of as to "what promise hee made when he came first to y[t] Societie he annswereth & sayth that he made y[e] Protestation: that he wold walke with the rest of y[m] so longe as they did walke in the way of the Lorde, & so farr as might be warranted by the Word of God." Harleian MS. 7042, communicated to me by Dr. Dexter. See also his *Cong. as seen*, p. 265; and Strype, *Annals* IV. No. CXV, ed. 1824, p. 244. A suggestion as to the possible original covenant of the Mayflower church has already been made, see *ante*, p. 83. The covenant of Henry Jacobs' church organized in 1616 in London, and the first Congregational church to gain a permanent foothold in that city, is thus described; they "solemnly covenanted with each other in the presence of Almighty God, to walk together in all God's ways and ordinances, according as he had already revealed, or should further make them known to them." Neal, *Hist. of the Puritans*, Toulmin's ed., Bath, 1794, II: 100. Hanbury, *Memorials*, I: 292, 293. No covenant of the Dorchester company, whose church was organized in March 1630, at Plymouth, Eng., and emigrated bodily to our shores, has been preserved earlier in date than 1647 (given later in this work). But the next in order of our New England churches, that of Boston, had a covenant as simple as that of Salem. (See Ch. VII of this work.) The Charlestown church, of Nov. 2, 1632, has the following covenant: "Wee whose names are heer written Being by his most wise and good providence brought together, and desirous to vnite o[r] selus into one Congregation or Church, vnder o[r] Lord Iesus Christ our Head: In such sort as becometh all those whom he hath Redeemed and sanctified vnto himselfe, Doe heer sollemnly and Religeously as in his most holy presence, Promice and bynde o[r] selus to walke in all o[r] wayes according to the Rules of the Gospell, and in all sinceer conformity to his holy ordinances: and in mutuall Love and Respect each to other; so near as God shall give vs grace." Photographic fac-simile in *The Commemoration of the 250th Anniversary of the First Church, Charlestown, Mass.* Privately Printed, 1882. It is evident, therefore, that in simplicity and brevity the Salem covenant conforms to the general custom of our earliest Congregational churches. A seeming exception is perhaps the covenant of the Watertown church of July 30, 1630 (*Magnalia*, ed. 1853–5, I: 377; Punchard, IV: 43, 44); but the exception is more apparent than real, for though the form is long and descriptive, the content is simple.

[2] From White's text of the copy in the church-book of 1660–1.

[3] Fiske's copy, *Hist. Coll. Essex Inst.*, I. 37, 38, inserts *yos*, i. e. those. I have not noticed variations in spelling between Fiske and the church-book.

[4] A favorite text, John Higginson preached on it at the renewing of this covenant in 1661. Ch. records, White, p. 48.

ence how dangerous it is to sitt loose to the Covenant wee make with our God : and how apt wee are to wander into by pathes, even to the looseing of our first aimes in entring into Church fellowship : Doe therefore solemnly in the presence of the Eternall God, both for our own comforts, and those which[1] shall or maye be joyned unto us, renewe that Church Covenant we find this Church bound unto at theire first beginning, viz: That We Covenant with the Lord and one with an other; and doe bynd our selves in the presence of God, to walke together in all his waies, according as he is pleased to reveale himself unto us in his Blessed word of truth.[2] And doe more explicitely in the name and feare of God, profess and protest to walke as followeth through the power and grace of our Lord Jesus.[3]

1 first wee avowe the Lord to be our God, and our selves his people in the truth and simplicitie of our spirits.

2 We give our selves to the Lord Jesus Christ, and the word of his grace, fore the teaching, ruleing and sanctifyeing of us in matters of worship, and Conversation, resolveing to cleave to him alone for life and glorie ; and oppose all contrarie wayes, cannons and constitutions of men in his worship.

3 Wee promise to walke with our brethren and sisters in this Congregation with all watchfullnes and tendernes, avoyding all jelousies, suspitions, backbyteings, censurings, provoakings, secrete risings of spirite against them; but in all offences to follow the rule of the Lord Jesus, and to beare and forbeare, give and forgive as he hath taught us.

4 In publick or in private, we will willingly doe nothing to the ofence of the Church but will be willing to take advise for our selves and ours as ocasion shalbe presented.

5 Wee will not in the Congregation be forward eyther to shew oure owne gifts or parts in speaking or scrupling, or there discover the fayling of oure brethren or sisters butt atend an orderly cale there unto ; knowing how much the Lord may be dishonoured, and his Gospell in the profession of it, sleighted, by our distempers, and weaknesses in publyck.

6 Wee bynd our selves to studdy the advancement of the Gospell in all truth and peace, both in regard of those that are within, or without, noe way sleighting our sister Churches, but useing theire Counsell as need shalbe : nor laying a stumbling

1 Fiske reads *who*.

2 This sentence, the original covenant of the church, ends in Fiske's copy with a comma.

3 Fiske reads *ye helpe & poux of ye Lord Jesus*.

block before any, noe not the Indians, whose good we desire to promote, and soe to converse, as we may avoyd the verrye appearance of evill.

7 We hearbye promise to carrye our selves in all lawfull obedience, to those that are over us, in Church or Commonweale,[1] knowing how well pleasing it will be to the Lord, that they should have incouragement in theire places, by our not greiveing theyre spirites through our Irregularities.[2]

8 Wee resolve to approve our selves to the Lord in our perticular calings, shunning ydleness as the bane of any state, nor will wee deale hardly, or oppressingly with any, wherein we are the Lord's stewards :[3]

9 alsoe promyseing to our best abilitie to teach our children and servants, the knowledg of God[4] and his will, that they may serve him also ; and all this, not by any strength of our owne, but by the Lord Christ, whose bloud we desire may sprinckle this our Covenant made in his name.[5]

THE ANTI-QUAKER ARTICLE OF 1660–1[6]

This Covenant[7] was renewed by the Church on a sollemne day of Humiliation 6 of 1 moneth 1660.[8] When also considering the power of Temptation amongst us by reason of ye Quakers doctrine to the leavening of some in the place where we are and endangering of others, doe see cause to remember the Admonition of our Saviour Christ to his disciples Math. 16. Take heed and beware of ye leaven of the doctrine of the Pharisees and doe judge so farre as we understand it y^t^ ye Quakers doctrine is as bad or worse than that of ye Pharisees ; Therefore we doe Covennant by the help of Jesus Christ to take heed and beware of the leaven of the doctrine of the Quakers.

1 Fiske reads *common wealth*.

2 This is the article to which Morton refers (*Memoriall*, p. 75 ; Davis ed, pp. 145, 146) : "And because they foresaw that this Wilderness might be looked upon as a place of Liberty, and therefore might in time be troubled with erroneous spirits, therefore they did put in one Article into the *Confession of Faith* on purpose about *the Duty and Power of the Magistrate in Matters of Religion*." He attributes its adoption, mistakenly, to 1629 — his own work was published 40 years later — but it fits in admirably with the repentant spirit of the church for its actions under the lead of Roger Williams. See *ante*, p. 109.

3 In Fiske's copy this article and the following are joined in one.

4 Fiske reads *ye Lord*.

5 Fiske reads *we desire should be sprinkle*. *This our covenant*, etc.

6 From White's text of the copy in the church-book of 1660–1. *N. E. Cong.*, p. 14.

7 I.e., the enlarged covenant of 1636, to which it is immediately appended.

8 In modern reckoning 1661. See *ante*, p. 113. The article was prepared in 1660 and "added"

THE DIRECTION OF 1665[1]

A

DIRECTION

FOR

A PUBLICK PROFESSION

In the CHURCH ASSEMBLY, after private Examination by the *ELDERS.*

Which Direction is taken out of the Scripture, and Points unto that Faith and Covenant contained in the Scripture.

Being the same for Substance which was propounded to, and agreed upon by the Church of *Salem* at their beginning. *the sixth of the sixth Moneth,* 1629.

In the Preface to the Declaration *of the* Faith *owned and professed by the Congregationall* Churches *in* England.

The Genuine use of a Confession of Faith is, that under the same Form of Words they express the substance of the same common Salvation or unity of their Faith. Accordingly it is to be looked upon as a fit meanes, whereby to express that their Common Faith and Salvation, and not to be made use of as an imposition upon any.[2]

[2] VV*E Beseech you Brethren to know them that labour among you, and are over you in the Lord, and admonish you and to esteem them very highly in love for their work sake and be at peace among your selves.* 1 Thess. 5. 12, 13.

Obey them that have the rule over you and submit your selves, for they watch for your soules, as they that must give an account, that they may do it with joy and not with grief, for that is unprofitable for you, Heb. 13. 17.

Who is that wise and faithfull steward, whom his Lord shall make Ruler over his houshold, to give them their portion of meat in due season, Luk. 12. 42.

March 6–16, 1661. Church-records, White, p. 48. The date in the text is not an error, however. The year was held to begin March 25, and March was therefore the first month, though its first 24 days were held to belong to the previous year. Yet the usage in dating during the early days of March was not absolutely uniform, some even then would have written 1661. See Preface to Savage's Winthrop's *Journal*, I : xi.

[1] Text from original.

[2] Savoy Declaration, ed. 1658. Preface, pp. iii, iv.

One Faith, one Baptism. Eph. 4. 5.
The Common Faith. Tit. 1. 4.
The common Salvation. Jude Ver. 3.
Christ Jesus the high priest of our Profession, Heb. 3. 11.
The profession of our Faith. Heb. 10. 22.
One shall say I am the Lords, Isai. 44. 5.
Hold fast the form of sound words. 2 Tim. 1. 13.
The form of Knowledge, and of the truth, Rom. 2. 20.
The form of Doctrine delivered unto you, Rom. 6. 17.

[3] *THE CONFESSION OF FAITH.*

I do believe with my heart and confess with my mouth.

Concerning God.

THat there is but one only true God in three persons, the Father, the Son, and the Holy Ghost. each of them God, and all of them one and the same Infinite, Eternall God, most Wise, Holy, Just, Mercifull and Blessed for ever.

Concerning the Works of God.

THat this God is the Maker, Preserver, and Governour of all things according to the counsel of his own Will, and that God made man in his own Image, in Knowledge, Holiness and Righteousness.

Concerning the fall of Man.

THat *Adam* by transgressing the Command of God, fell from God and brought himself and his posterity into a state of Sin and death, under the Wrath and Curse of God, which I do believe to be my own condition by nature as well as any other.

[4] *Concerning Jesus Christ.*

THat God sent his Son into the World, who for our sakes became man, that he might redeem and save us by his Obedience unto death, and that he arose from the dead, ascended unto Heaven and sitteth at the right hand of God, from whence he shall come to judge the World.

Concerning the Holy Ghost.

THat God the holy Ghost hath fully revealed the Doctrine of Christ and will of God in the Scriptures of the Old and New Testament, which are the Word of God, the perfect, perpetuall and only Rule of our Faith and Obedience.

Concerning the Benefits we have by Christ.

THat the same Spirit by Working Faith in Gods Elect, applyeth unto them Christ with all his Benefits of Justification, and Sanctification, unto Salvation, in the use of those Ordinances which

God hath appointed in his written word, which therefore ought to be observed by us until the coming of Christ.

Concerning the Church of Christ.

THat all true Believers being united unto Christ as the Head, make up one Misticall Church which is the Body of Christ, the members wherof having fellowship with the Father Son and Holy-Ghost by Faith, and one with an other in love, doe receive here upon earth forgiveness of Sinnes, with the life of grace, and at the Resurrection of the Body, they shall receive everlasting life. *Amen.*

[5] *THE COVENANT:*

I do heartily take and avouch this one God who is made known to us in the Scripture, by the Name of God the Father, and God the Son even Jesus Christ, and God the Holy Ghost to be my God, according to the tenour of the Covenant of Grace; wherein he hath promised to be a God to the Faithfull and their seed after them in their Generations, and taketh them to be his People, and therfore unfeignedly repenting of all my sins, I do give up myself wholy unto this God to believe in love, serve & Obey him sincerely and faithfully according to his written word, against all the temptations of the Devil, the World, and my own flesh and this unto the death.

I do also consent to be a Member of this particular Church, promising to continue stedfastly in fellowship with it, in the publick Worship of God, to submit to the Order Discipline and Government of Christ in it, and to the Ministerial teaching guidance and oversight of the Elders of it, and to the brotherly watch of Fellow Members: and all this according to Gods Word, and by the grace of our Lord Jesus Christ enabling me thereunto. *AMEN.*

[1] It has been pointed out, *ante*, p. 115, that one of the uses of this confession and covenant was when a baptized child of the church wished to pass from its baptismal fellowship to its full communion. For such use its expressions of personal piety seem natural. But there is every reason to suppose, also, that this creed and covenant were employed for those who could not claim a work of grace sufficient to enable them to ask for full communion, but who simply "owned the covenant" and had their children baptized. Yet New England custom sanctioned as strenuous a covenant as this in their cases. That used by the First Church of Hartford for "half-way" members in 1696 is as follows: "We do solemnly in ye presence of God and this Congregation avouch God in Jesus Christ to be our God one God in three persons ye Father ye Son & ye Holy Ghost & y^{t} we are by nature childr^{n} of wrath & y^{t} our hope of Mercy with God is only thro' ye righteousnesse of Jesus Christ apprehended by faith & we do freely give up ourselves to ye Lord to walke in communion with him in ye ordinances appointed in his holy word & to yield obedience to all his co͞mands & submit to his governm^{t}. & wheras to ye great dishon^{r} of God, Scandall of Religion & hazard of ye damnation of Souls, ye Sins of drunkenness & fornication are Prevailing amongst us we do Solemnly engage before God this day thro his grace faithfully and conscientiously to strive against those Evills and ye temptations that May lead thereto." *Church records*, G. L. Walker, *Hist. First Ch. in Hartford*, Hartford, 1884, p. 248. Like this Salem *Direction* the Hartford covenant was not formally adopted by the church, though prepared by its pastor and used by its services. For a century, at Hartford, each pastor wrote his own form.

[6] Questions to be Answered at the Baptizing of Children, or the substance to be expressed by the Parents.

Quest *Doe you present and give up this child, or these children, unto God the Father, Sonne and Holy Ghost to be baptized in the Faith, and Engaged in the Covinant of God professed by this Church?*

Quest. *Doe you Sollemnly Promise in the Presence of God, that by the grace of Christ, you will discharge your Covinant duty towards your Children, soe as to bring them up in the Nurture and Admonition of the Lord, teaching and commanding them to keep the way of God, that they may be able (through the grace of Christ) to make a personall profession of their Faith and to own the Covinant of God themselves in due time.*

FINIS

VII

THE COVENANT OF THE CHARLESTOWN-BOSTON CHURCH, 1630

The Covenant is preserved in the Records of the First Church in Boston.

PRINTED TEXTS

I. Foxcroft, *Observations, Historical and Practical, on the Rise and Primitive State of New England*, Boston, 1730, p. 3.[1]

II. Emerson, *Historical Sketch of the First Church in Boston*, Boston, 1812, pp. 11, 12.[2]

III. Budington, *History of the First Church, Charlestown*, Boston, 1845, pp. 13, 14.

IV. Drake, *History and Antiquities of Boston*, Boston, 1856, p. 93.

V. Elliott, *New England History*, New York, 1857, I : 398.

VI. R. C. Winthrop, *Life and Letters of John Winthrop*, Boston, 1864–7, II : 45.

VII. Waddington, *Congregational History, 1567–1700*, p. 269.

VIII. Punchard, *History of Congregationalism*, Boston, 1880, IV : 42.

IX. *Commemoration by the First Church . . of the Completion of 250 years since its foundation*, Boston, 1881, p. 201.

X. A. B. Ellis, *History of the First Church in Boston*, Boston, 1881, p. 3.

XI. R. C. Winthrop, *Boston Founded*, in Winsor's *Memorial History of Boston*, Boston, 1882, p. 114.

XII. G. E. Ellis, *Puritan Age in . . Massachusetts*, Boston, 1888, p. 58.

LITERATURE

The circumstances of the adoption of this covenant are described in two contemporary letters to Gov. Bradford of Plymouth, from Samuel Fuller and Edward Winslow, preserved in Bradford, *History of Plymouth Plantation*, pp. 277–279; and in Bradford's Letter-Book, *1 Coll. Mass. Hist. Soc.*, III : 74–76. The essential portions of these letters were given in abstract by Prince, *Chron. Hist. of New England*, I : 242–244. The facts, thus preserved, have been treated with more or less fullness in each of the works from which texts of the covenant have been cited. I will only add to the list there given, Felt, *Eccles. Hist. N. E.*, I : 138, 139; Palfrey, *Hist. N. E.*, I : 316; Dexter, *Congregationalism as seen*, 417. Governor Winthrop gives no account of the adoption of this covenant, his *History of New England* (or *Journal*) having a large blank at this point; though he describes the election and installation of the officers of the church four weeks after (Savage's 2d. ed. Boston, 1853, I : 36–39). Hubbard (*Gen. Hist. N. E.*, ed. Boston, 1848, p. 135) and Mather (*Magnalia*, ed. 1853–5, I : 79) observe the same silence.

---

[1] Century Sermon. Thomas Foxcroft was minister of the First Church, Boston, from 1717 to his death in 1769.

[2] William Emerson was pastor of the First Church, 1799–1811; father of Ralph Waldo Emerson.

IN the previous chapter[1] the story was told of the rapid growth of the enterprise for Puritan colonization in New England under the fostering care of Rev. John White, the securing of a large land grant from the Plymouth Council in March, 1628, and the sending of Endicott to Salem as representative of the new company in the summer of the same year; and, finally, the grant of a patent by the crown to the now much enlarged body of adventurers, on March 4, 1629, organizing it into the "Governour and Company of the Mattachusetts Bay." The first governor of the corporation thus created was Matthew Cradock,[2] a London merchant of wealth; and the evident intention was that the control of the Company should remain in England and its authority be exercised through agents like Endicott. But as the tyranny of church and crown pressed with increasing severity upon the Puritans of England, men of so great prominence and in such numbers announced their intention of casting in their lot with the Company as actual settlers on the shores of New England, that a change of policy seemed advisable. Accordingly, on July 28, 1629, Cradock himself proposed that the government of the Company be transferred to New England soil.[3] Decision was not immediately given by the Company as a whole, but the desires of a prominent body of Puritans, embracing such men as Winthrop, Saltonstall, Dudley, Pynchon, and Nowell, who entered into a mutual covenant at Cambridge, Eng., August 26, 1629, to emigrate to New England provided the government and patent should be legally carried thither,[4] caused matters to come to a head; and on August 29 the transfer was voted.[5] Since Cradock and others of the old officers of the Company could not leave England, they naturally resigned; and the vacant governorship

1 See *ante*, p. 100.

2 Some biographical facts regarding him may be found in Young, *Chron. . . Mass.*, pp. 137, 138.

3 *Records . . of Massachusetts*, Boston, 1853, I: 49. Young, *Chron. . . Mass.*, pp. 85, 86.

4 Young, *Ibid.*, pp. 281, 282.

5 *Records*, I: 50, 51. Young, *Ibid.*, pp. 86–88. Compare Palfrey, I: 301, 302, and G. E. Ellis, *Puritan Age . . in . . Mass.*, pp. 46–49.

was filled, October 20, 1629,[1] by the choice of John Winthrop.[2] Preparations for departure now went on apace, and hundreds of emigrants decided to avail themselves of the facilities afforded by the Company. With the opening spring of 1630 these colonists now began pouring across the Atlantic. First of all to leave England was a body organized by the influence of John White of Dorchester, England, and which had been joined together into Congregational church-estate at Plymouth, England, in March, 1630, just before sailing, and had there chosen John Warham and John Maverick its ministers.[3] Arrived in Massachusetts Bay on May 30 of that year, they named their new settlement Dorchester, in memory of their English home. These Dorchester emigrants did not much anticipate, either in sailing or arrival, their companions in the great emigration[4] of 1630. Winthrop and his immediate company got away from English shores April 8, and reached Salem, June 12.[5] But Salem proved not to their liking,[6] and they almost immediately removed to Massachusetts Bay, where the majority of Winthrop's immediate associates settled on the north side of Charles river at Charlestown, but a few took up their abode on the south side at what was soon to be named Boston.[7]

[1] *Records*, I: 59, 60; Young, *Ibid.*, pp. 104, 105.

[2] Of Winthrop, one of the greatest names in New England history, little need here be said. Born at Edwardston, Suffolk, Jan., 1588, of a family of considerable prominence, he studied at Cambridge for two years, beginning with 1602; but left without taking a degree. He practiced law, and discharged the duties of a justice, coming also into connection with many who were in Parliament; but repeated domestic bereavement in early life increased the always serious bent of his spirit and inclined him to a profound interest in religious things. Precisely how his thoughts were turned toward New England we know not, but by May, 1629, he was seriously weighing the advisability of going thither. His agreement with others to undertake the voyage followed in August, and in October he was chosen governor of the Company. He arrived at Salem June 12, 1630; and thenceforward, till his death in March, 1649, he lived in New England, and was intimately concerned with its affairs. From the foundation of Boston he was identified with that town. He held the governorship till 1634, and again 1637–1640, 1642–1644, 1646–1649. Strong, patient, courageous, and above all profoundly religious, the influence which he exercised in moulding the infant colony can hardly be over estimated. The best work regarding him is that of his descendant Robert C. Winthrop, *Life and Letters of John Winthrop*, 2 vols., Boston, 1864–1867. Of the many other sketches of him I will refer only to one of the earliest, Mather, *Magnalia*, ed. 1853–5, I: 118–131; and the latest, Appleton's *Cyclopædia of Am. Biography*, 1889, VI: 572–574, and J. H. Twichell, *John Winthrop*, New York, 1891.

[3] The circumstances of their organization, and the later removal of a portion of this Dorchester Company to what is now Windsor, Conn., will be related in a subsequent chapter.

[4] Prince, *Chron. Hist. N. E.*, p. 240; Hutchinson, *Hist. . . Mass. Bay*, I: 19; and Young, *Chron . . Mass.*, p. 127, estimate the number of Puritan emigrants to New England in 1630 at 1500.

[5] Winthrop, *History (Journal)*, Savage's 2d ed., I: 6–29.

[6] Dudley's Letter to the Countess of Lincoln, Young, *Chron. . . Mass.*, p. 312.

[7] *Ibid.*, 313. This settlement took place about July 10 or 12. See Prince, *Chron. Hist. N. E.*, p. 240.

If Samuel Fuller, the physician and deacon of Plymouth, was correctly informed the attention of Winthrop's company had already been drawn by a minister whom they held in high esteem and who was later to fill a distinguished teachership in the Boston church, John Cotton, then of Boston, England, to the model set by Plymouth.[1] It was on ready soil, therefore, that the seeds fell when Fuller, who had been called to the medical aid of Winthrop's company and the Dorchester emigrants before the governor had been three weeks on the New England shores, expounded the Plymouth church-way in public and private.[2] We may be sure also that Fuller's earlier friend and sympathizer, Endicott, was of material aid in setting forth Congregational principles since Fuller speaks of him at this time as a second Barrowe.[3] But the Plymouth church was to have a yet more active share in directing the affairs of Winthrop's company toward church organization. On Sunday, July 25, Isaac Johnson, Winthrop's companion, being then at Salem, received a letter[4] from the governor at Charlestown entreating the

[1] Fuller to Bradford. Dated Massachusetts, June 28, 1630. Bradford's Letter-Book, *1 Coll. Mass. Hist. Soc.*, III: 74, 75. "Here is a gentleman, one Mr. Cottington, a Boston [Eng.] man, who told me that Mr. Cotton's charge at Hampton was, that they should take the advice of them at Plymouth, and should do nothing to offend them." *i. e.*, at Southampton before sailing.

[2] *Ibid.* "We have some privy enemies in the bay, but (blessed be God) more friends; the Governour hath had conference with me, both in private and before sundry others . . . the Governour hath told me he hoped we will not be wanting in helping them, so that I think you [*i. e.*, Bradford and his associates] will be sent for."

[3] *Ibid.*, "a second Burrow."

[4] This letter and the consequent action, is made known to us in a letter to Gov. Bradford, Pastor Ralph Smith and Elder William Brewster, of Plymouth, written from Salem, July 26, 1630, by Winslow, and signed by Winslow and Fuller. Text in Bradford, *Hist. Plym. Plant.*, pp. 277, 278; and Letter Book, *1 Coll. Mass. Hist. Soc.*, III: 75, 76. Some important parts of Winslow's letter are as follows: "Sr: Being at Salem yᵉ 25. of July, being yᵉ saboath, after yᵉ evēing exercise, Mʳ. Johnson received a letter from yᵉ Govʳ, Mʳ. John Winthrop, manifesting yᵉ hand of God to be upon them, and against them at Charles-towne . . . It was therfore by his desire taken into yᵉ Godly consideration of yᵉ best hear, what was to be done to pacifie yᵉ Lords wrath. [And they would do nothing without our advice, I mean those members of our church, there known unto them, viz. Mr. Fuller, Mr. Allerton, and myself, requiring our voices as their own.] Wher it was concluded, that the Lord was to be sought in righteousnes; and to that end, yᵉ 6. day (being Friday) of this present weeke, is set aparte, that they may humble them selves before God, and seeke him in his ordenances; and that then also such godly persons that are amongst them, and knoŵ each to other, may publickly, at yᵉ end of their exercise, make known their Godly desire, and practise yᵉ same, viz. solem̄ly to enter into covenante with yᵉ Lord to walke in his ways. And since they are so disposed of in their outward estats, as to live in three distinct places, each having men of abilitie amongst them, ther to observe yᵉ day, and become 3. distincte bodys; not then intending rashly to proceed to yᵉ choyce of officers, or yᵉ admitting of any other to their societie then a few, to witte, such as are well knowne unto them; promising after to receive in such by confession of faith, as shall appeare to be fitly qualified for y estate. They doe ernestly entreate that yᵉ church of Plimoth would set apparte yᵉ same day, for yᵉ same ends, beseeching yᵉ Lord, as to withdraw his hand of correction from them, so also to establish and direct them in his wayes." From Bradford's *History*, clause in brackets added in *Letter Book*.

advice of the Salem church in view of the severe mortality which was afflicting the new settlers on the Charles river. Deacon Fuller, Edward Winslow, and Isaac Allerton, of the Plymouth church, were at Salem, and the good people of that church sought their counsel also in the weighty matter laid before them.[1] Possibly Winthrop had outlined, in the letter to Johnson, a plan for which he desired the approval of the Salem brethren; more probably Johnson was himself sufficiently identified with Winthrop and his company to accept counsel in their behalf and to agree to a definite line of action in their stead. At all events, it was determined that Sabbath evening at Salem that the three settlements into which Winthrop's immediate company had already divided, Charlestown, Watertown, and probably either Roxbury or Medford,[2] should observe the coming Friday, July 30, as a fast; and that those who were fit among their inhabitants should enter into church-estate by covenant. At the same time the Plymouth church, in the persons of its three members at Salem, was entreated to "set apparte y[e] same day, for y[e] same ends," beseeching God's mercy on the afflicted people of Massachusetts Bay and His blessing on their new church insti-

1 The letter just quoted is indeed obscure. Prince, *Chron. Hist. N. E.*, pp. 242, 243, represents it as conveying information to Johnson at Salem, rather than asking advice. I have interpreted it as seems more probable to me. Winslow's letter to Bradford certainly implies that the advice of the Salem people was sought, and given. That advice seems to include the establishment of covenant church relationships, as one means of seeking the Lord in righteousness. There was not time between Sunday evening, when Winthrop's letter was received, and Monday, when Winslow's letter was written, for any action embodying the Salem advice to be taken at Charlestown and reported back to Salem. Hence the setting apart of Friday must have been definitely determined upon at Salem, and probably that Sabbath evening. As representative of the only other church which had had experience on New England soil (that of Dorchester had only just arrived) it was natural for Johnson and the Salem brethren to consult the men from Plymouth. Probably Winthrop may have suggested such a course, though it is hard to assert that to be the case from Winslow's letter. We may assume also, though it does not appear on the record, that Salem observed the day in prayer for Winthrop's company in the same way that was urged upon Plymouth.

2 What are signified by the "three distinct places" and "3. distincte bodys" of Winslow's letter is hard to say with certainty. Prince, *Chron. Hist. N. E.*, p. 243, interprets them as Salem, Dorchester, and Charlestown. This view is, however, obviously incorrect, as Winslow's letter clearly implies that the three places were inhabited by Winthrop's immediate company, and by persons not yet gathered in church-estate; while Salem and Dorchester already had well-established churches. Of course one of the places is Charlestown, where Winthrop then was. Another is clearly Watertown, where a church was to be formed on the same day as the Charlestown-Boston church, and doubtless as a result of the same Salem advice. The third place is more obscure; but it can hardly have been Boston, which was regarded for two years longer as ecclesiastically one with Charlestown. Reasons which space does not permit me to elaborate incline me to think that either Roxbury or Medford is the third. The question is of little importance, for, whatever the third place may have been, we have no evidence of the formation of a church at this time elsewhere than at Charlestown and Watertown.

tutions. Thus, though the Boston church was to remain Nonconformist rather than Separate in its attitude toward the Church of England, it from the very first held out the hand of brotherhood, really if a little indirectly, to the Separatist body at Plymouth. In accordance with this advice, and upon the day designated, Congregational churches were gathered at Charlestown and at Watertown,[1] by the solemn adoption of a covenant. Agreeably also to the counsel that there should be no rashness or haste in the admission of members, the church at Charlestown was formed, on this initial day of its history,[2] by four men only, John Winthrop, Isaac Johnson,[3] Thomas Dudley,[4] and Rev. John Wilson[5]—the four most considerable personages in the little com-

[1] Mather, *Magnalia*, ed. 1853–5, I : 377, gives the text of the Watertown covenant, and its date as July 30, 1630. Some unsuccessful attempts have been made to dispute the correctness of this date, but there can be no reasonable doubt as to its accuracy. See Francis, *Hist. Sketch of Watertown*, Cambridge, 1830, appendix, pp. 132–135 ; Note, by Savage, to Winthrop's *Hist. N. E. (Journal)*, ed. 1853, I : 112–114 ; Bond, *Genealogies . . Early Settlers of Watertown*, Boston, 1855, pp. 979–982 ; Dexter, *Cong. as seen*, p. 413.

[2] Our knowledge of the circumstances under which the formation of the Charlestown-Boston church was effected is based on a letter of Samuel Fuller to Gov. Bradford, dated Charlestown, Aug. 2, 1630. *Letter Book*, *1 Coll. Mass. Hist. Soc.*, III : 76 ; and Bradford, *Hist. Plym. Plant.*, pp. 278, 279 ; in which he says : "Some are here entered into church covenante ; the first were 4. namly, ye Govr, M^r^. John Winthrop, M^r^. Johnson, M^r^. Dudley, and M^r^. Willson ; since that 5. more are joyned unto them, and others, it is like, will adde them selves to them dayly."

[3] Isaac Johnson, the largest subscriber to the stock of the Mass. Company, and a man of prominence in every way, was from Clipsham, County of Rutland. His wife was the daughter of the Earl of Lincoln. Both were victims of the sickness which swept away so many of the first settlers of Charlestown, she dying in Aug. and he Sept. 30, 1630. See Dudley, *Letter to Countess of Lincoln*, Young, *Chron. . . Mass.*, pp. 317, 318 ; Hutchinson, *Hist. . . Colony of Mass. Bay*, I : 16 ; Eliot, *Biog. Dict.*, pp. 281–283 ; Savage's Winthrop, ed. 1853, I : 5 ; Allen, *Am. Biog. Dict.*, ed. Boston, 1857, p. 477, etc.

[4] Thomas Dudley, born at Northampton, Eng., 1576, gained some knowledge of law, served as the captain of a company of volunteers under Henry IV. of France in 1597. Then after some time became steward to the Earl of Lincoln, and embraced Puritan sentiments. Lived for a time at Boston, Eng. He united with Winthrop in the Cambridge Agreement, Aug. 26, 1629. On March 23, 1630, he was chosen deputy governor of the Company. He was always prominent in the colony, being elected governor four times, deputy thirteen times, and major-general. He died July, 1653. See Mather, *Magnalia*, ed. 1853–5, I : 132–135 ; Hutchinson, I : 14–15 ; Young, *Chron. . . Mass.*, p. 304 ; Savage's Winthrop, I : 60–62 ; *1 Proc. Mass. Hist. Soc.*, XI : 207–222.

[5] John Wilson, at first teacher, then pastor of the Charleston-Boston church, was born at Windsor, Eng., 1588, his father being canon of the castle chapel. His mother was a niece of Archbishop Grindall. Wilson was educated at Eton, and then at Cambridge, where he graduated A. B., 1605, and A. M., 1609. His father persuaded him to study law, not approving of his Puritan tendencies, but Wilson's bent was for the ministry. After serving as chaplain in Puritan families and preaching in various places, he settled at Sudbury, Suffolk, where he came to know Winthrop. Here, though a minister of the Church of England, his Puritan inclinations were so marked as to lead the bishop of Norwich to suspend and silence him. The prohibition was removed, through influence, but Wilson preferred to go to New England and therefore joined with Winthrop. He was chosen teacher of the Boston church at Charlestown, Aug. 27, 1630; and pastor Nov. 22, 1632 (Winthrop, Savage's ed. 1853, I : 36–39, 114, 115). He remained in office till his death, Aug. 7, 1667. Though inferior in ability to his ministerial associate, John Cotton, he was a man of mark, well liked for his sweet temper, and popular in the community. He wrote little.

munity.[1] Within three days five more had been admitted to fellowship, and other members joined in rapid succession.

The church so begun was not yet equipped with officers; though all men knew who was to be its minister, and preaching was doubtless maintained. The next step was taken by the General Court of the Company, on August 23, 1630, when support, to be raised by taxation from those places under the Massachusetts jurisdiction where churches had not been formed previous to July 30, was voted to Mr. Wilson of Charlestown-Boston and Mr. Phillips of Watertown.[2] It was not till after the salary of its minister had thus been provided, that the Charlestown-Boston church held another fast, and solemnly chose and installed its officers August 27, 1630. At that time John Wilson was elected teacher, Increase Nowell ruling-elder, and William Gager and William Aspinwall deacons.[3] The officers thus selected were then installed by the laying on of hands, but with the express reservation, in the case of Mr. Wilson, that the act was not to be construed as a denial of the validity of his English and Episcopal ordination.[4]

But Charlestown was not to be the permanent home of the majority of its early settlers; by the time that the officers were chosen the exodus to Boston was well begun, by November the governor himself had removed thither,[5]—soon Boston was more populous than Charlestown. Naturally services began to be held

---

See Mather, *Magnalia*, ed. 1853–5, I: 302–321; Eliot, pp. 496–499; Emerson, *Hist. Sketch First Ch. in Boston*, Boston, 1812, *passim;* Young, *Chron. . . Mass.*, pp. 325, 326; Savage's Winthrop, *passim;* A. W. M'Clure, *Lives of the Chief Fathers of N. E.*, Boston, (1846) 1870, II: 7–172; Sprague, *Annals Am. Pulpit*, I: 12–15; A. B. Ellis, *Hist. First Ch. Boston*, Boston, 1881, pp. 4–6, 98–102; Appleton's *Cyclop. Am. Biog.*, VI: 553, etc.

[1] Their only rivals in station, Sir Richard Saltonstall and Rev. George Phillips, were the leaders of the branch of the settlement at Watertown.

[2] *Mass. Colonial Records*, I: 73. Both were to have houses built at public expense. Mr. Phillips was to have also specified provisions and £20 *per annum*, or £40 without provisions, at his option. Mr. Wilson £20 "till his wife come ouer." "All this to be att the comon charge, those of Mattapan [Dorchester] & Salem onely exempted," *i. e.*, because these two places had churches of their own.

[3] Winthrop, *Hist. N. E.* (*Journal*), Savage's ed. 1853, I: 36–39.

[4] *Ibid.* See *ante*, p. 99.

[5] Winthrop's letter to his wife is dated "Boston . . . Nov. 29, 1630." *Ibid.*, I: 456. The *Early Records of Charlestown*, given in Young, *Chron. . . . Mass.*, 371–387, contain a picturesque and circumstantial account of the settlement of Charlestown and Boston. Doubtless it rests upon good traditional evidence, and is accurate in general impression; but it was compiled in 1664, and should by no means be treated as a contemporary authority, as many historians have done.

on the Boston side,[1] though the two peoples were looked upon as one congregation. The preponderance of Boston so increased that, in August, 1632, a meeting-house was begun there at the joint expense of the people of both places.[2] But the river was a barrier difficult to cross in bad weather, and it is no wonder that the people of Charlestown amicably withdrew from their brethren at Boston in October, 1632, and were formed into a church of their own on November 2 of that year.[3] Thenceforward the Boston and Charlestown congregations pursued independent paths. The eminence already attained by the Boston church was crowned when its ministerial equipment was completed according to the ideas of the time, by the ordination of John Cotton, certainly the ablest of the early Massachusetts ministry, to the office of teacher, October 10, 1633.[4]

The Charlestown-Boston covenant is a plain, sweet, simple promise of obedience to God and of aid to one another.[5] It does not touch upon doctrinal questions for the same reason that the early covenant of Salem does not treat of them,— such questions were not yet mooted in Winthrop's company. But it was of the highest importance for the development of Congregationalism on our shores; for it was the work of men who were essentially conservative, who had no desire to break with the Church of England and did not regard themselves as separating from her. And it was the work, too, of those who were, and were to be, above all others, the leaders and founders of civil institutions in Massachusetts. In thus heartily embracing Congregationalism at the outset

---

[1] Probably the services were thenceforth held chiefly in Boston, as the pastor and governor moved thither. Hunnewell, *Commemoration of the 250th Anniversary First Ch., Charlestown*, p. 30, records a tradition that preaching was had at first alternately in Boston and Charlestown.

[2] Winthrop, as cited, I: 104. While at Charlestown the services were held in part in the open air and in part in the "great house" built at the expense of the Company in 1629. Hunnewell, as cited, p. 30.

[3] Winthrop, as cited, I: 112. Hunnewell, as cited, p. 31. For the covenant then adopted, see *ante*, p. 116.

[4] Winthrop, as cited, I: 135–137. The church had advanced in its opposition to Episcopal rites and ordinances since the days of Wilson's election, for though Cotton had long been a minister of the Church of England, he was now explicitly *ordained* to his Boston office, by the imposition of the hands of the pastor and elders and prayer.

[5] Dr. McKenzie, in his *Discourse* printed in connection with the address of Mr. Hunnewell, just cited, p. 8, suggests that the covenant is propably from the pen of Winthrop. It is still in use by the First Church in Boston (now Unitarian).

the Charlestown-Boston Christian community made it certain that Congregationalism was to be the polity of Puritan New England.

THE CHARLESTOWN-BOSTON COVENANT.[1]

In the Name of our Lord Jesus Christ, & in Obedience to His holy will & Divine Ordinaunce.

Wee whose names are herevnder written, being by His most wise, & good Providence brought together into this part of America in the Bay of Masachusetts, & desirous to vnite our selves into one Congregation, or Church, vnder the Lord Jesus Christ our Head, in such sort as becometh all those whom He hath Redeemed, & Sanctifyed to Himselfe, do hereby solemnly, and religiously (as in His most holy Proesence) Promisse, & bind o^r^selves, to walke in all our wayes according to the Rule of the Gospell, & in all sincere Conformity to His holy Ordinaunces, & in mutuall love, & respect each to other, so neere as God shall give vs grace.

---

[1] Text from A. B. Ellis, *History of the First Church in Boston*, p. 3. Mr. Ellis, now clerk of the First Church, has kindly verified the text in his *History* by a fresh comparison with the copy of the Records of the First Church made by David Pulsifer in 1847.

VIII

HOOKER'S SUMMARY OF CONGREGATIONAL PRINCIPLES, 1645

I. These articles were originally published in Hooker's preface to his *Survey of the Summe of Church-Discipline*, etc., London, . . 1648, pp. [xvii–xix.] Thence they were reproduced in

II. Hanbury, *Historical Memorials*, etc., London, 1839–44, III: 266, 267; and

III. Felt, *Ecclesiastical History of New England*, Boston, 1855, I: 566; and

IV. G. L. Walker, *History of the First Church in Hartford*, Hartford, 1884, pp. 144, 145.

THE coming of Winthrop's company was but the beginning of a great outpouring[1] from Old England to the New,—an emigration which continued in full force till the changes in the English political horizon at the opening of the Long Parliament gave promise to the Puritans of satisfactory reforms at home, and thus removed the chief impulse toward the planting of Puritan colonies beyond the Atlantic. As a whole, this great emigration was remarkably homogeneous in character and united in habits of religious thought. But it was impossible that in so large a body some degree of diversity should not be found. It is remarkable that, freed as the emigrants were from the restraints of the English Establishment, their divisions were so few and so comparatively unimportant.

The first really serious question to disturb the peace of our rising churches was that occasioned by the coming of Mrs. Anne

[1] Johnson, *Wonder-Working Providence*, London, 1654, Poole's reprint, Andover, 1867, p. 31, estimated the number who had come to New England by 1643 as 21,200. These figures were approved by Pres. Stiles in a glowing sermon preached Apl. 23, 1760, at Bristol, R. I., before the Congregational Convention of that province—a sermon in which the preacher indulged in predictions as to the growth of New England's population during the next 100 years which far exceed anything which has been realized on New England soil. Pres. Stiles added the observation that between 1643 and 1760 more persons probably left New England than came to her shores. Palfrey, *Hist. N. E.*, I: vii (Preface), substantially accepts these statements; and doubtless they are approximately true, though Savage in a note to Winthrop, ed. 1853, II: 403, 404, intimates that the figures may not be taken as final.

Hutchinson to Boston in 1634, Mr. Henry Vane in 1635, and Mrs. Hutchinson's husband's brother-in-law, Rev. John Wheelwright, in 1636. The views of Mrs. Hutchinson, embraced as they were in large degree not only by the two whose names have been associated with hers, but by a majority of the Boston church, were stigmatized by her opponents as "Antinomian"; and certainly laid far too much stress on the believer's confidence in his good estate, rather than visible betterment in his character, as evidence of his acceptance with God. However worthy of respect Mrs. Hutchinson herself may have been, there can be no doubt that the controversy raised by her came perilously near wrecking the infant colonies; and the greatness of the danger explains in part, without justifying, the severe measures of repression employed by the churches and the government.[1] The dispute occasioned the calling by the Massachusetts General Court[2] of the first Synod ever held in New England, an assembly which met on Aug. 30, 1637,[3] at what is now Cambridge, and continued in session, with Thomas Hooker[4] and Peter Bulkeley,[5] as moderators, for twenty-four days. By this Synod some eighty-two opinions, ascribed to or said to be deducible from the teachings of Mrs. Hutchinson, and other disturbers of the churches at the time, were condemned.[6]

---

[1] The sources and literature of this controversy are presented in an admirable bibliographical note by Winsor in the *Memorial History of Boston*, Boston, 1882, I: 176, 177. To the summary there given the writer may add as having appeared since the publication of the *History*, a contemporary document of the first importance, communicated by Prof. F. B. Dexter, to the *2 Proc. Mass. Hist. Soc.*, IV: 159–191, from the MSS. collected by Pres. Stiles, and giving a report of the trial of Anne Hutchinson. The controversy has been discussed from various points of view by G. L. Walker, *Hist. First Ch. in Hartford*, Hartford, 1884, pp. 97–103; Brooks Adams, *Emancipation of Mass.*, Boston, 1887, pp. 44–78; Doyle, *The English in America, Puritan Colonies*, London, 1887, I: 173–189; G. E. Ellis, *Puritan Age . . in . . Mass.*, Boston, 1888, pp. 300–362. Dr. Winsor does not include Punchard, *History of Congregationalism*, Boston, 1880, IV: 196–248, who gives a good sketch of the controversy and its results; and since Winsor's note was written Charles Francis Adams has published a picturesque and valuable narrative of the dispute in his *Three Episodes of Mass. History*, Boston, 1892, pp. 363–578.

[2] The fact of this call is not mentioned in the Colony Records or Winthrop, but may be deduced from the latter's statement that the diet of the Synod and the traveling expenses of the delegates from Connecticut were paid by the government. Savage's ed. 1853, I: 288.

[3] A contemporary account of its proceedings is to be found in Winthrop, *Ibid.*, I: 284–288. In attendance "were all the teaching elders through the country, and some new come out of England."

[4] Of Hartford, Conn.

[5] Of Concord, Mass.

[6] These opinions are given in Winthrop and Welde's *Short Story of the Rise, reign, and ruine of the Antinomians, Familists & Libertines, that infected the Churches of Nevv England*, London, 1644; but are more accessible in Felt, *Ecclesiastical History of N. E.*, Boston, 1855, I: 313–319.

But the most effective, if least creditable, termination to the dangerous dispute was given not by the Synod, but by the Court, in banishing Wheelwright and Mrs. Hutchinson and some of their prominent supporters from the Massachusetts jurisdiction, by its sentence on November 2, 1637.[1]

These internal conflicts were, however, only a portion of the difficulties in which the early New England churches found themselves involved. As has already been pointed out, though the churches of Massachusetts Bay and of Connecticut had left England as Non-Conformists rather than Separatists, and though influential churches, like that of Boston, still refused to reject the Church of England as anti-Christian, they had all of them nevertheless organized on the model set by Separatist Plymouth. It was natural that such action should excite a degree of alarm in the minds of those Puritans in England who still hoped for the reformation of the Establishment, and especially that dominant wing of English Puritanism whose non-conformity looked rather in the direction of Presbyterianism than Congregationalism. Such alarm found expression in 1636 or 1637 in *A Letter of Many Ministers in Old England, requesting The judgement of their Reverend Brethren in New England concerning Nine Positions, written Anno Dom.* 1637.[2] These questions have to do with the use of a liturgy, admission to the sacraments, church-membership, excommunication, and ministerial standing. To this letter of inquiry the ministers of New England responded at some length in 1638 and 1639, by the pen of John Davenport,[3] pastor of the church at New Haven.

[1] *Records*, . . *Mass. Bay*, I: 207.

[2] So the title page of the first edition of this document, 1643; but Shepard and Allin credit its sending to 1636. See Felt, *Eccles. Hist. N. E.*, I: 277. The Letter to New England, the Reply, and Ball's Rejoinder were printed in one small volume in London in 1643. The same year, also, the New England answers were printed at London, together with Richard Mather's Answer to the XXXII Questions, about to be noted, and his reply to Bernard regarding Church-Covenant — the whole under the title of *Church-Government and Church-Covenant Discvssed*, etc., and furnished with a preface by Hugh Peter. The Letter, Replies, and Rejoinder are given in copious extract by Hanbury, *Historical Memorials*, II: 18–39; and the Positions may be found also in Felt, *Eccles. Hist. N. E.*, I: 277; and a summary of the Answers, *Ibid.*, 366–368.

[3] On its authorship see I. Mather, *Discourse Concerning the Unlawfulness of Common Prayer*, [1689] p. 14. The first copy miscarried, 1638, and the reply was sent anew in 1639. See *Church-Government*, as cited, pp. 24, 28; and Shepard and Allin's *Defence* (Hanbury, *Memorials*, III: 36).

A rejoinder, by Rev. John Ball on the part of the English critics, followed in 1640; and a defense of the New England answers by Rev. Thomas Shepard of Cambridge, Mass., and Rev. Thomas Allin of Charlestown, in 1645.[1]

About the time[2] that the *Nine Positions* were sent over to New England the English Puritans also forwarded to their brethren across the sea a list of *Thirty-two Questions* for answer.[3] These inquiries covered the whole field of church polity and procedure, treating of such matters as the constitution of a church, the conditions of membership therein, the churchly character of English parishes, the ministry, the brethren and their methods of procedure, ministerial settlement and standing, and lay-preaching; as well as of doctrinal symbols and the legislative powers of synods and councils. And to these questions also the churches of New England sent a full and candid reply by the pen of Rev. Richard Mather, of Dorchester, in 1639.[4]

The Congregationalism of both these replies is of the type of Barrowe rather than that of Browne. It gives practically all power into the hands of the officers of the church, and leaves to the brethren little more than a bare right to consent.[5] But if this

---

[1] *A Defence of the Answer made unto the 9 questions . . . against the Reply thereto of John Ball*, etc., London, 1645. The more essential portions are reprinted in Hanbury, *Memorials*, III: 33–43.

[2] Felt, *Eccles. Hist. N. E.*, I: 278.

[3] These Questions were published, with Mather's Answers, at London in 1643, in the book entitled *Church-Government and Church-Covenant Discvssed*, etc., cited in note, p. 134. The Questions are also given in Felt, *Ibid.*, I: 278–282; and the Answers are epitomized, *Ibid.*, pp. 380–386.

[4] Mather speaks in the name of the New England ministers throughout his tract, and his son, Increase Mather, expressly affirmed that "what he wrote was approved of by other Elders, especially by *Mr. Cotton*, unto whom he Communicated it." *Order of the Gospel*, Boston, 1700, p. 73. See also Dexter, *Cong. as seen*, p. 426. But a passage in Cotton's *Reply to Mr. Williams his examination* (printed in 1647, reprinted in *Pub. Narragansett Club*, Providence, 1867, II: 103), which Dr. Dexter seems to have overlooked, makes it evident that though Mather's sentiments had the approval of the New England ministry, the Answers were not submitted to them. "Though he [R. Williams] say, that M[r]. *Cotton*, and the New-English Elders returned that Answer [the 31st]: yet the answer to that Question, and to all the other thirty-two Questions, were drawne up by M[r]. *Mader*, and neither drawne up nor sent by me, nor (for ought I know) by the other Elders here, though published by one of our Elders [Hugh Peter] there." But though Cotton had no share in the composition of the Answers, he approved them, for he goes on, in the next paragraph, to say: "I have read it, and did readily approve it (as I doe the substance of all his Answers) to be judicious, and solide." The same fact is attested by the Preface to the *Disputation concerning Church Members*, London, 1659 (*i. e.*, result of Half-Way Covenant Convention of 1657): "The 32 Questions, the Answerer whereof was Mr. Richard Mather, and not any other Elder or Elders in New England."

[5] See Davenport's answer to the 5th Position, *Church-Government and Church-Covenant Discvssed*, p. 72; and Richard Mather's reply to the 15th Question; *Ibid.*, pp. 47–60. Compare also Dexter, *Cong. as seen*, pp. 425–430.

type of Congregationalism was not far removed from Presbyterianism in the administration of the internal affairs of the individual church by its officers, it was widely at variance with the Presbyterian model in regard to the power of synods over the churches and the right of each church to set apart its ministry.[1] In these matters the New-England apologists asserted a much larger liberty than Presbyterianism would countenance.

But Presbyterianism had always been popular among the Puritans of England, and as the struggle with Charles wore on, and Scotch influence grew in English counsels, Presbyterian predominance in the mother-land became more marked. The first of July, 1643, saw the meeting of the Westminster Assembly, the great ecclesiastical council which Parliament had summoned by an ordinance of June 12, of that year, to give advice as to the reformation of the Church of England.[2] This body, as is well known, was overwhelmingly Presbyterian in sentiment, the Congregationalists being represented by only five men of prominence and a few of comparative insignificance in the Assembly; though this proportion, fair enough perhaps at the time when the Assembly was called, was far from representing the strength of Congregationalism in

---

[1] See answers to the 7th and 8th Positions, *Ibid.*, pp. 76–78; and to the 18th Question, *Ibid.*, pp. 62–66.

[2] The Westminster Assembly was in regular session from July 1, 1643, to Feb. 22, 1649. It never formally adjourned, and continued to meet, in some sort, till March 25, 1652. Its work embraced (*a*) *Directory for the Publique Worship of God*, etc., prepared in 1644, and approved by Parliament Jan. 3, 1645. (*b*) Advice for Ordination of Ministers and the Settling of Presbyterian Government; modified and approved by Parliament in November, 1645, June, 1646, and June, 1647 (see also Dexter, *Cong. as seen.* Bibliog. Nos. 1233, 4, 96). By the approval of these recommendations, and by express ordinances in August, 1645, Presbyterianism became the legal form of church-government in England, though actually put into complete practice only in London and Lancashire. (*c*) *Humble Advice . . . concerning a Confession of Faith* (the Westminster Confession), presented to Parliament Dec. 4, 1646; adopted by the Scotch General Assembly, Aug. 27, 1647; somewhat amended by Parliament in the governmental articles, and issued for England June 20, 1648. (*d*) *A Larger Catechism*, and *A Shorter Catechism*, presented to Parliament in October and November, 1647, and by it approved Sept. 15, 1648. The Scotch General Assembly approved July 20 and 28, 1648, respectively.

It is hardly necessary to observe that this great council, which formulated the beliefs of Scotland and Presbyterian America, was essentially Puritan in composition. One hundred and fifty persons were called to it by Parliament (149 only appear in the Lord's Journal, but Prof. Masson has shown this to be a probable error. See his *Life of John Milton*, II: 515–525, where the full list of members is given, with biographical notes). Of this 150, 30 were laymen, the remaining 120 being almost to a man clergymen of the Church of England. A considerable proportion absented themselves. To this body, eight Scotch commissioners, five clerical and three lay, had the right to add their presence and their voices in debate. They were chosen by the Scotch General Assembly, Aug. 19, 1643. The composition and work of the Assembly is well described, and its literature pointed out, by Schaff, *Creeds of Christendom*, I: 727–820; see also Masson, *Life of John Milton*, II: 609—IV: 63, *passim*.

the nation after the acceptance of its main principles by Cromwell and the army.[1]

It was natural that, though New England had embraced Congregationalism of the Barrowist type, this growth of Presbyterianism in England should not be without its influence on this side of the water. Particularly was this the case at Newbury, where Thomas Parker and James Noyes were pastor and teacher. These honored ministers wished to do away with the right of consultation and assent which the Barrowist Congregationalism of New England left to the brethren in matters of church discipline. They would gladly see partial Presbyterianism introduced, and looked to the Westminster Assembly as a hopeful means for the accomplishment of this result. These views brought trouble into the church at Newbury, and the result was the assembly of a general meeting of the ministers of the colonies, a body which has sometimes, though erroneously, been styled a Synod,[2] and ranked the second in date among the Synods of New England. But the testimony of Richard Mather, himself a member, to its non-synodical character is too strong to be set aside,[3] and is supported by Winthrop's statement

[1] The Congregationalists or Independents in the Westminster Assembly, though few, vigorously sustained their views and were, on the whole, treated with much respect, though outvoted at all points. As early as Dec. 30, 1643 (on date see Masson's *Milton*, III: 23, 24), Rev. Messrs. Thomas Goodwin, Philip Nye, Sidrach Simpson, Jeremiah Burroughes, and William Bridge, joined in a sweet-tempered and modest publication, under the title of *An Apologeticall Narration hvmbly svbmitted to the Honourable Houses of Parliament*, London, 1643. In this tract they declare their entire agreement in points of doctrine with the Presbyterian wing of the Assembly, but desire permission to exercise a degree of liberty in matters of church-government. In 1645 we find these men, with William Greenhill and William Carter, uniting in *A Remonstrance Lately Delivered in to the Assembly*, London, 1645, in which they excuse themselves for not presenting a full model of Congregational church-government, on the ground that in view of recent votes of Parliament and the tone of the Assembly it would be useless. A few other names of Congregationalists in the Assembly, making perhaps a dozen in all, may be found in Schaff, *Creeds*, I: 737. See also Dexter, *Cong. as seen*, pp. 647–659. Of the New England ministers, Cotton, Davenport, and Hooker were offered elections to the Assembly, but declined to go.

[2] So Dexter, *Cong. as seen*, p. 432.

[3] Samuel Rutherford, in his *Due right of Presbyteries*, London, 1644, pp. 476–481, gives some "Synodicall propositions" which he had received by letter from New England. Richard Mather, in his *Reply to Mr. Rutherfurd*, London, 1647, pp. 77, 78 (the pages should have been numbered 87, 88, the figures 71–80 being repeated), thus comments upon them: "There was indeed at *Cambridge* in the year 1643, a printed [private?] conference of some of the Elders of that Country; where sundry points of Church judgement were privatly discoursed of, and this was all. But as the meeting was not any Synod, as Synods are usually understood, so neither were there any Synodicall propositions there agreed upon. . . . This I am able to testifie, having been present at that meeting from the beginning thereof unto the end: . . . What information he goeth upon, I know not: peradventure some notes may have come to his view, which one or other might gather at that conference for his own private use: Peradventure some in their simplicity meaning no hurt,

that it "was an assembly . . . of all the elders in the country, (about 50 in all,) such of the ruling elders as would were present also, but none else."[1] It lacked the presence of representatives of the brethren of the churches which distinguishes a Synod from a ministerial Convention.

The sessions of the meeting were held at Cambridge, and the participants were entertained in the recently erected college building much after the manner of students.[2] The Convention opened on September 4, 1643, and had for its moderators Cotton and Hooker.[3] How long its sessions lasted we do not know, but it ended in a presentation of arguments on both sides and a disapproval of some features of Presbyterianism. The positive action of the meeting was summed up by a contemporary observer, doubtless a member of the assembly, as follows:—[4]

> "We have had a Synod lately, in our College, wherein sundry things were agreed on gravely; as, 1. That the votes of the People are needful in all admissions and excommunications, at least in way of consent; all yielding to act with their consent. — 2. That those that are fit matter for a church, though they are not always able to make large and particular relations of the work and doctrine of Faith, yet must not live in the commission of any known sin, or the neglect of any known duty. — 3. That Consociation[5] of churches, in way of more general meetings, yearly; and more privately, monthly, or quarterly; as Consultative Synods; are very comfortable, and necessary for the peace and good of the churches.— 4. It was generally desired That the *exercitium* of the churches' power might only be in the Eldership in each Particular Church;[6] unless their sins be apparent in their work. — 5. That Parish Churches in Old England could not be right without a renewed Covenant at least, and the refusers excluded."

The grounds of these decisions, in so far as they were anti-Presbyterian, were referred to the brethren of Newbury for their further consideration;[7] but, unfortunately, the work of the minis-

---

may have called that private conference by the name and tearme of a Synod . . . But however they [the] mistake a Rose [arose], sure I am, Synodicall propositions there were none; nor any Synod at all."

[1] Winthrop, ed. 1853, II: 165. [2] *Ibid.* [3] *Ibid.*

[4] This statement of the result of the meeting was contained in a letter from an unnamed writer in New England to a minister in England, quoted in *A Reply of two of the Brethren to A. S. . . , and some modest and innocent touches on the Letter from Zeland, and Mr. Parkers from New England*, etc., London, 1644, p. 7. The passage is quoted by Hanbury, *Memorials*, II: 343.

[5] This word was not yet used in the technical sense in which it was afterward employed in Connecticut — a modern "conference" is more the thought here.

[6] This is pure Barrowism.

[7] Winthrop, II: 165: "The assembly concluded against some parts of the presbyterial way, and the Newbury ministers took time to consider the arguments, etc." We are fortunately in pos-

ters neither changed the opinions of Noyes and Parker nor healed the trouble in the Newbury church.[1]

But Presbyterianism was rapidly gaining ground in England since Scotch military support seemed indispensable to the maintenance of the Parliamentary side in the conflict with the King. The same month in which the ministers' Convention of 1643 held its sessions at Cambridge saw the adoption of the Scotch Covenant by Parliament and the army, and the completion of the alliance between Parliament and the northern kingdom. The political and religious activity of the period was productive of a flood of pamphlets and books, many of which bore upon questions of deep interest to the Congregationalists of New England; and some directly criticized the New England polity from a Presbyterian standpoint. Such a work was Prof. Samuel Rutherford's *Due right of Presbyteries*, etc.,[2] a treatise in favor of the government of the Church of Scotland, of which the author was one of the brightest ornaments. Rutherford here opposed, in kindly spirit and with much learning, the New England view, as set forth in Cotton's *Way of the Churches*,[3] then being circulated in England in manu-

session of Mr. Parker's own version of the difficulty and the result. Under date of Dec. 17, 1643, he wrote to a friend in the Westminster Assembly as follows: "I assure you we have a great need of help in the way of Discipline, and we hope that we shall receive much light from you although we [Parker and Noyes] hold a fundamental power of Government in the People, in respect of election of ministers, and of some acts in cases extraordinary, as in the want of ministers · yet we judge, upon mature deliberation, that the ordinary exercise of Government must be so in the Presbyters as not to depend upon the express votes and suffrages of the People. There hath been a convent, or meeting, of the Ministers of these parts, about this question at Cambridge, in the Bay; and there we have proposed our arguments, and answered theirs; and they proposed theirs, and answered us: and so the point is left to consideration." *Trve Copy of a Letter written by Mr. T[homas] P[arker] . . . Declaring his Judgement touching the Government practised in the Chs. of N. E.*, London, 1644.

[1] Noyes published "what are the points he holds, and wherein he can or cannot concur with them [his fellow-ministers in N. E.], and the Reasons why," in *The Temple Measured*, etc., London, 1647. In this work he takes Presbyterian ground, save on the matter of governing elders, who are not to be distinct in office but are the ministers. For the later troubles in Newbury church, see Coffin, *Sketch of the Hist. of Newbury*, Boston, 1845, pp. 44, 54, 72–115.

[2] Printed at London, 1644. Rutherford — 1600?–1661 — was born at Nisbet, Scotland, and studied at Edinborough, where he taught after graduation. In 1627 he settled at Anworth, but was deprived in 1636 for opposition to the attempts to introduce Episcopacy into Scotland. In 1639 the Presbyterian reaction made him professor of divinity at St. Andrews. He sat as a Scotch commissioner in the Westminster Assembly. In 1661 he died, just as the restored monarchy was proceeding against him for treason.

[3] Cotton's *Way of the Churches of Christ in New-England. Or the VVay of Churches walking in Brotherly equalitie, or co-ordination, without Subjection of one Church to another*, got to England in manuscript and was published in 1645, the year after Rutherford's work appeared, by "a *Brownistical Author*, without Mr. *Cotton*'s Consent or Knowledge"; though exactly why

script, and in the recent works of Richard Mather in reply to the XXXII Questions, on Church-Covenant,[1] and in answer to Herle.[2] He also controverted the positions of Robinson's *Ivstification of Separation from the Church of England*,[3] and *The Peoples Plea for the Exercise of Prophesie*,[4] both of which had recently been reprinted. In general, Rutherford proved himself familiar with a wide range of Congregational literature, and showed himself able to put his own case clearly and effectively. Such a critic was not to be despised, nor was he alone in attacking the New England system. In spite of the publication of Cotton's great exposition of Congregational principles, *The Keyes of the Kingdom of Heaven*, in the same year that Rutherford's work appeared, it was felt that a direct rejoinder must be made. And for this task no fitter pen could be found than that of Thomas Hooker[5] of Hartford, the peer

Cotton should have seriously objected is not very evident to a modern reader. See Owen, *Defence of Mr. John Cotton*, etc., 1658, pp. 36–38; Mather, *Ratio Disciplinæ*, p. ii; Dexter, *Cong. as seen*, 434. Rutherford quotes from the manuscript, and with some verbal freedom, as tested by the printed text.

[1] See *ante*, p. 134, note 2.

[2] Mather and Tompson, *Modest & Brotherly Ansvver to Mr. Charles Herle his Book, against the Independency of Churches.* London, 1644.

[3] 1610. [4] 1618. The works were reprinted in 1639 and 1641 respectively.

[5] Thomas Hooker, probably the ablest of the early New England ministers, was born at Marfield, Leicester County, England, probably July 7, 1586. After preparation, probably at Market Bosworth, he entered Queen's College and then Emmanuel at Cambridge, graduating A.B. in 1608 and A.M. in 1611, and holding a fellowship after graduation. About 1620 he became rector of Esher, Surrey, a "donative" living, or one which could be given without the necessity of an order from a bishop inducting the candidate. He then became "lecturer," or supplementary Puritan preacher, at St. Mary's, Chelmsford, about 1625 or 1626; preaching there with great popular success. This of course attracted the unfavorable notice of Laud, who, as bishop of London, compelled him to relinquish his place, apparently in 1629. Hooker then opened a school, in connection with John Eliot, the later Indian missionary, at Little Baddow, near Chelmsford; but he was not long allowed to remain in peace. In 1630 he was summoned before the High Commission, and fled to Holland to avoid appearance. Here he lived for a short time at Amsterdam, and then for two years as associate minister of the English (Non-conformist) church at Delft. He went thence to Rotterdam, where he was associated in the ministry, over the Puritan church at that place, with Dr. William Ames. Meanwhile his English friends in considerable numbers had gone to New England, and settled first at Mt. Wollaston and then at Newtown—soon to be called Cambridge—and there awaited his ministry. He therefore came to New England in 1633, with Samuel Stone of Hertford and Towcester who was to be teacher of Mr. Hooker's congregation. On Oct. 11, 1633, Hooker and Stone were chosen pastor and teacher by the waiting congregation at Newtown. In 1636 they, with a majority of their church, removed to what was to be known as Hartford. Hooker was from his first coming prominent in all colonial affairs. He was a moderator at the Synod of 1637 and the Convention of 1643. He was instrumental in preparing the "Fundamental Laws," the first written constitution not only of Connecticut, but of English-speaking peoples, in 1639. He was invited by the Independents in Parliament to be one of three (with Davenport and Cotton) to enter the Westminster Assembly from New England. Hooker died at Hartford, July 7, 1647. His preaching was effective; his power in argument great. His theology was strongly Calvinistic, of the type later known as Hopkinsian.

Among many sources of information respecting Hooker, the following may be mentioned:

of Rutherford in learning and inferior to none of the New England ministry in ability. His answer, *A Survey of the Summe of Church-Discipline*, was presented for the approval of a meeting of the ministers of all the New England colonies held at Cambridge, July 1, 1645, expressly to consider what action should be taken in view of the attacks of Presbyterians and Anabaptists.[1] But the original draft of the work was lost on its way to England, by the foundering of the ship which carried it,[2] and it was only after Hooker's death that a second, and somewhat imperfect, copy was put into print by his Hartford friends.[3]

Able as the *Survey* unquestionably is, it may well be regretted, on the score of readableness and permanent influence, that the author did not produce a direct treatise on Congregationalism, cast in the mold of his own systematized thought, rather than the repetitious work which his minute method of answering Ruther-

---

Mather, *Magnalia*, ed. 1853-5, I: 332-352; Trumbull, *Hist. of Connecticut*, New Haven, 1818, I: 293, 294; Edward W. Hooker, *Life of Thomas Hooker*, Boston, 1849, 1870; Sprague, *Annals of the Am. Pulpit*, New York, 1857, I: 30-37; Allen, *Am. Biog. Dict.*, 3d ed., Boston, 1857, p. 442; *Appleton's Cyclopædia of Am. Biog.*, III: 251; Goodwin, in *Dict. National Biog.*, XXVII: 295. By far the fullest lives of Hooker are two by G. L. Walker, one in his *Hist. First Church in Hartford*, Hartford, 1884, pp. 20-145; and the other in the "Makers of America" Series, New York, 1891. Hooker's will, and a complete bibliography of Hooker's writings by Dr. J. H. Trumbull, are given in connection with both of these biographies.

[1] Winthrop, Savage's ed., 1853, II: 304, 305, records: "Many books coming out of England, some in defence of anabaptism and other errors, and for liberty of conscience as a shelter for their toleration, etc., others in maintenance of the Presbyterial government (agreed upon by the assembly of divines in England) against the congregational way, which was practised here, the elders of the churches throughout all the United Colonies agreed upon a meeting at Cambridge this day [July 1, 1645], where they conferred their councils and examined the writings which some of them had prepared in answer to the said books, which being agreed and perfected were sent over into England to be printed. The several answers were these: Mr. Hooker in answer to Mr. Rutterford the Scotch minister about Presbyterial government, (which being sent in the New Haven ship was lost)." What some of these "many books" may have been the reader may judge by consulting the crowded titles under 1643 and 1644 in the bibliographical portion of Dexter's *Cong. as seen.* So little is known of this meeting that the following note of a deacon of the Dorchester church is of value: "1[d] July 1645 in this mo: the elders did meet at Cambridge in mattachusets baye in N: E to Consider of the motion made amonge the Comissioners of the 4 Confederate Colloneyes: when they did meet at Conecticute viz to thinke of some things that might in ffuture give some testimony from new Engl about the great questiō now in debate about church-Goverment [*i. e.*, in the Westminster Assembly, then in session]: & notice hereof was given publikely in the Assembly at Dorchester vicesimo nono Junii anno 45 that it was intended nothinge to bind the churches or iñovate the practice there of but only private amonge the elders & was no Synod but in such case the churches ought to have notice & to send their comissioners: & so might express at any tyme, but the p[r]sent notice was that the church might know how to direct their prayer written y[e] daye abovesaid by me Jo Wiswall." *Records . . . First Ch. at Dorchester*, Boston, 1891, pp. 253-4.

[2] The celebrated "phantom ship," *Magnalia*, ed. 1853-5, I: 84.

[3] Printed at London 1648. The circumstances are narrated by Edward Hopkins and William Goodwin of Hartford, in an epistle prefixed to the *Survey*.

ford seemed to him to require.[1] But in the preface, which he prepared, it would appear before sending the first draft to England in January, 1646,[2] Hooker has drawn up as clear a presentation of Congregational principles as has ever been given in the brief space of little more than a page of print, and one which has a special value as having been approved by all the ministers of Connecticut and a large portion of those of other colonies.

This statement, compact as it is, shows a decided advance in Congregational development beyond anything yet reached in England or Holland. And nowhere is this more manifest than in its theory of the relation of churches one to another, a subject on which it exhibits a definiteness of view to which English Congregationalists, even of the present day, have not yet attained. Councils, or "consociation of churches," are the proper expedients by which the advisory and admonitory relations of church to church may be expressed. Such councils may advise and entreat an erring church; if the church persist in error, the churches composing the council may renounce fellowship with the offending congregation. But excommunication of the erring, or the publication of sentences of a judicial character, are beyond the proper powers of a council. Here, then, is the historic New England theory of the authority of church councils clearly expressed, and as fully representative of present American usage as of the customs of 1645. It need scarcely be pointed out that this view of Hooker differs widely from the judicial theory of consociations afterwards adopted in Connecticut.

In regard to ministerial standing, Hooker was clear, as were the New England Congregationalists of his day, that a man was a minister only in connection with a local church. On this point the usage of the church universal, which regards a man once set apart to the pastoral calling as permanently enrolled in ministerial ranks, has overcome the more logical theory of early Congregationalism. In spite of the protests of some of the most earnest of

[1] See observations by G. L. Walker, *Hist. First Church in Hartford*, pp. 143, 144.

[2] There is nothing in the preface which implies that a copy of the work had been lost, or that this was a new draft. The conclusion therefore seems plain that this is the original preface, and if so, written between the meeting of July 1, 1645, and January, 1646.

our modern exponents of Congregational polity,[1] the theory of Hooker on this matter does not represent present usage, and American Congregationalists view one who has been ordained to the ministry, whether over a local church or not, as possessed of an abiding ministerial character.

THE PRINCIPLES OF 1645

"*If the Reader* shall demand how far this way of Church-proceeding receives approbation by any common concurrence amongst us: *I shall plainly and punctually expresse my self in a word of truth, in these following points*, viz.

Visible Saints[2] are the only true and meet matter, whereof a visible Church should be gathered, and confœderation is the form.[3]

The Church as *Totum essentiale*, is, and may be, before Officers.[4]

---

[1] See a forcible defence of the older New England view by the late Dr. Dexter, *Congregationalism: What it is; Whence it is; How it works.* Boston, 1865, pp. 154–159.

[2] This subject is treated at length in the *Survey*, Pt. I: pp. 13–34. Hooker understands by Visible Saints persons who give evidence of regeneration, and their infant offspring. "*Saints* as they are taken in this controversie . . . were members of the Churches, comprehending the Infants of confœderate believers under their Parents Covenant, according to 1 *Cor*. 7. 14 . . . *Saints* come under a double apprehension. *Some* are *such* according to *Charity: Some* according *to truth*. *Saints* according to *charity* are such, who in their practice and profession (if we look at them in their course, according to what we see by experience, or receive by report and testimony from others, or lastly, look we at their expressions) *they savour so much, as though they had been with Jesus*. . . . *These* we call *visible Saints* (leaving *secret things to God*)." *Survey*, Pt. I: pp. 14, 15.

[3] *I. e.*, union in a church-covenant. Hooker defines a church as having God for its efficient cause, "visible saints" as its "materiall cause," and the church-covenant as its "formall cause." *Survey*, Pt. I: 12, 45. But Hooker is far from declaring that this covenant must be formally expressed, though "Its most according to the *compleatnesse of the rule*, and for the better being of the Church, *that there be an explicite covenant*." A covenant may be "*implicite*" "when in their practice they *do that*, whereby they *make* themselves *ingaged* to walk in such a society, according to such rules of government, which are exercised amongst them, and so submit themselves thereunto: but doe *not* make any *verball profession* thereof. Thus the people in the *parishes in* England, when there is a *Minister* put upon them by the *Patrone* or *Bishop*, they *constantly* hold them to the *fellowship* of the people in such a place, *attend* all the *ordinances* there used, and the *dispensations* of the *Minister* so imposed upon them, *submit* thereunto, perform all *services* that may give countenance or incouragement to the person in this work of his Ministery. By *such actions*, and a *fixed* attendance upon *all such services* and duties, they declare *that* by their *practices*, *which* others do hold forth by publike *profession*. This . . . I would intreat the *Reader* to observe once for all: that if he meet with such accusations, that we nullifie all Churches beside our own: that upon our grounds received there must be no Churches in the world, but in N. *England*, or some few set up lately in old: that we are rigid *Separatists*, &c . . . a wise meek spirit passeth by them, as an unworthy and ungrounded aspersion." *Survey*, Pt. I: pp. 47, 48.

[4] This matter is discussed in the *Survey*, Pt. I: pp. 89–93. The position taken is that while the church as an organized body — a *Totum organicum* — must have officers, these officers exist by virtue of the choice of the church, which must therefore precede them and have an existence independent of them. To deny this is "As if one should say, It is *not a Corporation* of Aldermen, or freemen *before the Maior* be chosen. It is true, it is *not* a *compleat corporation* of Maior and Freemen, unlesse there be both: but that hinders not, but they be a *corporation of Free-men* united amongst themselves, though there be no Maior. Nay, they *must* be a corporation, *before* they can chuse a Maior. . . . Doth a Corporation, when it puts out a wicked Maior out of his place . . . nullifie their Corporation by that means . . .?" *Survey*, Pt. I: p. 92.

There is no Presbyteriall Church (*i. e.* A Church made up of the Elders of many Congregations appointed Classickwise, to rule all those Congregations) in the N. T.[1]

A Church Congregationall is the first subject of the keys.[2]

Each Congregation compleatly constituted of all Officers, hath sufficient power in her self, to exercise the power of the keyes, and all Church discipline, in all the censures thereof.[3]

---

[1] Discussed in *Survey*, Pt. I: pp. 94–139. The argument is varied and minute, but Hooker affirms that all offices and officers are the gift of Christ; that where there is no office there is no right to rule, that a church officer is to rule only over his particular congregation, and that no combination with other church officers can give him any right to rule over a congregation not his own, for he has no office over that congregation. If Presbyterianism be true the following points must be proved: "1. *That a person may be a Pastour to a people, by whom he was never chosen.* 2. And that he may be a *Pastour* (as the Office of a Pastour is appointed by Christ) *to such, to whom he neither can nor should preach constantly.* 3. And that he is bound to exercise *Jurisdiction of censure*, and decision of doubts to such, to whom he neither needs, nor indeed is bound *to feed by the word.* 4. or Lastly, that the Churches may give power to a man or men that Christ never appointed." *Survey*, Pt. I: p. 124.

[2] This technical expression of XVII century theology is thus defined by Hooker: "Ecclesiastical power made known unto us usually in Scripture under the name of *Keyes*, the signe or adjunct being put for the thing signified, the ensigne of authority for the authority it selfe.

This power is double, { Supreme and Monarchicall,
Delegate and Ministeriall.

1. The *Supreme* and *Monarchicall* power resides onely in our Saviour. . . .

2. There is also *a subordinate and delegated power*, which is proper to our present disquisition, and is nothing else, but *A right given by commission from* Christ *to fit Persons, to act in his house, according to his order.*" *Survey*, Pt. I: p. 185. Cotton thus expresses the idea: "The keys of the kingdom are the Ordinances which Christ hath instituted, to be administred in his Church; as the preaching of the Word, (which is the opening and applying of it) also the administring of the Seals [sacraments] and censures." *Keyes*, p. 2. Hooker's conclusion is that "*The power of the Keyes is committed to the Church of confederate Saints.*" *Survey*, Pt. I: p. 192. "In the Church, and by vertue of the Church, they are communicated to any that in any measure or manner share therein." *Ibid*, 195. "*The power of the Keyes* take it in the compleat nature thereof, its in the Church of beleevers, as in the first subject, *but every part of it is not in the same manner and order to be attended for its ruling in the Church; but in the order and manner which Christ hath appointed.*" *Ibid.* "It is not beleevers, as beleevers, that have this power, but as beleevers Covenanting and fitly capable according to Christs appointment, that are the first subject of this power. For beleevers that are as scattered stones, and are not seated in a visible Church or Corporation, as setled in the wall, these have not any Ecclesiasticall power." *Ibid.*, 203. But even within the church all believers do not share in the power of the Keys. "This power is given to *such beleevers*, who are counted fit by Christ and capable, which women and Children, deafe, and dumbe, and distracted are not." *Ibid.*, 204.

[3] "These keyes, and the power signified by them, must be given to such, who have some of this power *firstly*, and *formally*, and *originally*, and *virtually* can give the rest of the power, which so given, may be fully exercised in all the acts of binding and loosing, according to all the necessities of the Church and intendment of our Saviour Christ. And this may readily be accomplished and easily apprehended to be done by a Church of beleevers: They can admit, elect; this *formally* belongs to them: and officers being elected by them, the whole government of the Church, will then go on in all the operations thereof, and be fit to attain the ends, attended by our Saviour." *Ibid.*, 216.

The Officers appointed by the Gospel are as follows: *Survey*, Pt. II: p. 4.

"Officers of the Gospel may be considered with reference to their
- Number
  - Ruling
    - Ruling onely, as Elders.
    - Ruling and Teaching both, as
      - Pastors.
      - Doctors [Teachers].
  - Supporting the
    - State of the body, as Deacons.
    - Health, as Widowes.
- Institution, in
  - Election.
  - Ordination.

Ordination is not before election.[1]

There ought to be no ordination of a Minister at large, *Namely, such as should make him Pastour without a People.*[2]

The election of the people hath an instrumentall causall vertue under Christ, to give an outward call unto an Officer.[3]

Ordination is only a solemn installing of an Officer into the Office, unto which he was formerly called.[4]

Children of such, who are members of Congregations, ought only to be baptized.[5]

The consent of the people gives a causall vertue to the compleating of the sentence of excommunication.[6]

---

[1] Discussed in *Survey*, Pt. 2, pp. 39–41, "*Ordination* doth depend upon the *peoples lawfull Election*, as an *Effect* upon the *Cause*, by vertue of which it is fully Administred." *Ibid.*, 41.

[2] See *Ibid.*, Pt. 2, Ch. 2. "I shall by way of prevention, desire to settle that which *is our tenet: That Doctors* [Teachers] *and Pastors may preach, to all sorts, upon all occasions, when opportunity and liberty is offered, nay they ought so to do.* But this they do *not as Pastors, but as gifted and inabled Christians.* Pt. 4, pp. 31, 32.

[3] "*Election of the People rightly ordered by the rule of Christ, gives the essentials to an Officer, or leaves the impression of a true outward call, and so an Office-power upon a Pastor.*" *Ibid.*, Pt. 2, p. 66. See *Ibid.*, 66–75.

[4] ORDINATION is an *approbation of the Officer, and solemn setling and confirmation of him in his Office, by Prayer and laying on of hands.*" *Ibid.*, p. 75. "The maine weight of the worke [ordination] lyes in the *solemnity of Prayer;* which argues no *act of jurisdiction* at all." *Ibid.*, 74 [75]. "1. *When the Churches are rightly constituted*, and *compleated with all the Orders and Officers of Christ, the* RIGHT [perhaps *rite* or *right use*, the editors were undecided] *of Ordination belongs to the Teaching Elders; the Act appertaines to the Presbyters constituted of Ruling and Teaching.* . . . 2. Though the *act* of Ordination belong to the *Presbytery*, yet the jus & *potestas ordinandi*, is conferred *firstly* upon the *Church* by Christ, and resides in her. . . . Thirdly, in case . . . the condition of the Church is such, that she is *wholly destitute of Presbyters*, she may then out of her *own power*, given her by Christ, provide for her own comfort, *by ordaining her own Ministers.*" *Ibid.*, pp. 76, 77.

[5] Discussed in *Survey*, Pt. 3, pp. 10–28. Hooker holds that all children of church-members, i. e., of persons in covenant church relationship, are to be baptized irrespective of the moral character of the parents, so long as the parents are not excommunicate. "The *pinch* then of the *Question* lyes here, Whether persons *non confederate*, and so (in our sense not *Members of the Church*) do entitle their children to the seal of Baptisme, being one of the Priviledges of the Church, their Parents (though godly) being yet unwilling to come into Church-fellowship." This he answers in the negative, for "Children as children have not right unto Baptisme"; and "It belongs not to any Predecessors, either neerer or further off removed from the next Parents, καθ αὐτὸ and firstly, to give right of this priviledge to their Children." A child cannot be baptized on its grandparent's church membership. Hooker is far from favoring what was afterwards to be known as the *half-way covenant* position.

[6] *Survey*, Pt. 3, pp. 33–46. Hooker holds that the offence must first be laid before the elders and it rests with them to decide whether it is of sufficient importance to lay before the church. If unimportant, the elders may dismiss the complaint, though the complainant may, at risk of personal censure if unsustained, appeal from them to the brethren. But if weighty, the elders are to examine into the case, recording the accusation exactly and confining the disputants to the points at issue. This preliminary sifting of evidence is to be made by the elders "because *the body of the people*, if numerous, they will be unable with any comely conveniency, to *consider* and weigh *all the circumstances, with all the emerging difficulties*," p. 36, 37. But the elders are not to pass sentence without the consent of the brethren. "Thus the preparation is done, the cause rightly stated and cleered, doubts answered, mistakes removed, and by proofs fair and sufficient, the truth confirmed [all this by the elders]; now the cause is ready and ripe for judgement, and may easily

Whilst the Church remains a true Church of Christ, it doth not loose this power, nor can it lawfully be taken away.[1]

Consociation of Churches should be used, as occasion doth require.[2]

---

be determined in half an hour, which cost many weeks [to the elders] in the search and examination thereof.

The EXECUTION of the sentence issues in four things.

First, the *cause* exactly recorded, is as *fully* and *nakedly* to be *presented to the* consideration of *the Congregation.*

Secondly, the *Elders* are to goe before the Congregation in *laying open the rule*, so far as reacheth any particular now to be considered, and to *expresse their judgement* and *determination* thereof, *so far as appertains to themselves.*

Thirdly, unlesse the people be able to convince thẽm of errour and mistakes in their sentence, they are *bound to joyn their judgement with theirs, to the compleating of the sentence.*

Fourthly, *the sentence*, thus compleatly issued, is to be *solemnly passed and pronounced* upon the Delinquent *by the ruling Elder*, whether it be the censure of *admonition* or *excommunication*," p. 38. It will be seen that Hooker's position is distinctly, though mildly, Barrowist.

[1] *Survey*, Pt. 3, pp. 40–46. Some of his considerations are the following: "*The fraternity have no more power to oppose the sentence of the censure, thus prepared and propounded by the Elders, then they have to oppose their doctrine which they shall publish.* But they have as much power to oppose the one as the other. . . . Since then it is yeelded on all hands, *that the fraternity may renounce and condemn the false, erronious and hereticall Doctrines of an Elder . . . and take away his Office from him:* they may do *as much* by parity of reason *against his false and unjust censures* propounded and concluded, and so interpose and oppose proceeding, as that they shall never take place and be established in the Congregation . . . The conclusion then is, The *fraternity* put for th a [forth a] *causall power* in the censure of excõmunication, whence it receives its compleat being, *and here lyes the supream Tribunal in poynt of judgement.*" pp. 41–43. Hooker holds that the church may proceed against any of its elders as against any other of its membership, though what preliminary steps shall be taken in the "preparation" of the case he does not explain. "In case the Elders offend, and are complained of, to whom must the complaint be carried? the text saith, To the Church . . . and let it be supposed that where there be three Elders, two of them should turn Hereticks and continue so; how could the Church proceed against them, unlesse there was a *causall power in the fraternity* to accomplish this censure?" p. 44. Perhaps Hooker's view of the relation of the church to its officers is most clearly brought out in a comparison which he draws between it and a city corporation: "*The power of judgement* and *power of office* are apparently *distinct* and different *one from another*: The Elders in *poynt of rule* and exercising the act of their Office, are supream, and *above the Congregation;* none have that Office-authority, nor can put forth the acts thereof but themselves: But in *poynt of power of judgement or censure*, the *fraternity* they *are supream*, and above any member or Officer, in case of offence or delinquency: nor need any man strange at this distinction, when the like is daily obvious in paralel examples presented before our eyes. The Lord *Major* is above the *Court*, as touching the wayes and works of his Office, none hath right, nor can put forth such acts, which are peculiar to his place, and yet the *Court* is *above in poynt of censure*, and can answerably proceed to punish in a just way, according to the just desert of his sin. Thus the Parliament is above the King, the Souldiers and Captains above their Generall." Pt. 3, p. 45.

[2] The whole matter of Synods and Councils is discussed in part 4 of the *Survey*. Unfortunately the author left this portion of his work in a fragmentary condition, but his meaning is clear. By "consociation of churches," Hooker did not signify the peculiar institution later known by that name in Connecticut, but what modern Congregationalism calls *advisory councils.* His views are summed up in the following statement: "The truth is, *A particular Congregation is the highest Tribunall, unto which the greived party may appeal in the third place;* [omit ;] if private Councell, or the witnesse of two have seemed to proceed too much sharpely and with too much rigour against him [;] before the Tribunal of the Church, the cause may easily be scanned and sentence executed according to Christ. *If difficulties* arise in the proceeding, the *Counsell of other Churches* should be sought to clear the truth: but the *Power of Censure* rests still in the Congregation where Christ plcaed [placed] it." Pt. 4, p. 19.

Such consociations and Synods[1] have allowance to counsell and admonish other Churches, as the case may require.

And if they grow obstinate in errour or sinfull miscarriages, they should renounce the right hand of fellowship with them.[2]

But they have no power to excommunicate.[3]

Nor do their constitutions binde formalitèr & juridicè.[4]

---

[1] In a paper of Hooker's composition, found in his study, and printed as an appendix to the *Survey*, a Synod is thus defined: "A Synod is an Ecclesiasticall meeting, consisting of fit persons, called by the Churches, and sent as their messengers, to discover and determine of doubtfull cases, either in Doctrine or practise, according to the truth." Pt. 4, p. 45. In such a Synod or council, "all have equall power, because equally sent and chosen, which are the substantiall ingredients to make up Synodicall members." *Ibid.*, 46.

[2] "The *renouncing the right hand of fellowship*, which other Churches may do, and should do as occasion requires, is *another thing from excommunication . . . any Christian man or woman may, upon just grounds, reject the right hand of fellowship wiih* [*with*] *others, whom they cannot excommunicate.* In a word, there may be a *totall separation*, where there is *no excommunication*, Because *excommunication is a sentence judiciall*, presuppoung [presupposing] ever a *solemn and superior power* over the party sentenced; but no such thing in separation, or *rejection.*" Pt. 4, pp. 23, 24.

[3] That there should be Synods, which have *Potestatem juridicam*, is no where proved in Scripture, because it is not a truth." Appended paper, *Survey*, Pt. 4, pp. 48, 49.

[4] "*They* [*Synods and Councils*] *have no power to impose their Canons or Conclusions upon them* [*the Churches*]. 1. Because the Churches power is above them, in that they sent them. 2. Because the Churches have power to call another Synod, and send other Messengers, and passe sentence against them [i. e., decide against the members of the first council]. 3. Because in many cases it may injoyne a man to beleeve contradictions. As suppose a man under one Province, which hath determined a case one way, and therefore he must beleeve that [provided Synods can "binde formaliter"]: He removes himselfe the next month or week into another Province, and they have determined a contrary Conclusion, and he must beleeve that." *Ibid.*, 54. "But if Synods and such meetings be attended onely in way of consultation, as having no other power, nor meeting for any other end: Then as they are lawfull, so the root of them lyes in a common principle which God in providence hath appointed for humane proceeding, and that is, He that hearkens to counsell shall be safe. In the multitude of councellers there is safety. Hence all conditions and callings, as they need, so they use a Combination of counsell, for the carrying on of their occasions under their hand. Hence arise the Companies of Merchants, and all men of all Crafts. Hence Common Councels in all Kingdomes and States. And therefore in the Course of Christianity also the Churches of Christ should use the means, which God hath appointed for their more confortable and succesfull proceeding in a Church-way. And hence one Church may send to another, or to many, and that severally or joyntly meeting." *Ibid.*, p. 61. Hooker's general theory of the independence and communion of churches is perhaps best expressed in the following passage: "When this Church is said to be *Independent*, we must know

That INDEPENDENCY implies two things; } 1. Either an *absolute Supremacy*, and then it is opposed to *subordination.* 2. Or else a *sufficiency* in its kind, for the attainment of its end, and so its opposed to *imperfection.*

Take *that* word in the *first sence, so a particular Church or Congregation is not absolutely supreame*: For its subject unto, and under the supreme power politicke in the place where it is; so that the *Magistrate hath a coactive power* to compel the Church to execute the ordinances of Christ, according to the order and rules of Christ, given to her in that behalfe in his holy Word; and in case she swerves from her rule, by a strong hand to constraine her to keepe it. Hee is a nursing Father thus to the Church, to make her attend that wholesome dyet which is provided and set out, as her share and portion in the Scripture. Nay, should the supream Magistrate unjustly oppresse or persecute, she must be subject, and meekly according to justice, beare that which is unjustly inflicted. Againe, she is so farre *subject to the consociation of Churches*, that she is bound, in case of doubt and difficulty, to crave their counsell, and if it be according to God, to follow it: and if she shall erre from the rule, and continue obstinate therein, *they have authority to renounce the right hand of fellowship* with her. In the *second sence*, the Church may be said to be *Independent*, namely *sufficient to attaine her end;* and therefore hath *com-*

In all these I have leave to professe the joint judgement of all the Elders upon the river :[1] *Of* New-haven,[2] Guilford,[3] Milford,[4] Stratford,[5] Fairfield[6] : *and of most* of the Elders of the Churches in the Bay,[7] *to whom I did send in particular, and did receive approbation from them, under their hands : Of the rest* (*to whom I could not send*) *I cannot so affirm ; but this I can say, That* at a common meeting,[8] *I was desired by them all, to publish what now I do.*

---

pleat power, being rightly constituted, to exercise all the ordinances of God. As *all Arts* are thus *compleat* in their *kinde*, and have a compleat sufficiency in themselves to attaine their owne end ; and *yet* are truely said to be *subordinate* each to the other in their workes. *The* Word, then, in its faire and inoffensive sence, imports *thus much*, *Every particular Congregation, rightly constituted and compleated, hath sufficiency in it selfe, to exercise all the ordinances of Christ.*" Pt. 2, pp. 79, 80.

[1] I. e., on the Connecticut. These churches were Hartford, under Hooker and Samuel Stone ; Windsor, under John Warham ; Wethersfield, under Henry Smith ; Springfield, Mass., under George Moxon ; and Old Saybrook, under James Fitch.

[2] Under John Davenport and William Hooke.

[3] Under Henry Whitfield and John Higginson, the latter later of Salem.

[4] Under Peter Prudden.

[5] Under Adam Blakeman.

[6] Under John Jones.

[7] I. e., of Massachusetts Colony.

[8] At Cambridge, July 1, 1645 ; see *ante*, p. 141.

IX

THE WINDSOR CREED-COVENANT, 1647

The extant contemporary record of this document is contained in a note-book of Deacon Matthew Grant of Windsor, now in the possession of Dr. J. H. Trumbull of Hartford. It has been printed in the *Congregational Quarterly*, Vol. IV, pp. 168, 169 (April, 1862).

THE members of the church which ultimately found its resting place at Windsor, Connecticut, were originally part of a company organized in the west-of-England counties of Devon, Dorset, and Somerset, in 1629 and 1630.[1] This was a region where the influence of Rev. John White, the distinguished Puritan of Dorchester, had long been felt; and he was doubtless largely instrumental in bringing together the adventurers in the enterprise. The personal following of Rev. John Warham, a Puritan minister of the Established Church at Exeter, formed a considerable portion of the body.[2] Their church organization was effected, unlike that of any other of the Puritan churches of New England, before leaving English shores, at Plymouth, where the company had gathered preparatory to sailing;[3] and there John Warham

---

1 Our informant regarding the early history of this company is Capt. Roger Clap, one of its original members, whose *Memoirs*, written after 1676, in his old age, for the instruction of his children, were first printed at Boston in 1731. They have since been a number of times republished; in 1844 by the Dorchester, Mass., Antiquarian and Historical Society, at Boston. The more essential portions are given by Young, *Chron.* . . . *Mass.*, pp. 344–367.

The general history of the company and the church, both in their early experiences and later story, may be found in the Dorchester Ant. and Hist. Society's *Hist. of the Town of Dorchester*, Boston, 1859; Stiles' *Hist. of Ancient Windsor*, New York, 1859 (a new edition is just out); and Messrs. Tuttle, Wilson, and Hayden's contributions to the history of Windsor in Trumbull's *Memorial History of Hartford County*, Boston, 1886, II: 497–560. The 250th Anniversary of the church in 1880 was commemorated by a sketch of the church's history by its late pastor, Rev. G. C. Wilson, *Record of the Services held at the Cong. Ch. of Windsor, Conn., in celebration of its 250th Anniv. Mch. 30, 1880*, [Hartford] 1880, pp. 8–35.

2 Roger Clap's *Memoirs*, pp. 18, 19. Young, *Chron.* . . . *Mass.*, p. 346.

3 *Ibid.*, p. 39: "These godly People resolved to live together; and therefore as they had made choice of those two Revd. Servants of God, Mr. *John Warham* and Mr. *John Maverick* to be their Ministers, so they kept a solemn *Day of Fasting* in the *New Hospital* in *Plymouth, in England*, spending it in Preaching and Praying: where that worthy Man of God, Mr. *John White* of *Dorchester*, in *Dorset*, was present, and Preached unto us the Word of God in the fore-part of the Day; and in the latter part of the Day, as the People did solemnly make *Choice* of,

was chosen and installed as pastor, and John Maverick as teacher.[1] After a voyage lasting from March 20 to May 30, 1630, the company landed at Nantasket, and within a few days after their arrival took up their abode at Mattapan, soon to be known as Dorchester, in memory of the home of their friend and promoter, Rev. John White.

The coming of the Dorchester company was followed in a few days by the arrival in Massachusetts Bay of the emigrants who accompanied Winthrop, and the settlements thus begun were rapidly multiplied by fresh Puritan arrivals during the years following 1630. One of the chiefest of these later companies was that which settled at Mt. Wollaston and then at Newtown (the later Cambridge, Mass.). This company, like that of Dorchester, had a distinct unity and character. Its church enjoyed, from 1633 onward, the ministrations of Thomas Hooker and Samuel Stone;

---

and call these godly Ministers to be their *Officers*, so also the Revd. Mr. *Warham* and Mr. *Maverick* did *accept* thereof, and expressed the same." When Dr. Samuel Fuller of Plymouth, Mass., met Warham soon after his landing on these shores, he found Warham's views as to the composition of a church not quite so strenuous as those of the majority of Puritans who came to New England: "Mr. Warham holds that the invisible [visible] church may consist of a mixed people, godly and openly ungodly." Bradford's Letter-book, *1 Coll. Mass. Hist. Soc.*, III: 74. But the practice of the church cannot have much differed from that of other New England churches, for it was not till after the settlers had arrived at Dorchester that Roger Clap, though a member of the company before leaving England, was admitted to the church: "After God had brought me into this Country, He was pleased to give me Room in the Hearts of his Servants, so that I was admitted into the Church Fellowship at the first beginning in *Dorchester*, in the year 1630." *Memoirs*, p. 24.

[1] John Warham, for one so prominently associated with the early history of a company of settlers of mark in Massachusetts and Connecticut, is very little known. The fact that he lived till 1670 shows that he must have been comparatively young when he came to America. Before leaving England he had been a successful minister of the Establishment at Exeter. Mather, in one of his most padded biographies, records his supposition that Warham was "the first preacher that ever thus preached with notes in our New-England": but the passage is so obscure that the writer feels by no means clear whether Mather meant that Warham was the first to preach from notes, or as Judge Davis interpreted it, the first to preach from notes in a free and natural manner (Davis' ed. Morton's *Memorial*, Boston, 1826, p. 482); Mather also declares that he was so subject to melancholy as to deny himself the Lord's Supper when offering it to others. He attended at least one of the sessions of the Cambridge Synod of 1646–48; and was sent to the meeting of 1657 at Boston, by the Connecticut General Assembly. He died April 1, 1670. See Mather, *Magnalia*, ed. 1853–5, I: 441, 442; Young, *Chron. . . . Mass.*, pp. 347, 348 (where a few further references may be found); Allen, *Am. Biog. Dict.*, 3d ed., p. 820; Sprague, *Annals Am. Pulpit*, I: 10, 11; Wilson, in *Memorial Hist. Hartford County*, Boston, 1886, II: 534–538.

John Maverick is even less known than Warham. Roger Clap, in his *Memoirs*, speaks of him as "Mr. Maverick, who lived forty miles off" [i. e., from Exeter, England], Young, *Chron. . . . Mass.*, p. 347; and Winthrop in recording his death under date of Feb. 3, 1636, speaks of him as "being near sixty years of age." Savage's ed., I: 216. He must therefore have been considerably older than Warham. Winthrop fixes his office as that of "teacher of the church of Dorchester," and speaks of him as "a man of a very humble spirit, and faithful in furthering the work of the Lord here, both in the churches and civil state." *Ibid.* His death prevented his emigration to Conn. The facts regarding Maverick may be found in W. H. Sumner's *Hist. of East Boston*, Boston, 1858, pp. 57–68.

and its chief layman, John Haynes, was of sufficient honor to be chosen governor of the Massachusetts Colony in 1635. It need be no matter of surprise therefore that, united as were all the Puritan settlements about the Bay in the main purpose of their enterprise, a certain degree of restlessness should be felt on account of the close proximity in location of different companies, each possessing a distinct individuality and each believing its ministers and prominent laymen to be the superiors of any in the Colony. In the case of the Newtown company, at least, there is much reason to believe that the views of Hooker led to a more democratic conception of the true character of civil government, and an unwillingness to limit the franchise to church-members, which put the company in a measure out of sympathy with most of its fellows in Massachusetts. Whether their divergences were publicly expressed or not, unrest existed.[1] By May, 1634, the Newtown (Cambridge) people were complaining to the General Court of insufficiency of land, and during the following months were sending spies to examine into the character of the soil along the Connecticut.[2] In September of that year the people of Newtown were before the General Court once more, this time with a formal demand to be allowed to go to Connecticut.[3] The matter was compromised at the time, and the proposed emigration delayed; but adventurous spirits were already finding their way to the river,[4] and by 1635 the outflow of permanent settlers from Massachusetts to Connecticut was large. In the autumn of that year many of the people of Dorchester journeyed across the wilder-

---

[1] Compare G. L. Walker, *Hist. First Ch. in Hartford*, pp. 73–83; *Thomas Hooker*, pp. 82–90; I. N. Tarbox in *Memorial Hist. Hartford County*, I: 19–28; Palfrey, *Hist. of New England*, I: 446.

[2] Winthrop, Savage's ed., 1853, I: 157, 162; *Records of . . . Mass. Bay*, I: 119.

[3] Winthrop, I: 166–170. Winthrop notes "the main business, which spent the most time, and caused the adjourning of the court [to Sept. 25], was about the removal of Newtown." It did not get into the Colonial Records, probably because compromised for the time-being. "This matter was debated divers days, and many reasons alleged pro and con. The principal reasons for their removal were: 1. Their want of accommodation for their cattle . . . 2. The fruitfulness and commodiousness of Connecticut, and the danger of having it possessed by others, Dutch or English. 3. The strong bent of their spirits to remove thither." Doubtless the last-mentioned was the most important.

[4] The beginnings of settlement from Watertown in what is now Wethersfield were made in 1634. S. W. Adams, in *Memorial Hist. Hartford County*, II: 435, 436. Andrews, *River Towns of Connecticut*, *Johns Hopkins Hist. Studies*, Ser. VII: 7–9, pp. 13–17.

ness and settled in what is now Windsor, Conn.; and with them came, it would appear, some of Hooker and Stone's congregation from Newtown to join those straggling settlers who had begun, during the summer of 1635, to break the soil of the later Hartford.[1] The prior claims of the Dutch and of Plymouth Colony were practically disregarded,[2] the new settlers, though still viewed as under the jurisdiction of Massachusetts,[3] felt that they were building for themselves and their kindred. But the year 1636 was the time of greatest exodus. With the opening spring Hooker and Stone, with the major portion of the Newtown church, made their way to Hartford,[4] while not far from the same time, perhaps a little earlier than those of Newtown, many of the Dorchester colonists,[5] and with them probably their pastor, John Warham,[6] joinèd those of their number who had wintered on the Windsor soil. It would be clearly too much to affirm, as some have done, that there was here the emigration of three organized towns to

---

[1] Winthrop, I: 204, under date of Oct. 15. For the return of some see *Ibid.*, p. 207 (Nov. 26), and 208, 209 (Dec. 10). Winthrop does not expressly describe this company as from Dorchester, hence some have held it to be from Newtown. It was probably from both, but largely from the former, since under date of April 1, 1636, Winthrop records that a great part of the church at Dorchester had already gone to Connecticut, and that those who had taken their cattle before winter had lost nearly the value of £2,000, p. 219. These in all probability are the "cows, horses, and swine," to which he refers under date of Oct. 15. See Tarbox, in *Memorial Hist. Hartford County*, I: 34, 35. Andrews, *River Towns*, 19–23.

[2] The Dutch captain, Adriaen Block, had sailed up the Connecticut as far as Windsor in 1614. A doubtful tradition had it that the Dutch had begun a fort at Hartford as early as 1623. They certainly purchased land of the Indians June 8, 1633, and completed their fort. In the same year, 1633, the people of Plymouth erected a trading post in Windsor. See Savage's Winthrop, I: 134, 135; Bradford, *Hist. Plym. Plant.*, 311–314; O'Callaghan, *Hist. of New Netherland*, 2d ed., New York, 1855, I: 150–155; Brodhead, *Hist. of State of New York*, 1853, I: 56, 234, 235; Tarbox, in *Memorial Hist. Hartford County*, I: 15–18.

[3] The Mass. General Court, at its session of March 3, 1636, issued a commission in which it rehearsed the facts that "dyv [divers] of or loveing ffriends, neighbrs, ffreemen & members of Newe Towne, Dorchestr, Waterton, & other places, whoe are resolved to transplant themselues & their estates vnto the Ryver of Conecticott, there to reside & inhabite, & to that end dyvrs are there already, & dyvrs others shortly to goe" and appointed a commission of eight to govern the settlements on the river for a year from date. *Records . . . Mass. Bay*, I: 170, 171. As these eight commissioners were all settlers upon the river, their rule naturally passed without friction into self-government on or before the expiration of the allotted year, it having become evident that however it might be with Springfield (to which colony of 1636 two of the commissioners belonged) the three lower settlements were outside of Massachusetts jurisdiction.

[4] Winthrop, I: 223, under date of May 31, 1636, records: "Mr. Hooker, pastor of the church of Newtown, and the most of his congregation, went to Connecticut. His wife was carried in a horse litter; and they drove one hundred and sixty cattle, and fed of their milk by the way."

[5] See above, note 1.

[6] Whether Warham came to Connecticut in the autumn of 1635 or the spring of 1636 is a disputed point; the probabilities seem to favor the latter supposition. See Andrews, *River Towns*, 21, 22. Maverick would doubtless have joined in the emigration had he not been prevented by death, Feb. 3, 1636. Winthrop, I: 216.

Connecticut;[1] but in the case of two of the three companies, Windsor and Hartford, there was a transfer of church organization, so that new ecclesiastical institutions had to be established on the soil which they had left.[2] The present first churches of Windsor and Hartford are no product of Connecticut soil, the one traces its continuous existence back to the shores of Massachusetts Bay, the other beyond the ocean to the New Hospital at Plymouth.

The colony thus established showed itself from the first self-reliant and creative. Though closely allied to Massachusetts, its civil and ecclesiastical development has always had a distinct character.[3] And though by reason of numbers, wealth, and the ability of its inhabitants, Hartford became the leader of the three original river towns, Windsor has shared in all that is peculiar in Connecticut story.

It was eleven years after the full establishment of the Windsor church in its Connecticut domicile that the Creed-Covenant now under consideration was adopted. Of the immediate circumstances we know nothing, and we are ignorant also as to the possession by the church of any statement of belief previous to this time. Had any been in use (a matter more than doubtful), it has completely disappeared. The Creed-Covenant of Oct. 23, 1647, is the oldest symbol of the Windsor church which exists; not only so, it is the oldest symbol at all answering to what modern usage

---

[1] The view that the settlers of Connecticut came into the land as "three distinct and individual town organizations" was advocated by the late Prof. Alexander Johnston in his *Genesis of a New England State*, *Johns Hopkins Studies*, I Series, 11 (Sept., 1883); and his *Connecticut*, *American Commonwealths* Series, Boston, 1887, pp. 11, 12. It has, however, been successfully challenged by Hon. Mellen Chamberlain in his *Remarks on the New Historical School*, *Proc. Mass. Hist. Soc.*, Jan., 1890; and Dr. Charles M. Andrews in his *Origin of Connecticut Towns*, *Annals Am. Acad. Political and Social Science*, Oct., 1890.

[2] The learned introduction to the *Records of the First Ch. at Dorchester*, Boston, 1891, shows that only a part of the Dorchester members went to Windsor, and holds that "whether the Windsor party went as a church organization or simply as a colony of fellow church members is not known." But it does not set aside the fact that a reorganization of the Dorchester church had to take place after the Windsor emigration. The Newtown emigrants certainly went to Hartford as an organization, and it would need considerable evidence in rebuttal to show that the Windsor settlers did not also. The presumption is certainly that they did.

[3] As illustrations of some of these peculiarities I may cite the fact that Connecticut (as distinct from Massachusetts and New Haven), never made church-membership a condition of voting citizenship; the Consociational system of Connecticut church government never found a home in Massachusetts; on the other hand, Connecticut has never welcomed Massachusetts Unitarianism.

calls a "confession of faith," to be found in Connecticut ; and one of the earliest church creeds of New England. But while we do not know the exact circumstances of its adoption, we have various hints which enable us to form a conjecture as to what was passing in the pastor's mind. The growing Presbyterianism of England and the need of some recognized standards of doctrine and polity at home had led to the calling of the celebrated Cambridge Synod in 1646,— the body which was to put forth, in 1648, the Cambridge Platform.[1] Two sessions of that assembly had already been held, in Sept., 1646, and in June, 1647 ; and Mr. Warham had been present at the latter.[2] On his return he had preached, August 15, a sermon based in large part on Hooker's then unpublished *Survey*,[3] in which he had entered at length into discussion of the constitution of a true church. It is plain, therefore, that questions of doctrine and polity were uppermost in the Windsor pastor's mind during the summer and autumn months of 1647, and this Creed-Covenant was the natural outcome.

The Creed-Covenant is of course Calvinistic in point of view, but its non-polemic tone is noticeable. Of the distinctive doctrines of Calvinism only that of the perseverence of the saints is made at all conspicuous. It is distinctly Congregational in its assertion of the necessity of the local organization by covenant ; while its concluding section is the covenant proper, by which the believers at Windsor promised to walk in fellowship with one another. Probably Warham would have been far from claiming that this creed covered the range of Christian doctrine. But it certainly contains, in simple phrase, the essentials of the Gospel, redemption from sin through repentance and faith in the atoning work of Christ, and a life of love toward God and our neighbor through the strength which comes from Him.

THE WINDSOR CREED-COVENANT, 1647.

1. We believe though God made man in an holy and blessed condition, yet by his fall he hath plunged himself and all his posterity into a miserable state.— Rom. iii: 23; v: 12.

---

[1] See following chapter.

[2] See note by Dr. Trumbull, *Cong. Quarterly*, IV: 168 (April, 1862).

[3] *Ibid.*

2. Yet God hath provided a sufficient remedy in Christ for all broken hearted sinners that are loosened from their sins and selves and world, and are enabled by faith to look to Him in Christ, for mercy, inasmuch as Christ hath done and suffered for such whatever His justice requires to atonement and life; and He doth accept His merits and righteousness for them that believe in Him, and imputeth it to them to their justification, as if they had satisfied and obeyed, themselves.— Heb. vii: 25; Mat. xi: 28; xxii: 24; v: 4, 6; 1 Cor. i: 30; Rom. iv: 3, 5; v: 19.

3. Yet we believe that there is no other name or means to be saved from guilt and the power of sin.— John xiv: 6; Acts iv: 12.

4. We believe God hath made an everlasting covenant in Christ with all penitent sinners that rest on him in Christ, never to reject, or cease to do them good.— Heb. viii: 6; vii: 22; 1 Sam. xii: 22; Jere. xxxii: 40.

5. We believe this covenant to be reciprocal, obliging us to be his people, to love, fear, obey, cleave to him, and serve him with all our heart, mind, and soul; as him to be our God, to love, choose, delight in us, and save and bless us in Christ: yea, as his covenant binds us to love him and his Christ for his own sake, so to love our brethren for his sake.— Deut. x: 12; Hos. iii: 3; ii: 21; Deut. xxvi: 17–19; John iv: 21.

6. We believe that God's people, besides their general covenant with God, to walk in subjection to him, and Christian love to all his people, ought also to join themselves into a church covenant one with another, and to enter into a particular combination together with some of his people to erect a particular ecclesiastical body, and kingdom, and visible family and household of God, for the managing of discipline and public ordinances of Christ in one place in a dutiful way, there to worship God and Christ, as his visible kingdom and subjects, in that place waiting on him for that blessing of his ordinances and promises of his covenant, by holding communion with him and his people, in the doctrine and discipline of that visible kingdom, where it may be attained.— Rom. xii: 4, 5, 6; 1 Cor. xii: 27, 28; Ephes. iv: 11, 12; Acts ii: 47; Exod. xii: 43, 44, 45; Gen. xvii: 13; Isa. xxiii: 4.

7. We for ourselves, in the sense of our misery by the fall and utter helplessness elsewhere, desire to renounce all other saviours but his Christ, and to rest on God in him alone, for all happiness, and salvation from all misery; and do here bind ourselves, in the presence of men and angels, by his grace assisting us, to choose

the Lord, to serve him, and to walk in all his ways, and to keep all his commandments and ordinances, and his Christ to be our king, priest and prophet, and to receive his gospel alone for the rule of our faith and manners, and to [be] subject to the whole will of Christ so far as we shall understand it; and bind ourselves in special to all the members of this body, to walk in reverend subjection in the Lord to all our superiours, and in love, humility, wisdom, peaceableness, meekness, inoffensiveness, mercy, charity, spiritual helpfulness, watchfulness, chastity, justice, truth, self-denial, one to another, and to further the spiritual good one of another, by example, counsel, admonition, comfort, oversight, according to God, and submit or[selves] subject unto all church administration in the Lord.

FINIS.

X

THE CAMBRIDGE SYNOD AND PLATFORM, 1646–1648

Text and Reprints

A. THE TENTATIVE CONCLUSIONS RESPECTING THE POWER OF MAGISTRATES AND THE NATURE OF SYNODS, 1646

I. *The Result | of a | Synod | at | Cambridge | in | New-England, | Anno. 1646. | Concerning | The Power of Magistrates in mat- | ters of the First Table. | Nature & Power of Synods ; | and other matters thereun- | to belonging. | London | Printed by M. S, for John Allen | and Francis Eglesfield in Pauls | Church-yard. 1654.* 16° pp. ii, 76.

II. A second edition was issued at London in 1655.

B. THE CAMBRIDGE PLATFORM, 1648

The manuscript is in the possession of the American Antiquarian Society, Worcester, Mass.

I. *A Platform of Church Discipline . . . Printed by S*[*amuel*] *G*[*reen*] *at Cambridge in New England . . . 1649.*[1] 4° pp. x, 32.

II. *A Platform of Church Discipline* [etc.] London, 1653? (Suppressed as incorrect by Edward Winslow.)[2]

III. *A Platform of Church Discipline* [etc.] *Printed in New-England ; and Reprinted in London* [etc.] *1653.* (With two pages of preface by Edward Winslow.) 4° pp. vi, viii, 30.

IV. *A Platform* [etc.] *Cambridge : Printed by Marmaduke Johnson, 1671.* 4° pp. xii, 34.

V. At Boston in 1680, with the first edition of the *Confession* of that year.

VI. At Boston in 1699 in English and Indian, with the *Confession* of 1680.[3]

VII. At Boston 1701. With an appendix of five pages on Congregational practices and principles.[4] 8° pp. xxv, 64, 6. Reprinted for Boston First Church.

VIII. In Mather, *Magnalia*, London, 1702. Ed. Hartford, 1853–5, II: 211–236.

IX. In Indian, 1704.[5]

X. At New York, 1711. A reprint of the Boston edition of 1701.[6]

XI. 1713. Boston?[7]

XII. Boston, 1717, 8° pp. xvi, 40.[8]

---

[1] Full title in connection with the reprint of the text of the *Platform*, at the close of this chapter.

[2] Dexter, *Cong. as seen*, Bibliography No. 1631.

[3] Catalogue of Coll. of Mr. Brayton Ives, New York, 1891, No. 145.

[4] Brinley Sale Catalogue, Hartford 1878, Nos. 737, 5878.

[5] Dexter, *Ibid.*, No. 1507.

[6] Brinley Cat., 3382.

[7] Dexter, *Ibid.*, No. 1635.

[8] Brinley Cat., 5879.

XIII. In *The Results of Three Synods* (*i. e.*, 1646–8, 1662, 1679). Boston, 1725. 16° pp. ii, vi, 118. [Platform, pp. 1–49.]

XIV. Boston, 1731.[1]

XV. Boston, 1749. 16° pp. 83.

XVI. Boston, 1757, with *Confession* of 1680.[2]

XVII. Boston, 1772, with Wise, *Vindication of the Government of N. E. Churches*.

XVIII. Boston, 1808, 12° pp. 70.

XIX. Boston, 1819, 12° pp. xvi, 52.

XX. In *The Discipline Practised in the Churches of New England*, Whitchurch, Shropshire, Eng., 1823. 12° pp. xxiv, 130.

XXI. In *The Cambridge and Saybrook Platforms . . . with the Confession of . . . 1680; and the Heads of Agreement . . . 1690*. Boston, 1829, 12° pp. iv, 132; Platform, 13–67.

XXII. In *Congregational Order. The Ancient Platforms of the Congregational Churches of New England* [etc.] *Published by Direction of the General Association of Connecticut*. Middletown, 1843, 12° pp. x, 351; with Saybrook Confession, Articles, and the Heads of Agreement, etc. Platform, pp. 73–152.[3]

XXIII. In *Report on Congregationalism, including a Manual of Church Discipline, together with the Cambridge Platform, adopted in 1648, and the Confession of Faith, adopted in 1680*. Boston, 1846, 18° pp. vi, 128. Platform, pp. 47–85.[4]

XXIV. Reprint of the *Platform* and *Confession* from the edition of 1846. Boston, 1850.

XXV. *The Cambridge Platform* [etc.] *and the Confession . . . 1680, to which is prefixed a Platform of Ecclesiastical Government, by Nath. Emmons*. Boston, 1855, 12° pp. ii, 20, 84.

SOURCES

I. *Records of the Governor and Company of the Massachusetts Bay*. Boston, 1853–4, II: 154–156, 200, 285; III: 70–73, 177, 178, 204, 235, 236, 240.

II. Winthrop, *History of New England* (*Journal*), Savage's ed. Boston, 1853, II: 323, 324, 329–332, 338, 376, 402, 403.

III. The sources are well epitomized in Felt, *Ecclesiastical History of New England*, Boston, 1855, 1862, I: 570–574, 577–579, 597, 598, 601, 602, 613; II: 5, 6, 16, 18, 19, 45, 46, 96, 97.

LITERATURE

Among the various accounts of the Synod and Platform by later writers the following may be pointed out:

I. Hubbard, *General History of New England* (written about 1680). Boston, 1848, pp. 532–540.

II. Mather, *Magnalia*, London, 1702, Ed. Hartford, 1853–5, II: 207–211, 237–272 *passim*.

---

[1] *Ibid.*, 7465. [2] *Ibid.*, 7466.

[3] Dexter notes 3 editions of *Cong. Order*. Hartford, [1842]; Middletown, 1843; 1845. *Cong. as seen*, Bibl. No. 5633.

[4] By a Committee of which Drs. Leonard Woods, Heman Humphrey, Thomas Snell, Thomas Shepard, Timothy Cooley, R. S. Storrs, and Rev. Parsons Cooke were the members, appointed in May, 1844, by a meeting of Congregational ministers in Boston. The story is told by Dexter, *Cong. as seen*, pp. 514, 515; and in the report itself.

III. Neal, *History of New-England*, London, 1720, I: 272–275 (largely from Mather). Neal gives an abridgment of the Platform, II: 643–655.

IV. Historical Preface to *The Cambridge and Saybrook Platforms*, etc., Boston, 1829, pp. 5–12.

V. Clark, *Historical Sketch of the Congregational Churches in Massachusetts*, Boston, 1858, pp. 39–43.

VI. Palfrey, *History of New England*, Boston, 1858–64, II: 165–186.

VII. Dexter, *Congregationalism . . . as seen in its Literature*, New York, 1880, pp. 435–448.

VIII. A very unsympathetic presentation of the motives of the framers of the Cambridge Platform, though with but little account of the work itself, may be found in Mr. Brooks Adams's *Emancipation of Massachusetts*, Boston, 1887, pp. 79–104.

IX. Doyle, *The English in America, The Puritan Colonies*, London, 1887, II: 91–94.

AS has already been pointed out in a previous chapter,[1] the course of events during the first half of the fifth decade of the seventeenth century in England was strongly in favor of Presbyterianism. Politics had forced Parliament into a union with the Scotch, when the arduous nature of the military struggle with the king had become evident; and union had signified the adoption of the Scotch type of church polity,—a Presbyterianism not unwelcome at first to a large portion of the English Puritans. The Westminster Assembly had begun its sessions in July, 1643. Its Presbyterian complexion had been evident even before its coming together,[2] and by the close of 1645 it had prepared a full scheme of Presbyterian government, which soon received the approval of Parliament in its substantial entirety.[3] These were indeed momentous changes, and it might well be anxiously questioned by the Congregationalists of New England whether a Parliament which had seemingly brought the ecclesiastical institutions of England into conformity with those of Scotland[4] might not next proceed to enforce a similar uniformity in New England.

Nor were there those wanting in New England itself who

---

[1] See *ante*, p. 136.

[2] When Cotton, Davenport, and Hooker were sounded by the Independents in Parliament in 1642 as to whether they would put themselves in the way of appointment to the Assembly, "Mr. Hooker liked not the business, nor thought it any sufficient call for them to go 3,000 miles to agree with three men (meaning those three ministers who were for independency)." Winthrop, II: 92.

[3] See *ante*, p. 136, note 2.

[4] "Seemingly," because, though adopted by Parliament, Presbyterian institutions were never successfully established in most parts of the Kingdom.

would have been glad to welcome Parliamentary interference in affairs of church and state alike. The Presbyterian movements at Newbury, which resulted in the meeting of ministers at Cambridge in 1643, have already been pointed out;[1] and the futility of the attempts made to change the views of Noyes and Parker shows that their convictions were such that they would be likely to look with favor upon Parliamentary limitation of the "New England way." Nor were they the only ministers who advocated Presbyterian views. Peter Hobart, the pastor at Hingham, was essentially a believer in the Scotch polity, at least in the internal management of the affairs of his own congregation.[2] And, in addition to these conscientious supporters of Presbyterianism, there is ample evidence that there were many in the Massachusetts Colony, and some of them men of weight in the community, who felt the limitation of the franchise[3] and of the rights of baptism to those in church-covenant to be a grievous burden, and one which Parliamentary interference, or the free allowance of Presbyterianism, would speedily remove.

An illustration of this temper of mind, and of the curiously mixed motives which made some look with favor on Parliamentary interference in the affairs of the Colony, occurred in 1645. The people of Hingham,[4] tiring of their former commander of militia, chose another and presented his name to the magistrates of the General Court for confirmation. The magistrates thought the action inexpedient, and ordered the affair to rest till further consideration could be had by the Court. But the Hingham soldiery were not so to be put off, and again chose their new captain, Allen. Of course this action was opposed by the former commander, Eames, and some discussion took place as to the exact nature of the magistrate's order. The Allen party charged Eames, before

---

[1] See *ante*, p. 137.

[2] "Mr. Hubbert, the pastor there [at Hingham], being of a Presbyterial spirit, did manage all affairs without the church's advice, which divers of the congregation not liking of, they were divided into two parts." Winthrop, II: 288.

[3] This limitation of the franchise to church-members was peculiar to Massachusetts and New Haven. It did not obtain in Plymouth and Connecticut.

[4] The story is told at length by Winthrop, II: 271–313. See also *Records of . . . Massachusetts Bay* (Colonial Records), III: 17–26.

the church, with untruth, and the minister, Peter Hobart, urged his instant excommunication. Eames appealed to Winthrop and three other magistrates for redress, and they, lending a willing ear to his complaints, ordered the five leaders in the renewed choice of Allen and the subsequent attack upon Eames, to appear and give surety for trial before the next General Court. It so happened that the Rev. Mr. Hobart was brother to three of the five accused, a fact which doubtless accounts in part for his eagerness to see Eames cast out of church-fellowship; and he now presented himself before the magistrates and protested in no measured terms against their recent action. But matters did not rest here. Five more of the Hinghamites were summoned, "for speaking untruths of the magistrates in the church," and appeared, this time before Winthrop alone. They refused to give bonds, and two of them repeating the refusal at a later appearance, Winthrop ordered the two committed. This step was warmly resented by the people of Hingham, who now, under the lead of their minister and to the number of "about ninety,"[1] presented a petition to the next General Court asking that body to take cognizance of Winthrop's acts, —though avoiding the mention of his name in the document. The matter being thus presented before the highest colonial tribunal, and Winthrop being thus charged with having exceeded the rightful powers of a magistrate, the case was tried by the General Court. The Legislature itself was much divided, but the outcome of the trial was that Winthrop was acquitted and the petitioners fined. But the sympathy of the lower house—the deputies of the towns—was largely against the magistrates of the upper house, who were felt by very many, even of the Legislature, to be too high handed in their general administration.

While these proceedings had been taking place in the Court, the meeting of ministers from the various colonies, of which mention has been made as approving Hooker's *Survey*, occurred at Cambridge.[2] Their sympathies were declaredly on the side of the magistrates, who had therefore proposed that their advice should

[1] The Colonial Records (Vol. III: 17) say "to the noumber of 81."

[2] July 1, 1645, see *ante*, p. 141.

be taken in the dispute; but this the deputies of the towns opposed so firmly that the proposition failed.[1] But the ministers were brought into the dispute, nevertheless, for when Rev. Mr. Hobart perceived that matters were going against him, and that his opponents at Hingham were withdrawing from his congregation, he called in the advice of the "elders," who, as might be expected, found him to be in the wrong and sustained the magistrates.

Under these circumstances the temper of Rev. Mr. Hobart and his friends at Hingham rose; and when attempt was made to levy the fines imposed, it was forcibly resisted. For this Rev. Mr. Hobart and his associates were proceeded against by the magistrates, in March, 1646, and in due time brought before the "court of assistants."[2] Here it was proved that Mr. Hobart had publicly attacked the authority of the Colony by declaring, among other things, "That we were but as a corporation in England"; and "That by our patent (as he understood it) we could not put any man to death, nor do divers other things which we did."[3] For this he was fined £20.

Doubtless it has seemed to the reader that the measure dealt out to Mr. Hobart was hard. But the situation was certainly one to excite serious alarm. The danger of Parliamentary interference in the affairs of church and state in New England was great. A division at home at such a time was most unfortunate; and the state of affairs was rendered doubly perilous by the evidence which the Hingham quarrel revealed, even among the church-members of the lower house, of restiveness under the existing state of affairs.

---

[1] "The deputies would by no means consent thereto, for they knew that many of the elders understood the cause, and were more careful to uphold the honor and power of the magistrates than themselves well liked of." Winthrop, II: 278.

[2] It need hardly be pointed out that according to the charter of 1629 the government of the Mass. Company consisted of a governor, deputy-governor, and assistants (the whole body popularly known as magistrates), chosen by the magistrates and freemen assembled in General Court each spring. As the freemen grew in number, their presence as a whole became impossible; in 1634, therefore, they were allowed to appear by deputies from each town. In 1644 the deputies and magistrates were separated into two houses. In accordance with the charter the governor, deputy-governor, and assistants (*i. e.*, the magistrates), could hold a judicial and legislative court whenever necessary between the meetings of the General Court. There was at this time no sharp distinction between the enactment of laws and the administration of justice in any of these courts. See, *inter alia*, *Records Mass. Bay*, I: 11, 12, 118, 119; II: 58, 59; Hutchinson, *Hist. Mass. Bay*, I: 25, 26, 35–37; Palfrey, *Hist. N. E.*, I: 371–382, 617–623; II: 8–18.

[3] Winthrop, II: 313.

Nor were matters bettered by the denunciations of the acts of the colonial government as unauthorized, and their whole body of liberties as subject to Parliamentary revision, in which one of the ministers of the Colony had indulged. Having thus declared himself, the next logical step for Mr. Hobart to take was to appeal for the same Parliamentary redress which might have been invoked against the proceedings of any English corporation; and if Parliament once began interference no man could predict where it would end.

The further step which Hobart did not take was actually taken by others of more determination, in a movement inimical to the Colony, and at one time exceedingly formidable. It is perhaps unwarrantable to say that this more serious attack upon the government would not have been made had the Hingham affair never occurred, but it seems not too much to affirm that its immediate occasion was the excitement aroused by the course of events at Hingham. And while it is doubtful whether any very determined love of Presbyterianism, as a system of church polity, moved these opponents of the Massachusetts system, they were willing enough to welcome those features of Presbyterianism[1] and of Parliamentary interference which would aid them in their main purpose, the overthrow of existing institutions.

This new movement[2] began with a neighbor of Mr. Hobart, William Vassall, one of the assistants of the Company named in the charter of 1629; but apparently a man of discontented spirit always.[3] For some years Vassall had been a resident of Scituate, under the Plymouth jurisdiction; where, indeed, no necessity of church-membership laid restriction upon suffrage, but where the usual New England customs prevailed in religious matters. His plan of action was simple and promised success. Taking ad-

---

[1] Palfrey, II: 166, calls the movement a "Cabal of Presbyterians," but as Brooks Adams has pointed out, *Emancipation of Mass.*, p. 95, the proof that this was primarily a religious movement seems wanting.

[2] For its history, see Winthrop, II: 319–392, *passim;* Hubbard, 499–518; Hutchinson, I: 145–149; Palfrey, II: 166–179.

[3] Winthrop, II: 319, speaks of him as: "a man of a busy and factious spirit, and always opposite to the civil governments of this country and the way of our churches"; and Palfrey, I: 167, declares that this view has "some confirmation" from other sources. Savage gives an account of him in a note to Winthrop, II: 319.

vantage of the political situation on both sides of the Atlantic, he determined that petitions should be presented to the General Courts of[1]

"Massachusetts and of Plimouth, and (if that succeeded not) then to the parliament of England, that the distinctions which were maintained here, both in civil and church estate, might be taken away, and that we might be wholly governed by the laws of England."

As a first step, Vassall had the case laid before the Plymouth Court, in October, 1645, and proposed, so Winslow records,[2]

"to allow and maintaine full and free tollerance of religion to all men that would preserve the civill peace and submit unto government."

Nor did the proposition meet a wholly unfavorable hearing on the part of some of the Court; but Bradford refused to let the matter come to a vote and thus brought the petition to naught. The next step seems to have been the preparation of a petition[3]

"to the parliament, pretending that they being freeborn subjects of England, were denied the liberty of subjects, both in church and commonwealth, themselves and their children debarred from the seals of the covenant, except they would submit to such a way of entrance and church covenant, as their consciences could not admit, and take such a civil oath as would not stand with their oath of allegiance."

But Vassall was not working alone in the matter. His sympathizers in Massachusetts were numerous; and now, at the General Court held at Boston in May, 1646, some seven of them, Dr. Robert Child, Thomas Fowle, Samuel Maverick, Thomas Burton, John Smith, David Yale, and John Dand[4]—the first-named a reputed graduate of Padua, and all the others of sufficient standing to be given the title of "Mr." by Winthrop,—presented a petition[5] in which the statements of the proposed memorial to Par-

1 Winthrop, II: 319.

2 Our information is derived from a letter of Winslow to Winthrop preserved in Hutchinson, *Hist. . . . Mass. Bay*, III (*Collection*): 153–155, under date of Nov. 24, 1645. The letter carefully omits the names of the petitioners.

3 Winthrop, II: 319, 320.

4 Brief biographical notes regarding most of the signers, by Savage, will be found in his second edition of Winthrop, II: 320, 321.

5 The text of the petition may be found in Hutchinson, III (*Collection*): 188–196. Some of its more important passages are the following: "1. Whereas this place hath been planted by the incouragement, next under God, of letterts patent given and granted by his Majesty of England . . . . we cannot, according to our judgments, discerne a setled forme of government according to the lawes of England, . . . 2. Whereas there are many thousands in these plantations, of the English nation, freeborne, quiett and peaceable men, righteous in their dealings, forward with hand, heart and purse, to advance the publick good . . . who are debarred from all civill imployments (without any just cause that we know) not being permitted to bear the least office

liament were amplified and strengthened, and formal notice was given that, unless the prayer was heard, recourse would be had to Parliament.

It is impossible not to have a high degree of sympathy with these men in their complaint. The formidable barriers which stood in the way of church-membership have already been pointed out,[1] and justifiable as they seemed from a Congregational standpoint as to the proper composition of a church, they were a departure from the practice of all ecclesiastical bodies of importance then to be found in the Protestant world. The matter of the franchise was even more galling. Though the population of Massachusetts was probably over 15,000 at the time of the petition, up to 1643 only 1,708 persons had become citizens in the Colony, and of them a number had removed to Connecticut. If the ecclesiastical test was not applied in Plymouth, the case was even worse there; so difficult was it to obtain citizenship that out of some 3,000 inhabitants only about 230 had been enfranchised by 1643.[2] Not only were the majority of the male inhabitants thus shut out from any active share in the government, the ranks of the excluded contained many of wealth, character, and influence in the community. But while it must be admitted that the complaints of the disfranchised had much justification, the time was no fit season for a change in the constitution. The leaders

(though it cannot be denyed but some are well qualifyed) no not so much as to have any vote in choosing magistrates, captains or other civill and military officers; notwithstanding they have . . . paid all assessments, taxes, rates. . . . We therefore desire that civill liberty and freedom be forthwith granted to all truely English, equall to the rest of their countrymen. . . . . 3. Whereas their are diverse sober, righteous and godly men, eminent for knowledge and other gracious gifts of the holy spirit, no wayes scandalous in their lives and conversation, members of the church of Endland . . . not dissenting from the latest and best reformation of England, Scotland, &c. yet they and their posterity are deteined from the seales of the covenant of free grace, because, as it is supposed, they will not take these churches covenants, for which as yet they see no light in Gods word . . . They are compelled, under a severe fine, every Lords day to appear at the congregation, and notice is taken of such who stay not till baptism be administred to other mens children, though deneyed to their owne; . . . We therefore humbly intreat you . . . to give liberty to members of the church of England, not scandalous in their lives and conversations . . . to be taken into your congregation and to enjoy with you all those liberties and ordinances Christ hath purchased for them . . . or otherwise to grant liberty to settle themselves here in a church way, according to the best reformations of England and Scotland, if not, we and they shall be necessitated to apply our humble desires to the honourable houses of parliament."

[1] See *ante*, p. 106.

[2] These figures may be found in Palfrey, *History of New England*, II: 5–8.

of New England felt that they were the champions of a religious cause not only in their own land but in England,—a cause, too, which was unpopular in the eyes of the majority of Parliament. They feared that their system was to be attacked by the English authorities in its political and ecclesiastical features; and they felt, therefore, that instead of effecting any changes, the result of which it was impossible to foresee, they must strengthen the foundations of existing institutions and prepare to meet opposition. The petition was therefore laid over till the next session.[1]

But though the petition was not dealt with at this time, the movement which led to the petition, rather than the petition itself,[2] had determined the ministers and magistrates of the Colony to secure, if possible, a united ecclesiastical constitution. Congregationalism had passed the experimental stage. It was no longer the polity of small and isolated congregations, like those of Amsterdam or Scrooby. It was now substantially the established church of New England, and as such was united by common interests, and bound together by the necessarily conservative attitude toward other polities which such a position implied. As yet this essential unity had had no expression. Its features had been delineated in many works of recognized value, but they had found no authoritative statement. There was no standard by which the relations of one church to another could be determined; none which decided whether a certain course of action was Congregational or not. Whether the creation of such a standard was strictly in accordance with the original principles of Congregationalism may be questioned; but there can be no doubt that it was a logical and necessary step in development if Congregationalism was to be enforced by the civil government as an exclusive polity. The difference between English and American Congregationalism is chiefly due to this unlikeness of re-

[1] Winthrop, II: 321.

[2] Whether the order for a Synod followed the presentation of the petition is doubtful—the Court began May 6, 1646, and lasted "near three weeks" (i. e., till about the 25th). The order for the Synod is entered in the *Colony Records* (II: 154), under date of May 15. It was the subject also of considerable discussion before its passage. But Winthrop (II: 321), declares that the petition was presented, "the court being then near at an end."

lationship to the state and to other ecclesiastical bodies. English Independency has always occupied a more or less conscious position of protest against the established Episcopacy. It has never had state support. It has therefore always had a certain radical and innovating character, and the necessity of fixing its own standards has never been sharply impressed upon it; rather its whole course has been one of protest against standards erected and imposed by authority. But New England Congregationalism, in becoming a dominant church-system enjoying the support of the state, took of necessity a conservative position. Other bodies, including the Church of England itself, when they appeared on New England soil, were the innovators who were to show cause for their departure from the New England way. Such a position demands the establishment of standards and the recognition of certain uniform methods of procedure, that the established polity may maintain its integrity.[1]

The natural and Congregational way to arrive at any such agreement in regard to the common polity of the churches was by means of a Synod, or, as modern Congregationalism would prefer to call it, a Council. But as the Congregationalism of the seventeenth century was largely imbued with the feeling that the officers of civil government were to be consulted in all affairs of moment concerning the churches, the motion toward this Synod took the form of an application by some of the ministers to the General Court of the Massachusetts Colony, at its May session in 1646, for the summons of such a meeting.[2] The bill, which would appear to have been drawn up in form for enactment by the ministers who presented it, encountered the same diversity of feeling which had been shown in the Hingham affair. The magistrates, in sympathy with the clerical applicants, passed the bill as presented; but the deputies of the towns objected to the mandatory form of the enactment:[3]

"First, because therein civil authority did require the churches to send their messengers to it, and divers among them [the deputies] were not satisfied of any

---

[1] See the suggestive remarks of Palfrey, *Hist. N. E.*, II: 179–183.

[2] Winthrop, II: 323.

[3] *Ibid.*

such power given by Christ to the civil magistrate over the churches in such cases; secondly, whereas the main end of the synod was propounded to be, an agreement upon one uniform practice in all the churches, the same to be commended to the general court, etc., this seemed to give power either to the synod or the court to compel the churches to practise what should so be established."

The magistrates were ready in the main to defend the positions to which the deputies objected. They declared the right of the magistrates to summon representatives from the churches when occasion demanded;[1] and though they were clear that the proposed Synod would have no power to command, but only to counsel, they were positive that the Court could enforce or reject the result, as it seemed to the mind of the Legislature to accord or not with the Word of God. Yet it was evident that something should be conceded to the deputies' scruples, and it was therefore decided that, though the Court would waive none of the theoretic rights asserted by the magistrates, the call should take the form of invitation rather than command. Agreement being thus reached, both houses united in a request for the desired Synod.

The length of the document which embodies this call might well seem to make its omission here desirable, was it not for the light which it sheds on the matters which the General Court supposed would form the topic of the Synod's discussions. A careful reading will show that the Court intended a more direct treatment of the questions raised by Vassall, Child, and their associates than the Synod actually gave; and it certainly shows that problems which have usually been associated with a later stage of New England history were uppermost in the minds of those who issued the call.

"Boston, ye 15th 3th m̊, 1646.[2]

The right forme of church gov^{r}mn^{t} & discipline being agreed[3] p̄t of ye kingdome of Christ upon earth, therefore ye establishing & settleing thereof by ye ioynt & publike agreem^{t} & consent of churches, & by ye sanction of civill authority, must

[1] The reason given is that God has laid on the civil rulers the duty of maintaining the purity of the churches, both in doctrine and discipline. *Ibid.*

[2] The call is recorded in the Journal of the upper house, *Records . . . Mass. Bay*, II: 154–156, and of the lower, *Ibid.*, III: 70–73. There are a few minor verbal differences, which will be noted only when they affect the sense. The text here given is that of the upper house.

[3] Deputies' Record, *a good pte.*

needs greatly conduce to ye honor & glory of or Lord Jesus Christ, & to ye settleing & safety of church and com̄on wealth, where such a duty is diligently[1] attended & p'formed; & in asmuch as times of publike peace, wch by ye mrcy of God are vouchsafed to these plantations, but how long ye same may continue wee do not know, are much more com̄odious for ye effecting of such a worke then those troublesome times of warr & publike disturbances thereby, as ye example of or deare native country doth witnes at this day, where by reason of ye publike com̄otions & troubles in ye state of[2] reformation of religion, & ye establishing of ye same is greatly retarded, & at ye best cannot be p'fected wthout much difficulty & danger, & whereas divers of or Christian country men & freinds in England, both of ye ministry & othrs, considering ye state of things in this country in regard of or peace & otherwise, have sundry times, out of their brothrly faithfulnes, & love, & care of our weldoing, earnestly by lettrs from thence solicited, & called upon us yt wee would not neglect ye oportunity wch God hath put in our hands for ye effecting of so glorious & good a worke as is mentioned, whose advertisemts are not to be passed over without due regard had thereunto, & considring wthall yt, through want of ye thing here spoken of, some differences of opinion & practice of one church from anothr do already appeare amongst us, & othrs (if not timely p'vented) are like speedily to ensue, & this not onely in lesser things, but even in pointes of no small consequence & very materiall, to instance in no more but onely those about baptisme, & ye p'sons to be received thereto, in wch one p̄ticular ye app'hensions of many p'sons in ye country are knowne not a little to differ; for whereas in most churches the ministrs do baptize[3] onely such children whose nearest parents, one or both of them, are setled membrs, in full com̄union wth one or other of these churches, there be some who do baptize ye children if ye grandfather or grandmother be such members, though the im̄ediate parents be not,[4] & othrs though for avoyding of offence of neighbor churches, they do not as yet actually so practice, yet they do much incline thereto, as thinking more liberty and latitude in this point ought to be yeilded then hath hitherto bene done,[5] & many p'sons liveing in ye country who have bene members of ye congregations in England, but are not found fit to be received at ye Lords table here, there be notwthstanding considerable p'sons in these churches who do thinke that ye children of these also, upon some conditions & tearmes, may & ought to be baptized likewise; on the othr side there be some amongst us who do thinke that whatever be ye state of ye parents, baptisme ought not to be dispensed to any infants whatsoever,[6] wch various app'hensions being seconded wth practices according thereto, as in part they already are, & are like to be more, must needs, if not timely remedied beget such differences as wilbe displeasing to the Lord, offensive to others, & dangerous to our selues, therefore[7] for the further healing & preventing of the further groth of the said differences, and upon other groundes, and for other ends aforementioned.

---

1 *Ibid.*, *dewly*. 2 *Ibid.* ye. 3 *Ibid.*, omits *baptize*.

4 Cotton had declared this to be the view held by him and the Boston church, in a letter written to the Dorchester church as early as Dec. 16, 1634. See Increase Mather, *First Principles of New England, Concerning The Subject of Baptisme*, etc., Cambridge, 1675, p. 2; Hooker took the opposite view. *Survey*, Pt. 3, pp. 9–27.

5 As early as 1645, Richard Mather had advocated what was substantially the half-way-covenant position. *First Principles*, etc., p. 11.

6 Instances of Baptist believers, at Salem and elsewhere in Massachusetts colony, previous to 1646, will be found in G. E. Ellis, *Puritan Age . . . in Mass.*, pp. 379–386. It is possible that some inkling of the views of Henry Dunster, which were to compel him to resign the presidency of Harvard College in 1654, had already got abroad.

7 In the Deputies' Record this clause beginning *therefore* opens the next paragraph.

Althrough this Courte make no question of their lawfull power by the word of God to assemble the churches, or their messeng^rs^, upon occasion of counsell, or any thing wch may concerne the practise of the churches, yet because all members of the churches (though godly & faithfull) are not yet clearely satisfied in this point, it is therefore thought expedient, for the p'sent occasion, not to make use of that power, but rather to exprese[1] o^r^ desire that the churches will answere the desire of this p'sent Generall Co^r^te, that there be a publike assembly of the elders & other messengers of the severall churches within this iurisdiction, who may come together & meete at Cambridge upon the first day of September now next ensuing, there to discusse, dispute, & cleare up, by the word of God, such questions of church governm^t^ & discipline in ye things aforementioned, or any oth^r^, as they shall thinke needfull & meete, & to continue so doing till they, or ye maior part of them, shall have agreed & consented upon one forme of gov^r^ment & discipline, for the maine & substantiall p̄ts thereof, as that wch they iudge agreeable to the Holy Scriptures, which worke, if it be found greater then can well be dispatched at one meeting, or session of ye said assembly, they may then, as occasion & neede shall require, make two sessions or more, for ye finishing of ye same; & what they shall agree upon they shall exhibite ye same in writing to ye Govern^r^, or Deputy Gov^r^n^r^, for ye time being, who shall p'sent ye same to ye Gen^r^all Courte then next ensuing, to ye end that the same being found agreeable to ye word of God, it may receive from ye said Gen^r^all Co^r^te such app'bation as is meete, that ye Lord being thus acknowledged by church & state to be o^r^ Iudge, o^r^ Lawgiver, & o^r^ King, he may be graciously pleased still to save us, as hith^r^to hee hath done, & glory may still dwell in o^r^ land, truth & peace may abide still in these churches & plantations, & o^r^ posterity may not so easily decline fro^m^ ye good way, when they shall receive ye same thus publikely & solemnly com̄ended to them, but may rath^r^ ad to such begin̄ings of reformation & purity as wee in o^r^ times have endeav^r^ed after, & so ye churches in Newe England may be Jehovahs, & hee may be to us a God from gen^r^ation to generation.

And as for ye cost & charges of ye said Assembly, its thought meete, iust, & equall that those churches who shall thinke meete to send their eld^r^s & messeng^r^s shall take such care as that, dureing their attendance at ye said Assembly, they may be p'vided for, as is meete, & what strangers or oth^rs^ shall, for their owne edification, be p'sent at the said Assembly, they to p'vide for themselues & bear their owne charge. And,[2] forasmuch as ye plantations w^th^in ye iurisdictions of Plimoth, Con̄ectecott, & Newe Haven are combined & united wth these plantations w^th^in ye Massachusets, in ye same civill combination & confederacy,—[3]

It is therefore hereby ordered & agreed, that ye churches w^th^in ye said iurisdictions shalbe requested to send their elders & messeng^rs^ to ye Assembly aforementioned, for wch end ye Secretary for ye time being shall send a sufficient number of coppies of this p'sent[4] declaration unto ye eld^r^s of ye churches w^th^in ye iurisdictions aforementioned, or unto ye governer or govern^rs^, com̄ission^r^ or com̄ission^rs^, for ye said confederate iurisdictions respectively, that so those churches, haveing timely notice thereof, may ye bett^r^ p'vide to send their eld^rs^ & messengers to ye Assembly, who, being so sent, shall be received as p̄ts & members[5] thereof, & shall have like

[1] Deputies' Record reads, *rather hereby declare it to be ye desire of this p̄sent Gennerall Courte, yt there be a publicke assem̄bly.*

[2] In the Deputies' Record this sentence begins the next paragraph.

[3] Reference is here made to the union effected between the four colonies in 1643.

[4] Deputies' Record, *p̄sent order or declarcon.*

[5] *Ibid.*, *p̄te memb's.*

lib^{r}ty & pow^{r} of disputing & voting therein, as shall ye messeng^{rs} & eld^{rs} of ye churches wthin ye iurisdiction of ye Massachusets."

It is evident that the Court intended that the Synod should pass upon the questions regarding baptism and church-membership which were already agitating the community, and which appeared in the petition of Dr. Child and his associates.

The summer between the adjournment of the Court and the time set for the meeting of the Synod was spent largely in discussion, in which that petition and its supporters came in for a full share of condemnation from the upholders of existing institutions.[1] But it is plain that the frequent sermons to which Massachusetts congregations listened that summer did not wholly remove the objections entertained by many as to the propriety of a Synod, and especially of a Synod called by the General Court, in spirit if not in letter. When the appointed first of September arrived, however, all the Massachusetts churches had sent their representatives, "except Boston, Salem, Hingham, Concord."[2] The absence of the latter was accidental, for Concord had not been able to find any brother fit to send and its pastor was hindered. Hingham, in view of recent events, would hardly have been likely to respond to an invitation of the General Court, even if the Presbyterian sympathies of its minister had been less pronounced. But with Boston and Salem the case was more serious. These churches, one the oldest and the other the largest in the Colony, took exception to the Synod[3]—

"1. Because by a grant in the Liberties the elders had liberty to assemble without the compliance of civil authority, 2. It was reported, that this motion came originally from some of the elders, and not from the court, 3. In the order was expressed, that what the major part of the assembly should agree upon should be presented to the court, that they might give such allowance to it as should be meet, hence was inferred that this synod was appointed by the elders, to the intent to make ecclesiastical laws to bind the churches, and to have the sanction of the civil authority put upon them."

---

[1] A defence of the petitioners was published at London in 1647 by J. Child, brother of the petitioner, under the title of *New-Englands Jonas cast up at London; or a Relation of the Proceedings of the Court at Boston in N. E.* etc., in which much complaint is made of pulpit attacks upon the petitioners. The work has been several times reprinted, *2 Coll. Mass. Hist. Soc.*, IV: 107–120; Force, *Tracts*, Washington, 1836–46, IV; and with prefatory matter by W. T. R. Marvin, Boston, 1869.

[2] Winthrop, II: 329.

[3] *Ibid.*

These views, Winthrop tells us, were chiefly advanced by those "who came lately from England, where such a vast liberty was allowed, and sought for by all that went under the name of Independents."[1] Their advocates were able to quote in their behalf not only such stout defenders of English Congregationalism as Goodwin, Nye, and Burroughes, but a positive order enjoining "that all men should enjoy their liberty of conscience," issued by the Commissioners for Plantations, a board recently established by Parliament,[2] to the English settlers in the West Indies and Bermuda,—an order which the Commissioners had sent to Massachusetts in the softened form of advice. This party of opposition to the Synod embraced some thirty or forty of the Boston church.

Here, then, was material for a serious division, the more so that some of the points raised were of a nature exceedingly difficult to answer. The first objection, for instance, was based on the provision of the Body of Liberties of 1641, that[3]—

> "The Elders of the Churches have free libertie to meete monthly, Quarterly, or otherwise, in convenient numbers and places, for conferences, and consultations about Christian and Church questions and occasions."

But the majority of the church, of whom Winthrop was doubtless the leader, had a ready reply to all the criticisms. That to the first demurrer is perhaps the most curious. They affirmed that the permission to ministers to meet upon their own motion,[4]

> "was granted only for a help in case of extremity, if, in time to come, the civil authority should either grow opposite to the churches, or neglect the care of them, and not with any intent to practise the same, while the civil authority were nursing fathers to the churches."

It was further urged, as an answer to the second objection, that it was really no concern of the churches[5]

---

[1] *Ibid.*

[2] The Commissioners for Plantations were a board of six lords and twelve commoners, created by Parliament Nov. 2, 1643; and designed to exercise whatever authority had been enjoyed by King Charles over these plantations. Among the commoners was Samuel Vassall, a brother of the New England agitator, William Vassall,—a fact which explains something of the confidence with which he and the petitioners proposed to appeal to English authority, and the dread with which the ministers and Court regarded his schemes. See Palfrey, I: 633, 634.

[3] The Body of Liberties was a code of laws drawn up chiefly by Rev. Nathaniel Ward of Ipswich, and adopted by the General Court, for trial and approval by use, in December, 1641. The code may be found in *3 Coll. Mass. Hist. Soc.*, VIII: 191–237. See also Winthrop, II: 66; and Felt, *Ecclesiastical History*, I: 439, 440. The law is section 95, clause 7.

[4] Winthrop, II: 330.

[5] *Ibid.*

"to inquire, what or who gave the court occasion to call the synod, . . . it was the churches' duty to yield it to them [the Court]; for so far as it concerns their command or request it is an ordinance of man, which we [the churches] are to submit unto for the Lord's sake, without troubling ourselves with the occasion or success."

To the third point of criticism it was answered that the language of the Court did not forbid the Synod to submit their finding to the churches for approval before returning it to the Court, and did not imply that the Court intended to make it penally binding.

But, spite of these reasonings, the objectors were not convinced; and after two Sabbaths spent in vain agitation, the pastor and teacher, Wilson and Cotton, "told the congregation, that they thought it their duty to go notwithstanding, not as sent by the church, but as specially called by the order of the court."[1] Meanwhile the Synod had met, and had sent an urgent appeal to the Boston church to choose delegates, since it was clear to the Synod that a refusal on the part of Boston and Salem would peril the whole enterprise. On the reception of these letters the ruling elders, Thomas Oliver and Thomas Leverett, hastily summoned such of the church as they could gather on Wednesday, September 2; but "nothing could be done."[2] On the following day, however, the regular Thursday lecture was given, and thither the greater part of the Synod repaired. It is probable that the Boston ministers felt that, under the circumstances, a stranger's voice would be more persuasive, and Rev. John Norton of Ipswich, later to be teacher of the Boston church, was well fitted for the task. He[3]

"took his text suitable to the occasion, viz., of Moses and Aaron meeting in the mount and kissing each other, where he laid down the nature and power of the synod, as only consultative, decisive, and declarative, not coactive, etc. He showed also the power of the civil magistrate in calling such assemblies, and the duty of the churches in yielding obedience to the same. He showed also the great offence and scandal which would be given in refusing, etc."

Norton's sermon was not without considerable effect, and when the question was next brought up by the Boston church, on Sunday, September 6, the matter was finally put to vote by show of hands. The majority was clearly in favor of representation in the Synod; but the minority objected that the church had hitherto

[1] *Ibid.* [2] *Ibid.*, 331. [3] *Ibid.*

required a unanimous vote for important decisions. The force of the objection was felt; but the majority replied that the case was one demanding action, unanimous if possible, if not, the majority must act. At this stage of proceedings the spirit of well meant but impracticable compromise took hold of some of the brethren, and it was seriously proposed that, instead of sending delegates, the church should attend the Synod in a body. Happily good sense prevailed, and "in the end it was agreed by vote of the major part, that the elders and three of the brethren should be sent as messengers."[1] The absence of records and of a chronicler like Winthrop make it impossible to follow the course of the discussion in the Salem church, but we may presume, since we hear nothing further regarding its opposition to the Synod, that arguments similar to those used at Boston overcame its reluctance. The Synod, therefore, was able to set about its work with the moral support of twenty-eight of the twenty-nine churches in the Massachusetts Colony (to which the two churches of New Hampshire should be added, that province being then under the protection of Massachusetts); and the good-will, together with a few representatives, of the twenty-two churches of Plymouth, Connecticut, and New Haven.[2]

Though ready for deliberation at last, a variety of causes prevented the doing of much of importance at this session of the Synod. The disputes at Boston had taken a number of days, the season was late,[3] and "few of the elders of other colonies [than

[1] *Ibid.*, 332.

[2] Under no claim of infallibility the following list of churches in the four confederate colonies is subjoined—the dates are those of organization. *Massachusetts*, Salem, 1629, Boston, 1630, Watertown, 1630, Roxbury, 1632, Lynn, 1632, Charlestown, 1632, Ipswich, 1634, Newbury, 1635, Hingham, 1635, Weymouth, 1635, Cambridge, 1636, Concord, 1636, Dorchester, 1636, Springfield, 1637, Salisbury, 1638, Dedham, 1638, Quincy, 1639, Rowley, 1639, Sudbury, 1640, Edgartown, 1641? Woburn, 1642, Gloucester, 1642, Hull, 1644, Wenham, 1644, Haverhill, 1645, Andover, 1645, Reading, 1645, Topsfield, 1645, Manchester, 1645. (*New Hampshire*, Hampton, 1638, Dover, 1638, Exeter, 1638, was dead.) *Plymouth*, Plymouth, 1602? Duxbury, 1632, Marshfield, 1632, Scituate [London, 1616], 1634 (removed to Barnstable 1639), Taunton, 1637, Sandwich, 1638, Yarmouth, 1639, Scituate (new), 1639, South Scituate, 1642, Rehoboth, 1644, Eastham, 1646. *Connecticut*, Windsor, 1630, Hartford, 1633, Wethersfield, 1636[41]? Saybrook, 1639[46]? Fairfield, 1639[50]? Stratford, 1640? South Hampton, L. I. (under Conn. jurisdiction), 1640? *New Haven*, New Haven, 1639, Milford, 1639, Stamford, 1641? Guilford, 1643, Branford, 1644 (from South Hampton, L. I.). The question mark indicates doubt as to date of organization. See Dexter, *Cong. as seen*, p. 412; and *Cong. Quarterly*, IV: 269, 270 (July, 1862); Clark, *Hist. Sketch of the Cong. Chs. in Mass.*, Boston, 1858; Punchard, *Hist. of Congregationalism*, IV, *passim*.

[3] It should be remembered that we have to do with old style dates—the day of meeting, therefore, corresponded with the modern Sept. 11.

Massachusetts] were present."[1] Yet substantial progress was made. A committee prepared and presented a paper of some length on the much debated problems regarding the power of the civil magistrate to interfere in matters of religion, the nature and powers of a Synod, and the right of the magistrates to call such assemblies.[2] The opinion expressed on the first and third points was strongly affirmative, while a Synod was declared to be, as Norton pictured it to the Boston church, an advisory rather than a judicial body. But the Synod treated the report with great caution, it "being distinctly read in the Assembly, it was agreed thus farre onely, That they should be commended unto more serious consideration against the next Meeting."[3]

A yet more important matter was the appointment by the Synod of Rev. Messrs. John Cotton of Boston, Richard Mather of Dorchester, and Ralph Partridge of Duxbury in Plymouth Colony, each to prepare a "model of church government" for submission to the assembly at its next session.[4] And so, having sat "but about fourteen days,"[5] the Synod adjourned to the eighth of June, 1647.

On October 7th, following the close of the Synod, the General Court met once more. To its thinking the outlook was serious enough. Samuel Gorton, who had successively turmoiled Massachusetts, Plymouth, and Rhode Island, and had received severe treatment in all, had gone to England with two followers, Greene and Holden, in 1644, and laid complaint against Massachusetts before the Commissioners for Plantations. Holden had returned,

[1] Winthrop, II: 332.

[2] Some extracts from this Report will be given at the close of this introduction. It cannot be too frequently pointed out that by a "Synod" the New England fathers meant what is now known as a council.

[3] Report—*Result of a Synod at Cambridge in N. E. Anno 1646*, p. 1. Hubbard, *Gen. Hist.*, 536, 537; and Mather, who follows him, *Magnalia*, ed. 1853–5, II: 210, quote a single passage from this report and imply that the Synod endorsed it. Such was not the case, save as represented above. The statement that it was "accompanied with a discourse of Mr. Tho. Allen, wherein this doctrine was further explained," is also erroneous. Allen wrote a simple preface to this tract and two others which he bound with it. On the joint title-page Allen attributed its authorship to John Cotton, but a careful reading of the preface fails to give certainty to this conjecture.

[4] *Magnalia*, ed. 1853–5, II: 211. Mather is doubtless correct in this statement. His grandfathers were two of the three designated, and the draft by Ralph Partridge still exists in the manuscript collections of the American Antiquarian Society at Worcester.

[5] Winthrop, II: 332.

arriving at Boston in September, 1646, armed with orders from the Commissioners directing that free passage should be granted to the three complainants through Massachusetts to Narragansett Bay,[1] and not obscurely intimating that an answer to the charges was expected from the Massachusetts government.[2] The situation was most embarrassing. To refuse to honor the orders of the Commissioners would mean a breach with the home government, but to admit their authority would be practically to abandon the local autonomy of the colonial government. It was clear, too, that Dr. Child and his fellow petitioners were alive to the fact that their prayer was to meet no favoring response in Massachusetts, and were about to carry out their threat and take the case before the Commissioners. If the authority of that board was admitted by the colonial government in one matter, what was to prevent the imposition by the Commissioners of all the changes desired by Vassall or Child? On Holden's coming the magistrates in Boston had consulted the ministers who happened to be in the town for the Thursday lecture, and they had decided, on the whole, to allow Holden free passage, without raising the question of the validity of his documents.[3] But it was impossible to temporize much longer. The court, therefore, at its October meeting took prompt steps. A committee of four was appointed to[4]

"examine all the answ^{rs} y^{t} are brought into this Co^{r}te to ye petition of Docto^{r} Child & Mr Fowle, etc, & out of all to draw up such an answ^{r} thereto as they thinke most meete, & p'sent ye same to this Co^{r}te, & furth^{r} to treate wth Mr Winslow,[5] & to agree wth him as an agent for us, to answer to what shalbe obiected against us in England."

Pending the labors of this committee the Court adjourned till November 4, following.

On its reassembling the Court adopted a most remarkable document, doubtless the work of the committee as authors or revisers. In a "Declaration,"[6] intended evidently for effect in Eng-

---

[1] To follow the story of these men, Antinomians whom the age hardly knew how to deal with, is aside from our purpose. Among many sources of information I may cite Winthrop, *passim;* Hutchinson, *Hist. . . . Mass. Bay*, I: 117–124; Allen, *Biographical Dict.*, Boston, 1857, pp. 390, 391; Palfrey, *Hist. N. E.*, II: 116–140, 205–220.

[2] Winthrop, II: 333, 342–344.

[3] *Ibid.*, 334.

[4] *Records . . . Mass. Bay*, II: 162.

[5] Edward Winslow, the Plymouth pilgrim.

[6] The text may be found in Hutchinson, *Collection:* 196–218.

land, they opposed the petition of Child and his associates, and justified the form and methods of the Massachusetts government. In parallel columns they placed the main provisions of the *magna charta* and English common law and the answering enactments of the charter, liberties and laws of Massachusetts. They denied that taxation had been unfair or burdensome, they claimed that the petitioners did not really represent the unenfranchised,[1] that admission to the church and its ordinances was readily attained by all who were fit,[2] while the right of baptism of their children was at that moment under discussion by the Synod.[3]

Before their agent should go to England, however, it seemed to the Court that some understanding as to the extent of their claims to local autonomy should be reached; and, therefore, "such of the elders as could be had were sent for, to have their advice in the matter."[4] After much discussion it was the conclusion of both ministers and magistrates that, though the Colony owed allegiance to the English authorities, its powers of self-government were so great that no appeals from its proceedings could be allowed.[5] These

[1] "These remonstrants would be thought to be a representative part of all the non-freemen in the countrie; but when we have pulled off theire vizards, we find them no other but Robert Child, Thomas Fowle, &c. For first, although their petition was received with all gentlenes, yet we heare of no other partners that have appeared in it, though it be four months since it was presented. . . . These [*i. e.*, the non-petitioning] non-freemen also are well satisfyed (as we conceive) and doe blesse God for the blessings and priviledges they doe enjoy under this government. They think it is well, that justice is equally administred to them with the freemen; that they have equall share with them in all towne lotts, commons, &c., that they have like libertie of accesse to the church assemblies, and like place and respect there, according to theire qualities . . . as also like freedome of trade and commerce." *Ibid.*, 210, 211.

[2] "These remonstrants are now come to the church doore. . . . They tell us, 'that divers sober, righteous, and godly men . . . are detained from the seales, because . . . they will not take these churches covenant.' The petitioners are sure mistaken or misrepresent the matter; for the true reasons why many persons in the country are not admitted to the seales are these: First, many are fraudulous in theire conversation; or 2dly, notoriously corrupt in their opinions; or 3dly, grossly ignorant in the principles of religion; or 4thly, if any have such knowledge and gifts, yet they doe not manifest the same by any publick profession before the church or before the elders, and so it is not knowne that they are thus qualified. . . . The truth is, we account all our countrymen brethren by nation, and such as in charity we may judge to be beleevers are accounted also brethren in Christ. If they [the petitioners] be not publickly so called (especially in the church assemblies) it is not for want of due respect or good will towards them, but only for distinction sake, to putt a difference betweene those that doe communicate together at the Lords table, and those who doe not." *Ibid.*, 213, 214, 217.

[3] "Concerning the baptisme of the children of such as are not members of our churches, there is an assembly of the elders now in being, and therefore we think fitt to deferr any resolution about that and some other pointes concerning the church discipline, untill we shall understand theire conclusion therein, for further light in these things." *Ibid.*, 217.

[4] Winthrop, II: 340.

[5] *Ibid.*, 341, 345. John Allin, of Dedham, was the spokesman of the ministers.

points being settled, and the ministers' views regarding the petition of Child and his associates having been heard, the Court now proceeded to deal with the petitioners without ministerial advice.[1] Two of their number, Fowle and Smith, were arrested, the former as he was about to set sail for England, and informed that the Court held them to account for the allegations of the petition.[2] This brought all the petitioners except Maverick into Court, and a scene followed in which much heated speech was indulged on both sides; and ending in an announcement by Child of appeal to the Commissioners, and a declaration by Winthrop that no appeal would be admitted.[3] A committee of the Court then drew up a list of some twelve particulars in which they declared the statements of the petition false and scandalous;[4] to which the petitioners replied *seriatim*, and the Court rejoined "extempore."[5] But through all this cloud of charge and countercharge it is easy to see that the real question in the minds of the Court was that which Massachusetts was to champion for all America a century and a quarter later, whether New England affairs were to be controlled by New England men, or by the will of Parliament. This local independence Child denied. The Court as stoutly affirmed it.[6] And in this resolution of the Court lay the future not only of the New England churches, but of New England liberty. Yet while we cannot but rejoice that the Court took this attitude, its own course of action was arbitrary enough; and it is with a feeling of regret that we learn that it proceeded to fine Child fifty pounds, Smith forty, Maverick ten, and the rest thirty each;[7] and that when, about a week later, Child attempted to go to England to prosecute his appeal, he was arrested, and Dand's study forcibly entered and searched. Here papers were found, designed for presentation to the Commissioners, setting forth the character and conduct of the

---

1 *Ibid.*, 346, 347.

2 *Ibid.* See also *Records*, III: 88, 89. The petitioners were all summoned by the Court.

3 *Ibid.* The petitioners were informed that they were arraigned not for petitioning but for the false statements of the petition.

4 *Ibid.*, 348–350. *Records . . . Mass. Bay*, III: 90, 91.

5 Winthrop, II: 350–354.

6 *Ibid.*, 354-355. "His [Child's] argument was this, every corporation of England is subject to the laws of England; but this was a corporation of England, ergo, etc."

7 *Ibid.*, 355; *Records*, III. 94. Fowle was "then at sea."

Massachusetts government in no favorable light, questioning whether the talk of the ministers and magistrates in the Colony did not amount to high treason, and whether the patent might not be forfeited; and also praying that a governor or commissioner should be appointed to rule the Colony, and that Presbyterian churches be established.[1] For this presentation and request, which struck at the foundations of church and state in the Colony, three of the petitioners were committed. But though the Court might imprison, the case was sure of a hearing in England for, before the close of 1646, Fowle and Vassall set sail. Those petitioners who were still in the Massachusetts jurisdiction, Child, Smith, Burton, Dand, and Maverick, were all condemned by the Court in May, 1647, to fines of one and two hundred pounds each.[2] Dand made his submission to the Court and was released without payment in May, 1648.[3] Maverick secured an abatement of one-half in 1650 when the matter had somewhat quieted,[4] but Child was in England by October, 1647, still a considerable debtor to the Colony.[5]

In the meanwhile Gov. Edward Winslow, of Plymouth, had sailed for England in December, 1646,[6] as the duly accredited agent of the Colony,[7] provided with a formal answer to the charges of Gorton for presentation to the Commissioners,[8] and a variety of secret instructions as to how to meet the questions raised by Child and his friends.[9] His position was at first anything but easy. The brother of Vassall, the New England malcontent, was one of the Commissioners; the brother of Child was an active and able opponent of the Massachusetts government, and some of the petitioners had come over to push their own cause. But Winslow went to work with vigor; in a few weeks after his landing, and pending the decision of the Commissioners, he published a sharp attack upon Gorton and his followers,[10] and not without

---

[1] Winthrop, II: 356-358; Hutchinson, *Hist. . . . Mass. Bay*, ed. London, 1765, I: 146-149.

[2] *Records*, III: 113. Maverick was fined £50 in addition, since he was a freeman, making a total for him of £150.

[3] *Ibid.*, II: 241. [4] *Ibid.*, III: 200. [5] *Ibid.*, II: 199. [6] Winthrop, II: 387.

[7] *Ibid.*, 364, 365; *Records*, III: 93, 94. The Court considered Winslow's mission of such general interest that letters were sent to Plymouth, Connecticut, and New Haven asking them to share in the expense. *Records*, II: 165.

[8] Winthrop, II: 360–364; *Records*, III: 95–98. [9] Winthrop, II: 365–367.

[10] *Hypocrisie Vnmasked: by A True Relation of the Proceedings of the Governour and Company of the Massachusets against Samvel Gorton*, etc., London, 1646 [in new style, 1647].

decided effect. In a similar way he replied, during the course of 1647, to the defence of the petitioners published by Child's brother in that year.[1] Yet it may well be questioned whether these efforts would have availed to save the Massachusetts government from serious defeat and the churches from dreaded interference had not an entire change come over the political situation in England. In 1645 and 1646, when Vassall and Child began their agitation, the Presbyterians were in the ascendant. But the influence of the army was constantly growing — an army which was predominantly Independent; and with the Independents the New Englanders were held in high esteem. Just before Winslow reached England the king had been surrendered to Parliament by the Scotch. It was a great Presbyterian triumph; that party seemingly secure in control of Parliament, appeared free to carry out whatever policy it wished. But the Presbyterians had scarcely begun to enjoy their apparent supremacy, when the scale turned against them. In March, 1647, just as Winslow's first pamphlet was appearing, Parliament tried to disband the army. The army refused to obey, and demanded arrears of pay. And, in June, 1647, it obtained possession of the person of the king by force. The same month the army compelled eleven prominent Presbyterians to leave Parliament, and the Independents came into power. Presbyterian London asserted itself in July, but was soon overawed. Presbyterianism as a political force had lost the day; by the dawn of 1648 its great defenders, the Scotch, were openly on the side of the king. Their defeat by Cromwell at Preston, August 17, 1648, put an end to any hope of their return to power till after Cromwell's death. The effect on the New England cause of these sudden overturnings was apparent at once. In May, 1647, the Commissioners saw their way clear to inform the Massachusetts authorities that they had neither intended to encourage appeals from colonial justice, nor limit colonial jurisdiction by anything that had been done in the Gorton case.[2] By July the Commission was satisfied to leave the ques-

[1] Child's book was, *New-Englands Jonas cast up at London*, London, 1647 (see *ante, p.* 171, *note* 1); that by Winslow, *New-Englands Salamander*, etc., London, 1647. (Reprinted in *3 Coll. Mass. Hist. Soc.*, II: 110–145).

[2] Winthrop, II: 389, 390.

tion of jurisdiction over the lands of the Gortonites to the New England colonial governments.[1] Nor was Winslow less successful against Child and his associates. The ships which arrived at Boston in May, 1648, informed the magistrates "how the hopes and endeavors of Dr. Child and other the petitioners, etc., had been blasted by the special providence of the Lord, who still wrought for us."[2]

This long negotiation formed the political background of the Cambridge Synod. Its perilous course was watched with anxiety, and when it was clear, by the autumn of 1647, that the existing institutions of New England were not to be disturbed, the relief was proportionately great. It produced one change of importance, however, in the work of the Synod. The prime questions propounded by the General Court had been those of baptism and church membership. These problems had been forced to the fore-front by the movement which had given rise to the petition. But they were questions regarding which there was much diversity of view, and therefore the Synod chose to pass them by, when they ceased to be pressing by reason of the defeat of the petitioners; and gave instead a merely subsidiary and somewhat ambiguous treatment to the topics which the Court had made chief.[3] No doubt most men in New England were glad to have it so at the time, yet the questions were such as could not be ignored, and half a generation later they demanded and obtained a solution. But it was fortunate indeed that the discomfort of their enemies gave the representatives of the New England churches opportunity to work out the declaration of their polity in peace.

---

[1] *Ibid.*, 387, 388. [2] *Ibid.*, 391, 392.

[3] The Preface to the Result of the Synod of 1662, *Propositions Concerning the Subject of Baptism*, etc., Cambridge, 1662, p. xii, says: "*And in the* Synod *held at* Cambridge *in the year 1648, that particular point of Baptizing the children of such as were admitted members in minority, but not yet in full communion, was inserted in some of the draughts that were prepared for that Assembly, and was then debated and confirmed by the like Arguments as we now use, and was generally consented to; though because some few dissented, and there was not the like urgency of occasion for present practise, it was not then put into the* Platform *that was after Printed.*" (See later page of this work.)

Allin, in his *Animadversions upon the Antisynodalia Americana*, Cambridge, 1664, p. 5, is more definite. He uses language which implies that Charles Chauncy of Scituate, later president of Harvard, was the opponent: "When this matter was under Consideration in the Synod, 1648, the Author of this Preface [Chauncy] knoweth well who it was that professed, *He would oppose it with all his might*: by reason whereof, and the dissent of some few more, it was laid aside at that time." For the statement in the draft submitted by Mather to the Synod, see *post*, p. 224.

The Synod which had adjourned in mid-September, 1646, re-assembled at Cambridge, on June 8, 1647. The attendance embraced men as far removed in residence from the place of meeting as Gov. Bradford of Plymouth, and Rev. Messrs. Stone of Hartford, and Warham of Windsor. On June 9, the Synod listened in the morning to a denunciatory sermon from Rev. Ezekiel Rogers of Rowley, in which the preacher inveighed against the late petitioners, and attacked the growing habit of the brethren in the churches "making speeches in the church assemblies," and found fault with various customs, such as the wearing of long hair. "Divers were offended at his zeal in some of these passages;" and doubtless the pleasure of the Synod was greater, if their comprehension of the sermon was less, when "Mr. [John] Eliot preached to the Indians in their own language before all the assembly," in the afternoon.[1] But the session did not long continue. An epidemic, which cost Hartford Thomas Hooker, and Boston Gov. Winthrop's wife, compelled it to break up before it had accomplished much of moment.[2]

As the Synod went on the conception of its possible functions magnified. The original thought of the Court had been a settlement of church polity, with special attention to the disputed questions of baptism and church membership. Circumstances had made those questions less pressing, and had brought into greater prominence the broader function of the Synod, that of giving a constitution to the churches. But it might do even more. The Westminster Assembly had prepared a Confession of Faith in regard to which much secrecy was still observed.[3] It had not yet been adopted by Parliament, though approved August 27, 1647, by the Scotch General Assembly. There was reason to fear that it might not be wholly satisfactory. And therefore, at its session on October 27, 1647, the Massachusetts Gen-

[1] Our account of this session is in Winthrop, II: 376. [2] *Ibid.*, 378, 379.

[3] The Confession was finished Dec. 4, 1646, and presented to Parliament. That body at once ordered that "600 copies, and no more be printed," and the printer was directed not to make any public. Matters then dragged on till April, 1647, when the Commons ordered proof texts furnished. This was done and the result printed under the same charge of secrecy. Discussion continued till the Confession, in slightly modified form, was adopted, June 20, 1648. See Schaff, *Creeds*, I: 757, 758; Dexter, *Cong. as seen*, *Bibliog.*, Nos. 1287, 1305.

eral Court added to the duties of the Synod that of preparing a Confession of Faith, by the following order :[1]

"Whereas there is a synode in being, & it is ye purpose, beside ye clearing of some points in religion questioned,[2] to set forth a forme of church govern^t^, accord^g^ to ye ord^r^ of ye gospell, & to that end there are certeine members of ye synode that have in charge to prepare ye same against the synode;[3] but this Co^r^te conceiving that it is as fully meete to set fourth a confession of ye faith we do p'fesse touching ye doctrinall p̄t of religion also, we do desire, therefore, these rev^r^end eld^r^s following to take some paines each of them to p'pare a breife forme of this nature, & p'sent ye same to ye next session of ye synode, that, agreeing to one, (out of them all,) it may be printed wth the oth^r^[4] Mr Norrice,[5] Mr Cotton,[6] Mr Madder,[7] Mr Rogers, of Ipswich,[8] Mr Sheopard,[9] Mr Norton,[10] & Mr Cobbet.[11]

Doubtless the matter was taken into consideration; but before the Synod again met copies of the Westminster Confession had been received and the nature of that symbol had become fully known. The Court's order regarding a Confession was obeyed, as will be seen, but in a somewhat different way from that which the Court suggested.

The final session of the Synod opened at Cambridge on August 15, 1648;[12] and, as at the previous meeting, the body began its work by listening to a sermon. This time the preacher was John Allin of Dedham, and the theme an exposition of the teaching of the fifteenth chapter of *Acts* in regard to the nature and power of Synods, a treatment which led the divine to expose and rebuke a number of errors which had appeared affecting this subject during the late discussions throughout the Colony. The sermon was "very godly, learned, and particular";[13] yet it may be questioned whether it awakened as decided an interest in the congregation as did a snake that wriggled into the elder's seat, behind the preacher, during its delivery. And when Rev. William Tompson of Braintree had effected the reptile's death, the members of the Synod, like all their generation, eager to discover signs and divine interpositions in the occurrences of life, felt that[14]

"it is out of doubt, the Lord discovered somewhat of his mind in it. The serpent," so they interpreted the imagined symbolism, "is the devil; the synod, the represent-

---

1 *Records,* . . . . *Mass. Bay*, II: 200.
2 *I. e.*, Baptism and church membership.
3 *I. e.*, Rev. Messrs. Cotton, Mather, and Partridge; see *ante*, p. 175.
4 *I. e.*, with the Platform of government.
5 Edward Norris, of Salem.
6 John Cotton, of Boston.
7 Richard Mather, of Dorchester.
8 Nathaniel Rogers.
9 Thomas Shepard, of Cambridge.
10 John Norton, of Ipswich, later of Boston.
11 Thomas Cobbett, of Lynn.
12 Winthrop, II: 402, 403.
13 *Ibid.*
14 *Ibid.*

atives of the churches of Christ in New England. The devil had formerly and lately attempted their disturbance and dissolution; but their faith in the seed of the woman overcame him and crushed his head."

The Synod went on harmoniously and rapidly with its work. The Platform of Church Discipline, drawn up by Richard Mather[1] of Dorchester, with large use of previous writings of his own and of Cotton, was preferred as the basis of the Synod's ecclesiastical constitution, and substantially adopted.[2] To it was prefixed a Preface by Rev. John Cotton of Boston,[3] designed to explain some

---

[1] *Magnalia*, ed. 1853–5, I: 453. Richard Mather, the first of a distinguished New England family, was born at Lowton, Lancashire, in 1596. He studied at Oxford for a brief time, and then was asked to settle as minister of the Puritan congregation at Toxteth Park, near Liverpool, where he had already taught school. He was ordained by the bishop of Chester in 1620, but his Puritanism was so pronounced that he was silenced in 1633 and 1634, having never worn the surplice. Obliged thus to relinquish his ministry at Toxteth, he came to New England in 1635. He was settled at Dorchester in 1636, and was from the first prominent in the affairs of the Colony. His answer to the XXXII Questions has already been noticed. He replied to the Presbyterian treatises of Herle and Rutherford; and, at a later period, took an active part in the half-way covenant controversy. He died at Dorchester, April 22, 1669. Of his sons, the youngest, Increase, was the most famous, and Increase's son, Cotton, kept the family name in prominence.

Only a few of the biographical sources need be mentioned. Increase Mather, *Life of Richard Mather* (1670), in *Coll. Dorchester Antiquarian Soc.*, Boston, 1850; *Magnalia*, I: 443–458; Allen, *Am. Biog. Dict.*, ed. 1857, pp. 555, 556; Sprague, *Annals Am. Pulpit*, I: 75–79; Appleton's *Cyclop. Am. Biog.*, IV: 251; H. E. Mather, *Lineage of Rev. Richard Mather*, Hartford, 1890, pp. 33–51 (with portrait). Mather's works are enumerated by Sprague and H. E. Mather.

[2] Valuable extracts from Partridge's draft, not adopted by the Synod, may be found in Dexter, *Cong. as seen*, pp. 444–447. He would not have given so much authority to the magistrates in matters of belief as the Synod did. Mather's first draft, which like that of Partridge is in the possession of the Am. Antiquarian Soc. at Worcester, a little more than twice as long as the form finally adopted, and was not only abridged, but a good deal modified by the Synod. The final form, also at Worcester, is in Mather's handwriting.

[3] See Increase Mather, *Order of the Gospel, Professed and Practised by the Churches of Christ in New England*, etc., Boston, 1700, p. 137. John Cotton, who might contest with Hooker the claim to rank as the ablest of the New England ministry, was born at Derby, Eng., Dec. 4, 1585. He was educated at Cambridge, entering Trinity College about 1598, and graduating A.M. in 1606. He became a fellow of Emmanual College, then the Puritan center, and later served as head lecturer, dean, and catechist. He became religiously awakened, and inclined toward Puritanism; and about 1612 was made minister of the fine old church of St. Botolph, at Boston in Lincolnshire. Here he remained for twenty years, in spite of one suspension for Puritanism. His work was laborious, but eminently successful. Beside his regular Sunday sermons and his exposition of "the body of divinity in a catechetical way" on Sunday afternoons, he preached four times in the week, and conducted a kind of theological seminary in his own home. Attracting the attention of Laud, he escaped serious consequences by flight, and arrived at the New England Boston in September, 1633. Here he immediately became teacher of the Boston church. He was the ecclesiastical leader of the Massachusetts colony, a part of about all that was done in church or state till his death at Boston, Dec. 23, 1652. His works were very numerous, and embrace doctrinal, devotional, ecclesiastical, and controversial treatises. His *Keyes of the Kingdom of Heaven*, London, 1644, has always been considered one of the most authoritative expositions of Congregationalism.

Cotton's life has been frequently treated. The earliest sketch is that of Rev. Samuel Whiting of Lynn, Young, *Chron. . . . Mass.*, 419–430; his successor, John Norton, published his life, *Abel being Dead yet speaketh; or the Life & Death of . . . Cotton*, London, 1658, reprinted Boston, 1834. See also Mather, *Magnalia*, ed. 1853–5, I: 252–286; A. W. M'Clure, *Life of John Cotton*, Boston, 1846 (1870); Allen, *Dict. Am. Biog.*, ed. 1857, 265–268; Sprague, *Annals Am. Pulpit*, I: 25–30; J. S. Clark, in *Cong. Quarterly*, III: 133–148 (April, 1861, with portrait); other references may be found in a note by Justin Winsor to *Memorial History of Boston*, I: 157, 158. A list of Cotton's writings is given by Allen and Clark.

features of New England church practices and to combat the charge frequently made by the Presbyterian party in England, as well as by the Episcopalians, that the churches of New England were of doubtful orthodoxy. And we may be sure that it was with especial pleasure, in view of the allegations of doctrinal unsoundness brought against them by some of their English brethren, that the Synod proceeded to fulfill the spirit rather than the letter of the Court's injunction in regard to a Confession of Faith by a hearty acceptance of the doctrinal part of the work of the Westminster Assembly ("for the substance therof") which had just received the approval of Parliament.[1] These things were quickly done, and as the Synod united in a parting hymn,[2] after a session of less than a fortnight,[3] it was doubtless with a feeling of satisfaction in their work. They had put the churches of New England, by formal declaration, where they had always been in fact, at one in doctrine with the Puritan party in England, whether Presbyterian or Independent. Their orthodoxy could not be impugned. They had formulated their polity in strict and logical order, and had given the churches a standard by which their practice might be regulated and innovation resisted. They had presented it, too, in a form not likely to arouse the jealousy of either faction in England or give excuse for Parliamentary interference.

The Cambridge Platform is the most important monument of early New England Congregationalism, because it is the clearest reflection of the system as it lay in the minds of the first generation on our soil after nearly twenty years of practical experience. The Platform is Barrowist. It does not recognize strongly the democratic element in our polity, because Congregationalism at that day was Barrowist. It urges the right of the civil magistrate to interfere in matters of doctrine and practice, because Congregationalism then believed that such rights were his. It upholds Congregationalism as a polity of exclusive divine warrant, because

[1] See Preface to the Platform, p. 195 of this volume.

[2] *Magnalia*, ed. 1853–5, II: 211. They sang "the song of Moses and the Lamb in the fifteenth chapter of the Revelation — adding another sacred *song* from the nineteenth chapter of that book; which is to be found metrically paraphrased in the New-England psalm-book."

[3] Winthrop, II: 403.

Congregationalism in the seventeenth century so regarded itself. But it affirms the permanent principles of Congregationalism with equal clearness and insistence. The autonomy of the local church, the dependence of the churches upon one another for counsel, the representative character of the ministry, are all plainly taught and have given to the Platform a lasting value and influence.

The Platform thus adopted was put forth in print by means of the rude press at Cambridge in 1649, and at the October session of the General Court of that year was duly presented to the Massachusetts authorities. The Court proceeded with its usual caution and adopted the following vote[1]—

"Whereas a booke hath bene presented to this Cour^t, intituled a Platforme of Church-Discipline out of the Word of God, etc., being the result of what the synod did in their assembling, 1647,[2] at Cambridge, for the[3] consideration & acceptance, the Court doth conceive it meet to be com̄ended to the judicious & pious consideration of the seuerall churches wth in this jurisdiction, desiring a returne from them at the next Gen̄ll Court how farr its suiteable to their judgmen^ts & approbations, before this Court proceed any furthe^r therein."

But, thus urged, the churches were slow in their compliance; and on June 19, 1650, the Court further voted that[4]—

"forasmuch as (it is sajd) that some of the churches were ignorant of the sajd order, & therefore little hath ben done in that p̄ticular, this Courte . . . doe hereby order, that the sajd booke be duly considered off of all the sayd churches within this pattent, & that they, without fayle, will returne theire thoughts and judgments touchinge the p̄ticulars thereof to the next session of this Court . . . and further, it is hereby desired, y^t euery church will, by the first oppertunity, take order for the p'cureinge of that booke, published by the synod at London, concerninge the doctrine of the gosple,[5] that the churches may consider of that booke, also, as soone as they can be gotten."

Thus admonished, the churches seem generally to have obeyed. If a judgment may be based on the instances in which records have come down to us, the books were read to the churches, and the opinion of the membership expressed by a vote.[6] Of course, as the

[1] *Records . . . Mass. Bay*, II: 285; III: 177, 178. The text is from the Magistrate's Record.

[2] A mistake for 1648.

[3] Deputies' Record reads more correctly *their*, i. e., the Court's.

[4] *Records*, III: 204; IV: 22.

[5] I. e., the Westminster Confession.

[6] A few examples are given by Felt, *Ecclesiast. Hist.*, II: 18, 19, 29. Some of the communications of the churches are in the MSS. Collections of the Am. Antiquarian Soc., Worcester, Mass. I have not seen them.

elders framed the proposition, their influence in the decision of each church would be great. When the Court came together once more, in May, 1651, it was moved to a vote, apparently on the 22d, expressing its thanks to the Synod now nearly three years adjourned; but declaring that[1]—

"many of whom [the churches of Massachusetts] were pleased to p'sent to the last session of the last Court, by the deputyes of the seuerall townes, seuerall objections against the s̄d confession of discipline, or seuerall p̄tyculers therein, wherevppon the Court judged it convenient & conduceinge to peace to forbeare to giue theire approbation therevnto vnles such objections as were p'sented were cleared & remoued; for which purpose this Court doth order the secritary to draw vp ye s̄d objections, or the princypall of them, & to deliuer the same to Reuerend Mr Cotten within one moneth, to be com̄unicated to the elders of the seuerall churches, who are desired to meete & cleare the s̄d doubts, or any other that may be imparted to them by any other p'son concerninge the s̄d draught of discipline, & to returne theire advice & helpe herein to the next session of this Generall Court, which will alwayes be zealous acording to theire duty to giue theire testimony to euery truth of Jesus Christ, though they cannot se light to impose any formes as necessary to be obserued by the churches as a bindinge rule."

Little as this cautious vote seems to indicate any disposition of the General Court to be domineering over the churches, there were four of the deputies, including the representatives of the town and church of Boston, who voted against it.[2]

The ministers met duly, at some uncertain date that summer, and having considered the objections referred to them by the Court, they "appointed Mr. Richard Mather to draw up an answer to them" [the criticisms]; and this "answer by him composed, and by the rest approved, was given in"[3] to the Court at its October session, 1651. And now, more than three years after the close of the Synod, the Court finally put the stamp of its approval on the Platform, yet in no mandatory way. On October 14 it voted:[4]

"Whereas this Court did, in the yeare 1646, giue encouragment for an assembly of the messengers of the churches in a synode, and did desire theire helpe to draw vpp a confession of the fayth & discipline of the churches, according to the word of God, which was p'sented to this Court, & com̄ended to the seuerall churches, many of whom returned theire approbation & assent to the s̄d draught in generall, & diverse of the churches p'sented some objections & doubtes agaynst some perticulers in the sd

[1] *Records . . . Mass. Bay*, III: 235, 236; IV: 54, 55.

[2] John Leverett and Thomas Clarke of Boston, William Tyng of Braintree, and Jeremiah Hutchins of Hingham. It is evident that at Boston and Hingham feeling against the Synod still continued.

[3] *Magnalia*, ed. 1853–5, II: 237. The manuscript, in Mather's handwriting, is at Worcester.

[4] *Records*, III: 240; IV: 57, 58.

draught, wherevppon, by order of this Court, the sd objections were commended to the consideracõ of the elders, to be cleared & remoued, who haue returned theire answer in writinge, which the Court, havinge p'vsed, doe thankfully acknowledge theire learned paynes therein, & account themselues called of God (especially at this time, when the truth of Christ is so much opposed in the world) to giue theire testimony to the sd Booke of Discipline, that for the substance thereof it is that we haue practised & doe beleeue."

The magistrates, always stronger than the deputies in their support of existing institutions in church and state, appear to have passed the resolution without dissent; but, spite of its inoffensive form, fourteen of the forty deputies voted against its adoption.[1] But with this action of the Court the Cambridge Platform became the recognized, if not the unquestioned,[2] pattern of ecclesiastical practice in Massachusetts. Endorsed, "for the substance of it," by the Reforming Synod in September, 1679,[3] it continued the legally recognized standard till 1780.

Unfortunately the absence of any mention of action concerning the Platform in the contemporary records of the colonies of Plymouth, Connecticut, and New Haven veils the story of its reception in those jurisdictions. But a considerable, though uncertain, number of the ministers and laymen of those colonies had taken part in the sessions of the Synod, and there is no reason to suppose that the result was any less acceptable to their churches than to those of Massachusetts. Though written a century and a half later, the affirmation of Trumbull is doubtless essentially true that[4]—

"the ministers and churches of Connecticut and New Haven were present [at the Cambridge Synod], and united in the form of discipline which it recommended. By this Platform of discipline, the churches of New-England, in general, walked for more than thirty years."

1 William Hawthorne, Henry Bartholomew,* Salem; Thomas Clarke, John Leverett,* Boston; Stephen Kinsley, William Tyng,* Braintree; Richard Browne, Watertown; John Johnson, Roxbury; Esdras Reede,* Wenham; William Cowdry,* Reading; Walter Haynes,* Sudbury; Roger Shaw,* Hampton, N. H.; John Holbrooke,* Weymouth; Jeremiah Hutchins, Hingham. Where marked * the whole delegation of the town voted negatively.

2 Mather, *Magnalia*, II: 237–247, gives four points, *a*, the Platform's lack of clearness regarding the right of a minister to dispense the sacraments to any congregation not his own; *b*, its assertion of the distinct office of ruling elders; *c*, the practice of ordaining at the hands of the brethren of the local church rather than of ministers of other churches; *d*, the use of personal relations and confessions in the admission of members; as cases in which the thought of the churches in his day varied from the Platform.

3 Result of Synod of 1679, in *Necessity of Reformation*, etc., Boston, 1679, Epistle Dedicatory, p. v; see also *Magnalia*, II: 237.

4 Trumbull, *History of Connecticut*, New Haven, 1818, I: 289.

THE CAMBRIDGE SYMBOLS

THE TENTATIVE CONCLUSIONS OF 1646 (*Extracts*)

The Result of the Disputations of the *Synod*, or *Assembly*, at *Cambridge* in *New England*, Begun upon the first day of the 7th Month, *An. Dom.* 1646. *About the power of the Civill Magistrate in matters of the first Table; and also about the grounds of Synods, with their power, and the power of calling of them.* Being drawn up by some of the Members of the Assembly, deputed thereunto, and being distinctly read in the Assembly, it was agreed thus farre onely, That they should be commended unto more serious consideration against the next Meeting.

TOuching the Question of the Civill Magistrate in matters of Religion, we shall crave leave to narrow and limit the state of it in the mannner of the Proposall of it, and shall therefore propound it thus.

Quest. Whether the Civil Magistrate in matters of Religion, or of the first [2] Table, hath power civilly to command or forbid things respecting the outward man, which are clearly commanded and forbidden in the word, and to inflict sutable punishments, according to the nature of the transgressions against the same, and all this with reference to godly peace?

Answ. The want of a right stating of this Question, touching the Civil Magistrates power in matters of Religion, hath occasioned a world of Errours, tending to infringe the just power of the Magistrate, we shall therefore explaine the termes of the Question, and then confirme it in the Affirmative.

By [[1]*Commanding, Forbidding, and Punishing*] we meane the coercive power of the Magistrate, which is seen in such acts. By [*Matters of Religion commanded or forbidden in the word, respecting the outward man*] we understand indefinitely, whether those of Doctrine or Discipline, of faith or practice; his power is not limited to such matters of Religion onely, which are against the light of Nature, or against the Law of Nations, or against the fundamentalls of Religion; all these are matters of Re-[3]ligion, which may be expressed by the outward man, but not onely these; therefore we say not barely thus [*In matters of the first Table*] but joyn therewith [*In matters of Religion*] that all ambiguity may be avoided, and that it may be understood as well of matters which are purely Evangelicall, so far as expressed by the outward man, as well as of other things. And we say, [*Commanded or forbidden in the word*] meaning of the whole word, both of the Old and New Testament; exception being onely made of such things which were meerly Ceremoniall, or otherwise peculiar to the *Jewish* polity, and cleered to be abolished in the New Testament: By which limitation of the Magistrates power to *things commanded or forbidden in the word*, we exclude any power of the Magistrate, either in commanding any new thing, whether in doctrine or discipline, or any thing in matters of Religion, which is beside or against the word, or in forbidding any thing which is according to the word.

[1] [ ] instead of " ".

1 Hence he is not to mould up and impose what Erastian forme of Church polity he pleaseth; because if there be [4] but one form commanded now of God, he cannot therefore command what forme he will.

2 Hence he is not to force all persons into the Church, or to the participation of the seals; because he is not thus commanded.

3 Hence he is not to limit to things indifferent, which are neither commanded, nor forbidden in the word, without apparent expediency or inexpediency of attending the same. By that expression [*cleerly*] *commanded or forbidden in the word*, we understand that which is cleer, either by express words, or necessary Consequence from the Scripture; and we say *cleerly commanded or forbidden in the word.* Not simply that which the Magistrate or others think to be cleerly commanded or forbidden; for they may thinke things commanded, to be forbidden, and things forbidden to be commanded; but that which is in it selfe in such sort cleer in the word, *de jure*, the Civil Magistrate in these days since Christs ascension, may and ought to command and forbid such things so cleared in the word, albeit *de facto*, oft-times he doe [5] not. [*Sutably inflicting punishments according to the nature of the transgressions*] This clause needeth not much explication, being so plaine of it selfe; some things commanded and forbidden in the Law of God, are of a smaller nature in respect of the Law of man, and in this respect 'tis true which is often said, that *De minimis non curat lex*, *i. e.* Mans Law looks not after small matters, but other things commanded or forbidden in Gods Law, are momentous, and of a higher nature, and though small in themselves, yet weighty in the consequence or circumstance. And in this case if he inflict a slight paper punishment when the offence is of an high nature; or contrariwise, when he inflicts that which is equivalent to a capitall punishment, when the offence is of an inferiour nature, he doth not punish sutably. There are sundry rules in the word in matters of this sort, as touching the punishment of Blasphemy, Idolatry, Heresie, prophanation of the Lords day, and sundry other like matters of Religion, according to wch Magistrates of old have held, and others now may observe proportions, in ma-[6] king other particular Laws in matters of Religion, with sanctions of punishments, and inflicting the same, they inflict sutable punishments. . . . . . [7] . . . . By this, which hath been already spoken touching the acts and rule of the Magistrates coercive power in matters of Religion, the impertinency and invalidity of many objections against this his power will appear, as . . . . [8] . . . . 3. That thereby tyranny is exercised over mens tender consciences, and true liberty of conscience is infringed; when as he *de jure* commands nothing but that which, if men have any tendernesse of conscience, they are bound in conscience to submit thereto, and in faithfull submitting to which is truest liberty of conscience, conscience being never in a truer or better estate of liberty here on earth, than when most ingaged to walke according to Gods Commandements. . . . . [9] . . . . [10] . . . . 7. That thereby the civill Magistrate is put upon many intricate perplexities & hazards of conscience, how to judge in and of matters of Religion.

But this doth not hinder the Magistrate from that use of his coercive power, in matters commanded or forbidden in the first Table, no more then it doth hinder him from the like power in matters of the second Table;[1] none being ignorant what perplexing intricacies there are in these as well as in the former; as conscientious Mag-

[1] It need scarcely be pointed out that what is signified are the actions, murder, adultery, theft, falsewitness, etc., which are the subjects of criminal law as well as of the second half of the Commandments, *Exodus*, xx: 12–17.

istrates finde by dayly experience. . . [11]. . . [12] . . [13] . . [14] 11. That thereby we shall incourage and harden *Papists* and *Turks* in their cruell persecutions of the *Saints;* whereas for the Magistrate to command or forbid according to God, as it is not persecution, so neither doth it of it selfe, tend to persecution. Power to presse the Word of God and his truth, doth not give warrant to suppresse or oppresse the same: the times are evill indeed when the pressing of obedience to the rule shall be counted persecution. . . . . [15–19] . . . Will not this *Thesis* arme and stir up the Civill power in Old *England*, against godly Orthodox ones of the Congregationall way: or exasperate Civill power in *New England*, against godly, moderate, and Orthodox Presbyterians, if any such should desire their liberty here? we conceive no,[1] except the civill disturbance of the more rigidly, unpeaceably, and corruptly minded, be very great; yet betwixt men godly and moderately minded on both sides, the difference upon true and due search is found so small, by judicious, Orthodox, godly, and moderate Divines, as that they may both stand together in peace and love; if liberty should be desired by either sort here or there so exercising their liberty, as the [20] publick peace be not infringed.

---

[48] . . . . W*Hat be the grounds from Scripture to warrant Synods?*

In answer to this Question, we shall propound to consideration three Arguments from Scripture, and five Reasons.

Arguments.

Augum: 1 Taken from *Acts* 15. An orderly Assembly of qualified Church-messengers (Elders and other Brethren) in times of controversie and danger, concerning weighty matters of Religion, for the considering, disputing, finding out and clearing of the truth, from the Scripture, and establishing of Peace amongst the Churches, is founded upon *Acts* 15.

But a Synod is an orderly Assembly [etc.] . . . [49] . . . *Ergo*, A Synod is founded upon *Acts* 15.

---

[63] . . . . W*Hat is the Power of a Synod?*

The Power of a Synod

Is { Decisive
Directive, &
Declarative } of the truth, by

clearing and evidencing the same out of the word of God, non *coactive*, yet more than *discretive*.

For the better understanding hereof, consider that Ecclesiasticall Power is

1 Decisive, in determining by way of discussion and disputation, what is truth, and so consequently resolving [64] the Question in weighty matters of Religion, *Acts* 15, 16, 28. & 16. 4. This belongs to the Synod.

2 Discretive, in discerning of the truth or falshood that is determined; this belongs to every Believer.

---

[1] It will be remembered that the Presbyterians were now in power in England. Yet the course of events in New England had made the statement not wholly without justification. Winslow in 1647 was able to cite the cases of the ministers of Newbury and Hingham as illustrations of toleration of Presbyterian views, *Hypocrisie Vnmasked*, pp. 99, 100.

3 Coactive or judicial (for we omit to speak in this place of Official judgement) in judging of the truth determined Authoritatively, so as to impose it with Authority, and to censure the disobedient with Ecclesiastical censure, 1 *Cor.* 5. 12. *Mat.* 18. 17. This belongeth to every particular Church.

The judgement of a Synod is in some respect superiour, in some respect inferiour to the judgement of a particular Church; it is superiour in respect of direction; inferiour in respect of jurisdiction, which it hath none.

Quere. *How, and how far doth the sentence of a Synod bind?*

Answ. We must distinguish between the Synods declaration of the truth, and the politicall imposition of the truth declared by the Synod.

The Synods declaration of the truth binds not *politically*, but *formally* onely, [65] (*i. e.*) *in foro interiori* (*i. e.*) it binds the conscience, and that by way of the highest institution that is meerly doctrinall. The politicall Imposition of the truth declared by the Synod, is Ecclesiasticall, or Civill: Ecclesiasticall, by particular Churches, and this binds not onely formally, but politically, *in foro exteriori, i. e.* it binds the outward man, so as the disobedient in matters of offence, is subject unto Church censure, affirmatively, towards their own Members; negatively, by non communion, as concerning others, whether Church or Members. Civil, by the Magistrate strengthening the truth thus declared by the Synod, and approved by the Churches, either by his meer Authoritative suffrage, assent, and testimony, (if the matter need no more) or by his authoritative Sanction of it by Civill punishment, the nature of the offence so requiring.

---

[66] . . *To whom belongeth the power of calling a Synod?*

Answ. For satisfaction to this Question, we shall propound one distinction, and answer three Queries.

Distin: The power of calling Synods is either

Single { Authoritative, belonging to the Magistrates.
Ministeriall, belonging to the particular Churches.

Mixt { When both proceed orderly and jointly in the use of their severall powers.

. . . . [70] *Queries.*

Querie 1 *In what case may the Magistrate proceed to call a* Synod *without the consent of the Churches?*

Answ. The Magistrate in case the Churches be defective, and not to be prevailed with, for the performance of their duty, (just cause so requiring) may call a Synod, and the Churches ought to yield obedience thereunto.

[71] But notwithstanding the refusall, he may proceed to call an Assembly, and that for the same end that a Synod meetes for, namely, to consider of, and clear the truth from the Scriptures, in weighty matters of Religion: But such an Assembly called and gathered without the consent of the Churches, is not properly that which is usually understood by a Synod, for though it be in the power of the Magistrate to Call, yet it is not in his power to Constitute a Synod, without at least the implicite consent of the Churches: Because Church-Messengers, who necessarily presuppose an explicite (which order calls for) or implicite consent of the Churches, are essentiall to a Synod.

Querie 2 *In what case may the Churches call a* Synod *without the consent of the Magistrate?*

[72] *Answ.* In case the Magistrate be defective, and not to be prevailed with for the performance of his duty; just cause, providence, and prudence concurring: The Churches may both Call and Constitute a Synod: The Reason why the Churches can Constitute a Synod without the consent of the Magistrate, although the Magistrate cannot constitute a Synod without the consent of the Churches, is because the essentialls of a Synod, together with such other cause, as is required to the being (though not so much to the better being) of a Synod, ariseth out of particular churches. . . . . . .

[74] *Querie* 3 *In case the Magistrate and Churches are both willing to proceed orderly in the joynt exercise of their severall Powers, whether it is lawfull for either of them to call a* Synod *without the Consent of the other?*

Answ. No; they are to proceed now by way of a mixt Call. . . . .

The Churches desire, the Ma-[75]gistrate Commands; Churches
act in a way of liberty, the Ma-
gistrate in a way of Authority.
Moses and *Aaron* should
goe together, and kiss
one another in
the Mount of
GOD.

* * *

THE CAMBRIDGE PLATFORM, 1648

A | PLATFORM OF | CHURCH DISCIPLINE | *GATHERED OUT OF THE WORD OF GOD:* | *AND AGREED UPON BY THE ELDERS:* | AND MESSENGERS OF THE CHURCHES | ASSEMBLED IN THE SYNOD AT CAMBRIDGE | *IN NEW ENGLAND* | To be presented to the Churches and Generall Court | for their consideration and acceptance, | in the Lord. | The Eighth Moneth Anno 1649 | —— | Psal: 84.1. *How amiable are thy Tabernacles O Lord of Hosts?* | Psal: 26.8. *Lord I have loved the habitation of thy house & the* | *place where thine honour dwelleth.* | Psal: 27. 4. *One thing have I desired of the Lord that will I seek* | *after, that I may dwell in the house of the Lord all the* | *dayes of my life to behold the Beauty of the Lord & to* | *inquire in his Temple.* | —— | Printed by *S G* at *Cambridge* in *New England* | and are to be sold at *Cambridge* and *Boston* | *Anno Dom: 1649.*

[ii Blank]

THE PREFACE[1]

THE *setting forth of the Publick Confession of the Faith of Churches hath a double end, & both tending to publick edification. first the maintenance of the faith entire within it self: secondly the holding forth of Unity & Harmony, both amongst, & with other Churches. Our Churches here, as (by the grace of Christ) wee beleive & profess the same Doctrine of the trueth of the Gospell, which generally is received in all the reformed Churches of Christ in Europe: so especially, wee desire not to vary from the doctrine of faith, & truth held forth by the churches of our native country. For though it be not one native country, that can breed vs all of one mind; nor ought wee for to have the glorious faith of our Lord Jesus with respect of persons: yet as Paul who was himself a Jew, professed to hold forth the doctrine of justification by faith, & of the resurection of the dead, according as he knew his godly countrymen did, who were Iewes by nature* (*Galat.* 2. 15. *Acts* 26. 6, 7.) *soe wee, who are by nature, English men, doe desire to hold forth the same doctrine of religion (especially in fundamentalls) which wee see & know to be held by the churches of England, according to the truth of the Gospell*

The more wee discern, (that which wee doe, & have cause to doe with incessant mourning & trembling) the unkind, & unbrotherly, & unchristian contentions of our godly brethren, & countrymen, in matters of church-government: the more ernestly doe wee desire to see them joyned

[1] This work, apparently the first specimen of the printing of Samuel Green of Cambridge, is thus truly characterized by Thomas, *History of Printing in America*, 2d ed., Albany, 1874, I: 63, 64, "This book appears to be printed by one who was but little acquainted with the typographic art . . . the press work is very bad, and that of the case no better . . . the compositor did not seem to know the use of points . . . Letters of abbreviation are frequently used . . The spelling is very ancient."

together in one common faith, & our selves with them. For this end, having perused the publick confession of faith, agreed upon by the Reverend assembly of Divines at Westminster, & finding the summ & substance therof (in matters of doctrine) to express not their own judgements only, but ours also: and being likewise called upon by our godly Magistrates, to draw up a publick confession of that faith, which is constantly taught, & generaly professed amongst us, wee thought good to present unto them, & with them to our churches, & with them to all the churches of Christ abroad, our professed & hearty assent & attestation to the whole confession of faith (for substance of doctrine) which the Reverend assembly presented to the Religious & Hononrable **Parlamet** *of England: Excepting only some sections in the* 25 30 & 31. *Chapters of their confession, which concern points of controversie in church-discipline; Touching which wee refer our* [2] *selves to the draught of church-discpline in the ensueing treatise.*

The truth of what we here declare, may appear by the unanimous vote of the Synod of the Elders & messengers of our churches assembled at Cambridg, the last of the sixth month, 1648: *which joyntly passed in these words*; This Synod having perused, & considered (with much gladness of heart, & thankfullness to God) the cōfession of faith published of late by the Reverend Assembly in England, doe judge it to be very holy, orthodox, & judicious in all matters of faith: & doe therfore freely & fully consent therunto, for the substance therof. Only in those things which have respect to church government & discipline, wee refer our selves to the platform of church-discipline, agreed upon by this present assēbly: & doe therfore think it meet, that this confession of faith, should be cōmended to the churces of Christ amongst us, & to the Honoured Court, as worthy of their due consideration & acceptance. *Howbeit, wee may not conceal, that the doctrine of vocation expressed in* Chap 10. S 1. & *summarily repeated* Chap, 13. & 1. *passed not without some debate. Yet considering, that the term of vocation, & others by which it is described, are capable of a large, or more strict sense, & use, and that it is not intended to bind apprehensions precisely in point of order or method, there hath been a generall condescendency therunto.*

Now by this our professed consent & free concurrence with them in all the doctrinalls of religion, wee hope, it may appear to the world, that as wee are a remnant of the people of the same nation with them: so wee are professors of the same common faith, & fellow-heyres of the same common salvation. Yea moreover, as this our profession of the same faith with them, will exempt us (even in their judgmēts) from suspicion of heresy: so (wee trust) it may exempt us in the like sort from suspicion of schism: that though wee are forced to dissent from them in matters of church-discipline: Yet our dissent is not taken up out of arrogancy of spirit in our selves (whom they see willingly condescend to learn of them:) neither is it carryed with uncharitable censoriousness towards them, (both which are the proper, & essentiall charracters of schism) but in meekness of wisdom, as wee walk along with them, & follow them, as they follow Christ: so where wee conceiv a different apprehention of the mind of Christ (as it falleth out in some few points touching church-

order) wee still reserve due reverence to them (whom wee judge to be, through Christ, the glorious lights of both nations:) & only crave leave (as in spirit wee are bound) to follow the Lamb withersoever he goeth, & (after the Apostles example) as wee beleive, so wee speake.

And if the example of such poor outcasts as our selves, might prevaile if not with all (for that were too great a blessing to hope for) yet with some or other of our brethren in England, so farr as they are come to mind & speake the same thing with such as dissent from them, wee hope in Christ, it would not onely moderate the harsh judging [3] *and condemning of one another in such differences of judgment, as may be found in the choysest saints: but also prevent (by the mercy of Christ) the perill of the distraction & destruction of all the churches in both kingdoms. Otherwise, if brethren shall goe on to bite & devoure one another, the Apostle feared (as wee also, with sadness of heart doe) it will tend to the consuming of them, & us all: which the Lord prevent.*

Wee are not ignorant, that (besides these aspertions of Heresy & Schism) other exceptions also are taken at our way of church-government: but (as wee conceive) upon as little ground.

As 1 That by admitting none into the fellowship of our Church, but saints by calling, wee Rob many parish-churches of their best members, to make up one of our congregations: which is not only, to gather churches out of churches (a thing unheard of in Scripture:) but also to weaken the hearts & hands of the best Ministers in the parishes, by dispoyling them of their best hearers.

2 That wee provide no course for the gayning, & calling in, of ignorant, & erronious, & scandalous persõs, whom wee refuse to receive into our churches, & so exclude from the wholsom remedy of church-discipline.

3 That in our way, wee sow seeds of division & hindrance of edificatiõ in every family: whilst admitting into our churches only voluntaries, the husbãd will be of one church, the wife of another: the parents of one church, the children of another the maister of one church, the servants of another. And so the parents & maisters being of different churches from their children & servants, they cannot take a just account of their profiting by what they heare, yea by this meanes the husbands, parents, & maisters, shall be chargable to the maintenãce of many other churches, & church-officers, besides their own: which will prove a charge & burden unsupportable.

But for Answer, as to the first. For gathering churches out of churches, wee cannot say, that is a thing unheard of in Scripture. The first christian church was gathered out of the Jewish church, & out of many Synagogues in that church, & consisted partly of the Inhabitants of Ierusalem, partly of the Galileans: who though they kept some communion in some parts of publick worship with the Temple: yet neither did they frequent the Sacrifices, nor repair to the Sanedrim for the determining of their church-causes: but kept entire & constant communion with the Apostles church in all the ordinances of the gospell. And for the first christian church of the Gentiles at Antoch, it appeareth to have been gathered & constituted partly of the dispersed brethren of the church at Ierusalem (wherof some were men of Cyprus, and Cyrene) & partly of the beleiving Gentiles. Acts. 11. 20, 21.

If it be said the first christian church at Ierusalem, & that at Antioch were gathered not out of any christian church, but out of the Jewish Temple and [4] Synagogues, which were shortly after to be abolished: & their gathering to Antioch, was upon occasion of dispersion in time of persecution.

Wee desire, it may be considered, 1 *That the members of the Jewish Church were more strongly and straitly tyed by express holy covenant, to keep fellowship with the Iewish church, till it was abolished, then any members of christian parish-churches are wont to be tyed to keep fellowship with their parish-churches. The Episcopall Canons, which bind them to attend on theier parish church, it is likely they are now abolished with the Episcopacy. The common Law of the Land is satisfyed (as wee concive) if they attend upon the worship of God in any other church though not within their own parish. But no such like covenant of God, nor any other religious tye lyeth upon them to attend the worship of God in their own parish church, as did lye upon the Iewes to attend upon the worship of God in their Temple and Synagogues.*

2 *Though the Iewish Temple Church at Ierusalem was to be abolished, yet that doeth not make the desertion of it by the members, to be lawfull, till it was abolished. Future abolition is no warrant for present desertiō: unless it be lawfull in some case whilest the church is yet in present standing to desert it; to witt, either for avoyding of present polutions, or for hope of greater edification, and so for better satisfaction to conscience in either [.] future events (or foresight of them) do not disolve present relations. Else wives, children, servants, might desert their husbands, parents, masters, when they be mortally sick.*

3 *What the members of the Iewish church did, in joyning to the church at Antioch, in time of persecution, it may well be concived, the members of any christian church may do the like, for satisfaction of conscience. Peace of conscience is more desirable, then the peace of the outward man: and freedome from scruples of consciēce is more comfortable to a sincere heart, then freedome from persecution.*

If it be said, these members of the Christian Church at Ierusalem, that joyned to the church at Antioch, removed their habitations together with their relations: which if the brethren of the congregationall way would doe, it would much abate the grievance of their departure from their presbyteriall churches.

Wee verily could wish them so to doe, as well approving the like removall of habitations, in case of changing church-relations (provided, that it may be done without too much detriment to their outward estates) and wee for our partes, have done the same. But to put a necessity of removall of habitation in such a case, it is to foment and cherish a corrupt principle of making civil cohabitation, if not a formall cause, yet at least a proper adjunct of church-relation; which the truth of the Gospel doeth not acknowledg. Now to foment an errour to the prejudice of the trueth of the Gospell, is not to walke with a right foot according to the truth of the Gospel, as Paul judgeth. Galat. 2. 14.

[5] 4 *Wee do not think it meet, or safe, for a member of a pres-*

byteriall Church, forthwith to desert his relation to his Church, betake himself to the fellowship of a Congregationall Church, though he may discern some defect in the estate, or government of his owne.

For 1. Faithfullness of brotherly love in Church-relation, requireth, that the members of the Church should first convince their brethren of their sinfull defects, & duely wait for their reformation, before they depart from them. For if wee must take such a course for the healing of a private brother, in a way of brotherly love, with much meekness, & patience: how more more ought wee so to walk with like tendrness, towards a whole church.

Again 2 By the hasty departure of sound members from a defective church, reformation is not promoted, but many times retarded, & corruption increased. Wheras on the contrary, while sincere members breathing after purity of reformation abide together, they may (by the blessing of God upon their faithfull endeavours) prevaile much with their Elders, & neighbours towards a reformation; it may be, so much, as that their Elders in their own church shall receive none to the Seales, but visible saints: and in the Classis shall put forth no authoritive act (but consultative only) touching the members of other churches: nor touching their own, but with the consent (silēt consent at least) of their own church: which two things, if they can obteyn with any humble, meek, holy, faithfull endeavours, wee cōceiv, they might (by the grace of Christ) find liberty of conscience to continue their relation with their own presbyteriall church without scruple.

5 *But to add a word farther, touching the gathering of Churches out of Churches, what if there were no express example of such a thing extant in the Scriptures? that which wee are wont to answer the Antipædobaptists, may suffice hear: it is enough, if any evidence therof may be gathered from just cōsequenc of Scripture light. Doctor Ames his judgmēt concerning this case, passeth (for ought wee know) without exceptiō, which he gave in his* 4 *booke of cōsciēce*[1] *in Ans to* 2 *Qu: C* 14. *Num* 16.

If any (saith he) wronged with unjust vexation, or providing for his own edificatiō or in testimony against sin̄ depart from a church where some evills are tollerated, & joyn himself to another more pure, yet without cōdemning of the church he leaveth, he is not therfore to be held as a schismatick, or as guilty of any other sinn. *Where the Tripartite disjunction, which the judicious Doctor putteth, declareth the lawfullness of the departure of a Church-member from his church, when either through wearyness of unjust vexation, or in way of provision for his own edification, or in testimony against sinn, he joyneth himself to another congregation more reformed. Any one of these, he judgeth a just & lawfull cause of departure,* [6] *Though all of them do not concurr together. Neither will such a practise dispoyle the best Ministers of the parishes of their best hearers.*

For 1 Sometimes the Ministers themselves are willing to joyn with their better sort of hearers, in this way of reformation: &

[1] Dr. William Ames, *De Conscientia*, Amsterdam, 1635. The reference should be Q. 3: C. 24.

then they & their hearers continue stil their Church relation together, yea & confirm it more straitly & strongly, by an express renewed covenant, though the Ministers may still continue their wonted preaching to the whole parrish.

2 If the Ministers do dislike the way of those, whom they otherwise count their best members, & so refuse to joyn with them therin; yet if those members can procure some other Ministers to joyn with them in their own way, & still continue their dwelling together in the same town, they may easily order the times of the publick assembly, as to attend constantly upon the ministery of their former Church: & either after or before the publick assembly of the parish take an opportunity to gather together for the administratiō of Sacramēts, & Censures, & other church ordinances amongst themselves. The first Apostolick church assembled to hear the word with the Jewish church in the open courts of the Temple: but afterwards gathered together for breaking of bread, & other acts of church-order, from house to house.

3 Suppose, Presbyteriall churches should cōmunicate some of their best gifted members towards the erecting & gathering of another church: it would not forthwith be their detriment, but may be their enlargment. It is the most noble & perfect work of a living creature (both in nature & grace) to propagate, & multiply his kind: & it is the honour of the faithfull spouse of Christ, to set forward the work of Christ as well abroad as at home. The church in Cant. the 8. 8. to help forward her little sister-church, was willing to part with her choyse-materialls, even beames of Cedar, & such pretious living stones, as weer fit to build a Silver pallace. In the same book, the church is compared sometime to a garden, sometime to an orchard, Cant 4. 12, 13. No man planteth a garden, or orchard, but seeketh to get the choysest herbes, & plants of his neighbours, & they freely impart them: nor doe they accoūt it a spoyle to their gardens, & orchards, but rather a glory. Nevertheless, wee go not so farr: we neither seek, nor ask the choyse-members of the parishes but accept them being offered.

If it be said, they are not offered by the Ministers, nor by the parish churches (who have most right in them) but only by themselves.

It may justly be demaunded, what right, or what powr have either the ministers, or parish church over them? Not by solemn church covenant: for that, though it be the firmest engagement, is not owned, but rejected. If it be, by [7] Their joyning with the parish, in the calling & election of a minister to such a congregation at his first comming, there is indeed just weight in such an ingagement: nor doe wee judge it safe for such to remove from such a minister, unless it be upon such grounds, as may justly give him due satisfactiō.. But if the uniō of such members to a parish Church, & to the ministery therof, be only by cohabitation within the precincts of the parish, that union, as it was founded upō humane law: so by humane law it may easily be released. Or otherwise, if a man remove his habitation, he removeth also the bond of his relation, & the ground of offence.

4 It need not to be feared, that all best hearers of the best ministers, no nor the most of them, will depart from them upon point of church-govermēt. Those who have found the presence & powr of the spirit of Christ breathing in their ministers, either to their conversion, or edification, will be slow to change such a ministry of faith, & holyness, for the liberty of church-order. Upon which ground, & sundry other such like, their be doubtless sundry godly & judicious hearers in many parishes in England that doe & will prefer their relation to their ministers (though in a presbyteriall way) above the Congregationall confœderation.

5 But if all, or the most part of the best hearers of the best ministers of parishes, should depart from them, as prefering in their judgments, the congregationall way: yet, in case the congregationall way should prove to be of Christ, it will never greiv the holy hearts of godly ministers, that their hearers should follow after Christ: yea many of themselves (upon due deliberation) will be reaedy to go along with them. It never greived, nor troubled John Baptist, that his best disciples, departed from him to follow after Christ. Joh. 3. But in case the congregationall way should prove to be, not the institution of Christ (as wee take it) but the invētion of men: then doubtless, the presbyteriall form (if it be of God) will swallow up the other, as Moses rod devoured the rods of the Ægyptians. Nor will this put a necessity upon both the opposite partyes, to shift for themselves, & to seek to supplant one another: but only, it will call upon them ἀληθεύειν ἐν ἀγάπῃ to seek & to follow the trueth in love, to attend in faithfullness each ūto his own flock, & to administer to them all the holy things of God, & their portiō of food in due season: & as for others, quietly to forbear them, & yet to instruct them with meekness that are contrary minded: leaving it to Christ (in the use of all good meanes) to reveal his own trueth in his own time: & mean while endeavouring to keep the unity of the Spirit in the bond of peace. *Philip.* 3. 15, 16. *Ephesians.* 4. 3.

[8] To the 2 Exception, That wee take no course for the gayning & healing & calling in of ignorant, & erronious, & scandalous persōs, whom wee refuse to receive into our churches & so exclude them from the rēmidy of church-disciplīe.

Wee conceive the receiving of them into our churches would rather loose & corrupt our Churches, then gain & heale them. A little leaven layed in a lump of dough, will sooner leaven the whole lump, then the whole-lump will sweeten it. Wee therefore find it safer, to square rough & unhewen stones, before the[y] be layed into the building, rather then to hammer & hew them, when they lye unevenly in the building.

And accordingly, two meanes (wee use to gayn & call in such as are ignorāt or scandalous. 1 *The publick ministery of the word, upon which they are invited by counsel, & required by wholsome lawes to attend. And the word it is, which is the powr of God to salvation, to the calling & winning of soules.* 2 *Private conference, & conviction by the Elders, & other able brethren of the church: whom they doe the more respectively hearken unto, when they see no hope of enjoying church-fellowship, or participation in the Sacraments for themselves, or their children, till they approve their judgments to be sound & orthodox, & their lives subdued to some hope of a godly conversation. What can Classical discipline, or excōmunication it selfe do more in this case.*

The 3 Exception wrappeth up in it a three fold domestical inconvenience: & each of them meet to be eschewed. 1 Disunion in families between each relation: 2 Disappointmēt of edificatiō, for want of opportunity in the governours of familyes to take accoūt of things heard by their children & servants. 3 Disbursments of chargeable maintenance to the several churches, wherto the several persons of their familyes are joyned.

All which inconveniences either do not fall out in congregationall-churches; or are easily redressed. For none are orderly admitted into congregational-churches, but such as are well approved by good testimony, to be duly observant of family-relations. Or if any otherwise disposed should creep in, they are either orderly healed, or duly removed in a way of Christ. Nor are they admitted, unless they can give some good account of their profiting by ordinances, before the Elders & brethren of the church: & much more to their parēts, & masters. Godly Tutors in the university can take an account of their pupills: & godly housholders in the Citty can take account of their children & servants, how they profit by the word they have heard in several churches: & that to the greater edification of the whole family, by the variety of such administrations. Bees may bring more hony, & wax into the hive, when they are not limited to one garden of flowers, but may fly abroad to many.

Nor is any charge expected from wives, children, or servants to the maintenance of congregationall churches, further then they be furnished with personall estates, or earnings, which may enable them to contribute of such things as they have, & not of [9] *Such as they have not. God accepteth not Robbery for a sacrifice. And though a godly housholder may justly take himselfe bound in conscience, to contribute to any such Church, wherto his wife, or children, or servants doe stand in relation: yet that will not aggravate the burden of his charge, no more then if they were received members of the same Church wherto himself is related.*

But why doe wee stand thus long to plead exemptions from exceptions? the Lord help all his faithfull servants (whether presbyteriall, or congregationall) to judge & shame our selves before the Lord for all our former complyances to greater enormityes in Church-government, then are to be found either in the congregationall, or presbyteriall way. And then surely, either the Lord will cleare up his own will to us, & so frame, & subdue us all to one mind, & one way, (Ezek. 43. 10, 11.) *or else wee shall learn to beare one anothers burdens in a spirit of meekness. It will then doubtless be farr from us, so to attest the discipline of Christ, as to detest the disciples of Christ: so to contend for the seameless coat of Christ, as to crucifie the living members of Christ: soe to divide our selves about Church communion, as through breaches to open a wide gap for a deluge of Antichristian & prophane malignity to swallow up both Church & civil state.*

What shall wee say more? is difference about Church-order becom the inlett of all the disorders in the kingdom? hath the Lord indeed left us to such hardness of heart, that Church-government shall become a snare to Zion, (as somtimes Moses was to Ægypt, Exod. 10. 7.) *that wee cannot leave contesting & contending about it, till the kingdom be destroyed? did not the Lord Jesus, when he dedicated his sufferings for his church, & his also unto his father, make it his earnest & only prayer for us in this world, that wee all might be one in him? John.* 17. 20, 21, 22, 23. *And is it possible, that he (whom the Father heard alwayes, John.* 11. 42.) *should not have this last most solemn prayer heard, & graunted? or, shall it be graunted for all the saints elsewhere, & not for the saints in England; so that amongst them disunion shall grow even about Church-union, & communion? If it is possible, for a little faith (so much as a grain of mustardseed) to remove a mountaine: is it not possible, for so much strength of faith, as is to be found in all the godly in the kingdom, to remove those Images of jealousie, & to cast those stumbling-blockes out of the way, which may hinder the free passage of brotherly love amongst brethren? It is true indeed, the National covenant*[1] *doth justly engage both partyes, faithfully to endeavour the utter extirpation of the Antichristiã Hierarchy, & much more of all Blasphemyes, Heresies, & damnable errours. Certainly, if congregational discipline be Independent from the inventions of men, is it not much more Independent from the delusions of Satan? what fellowship hath Christ with Belial? light with darkness? trueth with errour? The faithfull Iewes needed not the help of the Samaritans, to* [10] *Reedify the Temple of God: yea they rejected their help when it was offered. Ezra the* 1, 2, 3. *And if the congregationall way be a way of trueth (as wee believe) & if the brethren that walk in it be zealous of the trueth, & hate every false way (as by the rule of their holy discipline they are instructed,* 2 *John.* 10, 11.) *then verily, there is no branch in the Nationall covenant, that engageth the covenanters to abhore either Congregationall Churches, or their way: which being duely administred, doe no less effectually extirpate the Antichristian Hierarchy, & all Blasphemies, Heresyes, & pernicious errours, then the other way of discipline doeth, which is more generally & publickly received & ratifyed.*

But the Lord Jesus commune with all our hearts in secret: & he who is the King of his Church, let him be pleased to exercise his Kingly powr in our spirites, that so his kingdome may come into our Churches in Purity & Peace. Amen. Amen.

---

[1] *I. e.* The Scotch Covenant, adopted by Parliament, to secure Scotch aid in its struggle with the King, in Sept., 1643.

CHAPTER I.

Of the form of Church-Government; and that it is one, immutable, and prescribed in the Word of God.

I

Ecclesiasticall Polity or Church Government, or dis- Ezek 43, 11
cipline is nothing els, but that Forme & order that is to Col, 2, 5 1 Tim. 3, 15
be observed in the Church of Christ vpon earth, both for
the Constitution of it, & all the Administrations that
therein are to bee performed.

2 Church-Government is Considered in a double respect either in regard *of* the parts *of* Government themselves, or necessary Circumstances thereof. The parts of
Government are prescribed in the word, because the Lord Hebr 3, 5, 6
Iesus Christ the King and Law-giver of his Church, is no
less faithfull in the house of God then was Moses, who Exod 25 40
from the Lord delivered a *form &* pattern of Govern- 2 Tim 3 16
ment to the Children of Israel in the old Testament: And
the holy Scriptures are now also soe perfect, as they are
able to make the man of God perfect & thorough-ly furnished vnto euery good work; and therefore doubtless
to the well ordering of the house of God.

3 The partes of Church-Government are all of them 1 Tim 3 15 1 Chron 15
exactly described in the word of God being parts or 13 Ex 20 4 1 Tim 6 13
means of Instituted worship according to the second Com- v 16 Heb 12
mandement: & therefore to continue one & the same, 27 28. 1 Cor, 15 22
vnto the apearing of our Lord Iesus Christ as a kingdom
that cannot be shaken, untill hee shall deliver it up unto
God, euen the Father.[1] Soe that it is not left in the Deut 12 32. Ezek 43 8.
power of men, officers, Churches, or any state in the 1 Kings 12.
world to add, or diminish, or alter any thing in the least 31 32 33
measure therein.

4 The necessary circumstances, as time & place &c 1 Kings 12 v: 28 29
belonging unto order and decency, are not soe left unto Isai 29 13.

[1] The same idea is expressed, though not in identical language, by Mather, *Church-Government and Church-Covenant Discvssed*, (answer to XXXII Questions,) London, 1643, p. 83.

Col 2 22 23 Acts 15 28 — Matt 15 9 1 Cor 11 23 c 8 34. — 1 Cor 14 26 1 Cor 14 40 1 Cor 11 14 1 Cor 11 16 1 Cor 14 12 19. Acts 15 28.

men as that under pretence [2] of them, they may thrust their own Inventions vpon the Churches: Being Circumscribed in the word with many Generall limitations; where they are determined in respect of the matter to be neither worship it self, nor Circumstances seperable from worship: in respect of their end, they must be done vnto edification: in respect of the manner, decently, and in order, according to the nature of the things them selves, & Civill, & Church Custom. doth not euen nature it selfe teach you? yea they, are in some sort determined particularly, namely that they be done in such a manner, as all Circumstances considered, is most expedient for edification: so, as if there bee no errour of man concerning their determination, the determining of them is to be accounted as if it were divine.

CHAP: II.

Of the nature of the Catholick Church in Generall, & in speciall, of a particular visible Church.

Eph 1 22 23 & 5 25 26 30. Heb 12 23.

The Catholick Church,[1] is the whole company of those that are elected, redeemed, & in time effectually called from the state of sin & death vnto a state of Grace, & salvation in Iesus Christ.

Rom 8 17. 2 Tim 2 12 c 4 8. Eph 6 12 13.

2 This church is either Triumphant, or Militant. Triumphant, the number of them who are Gloryfied in heaven: Militant, the number of them who are conflicting with their enemies vpon earth.

2 Tim 2 19. Rev 2 17 1 Cor 6 17. Eph 3 17. Rom 1, 8 1 Thes 1 8 Isay 2, 2 1 Tim 6 12.

3 This Militant Church is to bee considered as Invisible, & Visible. Invisible, in respect of their relation wherin they stand to Christ, as a body unto the head, being united unto him, by the spirit of God, & faith in their hearts: Visible, in respect of the profession of their faith, in their persons, & in particular Churches: & so there may be acknowledged an universall visible Church.[2]

Acts 19 1 Colos 2, 5.

4 The members of the Militant visible Church,[3] con-

[1] Compare R. *Mather*, *Apologie . . . for Chvrch-Covenant*, London, 1643, p. 11.

[2] *I. e.*, The body of those who outwardly profess faith in Christ, viewed as brought into one class by that profession, but not as thereby organized into one visible body corporate.

[3] We may perhaps insert *are to be* in conformity to the preceding paragraph.

sidered either as not yet in church-order, or as walking according to the church-order of the Gospel. In order,[1] & so besides the spiritual union, & communion, common to all believers, they injoy more over an union & communion ecclesiasticall-Political:[2] So wee deny an universall visible church.[3] Matt 18 17. 1 Cor. 5 12

5 The state the members of the Militant visible church [3] walking in order, was either before the law, Oeconomical, that is in families; or under the law, National: or, since the comming of Christ, only congregational:[4] (The term Independent, wee approve not:[5]) Therfore neither national, provincial, nor classical.[6] Gen. 18 19 Exod: 19 6.

6 A Congregational-church, is by the institution of Christ a part of the Militant-visible-church, consisting of a company of Saints by calling, united into one body, by a holy covenant, for the publick worship of God, & the mutuall edification one of another, in the Fellowship of the Lord Iesus.[7] 1 Cor: 14, 23 1 Cor: 14, 36 1 Cor: 1 2. 1 Cor: 12 27 Exo: 19 5 6 Deut: 29: 1. & 9 to 15 Acts. 2. 42, 1 Cor 14 26.

CHAP: III.

Of the matter of the Visible Church Both inrespect of Quality and Quantity.

The matter of a visible church are *Saints* by calling.[8] 1 Cor: 1 2 Ephe 1 1. Hebr: 6. 1. 1 Cor. 1 5. Rom. 15 14. Psal: 50 16–17. Act 8 37. Matt: 3 6. Rom. 6 17

2 By Saints, wee understand,

1 Such, as haue not only attained the knowledge of the principles of Religion, & are free from gros & open scandals, but also do together with the profession of their faith & Repentance, walk in blameles obedience to the word, so as that in charitable discretion they may be

---

[1] *I. e.*, The members of the company of professed disciples of Christ on earth are to be considered in this treatise, not as isolated believers but as united in the corporate fellowships established by the Gospel.

[2] *I. e.*, This Gospel-order implies the union of Christians into local covenanted corporations.

[3] *I. e.*, There is no *corporate* union and communion of all the professed followers of Christ, only an association of local churches, if by the word *church* the organized body of believers is signified. Compare Mather, *Church-Government and Church-Covenant Discvssed*, (Answer to XXXII Questions,) London, 1643, pp. 9, 10.

[4] Compare Cotton, *Keyes*, p. 30.

[5] See Cotton's reasons why the fathers of New England disliked the name *Independent*, *Way of the Cong. Churches Cleared*, p. 11.

[6] Compare Cotton, *Way of the Churches*, p. 2.

[7] Compare Mather, *Apologie . . . for Chvrch-Covenant*, pp. 3–5.

[8] Compare Mather, *Church-Government and Church-Covenant Discvssed*, (Answer to XXXII Questions,) pp. 8, 9.

1 Cor. 1 2. Phillip. 1 1, Collos 1 2.

accounted Saints by calling, (though perhaps some or more of them be unsound, & hypocrites inwardly :) because the members of such particular churches are commonly by the holy ghost called Saints & faithfull brethren

Ephes. 1 1. 1 Cor 5 2 13 Rev. 1 14 15 & 20. Ezek. 44. 7 & 9. & chap. 23 38 39. Num 29 & 20. Hagg. 2 13 14. 1 Cor. 11 27 29. Psal. 37 21 : 1 Cor 5 6. 1 Cor. 7 : & 14.

in Christ, and sundry churches haue been reproued for receiving, & suffering such persons to continu in fellowship amongst them, as have been offensive & scandalous : the name of God also by this means is Blasphemed : & the holy things of God defiled & Prophaned. the hearts of godly grieved : & the wicked themselves hardned : & holpen forward to damnation. the example of such doeth endanger the sanctity of others. A litle Leaven Leaveneth the whole lump.

Ier. 2 21, 1 Cor. 5 12 Ier. 14. Gal. 5 4. 2 Cor. 12 21. Rev. 2 14 15, & 21 21.

2 The children of such, who are also holy.[1]

3 The members of churches though orderly constituted, may in time degenerate, & grow corrupt & scandalous, which though they ought not to be tolerated in the church, yet their continuance therein, through the defect of the execution of discipline & Just censures, doth not immediately dissolv the being of the church, as appeares in the church of Israell, & the churches of *Galatia & Corinth*, *Pergamus*, *& Thyatira*.

1 Cor 14 21

[4] 4 The *matter* of the Church in respect of it's *quantity* ought not to be of gteater number then may ordinarily

Matt. 18 17

meet together conveniently[2] in one place : nor ordinarily fewer, then may conveniently carry on Church-work. Hence when the holy Scripture maketh mention of the

Rom 16 1 1 Thes 1 1 Rev 2 8 c 3 7

Saints combined into a church-estate, in a *Town* or *Citty*, where was but one Congregation, it usually calleth those Saints [*the church*][3] in the singular number, as *the church* of the *Thessalonians* the church of *Smyrna*, *Philadelphia*, & the like : But when it speaketh of the Saints in a *Nation*, or *Province*, wherin there were sundry Congregations, It frequently & usually calleth them by the name of *churches*,

1 Cor 16 1 19 Gal 1, 2 2 Cor 8 1. 1 Thes 2, 14

in the plurall number, as the [*churches*] of *Asia*, *Galatia*, *Macedonia*, & the like: which is further confirmed by what is written of sundry of those churches in particular, how they were Assembled & met together the whole church in one place, as the church at *Jerusalem*, the church at *Antioch*,

---

[1] *Ibid.*, p. 20.

[2] Compare Cotton's remarks, *Way of the Churches*, London, 1645, pp. 53, 54.

[3] [ ] *sic*, and later.

the church at *Corinth*, & *Cenchrea*, though it were more Acts 2 46
neer to *Corinth*, it being the port thereof, & answerable to c 5 12. c 6 2. Acts 14,
a Village, yet being a distinct Congregation from *Corinth*, 27 c 15 38 1 Cor 5, 4.
it had a church of its owne as well as *Corinth* had.[1] c 14, 23. Rom 16, 1

5 Nor can it with reason be thought but that every church appointed & ordained by *Christ*, *had* a ministrie ordained & appointed for the same: & yet plain it is, that there were no ordinary officers appointed by Christ for any other, then *Congregational* churches: Elders being
appointed to feed, not all flocks, but the particular flock of Acts 20 28.
God over which the holy Ghost had made them the overseers, & that flock they must attend, even the whole flock: & one *Congregation* being as much as any ordinary Elders can attend, therfore there is no greater Church then a *Congregation*, which may ordinarily meet in one place.

CHAP: IV.

Of the Form of A Visible Church & of Church Covenant.

Saints by Calling, must have a Visible-Political-Union 1 Cor 12 27. 1 Tim 3 15.
amongst themselves, or else they are not yet a particular Ephe 2 22 1 Cor 12 15,
church: as those similitudes hold forth, which Scripture 16 17
makes use [5] of, to shew the nature of particular Churches: As a *Body*, A *building*, or *House*, *Hands*, *Eyes*, *Feet*, & other members must be united, or else, remaining seperate are not a body. *Stones*, *Timber*, though squared, hewen & pollished, are not an house, untill they are compacted & united: so Saints or believers in judgment of charity, are not a church, unless *Orderly* knit together.[2]

2 Particular churches cannot be distinguished one from another but by their formes. *Ephesus* is not *Smyrna*,
& *Pergamus Thyatira*, but each one a distinct society of it Rev 1
self, having officers of their owne, which had not the charge of others: Vertues of their own, for which others are not praysed: Corruptions of their owne, for which others are not blamed.[3]

3 This *Form* is the *Visible Covenant*, Agreement, or Exod 19 5 ver 8,
consent wherby they give up themselves unto the Lord, to Deu 29 12

[1] Compare Richard Mather and William Tompson's *Modest & Brotherly Answver to Mr. Charles Herle his Book*, London, 1644, pp. 32, 33.

[2] Compare Mather, *Apologie . . . for Chvrch-Covenant*, p. 5; *Church-Government*, p. 39.

[3] Compare *Ibid.*, *Apologie*, p. 14.

13. Zach 11 14. cap 9 11

the observing of the ordinances of Christ together in the same society, which is usually called the *Church-Covenant;* For wee see not otherwise how members can have *Church-power* one over another mutually.[1]

Ephe 2, 19 2 Cdr [Cor] 11 2

Gen 17 7. Deu 29 12 13. Ephe 2, 12 19

The comparing of each particular church unto a *Citty*, & unto a *Spouse*,[2] seemeth to conclude not only a Form, but that that Form, is by way of a *Covenant.*

The *Covenant*, as it was that which made the Family of Abraham and children of Israel to be a church and people unto God,[3] so it is that which now makes the severall societyes of Gentil believers to be churches in these dayes.

4 This Voluntary *Agreement*, *Consent or Covenant* (for all these are here taken for the same): Although the more express & plain it is, the more fully it puts us in mind of our mutuall duty, & stirreth us up to it, & leaveth lesse room for the questioning of the Truth of the *Church-estate* of a Company of professors, & the Truth of membership of particular persons: [6] yet wee conceive, the substance of it is kept, where there is a real Agreement & consent, of a company of faithful persons to meet constantly together in one Congregation, for the publick worship of God, & their mutuall edification: which real agreement & consent they doe express by their constant practise in comming together for the publick worship of God, & by their religious subjection unto the ordinances of God there: the rather, if wee doe consider how Scripture covenants have been entred into, not only expressly by word of mouth, but by sacrifice; by hand writing, & seal; & also somtimes by silent consent, without any writing, or expression of words at all.[4]

Exod 19 5 to 8 & 24 3 17. Iosh 24 18 to 24 Psal 50 5 Neh 9 38 c 10 1. Gen 17. Deu 29.

5 This forme then being by mutuall covenant, it followeth, it is not faith in the heart, nor the profession of that faith, nor cohabitation, nor Baptisme;[5] 1 Not faith in the heart? becaus that is invisible:[6] 2 not a bare profession; because that declareth them no more to be members

[1] Compare *Ibid.*, and Cotton, *Way of the Churches*, pp. 2–4.

[2] Compare Mather, *Apologie*, pp. 10–13.

[3] Compare *Ibid.*, 6, 7.

[4] Compare *Ibid.*, pp. 36-41; and Mather, *Church-Government and Church-Covenant Discvssed*, (Answer to No. 9, of the XXXII Questions,) pp. 24–28. The fathers of New England of Puritan education were careful to maintain the churchly character of English parish Assemblies.

[5] Insert *that constitutes a church.*

[6] Compare Mather, *Apologie*, pp. 16–20; and *Church-Government*, p. 24.

of one church then of another:[1] 3 not Cohabitation; *Atheists* or *Infidels* may dwell together with beleivers:[2] 4 not Baptism; because it presupposeth a church estate, as circumcision in the old Testament, which gave no being unto the church, the church being before it, & in the wildernes without it. seals presuppose a covenant already in being, one person is a compleat subiect of Baptism: but one person is uncapable of being a church.[3]

6 All believers ought, as God giveth them opportunity there unto, to endeavour to joyn themselves unto a particular church & that in respect of the honour of Jesus Christ, in his example, & Institution, by the professed acknowledgment of, & subiection unto the order & ordinances of the Gospel: as also in respect of their good of communion, founded upon their visible union, & containd in the promises of Christs special presence in the church: whence they have fellowship with him, & in him one with an other: also, for the keeping of them in the way of Gods commandments, & recovering of them in case of wandring, (which all Christs sheep are subiect to in this life), being unable to returne of themselves; together with the benefit of their mutual edification, and of their posterity, that they may not be cut off from the priviledges of the covenant. otherwis, if a believer offends, he remaines destitute of the remedy provided in that behalf. & should all believers neglect this duty of joyning to all particular congregations: it might follow thereupon, that Christ should have no visible political churches upon earth,[4]

Acts 2 47. & 9 26. Matt 3 13 14 15. & 28 19 20. Psal 133,, 2 3 & 87 7 Matt 18 20 1 Iohn 1 3.

Psal 119 last 1 Pet 2. 25 Eph 4 16 Ioh 22 24 25. Matt 18 15 16 17.

[7]

CHAP V. *Of the first subject of church powr or, to whom church powr doth first lelong.*[5]

The first subject of church powr, is eyther *Supream*, or *Subordinat*, & *Ministerial*. the *Supream* (by way of gift from the father) is the Lord Iesus Christ.[6] the *Ministerial*,

Matt 28 18. Rev 3, 7. Isai 9 6. John 20 21 23. 1 Cor 14 32.

---

[1] Compare Mather, *Church-Government*, (Answer to No. 3, of the XXXII Questions,) pp. 9–11.

[2] Compare Mather, *Apologie*, pp. 20, 21.

[3] Compare *Ibid.*, 32; and Mather, *Church-Government*, (Answer to Quest. 4,) pp. 12–20.

[4] *Ibid.* (Answer to Quest. 12,) pp. 38, 39.

[5] Read *belong*.

[6] Compare Cotton, *Keyes*, pp. 29–31.

Titus 1 5.
1 Cor 5 12.

is either extraordinary; as the *Apostles, Prophets, & Evangilists:*[1] or *Ordinary;* as every particular *Congregational* church.[2]

Rom 12 4 8.
Acts 12 3 C 6 3
4 C 14 23.
1 Cor 12 29 30.

2 *Ordinary* church powr, is either the power of office, that is such as is proper to the eldership:[3] or, power of priviledge, such as belongs unto the brotherhood.[4] the latter is in the brethren formally, & immediately from Christ, that is, so as it may according to order be acted or exercised immediately by themselves:[5] the former, is not in them formally or immediately, and therfore cannot be acted or exercised immediately by them, but is said to be in them, in that they design the persons unto office, who only are to act, or to exercise this power.[6]

CHAP VI.

Of the Officers of the Church, & especially of Pastors & Teachers.

Acts 14 23

A Church being a company of people combined together by covenant for the worship of God, it appeareth therby, that there may be the essence & being of a church without any officers, seeing there is both the form and matter of a church, which is implyed when it is said, the Apostles ordained elders in every church,

Rom 10 17
Ier 3 15.
1 Cor 12 28.
Ephe 4 11
Psal 68 18.
Eph 4, 8 11
Eph 4 12 13.

2 Nevertheless, though officers be not absolutely necessary, to the simple being of churches, when they be called: yet ordinarily to their calling they are, and to their well being: and therfore the Lord Iesus out of his tender compassion hath appointed, and ordained officers which he would not have done, if they had not been usefull & need full for the church; yea, being Ascended into heaven, he received gifts for men, and gave gifts to men, whereof officers for the church are Justly accounted no small parts; they being to continue to the end of the world, and for the perfecting of all the Saints.

1 Cor 12 28
Eph 4 II Ga 1
Act 8 6 26 19 C
11 28
Rom 11 7 8.

3 The officers were either extraordinary, or ordinary,

---

[1] Compare Cotton, *Way of the Churches*, p. 10.

[2] Compare Cotton, *Keyes*, pp. 31, 32.

[3] *Ibid.*, 20–23. [4] *Ibid.*, 12–19. [5] *Ibid.*, 33, 34.

[6] *Ibid.*, 34–37. Compare on whole paragraph Mather, *Church-Government* (Answer to Quest. 15), pp. 47–60.

extraordinary, as *Apostles, Prophets, Evangilists.*[1] ordinary
as *Elders & Deacons.*[2]

[8] The *Apostles, Prophets, & Evangelists*, as they were 1 Cor 4 9.
called extraordinarily by Christ, so their office ended with
them selves whence it is that *Paul* directing *Timothy* how
to carry along Church-Administrations, Giveth no direc- 1 Tim 3 1, 2 V 8 to 13
tion about the choice or course of *Apostles, Prophets*, or Tit 1, 5. Act 20 17 28
Evangelists, but only of *Elders & Deacons.* & when *Paul* 1 pet 5 1 2 3
was to take his last leave of the church of *Ephesus*, he
committed the care of feeding the church to no other, but
unto the Elders of that church. The like charge doth 1 Tim 3 2 Phil 1 1.
Peter commit to the Elders. Acts 20 17 28. 1 Tim 5 17..

4 Of *Elders* (who are also in Scripture called *Bishops*)
Some attend chiefly to the ministry of the word, As the *Pastors & Teachers Others*, attend especially unto *Rule*, who Eph 4 11 Rom 12 7 8.
are therfore called *Ruling Elders.*[3] 1 Cor 12 8

5 The office of *Pastor & Teacher*, appears to be distinct. The *Pastors* special work is, to attend to *exhortation:*
& therein to Administer a word of *Wisdom:* the *Teacher*
is to attend to *Doctrine*, & therein to Administer a word
of *Knowledg* :[4] & either of them to administer the *Seales* of 2 Tim 4 1 2. Tit 1 9
that Covenant, unto the dispensation wherof the[5] are alike
called: as also to execute the *Censures*, being but a kind
of application of the word, the preaching of which, to-
gether with the application therof they are alike charged Eph 4 11 12 Cap 1 22 23
withall.[6]

6 And for as much as both *Pastors & Teachers* are
given by Christ for the perfecting of the Saints, & edifying of his body, which Saints, & body of Christ is his
church; Therfore wee account *Pastors & Teachers* to be
both of them church-officers; & not the *Pastor* for the 1 Sam 10 12 v 19 20
church: & the *Teacher* only for the *Schools*, Though this 2 king 2 3 v 15,
wee gladly acknowledg, that *Schooles* are both lawfull,
profitable, & necessary for the trayning up of such in good
Litrature, or learning, as may afterwards be called forth
unto office of *Pastor* or *Teacher* in the church.

---

1 Compare Cotton, *Way of the Churches*, p. 10.

2 *Ibid.*

3 *Ibid.*, pp. 10, 14.

4 *Ibid.*, 11–13; and Mather, *Church-Government* (Answer to Quest. 22), pp. 74–76.

5 Read *they*, see errata.

6 Compare Mather, *Ibid.*, 74, 75.

CHAP VII. *Of Ruling Elders & Deacons.*

Rom 12 7 8 9. 1 Tim 5. 17. 1 Cor 12 28.

The *Ruling Elders*[1] office is distinct from the office of *Pastor & Teacher.* The *Ruling Elders* are not so called to exclude the *Pastors & Teachers* from *Ruling*, but because *Ruling & Governing* is common to these with the

Heb 13 17 1 Tim 5 17

other; wheras attending to teach and preach the word is peculiar unto the former.

1 Tim 5, 17.

2 The *Ruling Elders* work is to joyn with the *Pastor & Teacher* in those acts of spiritual *Rule* [9] which are distinct from the ministry of the word & Sacraments committed to them. of which sort, these be, as follow-

2 Chro. 23 19. Rev. 21 12. 1 Tim 4. 14 Matt 18 17. 2 Cor 2 7, 8 Acts 2. 6

eth.[2] I to *open & shutt* the dores of Gods house, by the *Admission* of members approved by the church: by *Ordination* of officers chosen by the church: & by *excommunication* of notorious & obstinate offenders renounced by the church: & by *restoring* of pœnitents, forgivē by the

Acts 21. 18 22, 23.

church. II To call the church together when there is occasion, & seasonably to dismiss them agayn. III To *prepare* matters in private, that in publick they may be carried an end with less trouble, & more speedy dispatch. IV To *moderate* the carriage of all matters in the church assembled. as, to *propound* matters to the church, to

Acts 6. 2, 3 c 13, v 15 2 Cor 8, 10 Heb 13. 7, 17 2 Thes 2. 10 11, 12

Order the season of speech & silence; & to *pronounce* sentence according to the minde of Christ, with the consent of the church. V To be *Guides & Leaders* to the church, in all matters what-soever, pertaining to church administrations & actions. VI To *see* that none in the church live inordinately out of rank & place; without a

[1] Of all church offices in early New England practice none were so much the subjects of discussion as the ruling eldership. Of no office was the theoretic necessity more stoutly maintained, and yet none was so speedily abandoned in practice. A moment's examination of the catalogue of duties here enumerated will show in large measure the reason of this neglect of the office. The functions are such as would tend to ill-feeling and they are not counter-balanced by any ordinary share in the more pleasing duties of preaching the word. In the Barrowist Congregationalism of the day, the ruling elder trenched on matters which Modern Congregationalism has left some to the brethren, others to the minister. He occupied a position between the minister and the brethren sure to be full of embarrassment and of no real use. See I. N. Tarbox, *Ruling Elders in the Early N. E. Chs.*, *Cong. Quarterly*, XIV: 401–416 (July, 1872).

The divine institution and antiquity of the ruling eldership is argued at length by Cotton, *Way of the Churches*, pp. 13–33.

[2] The duties here enumerated as belonging to the ruling elders are given by Cotton, *Ibid.*, 36, 37, in language so similar that the passage must have been under Mather's eye as he wrote this chapter, unless Cotton himself wrote it. Mather's original draft was much fuller.

calling, or Idlely in their calling. VII To *prevent* & heal such offences in life, or in doctrin; as might corrupt the church. IIX To *feed* the flock of God with a word of *admonition*. IX And as they shall be sent for, to *visit*, & to *pray* over their sick brethren. X & at other times as opportunity shall serve therunto. Acts 20, 28 v 32. 1 Thes 5. 12 Jam. 5. 14 Acts 20. 20

3 The office of a *Deacon* is Instituted in the church by the Lord Jesus. somtime they are called *Helps*.[1] Acts 6. 3. v 6 Phil 1. 1 1 Tim 3. 8 1 Cor 12, 28

The Scripture telleth us, how they should be qualified: *Grave, not double tongued, not given to much to wine, not given to filthy lucre.* they must first be *proved* & then use the office of a *Deacon*, being found *Blameless*. 1 Tim 3 8, 9.

The office and work of the *Deacons*[2] is to receive the offrings of the church, gifts given to the church, & to keep the treasury of the church: & therewith to serve the *Tables* which the church is to provide for: as the *Lords Table*, the table of the *ministers*, & of such as are in *necessitie*, to whom they are to distribute in simplicity. Acts 4, 35, c 6. 2, 3, c 6. 2 Rom 12. 8

4 The office therefore being limited unto the care of the temporall good things of the church, it extends not unto the attendance upon, & administration of the spirituall things thereof, as the word, and Sacraments, or the like. 1 Cor 7 17.

5 The ordinance of the Apostle, & practice of the church, commends the *Lords day* as a fit time for the contributions of the Saints. 1 Cor 16, 1, 2, 3

[10] 6 The Instituting of all these officers in the Church, is the work of God himselfe; of the Lord Jesus Christ; of the holy Ghost. & therefore such officers as he hath not appointed, are altogether unlawfull either to be placed in the church, or to be retained therin, & are to be looked at as humane creatures, meer Inventions & appointments of man, to the great dishonour of Christ Jesus, the Lord of his house, the King of his church, whether *Popes, Patriarkes, Cardinals, Arch-bishops, Lordbishops, Arch-deacons, Officials, Commissaries*, & the like. These & the rest of that *Hierarchy* & *Retinue*, not being plants of the Lords planting, shall all be certeinly be[3] rooted out, & cast forth. 1 Cor 12, 28 Eph 4, 8, 11 Acts 20, 28 Matt 15, 13

[1] Compare Cotton, *Way of the Churches*, p. 38.

[2] The paragraphs describing the duties of deacons closely follow the description given by Cotton, *Ibid.*, which Mather had before him.

[3] Omitted in errata.

1 Tim 5, 9, 10. 7 The Lord hath appointed *ancient widdows*, (where they may be had) to minister in the church, in giving attendance to the sick, & to give succour unto them, & others in the like necessities.[1]

CHAP: IIX.

Of the Election of Church-Officers.

Heb 5, 4 No man may take the honour of a Church-Officer unto himself, but he that was *called* of God, as was *Aaron*.[2]

Galat 1, I Acts 14. 23 cap 6. 3 2 *Calling* unto office is either *Immediate*, by Christ himself: such was the call of the Apostles, & Prophets: this manner of calling ended with them, as hath been said:[3] or *Mediate*, by the church.[4]

1 Tim 5. 22 cap 7, 10 Acts 16. 2 cap 6. 3 3 It is meet, that before any be ordained or chosen officers, they should first be *Tryed & proved*; because hands are not suddenly to be laid upon any,[5] & both *Elders & Deacons* must be of honest & good report.

4 The things in respect of which they are to be *Tryed*, are those *gifts & virtues* which the Scripture requireth in men, that are to be elected into such places. *viz*, that *Elders* must be *blameless, sober, apt to teach*, & endued with such other qualifications as are layd downe, 1 Tim: 3 & 2. Tit: 1, 6 to 9. *Deacons* to be fitted, as is directed, Acts. 6, 3. 1 Tim: 3. 8, to 11.[6]

Act 14, 23. c 1. 23. c 6. 3. 4. 5. 5 Officers are to be *called by such Churches*, where unto they are to minister. of such moment is the preservation of this power, that the churches exercised it in the presence of the Apostles.[7]

Gal 5, 13 6 A church being *free* cannot become *subject* to any, but by a free election; [11] Yet when such a people do chuse any to be over them in the Lord, then do they Hebr. 13, 17 becom subject, & most willingly submit to their ministry in the Lord, whom they have so chosen.

[1] Compare Cotton, *Way of the Churches*, p. 39.

[2] Compare Mather and Tompson, *Modest & Brotherly Answver*, p. 57.

[3] *Ibid.*

[4] *Ibid.*, 55–58. Compare Mather, *Church-Government*, (Answer to Quest. 20,) pp. 67, 68.

[5] Compare Cotton, *Way of the Churches*, p. 39. See also the *Modest & Brotherly Answver*, p. 51.

[6] *Way of the Churches*, p. 39. Here again the writer must have had Cotton's work before him.

[7] Compare Mather and Tompson, *Modest & Brotherly Answver*, pp. 55, 56.

7 And if the church have powr to *chuse* their offi- Rom. 16, 17
cers & ministers, then in case of manifest unworthyness, & delinquency they have powr also to *depose* them.[1] For to open, & shut: to chuse & refuse; to constitute in office, & remove from office: are acts belonging unto the same powr.

8 Wee judge it much conducing to the wel-being, & Cant. 8, 8, 9
communion of churches, that where it may conveniently be done, *neighbour-churches be advised withall*, & their help made use of in the triall of church-officers, in order to their choyce.[2]

9 The *choyce* of such Church-officers belongeth not to the civil-magistrates, as such, or diocesan-bishops, or patrones: for of these or any such like, the Scripture is wholly silent, as having any power therin.

CHAP: IX.

Of Ordination, & Imposition of hands.

CHurch-officers are not only to be chosen by the Acts. 13, 3 cap 14, 23
Church, but also to be *ordeyned* by *Imposition of hands*, & 1 Tim. 5, 22
prayer.[3] with which at ordination of Elders, *fasting* also is to be joyned.[4]

2 This *ordination* wee account nothing else, but the Num. 8, 10 Act. 6, 5, 6
solemn putting of a man into his place & office in the cap 13, 2, 3
Church wher-unto he had right before by election, being like the installing of a magistrat in the common wealth.[5]

Ordination therefore is not to go before, but to Acts. 6. 5. 6 cap 14. 23
follow *election*. The essence & substance of the outward calling of an ordinary officer in the Church, doth not consist in his ordination, but in his voluntary & free election by the Church, & in his accepting of that election.

---

[1] Compare Davenport, *Answer . . . unto Nine Positions*, London, 1643, pp. 76, 77, (Position 7).

[2] Compare Cotton, *Way of the Churches*, pp. 40, 45.

[3] Compare *Ibid.*, 40–42.

[4] "For our calling of *Deacons*, we hold it not necessary to ordaine them with like solemnitie, of fasting and prayers, as is used in the Ordination of *Elders*." *Ibid.*, 42. It was sufficient that they should be ordained by the hands and prayers of the ministers of the local church without a public invitation of neighboring churches, etc.

[5] From Mather, *Church-Government*, (Answer to Quest. 20,) p. 67. Compare the *Modest & Brotherly Answer*, p. 47.

wher-upon is founded the relation between Pastor & flock, between such a minister, & such a people.[1]

Ordination doth not constitute an officer, nor give him the essentials of his office. The Apostles were elders, without Imposition of hands by men: *Paul & Barnabas* were officers, before that Imposition of hands. Acts. 13. 3.[2] The posterity of *Levi* were Preists, & [12] Levits, before hands were laid on them by the Children of Israel.

1 Tim 4 14 Acts 13. 3 1 Tim 5. 22 3 In such Churches where there are Elders, *Imposition* of hands in ordination is to be performed by those Elders.[3]

4 In such Churches where there are no Elders,
Numb 8. 10 *Imposition of* hands may be performed by some of the Brethren orderly chosen by the church therunto. For if the people may elect officers which is the greater, & wherin the substance of the Office consists, they may much more (occasion & need so requiring) impose hands in ordination, which is the less, & but the accomplishment of the other.[4]

5 Nevertheless in such Churches where there are no Elders, & the Church so desire, wee see not why *Imposition of hands* may not be performed by the *Elders of other Churches.*[5] Ordinary officers laid hands upon the officers of many Churches: the presbytery of *Ephesus*
1 Tim 4 14 Acts. 13, 3 layd hands upon *Timothy* an Evangelist. The presbytery at *Antioch* laid hands upon *Paul & Barnabas.*[6]

1 Pet. 5. 2 Acts 20. 28 6 *Church Officers*, are officers to one church, even that particular, over which the Holy Ghost hath made them overseers. Insomuch as Elders are cōmanded to feed, not all flocks, but that flock which is cōmitted to their faith & trust, & dependeth upon them.[7] Nor can cōstant residence at one cōgregation, be necessary for

---

[1] Compare, *Church-Government*, 68; and Mather, *Reply to Mr. Rutherfurd*, London, 1647, pp. 102, 103.

[2] Compare the *Reply*, etc., pp. 104-106.

[3] Mather, *Church-Government* (Answer to Quest. 21), pp. 68, 69, 74. Compare Mather and Tompson, *Modest & Brotherly Answer*, pp. 45, 49.

[4] Mather, *Church-Government* (Answer to Quest. 21), pp. 69-74, Mather and Tompson, *Modest & Brotherly Answer*, pp. 45-53.

[5] *Ibid.*, 46, 48, 49, 53: Mather, *Reply to Mr. Rutherfurd*, p. 94. Cotton dissented, *Way of the Churches*, pp. 50, 51.

[6] *Modest & Brotherly Answer*, 45, 54.

[7] *Ibid.*, 48.

a minister, no nor yet lawfull, if he be not a minister to one cōgregation only, but to the church universall: because he may not attend one part only of the church, wherto he is a minister, but he is called to attend unto all the flock. Acts 20. 28

7. Hee that is clearly loosed from his office-relation unto that church wherof he was a minister, cānot be looked at as an officer, nor perform any act of *Office* in any other church, vnless he be again orderly called unto *Office*: which when it shall be, wee know nothing to hinder, but *Imposition of hands* also in his *Ordination* ought to be used towards him again.[1] For so Paul the Apostle received *Imposition of hands* twice at least, from Ananias. Acts. 9. 17. & Acts. 13, 3.

CHAP X.

Of the powr of the Church, & its Presbytery.

Supream & Lordly *power* over all the Churches upon earth, doth only belong unto Jesus Christ, who is King of the church, & the head therof. He hath the Governmēt upon his shoulders, & hath all powr given to him, both in heaven & earth.[2] Psal 2. 6 Eph 1. 21, 22 Isay 9. 6 Matt 28. 18

[13] 2 A Cōpany of professed believers *Ecclesiastically Confœderat*, as they are a church before they have officers, & without them; so even in that estate, *subordinate Church-power* under Christ deligated to them by him, doth belong to them, in such a mañer as is before expressed. C. 5. *S.* 2. & as flowing from the very nature & Essēce of a church: It being naturall to all bodyes, & so unto a church body, to be furnished with sufficient powr, for its own preservatiō & subsistāce. Acts 1. 23 c: 14, 23 c: 6. 3, 4 Mat: 18. 17 1 Co. 5. 4, 5

3 This *Government* of the church, is a mixt Goverment (& so hath been acknowledged long before the term of Indepēdency was heard of:) In respect of *Christ*, the head & King of the church, & the Soveraigne power residing in him, & exercised by him, it is a *Monarchy*: In respect of the body, or *Brotherhood* of the church, & powr from Christ graunted unto them, it resembles a *Democracy*, Rev: 3. 7 1 Cor 5. 12 1 Tim 5. 17

---

[1] See Mather, *Church-Government* (Answer to Quest. 21), pp. 69, 70. Compare Davenport, *Answer . . . unto Nine Positions*, pp. 76, 77 (Position 7).

[2] Compare Cotton, *Keyes*, 29, 30.

In respect of the *Presbyetry* & powr comitted to them, it is an *Aristocracy*.[1]

4 The *Soveraigne pown* which is peculiar unto Christ, is exercised, I In calling the church out of the world
Gal 1. 4. Rev 5. 8, 9 Matt 28. 20 Eph 4. 8. 12 Jam 4. 12 Isay 33. 22
unto holy fellowship with himselfe. II In instituting the ordinãces of his worship, & appointing his ministers & officers for the dispensing of them.[2] III In giving lawes for the ordering of all our wayes, & the wayes of
1 Tim 3, 15 2 Cor 10. 4, 5 Isay 32. 2 Luke 1. 51
his house:[3] IV In giving powr & life to all his Institutions, & to his people by them. V In protectĩg & delivering his church against & from all the enemies of their peace.

5 The power graunted by Christ unto the body of the church & *Brotherhood*, is a prerogative or priviledge which the church doth exercise: I In *Choosing* their own officers, whether Elders, or Deacons.[4] II In *admission* of their own members & therfore, there is great reason
Acts 6. 3, 5 c 14. 23 c 9. 26
they should have power to *Remove* any from their fellowship again. Hence in case of offence any one brother hath powr to convince & Admonish an offending brother:
Matt 18. 15, 16, 17
& in case of not hearing him, to take one or two more to sett on the Admonitiō, & in case of not hearing them, to proceed to tell the church: & as his offence may require
Tit 3. 10 Coll 4. 17 Mat 18. 17 2 Cor 2. 7, 8
the whole church hath powr to proceed to the publick Censure of him, whether by *Admonition*, or *Excōmunication:* & upon his repentance to restore him againe unto his former cōmunion.[5]

6 In case an Elder offend incorrigibly, the matter so requiring, as the church had powr to call him to office,
Collo 4. 17 Rom 16: 17
so they have powr according to order (the counsell of other churches where it may be had, directing therto[6] to remove him frō his Office:[7] & beĩg now but a mẽber,

---

[1] Quoted in substance by Mather, *Church-Government* (Answer to Quest. 15), p. 51 from Cartwright.

[2] Compare Cotton, *Keyes*, 30.

[3] Compare *Ibid.*

[4] Compare *Ibid.*, p. 12.

[5] Compare *Ibid.*, pp. 13-15; and *Way of the Churches*, 89-92.

[6] Insert).

[7] This subject is one on which Mather was more positive than Cotton. The latter in the *Keyes* (1644), pp. 16, 17, held that when all the ministry of a church were culpable the church could not excommunicate them, having no officers for the purpose; but only withdraw from them. But by the time of the publication of the *Way of the Chvrches* (1645), p. 101, Cotton had so far modified his views as to take substantially the position here given, and asserted the right of the church to discipline all its ministry. Davenport, *Answer . . . unto Nine Positions*, p. 77, agreed with the Platform. Cotton, *Keyes*, p. 43, suggested that in case all the elders of a church offended the "readiest course is, to bring the matter then to a Synod," i. e. council.

in case he add cōtumacy to his sin, [14] the Church that had powr to receive him into their fellowship, hath also the same powr to caſt him out, that they have concerning any other member. Matt. 18. 17

7 Church-government, or Rule, is placed by Christ in the officers of the church, who are therefore called *Rulers*, while they rule with God: yet in case of mal-administration, they are subject to the power of the church, according as hath been said before. the Holy Ghost frequently, yea alwayes, where it mentioneth Church-Rule, & church-government, ascribeth it to Elders: wheras the work & duty of the people is expressed in the phrase of obeying their Elders; and submiting themselves unto them in the Lord: so as it is manifest, that an organick or compleat church is a body politick, consisting of some that are Governors, & some that are governed, in the Lord.[1] 1 Tim. 5. 17 Hebr. 13. 17 1 Thes. 5, 12 Rom. 12. 8 1 Tim. 5. 17 1 Cor. 12. 28 29. Hebr. 13 7. 17

8 The powr which Christ has committed to the Elders, is to feed & rule the church of God,[2] & accordingly to call the church together upon any weighty occasion,[3] when the members so called, without just cause, may not refuse to come: nor when they are come, depart before they are dismissed: nor speak in the church, before they have leave from the elders: nor continue so doing, when they require silence,[4] nor may they oppose nor contradict the judgment or *sentence* of the Elders, without sufficient & weighty cause, becaus such practices are manifestly contrary unto order, & government, & in-lets of disturbance, & tend to confusion.[5] Acts. 20. 28 cap 6. 2 Num. 16. 12 Ezek. 46. 10 Acts. 13. 15 Hosh. 4. 4.

9 It belongs also unto the Elders to examine any officers, or members, before they be received of the church:[6] to receive the accusations brought to the Church, & to prepare them for the churches hearing.[7] In handling of offences & other matters before the Church they have powr to declare & publish the Counsell & will of God touching the same, & to pronounce sentence with the consent of the Church:[8] Lastly they Rev. 2. 2 1 Tim. 5. 19 Acts. 21. 18 22, 23 1 Cor. 5. 4, 5 Num. 6. 23, to 26.

[1] Compare Mather, *Church-Government* (Answer to Quest. 15), pp. 47–60; Cotton, *Keyes*, pp. 20–23; *Way of the Churches*, pp. 96–102.

[2] Cotton, *Keyes*, p. 20.

[3] Mather, *Church-Government*, 57; Cotton, *Keyes*, 21; *Way of the Churches*, 101.

[4] Mather, *Ibid.* Cotton, *Ibid.*, *Ibid.*

[5] Compare Mather, *Ibid.*, 58.

[6] Cotton, *Keyes*, 21.

[7] *Ibid.*, 22.

[8] *Ibid.*

have powr, when they dismiss the people, to bless them in the name of the Lord.[1]

10 This powr of Government in the Elders, doth not any wise prejudice the powr of priviledg in the brotherhood; as neither the powr of priviledg in the brethren, doth prejudice the power of government in the

Acts. 14. 15 ve. 23. c 6. 2 1 Cor. 5. 4 2 Cor. 2. 6, 7

Elders; but they may sweetly agree together. as wee may see in the example of the Apostles furnished with the greatest church-powr, who took in the concurrence & consent of the brethren in church-administrations. [15] Also that Scripture, 2 *Cor* 2. 9. & chap 10: 6 doe declare, that what the churches were to act & doe in

Hebr. 13. 17

these matters, they were to doe in a way of obedience, & that not only to the direction of the Apostles, but also of their ordinary Elders.[2]

11 From the premisses, namely, that the ordinary powr of Government belonging only to the elders, powr of priviledg remaineth with the brotherhood, (as powr of judgment in matters of censure, & powr of liberty, in matters of liberty:) It followeth, that in an organick Church, & right administration; all church acts, proceed after the manner of a mixt administration, so as no church act can be consummated, or perfected without the consent of both.[3]

CHAP: XI.

Of the maintenance of Church Officers.[4]

1 Cor. 9. 9 v 15. Matt. 9 38. c 10. 10 1 Tim. 5. 18

THE Apostle concludes, that necessary & sufficient maintenance is due unto the ministers of the word: from the law of nature & nations, from the law of Moses, the equity thereof, as also the rule of common reason. moreover the scripture doth not only call Elders labourers, &

Gala. 6. 6.

1 Cor. 9. 9 vers. 14. 1 Tim. 5. 18

workmen, but also speaking of them doth say, that the labourer is worthy of his *hire:* & requires that he which is taught in the word, should communicate to him, in all good things; & mentions it as an ordinance of the Lord, that they which preach the Gospel, should live of

[1] Mather, *Church-Government*, 58; Cotton, *Keyes*, 22; *Way of the Churches*, 100.

[2] Compare Mather, *Church-Government*, pp. 58–60.

[3] *Ibid.*, 57.

[4] Compare the brief paragraph, Mather, *Church-Government*, (Answer to Quest. 26,) pp. 76, 77.

the Gospel; & forbideth the muzling of the mouth of the ox, that treadeth out the corn.

2 The Scriptures alledged requiring this maintenance as a bounden duty, & *due debt*, & not as a matter of almes, & free gift therefore people are not at liberty to doe or not to doe, what & when they pleas in this matter, no more then in any other commanded duty, & ordinance of the Lord: but ought of duty, to minister of their *carnall things* to them, that labour amongst them in the word & doctrine, as well as they ought to pay any other work men their wages, or to discharge & satisfie their other debts, or to submit themselves to observe any other ordinance of the Lord. Rom 15 27 1 Cor. 9. 14

3 The Apostle, Gal: 6, 6. injoyning that he which is taught communicate to him that teacheth *in all good things*: doth not leave it arbitrary, what or how much a man shall give, or in what proportion, [16] but even the later, as well as the former, is prescribed & appointed by the Lord. Gala. 6. 6 1 Cor. 16. 2

4 Not only members of Churches, but *all that are taught in the word*, are to contribute unto him that teacheth, in all good things. In case that Congregations are defective in their contributions, the Deacons are to call upon them to doe their duty: if their call sufficeth not, the church by her powr is to require it of their members, & where church-powr through the corruption of men, doth not, or cañot attaine the end, the Magistrate is to see[1] ministry be duely provided for, as appeares from the commended example of Nehemiah. The Magistrates are nursing fathers, & nursing mothers, & stand charged with the custody of both Tables; because it is better to prevent a scandal, that it may not come & easier also, then to remove it when it is given. Its most suitable to Rule, that by the churches care, each man should know his proportion according to rule, what he should doe, before he doe it, that so his iudgment & heart may be satisfied in what he doeth, & just offence prevented in what is done. Galat. 6. 6. Act. 6. 3, 4 Neh. 13. 11 Isay. 49. 23 2 Cor. 8. 13 14

CHAP: XII.

Of Admission of members into the Church.

The *doors* of the Churches of Christ upon earth, doe not by Gods appointment stand so wide open, that all sorts 2 Chron. 23. 19. Mat. 13. 25. & 22, 12

[1] Insert *that the*.

of people good or bad, may freely enter therein at their
pleasure; but such as are admitted therto, as members
ought to be *examined* & *tryed* first; whether they be fit &
meet to be received into church-society, or not.[1] The
Acts. 8. 37 Evnuch of Æthiopia, before his admission was examined
by Philip,[2] whether he did beleive on Jesus Christ with all
Rev. 2. 2 his heart [3] the Angel of the church at Ephesus is com-
Acts 9. 26 mended, for trying such as said they were Apostles & were
not. There is like reason for trying of them that profess
themselves to be beleivers.

Rev. 21. 12 The officers are charged with the keeping of the doors
2 Chr. 23. 19 of the Church, & therfore are in a special mañer to make
tryall of the fitnes of such who enter. Twelve Angels are
set at the gates of the Temple, lest such as were Cere-
monially *unclean* should enter therinto.

Acts 2. 38 to 2 The things which are requisite to be found in all
42. c 8. 37 church members, are, *Repentance* from sin, & *faith* in Jesus
Christ. [17] And therfore these are the things wherof men
are to be examined, at their admission into the church &
which then they must profess & hold forth in such sort, as
may satisfie *rationall charity* that the things are there in-
Matt 3. 6. deed. Iohn Baptist admitted men to Baptism, confessing
Acts 19. 8. & bewayling their sinns: & of other it is said, that they
came, & confessed, & shewed their deeds.[5]

3 The weakest *measure* of faith is to be accepted in
those that desire to be admitted into the church: becaus
Rom 14. 1 weak christians if *sincere*, have the *substance* of that faith,
repentance & holiness which is required in church mem-
bers: & such have most *need* of the ordinances for their
Matt. 12. 20 confirmation & growth in grace.[6] The Lord Jesus would
Isay 40. 11. not quench the smoaking flax, nor breake the bruised reed,
but gather the tender lambes in his arms, & carry them
gently in his bosome. Such *charity* & tenderness is to be
used, as the weakest christian if sincere, may not be excluded, nor discouraged. Severity of examination is to be
avoyded.

---

1 Compare Mather, *Church-Government*, (Answer to Quest. 8,) pp. 23, 24; and Cotton, *Way of the Churches*, pp. 54–58.

2 See errata. 3 Cotton, *Way of the Churches*, pp. 5, 58. 4 See errata.

5 Mather, *Church-Government*, pp. 23, 24. Compare also Cotton, *Way of the Churches*, pp. 54, 55, 57, 58.

6 Cotton, *Ibid.*, p. 58.

4 In case any through excessive fear, or other infirmity, *be unable* to make their personal *relation* of their spirituall estate in publick, it is sufficient that the Elders having received private satisfaction, make *relation* therof in publick before the church, they testifying their assents therunto; this being the way that tendeth most to edification. But wheras persons are of better *abilityes*, there it is most expedient, that they make their *relations, & confessions* personally with their own mouth, as David professeth of himselfe. Psal 66. 16

5 A personall & publick *confession*, & declaring of Gods manner of working upon the soul, is both lawfull, expedient, & usefull, in sundry respects, & upon sundry grounds. Those three thousands. Acts. 2. 37. 41. Before they were admitted by the Apostles, did manifest that they were pricked in their hearts at Peters sermon, together with earnest desire to be delivered from their sinns, which now wounded their consciences, & their ready receiving of the word of promise and exhortation. Wee are to be ready to render a reason of the hope that is in us, to every one that asketh us: therfore wee must be able and ready upon any occasion to declare & shew our *repentance for sinn, faith unfagned;*[1] *& effectuall calling*, because these are the reason of a well grounded hope. I have not hidden thy righteousness from the great congregation. Psal: 40. 10. 1 Pet 3. 15 Hebr. 11. 1 Ephe 1. 18

[18] 6 This profession of faith & repentance, as it must be made by such at their *admission*, that were never in Church-society before: so nothing hindreth but the same way also be performed by such as have formerly been members of some other church, & the church to which they now joyn themselves as members, may lawfully require the same.[2] Those three thousand. Acts. 2. which made their confession, were mēbers of the church of the Jews before, so were they that were baptised by John. Churches may err in their admission: & persons regularly admitted, may fall into offence. Otherwise, if Churches might obtrude their members, or if church-members might obtrude themselves upon other churches, without due tryall, the matter so requring, both the lib- Matt. 3. 5, 6 Gallat. 2. 4 1 Tim. 5. 24

[1] Read *unfeigned.*

[2] Compare Mather, *Church-Government*, p. 30.

erty of churches would hereby be infringed, in that they might not examine those, conceřing whose fitness for communion, they were unsatisfied: & besides the infringing of their liberty, the churches themselves would ūavoidably be corrupted, & the ordinances defiled, whilst they might not refuse, but must receive the unworthy : which is contrary unto the Scripture, teaching that all churches are sisters, and therfore equall.

Cant. 8. 8

7 The like tryall is to be required from such members of the church, as were born in the same, or received their membership, & were baptized in their infancy, or minority, by vertue of the covenāt of their parents, when being grown up nnto[1] years of discretion, they shall desire to be made partakers of the Lords supper: unto which, because holy things must not be given unto the unworthy, therfore it is requisit, that these as well as others, should come to their tryall & examīation, & manifest their faith & repentance by an open profession therof, before they are received to the Lords supper, & otherwise not to be be[2] admitted there unto.[3]

Matt. 7. 6
1 Cor. 11. 27

Yet these church-members that were so born, or received in their childhood, before they are capable of being made partakers of full cōmunion, have many priviledges which others (not church-mēbers) have not: they are in covenant with God; have the seale therof upon them, *viz.* Baptisme ; & so if not regenerated, yet are in a more hopefull way of attayning regenerating grace, & all the spiritual blessings both of the covenāt & seal; they are also under Church-watch, & consequently subject, to the reprehensions, admonitions, & censures therof, for their healing and amendment, as need shall require.

[19] CHAP: XIII.

Of Church-members their removall from one Church to another, & of letters of recōmendation & dismission.

Church-members may not *remove* or *depart* from the Church, & so one from another as they please, nor with-

[1] Read *unto*.
[2] Omitted in errata.
[3] Compare Cotton, *Way of the Churches*, p. 5; Mather, *Church-Government*, pp. 20-22. Mather's first draft, now in the MSS. collections of the American Antiquarian Society at Worcester, read: "Such as are borne in ye ch: as members, though yet they be not found fitt for ye Lords Supper, yet if they be not culpable of such scandalls in Conversation as do justly deserve ch: Censures, it seemeth to vs, w^n they are marryed & have children, those their children may be recd to Baptisme." p. 63.

out just & weighty cause but ought to live & dwell to- Hebr. 10 25
gether : for as much as they are cōmanded, not to forsake the assembling of themselves together. Such *departure* tends to the dissolution & ruine of the body : as the pulling of stones, & peeces of timber from the building, & of members from the naturall body, tend to the destruction of the whole.[1]

2 It is therfore the duty of Church-members, in such times & places when counsell may be had, to consult with the Church wherof they are members, about their Prov. 11. 16
removall, that accordingly they have their approbation, may be incouraged, or otherwise desist. They who are joyned with consent, should not depart without consent, except forced therunto.[2]

3 If a members *departure* be manifestly unsafe, and sinfull, the church may not consent therunto : for in so Rom 14. 23. 1 Tim 5. 22.
doing, they should not act in faith : & should pertake Acts 21. 14.
with him in his sinn. If the case be doubtfull & the person not to be perswaded, it seemeth best to leave the matter unto God, & not forcibly to detayn him.[3]

4 Just reasōs for a mēbers *removal of* himselfe from the church are, I If a man canot continue without partakīg in *sinn.* II In case of *personall persecution*, so Paul Ephe. 5. 11 Acts 9. 25. & ver
departed from the disciples at Damascus. Also, in case 29. 30 chap 8. 1
of *generall persecution*, when all are scattered. III In case of real, & not only pretended, *want* of competent Nehe. 13. 20
subsistence, a door being opened for a better supply in another place, together with the meanes of spirituall edification. In these, or like cases, a member may lawfully remove, & the church cannot lawfully detayne him.

5 To *seperate* from a Church, eyther out of *contempt* of their holy fellowship, or out of *covetousness*, or for greater 2 Tim 4. 10
inlargements with just greife to the church; or out of *schisme*, or *want of love;* & out of a spirit of *contention* in Rom 16. 17
respect of some unkindness, or *some evill* only conceived, Jude . 19.
[20] or indeed, in the Church which might & should be Esh [Eph] 4. 2. 3
tolerated & healed with a spirit of meekness, & of which Coll 3. 13 Gala 6 . 1, 2
evill the church is not yet cōvinced, (though perhaps himselfe bee) nor admonished:[4] for these or the like rea-

[1] Compare Davenport, *Answer . . . . unto Nine Positions*, pp. 72-76.
[2] *Ibid.*, 74.
[3] *Ibid.*
[4] Compare Cotton, *Way of the Churches*, 105.

sons to withdraw from publick cōmunion, in word, or seales, or censures, is unlawfull & sinfull.

Isay 56. 8 Acts 9. 26 6 Such members as have orderly removed their habitation ought to joyn themselves unto the church in order, where they doe inhabit if it may bee: otherwise, they can neyther perform the dutyes, nor receive the priviledges of members; such an example tolerated in some, is apt to corrupt others; which if many should follow, would
1 Cor. 14. 33 threaten the dissolution & confusion of churches, contrary to the Scripture.[1]

Acts. 18. 27 7 Order requires, that a member thus removing, have letters *testimonial; & of dismission* from the church wherof he yet is, unto the church wherunto he desireth to be joyned, lest the church should be deluded; that the church may receive him in faith; & not be corrupted by receiving deceivers, & false brethren. Untill the person dismissed be *received* into another church, he *ceaseth not* by his letters of dismission to be a member of the church wherof he was.[2] The church cañot make a member no member but by excōmunication.[3]

Rom 16. 1, 2 8 If a member be called to remove *only for a time*,
2 Cor. 3. 1 where a Church is, letters of *Recommendation* are requisite, & sufficient for cōmunion with that church, in the ordinances, & in their watch: as Phœbe, a servãt of the church at Cenchrea, had letters writtē for her to the church of Rome, that shee might be received, as becōmeth saints.[4]

9 Such letters of *Recommendation & dismission* were written for Apollos: For Marcus to the Colosiãs; for
Acts. 18. 27 Coll 4. 10 Phœbe to the Romães; for sũdry others to other churches.
Rom. 16. 1 & the Apostle telleth us, that some persons, not sufficiently known otherwise, have special need of such letters,
2 Cor. 3. 1 though he for his part had no need therof.[5] The use of them is to be a benefit, & help to the party, for whom they are writtē; and for the furthering of his receiving amongst the Saints in the place wherto he goeth; & the due satisfaction of them in their receiving of him.

---

[1] Compare Mather, *Church-Government*, pp. 37–39.

[2] Compare Cotton, *Keyes*, pp. 17, 18; *Way of the Churches*, pp. 76, 103, 104.

[3] *Ibid.*, *Way*, p. 104.

[4] *Ibid.*, *Keyes*, p. 17; *Way*, p. 103.

[5] *Ibid.*, *Keyes*, p. 17.

CHAP : XIV.

Of excommunication & other Censures.

THE *Censures* of the church, are appointed by Christ, for the preventing, removing, [21] & healing of offences in the Church: for the reclayming & gayning of offending brethren: for the deterring others from the like offēces: for purging out the leaven which may infect the whole lump: for vindicating the honour of Christ, & of his church, & the holy profession of the gospel: & for preventing the wrath of God, that may justly fall upon the church, if they should suffer his covenant, and the seales therof, to be prophaned by notorious & obstinate offenders. 1 Tim. 5. 20 Deut 17. 12. 13 Jude 29 [23 ?] Deut. 13. 11 1 Cor. 5. 6 Rom . 2. 24 Rev. 2. 14. 15. 16. & 20

2 If an offence be *private* (one brother offending another) the offender is to goe, & acknowledg his repentāce for it unto his offended brother, who is then to forgive him, but if the offender neglect or refuse to doe it, the brother offēded is to goe, & cōvince & admonish him of it, between themselves privatly: if therupon the offender bee brought to repent of his offēce, the admonisher hath won his brother, but if the offender heare not his brother, the brother offended is to take with him one or two more, that in the mouth of two or three witnesses, every word may be established, (whether the word of admonition if the offender receive it, or the word of complaint, if he refuse it:) for if he refuse it, the offēded brother is by the mouth of the Elders to tell the church. & if he heare the church. & declare the same by penitēt confession, he is recovered & gayned; & if the church discern him to be willing to hear, yet not fully cōviuced[1] of his offence, as in case of heresy; They are to dispēce to him a publick admonition; which declaring the offēder to ly under the publick offence of the church, doth therby with-hold or suspend him from the holy fellowship of the Lords Supper, till his offence be removed by penitent cōfession. If he still continue obstinate, they are to cast him out by excōmunication.[2] Mat. 5. 23, 24 Luk. 17. 3. 4 Matt. 18. 15 V 16. V 17. Tit. 3. 10 Matt. 18. 17

3. But if the offēce be more *publick* at first, & of a more *heinous & criminall nature*, to wit, such as are con- 1 Cor. 5. 4, 5. & VII

[1] See errata.

[2] See Cotton, *Way of the Churches*, pp. 89–92; a passage which the writer had under his eye.

dēned by the light of nature; then the church without such graduall proceeding, is to cast out the offender, from their holy cōmunion, for the further mortifying of his sinn & the healing of his soule, in the day of the Lord Jesus.[1]

4 In dealing with an offēder, great care is to be takē, that wee be neither overstrict or rigorous, nor too indul-
Galat. 6. 1. gent or remiss; our proceeding herein ought to be with a spirit of meekness, considering our selves, lest wee also be tēpted; & that the best of us have need of much forgiv-
Matt 18. 34. 35 ness from the Lord. Yet the winīg & healīg of the offēders
c 6. 14, 15 Ezek. 13. 10 soul, being the end of these ēdeavours, wee must not daub
Jer. 6. 14 with ūtempered morter, nor heal the wounds of our brethren sleightly. on some have compassiō, others save with
Mat. 18. 17. fear.

1 Cor. 5. 11 2 The. 3. 6. 14 [22] 5 While the offender remayns excōmunicate, the Church is to *refrayn from all member-like communion* with him in spirituall things, & also from all familiar cōmuniō with him in civil things, farther then the necessity of natural, or domestical, or civil relatiōs doe require: & are therfore to forbear to eat & drīke with him, that he may be *ashamd.*[2]

6 Excōmunication being a spirituall punishment, it doth not prejudice the excōmunicate in, nor deprive him of his *civil rights*, & therfore toucheth not princes, or other magistrates, in point of their civil dignity or authority.
1 Cor 14. 24. 25 And, the excōmunicate being but as a publican & a heathen, heathens being lawfully permitted to come to hear the word in church assemblyes; wee acknowledg therfore
2 Thes 3. 14 the like liberty of hearing the word, may be permitted to persons excommunicate, that is permitted unto heathen. And because wee are not without hope of his recovery, wee are not to account him as an enemy but to admonish him as a brother.[3]

7 If the Lord sanctifie the censure to the offender, so as by the grace of Christ, he doth testifie his repent-
2 Cor 2. 7, 8 ance, with humble cōfession of his sinn, & judging of himselfe, giving glory unto God; the Church is then to *forgive* him, & to *comfort* him, & to *restore* him to the wonted brotherly communion, which formerly he injoyed with them.[4]

---

[1] *Ibid.*, pp. 92, 93.
[2] Compare *Ibid.*, p. 93.
[3] Compare *Ibid.*, pp. 93, 94.
[4] *Ibid.*, p. 94.

8 The suffring of prophane or scandalous livers to continue in fellowship, & partake in the sacraments, is doubtless a great sinn in those that have power in their hands to redress it; & doe it not. Nevertheless, inasmuch as Christ & his Apostles in their times, & the Prophets & other godly in theirs, did lawfully partake of the Lords commanded ordinances in the Jewish church, & neyther taught nor practiced *seperation* from the same, though unworthy ones were permitted therin; & inasmuch as the faithfull in the church of Corinth, wherin were many unworthy persons, & practises, are never commanded to absent themselves from the Sacramēts, because of the same: therfore the godly in like cases, *are not presently to seperate.*

Rev 2. 14. 15. ver. 20
Mat 23. 3. Acts 3. 1
1 Cor. 6 chap 15. 12 [12. 15?]

9 As *seperation* from such a Church wherin prophāe & scandalous livers are tolerated, is not presently necessary: so for the members therof, otherwise worthy, hereupon to *abstain* from communicating with such a church, in the participation of the Sacraments, is unlawfull. For as it were unreasonable for an iñocent person to be punished, for the faults of other, wherin he hath no hand, & wherunto he gave no consent: soe is it more unreasonable, that a godly [23] man should neglect duty, & punish himselfe in not cōming for his portion in the blessing of the seales, as he ought, because others are suffered to come, that ought not: especially, considering that himselfe doth neyther consent to their sinn, nor to their approching to the ordinance in their sinn, nor to the neglect of others who should put them away, & doe not: but on the contrary doth heartily mourn for these things, modestly & seasonably stirr up others to doe their duty. If the Church *cannot be reformed*, they may use their liberty, as is specified, chap: 13. sect: 4. But this all the godly are bound unto, even every one to do his indeavour, according to his powr & place, that the unworthy may be duly proceeded against, by the Church to whom this matter doth appertaine.

2 Chron. 30 18 Gen. 18. 25
Ezek 9. 4

CHAP: XV.

Of the cōmunion of Churches one with another.

ALthough Churches be distinct, & therfore may not be confoūded one with another: & equall, & therfore have

Rev 1. 4 Cant. 8. 8. Rom. 16. 16

1 Cor. 16. 19 Acts 15, 23 Rev 2, 1 not dominion one over another: yet all the churches ought to preserve *Church-communion* one with another,[1] because they are all united unto Christ, not only as a mysticall, but as a politicall head; whence is derived *a communion* suitable therunto.

2 The *communion* of Churches is exercised sundry wayes.

Cant. 8. 8 I By way of mutuall *care* in taking thought for one anothers wellfare.

II By way of *Consultation* one with another, when wee have occasion to require the judgment & counsell of other churches, touching any person, or cause wherwith they may be better acquainted then our selves. As the church of Antioch consulted with the Apostles, & Elders of the
Acts 15: 2 church at Ierusalem, about the question of circumcision of the gentiles, & about the false teachers that broached that doctrine. In which case, when any Church wanteth light or peace amongst themselves, it is a way of commun-
Acts 15. 6. ion of churches (according to the word) to meet together by their Elders & other messengers in a synod, to con-
: 22. 23 sider & argue the points in doubt, or difference;[2] & haveing found out the way of truth & peace, to commend the same by their letters & messengers to the churches, whom the same may concern. [24] But if a Church be rent with divisions amongst themselves, or ly under any open scandal, & yet refuse to consult with other churches, for healing or removing of the same; it is matter of just offence both to the Lord Jesus, & to other churches, as
Ezek 34. 4. bewraying too much want of mercy & faithfulness, not to seek to bind up the breaches & wounds of the church & brethren; & therfore the state of such a church calleth aloud upon other churches, to excertise a fuller act of brotherly communion, to witt, by way of *admonition.*

III A third way then of cõmunion of churches is by way of *admonition*, to witt, in case any publick offẽce be found in a church, which they either discern not, or are slow in proceeding to use the meães for the removing &
Gall 2. 11 to 14. healing of. Paul had no authority over Peter, yet when he saw Peter not walking with a right foot, he publickly

[1] Compare Cotton, *Way of the Churches*, pp. 102, 103.

[2] See Cotton, *Keyes*, 18, a passage which the writer must have had before him.

rebuked him before the church: though churches have no more authority one over another, then one Apostle had over another; yet as one Apostle might admonish another, so may one church admonish another, & yet without usurpation.[1] In which case, if the church that lyeth under offence, do not harken to the church which doth admonish her, the church is to acquaĩt other neighbour-churches with that offẽce, which the offending church still lyeth under, together with their neglect of the brotherly admonition given unto them; wherupon those other churches are to joyn in seconding the admonitiõ formerly givẽ: and if still the offẽding church continue in obstinacy & impenitency, they may forbear communion with them; & are to proceed to make use of the help of a Synod, or counsell of neighbour-churches walkĩg orderly (if a greater cañot conveniẽtly be had) for their conviction.[2] If they hear not the Synod, the Synod having declared them to be obstinate, particular churches, approving & accepting of the judgmẽt of the Synod, are to declare the sentence of non-cõmunion respectively concerning them: & therupon out of a religious care to keep their own communion pure, they may justly withdraw themselves from participation with them at the Lords table, & from such other acts of holy cõmunion, as the communion of churches doth otherwise allow, & require. Nevertheless, if any members of such a church as lyeth under publick offence; doe not consent to the offence of the church, but doe in due sort beare witness against it, they are still to be received to wonted communion: for it is not equall, that the innocent should suffer with the offensive. [25] Yea furthermore; if such innocent members after due wayting in the use of all good meanes for the healing of the offence of their own church, shall at last (with the allowãce of the counsel of neighbour-churches) withdraw from the fellowship of their own church & offer themselves to the fellowship of another; wee judge it lawfull for the other church to receive them (being otherwise fitt) as if they had been orderly dismissed to them from their own church.

Math 18. 15, 16, 17. by proportion

Gen 18. 25.

IV A fourth way of communion of churches, is by way of *participation*: the members of one church occasion-

[1] *Ibid.*, 19. Here, too, Cotton's language is closely followed.

[2] Compare *Ibid.*, pp. 18, 24, 25; also, *Way of the Churches*, 108, 109.

ally comming unto another, wee willingly admitt them to *partake* with us at the Lords table, it being the seale of our communion not only with Christ, nor only with the
1 Cor 12. 13 members of our own church, but also with all the churches of the saints: in which regard, wee refuse not to baptize their children presented to us, if either their own minister be absent, or such a fruite of holy fellowship be desired with us. In like case such churches as are furnished with more ministers then one, doe willingly afford one of their own ministers to supply the place of an absent or sick minister of another church for a needfull season.[1]

Rom 16. 1 V A fifth way of Church-communion is, by way of *recōmendation* when a member of one church hath occasion to reside in another church; if but for a season, wee cōmend him to their watchfull ffellowship by letters o*f* recommendation : but if he be called to settle his abode
Acts 18. 27 there, wee commit him according to his desire, to the ffellowship of their covenant, by letters of dismission.[2]

VI A sixt way of Church-communion, is in case of *Need*, to minister *reliefe & succour* one unto another :
Acts 11. 22 vers 29. either of able members to furnish them with officers; or of outward support to the necessityes of poorer churches;
Rom 13. 26, 27. as did the churches of the Gentiles contribute liberally to the poor saints at Ierusalem.[3]

3 When a cōpany of beleivers purpose to gather into church fellowship, it is requisite for their safer proceeding, & the maintaining of the communion of churches,
Galla 2. 1, 2, & 9 by proportion. that they signifie their intent unto the neighbour-churches, walking according unto the order of the Gospel, & desire their presence, & help, & right hand of fellowship which they ought readily to give unto them, when their[4] is no just cause of excepting against their proceedings.[5]

4 Besides these severall wayes of communion, there is also a way of propagation of churches ; when a church shall grow too nu- [26] merous, it is a way, & fitt season,
Isay 40. 20. Cant 8. 8, 9. to propagate one Church out of an other, by sending forth such of their mēbers as are willing to remove, & to pro-

[1] Here again the writer made considerable use of Cotton, *Keyes*, p. 17 ; though the communion by baptism and exchange of ministers is his own conception.

[2] Compare Cotton, *Keyes*, pp. 17, 18.

[3] Compare *Ibid.*, 18 ; *Way of the Churches*, pp. 107, 108.

[4] Read *there*. See errata.

[5] Compare Cotton, *Way of the Churches*, pp. 5, 6.

cure some officers to them, as may enter with them into church-estate amongst themselves : as Bees, when the hive is too full, issue forth by swarmes, & are gathered into other hives, soe the Churches of Christ may doe the same upon like necessity; & therin hold forth to thē the right hand of fellowship, both in their gathering into a church ; & in the ordination of their officers.[1]

CHAP : XVI.

Of Synods.

Synods orderly assembled, & rightly proceeding according to the pattern, Acts. 15. we acknowledg as the ordinance of Christ :[2] & though not absolutely necessary Acts 15. 2. to. 15.
to the being, yet many times, through the iniquity of men, & perversness of times, necessary to the welbeing of churches, for the establishment of truth, & peace therin.

2 Synods being spirituall & ecclesiasticall assemblyes, are therfore made up of spirituall & ecclesiasticall causes. The next efficient cause of them under Christ, is the powr of the churches, sending forth their Elders, [&] other messengers; who being mett together in the name Acts 15. ,2,3
of Christ, are the matter of a Synod :[3] & they in argueing, vers 6.
debating & determining matters of religion according to vers 7 to 23
the word, & publishing the same to the churches whom it concerneth, doe put forth the proper & formall acts of a Synod ; to the convictiō of errours, & heresyes, & the es- vers 31.
tablishment of truth & peace in the Churches, which is Acts 16 4. 15.
the end of a Synod.

3 Magistrates, have powr to call a Synod, by calling to the Churches to send forth their Elders & other mes- 2 Chron 29. 4. 5. to 11.
sengers, to counsel & assist them in matters of religion : but yett the constituting of a Synod, is a church act, & may be transacted by the churches, even when civil mag- Acts 15.
istrates may be enemyes to churches and to church assemblyes.[4]

4 It belongeth unto Synods & counsels, to debate &

[1] Here again the writer has made use of Cotton, *Keyes*, p. 19. See also *Way of the Churches*, pp. 109, 110.

[2] Cotton, *Keyes*, p. 23.

[3] *Result of a Synod at Cambridge . . . Anno, 1646*, p. 49.

[4] Compare *Ibid.*, pp. 70–72.

Acts 15. 1. 2. 6. 7. 1 Chro 15.13. determine controversies of faith, & cases of consciēce; to cleare from the word holy directions for the holy worship of God, & good government of the church; to beare wit-
2 Chron 29: 6, 7. Acts 15. 24 vers 28, 29. ness against mal-administration & [27] Corruption in doctrine or mañers in any particular Church, & to give directions for the reformation therof: Not to exercise Church-censures in way of discipline, nor any other act of church-authority or jurisdiction: which that presidentiall Synod did forbeare.

5 The Synods directions & determinations, so farr as consonant to the word of God, are to be received with reverence & submission; not only for their agreement therwith (which is the principall ground therof, & without which they bind not at all:) but also secondarily, for
Acts 15. the powr wherby they are made, as being an ordinance of God appointed therunto in his word.

6 Because it is difficult, if not impossible, for many churches to com altogether in one place, in all their mēbers universally: therfore they may assemble by their delegates or messengers, as the church of Antioch went
Acts 15. 2 not all to Ierusalem, but some select men for that purpose. Because none are or should be more fitt to know the state of the churches, nor to advise of wayes for the good therof then Elders; therfore it is fitt that in the choice of the messengers for such assemblies, they have
Acts 15: 2 vers 22, 23 special respect ūto such. Yet in as much as not only Paul & Barnabas, but certayn others also were sent to Ierusalem from Antioch. Acts. 15. & when they were come to Ierusalem, not only the Apostles & Elders, but other brethren also doe assemble, & meet about the matter; therfore Synods are to consist both of Elders, & other church-members, endued with gifts, & sent by the churches, not excluding the presence of any brethren in the churches.

CHAP: XVII

Of the Civil Magistrates powr in Matters Ecclesiastical.

It is lawfull, profitable. & necessary for christians to gather themselves into Church estate, and therin
Act 2. 41. 47. cap, 4. 1, 2, 3 to exercise all the ordināces of christ according unto the word, although the consent of Magistrate could

not be had therunto,[1] because the Apostles & christians in their time did frequently thus practise, when the Magistrates being all of them Jewish or pagan, & mostly persecuting enemies, would give no countenance or consent to such matters.

2 Church-government stands in no opposition to John 18, 36
civil govenment of cōmon-welths, nor any intrencheth upon the authority of [28] Civil Magistrates in their jurisdictions; nor any whit weakneth their hands in gov- John 18. 36 Acts 25. 8.
erning; but rather strengthneth them, & furthereth the people in yielding more hearty & conscionable obedience ūto them, whatsoever some ill affected persons to the wayes of Christ have suggested, to alienate the affections of Kings & Princes from the ordinances of Christ; as if the kingdome of Christ in his church could not rise & stand, without the falling & weakning of their government, which is also of Christ: wheras the contrary Isay 49. 23.
is most true, that they may both stand together & flourish the one being helpfull unto the other, in their distinct & due administrations.

The powr & authority of Magistrates is not for the restraīing of churches, or any other good workes, but for helping in & furthering therof; & therfore the consent & Rom 13. 4. 1 Tim 2. 2.
countenance of Magistrates when it may be had, is not to be sleighted, or lightly esteemed; but on the contrary; it is part of that honour due to christian Magistrates to desire & crave their consent & approbation therin: which being obtayned, the churches may then proceed in their way with much more encouragement, & comfort.[2]

4 It is not in the powr of Magistrates to compell their subjects to become church-members, & to partake at the Lords table:[3] for the priests are reproved, that brought ūworthy ones into the sāctuarie: then, as it was unlawfull Ezek 44. 7, 9
for the preists, so it is as unlawfull to be done by civil Magistrates. Those whom the church is to cast out if 1 Cor 5. 11
they were in, the Magistrate ought not to thrust into the church, nor to hold them therin.

---

[1] Cotton expresses the same view in different language, *Way of the Churches*, p. 6.

[2] Compare Cotton's statement of New England theory and practice, *Way of the Churches*, pp. 6, 7.

[3] Compare Cotton, *Keyes*, p. 51; the same idea is expressed in *The Result of a Synod at Cambridge . . . Anno*, *1646*, p. 4. See *ante*, p. 190.

5 As it is unlawfull for church-officers to meddle with
the sword of the Magistrate, so it is ūlawfull for the Magistrate to meddle with the work proper to church-officers.
Matth 20 25, 26. the Acts of Moses & David, who were not only Prīces, but
Prophets, were extraordinary; therfore not imitable.
2 Chron 26 16. 17. Against such usurpation the Lord witnessed, by smiting
Uzziah with leprosie, for presuming to offer incense

6 It is the duty of the Magistrate, to take care of
matters of religion, & to improve his civil authority for the
Psal 82. 2 observing of the duties commanded in the first, as well as
for observing of the duties commanded in the second
table.[1] They are called Gods. The end of the Magistrates
1 Tim 2. 1, 2 office, is not only the quiet & peaceable life of the subject,
in matters of righteousness & honesty, but also in matters
of godliness, yea of all godliness.[2] Moses, Joshua, David,
Solomā, [29] Asa, Jehoshaphat, Hezekiah, Josiah,[3] are
much commended by the Holy Ghost, for the putting forth
1 Kings 15. 14. c 22. 43 their authority in matters of religion: on the contrary,
2 Kings 12. 3 c 14. 4. c 15. 35. such Kings as have been fayling this way, are frequently
1 Kings 20. 42. taxed & reproved by the Lord. & not only the Kings of
Job 29, 25 c 31 26. 28. Judah, but also Job, Nehemiah, the king of Niniveh,
Neh 13 Jonah 3. 7. Darius, Artaxerxes, Nebucadnezar,[4] whom none looked at
Ezra 7. Dan 3. 29. as types of Christ,[5] (thouh[6] were it soe, there were no place
for any just objection,) are cōmēded in the book of God,
for exercising their authority this way.

7 The object of the powr of the Magistrate, are not
things meerly inward, & so not subject to his cognisance
& view, as unbeleife hardness of heart, erronious opinions not vented; but only such things as are acted by the
outward man;[7] neither is their powr to be exercised, in
1 Kings 20 28. vers 42 commanding such acts of the outward man, & punishīg the
neglect therof, as are but meer invētions, & devices of
men; but about such acts, as are commanded & forbidden in the word; yea such as the word doth clearly determine, though not alwayes clearly to the judgment of the
Magistrate or others, yet clearly in it selfe. In these he
of right ought to putt forth his authority, though oft-times
actually he doth it not.[8]

---

[1] Compare *Result of a Synod*, pp. 1 and following.
[2] *Ibid.*, pp. 34–36.
[3] *Ibid.*, p. 22.
[4] *Ibid.*, pp. 22, 23, 25–29.
[5] *Ibid.*
[6] Read *though*.
[7] Compare *Ibid.*, pp. 15, 16.
[8] This passage shows that Mather must have been familiar with the tentative *Result of a Synod* of 1646. (*Ante*, pp. 189–193.) See *Ibid.*, p. 4.

8 Idolatry, Blasphemy, Heresy, venting corrupt & pernicious opinions, that destroy the foundation, open contempt of the word preached, prophanation of the Lords day, disturbing the peaceable administration & exercise of the worship & holy things of God, & the like, are to be restrayned, & punished by civil authority.[1] Deut 13. 1 Kings 20. 28, vers 42. Dan 3. 29. Zach 13. 3. Neh 13. 21. 1 Tim 2. 2. Rom 13. 4.

9 If any church one or more shall grow schismaticall, rending it self from the communion of other churches, or shall walke incorrigibly or obstinately in any corrupt way of their own, contrary to the rule of the word; in such case, the Magistrate is to put forth his coercive powr, Joshua 22
as the matter shall require. The tribes on this side Jordan intended to make warr against the other tribes, for building the altar of witness, whom they suspected to have turned away therin from following of the Lord.

FINIS

[30 Blank]

[31] A TABLE OF THE CONTENTS [A simple list of the titles of the chapters, here omitted.]

Errata

The faults escaped in some of the bookes thus amended

Note that the first figures stands for page the next for line pag 8 19. r they. 10 11. r not, be. 13. 26. r admission. p 16. 28 r Philip. 17. 5. r Acts. 19. 18. 18. 28. r not bee adm. 19. r one. r to. 21. 21. r convinced. 25. 35. r there.

---

[1] Compare *Ibid.*, pp. 5, 6.

XI

THE HALF WAY COVENANT DECISIONS OF 1657 AND 1662

EDITIONS AND REPRINTS

A. THE CONCLUSIONS OF THE MINISTERIAL ASSEMBLY, 1657

The manuscript is in the possession of the *American Antiquarian Society*, Worcester, Mass.

A Disputation concerning Church-Members and their Children in Answer to XXI. Questions: London, 1659, 4° pp. [viii] 31.[1]

In abstract in I. Hubbard, *General History of New England*, ed. Boston, 1848, pp. 563–569.

II. Felt, *Ecclesiastical History of New England*, Boston, 1855–62, II: 154–158.

B. THE RESULT OF THE SYNOD OF 1662

The manuscript is in the possession of the *American Antiquarian Society*.

I. *Propositions Concerning the Subject of Baptism and Consociation of Churches, Collected and Confirmed out of the Word of God, by a Synod of Elders and Messengers of the Churches in Massachusets-Colony in New-England. Assembled at Boston, according to Appointment of the Honoured General Court, In the Year 1662*, etc., *Cambridge: Printed by S.*[*amuel*] *G.*[*reen*] *for Hezekiah Usher at Boston in New-England, 1662.* 4° pp. xvi, 32.

II. With same title, but without naming the place of publication, and with the addition of the *Answer of the Dissenting Brethren*, *i. e.*, Chauncy, *Anti-Synodalia Scripta Americana.* [London], 1662.

III. Mather, *Magnalia*, London, 1702. Ed. 1853–5, II: 279–301.[2]

IV. *Results of Three Synods*, etc. Boston, 1725, pp. 50–93.

V. *The Original Constitution, Order and Faith of The New England Churches*, etc. Boston, 1812, pp. 69–118.

VI. *Congregational Quarterly*, IV: 275–286. (July, 1862.)

Beside these publications of the full text of the result, the portion which has to do with Consociation of Churches was reprinted by Increase Mather, *A Disquisition Concerning Ecclesiastical Councils*, Boston, 1716, pp. 40–47; republished in *Congregational Quarterly*, XII: 366–369 (July, 1870).

An abstract of the result was given by Hubbard, *General History*, pp. 587–590.

SOURCES

Public Records of the Colony of Connecticut, Hartford, 1850, etc., I: 281, 288, 289, 293, 302, 437, 438; II: 53–55, 67, 69, 70, 84, 109, 516, 517.

---

[1] The publication was effected by Nathanael (and probably Increase) Mather. See *Brinley Catalogue*, I: 133.

[2] Dexter has pointed out that Mather's reprint is inaccurate; see *Cong. Quart.*, IV: 275.

Records of . . . Massachusetts, Boston, 1853–4, III: 419; IV, Pt. I: 280; Pt. II: 38, 60, 62.

Records of the Colony . . . of New Haven, Hartford, 1857–8, II: 195–198.

Acts of the Commissioners of the United Colonies, (in *Records of . . Plymouth*,) Boston, 1859, II: 328.

The sources are largely epitomized by Felt, *Ecclesiastical History of New England*, Boston, 1855, 1862, II: 153–159, 187, 189–191, 287–289, 291–296, 299–302, 310, 312, 333, 339–341, 365, 406, 407, 409.

CONTROVERSIAL PAMPHLETS

a. Opposed to the result. **1**. Charles Chauncy, *Anti-Synodalia Scripta Americana*, etc. [London] 1662; Printed in connection with the result of the Synod as issued at London;[1] **2**. *Answer of the Dissenting Ministers in the Synod, respecting Baptism and the Consociation of Churches*, Cambridge, 1662;[2] **3**. John Davenport, *Another Essay For Investigation of the Truth, in Ansvver to Two Questions, concerning* (a) *The svbject of Baptism.* (b) *The Consociation of Churches.* Cambridge, 1663, with preface by Increase Mather[3] and an appendix by Nicholas Street;[4]

b. In defense of the result. **1**. John Allin, *Animadversions upon the Antisynodalia Americana*, etc., Cambridge, 1664 [Reply to Chauncy]; **2**. Jonathan Mitchell and Richard Mather,[5] *A Defence of the Answer and Arguments of the Synod met at Boston in the year 1662 . . . Against the Reply made thereto by the Rev. Mr. J. Davenport* [this portion of the work by R. Mather][6] . . . *together with an Answer to the Apologetical Preface set before that Essay*, [here Mitchell answers Increase Mather,] Cambridge, 1664; **3**. *Collection of the Testimonies of the Fathers of the New England Churches respecting Baptism.* Cambridge, 1665?[7] **4**. Increase Mather, *The First Principles of New-England, Concerning the Subject of Baptisme & Communion of Churches. Collected partly out of the Printed Books, but chiefly out of the Original Manuscripts of the First and chiefe Fathers in the New-English Churches*, etc., Cambridge, 1675; **5**. Increase Mather, *A Discourse concerning the Subject of Baptisme, Wherein the present Controversies . . . are enquired into.* Cambridge, 1675.

LITERATURE

1. Hubbard, *General History of New England* [Account written soon after 1675],[8] ed. Boston, 1848, pp. 562–571, 587–591; **2**. Mather, *Magnalia*, London, 1702, ed. Hartford, 1853–5, II: 276–315; **3**. Neal, *History of New-England*, Lon-

[1] Thomas, *Hist. of Printing*, I: 255, believed this to have been issued also at Cambridge, Mass., in 1662. This is almost certainly a mistake. See Brinley Catalogue, I: 114.

[2] So given by Dexter, *Cong. as seen*, Bibl. No. 1935. May it not be identical with No. 1? I have not been able to find it, and am inclined to believe it a mistake.

[3] The youthful Mather soon changed his views, under the influence of Mitchell's arguments, and wrote in defense of the result. Compare *Magnalia*, ed. 1853–5, II: 310.

[4] Nicholas Street was teacher of the church at New Haven of which Davenport was pastor.

[5] The work was published anonymously.

[6] Davenport made rejoinder to R. Mather, but the reply was never printed. See *Cong. Quart.*, IV: 287.

[7] I know nothing of this work save the title as given in Thomas, *Hist. Printing in America*, II: 315. This classification is, therefore, purely conjectural. May this not be an erroneous description of I. Mather's *First Principles?*

[8] Hubbard speaks of Increase Mather's *First Principles*. etc., as "published not long since."

don, 1720, II: 335–337; **4**. Hutchinson, *History of the Colony of Mass. Bay*, ed. London, 1765, I: 223, 224; **5**. Trumbull, *History of Connecticut*, ed. New Haven, 1818, I: 296–313, 456–472; **6**. Upham, *Ratio Disciplinæ*, Portland, Me., 1829, pp. 221–228; **7**. Leonard Bacon, *Thirteen Historical Discourses, on the completion of 200 years, from the Beginning of the First Church in New-Haven*, New Haven, 1839, pp. 108, 139–146; **8**. Uhden, *Geschichte der Congregationalisten in Neu-England*, u. s. w., Leipzig, 1842, Conant's translation, *The New England Theocracy*, etc., Boston, 1858, pp. 163–200; **9**. Clark, *Historical Sketch of the Cong. Churches in Mass.*, Boston, 1858, pp. 44, 45, 69–73; **10**. Palfrey, *History of New England*, Boston, 1858–64, II: 486–493, III: 81–88, 116–119; **11**. Leonard Bacon, *Historical Discourse*, in *Contributions to the Ecclesiastical History of Connecticut*, New Haven, 1861, pp. 16–32; **12**. H. M. Dexter, *Two Hundred Years Ago, in New England*, in *Congregational Quarterly*, IV: 268–291 (July, 1862) [a most valuable and almost exhaustive monograph on the Synod of 1662]; **13**. D. T. Fiske, *The Half-Way Covenant*, in *Contributions to the Ecclesiastical History of Essex County, Mass.*, Boston, 1865, pp. 270–282; **14**. I. N. Tarbox, *Minutes of the General Association of Cong. Churches of Mass.*, Boston, 1877, pp. 35–42; **15**. Dexter, *Congregationalism . . . as seen in its Literature*, New York, 1880, pp. 467–476; **16**. G. L. Walker, *History of the First Church in Hartford*, Hartford, 1884, pp. 151–211 [corrects the misrepresentations as to the relations of the quarrel in the Hartford church to the Half-Way Covenant movement into which nearly all earlier writers have fallen]; **17**. G. L. Walker, *Jonathan Edwards and the Half-Way Covenant*, in *New Englander*, XLIII: 601–614 (Sept., 1884); **18**. Doyle, *English in America, The Puritan Colonies*, London, 1887, II: 94–100.

THE RECEPTION OF THE SYSTEM

a. By the Salem Church, White, *New England Congregationalism*, pp. 40–78 *passim* (original records); *b*. By the First Church, Boston, Hill, *History of the Old South Church*, Boston, 1890, I: 5–248 *passim*; *c*. By the Hartford Church, John Davenport, Letter to John Winthrop, Jr., in *3 Coll. Mass. Hist. Soc.*, X: 59–62; Walker, *History of the First Church*, Hartford, 1884, pp. 182–211; *d*. By the Stratford Church, Cothren, *History of Ancient Woodbury*, Waterbury, 1854, pp. 113–135; *e*. By the Dorchester Church, *Records of First Ch. at Dorchester*, Boston, 1891, pp. 35, 40, 49, 55, 70 [original records of value].

THE STODDARDEAN DISCUSSION

1. Increase Mather, *The Order of the Gospel*, Boston, 1700;[1] **2**. Stoddard, *The Doctrine of Instituted Churches Explained and Proved from the Word of God*, London, 1700;[2] **3**. [I. & C. Mather?] *The Young Man's claim unto the Sacrament of the Lords-Supper . . . by . . . John Quick . . . With a Defence*

---

[1] In general, a defense of the older New England views as to church-membership, rights of the brethren in church administration. "relations," covenants, synods, etc.

[2] Apparently drawn out by Mather's book, a large portion of the positions of which it traverses. Full presentation of the famous view on admission to the Supper, pp. 18–22. Stoddard affirms the existence of National Churches, denies the necessity of church covenants, and declares that the minister alone, without the intermeddling of the brethren, is to decide on fitness for admission to the sacraments.

of those Churches from what is Offensive to them in a Discourse lately Published, under the Title of, The Doctrine of Instituted Churches, 1700;[1] **4**. Stoddard, *The Inexcusableness of Neglecting the Worship of God, under A Pretence of being in an Unconverted Condition, Shewn in a Sermon Preached at Northampton, The 17th. Decemb. 1707*. Boston, 1708; **5**. Increase Mather, *A Dissertation, wherein the Strange Doctrine lately Published in a Sermon, the Tendency of which is to Encourage Unsanctified Persons (while such) to approach the Holy Table of the Lord, is Examined and Confuted*. Boston, 1708; **6**. Stoddard, *An Appeal to the Learned. Being A Vindication of the Right of Visible Saints to the Lords Supper, Though they be destitute of a Saving Work of Gods Spirit on their Hearts: Against the Exceptions of Mr. Increase Mather*. Boston, 1709; **7**. *An Appeal, Of some of the Unlearned, both to the Learned and Unlearned; Containing some Queries on S. Stoddard's Appeal*, Boston, 1709. An article of some value is that of [W. Bement], *Stoddardeanism*, in *New Englander*, IV: 350–355 (1846).

THE EFFORT FOR THE ABOLITION OF THE HALF-WAY SYSTEM

Opponents. **1**. Jonathan Edwards, *An Humble Inquiry Into the Rules of the Word of God, Concerning the Qualifications Requisite to a Compleat Standing and full Communion In the Visible Christian Church*. Boston, 1749, Edinburgh, 1790;[2] **2**. J. Edwards, *Misrepresentations Corrected, and Truth Vindicated*, Boston, 1752 [Reply to No. 26, below]; **3**. Bellamy, *Dialogue on the Christian Sacraments*, Boston, 1762;[3] **4**. Jacob Green, *Christian Baptism* ["Sermon Delivered at Hanover, in New-Jersey, Nov. 4. 1764"];[4] **5**. J. Green, *An Inquiry Into The Constitution and Discipline of the Jewish Church; In order to cast some Light on the Controversy, concerning Qualifications for the Sacraments of the New Testament*,[5] New York, 1768; **6**. J. Green, *A Reply to the Reverend Mr. George Beckwith's Answer*, New Haven [1769], [Reply to No. 31]; **7**. Bellamy, *The Half-Way-Covenant. A Dialogue*, New Haven, 1769;[6] **8**. Bellamy, *The Inconsistence of Renouncing The Half-Way-Covenant, and yet retaining the Half-Way-Practice. A Dialogue*,[7] New Haven [1769], [Reply to No. 30]; **9**. Bellamy, *That there is but one Covenant, whereof Baptism and the Lord's Supper are Seals, viz: the Covenant of Grace . . . and, the Doctrine of an External Graceless Covenant, Lately advanced, By the Rev. Mr. Moses Mather . . . Shewn to be an unscriptural Doctrine* [Reply to No. 27]. It has as preface, *A Dialogue between a Minister and his Parishioner, concerning the Half-Way-Covenant*,[8] New Haven, 1769 [Reply to

---

[1] Endorsed as a reply to the *Instituted Churches*, by John Higginson, William Hubbard, Zechariah Symmes, Sen., Samuel Cheever, Nicholas Noyes, Jeremiah Shepard, Joseph Gerrish, and Edward Paison.

[2] Primarily an attack on Stoddardeanism; opposes the Half-Way Covenant system on pp. 128–131. Edwards graduated at Yale in 1720. Pastor at Northampton, Mass.

[3] Yale, 1735, pastor Bethlem, Conn. Written soon after Edwards's dismission from Northampton, but not printed till 1762. A defence of Edwards. Opposed to the Half-Way Covenant by implication rather than explicitly.

[4] Harvard, 1744, pastor Hanover, N. J. A follower of Whitefield, Edwardean in spirit and opposed to seeking baptism for offspring when consciously unfit for the Lord's Table.

[5] A vigorous defence of Edwards's views.

[6] Bellamy's first Half-Way Covenant dialogue — a readable and forcible attack on the system.

[7] Bellamy's second dialogue.

[8] Bellamy's third dialogue.

No. 28]; **10.** Bellamy, *The Sacramental Controversy brought to a Point. The Fourth Dialogue between a Minister and his Parishioner.* New Haven [1770], [Reply to No. 33]; **11.** Bellamy, *A careful and strict Examination of the External Covenant . . . A Reply to the Rev. Mr. Moses Mather's Piece, entituled, The Visible Church in Covenant with God, further illustrated*, New Haven [1770], [Reply to No. 34]; **12.** Israel Holley, *A Letter to the Reverend Mr. Bartholomew of Harwinton: Containing A Few Remarks, Upon some of his Arguments and Divinity*,[1] Hartford, 1770, [Reply to No. 32]; **13.** *Rules of Trial: Or Half-Way Covenant Examined. In a letter to the Parishioner. By an Observer of the Dispute*, New London, 1770,[2] [Reply to No. 28]; **14.** Chandler Robbins, *A Reply to some Essays lately published by John Cotton, Esq. (of Plymouth) Relating to Baptism*,[3] Boston, 1773, [Reply to No. 37]; **15.** C. Robbins, *Some brief Remarks on A Piece published by John Cotton, Esq, of Plymouth*, Boston, 1774, [Reply to No. 38]; **16.** Cyprian Strong, *A Discourse on Acts II: 42. In which the Practice of Owning the Covenant is Examined*,[4] Hartford, 1780, 2d ed. 1791; **17.** C. Strong, *Animadversions on the Substance of Two Sermons preached at Stepney by John Lewis, A.M.*, Hartford, 1789, [Reply to No. 25]; **18.** C. Strong, *An Inquiry Wherein the end and design of Baptism . . . are particularly considered*,[5] Hartford, 1793; **19.** Nathanael Emmons, *Dissertation on the Scripture Qualifications for Admission and Access to the Christian Sacraments: comprising Some Strictures on Dr. Hemmenway's Discourse concerning the Church*,[6] Worcester, 1793, [Reply to No. 43]; **20.** Stephen West, *An Inquiry into the Ground and Import of Infant Baptism*,[7] Stockbridge, 1794; **21.** N. Emmons, *Candid Reply to Dr. Hemmenway's Remarks on his Dissertation*, Worcester, 1795, [Reply to No. 44]; **22.** C. Strong, *A Second Inquiry into the Nature and Design of Christian Baptism.*[8] Hartford, 1796; **23.** S. West, *A Dissertation on Infant Baptism in reply to the Rev. Cyprian Strong's Second Inquiry on that Subject*,[9] Hartford, 1798, [Reply to No. 22]; **24.** Timothy Dwight, *Sermon CLIX*, in *Theology; Explained and Defended in a Series of Sermons*, ed. New Haven, 1823, IV: 338–344.

Peculiar Views. **25.** John Lewis, *Christian Forbearance to weak Consciences a Duty of the Gospel. The Substance of Two Sermons*,[10] Hartford, 1789.

---

[1] Pastor at Suffield, Conn. Edwardean in view and friendly to Bellamy. Not very valuable.

[2] Anonymous. Unimportant. The writer asserts that conversion is a prerequisite to admission to the Sacraments.

[3] Yale, 1756, pastor Plymouth, Mass. A powerful argument against the system, which had been under discussion in the First Church since 1770.

[4] Yale, 1763, pastor Chatham, now Portland, Conn. A most vigorous attack on the system.

[5] One of the great works in opposition to the Half Way Covenant.

[6] Yale, 1767, pastor Franklin, Mass.

[7] Yale, 1755, pastor Stockbridge, Mass.

[8] Has to do only incidentally with the Half-Way Covenant. Strong's views is: "that the children of believers are not in covenant, and are not to be baptized in token of their title to the blessings of the covenant, but as a mark and token that their parents will keep covenant, and that their children are dedicated to God." p. 114.

[9] West combatted the Half-Way Covenant, but opposed Strong's view that baptism was only a seal of the parents' dedication of the child of God.

[10] Yale, 1770, pastor Stepney, now Rocky Hill, Conn. His view was that: "The same qualifications, which are necessary for an attendance on the Lord's Supper, are necessary to bring a child to baptism" . . . but: "the absenting of a person, who wishes to avoid every sin, and walk in newness of life, yet fears to approach the table of the Lord—is not such a breach of covenant as debars him from bringing his children to baptism." pp. 5, 6.

Defenders. **26**. Solomon Williams, *True State of the Question concerning The Qualifications Necessary to lawful Communion in the Christian Sacraments*,[1] Boston, 1751, [Reply to No. 1]; **27**. Moses Mather, *The Visible Church, in Covenant with God*,[2] New York, 1759, [error for 1769]; **28**. [Ebenezer Devotion], *The Half-way Covenant. A Dialogue between Joseph Bellamy, D.D., and a Parishioner, Continued, by the Parishioner*,[3] New London, 1769, [Reply to No. 7]; **29**. *The Parishioner having Studied the Point. Containing some Observations on the Half-Way Covenant, Printed* 1769,[4] [Reply to No. 7]; **30**. [Nathanael Taylor?] *A Second Dialogue, between a Minister and his Parishioner, Concerning the Half-Way-Covenant*,[5] Hartford, 1769, [Reply to No. 7]; **31**. George Beckwith, *Visible Saints lawful Right to Communion in Christian Sacraments, Vindicated*,[6] New-London, 1769, [Reply to No. 4]; **32**. Andrew Bartholomew, *A Dissertation, on The Qualifications, Necessary to A lawful Profession, and enjoying special Ordinances*,[7] Hartford [1769]; **33**. [E. Devotion?], *A Letter to the Reverend Joseph Bellamy, D.D., Concerning Qualifications for Christian Communion . . . From the Parishioner*,[8] New Haven [1770], [Reply to the preface of No. 9]; **34**. Moses Mather, *The Visible Church, in Covenant with God; Further Illustrated*, New Haven, 1770, [Reply to No. 9]; **35**. [E. Devotion?], *A Second Letter, to the Reverend Joseph Bellamy, D.D., Occasioned by his fourth Dialogue . . . From the Parishioner*, New Haven [1770], [Reply to No. 10]; **36**. Charles Chauncy, "*Breaking of Bread" in remembrance of the dying Love of Christ, a Gospel institution. Five Sermons*,[9] Boston, 1772; **37**. John Cotton, *The general Practice of the Churches of New-England, relating to Baptism, Vindicated: or, Some Essays . . . Delivered at several Church-Meetings in Plymouth*,[10] Boston [1772]; **38**. John Cotton, *The General Practice of the Churches of New England, Relating to Baptism Further Vindicated*, Boston, 1773, [Reply to No. 14]; **39**. William Hart, *A Scriptural Answer to this Question "What are the Necessary Qualifications for . . . Attendance upon the Sacraments of the New Covenant*,[11] New London, 1772; **40**. Moses Mather, *A Brief View of the Manner in which the Controversy About Terms of Communion . . . Has been conducted, in the present day*.[12] New Haven, 1772; **41**. Nathan Williams, *An Enquiry Concerning the Design and*

---

[1] Harvard, 1719, pastor Lebanon, Conn. Strongly Stoddardean, little *direct* reference to the system.

[2] Yale, 1739, pastor Middlesex, now Darien, Conn. A powerful Stoddardean treatise.

[3] Yale, 1732, pastor Scotland, Conn. Stoddardean.

[4] Anonymous and without place — Ultra-Stoddardean.

[5] Yale, 1745, pastor New Milford, Conn. Curiously enough Dr. H. M. Dexter, Bibliog. No. 3559, and the editors of Bellamy's Works, ed. Boston, 1850, II: 677–684, took this tract to be by Bellamy instead of against him. On the authorship see Israel Holly No. 12 above, and Prof. F. B. Dexter, *Yale Graduates*, p. 528.

[6] Yale, 1728, pastor Lyme, Conn. Stoddardean. An earnest defence of the Half-Way Covenant.

[7] Yale, 1731, pastor Harwinton, Conn. Opposed to Bellamy.

[8] Hot and personal.

[9] Harvard, 1721, pastor First Church, Boston. See pp. 106–113 for a strong presentation of a theory essentially Stoddardean.

[10] Harvard, 1730, pastor Halifax, Mass., but ill health had compelled retirement. Was now a member of the First Church, Plymouth, and the holder of civil offices (county treasurer, etc.). He strenuously resisted Robbins's attempt to induce the Plymouth church to abandon the Half-Way practice.

[11] Yale, 1732, pastor Saybrook, Conn. Stoddardean.

[12] A general reply to Bellamy and defence of the Stoddardean view. Mather is said to have adopted Edwards's view late in life. F. B. Dexter, *Yale Graduates*, p. 628.

Importance of Christian Baptism and Discipline, In way of a Dialogue Between a Minister and his Neighbour,[1] Hartford, 1778, Boston, 1792; **42.** Joseph Lathrop, *A Church of God described, the Qualifications for Membership stated, and Christian Fellowship illustrated, in two Discourses*,[2] Hartford, 1792; **43.** Moses Hemmenway, *A Discourse concerning the Church, in which . . . a Right of Admission and Access to Special Ordinances, in their Outward Administrations and Inward Efficacy*, [is] *Stated and Discussed*,[3] Boston, 1792; **44.** M. Hemmenway, *Remarks on Rev. Mr. Emmons' Dissertation*, Boston, 1794, [Reply to No. 19].

THE main purpose of the Massachusetts General Court in calling the Synod to meet at Cambridge in 1646 had been the settlement of the questions agitating the colonies as to baptism and church-membership.[4] The predominance of Presbyterianism at the time in England, and the machinations of those in New England who hoped by Presbyterian aid to overthrow the colonial churches and state, made these questions peculiarly pressing. But the cloud rolled away almost as quickly as it had arisen, and as the questions proposed by the Court encountered diversities of view among the representatives of the Congregational Churches assembled at Cambridge,[5] the more generally accepted features of the Congregational system were embodied in the Platform, and the vexed points regarding baptism, no longer pressing for immediate solution, were passed over in rather ambiguous phrases. This treatment of the subject was comparatively easy in 1648 because the opposition to the prevalent system had been largely championed by a defeated political party; but had the Cambridge Synod been pressed to a vote, the probability is that it would have substantially anticipated the decisions of 1662. The question was really far more religious than political. It was one sure to arise in the state of New England society. And as the leaders of the first generation passed rapidly away, soon after the close of the Cambridge

---

[1] Yale, 1755, pastor Tolland, Conn. Favors the Half-Way Covenant. The first edition bears the endorsements of Rev. Eliphalet Williams, East Hartford, Conn.; Rev. John Willard, Stafford, Conn.; Rev. Elizur Goodrich, Durham, Conn.; and Rev. Joseph Lathrop, West Springfield, Mass. The second edition has, in addition, Pres. Joseph Willard of Harvard; and Rev. Moses Hemmenway of Wells, Me.

[2] Yale, 1754, pastor West Springfield, Mass. An able defence of Stoddardeanism. In 1793 Lathrop was offered the professorship of Divinity in Yale College; see *N. H. Hist. Soc. Papers*, IV: 269.

[3] Harvard, 1755, pastor Wells, Me. Dislikes the name Half-Way Covenant; but strongly favors the system and inclines toward Stoddardeanism.

[4] See *ante*, pp. 168–171. [5] *Ibid.*, p. 181.

Synod, and the children of the emigrants grew to manhood and womanhood, the problem of baptism became every day more pressing as a question vitally affecting the churches themselves, whatever intermixture of political aspirations in regard to the franchise or taxation may have modified the discussions of 1645–8. The political element, slight at all times in comparison with the religious motive in the controversy, practically dropped out of sight after the defeat of Child and his associates. The second stage of the controversy on which we now enter was purely ecclesiastical. It was now solely as a problem of church polity that the position of the baptized but not regenerate members of the community was discussed.[1]

The original settlers of New England were men of tried religious experience. Most of those who occupied positions of prominence in the community could give a reason for the faith that was in them. They had been sifted out of the mass of the Puritans of England. The struggles through which they had gone, the type of piety which they had heard inculcated, and their efforts to overcome the spiritual inertia of the English Establishment, engendered prevailingly a deep, emotional, introspective faith, which looked upon a conscious regenerative work of the spirit of God in the heart as essential to Christian hope. And as the New England fathers held strongly to the doctrine that the visible church should consist of none but evident Christians,[2] none were admitted to the adult membership of the churches who could not relate some instance of the transforming operation of God in their own lives. The peculiar experience of the Puritans made the test a natural one for the first generation of New England settlers, and the preponderating weight of opinion in the community viewed those who could not meet it as unfit for a share in the ordinances of the Gospel.[3] This view involved a radical departure from the practice of the English Establishment; but the early Congregationalists clung

[1] See the forcible assertion of the non-political character of this discussion in D. T. Fiske, *Discourse*, in *Cont. Eccles. Hist. Essex Co., Mass.*, Boston, 1865, pp. 271, 272.

[2] See Mather, *Church-Government*, pp. 8, 9 (Answer to No. 2 of XXXII Quest.); Hooker, *ante*, p. 143, etc.

[3] See e. g. Lechford, *Plain Dealing*, Trumbull's reprint, p. 29.

to a regenerate membership as an absolute essential to the properly constituted church.

But there was one exception to this rule that none were accounted of the church save those who could claim a definite religious experience and who had taken covenant pledges to each other and to God. The constitutive element in the church was the covenant, and this covenant, like that made with the house of Israel by God, was held to include not only the covenanting adult but his children.[1] Hence, from the first, the fathers of New England insisted that the children of church members were themselves members, or in the covenant, and as such were justly entitled to those church privileges which were adapted to their state of Christian development, of which the chief were baptism and the watchful discipline of the church.[2] They did not enter the church by baptism; they were entitled to baptism because they were already members of the church.[3] Here then was an inconsistency in the application of the Congregational theory of the constitution of a church. While affirming that a proper church consisted only of those possessed of personal Christian character, the fathers admitted to membership, in some degree at least, those who had no claim but Christian parentage. They sought to avoid the inconvenience of this duality of entrance by insisting that none who

---

1 Cotton affirmed: "The same Covenant which God made with the *Nationall* Church of *Israel* and their Seed, It is the very same (for substance) and none other which the Lord maketh with any *Congregationall* Church and our Seed." *Certain Queries Tending to Accommodation . . . of Presbyterian & Congregationall Churches*, London, 1654, p. 13.

2 Morton recorded, under date of 1629: "The two ministers [Skelton and Higginson at Salem] . . . considered of the state of their children, together with their parents; concerning which, letters did pass between Mr. Higginson and Mr. Brewster, the reverend elder of the church at Plimouth, and they did agree in their judgments, namely, concerning the church membership of the children with their parents." *Memoriall*, ed. 1855, p. 101.

Mather in *Church-Government* (Answer to 5 & 6 of the XXXII Questions), pp. 20, 21, said: "Infants with us are Admitted Members in and with their Parents, so as to be Admitted to all Church priviledges of which Infants are capable, as namely to Baptisme." "They [the baptized children of the church] are also under Church-watch, & consequently subject, to the reprehensions, admonitions, & censures therof, for their healing and amendment, as need shall require." *Camb. Platform*. See *ante*, p. 224.

3 "The nature and use of Baptisme is to be a seale to confirme the Covenant of Grace between God and his Church, and the Members thereof, as circumcision also was, *Rom*. 4. 11. Now a seale is not to make a thing that was not, but to confirme something that was before; and so Baptisme is not that which gives being to the Church, nor to the Covenant, but is for confirmation thereof." . . . "Children that are borne when their Parents are Church Members, are in Covenant with God even from their birth, *Gen*. 17. 7. 12. and their Baptisme did seale it to them." Mather, *Church-Government* (Ans. to 4, 5, & 6 of XXXII Quest.), pp. 12, 20, 21.

came into the church by birth ought to go on to the great privilege of adult years, the Lord's Supper, without a profession of personal regeneration.[1] But the difficulties of the situation were not apparent in any marked degree till the children of the first settlers came to maturity.[2] Then, in addition to the two great divisions of early days, — the consciously regenerate and those who laid no claim to Christian character, — there arose a third class of the population, and one ever since familiarly known in every New England town, — a class of men and women whose parents had been actively Christian, who had themselves been baptized and educated in the Christian faith, were well grounded in the knowledge of Christian truth, were students of the Bible and interested listeners in the sanctuary, who were desirous of bringing up their families in the way in which they themselves had been trained, and who were moral and earnest in their lives; yet could lay claim to no such experience as that which their parents had called a change of heart, and when asked as to any conscious work of God in their souls were compelled to admit that they could speak with confidence of none. It was the rise of this class that thrust the Half-Way Covenant problem upon the New England churches.

Three courses of treatment were open to the churches in dealing with these persons, — each course liable to serious objections. They might have been admitted to all the privileges of communion; and a few in New England, whose inclination toward the Presbyterian or Episcopal customs of the old country was strong, leaned even at an early period toward the admission to the Lord's Supper of all who were intellectually familiar with the truths of the Gospel and of exemplary moral life.[3] But this position met with no general advocacy even among the class whom it would be

---

1 "But notwithstanding their Birthright, we conceive there is a necessity of their personall profession of Faith, and taking hold of Church-Covenant when they come to yeares . . . for without this it cannot so well be discerned; what fitnesse is in them for the Lords Table." *Ibid.*, p. 21.

2 Compare Preface to the *Propositions* of 1662, p. xiii, on a later page.

3 This was the view of Child and his fellow petitioners in 1646. See *ante*, p. 165. At an earlier time, 1641–2, Lechford recorded: "Of late some Churches are of opinion, that any may be admitted to Church-fellowship, that are not extremely ignorant or scandalous: but this they are not very forward to practice, except at *Newberry*." *Plain Dealing*, pp. 21, 22, Trumbull's reprint, p. 56.

supposed most to benefit. It was too positive an abandonment of the principle that the church should consist only of visible saints to be acceptable to those who had been trained by the fathers of New England. Yet, though advocated by but few, the fear that such a lowering of the terms of communion would take place did much to secure the acceptance of the Half-Way Covenant as the lesser of two evils.[1]

A second way of disposing of the problem would have been to have denied to this class any right to church membership or church privileges. But this method of dealing was open to grave objections, both theoretic and practical. The class thus cut off from the churches would be large, it would leave the membership of the churches in a minority, it would give substance to the criticisms freely offered by the Puritan party in England that too large a portion of the inhabitants of New England were outside the churches as it was.[2] But more serious was the objection that all New England authorities had held these men and women to be by birth church-members, and the Congregational system of the day knew no way out of church covenant save death, dismission to another covenant fold, personal withdrawal from a church in evident error, or excommunication. And how was this class to be excommunicated when they had, in general, tried to live upright and godly lives, and the only charge against them was a want of a regenerative change which none but God could effect? The principle that men could enter a Congregational church by birth as well as by profession once admitted, the membership of these persons was indubitable; and if members, why could they not enjoy and transmit the privileges of the church to their offspring, at least in so far as they themselves had received them? If church membership was a hereditary matter, what authority was there for limiting its descent to a single generation? Then, too, there was

[1] Compare Mitchell, *A Defence of the Answer* [of 1662] . . . *Against the Reply made thereto by* . . . *J. Davenport* . . . *together with an Answer to the Apologetical Preface set before that Essay*, Cambridge, 1664, p. 45 (Mitchell's reply to Increase Mather). See also *Magnalia*, ed. 1853–5, II: 309, 310.

[2] See Quest. 1 of the XXXII Quest. *Church-Government*, p. 1. Lechford, *Plain Dealing*, p. 73, Trumbull's reprint, pp. 150–152.

a well-grounded fear on the part of many of the best men in New England that if the membership of the children of the church was denied, no basis would be left on which they could be held amenable to church discipline, and discipline was greatly valued by early Congregationalists as a means of Christian training. To deprive a large class in the community of its benefits seemed like giving them up to heathenism. Probably a dread of the prevalence of Baptist views, limiting baptism to adult believers, had also something to do with the reluctance of the New England pastors to confine the rite to the children of visible saints.[1]

The objections to each of these two methods of dealing with the problem were so great that the New England churches at length settled down on what was practically a compromise. The standing of the unregenerate members in the church was held to entitle them to transmit church membership and baptism to their offspring; but their non-regenerate character made it impossible that they should become partakers of the Lord's Supper. Members of the church they were, but not in "full communion." At the same time, so solemn was the privilege of baptism believed to be, that none of the non-regenerate members of the church could claim it for their children without assenting to the main truths of the Gospel scheme and promising fidelity and submission to the discipline of the church of which they were members; in the phrase of the time, "owning the covenant." This was the result reached by the Ministerial Convention of 1657 and the Synod of 1662. It gave standing in the church for the class of moral but not regenerate people, it kept them under the influence of Christian obligation and discipline, it required from them the evidence of an intelligent comprehension of religious truth, and a public profession of willingness to guide their lives by Gospel principles and bring up their children in the fear of God. But it demanded no personal sense of a change of heart. It was an illogical and inconsistent position; and as such could not long be maintained.

[1] John Allin of Dedham, in his *Animadversions upon the Antisynodalia Americana*, Cambridge, 1664, preface p. [ii], says: "We see evidently, that the Principles of our Dissenting Brethren give great Advantages to the *Antipædobaptists*, which if we be silent, will tend much to their Encouragement and Encrease, to the Hazard of our Churches."

Greatly modified early in the eighteenth century, it was wholly abandoned in the nineteenth. Its effects were on the whole evil, not so much from what it encouraged worldly men to do, as from its tendency to satisfy those who might have come out into full Christian experience with an intellectual faith and partial Christian privileges. It made a half-way house between the world and full Christian discipleship, where there should be none, and hence deserved the nickname given by its opponents, the Half-Way Covenant. It can scarcely be doubted that it would have been better for the New England churches had they either received all reputable persons to baptism and the Lord's Supper, or rejected all from any membership in the church who could not give evidence of personal Christian character.[1] But the twofold theory of entrance into the church prevented the adoption of either method of dealing with the second generation on New England soil, and that inconsistent theory was the real source of the Half-Way Covenant.

The position formulated in 1657 and 1662 was reached only after a long discussion and by a gradual development of public thought. It was no part of the plan of the founders of New England at their coming. The class which was to make it seem needful was yet in childhood. Leading theologians, like Hooker, Cotton, Davenport, and Richard Mather, asserted that none but children of "visible saints" should be baptized,[2] and while they declared at the same time that the children of such saints were church members, the consequences of such membership by birth had not become apparent.

But it was not long before cases arose in which this strictness seemed to involve undue severity. In 1634 a godly grandfather, a member apparently of the Dorchester church, whose son or daughter could claim no regenerative work of God, desired baptism for his grandchild, since baptism was the outward witness to

[1] See the remarks of Leonard Bacon, *Discourse*, in *Cont. Eccles. Hist. Conn.*, New Haven, 1861, pp. 20–22; and D. T. Fiske, *Cont. Eccles. Hist. Essex Co., Mass.*, Boston, 1865, pp. 279, 280.

[2] For Hooker's views see e. g. *Survey*, Pt. 3, pp. 9–27; Cotton, *Way of the Churches*, p. 81: "Infants cannot claime right unto Baptisme, but in the right of one of their parents, or both: where *neither* of the *Parents* can claime right to the Lords Supper, there their *infants* cannot claime right to *Baptisme*." Davenport, *Answer of the Elders . . . unto Nine Positions*, pp. 61–71. R. Mather, *Church-Government* (Ans. to 5–7 of XXXII Quest.), pp. 20–23.

that interest in the covenant which children of visible saints were held to possess by birth. The advice of the Boston church was sought, and there the matter was publicly debated, with a result favorable to the grandfather's request. The teacher, Cotton, and the two ruling elders, Oliver and Leverett, wrote to the Dorchester church as follows:[1]

"Though the Child be unclean where both the Parents are Pagans and Infidels, yet *we may not account such Parents for Pagans and Infidels, who are themselves baptized, and profess their belief of the Fundimental Articles of the Christian Faith, and live without notorious Scandalous Crime, though they give not clear evidence of their regenerate estate*, nor are convinced of the necessity of Church Covenant. . . . *We do therefore profess it to be the judgement of our* [Boston] *Church . . . that the Grand-Father a member of the Church, may claim the privilege of Baptisme to his Grand-Child, though his next Seed the Parents of the Child be not received themselves into Church Covenant.*"[2]

This was indeed a modification of the original New England theory, and was disapproved in principle by Hooker and Richard Mather[3] within the next few years. But it will cause no surprise to learn that, holding such views in 1634, Cotton felt able, before his death in 1652, to say of the offspring of church members:[4]

"Though they be not fit to make such profession of visible faith, as to admit them to the Lords Table, yet they may make profession full enough to receive them to Baptisme, or to the same estate *Ishmael* stood in after Circumcision."

The same feeling of the necessity of an enlargement of the terms of baptism which characterized Cotton was soon shared by other New England ministers. By 1642, Thomas Allen of Charlestown argued in favor of the extension of the rite to the children of godly parents not yet gathered into church fellowship.[5] Within a year or two thereafter George Phillips of Watertown expressed in the most positive language the abiding church membership not only of the immediate offspring of visible saints, but of all de-

[1] The letter, dated Dec. 16, 1634, is preserved in Increase Mather's *First Principles of New England*, Cambridge, 1675, pp. 2–4. The absence of the signature of the Boston pastor, Wilson, is explained by his presence at the time in England.

[2] *Ibid.*, pp. 3, 4. The permission was coupled with the conditions that the grandfather undertake the education of the child, and that the parents make this no occasion for neglect.

[3] See p. 250, note 2.

[4] *First Principles*, p. 6. The letter is without date. Other examples of Cotton's views will be found in the preface to the *Propositions* of 1662, on a later page.

[5] Teacher at Charlestown 1639–1651. The passage is found in a letter to Cotton quoted in Felt, *Eccles. Hist. N. E.*, I: 480.

scended from them; and though he does not speak in the passage of their claim to baptism, his words leave little doubt as to what his attitude would have been.[1] In 1645 Richard Mather of Dorchester wrote as follows,[2] replying to the question:

> "When those that were baptized in Infancy by the Covenant of their Parents being come to Age, are not yet found fit to be received to the Lords Table, although they be married and have Children, whether are those their Children to be baptized or no;"—"I propound to Consideration this Reason for the *Affirmative*, *viz.* That the Children of such Parents ought to be baptized: the Reason is, the Parents as they were born in the Covenant, so they still continue therein, being neither cast out, nor deserving so to be, and if so, why should not their Children be baptized, for if the Parents be in Covenant, are not the Children so likewise? . . . If it be said the Parents are not *Confirmed members*, nor have yet been found fit for the Lords Table, I conceive this needs not to hinder their Infants from Baptisme so long as they, I mean the Parents do neither renounce the Covenant, nor doth the Church see just Cause to Cast them out from the same."

In view of the declarations just cited, it is no wonder that the Massachusetts General Court, in its call for the Synod of 1646–8, was moved to say that in regard to "baptisme, & y[e] p'sons to be received thereto," "y[e] apphensions of many p'sons in y[e] country are knowne not a little to differ;" and that, though the majority of churches baptized only the offspring of visible saints, there were some who were much inclined to extend the application of the rite "as thinking more liberty and latitude in this point ought to be yielded then hath hitherto bene done."[3]

These views were by no means confined to Massachusetts. Henry Smith of Wethersfield, Conn., wrote to Richard Mather, under date of August 23, 1647:[4]

> "We are at a Loss in our parts about members Children, being received into Communion, because it is undetermined, in the extent of it, at the *Synod*,[5] our thoughts here are that the promise made to the Seed of Confederates, *Gen.* 17, takes in all Children of Confederating Parents."

Samuel Stone, the teacher of the Hartford church, sympa-

---

[1] Pastor at Watertown 1630 to his death, July, 1644. His views are expressed in *A Reply to a Confutation of some Grounds for Infant Baptism; as also, Concerning the form of a Church, put forth against me by one T. Lamb*, London, 1645. Quotations were made in the Preface to the *Propositions* of 1662, p. x. See later page of this work.

[2] In a manuscript entitled *A plea for the Churches of Christ in New-England*, quoted by Increase Mather, *First Principles*, pp. 10, 11.

[3] For the whole of this valuable statement, see *ante*, pp. 168–171.

[4] Pastor at Wethersfield 1641–1648. His letter is in I. Mather, *First Principles*, p. 24.

[5] The Cambridge Synod was still in being, having just adjourned for the second time.

thized with his Wethersfield neighbor,[1] and John Warham of Windsor, was of the same mind.[2]

Nor was Plymouth colony without its share of advocates for the larger practice. Ralph Partridge of Duxbury, one of the three ministers appointed to draw up a platform for the consideration of the Cambridge Synod,[3] inserted the following statement in the form which he laid before that body in 1648:[4]

"The persons unto whom the Sacrament of Baptisme is dispensed (and as we conceive ought to be) are such as being of years, and converted from their Sins to the Faith of Jesus Christ, do joyn in Communion and Fellowship with a particular visible Church, as also the children of such Parents or Parent, as having laid hold of the Covenant of grace (in the judgement of Charity) are in a *visible Covenant*, with his Church and all their Seed after them that cast not off the *Covenant* of God by some Scandalous and obstinate going on in Sin."

A similar position was advocated by Richard Mather in the form of the Platform presented by him.[5] These views were championed in the Synod by some influential members, and had the support of a majority; but were omitted from the final draft of the Platform owing to the opposition of a few led, it would seem, by Rev. Charles Chauncy.[6]

It must have been plain by 1650 in what direction the tide was running, and it could not be long before some church would begin to practice what so many eminent divines approved. Commendations of the larger view continued. The saintly Thomas Shepard of Cambridge declared himself in its favor just before his death in 1649.[7] By that time, Cotton was willing even to baptize adopt-

---

[1] Letter to R. Mather, June 6, 1650, *First Principles*, p. 9, in which he affirms "that Children of *Church members* have right to *Church membership* by virtue of their *Fathers Covenant* . . . . Hence, 1. If they be presented to a Church, and Claim their Interest, they cannot be denyed," and speaks as if he had long been of this mind.

[2] *Ibid.*, Warham changed his mind later on this question. As early as 1630, he told Fuller of Plymouth, that the visible "church may consist of a mixed people, godly and openly ungodly." He favored the Half-Way Covenant, and introduced its use into his own church in January, 1658. In March, 1665, he announced that he had been convinced that he was in error, and the practice was abandoned by the church till 1668. See *1 Coll. Mass. Hist. Soc.*, III : 74; Walker, *Hist. First Ch., Hartford*, pp. 189, 190.

[3] See *ante*, p. 175.

[4] *First Principles*, p. 23.

[5] See *ante*, p. 224, for Mather's own words.

[6] See *ante*, p. 181, and Preface to *Propositions* of 1662, p. xii *post*. Cotton Mather says that John Norton was one of the supporters of the larger view in the Synod, but "the fierce oppositions of one eminent person caused him that was of a *peaceable temper* to forbear urging them any further." *Magnalia*, ed. 1853–5, I : 291.

[7] Preface to *Propositions* of 1662, on later page; *First Principles*, p. 22.

ed children of church members, provided their parents had been religiously inclined, and John Eliot[1] and probably Richard Mather were of the same opinion.[2] The year 1650 saw Samuel Stone of Hartford fully committed to the Half-Way Covenant theory, anxious to have a new Synod called which might introduce uniformity of practice, and confident that, unless some such meeting was held that very year and reason to the contrary given, the Connecticut churches would begin the use of the new system.[3] In 1651, Peter Prudden of Milford, second only to Davenport in ability among the ministers of New Haven colony, declared in a letter of peculiar force of argument his hearty support of the Half-Way Covenant position.[4] Thus, more than ten years before the Synod of 1662, there were warm advocates of the larger application of baptism among the chief religious leaders of each of the New England colonies, and the affirmation is within the bounds of probability that even then the weight of opinion among ministers in every colony, with the possible exception of New Haven, was on that side. But while this was true of the elders of the churches as a body, there was a considerable degree of opposition to the new theories among the brethren of the churches. Just how much it is impossible to say, but there is reason to believe that the pastors were more ready to welcome the larger practice than the churches.[5] The ministers were, on the whole, keenly alive to the danger of losing hold of a large class of the population; their pastoral labors lent weight to those practical arguments which had much to do in convincing men of the desirability of the Half-Way Covenant; while in almost every church enough sticklers for the old ways would be found to make anything like unanimous action difficult to obtain in abandoning what

[1] The Apostle to the Indians, teacher of the Roxbury church.

[2] *First Principles*, pp. 5, 6.

[3] *Ibid.*, p. 9. Letter of June 6, 1650.

[4] Preface to *Propositions* of 1662, pp. xi, xii, on later page of this work; a selection is given in *First Principles*, pp. 25, 26.

[5] Cotton Mather, *Magnalia*, ed. 1853–5, II: 311, 312, says, speaking of the state of affairs after 1662, "Very gradual was the procedure of the churches to exercise that church-care of their children, which the synodical propositions had recommended; for, though the pastors were generally principled for it, yet, in very many of the churches, a number of brethren were so stiffly and fiercely set the other way, that the pastors did forbear to extend their practice unto the length of their judgment." This must have been as true of the decade before 1662.

some deemed the safeguards of church purity. This fact accounts for the slowness with which the Half-Way Covenant practice was introduced into the churches, long after it had been largely accepted by the ministers.

In what church the agitation of this question as a practical issue was first commenced is hard to say. Certainly the matter was under discussion at Salem in 1652, and by 1654, if not earlier, had resulted in the acceptance of Half-Way Covenant principles. But though this adhesion to the new views was reaffirmed in 1661, the opposition of a few prevented the actual administration of baptism there till July, 1665.[1] The church in Dorchester, of which that earnest advocate of the new methods, Richard Mather, was pastor, discussed the question in the opening weeks of 1655, and with the result that:[2]

"it came to vote & by divers was voted yt they were members & that haveinge children they should have ym baptized if ymselves did take hold of their ffathers Covenant (but wt that takeing hold of Covenant is, was not Clerely agreed upon) albeit ymselves beinge examinyed were ffound neither ffit ffor the Lords table nor voteing in the Church but this & other thinges seemed strange and unsaffe unto Divers in Conclusiō soe it was 4 Lres were sent to the churches of Boston, Roxbury, Dedham & Braintree to intimate unto ym wt was by us intended if in the space of a month or 6 weekes we did not heare Reasons from ym against or yt it would be offensive now ye 11, (1) 54[3] there came 3 Lres one frō Boston Dedham & Roxbury in all wch after kind and Religious salutations we ffind . . . Boston desires Rather our fforbearance & declares ther 2 votes upō wt we had done Dedham sees not Light to goe so farre as we & Roxbury though 'ivers of ym ffeare it might make th . . . [4] & bring in time the Corruption of old England wch we ffled ffrom yet have voted that they see noe cause to diswade us."

Thus dissuaded on the whole, the matter continued one of debate for years at Dorchester,[5] and it was not till January 29, 1677, when Richard Mather had been more than seven years in

[1] Church records in White, *N. E. Congregationalism*, pp. 49, 50, 60, 61; *First Principles*, p. 27.

[2] *Records First Ch. at Dorchester*, Boston, 1891, pp. 164, 165.

[3] *I.e.*, March 11, 1655.

[4] Illegible.

[5] See *Dorch, Records*, pp. 35, 36, 69–75. An illustration of the diversity of feeling at Dorchester is the exclamation of the writer in the church book: "27 7 57 . . . same daye Martha minott p'sented by her ffather — though he was noe memb accordinge to our church order: but a Corruptiō Creepinge in as an harbenger to old england practice viz. to make all members; (wch god prvent in mercye." *Ibid.*, p. 168. It does not appear that the child was baptized till 1665, after her mother had been admitted to full communion (p. 174); but one can sympathize with the deathbed lament of Richard Mather over his ill-success in introducing the Half-Way practice.

his grave, that the Dorchester church adopted the Half-Way practice.[1]

But other churches were meanwhile debating the subject also. A letter of Rev. Nathaniel Rogers, written from Ipswich, in January, 1653, declared of his church:[2]

"We are this week to meet in the Church about it, and I know nothing but we must speedily fall to practice. If we in this shall be Leaders, I pray beg wisdom from *the Father of Lights*."

But the discussions of that week dragged on, and it was not till 1656, when Thomas Cobbett was preaching in Rogers's room, that the Ipswich church became in truth the leader in the new practice. Its vote, which would seem to be the first actual adoption of the full system as the rule of a New England church, is in part as follows:[3]

"1. We look at children of members in full communion, which were about [i. e., not more than] fourteen years old when their father and mother joined the Church, or have been born since, to be members in and with their parents. . . . 4. We look upon it as the Elder's duty to call upon such children, being adults, and are of understanding, and not scandalous, to take the covenant solemnly before our Assembly. 5. We judge that the children of such adult persons, that are of understanding, and not scandalous, and shall take the Covenant, shall be baptized. 6. That notwithstanding the baptizing the children of such, yet we judge that these adult persons are not to come to the Lord's Supper, nor to act in Church votes, unless they satisfy the reasonable charity of the Elders or Church, that they have a work of faith and repentance in them." [4]

Naturally this debate was not confined to Massachusetts. The questions raised were of interest to the churches throughout New England, and nowhere more than in Connecticut, where Half-Way Covenant views had been advocated by Stone and Warham and Smith. It so happened, also, that from 1653 to 1659 one of the bitterest quarrels in New England ecclesiastical history raged at Hartford, and spite of the efforts of the ministers and legislature of Connecticut and the advice of elders from other colonies, caused the secession of a considerable body from the Hartford

---

1 *Ibid.*, pp. 69–75, vote of "29 11 76."

2 The letter is dated 18. 11. 1652, *i. e.*, Jan. 18, 1653. *First Principles*, pp. 23, 24.

3 Ipswich Ch. Rec. in Felt, *Eccles. Hist. N. E.*, II: 141.

4 Notice that voting is not a Half-Way Covenant privilege. This reservation is made equally clearly in the Decisions of 1657 and 1662. The statement of Prof. Johnston (*Connecticut*, p. 227) that the Half-Way system "gave every baptized person a voice in church government" is baseless.

church and the settlement of Hadley, Mass.[1] This quarrel has not infrequently been represented as the beginning of the Half-Way Covenant controversy in New England. No opinion is more erroneous. At a later period, from about 1666 to 1670, the question of baptism tore the Hartford flock, and at the latter date resulted in its division for the second time and the formation of the present Second Church in Hartford; but in the first division baptism was no factor. A quarrel between Samuel Stone, the teacher, and William Goodwin, the ruling elder, in regard to the choice of a successor to the pastorate made vacant by the death of Thomas Hooker, involved the whole church, and while essentially a personal dispute, raised some interesting questions as to the relations of the officers and brethren in a Congregational church. But while there is no evidence that the extent of baptism was one of the dividing issues between 1653 and 1659 in the Hartford church, this condition of turmoil existing in the leading church in the colony very probably led to a considerable discussion of all questions affecting church procedure throughout the little commonwealth. It was rather as the consequence of this general agitation than of the special problems at Hartford that a petition was presented to the Connecticut General Court, at its session May 15, 1656, by persons whose names have not been preserved, but desirous, it would seem, of some enlargement of the terms of baptism. The form of the petition is unknown to us, but the Court voted that :[2]

"Mr. Governo^{r} [John Webster], Mr. Deputy [Thomas Welles], Mr. [John] Cullick & Mr. Tailcoat [John Talcott] are desired in some convenient time to advise wth the elders of this Jurisdiction about those things y^{t} are p^{r}sented to this Courte as grevances to severall persons amongst vs ; (and if they judge it nessisary,) to crave their healpe & assistance in drawing up an abstract from the heads of those things, to be p^{r}sented to the Gen : Courtes of the severall vnited Collonyes, and to desire an answer thereunto as sone as conveniently may be." [3]

The work appointed to this committee was duly performed.

---

1 The story of this quarrel was told for the first time with fullness by G. L. Walker, *History of the First Church in Hartford*, pp. 146–175.

2 *Conn. Records*, I: 281.

3 How little this dispute was connected with the quarrel of 1653–9 in the Hartford church is illustrated by the fact that Webster and Cullick were among the most prominent of Stone's opponents.

A list of questions was drawn up[1] and sent to the General Court of Massachusetts during the summer of 1656. Whether the other colonies were also consulted, as the vote directed, it is perhaps impossible to say.[2] Thus overtured, the Massachusetts Court took prompt action at its session October 14, 1656, as follows:[3]

"A letter from the Generall Court of Conecticot was presented to this Court, (together wth seuerall quæstions of practicall concernment in the churches,) wherein they propound theire desires of our concurranc wth them in desiring the help of the elders, for the resolution and clearing the sajd quæstions, and for that end that a tjme and place of meeting be assigned by this Court, and notice thereof may be given to the rest of the colonjes, that they may haue the op'tunitje to contribute theire asistance to this worke. The Court, considering the premises, doth order, that Mr Mather,[4] Mr Allyn,[5] Mr Norton,[6] Mr Thatcher,[7] of the county of Suffolke, Mr Bulkely,[8] if he cann come, Mr Chauncey,[9] Mr Syms,[10] Mr Sherman,[11] Mr Michells,[12] of the county of Midlesex, Mr Norrice,[13] Mr Ezekiell Rogers,[14] Mr Whiting,[15] Mr Cobbet,[16] of ye county of Essex, be desired to meet at Boston the first fifth day of June[17] next following, to conferr and debate the sajd quæstions, or any other of like nature that shall or maybe propounded to them by this Court, either amongst themselves or wth such divines as shallbe sent to the sajd meeting from the other colonjes; and it is expected that the resolution of the sajd quæstions, together wth the grounds & reasons thereof, be presented to the Generall Court, to be comunicated and comended to such of ours that want information therein; and it is heereby ordered, that Robert Turner[18] take care to provide convenjent entertaynement for the sajd gent^n during theire attendance on the sajd meeting, and that the charges of those of this jurisdiccon be defrajed by the Tresurer; and it is further ordered, that, together wth the letter & quærjes from Conecticott, a coppy of this order be sent to all the confœderated colonjes, wth a letter from this Court desiring theire assistanc in this buisnes at the tjme & place aforesajd, y^t the secretary send a copy hereof, wth the quærjes, to one of the elders of each county."

Pursuant to this order the secretary, Edward Rawson, sent out the letters to the various colonial governments on October 22,

---

[1] These were doubtless substantially the XXI Questions answered by the Assembly at Boston in 1657. The list given by Trumbull, *Hist. Conn.*, I: 302, 303, is an error. It really belongs in 1666. See *Conn. Records*, II: 54, 55.

[2] The letter of the New Haven Court in reply to that of the Massachusetts body, February, 1657, seems to imply that they had not been directly consulted by Connecticut.

[3] *Records . . . Mass. Bay*, III: 419; IV: 1: 280.

[4] Richard Mather, Dorchester: all the names are those of ministers.

[5] John Allin, Dedham. [6] John Norton, Boston. [7] Thomas Thacher, Weymouth.

[8] Peter Bulkeley, Concord; nearly 74 years old.

[9] Charles Chauncy, Pres. Harvard Coll. 1654–1672. [10] Zechariah Symmes, Charlestown.

[11] John Sherman, Watertown. [12] Jonathan Mitchell, Cambridge.

[13] Edward Norris, Salem. [14] Of Rowley.

[15] Samuel Whiting, Lynn. [16] Thomas Cobbett, Ipswich.

[17] *i. e.*, June 4, 1657.

[18] Robert Turner was one of the licensed innkeepers of Boston. See *Mass. Records*, *passim*.

1656.[1] That to New Haven was thirty-six days on its way.[2] Their reception by the three lesser colonies was various. Plymouth appears to have taken no action. Connecticut of course responded favorably, the Massachusetts Court had carried into effect the Connecticut request, and on February 26, 1657, the Court of Connecticut voted:[3]

"This Court doth order that Mr. Warham,[4] Mr. Stone,[5] Mr. Blinman[6] & Mr. Russell[7] bee desired to meet, the first fifth day of June next, at Boston, to conferre & debate the questions formerly sent to the Bay Court, or any other of the like nature that shall bee p^r^pounded to them by that Court or by o^r^ owne, wth such divines as shall bee sent to the said meeting from the other Collonies; and that they make a returne to the Gen: Court of the issue of their consultations."

At the same time a proposition to send twelve questions in addition, the nature of which it is now impossible to determine, was defeated.[8] With regard to provision for the expenses of their representatives the Court of Connecticut was no less careful than that of Massachusetts:[9]

"It is also ordered, that the Deputies, wth the Deacons of the Church in each towne, take care that their said Eld^rs^ bee comely & honorably attended & suited wth necessaries in their journey to the Bay and home againe; and that the same, wth their p^r^portion of charge in the Bay, during their abode there vpon this seruice, bee discharged by the Treasurer; and also the Deputies are impowered to presse horses (if need bee,) for the end aforesaid."

And, not content with providing for the material wants of the Assembly, the Court ordered that Wednesday, March 25th, should:[10]

"bee obserued & kept a day of publicke humilliation, by all the Plantations in this [Connecticut] Jurisdiction, to seeke the presence, guidance & direction of the Lord in reference to the Synnod."

Two days before the Court of Connecticut had given its favorable response to the overtures from Massachusetts, the legislative body of New Haven colony had considered the same proposition and come to exactly opposite conclusions. In that colony the influence of John Davenport, the pastor of the New Haven church, was dominant and was set counter to the Half-Way Covenant

---

[1] *New Haven Records*, II: 196.

[2] *Ibid.*

[3] *Conn. Records*, I: 288.

[4] John Warham, Windsor; all were ministers.

[5] Samuel Stone, Hartford.

[6] Richard Blinman, New London.

[7] John Russell, Wethersfield.

[8] *Conn. Records*, I: 288.

[9] *Ibid.*, p. 289.

[10] *Ibid.*, p. 293.

theories. It was natural, therefore, that when the letter from Massachusetts was read to the Court at New Haven on February 24, 1657,[1] and "the help of such elders as were present" was taken, that colony should refuse to have part in the proposed Assembly. Their declinature was set forth in a long letter signed by their governor, Theophilus Eaton, and addressed to the Massachusetts Court.[2] They breathe not a little jealousy of their Connecticut neighbors, and hold that the Connecticut Court in dealing with its petitioners should have imitated the good example of Massachusetts as illustrated in the summary treatment of Child and his associates in 1646. They are fearful that a synod may bring in results of which they could not approve, but which they would find it hard to resist.[3] They are especially suspicious of the motives of the Connecticut petitioners, who, they tell the Massachusetts Court, they:[4]

"heare . . . are very confident they shall obteyne great alterations, both in ciuill gouernm^t^ and in church discipline, and that some of them haue procured or hyred one as their agent to maintayne in writing, (as is conceived) that parishes in England, consenting to and continewing their meetings to worship God, are true churches, and such persons comeing ouer hether, (w^t^hout holding forth any worke of faith, &c.,) haue right to all church priveledges."

For their own part the New Haven representatives counsel a firm adherence to the old ways. They:[5]

"hope the generall courts, who haue framed their ciuill polity and lawes according to the rules of Gods most holy word, and the elders and churches who haue gathered and received their discipline out of the same holy scriptures, will vnanimously improve their power and indeavours to preserue the same invyolably."

And finally they plead the recent removal or death of a number of their ministers as an excuse for non-representation in the Assembly, a representation which, it is easy to see, they were anxious to

---

1 *New Haven Records*, II: 195; the date is given in the old style as "24th 12th mo, 1656."

2 *Ibid.*, 196–198. Dated Feb. 25, 1656 [7].

3 "Though they [i. e. the N. H. Court] approved yor readines to afford help when the case requires it, yet themselues conceive that the elders of Connecticote colony, wth due assistance from their court, had bine fully sufficient to cleare and maintayne the truth and to suppress the boldness of such petitioners, (according to a good president you gaue ye colony, some yeares since, in a case not much differring,) wthout calling a synod, or any such meeting, wch in such times may prove dangerous to ye puritie and peace of these churches and colonies." For the case of Child see *ante*, pp. 164–181.

4 *Ibid.*

5 *Ibid.*, 197.

avoid. In order, however, that there should be no mistake regarding their conservative position on the points at issue, they accompanied their letter by a formal reply to the proposed Questions, drawn up by John Davenport, and bearing the approval of the Court,—a document designed for presentation to the Assembly, should it be held.[1]

The refusal of New Haven and the non-action of Plymouth had no effect on the meeting of the Ministerial Assembly.[2] Most of the thirteen ministers chosen by Massachusetts and the four representatives of Connecticut came together at Boston, June 4, 1657, and their debates lasted till the 19th of the month.[3] Of the course of discussion and the events of the meeting we know nothing. The result could not have been unanimous, if Chauncy, later the champion of the conservative view, was present. But there was doubtless substantial agreement in the conclusions at which the assembly arrived. The membership of the children of church members was affirmed. That membership was declared to be personal and permanent, and sufficient to entitle the member by birth, even though not personally regenerate, to transmit membership and a right to baptism to his children, on condition of an express acknowledgment on his part of at least an intellectual faith and a desire to submit to all the covenant obligations implied in membership. Yet though this membership is complete, as far as it goes, it is not sufficient to admit to full communion or to a vote in church affairs. For these further privileges a profession of personal regeneration is necessary. The result was drawn up in the form of answers to each of the twenty-one questions,[4] written in a clear and often forcible style; and was from the pen of Richard Mather of Dorchester.[5]

---

[1] *Ibid.*, 198.

[2] This meeting, even in the action of the legislatures of the time, is loosely called a "Synod." It lacked however the essential element of representatives of the churches to make it a properly constituted synod. See Cambridge Platform, *ante*, p. 234.

[3] The Result is thus dated. Regarding the attendance Nathanael Mather says: "There being but about twenty called . . . and of those twenty, two or three met not with the rest." Preface to *Answer to XXI Questions*, on later page.

[4] Large extracts are given at the conclusion of this chapter.

[5] See Dexter, *Congregationalism as seen;* Bibl., p. 287. The result was never officially published. A copy was taken over to England, probably by Increase Mather, and published at London, 1659, with a preface by Nathanael Mather.

The Assembly having fully accepted the Half-Way Covenant principles, its members went to their homes. Whether the conclusions were presented to the Massachusetts Court, as directed in the call, it is impossible to say. No action regarding them is entered in the Records of that commonwealth. But in Connecticut their reception was noted as follows:[1]

"A true coppy of the Counsells answere to seuerall questions sent to the Massachusets from o^r^ Generall Court, being p^r^sented to this Court, signed by the Reuerend Mr. Sam : Stone, in the name of the rest of the Counsell, They doe order that coppies should goe forth to the seu^r^all Churches in this Collony as speedily, & if any exceptions bee against any thing therein, by any Church that shall haue the consideration thereof, the Court desires they would acquaint the next Gen : Court in Hartford, in Octo^r^ : that so suitable care may bee had for their solution & satisfaction."

Yet though the churches were thus urged and though the church at Windsor, if no other, began practicing the recommendations of the Assembly on January 31, 1658,[2] no "exceptions" are known to have been presented to the General Court. That this was the case was not due to any such degree of unanimity in favor of the newer views among the brethren of the churches of Connecticut as existed among the ministers. It is scarcely probable that other churches immediately followed the example of Windsor.[3] Public attention in Connecticut was diverted from the baptismal question by the aggravated form which the dispute in the Hartford Church had assumed, and by the fact that the quarrel had provoked a similar personal disagreement between a portion of the Wethersfield church and its minister, John Russell.[4] This protracted controversy, in which baptism was not a prime factor, issued in 1659 and 1660, in the removal of ex-Gov. John Webster, William Goodwin, the ruling elder of the Hartford church, Rev. John Russell, and other persons of prominence in the community to Hadley, Mass. But though public attention was drawn

[1] *Conn. Records*, I: 302, Aug. 12, 1657.

[2] Church Records, in Stiles, *History of Ancient Windsor*, New York, 1859, p. 172.

[3] As late as 1666, John Davenport was able to affirm that, beside the churches in what had been New Haven colony and at Stratford and Norwalk, Farmington, "the sounder parte of Windsor," and, he thinks, Norwich favored the old way. 3 *Coll. Mass. Hist. Soc.*, X: 60. The Half-Way Covenant was probably first used at Hartford soon after 1666. Trumbull, *Hist. Conn.*, I: 471, fell into the great error of holding that the system was not introduced into practice in Conn. till 1696.

[4] See *Conn. Records*, I: 319; Trumbull, *Hist. Conn.*, I: 309, 310.

aside for a time, the Half-Way Covenant views steadily won ground in Connecticut, and when the controversy reappeared the opponents in the churches were clearly in the minority.[1]

In Massachusetts a similar division of sentiment, greater by far among the brethren than among the pastors of the churches, probably prevented any immediate action favorable to the Half-Way Covenant system from the General Court. Discussion continued, and brought with it danger of serious division. The situation was made more critical when the Restoration, in 1660, brought into power in England the party hostile to the New England church-way.[2] It seemed more than ever desirable that uniformity of practice should prevail; and the civil power, which had taken the initiative in securing the decisions of 1648 and 1657, once more interfered. The Assembly of 1657 had been a mere meeting of at most a score of ministers. The General Court of Massachusetts determined to call a proper Synod, composed of all the ministers and the representatives of all the churches in the colony. Its action would not affect Connecticut, New Haven, or Plymouth, save by example, since these colonies were not asked to share in the Synod; but for Massachusetts it was hoped the action would be definitive. The prime matter to be settled was that problem of baptism which the Cambridge Synod of 1646–8 had evaded, and which the Assembly of 1657 had answered so fully in the spirit of the Half-Way Covenant. Accordingly, on December 31, 1661, the Massachusetts Court issued this sharp and peremptory order:[3]

"This Court, hauing taken into consideration that there are seuerall questions & doubts yet depending in the churches of this jurisdiction concerning seuerall practicall poynts of church disciplyne, doe therefore order & hereby desire, that the churches aforesajd doe send theire messengers of elders & brethren to Boston the 2ᵈ Twesday of the first moneth,[4] then & there to discusse & declare what they

[1] The year 1657 saw a curious limitation of the franchise in Connecticut, the causes of which are not very evident. (*Conn. Records*, I: 293: "This Court doth order, that by admitted inhabitants, specified in the 7th Fundamentall [of the constitution of 1639], are meant only housholders that are one & twenty yeares of age, or haue bore office, or haue 30 *l.* estate.") But its connection with the Half-Way discussion, if any, is not apparent. See also Andrews, *River Towns of Connecticut*, pp. 85–89.

[2] See Palfrey, *Hist. N. E.*, II: 490.

[3] *Records . . . Mass. Bay*, IV: 2: 38.

[4] *I. e.*, March 11, 1662.

shall judge to be the minde of God, revealed in his word, concerning such questions as shall be propounded to them by order of this Court referring to church orders as aforesajd, and that the seuerall churches take care to make due provition for the messengers by them sent.

This Court doe further order, as a meete expedient for the furtheranc of th' ends proposed in calling a synod to be kept by the messengers of all ye churches in this jurisdiction the 2^d^ Twesday in March next, that the neighboring elders, wth as much convenient speed as may be, doe meete together & consider of such questions, besides what is here vnder proposed, as they shall judge necessary to be then & there discussed for the setling of peace & trueth in these churches of Christ, & make theire returne wth as much convenient speede as may be to y^r^ Gou'no^r^ or secretary, who is to speede away a copie thereof, wth the Generall Courts order, to the seuerall churches, requiring them to send theire messengers to attend the sajd meeting."

The hasty gathering of the ministers of Boston and the adjacent towns, thus peremptorily summoned, met at once, and added to the problem of baptism, which the Court had in mind, a second question, regarding councils and the mutual relations of the churches, for the consideration of the Synod. The Court recorded the two subjects for discussion on the same page on which it minuted the call for the deliberative body: [1]

Quæst 1. Who are the subjects of baptisme.

Quæst 2. Whither, according to the word of God, there ought to be a consociation of churches, & what should be ye manner of it.

This last question was returned to ye secretary by ye elders.

Thus issued by the civil authorities of the commonwealth, the call for the Synod went forth to the Massachusetts churches. Its reception in them as a whole may perhaps be judged from the records of the Salem church[2]—

"On the 26th of 12th month,[3] being the Sabbath day, was read an order from the Gen. Court, for calling of a Synod, this Church (as the rest of the Churches in the Colony) being desired to send their messengers of Elders and brethren to Boston on the 10th of the 1st month[4] [etc]. . . . It was left unto consideration till the

---

[1] *Ibid.* This paragraph immediately follows the call quoted above, though of course a day or two must have intervened between the two votes to allow for a meeting of the ministers of the Boston vicinage, which the second vote implies had already taken place. The explanation is in the fact that the arrangement of the records of business at any particular meeting of the Court was seldom strictly chronological. See the editor's remarks in the prefaces to various volumes of the *Records.*

[2] White, *N. E. Congregationalism*, p. 53.

[3] This date is an error. It should be Jan. 26, 1662, a Sunday; Feb. 26, as here given, was Wednesday.

[4] The day mentioned in the call falls on March 11 and not the 10th.

Lord's day following, when Major Hawthorne, Mr. Bartholmew, and the Pastor[1] were chosen to go to the Synod at the time appointed."

The second Tuesday in March, 1662, saw, therefore, the coming together in the meeting-house of the First Church[2] in Boston of more than seventy representatives[3] of the Massachusetts churches. We know nothing in detail of the organization of the body, nor are we able to identify more than a few of those who were probably present as actually there.[4] It has been said, but the statement lacks positive proof, that the presiding officer at the sessions was Samuel Whiting, the venerable pastor at Lynn[5]—a man in every way fitted for the task. In the ranks of the ministerial membership were such lights of the New England pulpit as John Wilson[6] and John Norton[7] of the First Boston Church, Richard Mather[8] of Dorchester, with his sons Eleazer[9] of Northampton, and Increase,[10] just beginning his ministry in the Second Church of Boston. John Allin[11] of Dedham was there, and Zechariah Symmes[12] of Charlestown; Salem sent John Higginson,[13] Newbury the Presbyterianly inclined Thomas Parker.[14] From Cambridge came the venerable Charles Chauncy,[15] president of Harvard College; and the young, gifted Jonathan Mitchell,[16] pastor of the Cambridge church; with them, also, was John Mayo,[17] of the Second Boston

---

1 About this proportion of two representatives of the brethren to each minister must have been general, since all the ministers then in regular service in the colony numbered only 34, of whom, judging from the usual history of Synods, some must have been absent, and the total attendance was "above seventy."

2 Dexter, in *Cong. Quart.*, IV: 274.

3 *Ibid.*, from Mitchell, *Answer* [to I. Mather] *Apologetical Preface*, p. 3.

4 A list, nearly complete, of those who would be entitled to a place in the Synod as ministers is given by Dexter, *Cong. Quart.*, IV: 274.

5 Dexter, *Ibid.* Drake, *History of Boston*, Boston, 1852–6, I: 361. His biography is in the *Magnalia*, ed. 1853–5, I: 501–511. Perhaps a hint of this is contained in Thompson's elegiac verses on Whiting, *Ibid.*,

"Profoundest *judgment*, with a *meekness* rare,
Preferr'd him to the Moderator's chair," etc.

6 *Records . . . Mass. Bay*, IV: 2: 60.

7 Dexter, *Cong. Quart.*, IV: 274, omits Norton from his list of those possibly present. He returned from England, however, in time to take an active part in the closing session. See Letter of Increase Mather to John Davenport, in Hutchinson, *Hist. Mass. Bay*, ed. 1765, I: 224.

8 *Records . . . Mass. Bay*, *Ibid.; Records First Ch. Dorchester*, p 39.

9 Hutchinson, *Ibid.*

10 Increase Mather was a delegate from his father's church at Dorchester, *Records*, etc., p. 39.

11 *Rec. Mass. Bay*, *Ibid.*

12 *Ibid.*

13 White, *N. E. Cong.*, p. 53.

14 Hutchinson, *Ibid.*

15 *Ibid.* Doubtless as a representative of the Cambridge church.

16 Mather, *Magnalia*, ed. 1853–5, II: 99.

17 Hutchinson, *Ibid.*

church. The gathering included many from the rapidly thinning ranks of the first generation on New England soil; it numbered also the brilliant names which adorn the story of their children. And as the result of the Synod was but the working out of principles inherent in the Congregationalism of the founders of New England, so the votes by which it was adopted came in no small measure from those who were among the pioneers in the settlement of our towns and churches.

Of all who were present, those most conspicuous in debate were Jonathan Mitchell[1] on the side favoring the Half-Way Covenant; and, probably, Pres. Chauncy[2] among its opponents. To the persuasive skill of Mitchell, more than to any other, the result in 1662 was due, and the form in which it was cast was largely the product of his pen.[3]

The Synod which assembled in March, 1662, found that it had a severe task. At least eight or nine of the seventy present,[4] and probably even more at the early sessions,[5] opposed any admission of Half-Way principles. This opposition included a man of great prominence, Pres. Chauncy, and the two ministers of the Second Church in Boston, Mayo and Increase Mather,[6] the latter joined by his brother Eleazer of Northampton. They made a force formidable for quality if not for numbers. Thomas Parker of Newbury was a Presbyterian free-lance, though he had little fol-

---

1 Jonathan Mitchell was born in England in 1624, graduated Harvard College 1647, settled at Cambridge 1650, died July 9, 1668. Of brilliant powers of mind, marked piety, and kindly in spirit, he was one of the most prominent of the second generation of New England ministers. His biography is given by Mather, *Magnalia*, II: 66–113. See also Sibley, *Harvard Graduates*, Cambridge, 1873, I: 141–157, where a full list of his writings and ample references to biographical sources will be found.

2 Charles Chauncy was born in England in 1589, educated at Cambridge, settled at Ware, Eng., in 1627, suspended by Laud 1635, came to Plymouth, Mass., 1638, and soon settled at Scituate. In 1654 he became the second president of Harvard, an office which he retained till his death, Feb. 19, 1672. For his biography see Mather, *Magnalia*, I: 463–476; Allen, *Am. Biog. Dict.*, ed. 1857, pp. 213–215.

3 Mather, *Magnalia*, II: 99.

4 Mitchell, *Answer* to Increase Mather's *Apologetical Preface*, p. 3. "We suppose there were not *Five twice told* that did in any thing Vote on the Negative." *Ibid.*

5 Chauncy says: "Diverse of the Messengers [in this case the lay messengers] being no Logitians, and so unable to answer Syllogismes, and discern Ambiguities, were over-born." *Anti-Synodalia*, p. 5.

6 Increase Mather was of course not yet settled, though preaching at Boston. He sat for Dorchester. He later changed his views through the influence of Mitchell, and supported the result of the Synod, which his father, Richard Mather, always approved.

lowing;[1] and others criticised various features of the existing usages of the churches.[2] So it came about that "the Synod continuing together almost a fortnight, finding the questions to be weighty, and that divers of them could not then stay longer together, they adjourned the Synod to the 10th of the 4th month next."[3]

The session thus suspended was resumed on June 10th; but was once more adjourned, this time to September 10th.[4] Soon after the close of the second session Eleazer Mather had written to John Davenport of New Haven,[5] and that champion of the older method was stirred, either by Mather's letter or the news of the Synod's doings which came to him through other channels, to send on in writing his objections to the views of the majority. This document, which, as emanating from a minister of another colony, had no pertinence in a Massachusetts Synod, Increase Mather attempted to read to the body on its reassembling in September. The opposition of John Norton of Boston prevented, but a copy was put in circulation by Increase Mather and attracted considerable attention.[6]

It was, we may suppose, at the September session that the Propositions in which the Synod embodied its conclusions took on their final form. Their exact phraseology was the subject of much debate and was fixed by the Synod itself in each case.[7] The most fiercely contested battle ground was the fifth Proposition, of which three draughts were submitted to the body.[8] Against this Chauncy

---

1 "Mr. Parker, of Newbury, was one of the great antagonists of the congregational way and order, though it not being the work of the present synod, his many motions, to consider whether we were in the right ecclesiastical order, were not attended." E. Mather to J. Davenport, Hutchinson, I: 224.

2 "There was scarce any of the congregational principles, but what were layen at, by some or other of the assembly; as relations of the work of grace, power of voting of the fraternity in admission," etc. *Ibid.*

3 Salem Ch. Records, in White, *N. E. Congregationalism*, p. 54. In each instance of adjournment "notice was given the [Salem] Church."

4 *Ibid.*

5 July 4, 1662, quoted by Hutchinson.

6 Letter of I. Mather to J. Davenport, Oct. 21, 1662, quoted in Hutchinson, I: 224.

7 "The Propositions . . . were (after much discussion and consideration from the Word of God) Voted and Concluded by the Assembly in *the particular terms* as they are here expressed." Preface to *Propositions* of 1662, on later page.

8 Chauncy said: "There hath been three expressions of this proposition, and this [in the Result] swerves further off from Scripture then both the former." *Anti-Synodalia*, p. 27.

and his friends energetically labored, since it granted baptism to all children of persons themselves baptized who professed an intellectual faith, owned the covenant, and submitted to church discipline. But it is with a little surprise that we learn that the third Proposition, declaring the membership by birth of the children of visible believers, was brought forward by one of the leaders of the minority, possibly Chauncy himself.[1] No wonder that Mitchell could say of this proposition "some think [it] *carries the whole cause;*"[2] and the championing of this view of the status of the children of church members, while their right to bring their offspring to baptism was denied, is an illustration of the inconsistency of the position taken throughout the controversy by the opponents of the Half-Way Covenant, an inconsistency which gave them less weight than the general merits of their criticisms deserved. Having carefully formulated the Propositions regarding baptism, the Synod listened to several readings of the arguments by which they were supported, and voted their approbation.[3]

The first of the two Questions propounded by the Court having thus been disposed of by a vote of more than seven to one[4] in favor of the Half-Way Covenant system, the Synod hastily[5] took up the second Question, that in relation to "Consociation of Churches," or, as modern usage would say, Fellowship between Churches. Here the Synod, wearied with its work, and deeming the query of comparatively minor importance, did little more than reaffirm by a vote lacking but one of unanimity,[6] the principles laid down in the Cambridge Platform.

Soon after the termination of the Synod,[7] its conclusions were reported to the Massachusetts Court, October 8, 1662, by a committee consisting of four ministers, John Wilson, Richard Mather,

---

1 "One of the chief of our Dissenting Brethren did propound, and earnestly promote the third Proposition," Allin, *Animadversions upon the Anti-Synodalia*, p. 13.

2 Mitchell, *Answer* to Increase Mather's *Apologetical Preface*, p. 3, margin.

3 Preface to *Propositions* of 1662, on later page.

4 Mather, *Magnalia*, ed. 1853–5, II: 302.

5 "The Answer to the *second Question* is here given with great brevity . . . partly by reason of great straits of time," Preface to *Propositions* of 1662.

6 "There was a marvellous Unanimity; not one Elder, nor so much as two Brethren in all that Reverend Assembly dissenting." Increase Mather, *Disquisition Concerning Ecclesiastical Councils*, Boston, 1716, p. 37. Reprinted *Cong. Quart.*, XII: 365.

7 The day of adjournment is unknown.

John Allin, and Zechariah Symmes.[1] At the same time Increase Mather presented to the Court the objections formulated by John Davenport which the Synod had refused to hear. This he accompanied by a preface signed by Chauncy, Mayo, Eleazer Mather, and himself, in the name of the opposition.[2] The objectors' protest fared scarcely better than in the Synod; the utmost that the Court would grant was freedom from interference should the opponents see fit to print.[3] As for the Propositions voted by the majority, on the other hand:[4]

"the Court, on their pervsall, judged it meete to comēnd the same vnto the consideration of all the churches & people of this [Massachusetts] jurisdiction, and for that end ordered the printing thereof, the originall copie being left on file."

At the same time the Court advised that the committee should see to it:[5]

"that an epistle or p'face suiteable to the sajd worke be forthwith prepared, & sent to the presse, & that Mr Mitchell doe take the ouersight of the same at the presse, for the p'venting of any errata^rs."

The result was the publication of the Propositions by the press at Cambridge within a few weeks, while before the conclusion of the year an unofficial edition was brought out at London, having as an appendix the answer written by Chauncy and known as the *Anti-Synodalia Scripta Americana.*

These publications started a flood of controversial pamphlets heretofore unexampled in the history of the new world, and which must have taxed the capacities of the Cambridge press, though they added little light to the controversy. Chauncy and Davenport were promptly in the field urging that the new method would open the doors of the churches to the unworthy; and with them stood Increase Mather of Boston and Nicholas Street of New Haven. Mitchell, Allin, and Richard Mather were as forward to defend the result of the Synod;[6] and with more effect than is usual

---

1 *Records . . . Mass. Bay*, IV: 2: 60.

2 Letter to John Davenport, Hutchinson, *Hist. . . . Mass. Bay*, I: 224.

3 "Some of the court would fain have thrown them out [the objections] without reading, but the major part were not so violent. It was moved they might be printed. All the answer we could get, was, that we might do as we would. We count it a favour we were not commanded to be silent." *Ibid.*

4 *Records . . . Mass. Bay*, IV: 2: 60.

5 *Ibid.*, 62.

6 For details of these pamphlets see *ante*, p. 239.

in such controversies, for the arguments of Mitchell won over Increase Mather,[1] who became within less than ten years after the Synod the chief defender of its conclusions.[2] The Massachusetts Court left the question to the churches without further interference, and the Half-Way Covenant view, though the popular and growing theory, long met with disapproval among the brethren of many congregations.[3] Fifty years after the Synod there were still opposing churches[4] in Massachusetts.

The result of the Synod of 1662, being purely local in its application, called for no action on the part of the General Court of Connecticut. That colony had, at the moment, a most delicate question on its hands. The diplomatic ability of the younger Winthrop had secured from the recently restored Charles II. of England, in 1662, a charter not only granting practical local independence but adding the colony of New Haven to the Connecticut jurisdiction, much against the will of the former. The situation was made the more difficult because New Haven, owing to the influence of Davenport, was as much opposed to the Half-Way Covenant as the authorities of Connecticut were in its favor. No action on the part of the General Court for or against the new system took place at once.

But though the Connecticut Court took no immediate steps in favor of larger church privileges, the matter was agitated in the colony and with results that at last demanded the Court's interference. When Norton had returned, during the closing days of the Synod, from his embassy to England,[5] he had brought with him a

---

[1] *Magnalia*, ed. 1853-5, II: 310.

[2] Though not published till 1675, the Preface to Increase Mather's *First Principles* is dated May 1, 1671.

[3] *Magnalia*, II: 311, 312. Even so strong a favorer of the Half-Way Covenant as Richard Mather declared on his death-bed in 1669 to his son Increase: "A speciall thing which I would commend to you, is, Care concerning the Rising Generation in this Country, that they be brought under the Government of Christ in his Church; and that when grown up and qualified, they have Baptism for their Children. I must confess I have been defective as to practise, yet I have publickly declared my judgement, and manifested my desires to practise that which I think ought to be attended, but the Dissenting of some in our Church discouraged me." Increase Mather, *Life and Death of . . . Richard Mather*, Cambridge, 1670, p. 27.

[4] *Magnalia*, II: 313-315. The Boston First Church did not adopt the Half-Way Covenant practice till 1731, Emerson, *Hist. Sketch of the First Ch.*, Boston, 1812, p. 175.

[5] John Norton and Simon Bradstreet had been sent by Mass. to England to propitiate the restored monarchy. See Palfrey, *Hist. N. E.*, II: 520-531.

letter of Charles II. to the government of Massachusetts, directing that all who so chose and were peaceable should have freedom to worship according to the Prayer Book; and in general, that:[1]

"all persons of good and honest lives and conversations be admitted to the sacrament of the Lords supper, according to the said booke of common prayer, and their children to baptisme."

This letter had been received by the same Court which approved the result of the Synod, October 8, 1662;[2] and compliance had been avoided by a temporizing policy;[3] but in July, 1664, royal commissioners,[4] charged with a general revision of the affairs of the colonies arrived. There was from the first no doubt that their views favored a much broader admission to church privileges than the Half-way Covenant contemplated;[5] and at a later period they secured the consent of the colony of Plymouth to concessions substantially in accord with the king's letter to Massachusetts.[6] The known attitude of the English government and its commissioners doubtless increased the impatience in every colony of opponents of the strictness of early Congregationalism at the slow progress of the Half-Way Covenant practice, especially in view of the result of the Massachusetts Synod and the favor of many ministers.

This impatience found expression in Connecticut in a petition from William Pitkin[7] of Hartford and six other men of respectable position in the colony, presented to the General Court at its session in October, 1664, and setting forth much the same grievances that Child and his associates[8] had once preferred against the churches of Massachusetts. The petitioners declare that, though baptized members of the Church of England, they are refused com-

---

[1] Hutchinson, *Collection*, p. 379, dated June 28, 1662.

[2] *Records* . . . *Mass. Bay*, IV: 2: 58.

[3] *Ibid.* "Concerning liberty to use the common Prayer Book, none as yet among us have appeared to desire it; touching administration of the sacraments, this matter hath been under consideration of a synod, orderly called, the result whereof our last General Court commended to the several congregations, and we hope will have a tendency to general satisfaction." Answer to the king, 2 *Coll. Mass. Hist. Soc.*, VIII: 48.

[4] For their doings see Palfrey, II: 578–634.

[5] *I. e.*, admission of all respectable persons to the Lord's Supper.

[6] *Plymouth Records*, IV: 85–87. February, 1665.

[7] Some facts regarding Pitkin, who was a man of piety, and the names of his fellow-signers may be found in G. L. Walker, *Hist. First Church in Hartford*, pp. 195, 196.

[8] See *ante*, p. 164.

munion for themselves and baptism for their children, in contradiction of the king's letter to Massachusetts, and they beg the Court to compel the ministers of the colony to grant them such ordinances as they desire, or to relieve them from the necessity of contributing to the support of any minister who should refuse.[1]

This petition evidently met with some approval in the Connecticut Court, and determined that body to take action which, while not granting all that the petitioners desired, favored a large interpretation of the Half-Way Covenant:[2]

"This Court vnderstanding by a writing presented to them from seuerall persons of this Colony, that they are agrieved that they are not interteined in church fellowship; This Court haueing duely considered the same, desireing that the rules of Christ may be attended, doe commend it to the ministers and churches in this Colony to consider whither it be not their duty to enterteine all such persons, whoe are of honest and godly conuersation, haueing a competency of knowledg in the principles of religion, and shall desire to joyne wth them in church fellowship, by an explicitt couenant, and that they haue their children baptized, and that all the children of the church be accepted and acco^td^ reall members of the church, and that the church exercise a due christian care and watch ouer them; and that when they are growne up, being examined by the officer in the presence of the church, it appeares, in the judgment of charity, they are duely qualifyed to perticipate in that great ordinance of the Lords Supper, by theire being able to examine themselues and discerne the Lords body, such persons be admitted to full comunion.

The Court desires y^t^ the seuerall officers of ye respectiue churches, would be pleased to consider whither it be not the duty of the Court to order the churches to practice according to the premises, if they doe not practice w^th^out such an order.

If any dissent from the contents of this writing they are desired to help the Court wth such light as is wth them, the next Session of this Assembly.

The Court orders the Secret^ry^ to send a copy of this writing to the seuerall ministers and churches in this Colony."

Such an order, in the somewhat divided state of public opinion in regard to the Half-Way Covenant, could only produce further controversy and division. Adam Blakeman and Thomas Hanford, pastors of the churches of Stratford and Norwalk respectively, sent in to the Court a joint letter of earnest protest against the new way.[3] By June, 1666, the Hartford church was torn by contesting factions, of which the larger, led by the younger minister, Joseph Haynes, favored the larger practice;

---

[1] The full text is in Stiles, *Ancient Windsor*, ed. 1859, pp. 167, 168.

[2] *Conn. Rec.*, I: 437. Court of Oct. 13, 1664.

[3] The MS. is in the possession of Dr. J. H. Trumbull. Extracts are given by G. L. Walker *Hist. First Ch. Hartford*, p. 198.

while a strong minority, championed by Haynes's colleague, John Whiting, opposed.[1] In April of that year Abraham Pierson, the pastor of the church at Branford, with a majority of his flock, and some persons from Guilford, New Haven, and Milford, made arrangements to leave the colony for Newark, New Jersey, an agreement which they carried into execution the year following.[2] To this step they were led in part by dislike to the admission of non-church-members to the franchise, which was one of the consequences to New Haven colony of its absorption by Connecticut; but hostility toward the Half-Way Covenant added strength to their desire to remove.[3] At about the same time the church in Stratford was torn by a quarrel regarding the allowance of the Half-Way principles which resulted eventually in the division of the church and the settlement of Woodbury.[4] The Windsor church was in a chronic state of controversy, to which the question of baptism only added fuel.[5]

No wonder the General Court of Connecticut felt that it was time to bring these matters to a settlement, and therefore, at its session, October 11, 1666, it voted to call a "Synod" to meet at Hartford, May 15, 1667, to discuss seventeen questions propounded by the Court "to an issue."[6] As to the composition of the "Synod":[7]

> "This Court orders that all ye Preacheing Elders and Ministers that are or shalbe setled in this Colony at ye time of ye meeting of the Synod shalbe sent to attend as members of ye Synod. This Court orders that Mr. Michil,[8] Mr. Browne,[9] Mr. Sherman[10] and Mr. Glouer,[11] shalbe desired as from this Court to assist as members of this Synod."

---

[1] See *Ibid.*, pp. 184–211.

[2] See T. P. Gillett, *Hist. Cong. Ch. . . . of Branford. A Semi-Centennial Discourse*, New Haven, 1858, pp. 7–9.

[3] Felt, *Eccles. Hist. N. E.*, II: 412.

[4] See Cothren, *Hist. Ancient Woodbury*, Waterbury, 1854, pp. 113–134. The first document in the dispute is of Jan., 1666.

[5] See Stiles, *Hist. Ancient Windsor*, New York, 1859, pp. 163–193.

[6] *Conn. Records*, II: 53–55.

[7] *Ibid.*

[8] Jonathan Mitchell of Cambridge, Mass., one of the chief leaders in the Half-Way Covenant movement. All were ministers, distinguished for learning, and presumably favorable to the newer view.

[9] Edmund Browne, Sudbury, Mass.

[10] John Sherman, Watertown, Mass.

[11] Pelatiah Glover, Springfield, Mass.

The Court then declared that the body should proceed with the prescribed business: "Provided that ye maior part of ye Teacheing Elders[1] of ye Churches be present;"[2] and that in the meantime every minister in the colony should be provided with a copy of the questions, and all the churches be recommended to abstain from controversy pending the result of the "Synod."

The questions[3] thus sent forth cover a far greater range of topics than those communicated to the Massachusetts Court in 1656. Those which head the list are substantially a repetition of the queries addressed by the Massachusetts legislature to the Synod of 1662, viz.:

"1. Whether federall holines or couen^t^ interest be not ye propper ground of Baptisme. 2. Whether Com̄union of Ch^s^, as such, be not warrantable by the word of God."

But others bear directly on the questions raised by Pitkin and his friends, and show the dawnings of that system by which those who contributed to support of a minister, though not themselves church members, claimed a voice in his election, — a system which has been so peculiar a feature of New England Congregationalism:[4]

"4. Whether ministeriall officers are not as truly bound to baptize the visible disciples of X^t^ providentially setled amongst them, as officially to preach the Word. 5. Whether setled inhabitants of the Countrey, being members of other Churches, should haue their children baptized amongst vs w^th^out themselues first ord^r^ly ioyneing in Churches here. 9. Whether it doth not belong to ye body of a Towne collectiuely, taken joyntly, to call him to be their minister whom the Church shal choose to be their officer. 13. Whether the Church her invitation and election of an officer or preacheing Elder necessitates the whole Congregation to sit downe satisfied, as bound thereby to accept him as their Minister though invited and setled w^th^out ye Townes consent."

Here then were matters enough for a general discussion of a great part of what had heretofore been Congregational usage. It is easy to see that Connecticut was in a ferment, and that the

---

[1] *I. e.*, ministers in relationship to particular Conn. churches — the Court drew no distinction between pastors and teachers. Its purpose was to secure a representation of a majority of the churches.

[2] *Conn. Rec.*, *Ibid.*

[3] Text, *Ibid.*, 54, 55. Trumbull, *Hist. Conn.*, I: 302, 303, 457. He makes the mistake of attributing the same questions to 1656.

[4] An interesting account of the development of the parish system in Massachusetts is that of D. T. Fiske, *Cont. Eccles. Hist. Essex County*, pp. 262–269.

process had begun which was to lead to the erection of an ecclesiastical constitution imposed by state authority at Saybrook in 1708. Indeed, the main question which the Saybrook Platform was to attempt to answer was already asked in the thirteenth of this series of 1666:

> "Vnto whom shal such persons repaire that are grieued at any Church process or censure, or whether they must acquiesce in the Churches sentence vnto wch they doe belong."

But though of great importance, these questions never came to discussion in the way planned by the Court. Opposition to the proposed meeting manifested itself strongly. The stricter Congregationalists, doubtless, objected to the gathering as likely to impose the Half-Way Covenant upon them, and to its title of "Synod" as a misnomer for an assemblage of ministers only.[1] At all events the Court, at its session May 9, 1667, while reaffirming the summons, changed the title of the meeting to "Assembly."[2] Thus softened in title the body met,[3] but before it could do any business except discuss whether its debates should be public or private, it adjourned to the following October. Pending the reassembly a shrewd move was made by the leaders of the opposition to the Half-Way Covenant,—Rev. Messrs. John Whiting of Hartford, John Warham of Windsor, and Samuel Hooker of Farmington,—a move which abruptly terminated the Assembly. The Commissioners of the United Colonies met at Hartford, September 15, 1667,[4] and were induced to vote to:[5]

> "propound that wher any questian may or doth arise . . . that are of comon concernment whether in the Matters of faith or order and any of the Collonies shall apprehend it needfull to call in the helpe of a Councell or Synode for the orderly Desision therof; That the Members of such Councell or Synode May consist of the Messengers of the Churches called Indifferently out of all the vnited Collonies by an orderly agreement of the severall Generall Courts and the place of meeting to be att or neare Boston."

---

1 See remarks of G. L. Walker, *Hist. First Ch. Hartford*, p. 201.

2 *Conn. Records*, II: 67.

3 *Ibid.*, 70. Trumbull, I: 457, 458.

4 The Commissioners, two from each colony, had met annually from 1643 till the union of Conn. and New Haven. Their importance was now little and they met triennially.

5 *Acts of Comm. of United Colonies*, II: 328, in *Records of Plymouth*, Boston, 1859, X. See also *Conn. Records*, II: 69, 70.

On the strength of this vote the three ministers named approached the Connecticut Court at its meeting October 10, 1667, and declared that the Assembly wished the Court to lay the questions before a larger Council, composed of representatives of the other colonies as well as of Connecticut.[1] To this Rev. Messrs. Joseph Haynes of Hartford, and Gershom Bulkley of Wethersfield, the former Whiting's colleague and rival, responded in an address to the Court, in which they denied that the Assembly had desired a larger Council.[2] In this they doubtless represented the sentiment of their Half-Way Covenant friends. But to the Court the idea of a Council of all the colonies proved attractive, and it therefore voted requesting the churches to send their ministers to meet with those of Massachusetts and Plymouth, and asking the Massachusetts Court to appoint the time and place of meeting[3]—a desire which the Connecticut Court expressed by letter to the authorities in Boston, October 16, and transmitted by John Whiting.[4] But the Massachusetts Court was disinclined to move and made an evasive reply.[5] Thus all the elaborate preparations for such a settlement of disputed points in Connecticut as Massachusetts had attempted in 1662 ended in failure.

The Court recognized the unavailing character of its attempts, but the quarrels still continued at Hartford and elsewhere. As a last resort, therefore, on May 16, 1668, the Connecticut legislature requested Rev. Messrs. James Fitch of Norwich, Gershom Bulkley of Wethersfield, Joseph Eliot of Guilford, and Samuel Wakeman of Fairfield, to meet at Saybrook or Norwich on the following 8th or 9th of June, and:[6]

"Consider of some expedient for our peace, by searching out the rule and thereby cleareing up how farre the churches and people may walke together within themselues and one wth another in the fellowship and order of the Gospel, notwithstanding some various apprehensions amonge them in matters of discipline respecting membership and baptisme &c."

---

[1] *Conn. Records*, II: 69, 70. [2] Trumbull, *Hist. Conn.*, I: 458.

[3] *Conn. Records*, II: 70. [4] *Ibid.*, 516, 517.

[5] *Ibid. Records . . . Mass. Bay*, IV: 2: 354.

[6] *Conn. Records*, II: 84. Bacon, *Discourse*, in *Cont. Eccles. Hist. Conn.*, p. 27, has pointed out that one of the ministers was chosen from each of the four then newly established counties of the colony.

It was a confession of failure to secure union and a declaration of a willingness to admit variety in ecclesiastical practice.

In accordance with the request of the Court the four ministers met, and at the session of the legislature, May 13, 1669, presented their "returne." Exactly what this was we do not know, but it appears to have been of a conciliatory nature. The same Court voted thereupon as follows, a vote which was the practical solution of the Half-way Covenant dispute as far as the government of Connecticut was concerned:[1]

> "This Court . . . doe declare that whereas the Congregationall Churches in these partes for the generall of their profession and practice haue hitherto been approued, we can doe no less than still approue and countenance the same to be w^th^out disturbance vntill better light in an orderly way doth appeare; but yet forasmuch as sundry persons of worth for prudence and piety amongst us are otherwise perswaded, . . . This Court doth declare that all such persons being allso approued according to lawe as orthodox and sownd in the fundamentalls of Christian religion may haue allowance of their perswasion and profession in church wayes or assemblies w^th^out disturbance."

Here was a formal toleration for both the supporters of the Half-Way Covenant and its opponents, and permission also for churches hopelessly split upon the question to divide. Of this latter privilege the minority in the church at Hartford availed themselves at once.[2] But it curiously illustrates the strength of the Half-Way Covenant movement, in spite of the brave and in many ways successful fight made against it, that the withdrawing party at Hartford should, apparently on the very day of their formation into a separate church, have begun the use of the system hostility toward which had been their original ground of quarrel with the majority of the old church.[3] From this permission that both systems should exist side by side in Connecticut, interest in the dispute waned. In Massachusetts similar toleration had come to be practiced, though without leaving so distinct a mark upon the records of the colony. In Connecticut and Massachusetts alike the supporters of the Half-Way Covenant were the

---

[1] *Conn. Records*, II: 109.

[2] *Conn. Records*, II: 120. Walker, *Hist. First Ch. Hartford*, pp. 204–209. The Second Ch. Hartford was organized Feb. 12–22, 1670.

[3] *Ibid.*

growing party. Yet the stricter usage continued to have its representatives and was never wholly abandoned for the larger.[1]

Though aside from the main purpose of this introduction to the results of 1657 and 1662, a few words as to the later history of the Half-Way Covenant may not be inappropriate. The theory on which the action of the Ministerial Assembly of 1657, and the Synod of 1662, was based, was that only children of church members were entitled to baptism, because they alone had inherited membership. Children of those who were not in covenant were not to be baptized, they were not members of the church, and could only become so (save in the case of adoption into the household of a church member) by a profession of personal piety. So too "owning the covenant" was, in the view of the originators of the Half-Way Covenant practice, a solemn personal acceptance, as far as it lay in a man's power unaided by divine grace, of his place in the visible Kingdom of God, and a formal declaration of his intention to do his best to lead a Christian life by association in worship and discipline with the recognized people of God. He who was himself by birth one in covenant with God, and who made that covenant his own by a public declaration, was deemed to be in a state where he might hopefully expect that work of grace in the heart which it was believed God alone could effect. But as the seventeenth century closed, and the eighteenth with its prevailingly low type of piety wore on, the original basis of the baptismal right in the existing membership of the recipient was less and less insisted upon, though never absolutely forgotten. To "own the covenant" and to present one's children for baptism became less a solemn claiming of rights already possessed, and more an act deemed of value in itself. The membership of the claimant sank into the background; the rite, which was at first but a symbol of that membership, became the important thing, and to receive it was looked upon as a duty, something to be done for one's

[1] Bellamy was able to write in 1769, when the reaction against the system was beginning: "Even to this day the custom is not universal." *The Half-Way-Covenant, a Dialogue*, New Haven, 1769, p. 3.

children just as it was a duty to teach them to pray. So it came about that, by the time Cotton Mather wrote the *Ratio Disciplinæ*, many ministers admitted all applicants of good moral character to the covenant and granted them and their children baptism, without question as to whether the recipients were members by birth or not.[1] This was a wide departure from the original Half-Way Covenant practice, and one which tended vastly more than that to cheapen the Gospel ordinances. Indeed, there is reason to believe that in many places admission to the covenant came to be looked upon much as signing a temperance pledge has frequently been regarded in our day,—as a means by which large bodies of young people might be induced to start out in the right path in life.[2] And while some churches admitted to baptism those who had no other claim than a respectable life and a willingness to take the covenant obligations, others granted the rite to the children of those who had themselves been baptized, without requiring any covenant promises from the parents at all.[3]

It was natural that when the barriers which the Ministers' Convention and the Synod had erected between the non-church member and baptism were so broken down, that those other obstacles which they had placed between the member by birth who could not claim to be personally regenerate and the Lord's Supper should be lightly regarded in many quarters. If a man was member enough to be presumed fit for one sacrament in the absence of flagrant immorality, why was he not competent to

---

[1] Published 1726, Preface dated 1719. "It may be added, There having been some Insinuations made unto the World, as if the *Streets* here were crouded with *Unbaptized People*, because the Churches have not such *Terms of Initiation* here, as are practised in *other* Protestant Churches, 'tis to be now declared, that this is a most unaccountable *Calumny*, for 'tis well known there is not one Person in all the Country free from a scandalous and notorious disqualifying *Ignorance* and *Impiety*, but what may repair to some Hundred Ministers in these Colonies and be Baptised," p. 80.

[2] Compare Dexter, *Cong. as seen*, p. 475.

[3] On April 30, 1789, the First Church, Haverhill, Mass., voted: "Whereas it has been customary for persons in order to obtain baptism for their children, to make a public profession of faith called 'owning the Covenant,' and as this condition may hinder some persons (though otherwise qualified) from complying with the institution; voted that it be no longer required, but the children of all baptized persons may be admitted to this holy ordinance unless they (the parents) have forfeited this privilege by scandalous immorality." Quoted by D. T. Fiske, *Cont. Eccles. Hist. Essex Co., Mass.*, p. 279.

receive the other? So some men in New England reasoned, and the result was what may be called "Stoddardeanism," from the name of its chief exponent, though Stoddard was by no means the originator of the view. Its essence was that it was the duty of all who were sincerely desirous of living a Christian life, and who were church members by birth, even though not consciously regenerate, to partake of the Lord's Supper. Though never adopted by a majority of the New England churches, it was wide-spread in Western Massachusetts and Connecticut during the eighteenth century.

As early as 1677, Increase Mather, in a sermon before the Massachusetts General Court, complained of the spread of Stoddardean principles[1] in the ranks of the ministry. Nor was the region about Boston the only section of New England where such views were taught. They came into debate at the so-called Reforming Synod of 1679, where they exercised some influence on the result.[2] They were widely prevalent during the last quarter of the seventeenth century. But it is in the writings of Solomon Stoddard[3] that they have their sharpest expression.

---

[1] "I wish there be not teachers found in our Israel, that have espoused loose large principles here, designing to bring all persons to the Lord's Supper, who have an historical faith, and are not scandalous in life, though they never had experience of a work of regeneration in their souls." *A Call from Heaven To the Present and Succeeding Generations*, Boston, 1679, quoted by L. Withington, *Cont. Eccles. Hist. Essex Co., Mass.*, pp. 389, 390.

[2] Stoddard, in his *Appeal to the Learned*, pp. 93, 94, tells the following story: "The words of the Synod [of 1679] are these, *It is requisite that Persons be not admitted unto Communion in the Lords Supper without making a Personal and Public Profession of their Faith and Repentance*, [etc., The passage is in *Necessity of Reformation*, p. 10; to be found later in this work.] I shall give the World an Account how the matter was acted. Some of the Elders in the Synod had drawn up a Conclusion, That persons should make a Relation of the work of Gods Spirit upon their hearts, in order to coming into full Communion. Some others of the Elders objected against it, and after some discourse it was agreed to have a dispute on that question, Whether those Professors of Religion as are of good Conversation, are not to be admitted to full Communion, provided they are able to Examine themselves, and discern the Lords body. Mr. [Increase] *Mather*, held the Negative; I laboured to make good the Affirmative; The result was, That they blotted out that clause of Making a Relation of the work of Gods Spirit, and put in the room of it, *The Making a Profession of their Faith and Repentance;* and so I Voted with the Rest, and am of the same judgment still." To this statement of Stoddard the anonymous writer of the *Appeal of Some of the Unlearned* replied, p. 17: "The Story told of the blotting out a Passage in the result of the Synod, we are upon good Information from the Moderator [Increase Mather] himself, who drew up that Result, assured it is a mistake, and a gross one." But the definite statement of Stoddard over his own name is to be preferred to the hearsay of a nameless writer. Further confirmation of Stoddard's accuracy may be found in Thacher's account of the Reforming Synod quoted in chapter xiii of this volume.

[3] Solomon Stoddard was born at Boston in 1643, educated at Harvard, where he graduated in 1662, and after serving the college as tutor and librarian, he accepted an invitation to preach at Northampton in 1669, and a formal call in 1672. Here he remained till he died, Feb. 11, 1729. Of

That able and devout minister left the impress of his thought throughout the Connecticut valley. In 1700 he published his *Doctrine of Instituted Churches*,[1] a treatise which is widely at variance with the theories of early Congregationalism and is essentially a step in the direction of the parish systems of Europe. Not only did he assert the desirability of National Churches,[2] a doctrine against which the founders of New England set their faces; he denied the necessity of local covenants, in which they firmly believed;[3] while his views as to the authority of the minister in church administration would have suited the Presbyterian Parker of Newbury had he lived a generation earlier.[4] But his theory of access to the Supper is more important. He asks the question and gives the answer:[5]

> "Whether such Persons as have a good Conversation and a Competent Knowledge, may come to the Lords Supper, with a good Conscience, in case they know themselves to be in a Natural Condition?
>
> Answ. They may and ought to come tho they know themselves to be in a Natural Condition; this Ordinance is instituted for all the adult Members of the Church who are not scandalous, and therefore must be attended by them; as no Man may neglect Prayer, or hearing the Word, because he cannot do it in Faith, so he may not neglect the Lords Supper."

Increase Mather's *Order of the Gospel*[6] had apparently called out the treatise of Stoddard, and Mather now hastened to reply, reasserting his well known views, which were essentially a conserv-

---

his piety and pastoral zeal there can be no doubt, both were conspicuous, and his ministry was marked by at least five revivals. A man of much personal modesty, he was one of the great preachers of his day and easily the foremost minister in western Massachusetts, indeed Pres. Dwight declared that he "possessed, probably, more influence than any other Clergyman in the province, during a period of thirty years." An excellent sketch of him may be found in Sibley, *Graduates of Harvard*, II: 111–122, where a list of his writings and a considerable bibliography of his life is given. For the tradition as to Stoddard's conversion at the Supper, see I. N. Tarbox, in *New Englander*, XLIII: 624–626 (Sept., 1884).

1 For the writings of Stoddard and his opponents see *ante*, p. 240.

2 *Instituted Churches*, p. 25.

3 *Ibid.*, p. 8.

4 "The Teaching Officer is appointed by Christ to Baptize and Administer the Lords Supper, and therefore he is made Judge by God, what Persons those ordinances are to be Administred to, and it is not the work either of the Brethren or Ruling Elders, any ways to intermeddle in that Affair or Limit him . . . The Teaching Elders with the Ruling Elders, make the Presbytery of the Church; with whom the Government of the Church is entrusted: The Power of Censuring offenders in the Church and absolving of Penitents, doth belong alone to these, the Brethren of the Church are not to intermeddle with it." *Ibid.*, p. 12.

5 *Ibid.*, p. 21. Exactly when Stoddardeanism was adopted by the Northampton church is uncertain. The records show that as late as 1706 a distinction was made between covenant members and those in full communion.

6 Boston, 1700. See *ante*, p. 240.

ative presentation of the general positions of the leaders of the Half-Way Covenant movement forty years before. Stoddard made no immediate answer, but did not change his opinion, which he reasserted after a time in a published sermon, printed in 1708, which again called out Mather and led to Stoddard's elaborate defense of his theory in his *Appeal to the Learned.* In this work he affirms:[1]

> "This Ordinance [Supper] has a proper tendency in its own nature to Convert men. Herein men may learn the necessity & sufficiency of the Death of Christ in order to Pardon. Here is an affecting offer of Christ crucifyed; here is a Sealing of the Covenant, that if men come to Christ, they shall be Saved, which is a great means to convince of safety in coming to Christ.
>
> All Ordinances are for the Saving good of those that they are to be administred unto. This Ordinance is according to Institution to be applyed to visible Saints,[2] though Unconverted, therefore it is for their Saving good, and consequently for their Conversion."

These views of Stoddard spread widely and were adopted by many good men. The majority of the churches in Western Massachusetts accepted them, they were largely entertained in Connecticut, and the region about Boston was not without their representatives.[3] But though they might be held by devoted ministers and in earnest communities, they were a nullification of the conception of a church entertained by the founders of New England.[4] Yet the root of Stoddardeanism is to be found in the dual and inconsistent

---

1 Page 25.

2 Stoddard's conception of "visible saints" was "Such as make a serious profession of the true Religion, together with those that do descend from them, till rejected of God." *Instituted Churches*, p. 6.

3 In 1750, at the time of Edwards's dismission from Northampton, the old Hampshire Association might be divided as follows; *Stoddardean*, Amherst, Brimfield, Deerfield, East Granville, Great Barrington, Greenwich, Hadley, South Hadley, Longmeadow, New Marlborough, Northfield, Northampton, Sheffield, Shutesbury, Southampton, Springfield, West Springfield, Sunderland, Westfield, Wilbraham; Somers, Conn.; Suffield, Conn.; *Anti-Stoddardean*, Belchertown; Enfield, Conn.; Pelham. Hatfield was doubtful. See *New Englander*, IV: 353. The following ministers defended these views at various times in print, George Beckwith, Lyme, Conn.; Charles Chauncy, First Church, Boston; Ebenezer Devotion, Scotland, Conn.; Moses Hemmenway, Wells, Me.; Joseph Lathrop, West Springfield, Mass.; Moses Mather, Darien, Conn.; Solomon Williams, Lebanon, Conn. These of course represent but a few of the real number of adherents. Their geographical distribution may suggest something as to the wide spread of these opinions; while the later history of most of the churches represented may also suggest a degree of hesitation in claiming, as has often been done, that Unitarianism was the direct fruit of Stoddardeanism and the Half-Way Covenant.

4 Could anything much more foreign to the ideas of Hooker or of Cotton be imagined than the following church-act? "At a church meeting holden in Westfield [Mass.] Feb. 25th, 1728, voted, that those who enter full communion, may have liberty to give an account of a work of saving conversion or not. It shall be regarded by the church as a matter of indifference." *New Englander*, IV: 354.

theory of those founders as to church-membership, by experience and by birth. It is the complete demonstration of that original incongruity.

Perhaps the best illustration of the change of feeling which had come over New England in regard to the privileges of church membership is the statement of Cotton Mather in the *Ratio Disciplinæ*, where he speaks of the Stoddardean view as held by "some eminent *Pastors* (and some of their Churches)," and then describes the more conservative theory, defended by his father, that none should be admitted to the Supper but those who could testify to "*Experimental Piety*." He declares:[1]

"Indeed there is a *Variety* both of *Judgment* and *Practice* in the Churches of *New-England* upon this Matter; However it produces no troublesome *Variance* or *Contention* among them."

Fortunately this condition of apathy was not of long duration. The rise of a new type of theology led to an earnest and ultimately successful effort to overthrow not only Stoddardeanism but the Half-Way Covenant; and the struggle began where Stoddardeanism was most intrenched, at Northampton, Mass. Stoddard's successor was his grandson, Jonathan Edwards,[2] who became pastor of the Northampton church February 15, 1727. For nearly twenty years after the commencement of his ministry Edwards practiced the system introduced by his grandfather. But Edwards was deeply moved by the revival spirit of the second quarter of the eighteenth century. Though essentially Calvinistic, the prevailing type of theology in New England during the second half of the seventeenth century had laid great stress on the external means of grace. It was an unemotional age in religion. Revivals were almost unknown. No very sharp distinction was drawn, either in

---

[1] Pp. 84, 85.

[2] Born at East Windsor, Conn., Oct. 5, 1703, graduated at Yale 1720, studied theology at Yale till 1722, preached till April, 1723, in New York, became tutor at Yale May, 1724, and held the post till September, 1726. Settled at Northampton February, 1727, dismissed June, 1750. Settled at Stockbridge August, 1751, dismissed to become president of Princeton, January, 1758. Died March 22, 1758. Among the numerous biographies of Edwards perhaps the most valuable is S. E. Dwight, *Life of President Edwards*, New York, 1830. It is amply illustrated with letters and documents. A suggestive sketch is that of Prof. A. V. G. Allen, *Jonathan Edwards* (American Religious Leaders Series), Boston, 1889 (Reviewed by Dr. J. W. Wellman, Boston, 1890). A complete bibliography of Edwards's writings and a list of biographical authorities will be found in Prof. F. B. Dexter, *Biog. Sketches of the Grad. of Yale*, pp. 221-226.

experience or teaching, between the converted and unconverted. Though believed to be clearly distinguished by the eye of God, to human vision a careful discrimination was difficult. Hence great value was set on those means by which a soul might be nurtured in the Kingdom of God. As the eighteenth century opened this tendency increased, and to a considerable extent the type of preaching became "Arminian," as it was termed,—that is, increasing weight was laid upon the cultivation of morality as a means to a Christian life, rather than upon an insistance on the prime necessity of a divinely wrought change in a man's nature, a change of which morality should not be the means, but the fruit. It was the prevalence of these views in greater or less degree which made the acceptance of the Half-Way Covenant easy, and it is from them, rather than directly from that Covenant, that New England Unitarianism derives, in large part, its origin. But the revival movements in the fourth and fifth decades of the eighteenth century reproduced in large degree the type of preaching and experience which characterized the Puritans at their exodus from England. Conversion, that is, a conscious sense of a change in a man's relations to God, was insisted on as the prime test of Christianity. Such an experience is individual, not corporate; and in proportion as conscious regeneration was made the standard of trial, the corporate theory of hereditary covenant relationship to God sank into the background. And, as nothing short of a distinct sense of reconciliation with God's plans was held to give ground for a valid Christian hope, the supporters of the revival movements insisted that any dependence on means, however good in themselves, was illusory and dangerous,—many going so far as to say that no action of an unconverted man, not even prayer, could be acceptable in the sight of God. The "Great Awakening" under the preaching of Whitefield in 1740–41, led to a sharp division between the holders of the two positions, nicknamed at that time the "Old Lights" and the "New Lights." The principles of the school of theology which came out of the revivals were thus of necessity opposed to the Half-Way Covenant, and to that school its destruction was due. Of that school the founder and pioneer was Jonathan Edwards.

As has been seen, Edwards practiced Stoddardeanism far into his Northampton ministry, and at first without very serious scruples. But the revivals in which he bore a large share gradually produced a change of feeling in him, and by 1744 he was fully convinced that the theory of Stoddard was wrong.[1] No opportunity, however, permitted him to put his changed ideas into practice till December 1748, when he denounced the system in vogue in the Northampton church with his accustomed courage, and the controversy began between him and his people which led to his dismission in June 1750.[2] In the heat of this discussion he published, in August, 1749, his *Humble Inquiry . . . Concerning the Qualifications Requisite to . . . full Communion.*[3] The work was primarily an argument against Stoddardeanism, that was the point under debate between Edwards and the Northampton church; but it contained, in a subsidiary paragraph, a vigorous and consistent attack on the Half-Way Covenant system as conducive to a false sense of security and the neglect of a true seeking for conversion.[4] To this tract Rev. Solomon Williams of Lebanon, Conn., replied,[5] touching, of course, chiefly on the Stoddardean problem involved in the dispute; but in his rejoinder to Williams, Edwards did not fail to make clear once more his opposition not only to Stoddardeanism, but to the Half-Way Covenant.

With this reply the discussion of the subject in print ceased for a number of years, but Edwards's criticisms had their direct fruitage. Probably no disciple of Edwards more fully shared his views regarding conversion than Joseph Bellamy,[6] from 1738 to

---

[1] See Dwight, *Life of Pres. Edwards*, pp. 435–438.

[2] For a full account of the circumstances leading to the dismission see *Ibid.*, pp. 298–403.

[3] See *ante*, p. 241.

[4] Dr. D. T. Fiske in his valuable account of the Half-Way Covenant, *Cont. Eccles. Hist. Essex Co.*, p. 281, has fallen into the error of affirming that Edwards opposed Stoddardeanism, but not directly the Half-Way Covenant. Dr. Dexter, *Cong. as seen*, p. 487, quotes Dr. Fiske's statement with approval, and cites in confirmation the fact that Edwards administered the covenant in 1742. But neither writer has made allowance for the change in Edwards's views, and both must have overlooked pp. 126–131 of the *Humble Inquiry*. Compare G. L. Walker, *New Englander*, XLIII: 611.

[5] See *ante*, p. 243.

[6] Bellamy was born in Cheshire, Conn., Feb. 20, 1719; graduated at Yale 1735; studied theology to some extent under Edwards. Began preaching at Bethlem in November, 1738, and was

1790 the minister at Bethlem, Conn. On him and the church under his charge the effect of Edwards's tracts was decisive. The Bethlem Church Records bear testimony that:[1]

"Upon the publishing of Mr. Edwards' Book on the Sacrament, this Practice [the Half-Way Covenant] was laid aside, as not warranted by the holy scriptures — there being no other scriptural owning the covenant, but what implies a profession of Godliness."

But, in spite of this vote, and in spite of a defense of Edwards which shows that Bellamy was fully in sympathy with the Northampton pastor's opposition to Stoddardeanism and could logically hold no other position than that of hostility to the Half-Way Covenant,[2] it was not till nearly twenty years after Edwards's dismission that Bellamy began his determined public attack on the system. In January 1769, he published his first dialogue against the Half-Way Covenant.[3] Its homely but vigorous putting of the case had an immediate effect. Within the next few months three replies, two of which are of considerable ability, appeared. In April, Bellamy issued a second dialogue, and soon followed it by a third, with which he combined an attack upon a Stoddardean treatise on the *Visible Church, in Covenant with God*,[4] which had just been put forth by Rev. Moses Mather of Darien, Conn. Answers followed from Mather and others, and the fight of pamphlets waxed hotter and more personal. A fourth dialogue and a reply to Mather came from Bellamy's pen. Meanwhile a second controversy on the same subject was in progress between Jacob Green, an Edwardean pastor at Hanover, New Jersey, and Rev. George Beckwith of Lyme, Conn. At the same time the question rose, apparently independently, to prominence in the church at Plymouth, Mass.,[5] of which Chandler Robbins, a pupil of Bellamy, was pastor.

---

settled there in April, 1740. He remained in Bethlem till he died, Mch. 6, 1790. He was a prolific writer and a keen, if not always very generous, controversialist. His home was a Theological School, in which a number of New England theologians were trained, *e. g.*, the younger Jonathan Edwards, Samuel Spring, and Joseph Eckley. His works were published in 3 vols., New York, 1811, and 2 vols., Boston, 1850. A valuable biographical sketch, with a list of authorities, is that of F. B. Dexter, *Biog. Sketches Grad. Yale*, pp. 523–529. Lives in Sprague, *Annals Am. Pulpit*, I: 404–412; and by Prof. Park, *Schaff-Herzog Religious Encyclopædia*, may be mentioned.

[1] In Cothren, *Hist. Ancient Woodbury*, p. 244.

[2] *Dialogue on the Christian Sacraments*, Boston, 1762, but apparently written not long after Edwards's dismission.

[3] For the treatises in this controversy, see *ante*, pp. 241–244.

[4] See *ante*, p. 243. [5] *Ibid.*, pp. 243, 244.

The controversy thus begun continued, though with less frequency of publication, throughout the rest of the century. After Bellamy had laid down his pen forever, the battle was waged with most vigor by Rev. Cyprian Strong of Portland, Conn., who attacked the system as early as 1780, but whose most powerful work dates from 1793.[1] Strong went so far as to deny that the children of believers are personally in covenant. Their baptism is not a right, but an act of dedication and a pledge of parental faithfulness. At the same time, Rev. Nathanael Emmons, of Franklin, Mass., and Rev. Stephen West of Stockbridge, Mass., two of the leaders of the school of so-called "New Divinity" of which Jonathan Edwards was the founder, engaged in the attack. From the representatives of the Edwardean theology and its later modifications came the overthrow of the system. Able supporters of the older type of New England theology, like Rev. Messrs. Joseph Lathrop of West Springfield, Mass., and Moses Hemmenway of Wells, Maine, defended the Half-Way Covenant, and even Stoddardeanism, with vigor during the last decade of the eighteenth century; but the gradual dominance of the idea of conversion held by the representatives of the "New Divinity" throughout the Trinitarian body of the churches, emphasized by the remarkable series of revivals which began in the closing years of the last century and lasted well into the present, brought the system to an end. In most of the New England churches the change of feeling caused it to be quietly laid aside. At the Old South Church, Boston, it has never been formally voted out, though last administered in 1818,[2] and there is reason to believe that this tacit disuse of the system was not unusual. At Windsor, Conn., it was in use as late as 1822,[3] in Essex County, Mass., it lasted till about 1825,[4] while the church at Charlestown, Mass., continued the practice till 1828.[5]

---

[1] See *ante*, p. 242. [2] See H. A. Hill, *Hist. Old South Ch.*, II: 235.

[3] *New Englander*, XLIII: 614. See also Stiles, *Ancient Windsor*, p. 173. A prominent member of the Conn. Hist. Society at the present time, 1893, Dea. Jabez H. Hayden, was baptized under the Half-Way Covenant at Windsor. Mr. Hayden informs me that about the beginning of this century there was a general understanding among the ministers of central Connecticut not to practice the system except in families in which it had already been begun.

[4] *Cont. Eccles. Hist. Essex Co.*, p. 279.

[5] *New Englander*, *Ibid.*

THE DECISIONS OF 1657 AND 1662

Result of the Assembly of 1657 (Extracts)

A | DISPUTATION | CONCERNING | Church--Members | AND THEIR | CHILDREN, | IN | ANSWER | TO | XXI. QUESTIONS: | Wherein the State of such *Children* when *Adult,* | Together with their Duty towards the Church, | And the Churches Duty towards them | is DISCUSSED. | BY AN | ASSEMBLY of DIVINES | meeting at Boston in | *NEW ENGLAND,* | *June* 4th. 1657. | —— | Now Published by a Lover of Truth. | —— | *London,* Printed by *J. Hayes,* for *Samuel Thomson* at the Bishops | Head in *Pauls* Church-yard. 1659

[ii blank]
[iii]

To the READER.[1]

IT is justly accounted one of the glories of the English Nation, *that God hath honoured them with special light in some momentous Truths, above what he hath other* Protestant Churches *round about them. The morality of the Christian Sabbath, deep and spiritual insight into those secret transactions between the Lord and the soules of his elect at their first conversion, & also in their after walking in communion with God, are usually observed as instances hereof. And of the same kind, though perhaps in a lower rank, are those Truths about* [*t*]*he* instituted Worship *of God, which have been now for some years a considerable part of those disquisitions, which do also at this day exercise the most searching thoughts and ablest pens that are amongst us.* . . . [iii line 13–v line 26] *It is true indeed the* CivilMagistrates *of that* Jurisdiction *of the* English *in* New-England *that lies upon the River* Connectiquot, *sent these Questions to the* Magistrates *of the* Massachusets, *and they mutually called together sundry of the ablest* Ministers *of each* Colony, *and recommended to their search and considerations these enquiries thus stated, thus framed: And this was the happy rise of this* Disputation;

[1] The reader should be warned that this Preface is no part of the official result of the Assembly of 1657. It is simply a private explanation written by Nathanael Mather. On its authorship, see Increase Mather, *The Life and Death of . . . Mr. Richard Mather*, Cambridge, 1670, p. 32. Nathanael Mather was the third son of Richard Mather, born 1630, graduated at Harvard, 1647, went to England about 1650, and received a living at Harberton in 1655. In 1656 Cromwell gave him a living at Barnstaple, which he held till 1662, when, debarred from preaching in England, he became minister at Rotterdam, Holland. In 1671 he became Congregational pastor at Dublin, Ireland, and in 1688 went to London, where he preached till he died, July 26, 1697. See Sibley, *Biog. Sketches Graduates Harvard*, I: 157–161, where a list of biographical sources will be found.

what is here thus tendered to the world, being the result and product of the consultations and debates on this occasion had, which was by the Elders met together agreed to, and accordingly presented, to the Magistrates *of the aforesaid* Jurisdictions *respectively. But neverthelesse, it was especially and nextly for the service of the* Churches, *the pious and careful* Magistrates *being herein indeed nursing Fathers to them, for they finding doubts, and* [vi] *perhaps some differences about these points, likely to arise and disquiet the* Churches, *took this prudent and happy course, timely to bring forth such light, as might be to universal satisfaction, before darknesse had brought forth difference in judgment and perhaps practise also, and that contentions, and they such animosities and paroxysmes as would afterwards more hardly be healed, than* [then][1] *prevented.*

These Papers came some moneths ago to England, *and it was then in his thoughts that had them in his hands, to have made them publick; but for some reasons which then prevailed with him he forbore, yet hath since given way thereto, partly expecting, according to some intimation which he had from* New-England, *that the* Magistrates *there would have ordered the printing of them. But, not hearing since that it is there done, he hath given way to the desires of some Friends here, who were acquainted with them, and with his having of them, that they should now thus be made publick; hoping withall, that what is done herein, will not be unacceptable to those* Reverend persons, *that were the* authors *of this* Disputation. *Especially considering, that God who formes the Spirit of man within him, and in an especial manner guides the hearts and studies of his servants, hath of late set awork some of them in* Old England *also, to search into these* Questions, *and communicate the issue of their enquiries to the world in print; whence likewise many more, are awakened to desire and long, for further light in these points about which the main part of this disputation is.* . . . [vi line 24–vii line 6] . . . *And these Papers with the truths therein, having in themselves a tendency to this happy end, the midwifeing of them by the press into the publick and common light, in compliance with the aforesaid providence (they being likely otherwise to have lien hid in a private hand or two) cannot be lookt upon as at all injurious to those* honoured *and* reverend Elders *that were the Authors of them, much lesse to any others; for 'tis here done, (saving the Errata of the press) with such faithfulnesse as cannot be impeached.*

And this is the rather said, because perhaps the Reader may have been deceived in some other Treatises, which have gone abroad, and generally been look't upon, as the compilement of the Elders *in* New-England; *whereas they had but one private person for their Author. So it is indeed in the* 32 Questions, *the Answerer whereof was* Mr. Richard Mather, *and not any other Elder or Elders in* New-England, *who likewise is the Author of the* discourse concerning Church-Covenant *printed therewith, which latter he wrote for his private use in his own Study, never intending, nor indeed consenting to its publication, nor so much as knowing unto this day how the copy of it came abroad into those hands by*

[1] MS. addition (by Increase Mather?).

whom it is made publick, save that he conjectures some procured a copy of it from Mr. Cotton, *to whom (such was their intimacy in his life time) he communicated it, as he writes in a late Letter to a Son of his now in* England *who it seems had enquired of him concerning those Treatises; and much lesse is there any truth in that which is said in the Title page prefixed to the* Discourse *of* Church-Covenant, *as if it were sent over to* Mr. Barnard Anno 1639; Mr. Mather *having neither acquaintance nor any intercourse by Letters with* Mr. Barnard.

Nor indeed, are these Papers, now in thy hands, the declared judgment of all the Elders in New-England, *there being but about twenty called together by the* Magistrates *to consult of these things, and declare their judgments in them, and of those twenty, two or three met not with the rest. They are neverthelesse the genuine product of that* [viii] Meeting of Elders *which on the forementioned occasion was held in the* 4th Moneth 1657 *at* Boston *in* New-England.

What entertainment they will meet with now they are abroad it is not for me to say. They must now run the same hazard with other writings of this kind. Some passages there are which I fear will be wrested by one kind of men or other to serve their own hypothesis. It was in my thoughts, having some special advantages for it, here to have inserted somthing as to those particulars for the prevention of such an abuse. But I shall only say this, let but such passages in this short tract as seem most to vary from what the Elders *and* Churches *of* New-England *have been accounted to professe and practise, receive an interpretation as they will bear, from their own declared judgment, either in their* platform of Church Discipline, *or in other writings of their own, and I doubt not but it will be found, they are not warped from their former Faith and Order: Whatever some may think from this Treatise, or whatever* Mr. Giles Firmin[1] *hath born the world in hand, in any of his late misrepresentations of them; whom I rather chuse to instance in, for that his reports of* New-England *have perhaps therefore found the more credit, because he above others is not without advantages to know* New-England, *and the waies of the Churches there, better than it seems he doth.*[2] . . .

---

[1] Giles Firmin (1614–1697) was a Puritan of much mark both as a preacher and as a physician. He came to Boston in 1632, practiced medicine and was a deacon of the First Church. In 1647 he returned to England and became pastor at Shalford, Essex, an office which he held till 1662. His views on church-government were substantially those of Baxter, and led him to critise the Congregational system. See *Dict. National Biog.*, xix · 45, 46.

[2] The 18 concluding lines of the Preface are omitted.

[1]

A
DISPUTATION
CONCERNING
Church--Members
AND THEIR
CHILDREN
IN
ANSWER TO 21 QUESTIONS.

Quest. 1. W*Hether any Children of confederate Parents be under their Parents Covenant and members with them.*

Answ. Some Children of confederate Parents are by meanes of their Parents Covenanting, in Covenant also, and so Members of the Church by divine Institution. For, [2] *Arg.* 1. They that are in that Covenant for substance which was made with *Abraham, Gen.* 17. 7. they are in Covenant, and Members of the Church, by divine Institution, because that Covenant doth inferre Church-Membership, as being the formall cause thereof; For 1. A people that are in that Covenant, are thereby the visible People or Church of God, *Gen.* 17. 7. compared with *Deut.* 29. 12, 13. by this Covenant the Family of *Abraham*, and so afterwards the People of *Israel*, was made and established the visible Church of God. 2. Many were in that Covenant, which never were in saving state of grace; Therefore that was the externall or Church Covenant, which God makes with his visible Church or People. 3. Circumcision sealed that Covenant, which was the distinguishing mark between those within and those without the Church.

But some children are in that Covenant for substance which was made with *Abraham, Gen.* 17. 7. as appears by sundry Scriptures, which being rightly considered, and compared, do inferre the continuance of the substance of that Covenant, whereby God is a God to his People and their seed, under the new Testament, *Acts* 2. 39. *Gal.* 3. 14. with *Gen.* 28. 4. *Rom.* 11. 16, 17 . . . [p. 2 line 23—p. 3, line 12.] . . .

Arg. 2. Such children as are by Christ, affirmed to have a place and portion in the Kingdome of Heaven, they have a place and portion in the visible Church, and so consequently are members thereof. . . . [p. 3. l. 15—p. 4. l. 4.]

Arg. 3. If no children be members of the visible Church, then was not the Lord Jesus (when a child) a member of the visible Church, but none (we presume) will venture to say so of Christ.

Arg. 4. If it were not so, no children might be Baptized: For Baptisme being a Church Ordinance, and a seal of being incorporated into the Church, 1 *Cor*. 12. 13. and succeeding circumcision, which was proper to the Church, none can be subjects immediately capable thereof, but Church-Members; Nor doth the Power of Officers, as such, extend further then to the Churches; as they cannot judge, so they may not Baptize them that are without, or non-members.

Arg. 5. They that are some of the Disciples intended in *Mat*. 28. 19. are Church-members. . . . [l. 18—l. 31.] But some children are some of the Disciples intended in *Mat*. 28. 19. For 1. some children were some of those whom the Apostles in accomplishing that com-[5] mission, did Disciple, *Acts* 15. 20. . . . [l. 1.—l. 9.] And that the Apostles took in children with Parents when they were conversant in the work of Discipling, further appears from *Acts* 2. 39. & 16. 15, 31, 33. 1 *Cor*. 7. 14. . . . [l. 13–l. 23.]

Arg. 6. They that are subjects of the Lords visible Spiritual Kingdom, servants and children of the Lords Family, they are Members of the Church, which is called the Lords Kingdom, and House and Family in the Scripture: But so are some children, *Ezek*. 37. 25, 26, 27 . . [l. 28—p. 6. l. 18.]

Arg. 7. If no children be members of the visible Church, then we have no well-grounded hope according to ordinary course of dispensation, of the salvation of any dying Infants: And the reason is, because salvation pertains to the Church, *Isa*. 45. 17. *Eph*. 2. 12. & 5. 23, 26. *Joh*. 4. 22. *Act*. 2. 27. *Luke* 19. 9. . . . [l. 23—p. 7. l. 3.]

Arg. 8. If some children were Members of the Church of God in the old Testament, then some children are Members of the Church of God in the daies of the new Testament: But some children were Members of the Church in the time of the old Testament. . . . [l. 7—p. 8. l. 4.]

But all the Question will be about the consequence of the Proposition, and that may be cleared thus.

1. If the Church of the old Testament and the Church of the Gentiles under the new Testament, be for kind essentially the same, then if children were Members of that Church, they are also Members of these: [modern Gentile churches] . . . [l. 9.—p. 9. l. 3.]

2. Again, If the consequence be not good, then it will follow

that such *Jews* as were brought in by the Gospel into Church-estate, were great losers by embracing the Gospel; and the children losers by their Parents Faith, inasmuch as though in the former state, the children were Members with the Parents. . . . [l. 8.—p. 11. l. 4.]

5. If children were once Church-members and do not continue to be Church-members still, then their Membership must have been repealed by the Lord, who alone could make such an alteration. . . . [l. 7—l. 15.]

1. If the Lord had made such an alteration . . . then in all likelihood Christ or his Apostles would have made mention of it. . . . but now Christ and his Apostles in stead of mentioning any such thing, do confirm the contrary, *Mark* 10, 13, 14, 16. *Acts* 2. 39. 1 *Cor*. 7. 14. . . . [p. 11. l. 23—p. 12. l. 13.]

Quest. 2. *Whether all children of whatever years or condition be so, as,* 1. *Absent children never brought to the Church.* 2. *Born before their Parents Covenanting.* 3. *Incorrigible of seven, ten, or twelve years old.* 4. *Such as desire not to be admitted with their Parents, of such an age.*

Ans. Onely such children as are in their minority, covenant with their Parents; therefore not all children of whatsoever years and conditions. We do not hereby exclude such as being defective in their intellectuals, are as children in respect of their incapacity. . . . 2. Children in their minority, though absent, covenant in their Parents. . . . 3. Children born before their Parents covenanting, yet if in their minority when their Parents enter into covenant, do covenant with them. . . . [p. 4. l. 1.] 4. There is no sufficient reason (at least ordinarily) to conclude a child of seven, ten, or twelve years old to be incorrigible. . . . [l. 4—l. 15.]

Quest. 3. *Till what age shall they enter into Covenant with their Parents, whether sixteen, twenty one, or sixty?*

Ans. As long as in respect of age or capacity they cannot according to ordinary account, be supposed able to act in a matter of this nature for themselves, . . . much is to be left unto the discretion of Officers and Churches in this case.

Quest. 4. *What Discipline a child is subject to, from seven to sixteen years old?*

[14] *Ans.* 1. Church Discipline is taken either more largely for the act of a Church-member dispensed to a Church-member as such, by way of Spiritual watch, rebuke, *&c*. . . . Or more strictly, for the act of the whole Church, dispensed by a Member

thereof; as in case of publick rebuke, admonition, excommunication. . . . In the first sense, children in their minority, are subject to Church Discipline immediately, but not in the second.

2. It is the Duty of the Elders and Church to call upon Parents to bring up their children in the nurture and admonition of the Lord, and to see as much as in them lieth, that it be effectually done, . . .

3. Besides their subjection to Ecclesiastical Discipline, they are also subject to civil Discipline respectively according to their capacity, whether Domesticall, Scholasticall, or Magistraticall.

Quest. 5. *Whether a Father may twice Covenant for his Children in Minority in several Churches?*

Ans. 1. When a Parent is called to remove from one Church to another, he is also called to enter into covenant in that Church to which he removes. . . . [p. 14. l. 25—p. 15. l. 2.]

2. When the Parent thus removing, entreth into covenant, his children then in minority covenant in him: . . .

3. Hence it is the duty of Churches when they give Letters dimissory unto Parents, to insert the dismission of the children then in minority with them.

4. Adult children yet under the power of the Parents and removing with them, are to give their personal consent unto this translation of their Membership, and so to be orderly dismissed and received with their Parents, otherwise they remain Members of the Church of which they were before.

Quest. 6. *Whether the end of a Deputy Covenant, be not to supply personall incapacity, or whether Children ripe for personall Covenanting in regard of age, should Covenant by a Deputy, as others that are unable thereunto?*

Ans. 1. Children in their minority, whose immediate Parents are in Church-Covenant, do covenant in their Parents; . . .

2. Children adult ought to covenant in their own Persons. To covenant in our own persons according to the sense of this Question, is nothing else but an orderly and Church profession of our Faith, or a personall publick and solemn avouching of God, in an Ecclesiasticall way, to be our God, according to the covenant of his Grace, . . . [p. 15. l. 30—p. 17. l. 12.]

Quest. 7. *Whether as large Qualifications be not required of a Members child to the participation of the Lords Supper, and the priviledges of votes and censures, as were requirable of his Parents at their first entrance?*

Ans. The holding forth of Faith and Repentance with an

ability to examine themselves, by way of confession, to the judgment of Charity, were all requirable in the Parent for admission into the Church to full communion, and the same is requisite for the regular admission of the Parents child being grown adult, unto his full communion with the Church. . . . [p. 17. l. 22—p. 18. l. 29.] . . . Concerning the power of voting, it is not rational that they should exercise a Church-power as to the administration of Church-Ordinances, which voting implies, who themselves are unfit for all Ordinances. . . . [p. 18. l. 33—p. 19. l. 6.]

Ques. 8. *Whether by Covenant seed, is meant the seed of immediate Parents onely, or of remote also?*

Ans. The Gospel by Covenant seed, intends only the seed of immediate Parents in Church Covenant, as appears from 1 *Cor.* 7. 14. The Parents there spoken of are immediate Parents, their Progenitors were Heathens. The Gospel extends not the external Covenant beyond the immediate Parents. . . . [l. 13—l. 26.]

Ques. 9. *Whether adopted Children and bond servants be Covenant-seed?*

Ans. Adopted children and Infant-servants, regularly and absolutely subjected to the Government and dispose of such heads of Families as are in Church-covenant, though they cannot be said to be their natural seed, yet in regard[1] the Scriptures (according to the judgment of many Godly Learned) extend to them the [20] same Covenant priviledges with their natural seed, we judge not any Churches who are like-minded with them, for their practise herein: All which nothwithstanding, yet we desire at present to leave this Question without all prejudice on our parts to after free disquisition.

Ques. 10. *Whether the child admitted by his Fathers Covenant, be also a Deputy for his seed, without or before personal Covenanting, or without & before like personal qualifications in kind, as his Father was to enjoy when he became a Deputy?*

Ans. The meaning of this Question in other terms we conceive to be this; whether the child of a person joyned in Church-Covenant by means of his or her immediate Parents Covenant, though such a Parent be not admitted to, nor qualified for full communion, nor have covenanted in their own person, whether we say, the child of such a person is to be baptized: Whereunto we answer, in these following propositions.

Propos. 1. Infants either of whose immediate Parents are in Church-Covenant, do confæderate with their Parents, and are therefore Church-members with them. See Ans. to Quest. 1.

[1] Perhaps *to such children* should be inserted.

Propos. 2. It is the duty of those Infants when grown up to years of discretion, though not yet fit for the Lords Supper, to own the Covenant they made with their Parents, by entring thereinto in their own persons, and it is the duty of the Church to call upon them for the performance thereof; as appeareth by Scripture examples of persons both called to, and entring into Covenant, many of whom could not be looked upon as personally Gracious, and therefor not fit for all Ordi- [21] nances and full communion, *Deut.* 29. 12, 14. 2 *Chron.* 15. 12. 2 *Chron.* 34. 31, 32. . . .

Propos. 3. Being accordingly called thereunto, if after Church-admonition and other due means with patience used, they shall refuse the performance of this great duty, or in case they shall (notwithstanding like means applied) any otherwise continue scandalous, it is the part of the Church to proceed with them to the censure of excommunication . . . [p. 21. l. 11—l. 24.]

Propos. 4. In case they understand the grounds of Religion, are not scandalous, and solemnly own the Covenant in their own persons, wherein they give up both themselves and their children unto the Lord, and desire Baptism for them, we (with due reverence to any Godly Learned that may dissent) see not sufficient cause to deny Baptism unto their children, these reasons for the affirmative being proposed to consideration.

1. Church-Members without offence and not bapti- [22] zed, are to be baptized.

The children in Question are Church-Members without offence and not baptized.

Therefore the children in Question are to be baptized.

2. Children in the covenant of *Abraham*, as to the substance thereof, *i. e.* To whom the promise made to *Abraham*, as to the substance thereof doth belong, are to be baptized.

The children in Question are children in the covenant of *Abraham*, as to the substance thereof.

Therefore the children in Question are to be baptized.

3. Children in the same estate with those children under the Law, unto whom the seal of the righteousnesse of Faith, because in that estate was by Institution Divine to be applied, the Precept for so doing not repealed, and the reason for so doing still remaining are to be baptized.

But the children in Question are children in the same estate [etc.]

Therefore the children in Question are to be baptized.

4. Either the children in question are to be baptized, or the Gospel dispensation forbids the application of the seal unto children regularly in Church-covenant, unto whom the Mosaical dispensation commanded it to be applied.

[23] But the Gospel dispensation forbids not [etc.] . . .

Therefore the children in question are to be baptized. [l. 6–l. 16.]

5. Children unto whom the Gospel testifieth both the promise and baptisme by vertue of that promise, to belong, ought to be baptized.

The children in question are children unto whom [etc.]

Therefore the children in Question ought to be baptized.

Obj. The Parent though a Church-member, owning the Covenant in his own person, and qualified according to the premises, is not admitted to full communion, therefore the child ought not to be baptized.

Ans. The Church-act onely, and not any other act (much lesse defect) of the Parent is by Divine Institution, accounted to the child. The membership of the child is a distinct membership, from the membership [24] of the Parent. In case the Parents membership ceaseth by death or censure, the membership of the child remaineth still. The membership of the child is the same in kind with, and not inferiour to the membership of the Parent. Membership is a Relation, and therefore admits not of *magìs* and *minùs*, more or lesse: Members are better or worse, and communion is more or lesse; but membership admits not of degrees. *Benjamin* an Infant, but an hour old, is as truly a son as *Reuben*, a man of twenty two years of age. The child is baptized by vertue of his own membership, and not by vertue of his Parents membership. The Parents death is not with us an obstacle of the Childs Baptism.

Propos. 5. The same may be said concerning the children of such persons in question, who being dead or necessarily absent, either did or do give the Churches cause in judgment of charity, to look at them as thus qualified, and such, as had they been called thereunto would so acted: For in Charity that is here done interpretatively, which is mentioned in the fourth Proposition expresly.

Propos. 6. Though the persons forementioned own the Covenant according to the premises, yet before they are admitted to full communion (*i. e.* To the Lords Supper and voting) they must so hold forth their Faith and Repentance, unto the judgment of Charity by way of confession in the congregation, as it may appear unto the Church, that they are able to examine themselves and to discern the Lords body. See the proof hereof in *Ans.* to *Quest.* 7th.

Quest. 11. *Whether children begotten by an excommunicate person are to be baptized, he so remaining?*

[25] *Ans.* We cannot for the present answer the following Arguments for the Negative. 1. Persons excommunicate are not members . . . 2. Excommunicate Parents are to be looked at in Church-account as Heathens and Publicans. . . . 3. To baptize the children of the excommunicate, is to have Church-communion with the excommunicate: . . . [p. 25. l. 12—l. 16.]

Quest. 12. *Whether a Child born of a justly censurable person, yet not actually excommunicate, be to be baptized?*

Ans. We answer affirmatively. . . . [l. 19—l. 25.]

Quest. 13. *Whether a Members Childs unfitness for seals, disableth not his seed for Membership or Baptism?*

Ans. This question agreeing in scope with *Quest.* 10. We refer thither for Answer thereunto.

Quest. 14. *Whether a Members Child be censurable for any thing but scandalous actions, and not also for ignorance and inexperience?*

Ans. A Members child (like as it is with all other [26] members) is censurable only for scandalous sins, *Mat.* 18. 15, 18. 1 *Cor.* 5. 11. . . . [l. 2—l. 6.]

Quest. 15. *Whether a Members Child must only examine himself, and may not be examined by others, of his fitnesse for seals?*

Ans. It is a duty of a Members child to examine himself, and yet he is also subject to the examination of others. . . . [l. 11—l. 24.]

Quest. 16. *Whether only Officers must examine in private or else publike before the Church?*

Ans. Concerning their examination by the Elders in private, the former reasons conclude affirmatively. . . .

[27] Publick examination we also conceive to be regular, . . . [p. 27. l. 2.–l. 7.]

Quest. 17. *Whether the same grown Members Child must not be examined of his Charitable experience, before Baptism, as well as before the Lords Supper?*

Ans. We think the Elders do well to take an account of children, concerning the Principles of Religion according to their capacity, before they be baptized. . . . [l. 13—l. 23.]

Quest. 18. *Whether baptized Children sent away from the Church for settlement, and not intending return, are continually to be accounted Members?*

Ans. Baptized children though locally removed from the Church unto which they belong, are to be accounted Members, until dismission, death or censure dissolve that Relation, because Christ the Institutor of this Relation, onely by these waies dissolveth the same.

Quest. 19. *Whether Historical Faith and a blamelesse life fit a Members Child for all Ordinances and* [28] *Priviledges, and he must be examined only about them?*

Ans. Not only historical Faith, *i. e.* The meer knowledge of the fundamental Doctrine of Faith and a blamelesse life, but also such an holding forth of Faith and Repentance, as unto judgment of Charity sheweth an ability to examine themselves and to discern the Lords body, is requisite to fit a Members child for all Ordinances and Priviledges, and his blamelesse life notwithstanding, a Members child is to be examined concerning the other qualifications. . . . [p. 28. l. 11.—l. 32.]

Quest. 20. *Whether if a Church-Member barely say, it repents me, though seventy times seven times follow-*[29]*ing he relapse into the same gross evils, as lying, slander, oppression,* &c. *He be to be forgiven, and not censured?*

Ans. . . . Without the fruits meet for repentance, we are not called to forgive, *Mat.* 3. 8. *Luk.* 17. 3.

Notwithstanding a Brother offends seventy times seven times, that is, many times, a definite number being put for an indefinite, yet whilst God enables him to repent, it is our duty to forgive. 'Tis not the number of offences, but the holding forth of repentance in the offender, that is the measure of our forgivenesse. . . . [p. 29. l. 17—l. 29.]

Quest. 21. *Whether a Member under offence and not censured, or not with the highest Censure, can authoritatively be denied the Lords Supper or other Church-priviledges?*

Ans. 1. None but the Church can Authoritatively [30] deny to the Member his accesse unto the Lords Supper, because the power thereof is only delegated to that subject, *Mat.* 18. 17.

2. The Church cannot deny unto a Member his accesse unto the Lords Supper, untill she hath regularly judged him to be an offender.

3. The censure of admonition is the first act whereby a Church doth judicially declare a Member to be an offender; therefore till the censure of admonition be past, a Member cannot Authoritatively be denied communion in the Lords Supper, or other Church-priviledges, because of offence.

4. After the sentence of Admonition is past, the offender now admonished, may be (yea thereby is) Authoritatively denied to come unto the Lords Supper, and to vote in the Church, because he is judicially unclean, *Lev.* 22. 3, 4. & 7. 20, 21. *Mat.* 5. 23, 24. Though he be not yet Censured with the Censure of Excommunication.

5. All which notwithstanding, there are cases wherein a Brother apparently discerned to be in a condition rendring him (should he so proceed to the Lords Supper) an unworthy Communicant, may and ought regularly to be advised to forbear, and it is his duty to hearken thereunto.

6. Yet two things are here carefully to be attended.

1. That Brethren be not many Masters, taking upon them to advise and to admonish others to abstain without cause, or before the time, *Jam.* 3. 1.

2. That none forbear to come worthily, which is their duty, because to their private apprehension, another is [31] supposed (at least) to come unworthily, which is their sin.

7. In case the Church shall see cause to advise a Member to forbear, and he shall refuse to hearken thereunto, his refusal being also a violation of Church Order, addeth contumacy to his offence, and thereby ripens the Offender for Censure.

19 4th. 1657.
Boston. N. E.

Result of the Synod of 1662

PROPOSITIONS | concerning the | SUBJECT of BAPTISM | and | *CONSOCIATION* of *CHURCHES*, | Collected and Confirmed out of the WORD of GOD, | by a | SYNOD of ELDERS | *AND* | messengers of the churches | in *Massachusets*-Colony in *New-England*. | Assembled at *BOSTON*, according to Appointment of the | Honoured *GENERAL COURT*, | In the Year 1662. | ——— | *At a* General Court *held at* Boston *in* New- | England *the* 8th *of* October, 1662. | T*He Court having Read over this Result of the Synod, judge meet to* | *Commend the same unto the Consideration of all the Churches and* | *People of this Jurisdiction*; *And for that end doe Order the Printing* | *thereof*. | By the Court. *Edward Rawson* Secret'. | ——— | *CAMBRIDGE* : | Printed by *S. G.* for *Hezekiah Usher* at *Boston* in | *New-England*. 1662.

[ii Blank]

[iii]

THE PREFACE[1]

TO THE

CHRISTIAN READER;

And especially to the Churches of *Massachusets*-Colony in *NEW-ENGLAND*.

T*Hat one end designed by God's All-disposing Providence, in leading so many of his poor people into this Wilderness, was to lead them unto a distinct discerning and practise of all the Wayes and Ordinances of his House according to Scripture-pattern, may seem an Observation not to be despised. That we are fit or able for so great a service, the sense of our own feebleness forbids us to think. But that we have large and great opportunity for it, none will deny. For, besides the useful Labours and Contemplations of many of the Lords Worthies in other places, and in former times, contributing to our Help, and shewing our Principles to be neither novell nor singular, the advantage of Experience and Practise, and*

[1] This Preface was prepared after the close of the Synod, by order of the Massachusetts General Court, by the Committtee appointed by the Synod to report the results to the Court. It is probably from the pen of Jonathan Mitchell. See *ante*, p. 269.

the occasion thereby given for daily searching into the Rule, is considerable. And He that hath made the path of the just as a shining light, *is wont still to give unto them further light, as the progress of their path requires further practise, making his* Word a Lanthorn to their feet, *to shew them their way from step to step, though haply sometimes they may not see far before them. It is matter of humbling to us, that we have made no better improvement of our opportunities this way; but some Fruits God hath given, and is to be praised for.*

In former years, and while sundry of the Lords eminent Servants, now at rest from their labours, were yet with us, A Platform of Church-Discipline, *comprizing the brief summe thereof, especially in reference to the* Constitution *of Churches (which was our first work when we came into this Wilderness) was agreed upon by a* Synod *held at* Cambridge, *and published to the world: From which (as to the substance thereof) we yet see no cause to recede. Some few particulars referring to the* Continuation and Combination *of Churches, needed yet a more ex-*[iv]*plicite stating and reducing unto practise. For though the Principles thereof were included in what is already published, yet that there hath been a defect in practise (especially since of late years there was more occasion for it) is too too apparent: For the rectifying whereof, a more particular Explication of the Doctrine also about these things, is now necessary.*

In order hereunto, by the Care and Wisdome of our Honoured General Court, *calling upon all the* Churches *of this Colony, to send their* Elders *and* Messengers, *this* Synod *was assembled, who after earnest Supplications for Divine Assistance, having consulted the holy Scriptures touching the Questions proposed to them, have proceeded to the following Issue; hoping that if it might seem meet to the Father of Lights to guide the Churches unto a right Understanding and Practice of his Will in these things also, the beauty of Christ's wayes and Spiritual Kingdome among us would be seen in some more compleatness then formerly. For that which was the prayer of* Epaphras *for the* Colossians, *ought to be both the prayer and labour of us all;* viz. that we might stand perfect and compleat in all the will of God: *And we trust it is our sincere desire, that his Will, all his Will, and nothing else but his Will, might be done among us.* To the Law and to the Testimony *we do wholly referre our selves, and if any thing in the following Conclusions be indeed found not to speak according thereunto, let it be rejected.*

We are not ignorant that this our Labour will by divers be diversly censured; some will account us too strict in the Point of Baptism, *and others too laxe and large: But let the Scriptures be Judge between us all. There are two things, the Honour whereof is in a special manner dear to God, and which He cannot endure to be wronged in;* viz. *His* Holiness, *and His* Grace. *The Scripture is often putting us in minde how much the Lord loveth Holiness, and that in his House, and in the holy Ordinances thereof, and how he abhorreth the contrary,* Mal 2. 11. Psal. 93. 5. & 2. 6. Lev. 11. 44, 45. Ezek 22. 26. & 44. 7, 8. *And hence neither dare we admit those unto the holy Table of the Lord, that are short of Scripture-qual-*

ifications for it; viz. *Ability to* examine themselves, *and* discern the Lords body; *Nor yet receive or retain those in Church-estate, and own them as a part of the Lords holy People, that are visibly and notoriously unholy, wicked and prophane: such we are bidden to* put away from among us, 1 *Cor.* 5. 13. *and therefore ought not to continue* [v] *among us. Neither may we administer Baptism to those whose parents are not under any Church-power or Government any where. To baptize such, would be to give the Title and Livery to those that will not bear the yoke of Christs Disciples, and to put the holy Name of God upon them, touching whom we can have no tolerable security that they will be educated in the wayes of Holiness, or in the knowledge and practise of Gods holy Will.* Baptism, *which is the Seal of Membership in the Church* the Body of Christ, *and an* engaging Sign, *importing us to be the devoted* Subjects *of Christ, and of all his holy Government, is not to be made a common thing, nor to be given to those, between whom and the God-less licentious world there is no visible difference: This would be a provocation and dishonour to* the Holy One of Israel.

On the other hand, we finde in Scripture, that the Lord is very tender of his Grace; *that he delighteth to manifest and magnifie the Riches of it, and that he cannot endure any straitning or eclipsing thereof, which is both dishonourable unto God, and injurious unto men,* Gal. 2 21. Eph. 2. 7. & 3. 2, 6, 8 Rom 11. 1, 5. Acts 15. 10, 11. & 10. 15 & 20. 24, 26, 27. *And in special he is large in the* Grace of his Covenant *which he maketh with his* visible Church *and People, and tender of having the same straitned. Hence when he takes any into Covenant with himself, he will not only be* their God, *but* the God of their seed after them in their generations, *Genes.* 17, 7, 9. *And although the apostate wicked parent (that rejecteth God and his Wayes) do cut off both himself and his Children after him,* Exod. 20. 5. & 34. 7. *Yet the Mercy and Grace of the Covenant is extended to the faithful and their seed unto* a thousand generations, *if the successive parents do but in the least degree shew themselves to be* lovers of God, and keepers of his *Covenant and* Commandments, *so as that the Lord will never reject them till they reject him,* Exod 20. 6. Deut. 7. 9. Psal 105. 8, 9. Rom. 11. 16 - - 22. *Hence we dare not (with the Antipædobaptist) exclude the* Infant-children of the faithful *from the* Covenant, *or from* Membership *in the visible Church, and consequently not from* Baptism *the Seal thereof. Neither dare we exclude the same children from Membership (or put them out of the Church) when they* are grown up, *while they so walk and act, as to keep their standing in the Covenant and doe not reject the same. God owns them still, and they doe in some measure* [vi] *own him: God rejects them not, and therefore neither may we; and consequently* their children *also are not to be rejected. Should we reject or exclude any of these, we should shorten and straiten the grace of God's Covenant, more then God himself doth, and be injurious to the Souls of men, by putting them from under those Dispensations of Grace, which are stated upon the visible Church, whereby the children of God's visible people are suc-*

cessively in their Generations to be trained up for the Kingdome of Heaven, (whither the Elect member shall still be brought in the way of such means) and wherein he hath given unto Officers and Churches a solemn charge to take care of, and train up such, as a part of his flock, to that end; saying to them, as sometimes to Peter, If you love me, feed my lambs. *In obedience to which charge we hope it is, that we are willing and desirous (though with the inference of no small labour and burthen to our selves) to commend these Truths to the Churches of Christ; that* all the Flock, *even the Lambs thereof, being duly stated under* Pastoral *Power, we might after a faithfull discharge of our Duty to them, be able to give up our* account *another day* with joy and not with grief.

How hard it is to finde and keep the right middle way of Truth in these things, is known to all that are ought acquainted with the Controversies there-about. As we have learned and believed, we have spoken; but not without remembrance that we are poor feeble frail men, and therefore desire to be conversant herein with much humility and fear before God and man. We are not ignorant of variety of judgements concerning this Subject; which notwithstanding, with all due reverence to Dissenters, after Religious search of the Scriptures, we have here offered what seems to us to have the fullest Evidence of Light from thence; if more may be added, and may be found contained in the Word of God, this shall be no prejudice thereunto. Hence also we are farre from desiring that there should be any rigorous imposition of these things (especially as to what is more narrow therein, and more controversal among godly men.) If the Honoured Court see meet so farre to adde their countenance and concurrence, as to commend a serious consideration hereof to the Churches, and to secure those that can with clearness of judgement practise accordingly, from disturbance, that in this case may be sufficient. To tolerate, or to desire a Toleration of damnable Heresies, or of Subverters of the Fundamentals of Faith or Order, were an [vii] *irreligious inconsistency with the love of true Religion: But to bear one with another in lesser differences, about matters of a more difficult and controversal nature, and more remote from the Foundation, and wherein the godly-wise are not like-minded, is a Duty necessary to the peace and wel-fare of Religion, while we are in the state of infirmity. In such things let not him that practiseth* despise him *that forbeareth, and let not him that forbeareth* judge him *that practiseth,* for God hath received him.

But as we do not thus speak from doubting of the Truth here delivered (Paul knows *where the Truth lyes, and* is perswaded of it, *Rom.* 14. 14. *yet he can lovingly bear a Dissenter, and in like manner should we*) *So we do in the bowels of Christ Jesus commend the consideration of these things unto our Brethren in the several Churches. What is here offered is farre from being any declining from former Principles, it is rather a pursuance thereof; for it is all included in, or deducible from what we unanimously professed and owned in the fore-mentioned* Platform of Discipline, *many years since. There it is asserted, that* Children are Church-members; That they have many priviledges which others (not Church-members) have not; and that they are under Discipline in the Church, *chap.* 12. *sect.* 7. *and that will infer the right of their children, they continuing to walk orderly. And the other matter of* Consociation, *or exercise of* Communion of Churches, *is largely held forth* Chap. 15. & 16.

It may be an Objection lying in the mindes of some, and which many may desire a fuller Answer unto; That these things, or some of them, are Innovations *in our Church-wayes, and things which the Lord's Worthies in* New-England, *who are now with God, did never teach nor hold, and therefore why should we now, after so many years, fall upon new Opinions and Practises? Is not this* a declining *from our first Purity, and a blameable Alteration? To this: Although it were a sufficient Answer to say, That in matters of Religion, not so much what* hath been *held or practised, as what* should be, *and what the Word of God prescribes, ought to be our Enquiry and our Rule. The people in* Nehemiah's *time are commended for doing as* they found written in the Law, *though* from the dayes of Joshua the son of Nun, unto that day, the children of Israel had not done so, *Nehem.* 8. 14, 17. *See the like* 2 Chron. 30. 5, 26. 2 Kings 23. 21, 22. *they did not tye themselves to former use and custome, but to the Rule of Gods written Word, and so* [viii] *should we. It was* Thyatira's *praise, that their good works were* more at the last then at the first, *Rev.* 2. 19. *The Lord's humble and faithfull Servants are not wont to be forward to think themselves* perfect *in their attainments, but desirous rather to make* a progress *in the knowledge and practise of God's holy Will. If therefore the things here propounded concerning the children of Church-members, and the Consociation of Churches, be a part of the Will of God contained in the Scriptures, (as we hope the Discourse ensuing will shew them to be) that doth sufficiently bespeak their entertainment, although they had not formerly been held or heard of amongst us. Yet this must not be granted, the contrary being the Truth,* viz. *that the Points herein which may be most scrupled by some, are known to have been the judgement of the generality of the Elders of these Churches for many years, and of those that have been of most eminent esteem among us. As (besides what was before mentioned from the* Platform of Discipline) *may appear by the following* Testimonies *from sundry Eminent and Worthy* Ministers of Christ *in* New-England, *who are now with God.*

First, Touching the children of Church-members.

Mr. Cotton *hath this saying*; The Covenant and Blessing of *Abraham* is that which we plead for, which the Apostle saith is come upon us Gentiles, *Gal.* 3. 14. which admitteth the faithful and their Infant-seed, not during their lives, in case their lives should grow up to Apostacy or open Scandal, but during their infancy, and so long after as they shall continue in a visible profession of the

Covenant and Faith, and Religion of their fathers: otherwise, if the children of the faithful grow up to Apostacy, or any open Scandal, (as *Ishmael* and *Esau* did) as they were then, so such like now are to be cast out of the fellowship of the Covenant, and of the Seals thereof. *Grounds and Ends of Baptism of Children.*[1] p. 106. *see also* p. 133, 134. *Again*, The seed of the Israelites, though many of them were not sincerely godly, yet whilest they held forth the publick profession of God's people, *Deut.* 26. 3 – – 11. and continued under the wing of the Covenant, and subjection to the Ordinances, they were still accounted an holy seed, *Ezra* 9. 2. and so their children were partakers of Circumcision. Yea further, though themselves were sometimes kept from the Lords Supper (the Passeover) for some or other uncleanness, yet that debarred not their children from [ix] Circumcision. Against this may it not seem vain to stand upon a difference between the Church of Israel and our Churches of the New-Testament— For the same Covenant which God made with the National Church of Israel and their seed, it is the very same for substance, and none other, which the Lord makes with any Congregational Church, and our seed. *Quæry* 9th *of Accommodation and Communion of Presbyt. and Congregat. Churches.*[2] *And the same for substance with those Quæries, was delivered by him in* 12. *Propositions, as Mr.* Tho: Allen *witnesseth in Epist. to the Reader before Treat. of Covenant and those Quæries.*[3] *Now in the* 8th *of those Propositions he hath these words:* The children of Church-members with us, though baptized in their infancy, yet when they come to age they are not received to the Lords Supper, nor admitted to fellowship of Voting in Admissions, Elections, Censures, till they come to profess their Faith and Repentance, and to lay hold of the Covenant of their parents before the Church; and yet their being not cast out of the Church, nor from the Covenant thereof, their children as well as themselves being within the Covenant, they may be partakers of the first Seal of the Covenant.[4] *Lastly, speaking to that Objection*, That the Baptism of Infants overthrows and destroys the Body of Christ, the holy Temple of God; and that in time it will come to consist of natural and carnal Members, and the power of Government rest in the hands of the wicked. *He Answers*, That this puts a fear where no fear is, or a causless fear. *And in prosecution of his Answer he hath these words*; Let the Primitive Practise be restored to its purity, (*viz. that due care be taken of baptized members of the Church for their fitting for the Lords Table*) and then there will be no more fear of pestering Churches with a carnal generation of members baptized in their infancy, then of admitting a carnal company of hypocrites confessing their Faith and Repentance in the face of the Congregation. Either the Lord in the faithfulness of his Covenant will sanctifie the hearts of the baptized

---

1 London, 1647.

2 *Certain Queries Tending to Accommodation and Communion of Presbyterian and Congregational Churches*, London, 1654, pp. 12, 13.

3 Allen's "To the Reader," p. [xiv]; prefaced to Cotton, *Covenant of Grace*, etc. London, 1659.

4 Doubtless from a manuscript.

Infants to prepare them for his Table, or else he will discover their hypocrisie and profaneness in the presence of his Church before men and Angels, and so prevent the pollution of the Lords Table, and corruption of the Discipline of the Church by their partaking in them. *Grounds and Ends of Baptism, &c.* p. 161, 163. *See also Holiness of Church-* [x] *members,*[1] p. 41, 51, 56, 57, 63, 87. *Bloody Tenent washed,*[2] p. 44, 78.

Mr. Hooker *saith,* Suppose a whole Congregation should consist of such who were children to Parents now deceased who were confederate, their children were true members according to the Rules of the Gospel, by the profession of their fathers Covenant, though they should not make any personal and vocal expression of their engagement as the fathers did. *Survey,*[3] *part* 1. p. 48. *Again,* We maintain according to truth, that the believing parent covenants and confesseth for himself and his posterity, and this covenanting then and now is the same for the kinde of it. *Part* 3. *p.* 25. *See* p. 17, 18. *&* part 1. p. 69, 76, 77. *And in the Preface, setting down sundry things, wherein he consents with Mr.* R.[4] *he expresseth this for one, that* Infants of visible Churches born of wicked parents, being members of the Church, ought to be baptized. In these (*saith he*) and several other particulars, we fully accord with Mr. *R. And Part* 3. p. 11. It is not then the Question, whether wicked members while they are tolerated sinfully in the Church they and their children may partake of the Priviledges? for this is beyond question, nor do I know, nor yet ever heard it denied by any of ours.

Mr. Philips, *speaking of* a people made partakers of Gods Covenant, and all the priviledges outwardly belonging thereto, *he saith,* Themselves and all that ever proceed from them, continue in the same state, parents and children successively, so long as the Lord continues the course of his Dispensation; nor can any alteration befall them, whereby this estate is dissolved, but some apparent act of God breaking them off from him. *Reply,*[5] p. 126. *Again, speaking of that Holiness,* 1 Cor. 7. 14. *he saith,* I take it of fœderal holiness, whereby the children are with the believing parents taken by God to be his, and by him put under his covenant, and so they continue when men of years, though they never have any further grace wrought in them, nor have any other state upon them, then what they had when they were born. *Ibid.* p. 131. Again, a company become or are a Church, either by conversion and initial constitution, or by continuance of the same constituted Churches successively by propagation of members, who all are born in Church-state, and under the covenant of God, and belong unto the Church, and are a Church successively so long as God shall continue his begun dispensation, even as well & as fully as the first. Ibid. p. 145.

---

[1] London, 1650.

[2] London, 1647.

[3] *Survey of the Summe of Church-Discipline*, London, 1648.

[4] Prof. Samuel Rutherford. See *ante*, p. 139.

[5] George Phillips, pastor at Watertown, Mass. *A Reply to a Confutation of some Grounds for Infant Baptism . . . put forth against me by one T. Lamb.* London, 1645.

[xi] *Mr.* Shepard in *Defence of the Nine Positions,*[1] p. 143. *hath this expression,* Concerning the Infants of Church-members, they are subject to Censures whensoever they offend the Church, as others are, though so long as they live innocently they need them not. *And in the year* 1649, *not three moneths before his Death,*[2] *he wrote unto a friend a large Letter (yet extant under his own Hand) concerning the Membership of Children, wherein he proveth by sundry Arguments* that they are Members, *and answereth sundry* Objections *against it, and sheweth at large* what great good there is in children's Membership. *In which Discourses he asserteth,* That as they are Members in their infancy, so they continue Members when they are grown up, till for their wickedness they be cast out; and that they being Members, their seed successively are members also, until by Dissolution or Excommunication they be unchurched: That though they are Members, it follows not that they must come to the Lords Supper, but they must first appear able to examine themselves, and discern the Lords Body: That the children of godly parents, though they do not manifest faith in the Gospel, yet they are to be accounted of Gods Church, until they positively reject the Gospel, *Rom.* 11. That this Membership of children hath no tendency in it to pollute the Church, no more then in the Old Testament, but is a means rather of the contrary; And that there is as much danger (if not more) of the degenerating and apostatizing of Churches gathered of professing Believers, as of those that rise out of the seed of such.

Mr. Prudden[3] *in a Letter to a friend written in the year* 1651. *doth plainly express it to be his judgement,* That the children of Church-members, are Members, and so have right to have their children baptized, though themselves be not yet admitted to the Lords Supper. *His words are these:*

Touching the desire of such Members children as desire to have their children baptized, it is a thing that I do not yet hear practised in any of our Churches. But for my own part, I am inclined to think, that it cannot justly be denied, because their next Parents (however not admitted to the Lords Supper) stand as compleat Members of the Church, within the Church-Covenant, and so acknowledged that they might have right to Baptism. Now they being in Covenant, and standing Members, their Children also are Members by virtue of their Parents Covenant and Membership, as well as they themselves were by virtue of their Parents Covenant and Membership; And they have not renounced that Covenant, nor are justly censured for breach of that Covenant, but do own it and profess it, and by virtue of it claim the priviledge of it to their Children. *Then he puts this his Argument into form thus:* Those Children who are within the Covenant of the C[h]urch, and so Members of it, Baptism cannot be denied unto. But the Children in question are within the Covenant of the Church, and so Members of it. Therefore Baptism cannot be denied unto them. The Assumption is proved thus: The [xii] Children of such Parents as are within the Covenant of the Church, and so Members of the Church, are themselves within the Covenant of the Church, and so Members of it. But the Children in question are Children of such Parents as are in Covenant, and so Members of the

---

1 Thomas Shepard, pastor at Cambridge, Mass. T. Shepard & T. Allin, *A Defence of the Answer made* [by John Davenport] *unto the 9. Questions . . . against the Reply thereto by John Ball.* London, 1645.

2 He died Aug. 25, 1649.

3 Peter Prudden, minister at Milford, Conn., died 1656.

Church. Therefore they are so themselves. The Proposition is clear, because the Parents Covenant for themselves, and for their Children, *Deut.* 29. 10,—16. *Ezek.* 16. 8, 13. And God accepts both, *Gen.* 17. 12, 13. the whole Nation is fœderally holy, *Ezra* 9. 2. they are expresly said to be in Covenant with their fathers, *Deut.* 29. not partly or partially in Covenant, *Rom.* 9. 3, 4. *Acts* 2. 39. and God styles himself their God as well as their fathers, *Gen.* 17. 7, 8, 9. and to have God to be our God, is to be in compleat Church-Covenant with him. The Assumption is evident, because else such their Parents had not had right to Baptism the Seal of the Covenant, but that they had right unto, and so received it; and the same right that they had, their Children have, who are included in their Covenant, as they were in their fathers — and are not less truely or less compleatly in Covenant.

Lastly, (to adde no more) Mr. Nath. Rogers,[1] *in a Letter to a Friend, bearing date* 18. 11. 1652. *hath these words:*

To the Question concerning the Children of Church-members, I have nothing to oppose, and I wonder any should deny them to be Members. They are Members *in censu Ecclesiastico*; God so calls them, the Church is so to account of them: And when they are *adultæ ætatis*, though having done no personal act, yet are to be in Charity judged Members still, and till after due calling upon, they shall refuse or neglect to acknowledge and own the Covenent of their Parents, and profess their belief of, and subjection to the contents thereof — For Practise, I confess I account it our great default, that we have made no more real distinction between these and others, that they have been no more attended, as the lambs of the Flock of Christ: and whether it be not the cause of the corruption and woeful defection of our youth, *disquiri permittimus.*

So that it was the judgement of these Worthies in their time, that the children of Church-members are members of the Church as well as their parents, and do not cease to be members by becoming adult, but do still continue in the Church, untill in some way of God they be cast out; and that they are subject to Church-discipline, even as other members, and may have their children baptized before themselves be received to the Lords Supper; *and yet that in this way there is no tendency to the corrupting of the Church by unworthy members, or of the Ordinances by unworthy partakers. And in the* Synod *held at* Cambridge *in the year* 1648. *that particular point of Baptizing the children of such as were admitted members in minority, but not yet in full communion, was inserted in some of the draughts that were prepared for that Assembly, and was then debated and confirmed by the like Arguments as we now use, and was generally consented to*; *though because some few dissented, and there was not the like urgency of occasion for present practise, it was not then put into the* Platform *that was after Printed.*[2] *We need not mention the* Meeting *of* Elders *at* Boston *upon the Call of the Honoured* Court *in the year* 1657. *where in* Answer to XXI. Questions, *since Printed, this Point is particularly asserted. By all which it appeareth, that these are not things lately devised; or before unheard-of, nor can they justly be censured* [xiii] *as* Innovations *or* Declensions *from the received Doctrine in* New-England. *It is true, that in the beginning of these Plantations, and the Infancy of these Churches, there was not so much said touching these things as there hath been since*; *and the reason is, Because then there was not the like occasion as since hath been: Few children of Church-members being then adult, at least few that were then married,*

[1] Nathaniel Rogers, pastor at Ipswich, Mass., died 1655.

[2] See *ante*, p. 181.

and had children. Accordingly, when a Question was put about the priviledges of Members children, when come to years, these Churches then having been but of few years standing, our Answer was, That by reason of the Infancy of these Churches, we had then had no occasion to determine what to judge or practise in that matter.[1] Answer to the 5$^{th.}$ and 6$^{th.}$ of 32.Questions: *which may satisfie as to the Reason why in our first beginnings there was no more said touching these Questions. But afterwards, when there was more cause for it, many of the Elders in these Churches, both such as are now living, and sundry who are now deceased, did declare their judgements as aforesaid, and this many years ago.*

Secondly, Touching Consociation of Churches, take these few Testimonies, in stead of many more that might be alledged.

Mr. Cotton, Keyes,[2] p. 54, 55. It is a safe and wholsome and holy Ordinance of Christ, for particular Churches to joyn together in holy Covenant, or Communion & Consociation among themselves, to administer all their Church-affairs (which are of weighty, and difficult and common concernment) not without common consultation and consent of other Churches about them. *And how it is so, he there sheweth in all the particulars. See also* p. 24, 25, 47 59.

Mr. Hooker, Survey, *see* part 4. p. 1, 2. & p. 45. *And in the Preface he professeth his consent with Mr.* R. That Consociation of Churches is not only lawful, but in some cases necessary. That when causes are difficult, and particular Churches want light and help they should crave the assistance of such a Consociation. That Churches so meeting have right to Counsel, Rebuke *&c.* as the case doth require. And in case any particular Church shall walk pertinaciously, either in the profession of Errour or sinful Practise, and will not hear their counsel, they may and should renounce the right hand of fellowship with them. *And after he sets down this of* Consociation of Churches *amongst other things, wherein* he had leave to profess the joynt Judgement of all the Elders upon the River; of *New-haven, Guilford, Milford, Stratford, Fairfield, and most of the Elders in the Bay.*[3] *By* [xiv] *which it is clear, that this point of Consociation of Churches is no new invention of these times, but was taught and professed in* New-England *many years agoe, for so it was we see in Mr.* Hooker*'s time, and it is now above fifteen years since he departed this life.*

To these our own Ministers, we shall only adde a passage in the Apologetical Narration *of Dr.* Goodwyn, *Mr.* Nye, *Mr.* Sidrach Simpson, *Mr.* Burroughes, *and Mr.* Bridge;[4] *wherein, besides much more to this purpose, touching the Remedy provided in the Congregational-way for mal-Administrations, or other miscarriages in Churches,* p. 16–21. *They set it down* (*in* p. 21.) *as their past and present Profession,* That it *is* the most to be abhorred Maxime that any Religion hath ever

[1] R. Mather, *Church-Government*, London, 1643 (Answer to Nos. 2, 5, and 6 of the XXXII Questions), p. 22. (Written 1639.)

[2] London, 1644.

[3] See *ante*, p. 148.

[4] The chief Congregationalists in the Westminster Assembly.

made profession of, and therefore of all other the most contradictory and dishonourable unto that of Christianity, that a single and particular Society of men, professing the Name of Christ, and pretending to be endowed with a Power from Christ, to judge them that are of the same Body and Society within themselves, should further arrogate unto themselves an exemption from giving account, or being censurable by any other, either Christian Magistrate above them, or Neighbour-Churches about them.[1] *See also Mr.* Burroughes Heart-Divis.[2] pag 43, 44.

Brethren, bear with us: Were it for our own Sakes, or Names, or Interests, we should not be sollicitous to beg Charity of you. With us it is a small thing to be judged of man's day. *But it is for your sakes, for your children's sake, and for the Lord's sake, that we intreat for a charitable, candid, and considerate Acceptation of our labour herein. It is that the* Congregations *of the Lord might be* established *before Him in* Truth and Peace, *and that they might have* one heart and one way *in the fear of God*, for the good of them and of their children after them. *Do we herein seek our selves? our own advantage, ease or glory? Surely we feel the contrary! What is it we desire, but that we might do our utmost to carry your poor Children to Heaven*; *and that we might see these Churches bound up together in the Bonds of Truth and Peace?* Forgive us this wrong. *But should the Church-education of your children be by the want of your hearty concurrence, rendered either unfeizible or ineffectual*; *should they live as* Lambs in a large place, *for want of your agreement to own them* of the Flock, *we beseech you to consider how uncomfortable the account hereof would be another day*: *We* pray *with the Apostle*, that you do no evil, not that we should appear approved, [xv] but that you should do that which is *good and right*, though we be rejected. For we can do nothing against the truth, but for the truth: and this also we wish, even your perfection, 2 *Cor.* 13. 7, 8, 9. *However, we hope after-ages will bear witness, that we have been in some measure faithful to the Truth in these things, and to this part of Christs Kingdome also in our generation.*

But we may not let pass this opportunity, without a word *of Caution and Exhortation to the* Youth *of the Country, the* children *of our Churches, whose Interest we have here asserted. Be not you puffed up with Priviledges, but humbled rather, in the awful sense of the Engagement, Duty, and danger that doth attend them: It is an high favour to have a place in* Bethel, in the house of God, and in the gate of Heaven; *but it is a* Dreadful place: *God will be* sanctified *in all that* come nigh him. *A place nigh unto God* (*or among his people who are* near to him, Ps. 148. 14.) *is a place of great fear*, Psa. 89. 7. Take heed *therefore unto your selves, when owned as* the people of the Lord your God, (*Deut.* 27, 9, 10.) lest there should be among you any root that beareth gall and wormwood. *Take heed that you do not with a*

---

[1] *An Apologeticall Narration Hvmbly Svbmitted to the Honourable Houses of Parliament*, London, 1643.

[2] *Irenicvm, To the Lovers of Truth and Peace. Heart-Divisions opened in the Causes and Evils of them . . . . And Endeavours to heal them.* London, 1646.

spirit of pride and haughtiness, or of vanity and slightness, either challenge or use any of your Priviledges. Think not to bear the Name of Christians, without bearing the Yoke of Christ. Remember, that all Relations to God and to his people, do come loaden with Duty; *and all Gospel-duty must be done in* humility. *The wayes of the Lord are right, and the humble and serious shall walk in them, but proud Transgressors shall fall therein. Be not* sons of Belial, *that can bear no yoke: Learn subjection to Christs holy Government in all the parts and wayes thereof. Be subject to your godly Parents: Be subject to your spiritual Fathers and Pastors, and to all their Instructions, Admonitions and Exhortations: Be subject unto faithful Brethren, and to words of counsel and help from them*: Ye younger, submit your selves unto the elder; *and to that end*, be clothed with humility. *Lye under the Word and Will of Christ, as dispensed and conveyed to you by all his appointed Instruments in their respective places. Break not in upon the Lord's Table (or upon the Priviledges of full Communion) without due qualification, and orderly admission thereunto, lest you* eat and drink your own damnation. *Be ordered, and take not upon you to order the affairs of Gods Family; that is not the place of those who are yet but in the state of Initiation and Education in the Church of God. Carry it in all things with a spirit of humility, modesty, sobriety and* [xvi] *fear, that our soules may not weep in secret for your* pride, *and that God may not* resist & reject *you as a generation of his wrath. Oh that the Lord would pour out a spirit of Humiliation & Repentance upon all the younger sort in the Country, (yea & upon elder too, for our neglects) from* Dan *to* Beersheba! *Oh that we might meet at* Bochim, *because so many Canaanites of unsubdued, yea growing corruptions are found among us! Let it not be said, that when the first & best generation in New-England were* gathered to their fathers, there arose another generation after them that knew not the Lord. *Behold, the* Lord had a delight in your fathers to love them, *and he hath chosen you* their seed after them, *to enjoy these Liberties & Opportunities, as it is this day*: Circumcise therefore the fore-skin of your hearts, and be no more stiff-necked, *but* yield your selves to the Lord, *and to the Order of* His Sanctuary, *to seek him, and wait on him in all his wayes with holy fear and trembling: for the Lord your God is gracious and merciful, and will not turn away his face from you, if you return unto him; if you seek him he will be found of you, but if you forsake him, he will cast you off for ever.*

We shall conclude, when we have given the Reader a short account of the Work ensuing. The Propositions *in Answer to the* first Question, *were (after much discussion and consideration from the Word of God) Voted and Concluded by the Assembly in* the particular terms *as they are here expressed. The* Arguments *then used for their* Confirmation, *being drawn up by some deputed thereunto, after they had been several times read and considered in the Assembly, were Voted and Consented to, as* to the summe and substance *thereof. The answer to the* second Question *is here given with great brevity, partly because so much is already said there-about in the foresaid* Platform of Discipline, *and partly by reason of great straits of time:*

But what is here presented was the joynt conclusion *of the Synod. A* Preface *was desired by the Assembly to be prefixed by some appointed thereunto, which is here accordingly by them performed.*

Now the God of truth & peace guide us & all his people in the wayes, & give us the fruits thereof; *help us to* feed *his flock and his lambs, & to be* fed *by him as the sheep of his pasture, that when the* chief-Shepherd shall appear, *we may* receive *together* a Crown of glory that fadeth not away, *& may enter into the joy of our Lord, as those that have neither despised his* little ones, *nor denied to be our* Brother's keeper: *But having faithfully endeavoured to promote the continuation of his Kingdom, & Communion of his people, may Rest & Reign with all Saints in the kingdom of his glory:* Unto whom be glory in the Church by Christ Jesus throughout all ages world without end.

[1]

THE ANSWER *OF THE* ELDERS *AND OTHER* MESSENGERS

of the Churches, Assembled at Boston *in the Year* 1662, TO *The Questions Propounded to them by ORDER of the* Honoured GENERAL COURT.

Quest, 1. WHO *are the Subjects of Baptism?*

Answ:

The Answer may be given in the following propositions, briefly confirmed from the Scriptures.

1 *They that according to Scripture, are Members of the Visible Church, are the subjects of Baptisme.*

2 *The Members of the Visible Church according to scripture, are Confederate visible Believers, in particular Churches, and their infant-seed,* i. e. *children in minority, whose next parents, one or both, are in Covenant.*

3 *The Infant-seed of confederate visible Believers, are members of the same Church with their parents, and when grown up, are personally under the watch, discipline and Government of that Church.*

4 *These Adult persons, are not therefore to be admitted to full Communion, meerly because they are and continue* [2] *members, without such further qualifications, as the Word of God requireth therunto.*

5 *Church-members who were admitted in minority, understanding the Doctrine of Faith, and publickly professing their assent thereto; not scandalous in life, and solemnly owning the Covenant before the Church, wherin they give up themselves and their children to the Lord, and subject themselves to the Government of Christ in the Church, their children are to be Baptised.*

6 *Such Church-members, who either by death, or some other extraordinary Providence, have been inevitably hindred from publick acting as aforesaid, yet have given the Church cause, in judgment of charity, to look at them as so qualified, and such as had they been called thereunto, would have so acted, their children are to be Baptised.*

7 *The members of Orthodox Churches, being sound in the Faith, and not scandalous in life, and presenting due testimony thereof; these occasionally comming from one Church to another, may have their children Baptised in the church whither they come, by virtue of communion of churches: but if they remove their habitation, they ought orderly to covenant and subject themselves to the Government of Christ in the church where they settle their abode, and so their children to be Baptised. It being the churches duty to receive such unto communion, so farr as they are regularly fit for the same.*

The Confirmation of these Propositions from the Scripture followeth.

Proposition First.

They that according to Scripture are members of the visible Church, are the subjects of Baptisme.

The trueth hereof may appear by the following evidences from the word of God.

1. When Christ saith, *Go ye therefore and* teach, or (as the Greek is) *disciple all Nations, Baptising them, Mat.* 28. 19 [3] he expresseth the adequate subject of Baptisme, to be *disciples,* or *discipled ones.* But *disciples* there is the same with *members of the visible Church*:

For the visible Church is Christs *school,* wherein all the members stand related and subjected to him, as their Master and Teacher, and so are his *scholars* or *disciples,* and under his teaching, as *verse* 20. And it is that visible spiritual Kingdome of Christ, which he there from his Kingly power, *ver*: 18. sendeth them to set up and administer in *ver*: 19. the subjects whereof are under his Lawes and Government: *verse* 20. Which subjects (or members of that Kingdome *i. e.* of the visible church) are termed disciples *verse* 19. Also in the Acts of the Apostles (the story of their accomplishment of that commission) *disciples* are usually put for *members of the visible church*: *Acts* 1. 15. *In the midst of the disciples*: who with others added to them, are called *the church*, *Acts* 2: 47: The members whereof are again called *disciples*, *Acts* 6: 1, 2. *Acts* 9; 1, . . . *against the disciples of the Lord* i. e. against *the church of God.* 1 *Cor.* 15 9 *Gal* 1. 13 *Acts* 9 26 *He assayed to joyn himself to the disciples. The disciples at Lystra, Iconium and Antioch*, Acts 14 21, 22 are called *the church* in each of those places *verse* 23 So *the church verse* 27 *the disciples verse* 28. Acts 18. 22 *the church at Cesarea*; Acts 21. 16 the *disciples of Cesarea*: So Acts 18. 23 with *chap.* 15. 41. and *Gal.* 1. 2. Acts 18. 27 and *chap.* 20 1 with *verse* 17. 28. From all which it appeareth that *disciples* in *Mat.* 28. 19 and *members of the visible church*, are termes equivalent: and *disciples* being there by Christ himselfe made subjects of Baptism, it follows that the members of the visible Church are the subjects of baptisme.

2. Baptisme is *the seal of first entrance or admission into the visible church*; as appeareth from those texts 1 *Cor*: 12: 13. *Baptised into one body*, i. e. our entrance into the body or church of Christ, is sealed by Baptisme: and *Rom*; 6. 3, 5; *Gal.* 3: 27. where it is shewed that Baptisme is the Sacrament of *union* or of *ingrafting* into Christ the head, and consequently into the church his body & from the Apostles cōstant practise in baptising [4] persons upon their first comming in, or first giving up themselves to the Lord and them. *Acts* 8. 12. & 16. 15, 33. & 18. 8. and in *Acts* 2. 41, 42. they were baptized at their first *adding* to the church, or admission into the *Apostles fellowship*, wherin they afterward *continued.* And from its answering unto circumcision, which was a seal of initiation or admission into the church; Hence it belongs to all and onely those that are entred into, that are within, or that are members of the visible chuch.

3. *They that according to Scripture are members of the visible Church, they are in Covenant.* For it is the Covenant that constituteth the Church, *Deut* 29. 12, 13. They must *enter into covenant*, that they might be *established the people* or Church *of God.* Now, the initiatory seal is affixed to the Covenant, and appointed to run parallel therewith, *Gen.* 17. 7, 9, 10, 11. so circumcision was: and hence called *the covenant Gen.* 17. 13. *Acts* 7. 8. and so Baptisme is,

being in like manner annexed to *the promise* or Covenant, *Acts* 2. 38, 39. and being the seal that answereth to circumcision; *Col:* 2. 11, 12.

4. *Christ doth Sanctifie and cleanse the Church by the washing of water, i. e.* by Baptisme *Eph.* 5. 25, 26. Therefore the whole Church and so all the members thereof (who are also said in Scripture to be *Sanctified in Christ Jesus*, 1 *Cor*: 1. 2.) are the subjects of Baptisme: And although it is the *invisible church*, unto the spiritual and eternall good whereof, this and all other Ordinances lastly have respect, and which the place mentioned in *Eph*: 5. may in a special mañer look unto, yet it is *the visible Church* that is the next and immediate subject of the administration thereof. For the subject of visible external ordinances to be administred by men, must needs be visible. And so the Apostles Baptized sundry persons, who were of the visible, but not of the invisible Church, as Simon Magus, Ananias and Sapphira, and others. And these are visibly *Purchased* and *Sanctified* by the bloud of Christ, *the Bloud of the covenant*, *Acts* 20. 28. *Heb* 10. 29. Therefore the visible seal of the covenant and of cleansing by Christs bloud belongs to them.

[5] 5. *The Circumcision is often put for the whole Jewish Church or for the members of the visible Church under the Old Testament.* Those within are expressed by [*the circumcised*][1] and those without by [*the uncircumcised.*] *Rom:* 15. 8. & 3. 30. *Eph:* 2, 11, *Judg:* 14. 3. & 15. 18. 1 *Sam:* 14. 6 & 17. 26, 36. *Jer.* 9, 25, 26. Hence by proportion Baptisme (which is our Gospel circumcision, Col: 2. 11, 12.) belongs to the whole visible Church under the new Testament. Actual and personal circumcision was indeed proper to the males of old, females being but inclusively and virtually circumcised, and so counted of the circumcision: but the Lord hath taken away that difference now, and appointed Baptisme to be personally applied to both sexes*: Acts:* 8. 12. & 16. 15. *Gal:* 3 28. So that every particular member of the visible Church is now a subject of Baptisme. We conclude therefore that Baptisme pertaines to the whole visible Church, and to all and every one therein, and to no other.

Proposition 2[d].

The members of the visible Church according to Scripture, are confederate visible believers, in particular Churches, and their infant-seed, i. e. *children in minority, whose next parents, one or both, are in Covenant.*

Sundry particulars are comprised in this proposition, which wee may consider and confirme distinctly.

---

[1] [ ] in original.

Partic: 1. *Adult persons who are members of the visible Church, are by rule confederate visible beleevers: Acts:* 5. 14. *believers were added to the Lord.* The *believing* Corinthians were members of the Church there *Acts* 18: 8 with 1 *Cor.* 1. 2. & 12. 27. The inscriptions of the Epistles written to Churches, and calling the members thereof *Saints*, and *faithfull*, shew the same thing, *Eph* 1. 1. *Phi* 1. 1. *Col.* 1. 2. And that confederation, *i. e.* coventing explicite or implicite, [the latter preserveth the essence of confederation, the former is duety and most desireable] is necessary to make one a member of the visible Church, appears. 1. Because the Church is constituted by Covenant: for there is [6] between Christ and the Church the mutuall engagement and relation of King and subjects, husband and spouse; this cannot be but by Covenant (internall, if you speak of the invisible Church, external of the visible) a church is a company that can say, God is our God and we are his people, this is from the covenant between God and them. *Deut* 29, 12, 13, *Ezek:* 16, 8. 3. [2] The church of the old Testament was the church of God *by covenant Gen*: 17, *Deut* 29 and was reformed still by renewing of the covenant 2 *chron* 15, 12. & 23, 16: & 34, 31 32: *Neh*: 9 38: Now the churches of the Gentiles, under the new Testament stand upon the same basis or *root* with the church of the Old Testament, & therefore are constituted by *Covenant*, as that was *Rom*: 11. 17. 18. *Eph*: 2 11, 12, 19 & 3: 6. *Heb:* 8: 10, 3. Baptisme enters us into the Church Sacramentally, *i, e*, by sealing the Covenant. The *Covenant* therefore is that which constitutes the Church and inferrs membership, and is the *Vow* in *Baptisme* commonly spoken of.

Partic: 2. *The members of the visible Church are such as are confederate in Particular Churches.* It may be minded that we are here speaking of Members so stated in the visible Church, as that they are Subjects to whom Church ordinances may regularly be administred, and that according to ordinary dispensation. For were it graunted, that *the Apostles* and *Evangelists* did sometimes Baptize such, as were not Members of any Particular Church, yet their extraordinary office, large Power and commission renders them not imitable therein by *ordinary Officers.* For then they might Baptize in private without the presence of a Christian assemblie, as *Philip did the Eunuch.* But that in ordinary dispensation the Members of the visible Church according to Scripture, are such as are Members of some particular Church, appeares, 1. Because the visible beleever that professedly Covenants with God, doth therein give up himselfe to wait on God in all his ordinances.

Deut 26: 17, 18. *Math*: 28, 19, 20. But all the Ordinances of God are to be enjoyed onely in a particular Church. For how often do we find in the Scripture that they came *together into one place* (or met as a congregational particular Church) for the observation and enjoyment of the Ordinances. *Acts*: 2: 1, 44, 46. [7] & 4, 31: & 11. 26. & 20: 7. 1 *Cor*. 5: 4. & 11. 18. 20: 33. & 14: 23. 2. The Apostle in his Epistles, writing to *Saints* or *Beleevers*, writes to them as in *particular Churches*. 1 *Cor*. 1: 2. *Eph*: 1. 1. *Phil*: 1: 1. *Col*: 1. 2. And when the story of the Acts speakes of Disciples other places shew that those are understood to be *Members of particular Churches*, *Acts* 18. 23. *with* Gal: 1: 2. *Acts* 21 16. *with Chap* 18: 22. *Acts* 11. 26. & 14: 22, 23, 27, 28. All which shewes that the Scripture acknowledgeth no settled orderly estate of visible beleevers in Covenant with God, but onely in particular Churches. 3. The members of the visible Church are Disciples, as was above cleared: now *Disciples* are under *Discipline* and liable to Church-censures: for they are stated subjects of Christs Laws and Government, *Mat*: 28. 19, 20. but Church Government and censures are extant now in ordinary dispensation, onely in a particular Church. *Mat* 18. 17. 1 *Cor*: 5. 4.

Partic: 3. The Infant-seed of confederate visible beleevers are also members of the visible Church. The truth of this is evident from the Scriptures and reasons following.

Argum: 1. *The covenant of Abraham as to the substance thereof*, viz, *that whereby God declares himselfe to be the God of the faithfull & their seed*, *Gen*: 17. 7. *continues under the Gospel*, as appears. 1 Because the Beleeving inchurched *Gentiles* under the new Testament, do stand upon the same *root* of *covenanting Abraham*: which the *Jewes* were *broken off from*, *Rom* 11, 16, 17 18. 2 Because Abraham in regard of that Covenant was made a *Father of many nations*, *Gen*: 17. 4, 5. even of Gentiles as well as Jewes, under New-Testament as well as Old, *Rom*: 4. 16 17. *Gal* 3, 29. *i, e*, in Abraham as a patterne and root, God (not onely shewed how he Justifies the beleever, *Gal*: 3, 6,–9. *Rom*: 4. but also) conveied that covenant to the faithfull and their seed in all nations, *Luk*: 19. 9. If a Son of Abraham, then *Salvation i, e*: the Covenant dispensation, of Salvation is *come to his house*. 3. As that covenant was communicated to proselyte Gentiles under the Old Testament, so its communication to the inchurched Gentiles under the new Testament is clearly held forth in diverse places *Gal*: 3. 14 the blessing [8] of *Abraham* comprizeth both the internal benefits of Justification by faith &c: which the Apostle is there treating of; and the external dispensation of Grace in the visible church to the faithfull & their seed, *Gen*: 28 4. but the whole Blessing of Abraham (and so the whole covenant) *is come upon the Gentiles through Jesus Christ. Eph*: 2. 12, 19 They had been *strangers*, but now were *no more strangers* from *the covenants of promise*, *i, e*, from the covenant of grace, which had been often renewed, especially with Abraham and the house of Israel, and had been in the externall dispensation of it, their peculiar portion, so that the *Ephesians*, who were a farr off, being now called and made nigh, *v.* 13–17. they have the promise or the Covenant of promise to them and to their Children, according to *Acts*: 2, 39. and so are partakers of that Covenant of Abraham, that we are speaking of.

Eph : 3, 6. The inchurched Gentiles are put into the same *inheritance* for substance (both as to invisible & visible benefits, according to their respective conditions) are of the *same body*, and *partakers of the same promise* with the Jewes, the Children of Abraham, of old. The same may be gathered from *Gen* : 9, 27, *Mat.* 8. 11, *&* 21, 43. 4. Sundry Scriptures which extend to Gospel-times do confirme the same interest to the seed of the faithful which is held forth in the covenant of Abraham, and consequently do confirme the continuance of that covenant*:* as *Exod:* 20 : 6. there in the sanction of a moral and perpetual Commandement, and that respecting Ordinances, the portion of the church, God declareth himself to be a *God of mercy, to them that love him*, and to their seed after them *in their generations* : consonant to *Gen*: 17. 7. compare herewith *Psal.* 105. 8, 9 *&* *Deut.* 7. 9.

Deut : 30. 6. The grace signified by *circumcision* is there promised to Parents and children, importing the covenant to both, which circumcision sealed, *Gen:* 17. and that is a Gospel-promise, as the Apostles citing part of that context, as the voice of the Gospel, shewes *Rom* : 10, 6–8. with *Deut:* 30, 11–14. and it reacheth to the Jewes in the latter dayes, *ver.* 1–5.

Isay : 65, 23. In the most Glorious Gospel-state of the church, *ver.* 17–19. the blessing of the Lord is the promised portion of the *off-*[9]*spring* or Children, as well as of the faithfull parents, so *Isay* : 44. 3, 4. *Isai :* 59. 20, 21. *Ezek* : 37. 25, 26. at the future calling of the Jewes, which those texts have reference to, (*Rom :* 11. 26. *Ezek* : 37. 19–22, 23, 24.) *their Children* shall be under the promise or Covenant of special Grace to be conveyed to them in the Ordinances, *Isai* : 59. 21. and be subjects of *David, i, e,* Christ *their King Ezek* 37. 25. and have a portion in his *Sanctuary*, *vers* 26. and this according to the tenor of the ancient *covenant* of *Abraham*, whereby God will be *their God* (*viz.* both of parents and Children) *and they shall be* his *People*, *vers:* 26, 27. Now although more abundant fruits of the Covenant may be seen in those times, and the Jewes then may have more abundant Grace given to the body of them to continue in the Covenant, yet the tenor and frame of the Covenant itselfe is one and the same, both to Jewes, and Gentiles under the New-Testament; *Gal:* 3, 28. *Coll*: 3. 11. Heb. 8. 10. *The house of Israel*, *i*, *e*, the Church of *God*, both among *Jewes* and *Gentiles* under the new Testament, have that Covenant made with them, the summ whereof is, *I will be their God*, *and they shall be my people*: which is a renewing of that Covenant of *Abraham* in *Gen* 17. (as the same is very often over in those termes renewed in Scripture, and is distinguished from the Law, *Gal*: 3 16, 17. *Heb* 8. 9) wherein is implied Gods being *a God to the seed* as well as parents, and taking *both* to be his *People*, though it be not expressed: even as it is often plainly implied in that expression of the Covenant in other places of Scripture*:* *Deut.* 29. 13. *Jer.* 31. 1. *&* 32. 38, 39. *&* 24: 7, *&* 30 22, 20. *Ezek:* 37. 27, 25. Also the *writing of the Law in the heart*, in *Heb*: 8: 10. is that *heart circumcision* which *Deut*: 30. 6. extends both to parents and seed. And the terme, *House of Israel*, doth according to Scripture-use fitly expresse and take in (especially as to the externall administration of the Covenant) both parents and Children: among both which are found that elect and saved number, that make up the invisible Israel*:* compare *Jer:* 13. 11. *&* 9. 26. *Isai.* 5. 7. *Hos*: 1. 6. *Ezek*: 39. 25. Neither may we exclude the *least in age* from the good of that promise, *Heb* 8*:* 11. (they being sometimes pointed to by that phrase, *from the least* [10] *to the greatest*, *Jer.* 44. 12. with *verse* 7.) no more than the least in other respects; compare *Isa.* 54. 13.

In *Acts* 2. 39. at the passing of those Jews into New Testament Church-estate, the Lord is so far from *repealing the Covenant-interest* that was granted unto *children* in the former Testament, or from making the children there losers by their Parents faith, that he doth expresly *renew* the old grant, and tells them that *the promise* or covenant (for the promise and the covenant are terms that do mutually infer each other; compare *Acts* 3. 25. *Gal* 3. 16, 17, 18, 29. *Rom.* 4. 16. *Heb.* 6 17,) *is to them and to their children:* and the same is asserted to be the appointed portion of *the far off* Gentiles, when they should be *called.* By all which it appeareth that the *covenant of Abraham*, Gen. 17. 7. *whereby God is the God of the faithfull and their seed, continues under the Gospel.*

Now if the seed of the faithful be still in the covenant of *Abraham*, then *they are members of the visible Church*; 1. Because that covenant of *Abraham*, Gen. 17. 7. was properly *church-covenant*, or *the covenant which God makes with his visible church*, *i. e.* the covenant of grace considered in the external dispensation of it, and in the promises and priviledges that belong to that dispensation. For many were taken into that covenant, that were never of the *invisible* church: and by that covenant, the family of *Abraham*, as also by the renewing thereof, the house of Israel afterward were established the visible church of God, *Gen.* 17. and *Deut.* 29. 12, 13. and from that covenant men might be broken off, *Gen.* 17: 14. *Rom.* 11: 17, 19. and to that covenant, *Circumcision*, the badg of church-membership, was annexed. Therefore the covenantees therein were & are church-members. 2. Because in that covenant, the seed are spoken of in terms describing or inferring church-membership, as well as their parents: for they *have God for their God*, and are his *people*, as well as the parents, *Gen.* 17 7, 8. with *Deut*: 29: 11, 13. They have the covenant made *with them*, Deut 29: 14, 15. and the covenant is said to be *between God & them* (*between me & thee, and between thy seed after thee:* so the Hebrew runs) *Gen:* 17: 7. They are also in that covenant appointed to be the subjects of the *initiatory seal* of the covenant, [11] the seal of membership, *Gen.* 17: 9, 10, 11. Therefore the seed are according to that covenant, members of the visible church, as well as their parents.

Argum: 2. *Such seed or children are federally holy*, 1 Cor. 7. 14. The word [*holy*] as applied to any sort of persons, is never in Scripture used in a lower sense than for *federal* or *covenant-holiness*, (the covenant-holiness of the visible Church;) but very often in that sense, *Ezra* 9: 2. *Deut*: 7: 6. & 14: 2, 21: & 26: 19: & 28: 9: *Exod*: 19: 6: *Dan*: 8: 24: & 12: 7: *Rom*: 11: 16: So that to say they are *holy* in this sense, *viz.* by covenant-relation and separation to God in his Church, is as much as to say, *they are in the covenant of the visible church, or members of it.*

Argum: 3. From *Mark* 10: 14, 15, 16: Mat. 19: 14: childrens membership in the visible Church, is either the next and immediate sense of those words of Christ, *Of such is the kingdome of heaven*; and so *the kingdome of heaven, or of God*, is not rarely used in other Scriptures to express the visible church, or church-estate. *Mat:* 25: 1. & 21: 43: & 8. 11, 12: or it evidently follows from any other sense that can rationally be given of the words. For those may not be denied a place and portion in the *visible church*, whom Christ affirms to have a portion in the *kingdome* either of *invisible grace*, or of *eternal glory*: Nor do any in ordinary course pass into the Kingdome of Glory hereafter, but through the Kingdome of Grace in the visible Church here. Adde also, that Christ there graciously invites and calls *little children* to him, is *greatly displeased* with those that would hinder them, asserts them, notwithstanding their infancy, to be exemplary in *receiving the kingdome of God*, embraceth them *in his arms*, and *blesseth them*: all which shews Christ's dear affection to, and owning of the children of the Church, as a part of his kingdome; whom we therefore may not disown, lest we incurre his displeasure, as the Disciples did.

Argum: 4. *Such seed or children are disciples according to* Mat 28: 19: as appears, 1. Because subjects of Christ's Kingdome are equivalent with disciples there, as the frame of that Text shews, *verse* 18, 19, 20. but such children are subjects of Christ's Kingdome, or *of the kingdome of heaven, Mat*: 19: 14: In the discipling of all [12] Nations intended in *Mat.* 28. 19. *the kingdome of God*, which had been the portion of the Jews, was communicated to the Gentiles, according to *Mat.* 21. 43. But in *the kingdome of God* these children have an interest or portion, *Mark* 10. 14. 2. The Apostles in accomplishing that commission, *Mat.* 28. 19. did *disciple* some children, *viz.* the children of discipled parents, *Acts* 2. 39. *&* 15. 10. They are there called and accounted *disciples*, whom the false teachers would have brought under *the yoke of circumcision after the manner of Moses, verse* 1, 5. But many of those were children; *Exod.* 12. 48. *Acts* 21. 21. *Lydia* and *her houshold*, the Jaylor and *all his*, were discipled and baptized, *Acts* 16. 15, 31, 33. *Paul* at *Corinth* took in the children into the *holy school of Christ*, 1 *Cor* 7. 14. 3. Such children *belong to Christ*; for he calls them to him as his, to receive his blessing, *Mark* 10. 13--16. They are to be received in his Name, *Mark* 9. 37. Luke 9 48. They have *a part in the Lord, Josh.* 22. 24 25. therefore they are *disciples*: for to *belong to Christ*, is to be *a disciple of Christ, Mark* 9, 41. with *Mat.* 10. 42. Now if they be disciples, then they are *members of the visible church*, as from the equivalency of those terms was before shewed.

Argum: 5. *The whole current and harmony of Scripture shews, that ever since there was a visible church on earth, the children thereof have by the Lords appointment been a part of it.* So it was in the Old, and it is and shall be so in the New Testament. *Eve, the mother of all living*, hath a *promise* made *Gen.* 3. 15. not only of Christ the *head-seed*, but through him also of a *Church-seed*, to proceed from her in a continual lineal succession, which should continually be at visible *enmity with*, and stand at a distance, or be separated from *the seed of the Serpent.* Under that promise made to *Eve* and her seed, the children of *Adam* are born, and are a part of the Church in *Adam's* family: even *Cain* was so, *Gen.* 4. 1, 3. till *cast out of the presence of God* therein, *verse* 14. being now manifestly one of the seed of the Serpent, 1 *John* 3. 12. and so becoming the father of a wicked unchurched race. But then God *appointed* unto *Eve another*, viz: *Seth*, in whom to continue the line of her *Church-seed*, Gen 4. 25. How it did continue in [13] his seed *in their generations*, *Genes*: 5th sheweth. Hence the children of the Church are called *Sons of God*, (which is as much as members of the visible Church) in contradistinction to *the daughters of men*, *Gen.* 6. 2. If *righteous Noah* be taken into the *Ark* (then the onely preserving place of the Church) his *children* are taken in with him, *Gen.* 7. 1 though one of them, *viz. Ham*, after proved degenerate and wicked; but till he so appears, he is continued in the Church with his Brethren: So *Gen.* 9. 25, 26, 27. as the race of *Ham* or his son *Canaan* (parent and children) are *cursed*; so *Shem* (parent and children) *is blessed*, and continued in the place of blessing, the Church: as *Japhet* also, or *Iaphet's* posterity (still parent and children) shall in time be brought in. The holy line mentioned in *Gen.* 11. 10–26 shews how the Church continued in *the seed of Shem* from him unto *Abraham.* When that race grew degenerate, *Iosh.* 24. 2. then God called *Abraham* out of his countrey, and from his kindred, and *established his covenant with him*, which still took in parents and children, *Gen.* 17. 7, 9. So it did after in the house of Israel, *Deut.* 29. 11, 12, 13. and when any eminent restauration or establishment is promised to the Church, *the children* thereof are still taken in, as sharers in the same, *Psal* 102. 16, 28. & 69. 35, 36. *Jerem*; 32: 38, 39. *Isa*: 65: 18, 19, 23. Now when Christ comes to set up the Gospel-administration of his Church in the New Testament, under the term of *the kingdome of heaven*, *Mat*: 3: 2. & 11. 11. he is so far from taking away children's portion and membership therein, that himself asserts it, *Mat*: 19: 14. The *children* of the Gentile, but now *believing Corinthians*, *are holy*, 1 *Cor*: 7: 14. The Apostle writing to the Churches of *Ephesus* and *Colosse*, speaks to *children*, as a part thereof, *Eph*: 6: 1. *Col.* 3: 20. The inchurched *Romans*, and other *Gentiles*, stand on the *root of covenanting Abraham*, and in the *Olive* or visible Church, they and their children, till broken off (as the Jews were) by positive unbelief, or rejection of Christ, his Truth or Government, *Rom.* 11 13, 16, 17,–22. The children of the Jews, when they shall be called, shall *be as aforetime* in Church-estate, *Ier*: 30. 20. with 31. 1 *Ezekiel* 37. 25–28. From all which it appears, that the [14] series or whole frame and current of Scripture-expressions, doth hold forth *the continuance of childrens membership in the visible church* from the beginning to the end of the world.

Partic: 4. *The seed or children who become members together with their Parents* (*i. e.* by means of their parents covenanting) *are children in minority.* This appears, 1. Because such children are *holy* by their parents covenanting, who would *else be unclean*, 1 *Cor.* 7. 14 but they would not else necessarily be unclean, if they were adult; for then they might act for themselves, and so be holy by their personal covenanting: Neither on the other hand would they necessarily be *holy*, if adult, (as he asserts the children there to be) for they might continue Pagans: Therefore the Apostle intends onely infants or children in minority. 2. It is a principle that carries evidence of light and reason with it, as to all transactions, Civil and Ecclesiastical, that *if a man be of age he should answer for himself*, *John* 9. 21. They that are come to years of discretion, so as to *have knowledge and understanding*, fit to act in a matter of that nature, are to covenant by their own personal act, *Neh.* 10. 28, 29. *Isa.* 44 5. 3. They that are regularly taken in with their parents, are reputed to be visible *entertainers of the covenant*, *and avouchers of God* to be their God, *Deut*: 26. 17, 18. with *Deut.* 29. 11, 12. But if adult children should, without regard to their own personal act, be taken in with their parents, then some might be reputed *entertainers*, that are manifest *rejecters* of the covenant: for so an adult son or daughter of a godly parent may be.

Partic: 5. *It is requisite to the membership of children, that the next parents*, *one or both*, *be in covenant.* For although after-generations have no small benefit by their pious Ancestors, who derive federal holiness to their succeeding generations, in case they keep their standing in the covenant, and be not apostates from it ; yet the piety of Ancestors sufficeth not, unless the next parent *continue* in covenant, *Rom.* 11. 22. 1. Because if the next parent be cut or broken off, the following seed are broken off also, *Exod*: 20. 5. *Rom.* 11 17, 19, 20. as the Gentile believing parents and children were taken in; so the Jews, parents and children, were then [15] broken off. 2. One of the parents must be a believer, or *else the children are unclean*, 1 *Cor*. 7. 14. 3. If children may be accounted members and baptized, though the next parents be not in covenant, then the Church should be bound to baptize those whom she can have *no power over, nor hope concerning*, to see them brought up in the true Christian Religion, and under the Ordinances: For the next parents being wicked, and not in covenant, may carry away and bring up their children *to serve other Gods*. 4. If we stop not at the next parent, but grant that Ancestors may, notwithstanding the apostacy of the next parents, convey membership unto children, then we should want a ground where to stop, and then all the children on earth should have right to membership and Baptism.

Proposition 3[d].

The Infant-seed of confederate visible Believers, are members of the same Church with their parents, and when grown up, are personally under the Watch, Discipline and Government of that Church.

1. *That they are members of the same Church with their parents*, appears; 1. Because so were *Isaac* and *Ishmael* of *Abrahams* Family-church, and the children of the *Jews* and *Proselytes* of *Israels* National Church: and there is the same reason for *children* now to be of the *same Congregational Church* with their parents. Christ's care for children, and the scope of the Covenant, as to obligation unto Order and Government, is as great now, as then. 2. Either they are members of the same Church with their parents, or of some other Church, or Non-members: But neither of the latter; therefore the former. That they are not Non-members, was before proved in *Propos*. 2. *Partic*. 3. and if not members of the *same Church* with their parents, then *of no other*. For if there be not reason sufficient to state them members of that Church, where their parents have covenanted for them, and where ordinarily they are baptized and do inhabit, then much less is there reason to make them members of any other: and so they will be members of no particular Church at all; and it was be-[16]fore shewed, that there is no ordinary and orderly standing estate of Church-members but in some particular Church. 3. *The same covenant-act is accounted the act of parent and childe:* but the parents covenanting rendred himself a member of this particular Church; Therefore so it renders the childe also. How can children come in with and by their parents, and yet come into a Church, wherein and whereof their parents are not, so as that they should be of one Church, and the parents of another? 4. Children are in *an orderly and regular state:* for they are in that state, wherein the order of Gods Cove-

nant, and his institution therein, hath placed them; they being members by vertue of the Covenant of God. To say their standing is disorderly, would be to impute disorder to the order of Gods Covenant, or irregularity to the Rule. Now all will grant it to be most orderly and regular, that every Christian be a member in some particular Church, and in that particular Church, where his regular habitation is; which to children usually is, where their parents are. If the Rule call them to remove, then their membership ought orderly to be translated to the Church, whither they remove. Again, order requires that *the childe*, and the *power of government over the childe*, should go together. It would *bring shame* and confusion for the childe to be from under government, *Prov.* 29. 15. and Parental and Ecclesiastical government concurring, do mutually help and strengthen each other. Hence the parent and the childe must be members of the same Church; unless the childe be by some special providence so removed, as that some other person hath the power over him.

2. *That when these children are grown up, they are personally under the Watch, Discipline and Government of that Church*, is manifest: for, 1. Children were under *Patriarchal* and *Mosaical* discipline of old, *Gen.* 18 19. & 21. 7, 10, 12. *Gal.* 5. 3. and therefore under *Congregational* discipline now. 2. They are *within* the Church, or members thereof, (as hath been, and after will be further proved) and therefore subject to Church-judicature, 1 *Cor.* 5. 12. 3. They are *disciples*, and therefore under *discipline* in *Christ*'s school, *Matth.* 28. 19. 20. 4. They are [17] *in Church-covenant*, therefore subject to *Church-power*, *Gen*: 17. 7. with *Chap.* 18, 19. 5. They are *subjects of the kingdome of Christ*, and therefore under the laws and government of his Kingdome, *Ezek.* 37 25, 26. 6. *Baptism* leaves the baptized (of which number these children are) in a state of subjection to the *authoritative teaching* of Christ's Ministers, and to the *observation of all his commandments*, *Mat.* 28. 19, 20. and therefore in a state of subjection unto Discipline. 7. Elders are charged *to take heed unto, and to feed* (*i. e.* both to teach and rule, compare *Ezek.* 34. 3, 4) *all the flock* or Church, *over which the holy Ghost hath made them overseers*, *Acts* 20. 28. That children are a part of the flock, was before proved: and so *Paul* accounts them, writing to the same flock or Church of *Ephesus*, *Eph.* 6. 1. 8. Otherwise Irreligion and Apostacy would inevitably break into Churches, and no Church-way left by Christ to prevent or heal the same: which would also bring many Church-members under that dreadful judgement of being *let alone* in their wickedness, *Hosea* 4. 16, 17.

Proposition 4th.

These Adult persons are not therefore to be admitted to full Communion, meerly because they are and continue members, without such further qualifications, as the Word of God requireth thereunto.

The truth hereof is plain, 1. From 1 *Cor.* 11. 28, 29. where it is required, that such as come to the Lords Supper, be able *to examine themselves, and to discern the Lords body*; else they will *eat and drink unworthily, and eat and drink damnation* or judgement, *to themselves,* when they partake of this Ordinance. But meer membership is separable from such ability to examine one's self, and discern the Lords body: as in the children of the covenant that grow up to years is too often seen. 2. In the Old Testament, though men did continue members of the Church, yet for ceremonial uncleanness they were to be kept from full communion in the holy things, *Levit.* 7. 20, 21. Numb. 9. 6, 7. *&* 19. 13, 20. yea and the *Priests* and *Porters* in the Old Testament had [18] special charge committed to them, that men *should not partake in all the holy things,* unless duely qualified for the same, notwithstanding their membership, 2 *Chron.* 23. 19. *Ezekiel* 22. 26, & 44. 7, 8, 9, 23. and therefore much more in these times, where moral fitness and spiritual qualifications are wanting, *membership alone* is not sufficient for *full communion.* More was required to adult persons *eating the Passeover,* then meer membership: therefore so there is now to the Lords Supper. For they were to *eat to the Lord, Exodus* 12. 14. which is expounded in 2 *Chron.* 30. where, *keeping the Passeover to the Lord, verse* 5. imports and requires exercising Repentance, *verse* 6, 7. their actual giving up themselves to the Lord, *verse* 8. *heart-preparation* for it, *verse* 19. and *holy rejoycing before the Lord, verse* 21, 25. See the like in *Ezra* 6. 21, 22. 3. Though all members of the Church are subjects of Baptism, they and their children, yet all members may not partake of the Lords Supper, as is further manifest from the different nature of Baptism and the Lords Supper. Baptism firstly and properly seals *covenant-holiness,* as circumcision did, *Gen.* 17. *Church-membership,* Rom: 15. 8. *planting into Christ, Rom.* 6. and so members, *as such,* are the subjects of Baptism, *Matth.* 28. 19. But the Lords Supper is the Sacrament *of growth in Christ,* and of *special-communion* with him 1 *Cor.* 10. 16. which supposeth *a special renewal and exercise* of Faith and Repentance in those that partake of that Ordinance. Now if persons, even when adult, may be and continue members, and yet be debarred from the Lords Supper; until meet qualifications for the same do appear in them; then may they also (until like qualifications) be debarred from that power of *Voting* in the Church, which pertains to Males in full communion. It seems not rational that those who are not themselves fit for all Ordinances, should have such an influence referring to all Ordinances, as Voting in Election of Officers, Admission and Censure of Members, doth import. For how can they, who are not able *to examine and judge themselves*, be thought able and fit to *discern and judge* in the weighty affairs of the house of God? 1 *Cor.* 11. 28, 31. with 1 *Cor.* 5. 12.

[19]

Proposition 5th.

Church-members who were admitted in minority, understanding the Doctrine of Faith, and publickly professing their assent thereto; not scandalous in life, and solemnly owning the Covenant before the Church, wherein they give up themselves and their Children to the Lord, and subject themselves to the Government of Christ in the Church, their Children are to be Baptized.

This is evident from the Arguments following.

Argum: 1. *These children are partakers of that which is the main ground of baptizing any children whatsoever, and neither the parents nor the children do put in any barre to hinder it.*

1. *That they partake of that which is the main ground of baptizing any*, is clear; Because interest in the Covenant is the main ground of title to Baptism, and this these children have. 1. *Interest in the Covenant is the main ground of title to Baptism*; for so in the Old Testament this was the ground of title to Circumcision, *Gen* 17. 7, 9, 10, 11. to which Baptism now answers, *Col.* 2. 11, 12. and in *Acts* 2. 38, 39 they are on this ground exhorted to *be baptized*, because *the promise* or covenant *was to them and to their children.* That a member, or one in covenant, *as such*, is the subject of Baptism, was further cleared before in *Propos.* 1. 2, *That these children have interest in the covenant*, appears; Because *if the parent be in the covenant, the childe is also:* for the covenant is to parents and *their seed in their generations*, Gen: 17. 7, 9. *The promise is to you and to your children*, *Acts* 2. 39. If the parent *stands* in the Church, so doth the childe, among the Gentiles now, as well as among the Jews of old, *Rom*: 11. 16, 20, 21, 22. It is unheard of in Scripture, that the progress of the covenant stops at the infant-childe. But *the parents in question are in covenant*, as appears, 1. Because they were once in covenant, and never since discovenanted. If they had not once been in covenant, they had not warrantably been baptized; and they are so still, except in some way of God they have been

discovenanted, cast out, or cut off from their covenant-relation, which these have not been: neither are persons once in covenant, *broken off* from [20] it according to Scripture, save for notorious sin, and incorrigibleness therein, *Rom* 11. 20. which is not the case of these parents. 2. Because the tenor of the covenant is *to the faithfull and their seed after them in their generations*, *Gen:* 17. 7 even to a *thousand generations*, *i. e.* conditionally, provided that the parents successively do continue to be *keepers* of the covenant, *Exod*: 20. 6. *Deut:* 7: 9, 11 *Psalm* 105: 8. which the parents in question are, because they are not (in Scripture-account in this case) *forsakers or rejecters* of the God and Covenant of their fathers: see *Deut*: 29. 25, 26. 2 *Kings* 17: 15–20. 2 *Chron*: 7: 22 *Deut*: 7: 10.

2. That these parents in question *do not put in any barre to hinder* their children from Baptism, is plain from the words of the Proposition, wherein they are described to be such as *understand the doctrine of Faith, and publickly profess their assent thereto:* therefore they put not in any barre of gross Ignorance, Atheism, Heresie or Infidelity: Also they are *not scandalous in life, but solemnly own the covenant before the Church*; therefore they put not in any barre of Profaneness, or Wickedness, or Apostacy from the covenant, whereinto they entred in minority. That the infant-children in question do themselves put any barre, none will imagine.

Argum: 2. The children of the parents in question are *either children of the covenant, or strangers from the covenant*, Eph: 2: 12. *either holy or unclean*, 1 Cor: 7: 14 either *within* the Church or *without* 1 *Cor*: 5: 12, either such as *have God for their God*, or *without God in the world*, Eph: 2: 12. But he that considers the Proposition will not affirm *the latter* concerning these children: and *the former* being granted, infers their right to Baptism.

Argum: 3. To deny the Proposition, would be, 1. To straiten the grace of Christ in the Gospel-dispensation, and to make the Church in New Testament-times in a worse case, relating to their children successively, then were the Jews of old. 2. To render the children of the Jews when they shall be called, in a worse condition then under the legal administration; contrary to *Jer*: 30: 20. *Ezekiel* 37: 25, 26. 3. To deny the application of the initiatory Seal to such as regularly stand in the Church and Co-[21]venant, to whom the *Mosaical* dispensation, nay the first institution in the covenant of *Abraham*, appointed it to be applied, *Gen:* 17: 9, 10. *John* 7 22, 23. 4. *To break Gods covenant* by denying the initiatory Seal to those that are in covenant, *Gen:* 17: 9, 10, 14.

Argum: 4. *Confederate visible Believers, though but in the lowest degree such, are to have their children baptized*; witness the practice of *John Baptist* and *the Apostles*, who baptized persons upon the *first beginning* of their Christianity. But the parents in question *are confederate visible Believers*, at least *in some degree:* For, 1. Charity may observe in them sundry positive Arguments for it; witness the terms of the Proposition, and nothing evident against it. 2. *Children of the godly* qualified but as the persons in the Proposition, are said to be *faithfull*, *Tit*: 1. 6. 3. Children of the Covenant (as the Parents in question are) have frequently the beginning of grace wrought in them in younger years, as Scripture and experience shews: Instance, *Joseph*, *Samuel*, *David*, *Solomon*, *Abijah*, *Josiah*, *Daniel*, *John Baptist*, and *Timothy*. Hence *this sort* of persons showing nothing to the contrary, are in charity, or to Ecclesiastical reputation, visible Believers. 4. They that are regularly in the Church (as the Parents in question be) are *visible Saints* in the account of Scripture (which is the account of truth:) for the Church is, in Scripture-account, a company of *Saints*, 1 *Cor*: 14: 33. & 1. 2. 5. Being in covenant and baptized, they have Faith and Repentance *indefinitely given* to them in the Promise, and sealed up in Baptism, *Deut.* 30: 6. which continues valid, and so a valid testimony for them, while they do not reject it. Yet it doth not necessarily follow, that these persons are immediately fit for the Lords Supper; because though they are *in a latitude of expression* to be accounted visible Believers, or *in numero fidelium*, even as infants in covenant are, yet they may want that ability to examine themselves, and that special exercise of Faith, which is requisite to that Ordinance; as was said upon *Propos.* 4th.

Argum: 5. *The denial of Baptism to the children in question hath a dangerous tendency to Irreligion and Apostacy;* because it denies them, and [22] so the children of the Church successively, *to have any part in the Lord;* which is the way to make them *cease from fearing the Lord*, *Josh* 22. 24, 25, 27. For if they *have a part in the Lord*, *i. e.* a portion in Israel, and so in the Lord the God of Israel, then they are in the Church, or members of it, and so to be baptized, according to *Propos.* 1. The owning of the children of those that successively continue in covenant to be *a part of the Church*, is so far from being destructive to the purity and prosperity of the Church, and of Religion therein, (as some conceive) that this imputation belongs to the contrary Tenet. To seek to be more pure then the Rule, will ever end in impurity in the issue. God hath so framed his covenant, and consequently the constitution of his Church thereby, as to design a continuation and propagation of his Kingdome therein, from one generation to another. Hence the covenant runs *to us and to our seed after us in their generations.* To keep in the line, and under the influence and efficacy of this covenant of God, is the true way to the Churches glory: To cut it off and disavow it, cuts off the posterity of *Sion*, & hinders it from being (as in the most glorious times it shall be) *an eternal excellency, and the joy of many generations.* This progress of the covenant *establisheth* the Church, *Deut.* 29 13. *Jer.* 30. 20. The contrary therefore doth disestablish it. This obligeth and advantageth to the conveyance of Religion down to after-generations; the care whereof is strictly commanded, and highly approved by the Lord, *Psal*: 78. 4, 5, 6, 7. *Gen.* 18. 19. This continues a nursery still in Christ's Orchard or *Vineyard, Isa.* 5. 1, 7. the contrary neglects that, and so lets the whole run to ruine. Surely God was an holy God, and loved the purity and glory of the Church in the Old Testament: but then he went in this way of a successive progress of the covenant to that end, *Jer.* 13. 11. If some did then, or do now decline to *unbelief* and apostacy, that doth not make *the faith of God* in his covenant *of none effect*, or *the advantage* of interest therein inconsiderable: yea the more holy, reforming and glorious that the times are or shall be, the more eminently is a successive continuation and propagation of the Church therein designed, promised and intended, *Isa.* 60. 15 *&* 59. 21. *Ezek.* 37. 25--28. *Ps.* 102. 16--28. *Jer.* 32. 39.

[23] *Argum*: 6. *The parents in question are personal, immediate, and yet-continuing members of the Church.*

1. That they are *personal members*, or members in their own persons, appears, 1. Because they are personally *holy*, 1 *Cor.* 7 14: not parents onely, but [your children][1] are holy. 2. They are personally baptized, or have had Baptism, the seal of membership, applied to their own persons: which being regularly done, is a divine testimony that they are in their own persons members of the Church. 3. They are personally under discipline, and liable to Church-censures in their own persons; *vide Propos.* 3. 4. They are personally (by means of the covenant) in a visible state of salvation. To say they are not members in their own persons, but in their parents, would be as if one should say, They are saved in their parents, and not in their own persons. 5. When they *commit iniquity*, they personally *break the covenant*; therefore are personally in it, *Jer.* 11. 2, 10. *Ezek.* 16.

[1] [ ] in original.

2. By the like Reasons it appears that children are *immediate members*, as to the essence of membership, (*i. e.* that they themselves in their own persons are the immediate subjects of this adjunct of Church-membership) though they come to it by means of their parents covenanting. For as touching that distinction of *mediate and immediate*, as applied to membership, (which some urge) we are to distinguish 1. between the efficient and the essence of membership: 2. between the instrumental efficient or means thereof, which is the parents profession and covenanting; and the principal efficient, which is divine Institution. They may be said to be *mediate* (or rather *mediately*) members, as they become members *by means* of their parents covenanting, as an instrumental cause thereof: but that doth nothing vary or diminish *the essence* of their membership. For divine Institution giveth or granteth a real and personal membership unto them, as well as unto their parents, and maketh the parent a publick person, and so his act theirs to that end. Hence the essence of membership, *i. e. Covenant-interest, or a place and portion within the visible Church*, is really, properly, personally and immediately the portion of the childe by divine gift and grant, *Josh.* 22. 25, 27. their *children* [24] *have a part in the Lord*, as well as themselves. *A part in the Lord* there, and *Church-membership* (or *membership in Israel*) are terms equivalent. Now *the children* there, and *a part in the Lord*, are *Subject* and *Adjunct*, which nothing comes between, so as to sever the Adjunct from the Subject; therefore they are *immediate subjects* of that Adjunct, or *immediate members*. Again, their visible ingraffing into Christ the head, and so into the Church his body, is sealed in their Baptism: but in ingraffing nothing comes betwixt the graft and the stock: Their union is immediate; hence they are immediately inserted into the visible Church, or immediate members there of. The *little children* in *Deut.* 29. 11. were personally and immediately a part of *the people of God*, or members of the Church of Israel, as well as the parents. To be in covenant, or to be *a covenantee*, is the *formalis ratio* of a Church-member. If one come to be in covenant one way, and another in another, but both are in covenant or covenantees (*i. e.* parties with whom the covenant is made, and whom God takes into covenant) as the children here are, *Gen.* 17. 7, 8 then both are in their own persons the immediate subjects of the *formalis ratio* of membership, and so immediate members. To *act* in covenanting, is but the instrumental means of membership, and yet children are not without this neither. For the act of the parent (their publick person) is

accounted theirs, and they are said to *enter into covenant*, *Deut.* 29. 11, 12. So that what is it that children want unto an actual, compleat, proper, absolute and immediate membership? (so far as these terms may with any propriety or pertinēcy be applied to the matter in hand.) Is it *Covenant-interest*, which is the *formalis ratio* of membership? No, they are in covenant. Is it *divine grant and institution*, which is the *principal efficient?* No: he hath clearly declared himself, that he grants unto the children of his people a portion in his Church, and appoints them to be members thereof. Is it *an act of covenanting*, which is the *instrumental means?* No: they have this also reputatively by divine appointment, making the parent a *publick person*, and accounting them to covenant in his covenanting. A different manner and means of conveying the covenant to us, or of [25] making us members, doth not make a different sort of membership. *We* now are as truly, personally and immediately members of the body of faln mankinde, and by nature heirs of the condemnation pertaining thereto, as *Adam* was, though he came to be so by *his own personal act*, and we by *the act of our publick person*. If a Prince give such Lands to a man and his heirs successively, while they continue loyal; the following heir is a true and immediate owner of that Land, and may be personally dis-inherited, if disloyal, as well as his father before him. A member is one that is according to Rule (or according to Divine Institution) *within* the visible Church. Thus the child is properly, & personally or immediately. *Paul* casts all men into two sorts, those *within* and those *without*, i. e. *members* and *non-members*, 1 *Cor.* 5. 12. It seems he knew of no such distinction of *mediate* and *immediate*, as put a *medium* between these two. *Object.* If children be compleat and immediate members as their parents are, then they shall immediately have all Church-priviledges, as their parents have, without any further act or qualification. *Ans.* It followeth not. All priviledges that belong to members, *as such*, do belong to the children as well as the parents: But all Church-priviledges do not so. A member as such, (or all members) may not partake of all priviledges; but they are to make progress both in memberly duties and priviledges, as their age, capacity and qualifications do fit them for the same.

3. *That their membership still continues in adult age, and ceaseth not with their infancy*, appears, 1. Because in Scripture persons are *broken off*, onely for notorious sin, or incorrigible impenitency and unbelief, not for growing up to adult age, *Rom.* 11. 20. 2. *The Jew-children circumcised* did not cease to be members by growing

up, but continued in the Church, and were by virtue of their membership received in infancy, bound unto various duties, and in special unto those solemn personal professions that pertained to adult members, not as then entring into *a new membership*, but as making a progress in *memberly duties*, *Deut.* 26. 2–10. & 16. 16, 17 with *Gal.* 5. 3. 3. Those relations of *born-servants* and *subjects*, which the Scripture makes use of to set forth the state of children in the Church by, *Lev.* 25 41, 42. *Ezek.* 37. 25. do not, (as all men know) cease with infancy, but continue in adult age. Whence also it follows, that one special end of [26] membership received in infancy, is to leave persons under engagement to service and subjection to Christ in his Church, when grown up, when they are fittest for it, and have most need of it. 4. There is no ordinary way of cessation of membership but by *Death*, *Dismission*, *Excommunication*, or *Dissolution of the Society*: none of which is the case of the persons in question. 5. Either they are when adult, members or non-members: if non-members, then a person admitted a member, and sealed by Baptism, not cast out, or deserving so to be, may (the Church whereof he was still remaining) become a non-member, and out of the Church, and of the unclean world; which the Scripture acknowledgeth not. Now if the parent stand member of the Church, the childe is a member also: For now *the root is holy*, therefore *so are the branches*, *Rom.* 11. 16. 1 *Cor.* 7. 14. The parent is in covenant, therefore so is the childe, *Gen.* 17. 7. and if the childe be a member of the visible Church, then he is a subject of Baptism, according to *Propos* 1.

Proposition 6t.

Such Church-members, who either by death, or some other extraordinary Providence, have been inevitably hindred from publick acting as aforesaid, yet have given the Church cause in judgment of charity, to look at them as so qualified, and such as had they been called thereunto, would have so acted, their children are to be Baptized.

This is manifest. 1. Because the main foundation of the right of the childe to priviledge remains, *viz*: Gods institution, and the force of his covenant carrying it to the generations of such as contiue keepers of the covenant, *i. e.* not visible breakers of it. By virtue of which *institution and covenant.* the children in question are members, and their membership being distinct from the parents membership, ceaseth not, but continues notwithstanding the parents decease or necessary absence: and if members, then subjects of Baptism. 2. Because the parents not doing what is required in the *fifth Proposition*, is through want of opportunity; which is not to be imputed as their guilt so as to be a barre to the childes priviledge. 3. God reckoneth that as done in his service, to which there was a manifest desire and endeavour, albeit the acting of it was hindred; as in *David* to build the Temple, 1 *Kings* 8 18, 19. in *Abraham* to sacrifice his Son, *Heb.* 11. 17. according to that in 2 *Cor.* 8. 12. *Where* [27] *is a willing minde, it is accepted according to what a man hath, and not according to what he hath not:* which is true of this Church-duty, as well as of that of Alms. It is an usual phrase with the Ancients to style such and such Martyrs *in voto*, and baptized *in voto*, because there was no want of desire that way, though their desire was not actually accomplished. 4. The terms of the Proposition import that in charity, that is here done *interpretively*, which is mentioned to be done in the fifth proposition *expresly*.

Proposition 7th.

The members of Orthodox Churches, being sound in the Faith, and not scandalous in life, and presenting due testimony thereof; these occasionally comming from one Church to another, may have their children Baptized in the church whither they come, by virtue of Communion of Churches: but if they remove their habitation, they ought orderly to covenant and subject themselves to the Government of Christ in the Church where they settle their abode, and so their children to be Baptized. It being the churches duty to receive such unto communion, so farre as they are regularly fit for the same.

1. Such members of other Churches as are here described, occasionally coming from one Church to another, their children are to be baptized in the Church whither they come, by virtue of Communion of Churches: 1. Because he that is regularly a member of a true particular Church, is a subject of Baptism, according to *Propos.* 1st & 2d. But the children of the parents here described are such, according to *Proposition* 5th & 6th. therefore they are meet and lawful subjects of Baptism, or have right to be baptized. And *Communion of Churches* infers such acts as this is, *viz:* to baptize a fit subject of Baptism, though a member of another Church, when the same is orderly desired. (See *Platform of Discipline, chap.* 15. *sect.* 4) For look as every Church hath a double consideration, *viz.* 1. Of its own constitution and communion within it self; 2. Of that communion which it holds and ought to maintain with other Churches: So the Officer (*the Pastor or Teacher*) thereof, is there set, 1. To administer to this Church *constantly;* 2, To do acts of Communion *occasionally*, (*viz:* such as belong to his Office, as *Baptizing* doth) respecting the members of other Churches, with whom this Church holds or ought to hold communion.

2. To refuse Communion with a true Church *in law*-[28] *full and pious actions*, is unlawful, and justly accounted Schismatical. For if the Church be true, Christ holdeth some communion with it; therefore so must we: but if we will not have communion with it in those acts that are good and pious, then in none at all. *Total separation* from a true Church, is unlawful: But to deny communion in good actions, is to make a total separation. Now to baptize a fit subject, as is the childe in question, is *a lawfull and pious action*, and therefore *by virtue of Communion of Churches*, in the case mentioned to be attended. And if *Baptism lawfully administred*, may and ought to be *received* by us for our children, in another true Church, where Providence so casts us, as that we cannot have it in our own, (as doubtless it may and ought to be:) then also we may and ought in like case to *dispense Baptism*, when desired, *to a meet and lawfull subject*, being a member of another Church. To deny or refuse either of these, would be an unjustifiable refusing of Communion of Churches, and tending to sinful separation.

2. [3] *Such as remove their habitation, ought orderly to covenant and subject themselves to the Government of Christ in the Church, where they settle their abode, and so their children to be baptized*; 1. Because the regularly baptized *are disciples*, and under the *Discipline* and Government of Christ: But they that are absolutely removed from the Church whereof they were, so as to be uncapable of being under Discipline there, shall be under it no where, if not in the church where they inhabit. They that would have *Church-priviledges*, ought to be *under Church-power*: But these will be under no Church-power, but *as lambs in a large place*, if not under it there, where their setled abode is. 2. Every Christian ought to covenant for himself and his children, or professedly to give up himself and his to the Lord and that *in the way of his Ordinances*, *Deut.* 26 17 & 12. 5. and *explicite covenanting* is a duty, especially where we are called to it, and have opportunity for it: nor can they well be said to covenant *implicitely*, that do *explicitely* refuse a professed covenanting, when called thereunto. And especially this covenanting is a duty, when we would partake of such a Church-priviledge, as Baptism for our children is. But the parents in question will now be *professed covenanters* no where, if not in the Church where their fixed habitation is.

Therefore they *ought orderly to covenant there, and so their children* [29] *to be baptized.* 3. To *refuse* covenanting and subjection to Christ's Government in the Church where they live, being so removed, as to be utterly uncapable of it elsewhere, would be *a walking disorderly,* and would too much savour of *profaneness and separation* and hence to administer Baptism to the children of such as *stand in that way,* would be to administer Christ's Ordinances to such as are in *a way of sin and disorder* ; which ought not to be, 2 *Thess.* 3. 6 1 *Chron.* 15. 13. and would be contrary to that Rule, 1 *Cor.* 14. 40. *Let all things be done decently and in order.*

Quest. II W*Hether according to the Word of God there ought to be a Consociation of Churches, and what should be the manner of it?*

Answ. The answer may be briefly given in the Propositions following.

1. *Every church or particular Congregation of visible Saints in Gospel-order, being furnished with a Presbytery, at least with a Teaching Elder, and walking together in truth and peace, hath received from the Lord Jesus full power and authority Ecclesiastical within it self, regularly to administer all the Ordinances of Christ, and is not under any other Ecclesiastical Jurisdiction whatsoever.* For to such a Church Christ hath *given the Keyes of the Kingdome of Heaven, that what they binde or loose on earth, shall be bound or loosed in heaven,* Matt. 16. 19. & 18. 17, 18. Elders are *ordained in every Church,* Acts 14. 23. *Tit.* 1. 5. and are therein authorized officially to administer in the Word, Prayer, Sacraments and Censures, *Mat.* 28. 19, 20. *Acts* 6. 4. 1 *Cor.* 4. 1. & 5. 4, 12. *Acts* 20. 28. 1 *Tim.* 5. 17. & 3. 5. The reproving of the Church of *Corinth,* and of the *Asian* Churches severally, imports they had power, each of them within themselves, to reform the abuses that were amongst them, 1 *Cor.* 5. *Rev.* 2 14, 20. Hence it follows, that Consociation of Churches is not to hinder the exercise of this power, but by counsel from the Word of God to direct and strengthen the same upon all just occasions.

2. *The Churches of Christ do stand in a sisterly relation each to*

other, Cant. 8. 8., *being united in the same Faith and Order*, Eph. 4. 5. Col. 2. 5. *to walk by the same Rule*, Phil. 3. 16. *in the exercise of the* [30] *same Ordinances for the same ends*, Eph. 4 11, 12, 13. 1 Cor. 16. 1. *under one and the same political Head, the Lord Jesus Christ*, Eph. 1. 22, 23 & 4. 5. *Rev.* 2. 1. Which Union infers a Communion sutable thereto.

3. *Communion of Churches is the faithfull improvement of the gifts of Christ bestowed upon them for his service and glory, and their mutuall good and edification, according to capacity and opportunity.* 1 Pet. 4. 10, 11. 1 Cor. 12. 4, 7. & 10. 24. 1 Cor. 3. 21, 22. Cantic 8. 9. Rom 1. 15. Gal. 6. 10

4. *Acts of Communion of Churches are such as these:*

1. *Hearty Care and Prayer one for another*, 2 Cor. 11. 28. Cant. 8. 8 Rom. 1. 9. Collos. 1. 9. Eph. 6. 18.

2. *To afford Relief by communication of their Gifts in Temporal or Spiritual necessities.* Rom. 15. 26, 27. Acts 11. 22, 29. 2 Cor. 8. 1, 4, 14.

3. *To maintain Unity and Peace, by giving account one to another of their publick actions, when it is orderly desired*, Acts 11. 2, 3, 4–18. Josh. 22. 13, 21, 30. 1 Cor. 10 32. *and to strengthen one another in their regular Administrations*; *as in special by a concurrent testimony against persons justly censured*, Acts 15. 41. & 16. 4, 5. 2 Tim. 4. 15. 2 Thess. 3. 14.

4. *To seek and accept Help from, and give Help unto each other:*

1. *In case of Divisions and Contentions, whereby the peace of any Church is disturbed*, Acts 15. 2.

2. *In matters of more then ordinary importance*, [Prov. 24. 6. 15. & 22] as *Ordination, Translation, and Deposition of Elders, and such like*, 1 Tim. 5. 22.

3. *In doubtful and difficult Questions and Controversies, Doctrinal or Practical, that may arise*, Acts 15 2, 6.

4. *For the rectifying of mal-Administrations, and healing of Errours and Scandals, that are unhealed among themselves*, 3 *John ver*: 9, 10. 2 *Cor*. 2. 6–11. 1 *Cor*. 15. *Rev*: 2: 14, 15, 16. 2 *Cor*. 12. 20, 21, & 13 2. Churches now have need of help in like cases, as well as Churches then. Christ's care is still for whole Churches, as well as for particular persons; and Apostles being now ceased, there remains the duty of brotherly love, and mutual care and helpfulness, incumbent upon Churches, especially Elders for that end.

[31] 5. *In love and faithfulness to take notice of the Troubles and Difficulties, Errours and Scandals of another Church, and to administer help (when the case manifestly calls for it) though they should so neglect their own good and duty, as not to seek it*, Exod. 23. 4, 5. Prov. 24. 11, 12.

6. *To Admonish one another when there is need and cause for it: and after due means with patience used, to withdraw from a Church or peccant party therein, obstinately persisting in Errour or Scandal*; as in the *Platform of Discipline* (*chap.* 15. *sect.* 2. *partic.* 3.) is more at large declared: *Gal.* 2. 11–14. 2 *Thess.* 3. 6. *Rom.* 16. 17.

5. *Consociation of Churches, is their mutual and solemn Agreement to exercise communion in such acts, as aforesaid, amongst themselves, with special reference to those Churches, which by providence are planted in a convenient vicinity, though with liberty reserved without offence, to make use of others, as the nature of the case, or the advantage of opportunity may lead thereunto.*

6. *The Churches of Christ in this Countrey having so good opportunity for it, it is meet to be commended to them, as their duty, thus to consociate.* For 1. Communion of Churches being commanded, and Consociation being but an Agreement to practise it, this must needs be a duty also, *Psal.* 119. 106. *Nehem.* 9. 28. 2. *Paul* an Apostle sought with much labour the *conference*, concurrence, and *right hand of fellowship* of other *Apostles:* and ordinary Elders and Churches have not less need each of other, to prevent *their running in vain, Gal.* 2. 2, 6, 9. 3. Those general Scripture-rules touching the need and use of counsel and help in weighty cases, concern all Societies and Polities, Ecclesistical as well as Civil, *Prov.* 11. 14. & 15. 22. & 20 18. & 24. 6. *Eccles.* 4. 9, 10, 12. 4. The pattern in *Acts* 15 holds forth a warrant for Councils, which may be greater or lesser, as the matter shall require. 5. Concurrence and Communion of Churches in Gospel times, is not obscurely held forth in *Isa* 19. 23, 24, 25. *Zeph.* 3. 9. 1 *Cor.* 11. 61, & 14. 32, 36. 6. There hath constantly been in these Churches a profession of Communion, in giving the right hand of fellowship at the gathering of Churches, and Ordination of Elders: Which importeth a Consociation, and obligeth to the practice [32] thereof. Without which we should also want an expedient and sufficient Cure for emergent Church-difficulties and Differences: with the want whereof our Way is charged, but unjustly, if this part of the Doctrine thereof were duely practised.

7. *The manner of the Churches agreement herein, or entring into this Consociation, may be by each Church's open consenting unto the things here declared in Answer to this* 2[d]. *Question, as also to what is said thereabout in* chap. 15. & 16. *of the* Platform of Discipline, *with reference to other Churches in this Colony & Countrey, as in* Propos. 5th. *is before expressed.*

8. *The manner of exercising and practising that Communion, which this consent or agreement specially tendeth unto, may be, by making use occasionally of Elders or able Brethren of other Churches; or by the more solemn Meetings of both Elders and Messengers in lesser or greater Councils, as the matter shall require.*

FINIS.

XII

THE SAVOY DECLARATION, 1658

EDITIONS AND REPRINTS

I. *A | Declaration | of the | Faith and Order | Owned and practised in the | Congregational Churches | in | England; | Agreed upon and consented unto | By their | Elders and Messengers | in | Their Meeting at the Savoy, October 12. 1658.* | —— | —— | *London: | Printed by John Field, and are to be sold by | John Allen at the Sun Rising in Pauls | Church-yard, 1658.* 4° pp. [xxx], 64.

Four editions appeared in 1659, viz.

II. 1. The edition of 1658 with the date on the title-page altered to 1659, but without other changes.

III. 2. An edition with the same title page as No. II., and by the same publisher, but re-set in parts, and with minor variations.[1]

IV. 3. A small print edition, *London | Printed for D. L. And are to be sold in Paul's Church-yard, Fleet- | Street, and Westminster-Hall, 1659.*[2]

V. 4. Another small print edition, *London, | Printed by J. P. and are to be sold in S Pauls Church- | yard, Fleet-Street, and at Westminster-Hall, | 1659.*

VI. A Latin translation, by Prof. Johannes Hoornbeek of Leyden, appeared at Utrecht in 1662 under the title *Confessio nuper edita Independentium seu Congregationalium in Anglia.*[3]

Other editions appeared in English as follows,[4]

VII. 1677, 18°.
VIII. 1688, 18°.
IX. 1729, 8°.
X. Ipswich, 1745, 8°.
XI. Oswestry, 1812, 8°.

The revived interest in the history of Congregationalism has led to several reprints, more or less complete.

I. In Hanbury, *Memorials*, III : 517–548 ; entire.

II. By Dr. A. H. Quint, *Congregational Quarterly*, VIII : 241–261, 341–344, (July and October 1866); without the preface. Dr. Quint gives a full list of variations from the Westminster Confession and the Massachusetts Confession of 1680.

---

[1] This edition may be distinguished from No. II. by the presence, on an unnumbered page between pp. 53 and 54, of a list of books for sale. In Nos. I. and II. this page is blank, and is reckoned in the paging of the book. In No. III. the title to Ch. V. p. 10 is inverted, in Nos. I. and II. it is in the usual order. Many differences of punctuation may also be found.

[2] This is the text used by Dr. Quint in the *Cong. Quart.*, viii: pp. 241–261, 341–344 ; and Prof. Schaff in the *first* edition of his *Creeds*, III, p. 707.

[3] See Neal, *Puritans*, ed. New York, 1844, II : 178; Hanbury, *Memorials*, III : 517 ; Schaff, *Creeds*, I : 829.

[4] I am indebted for my information regarding Nos. VII–XI to William Orme's *Memoirs of . . . John Owen*, in *Works of John Owen*, London, 1826, I : 183.

III. By Prof. Philip Schaff, *Creeds of Christendom*, III : 707–729 ; the preface and the portions relating to church government are given in full, but only those sections of the Declaration of Faith which differ from the Westminster Confession, to be found earlier in the same volume.

SOURCES

Peck, *Desiderata Curiosa*, London 1779, II : 501–512 ; contains sixteen letters relating to the summons of the Synod.

LITERATURE

Neal, *History of the Puritans*, ed. New York, 1844, II : 177–180 ; Bogue & Bennett, *History of Dissenters*, London, 1808, 2nd ed. 1833, I : 181, 182 ; Orme, *Memoirs of . . . John Owen*, in *Works of John Owen*, London, 1826, I : 172–183 ; Price, *History of Protestant Nonconformity in England*, London, 1838, II : 619–623 ; Hanbury, *Memorials*, III : 515–548 ; Fletcher, *History of . . . Independency in England*, London, 1862, IV : 177–179 ; Schaff, *Creeds of Christendom*, New York, 1877, I : 829–833 ; Masson, *Life of John Milton*, London, 1859–80, V : 343–345 ; Dexter, *Congregationalism, as seen in its Literature*, pp. 661–663 ; Stoughton, *History of Religion in England*, ed. London, 1881, II : 488, 489. Some points of interest regarding this Declaration, and its relations to the New England Churches, may be found in Lawrence, *Our Declaration of Faith and the Confession*, in *Congregational Quarterly*, VIII : 173–190.

IT was the desire of the Puritans, from the opening of the Long Parliament, that there should be a general council of representatives of the English Church to consider and recommend such changes as seemed necessary, in the opinion of a great party in the nation, for that Church's further reformation. This wish found expression in the Grand Remonstrance ; and bills authorizing such an assembly were enacted in June, October, and December, 1642, but failed for lack of the king's assent.[1] But the increasing danger of the political situation, owing to the unexpected strength shown by the king after the outbreak of the civil war, induced Parliament to call the desired assembly by its own unsupported ordinance, on June 12, 1643,—a result doubtless hastened by the knowledge that such a council would be acceptable to the Scotch, whose military aid seemed indispensable. The composition of this celebrated body was determined by the Parliamentary call, which summoned one hundred and forty-nine persons[2] by name to a share in its proceedings; and, in spite of the prohibition of the Westminster Assembly by the king, sixty-nine of those invited gathered on the opening day,

[1] See Dexter, *Cong. as seen*, pp. 645–648.

[2] Really 150, see *ante*, p. 136.

July 1, 1643. Its average attendance was from sixty to eighty. Of the membership of the ecclesiastical council thus constituted the vast majority were, of course, *jure divino* Presbyterians, since Presbyterianism was not only the form of church polity approved in Scotland, but that to which the greater portion of the Puritans of England looked with hope at the outbreak of the civil war. Parliament, however, intended to be catholic in its call, and therefore invited certain Episcopalians[1] (though scarce any came), a few Erastians, like the scholars, Selden, Lightfoot, and Coleman, and, what attracts our chief attention, nearly a dozen Congregationalists,—all, even the Episcopalians summoned, being affiliated more or less closely with the great Puritan party.

Ten or eleven Congregationalists, or Independents[2] as they were more usually called, could have no decisive influence among so many Presbyterians, and of this number only about five could be accounted at all times thorough-going opponents of Presbyterian designs. These were Thomas Goodwin and Philip Nye, the most powerful debaters on the Congregational side, William Bridge, Jeremiah Burroughes, and Sidrach Simpson. They had all suffered persecution under Laud, and had all gone to Holland, where they had ministered to English congregations at Rotterdam,[3] and Arnheim;[4] and had returned to take positions of influence in England as soon as the tyranny of Laud was overthrown. With them were associated more or less intimately in the defense of Independency in the Assembly, William Carter of London, Joseph Caryl of Lincoln's Inn, William Green of Pentecomb, William Greenhill of Stepney, Peter Sterry of London, John Bond of the Savoy, London, and (possibly) Anthony Burgess of Sutton.[5] But though few in numbers, the Congregationalists in the Assembly were the peers of any of its membership in power of debate. They commanded respect much beyond that due to

1 A good account of these parties is given by Schaff, *Creeds of Christendom*, I: 734–747.

2 On the use of this name, compare Fletcher, *Hist. . . . of Independency*, London, 1862, IV: 23, 24.

3 Bridge and Burroughes as pastor and teacher.

4 Goodwin.

5 See Baillie, *Letters and Journals*, ed. Edinburgh, 1841-2, II: 110; Fletcher, *Hist. . . . Independency*, IV: 23, 24; Schaff, *Creeds*, I: 737. Of the laymen in the Assembly, Lord Say and Sele, Lord Wharton, and Sir Harry Vane, sided with the Independents.

their numerical weight.[1] Their disagreement with the Presbyterians was not on points of doctrine; the struggle between the two parties so unequally matched was over polity; and, later, over the degree of toleration to be granted to the minor differences of religious sects as well.[2]

Yet, while there can be no doubt as to the keenness and cogency of the Congregational champions in argument, it is hardly conceivable that they would have been listened to and answered with such patience by the great men of the Presbyterian majority, had it not early become evident that the progress of the war was resulting in the rapid spread of Independency in England. It was the consciousness that the Congregational debaters represented a party of unknown but increasing power in Parliament and the army that made the Presbyterian leaders bear with their arguments and objections.[3] It was the same consciousness on the part of the Congregational members that made them oppose and delay the Presbyterian models of Church-government, and, as early as January, 1644, led Goodwin, Nye, Bridge, Burroughes, and Simpson, to appeal from the Assembly to the Parliament which created it, and from which it derived all its right to be. This appeal, the *Apologeticall Narration*,[4] though claiming to be nothing more than a request that the government would not send the adherents of Congregationalism into a second exile,[5] was really an attempt to transfer the solution of the question between Presbyterianism and Congregationalism from the Assembly to a higher tribunal,—the opinion of Parliament and of the nation. As such, it was in some measure successful. Nine months after its publication, Cromwell, fresh from his victory at

---

[1] The work of the Independents in the Assembly is well described in Masson, *Life of John Milton*, III. *passim*. See also Dexter, *Cong. as seen*, pp. 656, 657.

[2] "Moreover, if in all matters of *Doctrine*, we [Congregationalists] were not as *Orthodoxe* in our judgements as our brethren [the Presbyterians] themselves, we would never have exposed our selves to this tryall and hazard of discovery in this Assembly. . . . But it is sufficiently known that in all *points of doctrine* . . . our judgements have still concurred with the greatest part of our brethren, neither do we know wherein we have dissented," *Apologeticall Narration*, pp. 28, 29. Regarding the growth of a spirit of toleration among the Independents in the Assembly see Fletcher, *Hist. . . . Independency*, IV: 29–74.

[3] Compare Masson, *Milton*, III: 20–26.

[4] *An Apologeticall Narration, Hvmbly Svbmitted to the Honourable Houses of Parliament*, London, 1643 (really January, 1644, see on date Dexter, *Cong. as seen*, p. 659.)

[5] *Apol. Narration*, pp. 30, 31.

Marston Moor, and well known to be a Congregationalist in sympathy, induced Parliament so far to recognize the rights of the Independents as to refer the general question of toleration to its most important committee, that of the "Two Kingdoms."[1]

But, spite of all they could do in debate, the weight of numbers gave the victory to the Presbyterians in the Assembly point by point. And something beside numbers favored the Presbyterians also. They were ready with the offer of a definite plan of church government. The Independents were not. They opposed the Presbyterian system in detail, but they could not be induced to present their own views in full systematic form. The Assembly justly complained of this unwillingness.[2] But the reason of it is not far to seek. The power behind the Congregationalists in the Assembly was the constantly growing ascendency of the Independents in the army. These army Independents were many shades of opinion,[3] and for their diversities of view the leaders, like Cromwell, claimed large toleration. To come out with a definite statement of their own theories was to expose the Congregationalists in the Assembly to the loss of a support that was very desirable, for though many were willing to unite with them in opposition to the proposed enforcement of Presbyterian uniformity, the diversity of opinion among the Independents in the army was too manifest to make union in anything but dissent probable. That this was the reason of the

[1] See Masson, *Milton*, III: 168, 169. The composition of the committee is given, *Ibid.*, p. 41.

[2] See *A Copy of a Remonstrance lately delivered in to the Assembly. By Thomas Goodwin. Ierem: Burroughs. William Greenhill. William Bridge. Philip Nie. Sidrach Simson. and William Carter. Declaring the Grounds and Reasons of their declining to bring into the Assembly, their Modell of Church-Government.* London 1645. The Assembly answered the same year. *The Ansvver Of the Assembly of Divines . . . Unto the Reasons given in to this Assembly by the Dissenting Brethren* [etc.] London 1645. They say: "The Assembly hath still great and just cause to expect a report from these Brethren: Those of their way having published in Print *that these Brethren are willing to do it.* The Assembly having Ordered it, the Brethren having held the Assembly six moneths in expectation of it. . . . Vpon which considerations we think . . . that they have some other cause then what they pretend to, and that something lies behinde the curtain. . . . Possibly they cannot *agree among themselves* (for it is easier to agree in dissenting, then in affirming) or possibly if they seven can agree, yet some other of their Brethren in the City, to whom it may be the Model was communicated, did not like it; or if so, yet possibly the Brethren might foresee, that if this Model should be published, there are some who at present are a strength to them, and expect shelter from them, may disgust it," p. 24.

[3] Some account of the sects in the army may be found in Masson, *Milton*, III: 84–91, 137–159.

refusal of the Congregationalists to formulate their views in the Assembly, the Presbyterians not obscurely hinted.[1] But these Congregationalists had conceptions definite enough, though they did not deem it politic to define them in their own words. They published and circulated with approval the works of the leaders of New England, like Cotton's *Keyes*,[2] and *Way of the Churches*, they assiduously propagated Congregational sentiments and opposed Presbyterian positions; but they did not expose themselves to condemnation in the Assembly, and the loss of needed, if somewhat uncertain, supporters without, by presenting their system in concrete and elaborated form.

But a few years brought great changes. The rise of the army to the real control in England, the falling away of the Scotch and their defeat in the second civil war,[3] the successive expulsions of the Presbyterians from Parliament,[4] the execution of the king, and the establishment of a Commonwealth under the control of Cromwell, removed the Congregationalists from the position of suppliants for Parliamentary toleration and placed them at least on a political equality with the Presbyterians; while their leaders enjoyed a greater degree of personal favor with Cromwell and the heads of his government than those of any other religious party. They were Cromwell's chaplains,[5] and the more distinguished Independents received educational and ecclesiastical livings at the hands of the government, the tenure of which, though agreeable, was not always very consistent with Congregational principles.[6] Such favor from the State, though it did not make Independency the State religion, placed the Con-

---

[1] Compare p. 344, note 2.

[2] It bears the inscription on the title page, "Published By THO. GOODVVIN and PHILIP NYE."

[3] Battle of Preston, Aug. 18, 1648.

[4] The dismissal of the eleven members, 1647, and "Pride's Purge," Dec. 6, 1648, brought Parliament wholly under the control of the army.

[5] Of Cromwell's chaplains Peter Sterry and John Howe were English Congregationalists, while Hugh Peter and William Hooke had had ministerial experience in New England, the one at Salem, the other at New Haven. William Bridge was offered the chaplaincy of the Council of State in Nov. 1649; but declined.

[6] Thomas Goodwin became Pres. Magdalen Coll., Oxford: John Owen was Dean of Christ Church and Vice-Chancellor at Oxford; Philip Nye, Rector of St. Bartholomew's, London; Joseph Caryl, Rector of St. Mary's Magnus. To accept the last named positions implied, in some degree at least, the acknowledgment of a National Church and of a right of appointment other than the will of the congregation.

gregationalists in a position where they naturally took a more conservative attitude than when they were simply struggling for a right to live, and were glad to accept aid from whatever source. Their numbers were multiplying, their preachers were respected, it seemed in every way desirable that they should now define their position doctrinally and ecclesiastically. Such action would bring them greater union, it would mark their separation from the various sectaries who sheltered themselves under the Independent name, and it was now open to none of the dangers which had threatened when Presbyterianism was all-powerful. The leading Congregationalists determined to have a Confession of their own; they would, without making their creed a test to which they required rigid conformity, bear testimony to their faith, and enjoy the fraternal communion to the existence of which no public declarations of Congregational ministers and churches in England had heretofore witnessed.[1]

Thus far we can trace the probable course of events which led to the gathering at the Savoy, but unfortunately, as one of the most learned of modern English Congregationalists has observed, "very much obscurity rests" on the preparations for that Assembly.[2] It seems certain, however, that the motion toward a Synod went out from the Independent divines in Cromwell's neighborhood, and probably took the form of a petition.[3] The Protector was naturally reluctant to summon a meeting which might possibly increase that friction between Presbyterians and Congregationalists which was the most threatening feature of the political situation,[4] but he gave his consent and allowed the proposed Synod to have the countenance, in an informal way, of his government. The call for the Assembly did not run in the name of the Commonwealth. It was not official in the same sense as the summons of the Westminster Assembly by Parliament; but the letters went forth from Henry Scobell, clerk

[1] See Preface to *Savoy Declaration*, pp. iii, iv, xiii.

[2] Dr. John Stoughton, *History of Religion in England*, II: 488, 489.

[3] Such is the view of Neal, Echard, Orme, Stoughton, Dexter, Schaff, Fletcher, etc. It is probably true, though it would be grateful if documents should be discovered illuminating this obscure part of the story.

[4] Neal, *Hist. of the Puritans*, ed. New York, 1844, II: 178.

of the Council of State, and were recognized by their recipients as having governmental approval. The first summons was for a meeting preparatory to the Synod. On June 15, 1658, Scobell wrote to the ministers of London and vicinity as follows:[1]

"Sir, the meeting of the elders of the congregationall churches in & about London, is appointed at Mr. Griffith's[2] on Monday next, at two of the clocke in the afternoone, where you are desired to be present. I am,

Sir, yours to love & serve you in the Lord,

Hen. Scobell."

June XV. MDCLVIII.

This preliminary meeting took place on the day appointed, June 21, and by its authorization letters were sent by Mr. Griffith, "in the name . . . of the congregationall elders in & about London,"[3] to leading Congregational ministers in the several counties where such churches were to be found, asking them to notify the churches in their respective neighborhoods to be present by pastors and delegates at the Savoy[4] in London on Wednesday, the 29th of September following. These letters, which were sent out on or about the 20th of August,[5] are not known to me to have been preserved, but the replies, returned not to Griffith but to Scobell, exist to the number of fifteen. An example or two may suffice:[6]

"Sir, Two dayes ago I received a letter from Mr. Griffith, giving notice of a meeting that is to be of pastours or messengers of the severall congregationall churches on xxix of September next at the Savoy, & of some other things.[7] I am therein directed to signify the receipt of it by the first post to you; which is the end of theis few lines from,

Sir, your humble servant,

Samuel Basnet, teacher of a church in Coventry.

---

[1] Peck, *Desiderata Curiosa*, London, 1779, II: 501.

[2] George Griffith, minister at the Charter House, London, 1648–1661. See Wilson, *Hist. . . . Dissenting Churches and Meeting Houses in London*, London, 1808, II: 516–518.

[3] Reply in Peck, *Desiderata Curiosa*, II: 510.

[4] The Savoy Palace was erected on the bank of the Thames by Peter, earl of Savoy and Richmond, in 1245. It passed through various vicissitudes, being the place of confinement of John II. of France, when a prisoner, 1357–63; John of Gaunt later made it his palace. It had been at one time a convent, and in 1505 was made a hospital by Henry VII. In Cromwell's time it sheltered various court officers; and it had the reputation of being a meeting place for Dissenters, and for representatives of the Continental Protestant churches.

[5] The replies, returned immediately on the receipt of the letters, are dated, with the exception of two belated epistles, between August 24 and Sept. 4. The letter to William Bridge at Yarmouth was dated Aug. 20.

[6] Peck, *Desiderata Curiosa*, II: 508, 509.

[7] The third point of Griffith's letter related to "subscription" — see Reply of Thomas Gilbert, Peck, II: 509. I am unable to say what was intended.

Theis to the honourable Henery Scobell esq; clerk of his hignes privy councill at Whitehall, present."

"Worthy Sir, I have lately received a letter from Mr. Griffith, in name of the brethren at London, whereby I am desired to certify you of the receipt thereof. This is then only to let you understand, that on the xxvi. of August I received his letters dated the xx. of August. And I shall take care that coppyes of the letters be sent unto all the churches in our countye;[1] continueing

your servant in the gospel of Christ Jesus,

Yarmouth, Aug. xxviii. William Bridge."

MDCLVIII.

In a similar way William Hughes of Marlborough promised to notify the churches of Wiltshire, Bankes Anderson of Boston and Edward Reyner of Lincoln those of Lincolnshire, Isaac Loeffs of Shenley the congregations of Hertfordshire, Thomas Gilbert of Edgemond those of Salop, Samuel Crossman of Sudbury those of Suffolk, Anthony Palmer and Carn[elms?] Helme of Bourton-on-the-water the churches of Gloucestershire, Thomas Palmer of Aston-upon-Trent those of Derby and Nottinghamshire, John Player of Canterbury those of Kent, while Vavasor Powell undertook to inform the churches of Wales. Most of the answers, though brief, are cordial, one or two are apparently guarded, and one slightly suspicious that some political design might be lurking behind the proposed Synod,[2] but, speaking in general, the letters make it evident that the response of the ministers as a whole was hearty.

Between the sending of the summons and the meeting of the Synod a momentous event occurred, the full political and ecclesiastical significance of which was not at once apparent, but which was to render futile much of the work of the Synod. The great Protector died, September 3, 1658, and was succeeded by his feeble son, Richard. In spite of this untoward event, however, the Synod met at the Savoy at the time appointed, September 29, having present the representatives of about a hundred and twenty churches.[3] It is probable that the majority were laymen,[4] as at

[1] Norfolk. [2] That of Thomas Gilbert of Edgemond, Peck, II: 509.

[3] Increase Mather, who was in England during the session of the Synod, said, writing in 1700 (*Order of the Gospel*, p. 75): "Messengers of One hundred and Twenty Congregational Churches in *England*, who met at the *Savoy* in *London*." Orme, *Works of John Owen*, I: 176, gives the total membership at the very probable figure of "about two hundred," and Dr. Dexter follows him.

[4] Neal, *Puritans*, ed. New York, 1844, II: 178, asserts this.

the Massachusetts Synod of 1662; but the leading Congregational ministers of England were of the membership. Who its moderators were it is impossible to say, but Thomas Goodwin, John Owen, and Philip Nye[1] were all prominent in its proceedings, and were each well fitted for such a duty; John Howe, the Protector's chaplain, though conspicuous, was probably too young to have any very important part.

The opening day was spent in discussion as to the course of procedure,[2] the question being, as reported by tradition when Neal wrote, whether they should amend the Westminster Confession, or draw up a new symbol on substantially the same lines.[3] The latter plan prevailed, and a Committee of the most influential divines that Congregationalism could boast, Thomas Goodwin, John Owen, Philip Nye, William Bridge, Joseph Caryl, and William Greenhill, were chosen to prepare and report the desired confession.[4] Every member of this Committee except Owen had borne his share in the Westminster Assembly. At the same time George Griffith was elected scribe of the Synod.[5] The work of the Committee, so far as completed, was reported each morning by the scribe to the whole Assembly,[6] and discussed, sometimes in speeches of considerable elaboration;[7] but so little was there of novelty in the result, that the Synod, having much time on its hands, was able to devote a large portion of its hours to hearing disputes in churches[8] and to the more devotional exercises of fasting and prayer.[9] Even thus the session was brief. The labors of the Committee were unanimously approved,[10] and the Savoy Synod adjourned on Tuesday,

[1] Of Nye, Calamy records, he "was a principal person in managing the meeting of the *congregational* churches at the *Savoy*." *Non-Conformist's Memorial*, ed. London, 1775, I: 87.

[2] The *Preface* says, p. xi, "The first days meeting, in which we considered and debated what to pitch upon." Neal recorded, *Puritans*, II: 178: "They opened their synod with a day of fasting and prayer." There is no necessary conflict between the two statements.

[3] Neal, *Puritans*, II: 178. Neal's work was originally published in 1732–38.

[4] *Ibid.* [5] *Ibid.* [6] *Ibid.*

[7] "Such rare elaborate speeches my ears never heard before, nor since. All along, there was a most sweet harmony of both hearts and judgments amongst them." Rev. James Forbes, a member, quoted by Orme, *Works of John Owen*, I: 181.

[8] Neal, *Ibid.*

[9] "We had some days of prayer and fasting, kept from morning till night," James Forbes, quoted by Orme.

[10] Calamy, *Account of the Ministers*, etc., ed. London, 1713, II: 444. See also *Preface* to the *Declaration* itself, p. xi.

October 12, 1658, after a session of twelve working days.[1] Shortly after, the result was formally presented to the new Protector, Richard Cromwell, by Rev. Thomas Goodwin, who had been delegated for that work by the Assembly.[2]

The Savoy Synod seem to have been almost surprised at the unanimity which they discovered among the representatives of the churches, a unanimity that was the more gratifying since these churches had never had any previous consultation;[3] and the writer of the Preface to the Declaration was convinced that such unity must be the direct work of the Spirit of God.[4] Without questioning his faith, however, it is easy to discover causes less clearly supernatural. There was very little that was original in the work of the Synod. The Committee which prepared the result had shared, for the most part, in the deliberations of the Westminster Assembly. Like the Congregationalists of New England, they had nothing but approval for most of the doctrinal work of that famous body. Some sections of the Westminster Confession they desired to omit; but even here their task had largely been mapped out for them, for Parliament in approving the Westminster result had struck out those sections most displeasing to the Independents.[5] The work of omission was thus comparatively easy; the Committee simply did more largely what Parliament had begun. But beside these omissions, the Savoy divines amended the phraseology of many passages, in general without important alteration of the sense; this is notably the case in the fifteenth chapter (on Repentance), which was wholly rewritten. They emphasized the

---

[1] Compare *Preface*, p. xi, where eleven working days are reckoned, omitting the opening day.

[2] See Orme, *Works of John Owen*, I: 182, 183, where a quotation is given from Goodwin's address to the Protector. Orme quotes from a *Catalogue of the places where Richard Cromwell was proclaimed*, p. 25.

[3] *Preface*, p. xiii.

[4] *Ibid.*, p. xii.

[5] The Westminster Confession was reported to Parliament Dec. 4, 1646, under the title of *Humble Advice of the Assembly of Divines*. But the Commons moved slowly. On April 22, 1647, they asked for proof-texts, which the Assembly furnished. Still they were not satisfied. The less reluctant General Assembly of Scotland adopted the Confession, as it came from the Assembly at Westminster, on Aug. 27, 1647; but Parliament still debated, and finally, on June 20, 1648, adopted the Confession, with the omission of Ch. XX, § 4 (relating to the punishment of heresy, etc.); Ch. XXIV, §§ 4 (in part), 5, 6 (on divorce); Ch. XXX entire (on church censures); and Ch. XXXI entire (on synods and councils). At the same time Parliament changed the title to *Articles of Christian Religion*. The fact that Scotland adopted the original form, and that Presbyterianism soon broke down in England, prevented the emendations of Parliament from acquiring permanency.

vicarious nature of Christ's sacrifice in chapters eight and eleven. They defined the nature of the law given to Adam in chapter nineteen. They asserted the rightfulness of toleration in non-essentials in chapter twenty-four. They omitted the declaration that baptism admits to the visible church in chapter twenty-nine. All these changes are of a minor nature. More important is the addition of a whole chapter, the twentieth, *Of the Gospel, and of the extent of the Grace thereof*, which though intensely Calvinistic, and in no way antagonistic to the Westminster Confession, is nevertheless a pleasing token of that readiness, always characteristic of Congregationalism, to hold forth the more gracious aspects of the religion of Christ, in at least as clear a light as the sanctions of law. Yet when these alterations in the Confession have been summed up, the impression remains that all that was really essential had been anticipated in the omissions made by Parliament. No wonder such slight emendations, suggested by men of such influence, found ready acceptance.

The really original work of the Savoy Synod was not upon the Confession, but is contained in the thirty sections relating to church-order appended to it. Here is a brief, compact, and lucid presentation of the main features of Congregationalism: — the headship of Christ, the constitution of the local church by the union of believers, its complete autonomy, its right to choose and ordain the officers appointed by Christ, the necessity of a call from a church to confer ministerial standing, the consent of the brethren as essential to all admissions and censures, synods or councils for advice but without judicial authority. But though these principles are made evident, and though they would hardly have been so fully formulated had it not been for the Cambridge Platform, the thirty sections adopted at the Savoy are far inferior as a working manual to the New England document. They breathe the hazy atmosphere of theoretic and non-consolidated Congregationalism, resembling in this respect the symbols of the closing years of the previous century. The grand outlines of the polity are rough-drawn, but the detail is not yet sketched in. The men who drew it had not beheld the workings of Congregationalism as an exclusive or even predominant polity.[1] Had they done so they would have attempted to answer some of the practical questions which such an experience would have raised. There is also not the slightest hint in the document that the divines at the Savoy felt any interest in those questions regarding baptism and church membership by which contemporary New England was being turmoiled.

As presented to the public, the result of the Savoy Assembly was preceded, it cannot be said fortified, by a long, dreary Preface, alleged to have been written by John Owen.[2] If that able man really wrote it, and it is not improbable that he did, it is certainly one of the weakest productions that ever came from his pen.[3] Its chief merit, aside from the few facts which it contains as to the course of events in the Synod, is its spirit of tolerance toward Christians of differing beliefs,—a tolerance as creditable as it was unusual in that age.[4]

The Savoy Synod and its Declaration faded quickly from men's minds in the turmoils of Richard Cromwell's protectorate and the ruin which overtook Independents and Presbyterians alike at the Restoration. It excited no controversy, save a bitter denunciation from Richard Baxter, who looked upon it as a menace to the union of Presbyterians and Independents which he desired to effect;[5] and a criticism, at a later period, upon its orthodoxy and consistency by Peter du Moulin, an Anglican minister of French

---

[1] A number of those who sat in the Assembly at the Savoy must have been in New England, but none such were of the committee to whom the formulation of the result was entrusted.

[2] Orme, *Works of John Owen*, I: 177. Owen is too well known to need any extended notice. He was born in 1616, graduated at Oxford B.A. in 1632 and M.A. in 1635, entered holy orders, but believed that he experienced conversion some time after through a chance sermon. He became identified with the Presbyterian wing of Puritanism, but was turned to Congregationalism by Cotton's *Keyes*, which he first read with the intention of refuting. In 1651 he was made dean of Christ Church Coll., Oxford, he sat in Parliament as representative of the University, in 1654 he became one of the "Tryers" for ministerial fitness. The returned Presbyterian Parliament put him out of office at Oxford in March, 1660. In 1663 he was invited to fill the place of Norton as teacher of the Boston, Mass., church, but declined, thinking himself more needed in England. He died Aug. 24, 1683. The best account of him is that by Orme, *Works of John Owen*, London, 1826, Vol. I., where a full list of his numerous writings will be found.

[3] Dexter, *Cong. as seen*, styles it: "over long and not over strong."

[4] See *Preface*, pp. iii, iv, viii–x.

[5] For the ungenerous criticisms passed by Baxter on the Declaration and its framers, see his autobiography, *Mr. Richard Baxter's Narrative of the Most Memorable Passages of his Life and Times*, Sylvester's ed., London, 1696, Pt. I: pp. 103, 104. Compare Neal, *Puritans*, ed. New York, 1844. II: 179, 180.

birth, who had misunderstood its teachings or obtained an erroneous copy of its Declaration. To the latter critic Owen replied with some asperity.[1] In England the course of events buried the Savoy Declaration in such oblivion that when Neal wrote, three-quarters of a century after its publication, he could affirm that even the Independents of his day had largely laid it aside for the more familiar works of the Westminster Assembly.[2] Had the Savoy Declaration never gone beyond the shores of the land of its birth it would have been one of the most ephemeral of symbols; but its lasting use was to be in New England. Adopted by a Massachusetts Synod at Boston in 1680 with a few immaterial modifications, and similarly accepted for Connecticut at Saybrook in 1708, its doctrinal confession long continued a recognized standard for the Congregational churches of America. They have never formally set it aside, and though in Congregational polity a general creed has binding authority only in so far as local churches accept it, this Savoy Confession, as slightly changed in 1680, was declared by the Council of 1865 — an assembly representative of the whole body of the Congregational churches of the United States — to embody substantially the faith to which those churches are pledged.[3] In its Saybrook form it was established by law as the recognized doctrinal standard of the churches of Connecticut, and so continued till 1784. The appended sections regarding church order were never ratified on this side of the Atlantic; in New England the ampler Platform adopted at Cambridge in 1648 rendered them superfluous, and it was, therefore, only the Savoy Synod's amended form of the Westminster Confession that survived the downfall of the English Commonwealth.

---

[1] The reply of Owen to Du Moulin gives us our knowledge of this controversy. It may be found in Orme's *Memoir*, *Works of John Owen*, I: 365–368. Though undated, a reference to Owen's *Doctrine of Justification* shows that the letter must be later than 1677.

[2] Neal, *Puritans*, II: 178.

[3] *Burial Hill Declaration*, on later page of this work: "We, Elders and Messengers of the Congregational churches of the United States in National Council assembled, . . . do now declare our adherence to the faith and order of the apostolic and primitive churches held by our fathers, and substantially as embodied in the confessions and platforms which our Synods of 1648 and 1680 set forth or reaffirmed."

THE SAVOY DECLARATION

A | DECLARATION | OF THE | FAITH and ORDER | Owned and practised in the | Congregational Churches | IN | ENGLAND; | Agreed upon and consented unto | By their | ELDERS and MESSENGERS | IN | Their Meeting at the *SAVOY*, *October* 12. 1658. | ——— | ——— | *LONDON*: | Printed by *John Field*, and are to be sold by | *John Allen* at the Sun Rising in *Pauls* | Church-yard, 1658.

[ii blank]

[iii]

A

PREFACE.

C*Onfession* of the *Faith* that is in us, when justly called for, is so indispensable a due all owe to the Glory of the Soveraign GOD, that it is ranked among the Duties of the first Commandment, such as Prayer is; and therefore by *Paul* yoaked with Faith it self, as necessary to salvation: *With the heart man believeth unto righteousness, and with mouth confession is made unto salvation.* Our Lord Christ himself, when he was accused of his Doctrine, considered simply as a matter of fact by preaching, refused to answer; because, as such, it lay upon evidence, and matter of testimony of others; unto whom therefore he refers himself: But when both the High Priest and *Pilate* expostulate his Faith, and what he held himself to be; he without any demur at all, cheerfully makes declaration, That he *was the Son of GOD*; so to the *High Priest*: And that he was a *King*, and *born to be a King*; thus to *Pilate*; though upon the uttering of it his life lay at the stake: Which holy profession of his is celebrated for our example, 1 *Tim.* 6. 13.

Confessions, when *made by a company* of professors of Christianity joyntly meeting to that end, the most genuine and natural use of such *Confessions* is, That under the same form of words, they express the substance of the same *common salvation*, or *unity of their faith*; whereby *speaking the same things*, *they shew themselves perfectly joyned in* [iv] *the same minde, and in the same judgement.* 1 Cor. 1.[1] 10.

And accordingly such a transaction is to be looked upon but as a meet or fit *medium* or *means* whereby to express *that* their *common faith and salvation*, and

[1] In the original these references are on the margin.

no way to be made use of as an *imposition* upon any: Whatever is of force or constraint in matters of this nature causeth them to degenerate from the *name* and *nature* of *Confessions*, and turns them from being *Confessions of Faith*, into *exactions* and *impositions of Faith.*

And such *common Confessions* of the Orthodox Faith, made in simplicity of heart by any such Body of Christians, with concord among themselves, ought to be entertained by all others that *love the truth as it is in Jesus*, with an answerable *rejoycing*: For if the unanimous opinions and (Acts 15.) assertions but in some few points of Religion, and that when by two Churches, namely, that of *Jerusalem*, and the *Messengers of Antioch* met, assisted by some of the *Apostles*, were by the Believers of those times received with so much joy, (as it is said, *They rejoyced for the consolation*) much more this is to be done, when the *whole* substance of Faith, and *form of wholesome words* shall be declared by the Messengers of a multitude of Churches, though wanting those advantages of counsel and authority of the *Apostles*, which *that Assembly* had.

Which acceptation is then more specially due, when these shall (to choose) utter and declare their Faith, in the same *substance* for matter, yea, *words*, for the most part, that other Churches and Assemblies, reputed the *most Orthodox*, have done before them: For upon such a correspondency, all may see *that* actually accomplished, which the Apostle did but exhort unto, and pray for, in those *two* more eminent Churches of the *Corinthians* and the (Rom. 15. 6, 8, 9.) *Romans*; [v] (and so in them for all the Christians of his time) that both *Jew* and *Gentile*, that is, men of different perswasions, (as they were) *might glorifie GOD with one minde and with one mouth.* And truly, the very turning of the Gentiles to the owning of the same Faith, in the substance of it, with the Christian Jew (though differing in greater points then we do from our brethren) is presently after dignified by the Apostle with this stile, That it is the *Confession of Jesus Christ* himself; not as the *Object* onely, but as the *Author* and *Maker* thereof: *I will confess to thee* (saith Christ to God) (V. 9.) *among the Gentiles.* So that in all such accords, *Christ* is the *great and first Confessor*; and we, and all our Faith uttered by us, are but the *Epistles*, (as *Paul*) and *Confessions* (as *Isaiah* there) of *their Lord and ours*; He, but expressing what is written in his heart, through their hearts and mouthes, *to the glory of God the Father*: And shall not we all *rejoyce* herein, when as Christ himself is said to do it upon this occasion: as it there also follows, *I will sing unto thy Name.*

Further, as the *soundness* and *wholsomness of the matter* gives the *vigor* and *life* to such *Confessions*, so the *inward freeness*, *willingness* and *readiness* of the spirits of the *Confessors* do contribute the *beauty* and *loveliness* thereunto: as it is in *Prayer* to God, so in *Confessions* made to men. *If two or three met, do agree*, it renders both, to either the more acceptable. The *Spirit of Christ* is in himself too *free*, great and generous a Spirit, to suffer himself to be used by any humane arm, to whip men into belief; he drives not, but *gently leads into all truth*, and *perswades* men to *dwell in the tents* of *like precious Faith*; which would lose of its preciousness and value, if that sparkle of freeness shone not in it: The character of his people is to be a *willing people in the day of his* [vi] *power*, (not Mans) *in the beauties of holiness*, which are the Assemblings of the Saints: one glory of which Assemblings in that first Church, is said to have been, *They met with one accord*; which is there in that Psalm prophesied of, in the instance of that first Church, for all other that should succeed.

And as this great Spirit is in himself free, when, and how far, and in whom to work, so where and when he doth work, he carrieth it with the same freedom, and is said to be a *free Spirit*, as he both is, and works in us: And where this *Spirit of the Lord is*, *there is Liberty*.

Now, as to this *Confession* of ours, besides, that a conspicuous conjunction of the particulars mentioned, hath appeared therein: There are also *four remarkable Attendants* thereon, which added, might perhaps in the eyes of sober and indifferent spirits, give the whole of this Transaction a room and rank amongst other many good and memorable things of this age; at least all set together, do cast as clear a gleam and manifestation of Gods Power and Presence, as hath appeared in any such kinde of *Confessions*, made by so numerous a company these later years.

The first, is the *Temper*, (or distemper rather) of the *times*, during which, these *Churches* have been gathering, and which they have run through. All do (out of a general sense) complain that the times have been *perillous*, or *difficult times*; (as the Apostle foretold) and that in respect to danger from *seducing spirits*, more perillous then the hottest seasons of Persecution. We have sailed through an Æstuation, Fluxes and Refluxes of great varieties of Spirits, Doctrines, Opinions and Occurrences; and especially in the matter of Opinions, which have been accompanied [vii] in their several seasons, with powerful perswasions and temptations, to seduce those of our way. It is known men have taken the freedom (notwithstanding what Authority hath interposed to the contrary) to vent and vend their own vain and accursed imaginations, contrary to the great and fixed Truths of the Gospel, insomuch, as take the whole round and circle of delusions, the Devil hath in this small time, ran, it will be found, that every truth, of greater or lesser weight, hath by one or other hand, at one time or another, been questioned and called to the Bar amongst Us, yea, and impleaded, under the pretext (which hath some degree of Justice in it) that all should not be bound up to the Traditions of former times, nor take Religion upon trust.

Whence it hath come to pass, that many of the soundest Professors were put upon a new search and disquisition of such truths, as they had taken for granted, and yet had lived upon the comfort of: to the end they might be able to convince others, and establish their own hearts against that darkness and unbelief, that is ready to close with error, or at least to doubt of the truth, when error is speciously presented. And hereupon we do professedly account it one of the greatest advantages gained out of the temptations of these times; yea the honor of the Saints and Ministers of these Nations, That after they had sweetly been exercised in, and had improved *practical* and *experimental Truths*, this should be their further lot, to examine and discuss, and indeed, anew to learn over every *Doctrinal Truth*, both out of the Scriptures, and also with a fresh taste thereof in their own hearts; which is no other then what the Apostle exhorts to, *Try all things*, *hold fast that which is good*. *Conversion* unto God at *first*, what is it else [viii] then a *savory* and *affectionate application*, and the bringing home to the heart with spiritual *light* and *life*, all *truths* that are necessary to salvation, together with other *lesser truths?* all which we had afore conversion taken in but notionally from common education and tradition.

Now that after this first gust those who have bin thus converted should be put upon a new probation and search out of the Scriptures, not onely of all principles explicitely ingredients to Conversion; (unto which the Apostle referreth the *Galatians* when they had diverted from them) but of all other superstructures as well as fundamentals; and together therewith, anew to experiment the power and sweetness of all these in their own souls: What is this but *tryed Faith* indeed? and equivalent to a new conversion unto the truth? *An Anchor* that is proved to be *sure* and *stedfast*, that will certainly hold in all contrary storms: This was the eminent seal and commendation which those holy Apostles that lived and wrote last; *Peter*, *John* and *Jude*; in their Epistles did set and give to the *Christians* of the latter part of those *primitive times*. And besides, it is clear and evident by all the other Epistles, from first to last, that it cost the Apostles as much, and far more care and pains to preserve them they had converted, *in the truth*, then they had taken to turn them thereunto at first: And it is in it self as great a work and instance of the power of God, that *keeps*, yea, *guards us through faith unto salvation*.

This perswasion cometh not of him that calleth you. Gal. 5. 8.

1 Pet. 1. 5.

Secondly, let this be added, (or superadded rather) to give full weight and measure, even to running over), that we have all along this season, held forth (though quarreled with for it by our brethren) this great principle of these times, *That amongst all Christian States and Churches, there* [ix] *ought to be vouchsafed a forbearance and mutual indulgence unto Saints of all perswasions, that keep unto, and hold fast the necessary foundations of faith and holiness*, in all other matters *extrafundamental*, whether of Faith or Order.

This to have been our constant principle, we are not ashamed to confess to the whole Christian world. Wherein yet we desire we may be understood, not as if in the *abstract* we stood indifferent to falsehood or truth, or were careless whether faith or error, in any Truths but fundamental, did obtain or not, so we had our liberty in our petty and smaller differences: or as if to make sure of that, we had cut out this wide cloak for it: No, we profess that the whole, and every particle of that Faith delivered to the Saints, (the substance of which we have according to our light here professed) is, as to the propagation and furtherance of it by *all Gospel-means*, as precious to us as our lives; or what can be supposed dear to us; and in our sphere we have endeavored to promote them accordingly: But yet withall, we have and do contend, (and if we had all the power which any, or all of our brethren of differing opinions have desired to have over us, or others, we should freely grant it unto them all) we have and do contend for this, That *in the concrete*, the persons of all such gracious Saints, they and their errors, as they are in them, when they are but such errors as do and may stand with communion with Christ, though they should not repent of them, as not being convinced of them to the end of their days; that those, with their errors (that are purely spiritual, and intrench and overthrow not civil societies), as *concrete with their persons*, should for Christs sake be born withall by all Christians in the world; and they notwithstanding be permitted to enjoy all Ordinances and spiritual Priviledges according to their light, as [x] freely as any other of their brethren that pretend to the greatest Orthodoxity; as having as equal, and as fair a right in and unto Christ, and all the holy things of Christ, that any other can challenge to themselves.

And this doth afford a full and invincible testimony on our behalf, in that whiles we have so earnestly contended for this just liberty of Saints in all the Churches of Christ, *we our selves have had no need of it*: that is as to the *matter* of the profession of *Faith* which we have maintained together with others: and of this, this subsequent Confession of Faith gives sufficient evidence. So as we have the confidence in Christ, to utter in the words of those two great Apostles, That *we have stood fast in the liberty wherewith Christ hath made us free* (in the behalf of others, rather then our selves) and having been *free, have not made* use of out [our] *liberty* for *a cloak of error or maliciousness* in our selves: And yet, loe, whereas from the beginning of the rearing of these Churches, that of the Apostle hath been (by some) prophecyed of us, and applyed to us, *That whiles we promised* (unto others) *liberty, we our selves would become servants of corruption, and be brought in bondage* to all sorts of fancies and imaginations; yet the whole world may now see after the experience of many years ran through (and it is manifest by this Confession) that the great and gracious God hath not onely kept us in that common unity of the Faith and Knowledge of the Son of God, which the whole Community of Saints have and shall in their generations come unto, but also in the same Truths, both small and great, that are built thereupon, that any other of the best and more pure Reformed Churches in their best times (which were their first times) have arrived unto: This Confession withall holding forth a professed opposition unto the common errors and heresies of these times.

[xi] These *two considerations* have been taken from *the seasons* we have gone through.

Thirdly, let the *space of time it self*, or days, wherein from first to last the whole of this Confession was framed and consented to by the whole of us, be duly considered by sober and ingenuous spirits: the whole of days in which we had meetings about it, (set aside the two Lords days, and the first days meeting, in which we considered and debated what to pitch upon) were but eleven days, part of which also was spent by some of us in prayer, others in consulting; and in the end all agreeing. We mention this small circumstance but to this end, (which still adds unto the former) That it gives demonstration, not of our *freeness* and *willingness* onely, but of our *readiness* and *preparedness* unto so great a work; which otherwise, and in other Assemblies, hath ordinarily taken up long and great debates, as in such a variety of matters of such concernment, may well be supposed to fall out. And this is no other then what the Apostle *Peter* exhorts unto, *Be ready always to give an answer to every man that asketh you a reason or account of the hope that is in you.* (1 Pet. 3, 15.) The Apostle *Paul* saith of the spiritual Truths of the Gospel, *That God hath prepared them for those that love him.* (8 Cor. 2. [1 Cor. 2:9]) The inward and innate constitution of the new creature being in it self such as is suted to all those Truths, as congenial thereunto: But although there be this mutual *adaptness* between these two, yet such is the mixture of ignorance, darkness and unbelief, carnal reason, preoccupation of judgement, interest of parties, wantonness in opinion, proud adhering to our own perswasions, and perverse oppositions and aversness to agree with others, and a multitude of such like distempers *common to believing man*: All which are not onely mixed with, but at times, (especially in [xii] such times as have passed over our heads) are ready to overcloud our judgements, and do cause our eyes to be double, and sometimes prevail as well as lusts, and do byass our wills and affections: And such is their mixture, that although there may be existent an habitual preparedness in mens spirits, yet not always a present readiness [is] to be found, specially not in such a various multitude of men, to make a solemn and deliberate profession of all truths, it being as great a work to finde the spirits of the just (perhaps the best) of Saints, ready for every truth, as *to be prepared for every good work.*

It is therefore to be looked at as a great and special work of the holy Ghost. that so numerous a company of Ministers, and other principal brethren, should so *readily*, *speedily* and *joyntly* give up themselves unto such a whole Body of *Truths that are after godliness*.

This argues they had not their faith to seek; but, as it said of *Ezra*, that *they* were *ready Scribes*, and (as Christ) *instructed unto the kingdom of heaven*, being as the good *housholders* of so many families of Christ, *bringing forth of their store and treasury New and Old*. It shews these truths had been familiar to them, and they acquainted with them, as with their *dailv food and provision*, (as Christs allusion there insinuates) in a word, that *so they had preached*, and that *so their people had believed*, as the Apostle speaks upon one like particular occasion. And the Apostle *Paul* considers (in cases of this nature) *the suddenness* or *length of the time*, either one way or the other; whether it were in mens *forsaking* or *learning* of the truth. Thus the *suddenness* in the *Galatians* case in leaving the truth, he makes a wonder of it: *I marvel that you are SO SOON* (that is, in so short a time) *removed from the true Gospel unto another*. Again on the contrary, in the *Hebrews* he aggravates their back-[xiii]wardness, *That when for the time you ought to be Teachers, you had need that one teach you the very first principles of the Oracles of God*. The Parable contrary to both these having fallen out in this transaction, may have some ingredient and weight with ingenuous spirits in its kinde, according to the proportion is put upon either of these forementioned in their adverse kinde, and obtain the like special observation.

Gal. 1. 6.

Heb. 5. 12.

This accord of ours hath fallen out without having *held any correspondency together*, or prepared consultation, by which we might come to be advised of one anothers mindes. We alledge not this as a matter of commendation in us: no, we acknowledge it to have been a great neglect: And accordingly one of the *first proposals* for union amongst us was, That there might be a constant correspondence held among the Churches for counsel and mutual edification, so for time to come to prevent the like omission.

We confess that from the first, every, or at least the generality of our Churches, have been in a maner like so many Ships (though holding forth the same general colours) lancht singly, and sailing apart and alone in the vast Ocean of these tumultuating times, and they exposed to every wind of Doctrine, under no other conduct then the Word and Spirit, and their particular Elders and principal Brethren, without Associations among our selves, or so much as holding out common lights to others, whereby to know where we were.

But yet whilest we thus confess to our own shame this neglect, let all acknowledge, that God hath ordered it for his high and greater glory, in that his singular care and power should have so watcht over each of these, as that all should be found to have steered their course by the same [xiv] Chart, and to have been bound for one and the same Port, and that upon this general search now made, that the same holy and blessed Truths of all sorts, which are currant and warrantable amongst all the other Churches of Christ in the world, should be found to be our Lading.

The whole, and every of these things when put together, do cause us (whatever men of prejudiced and opposite spirits may finde out to slight them) with a holy admiration, to say, That *this is no other* then *the Lords doing*; and which we with thanksgiving do take from his hand as a special *token upon us for good*, and

doth *shew that God is faithful* and *upright* towards *those that are planted in his house*: And that as the *Faith* was but *once* for all, and intentionally *first delivered unto the Saints*; so the *Saints*, when not abiding scattered, but gathered under their *respective Pastors* according to *Gods heart into an house*, and Churches unto the *living God*, such *together* are, as *Paul* forespake it, the most steady and firm *pillar* and *seat of Truth* that God hath any where appointed to himself on earth, where his truth is best conserved, and publiquely held forth; there being in such Assemblies weekly *a rich dwelling of the Word amongst them*, that is, a daily open house kept by the means of those good *Housholders*, their Teachers and other Instructers respectively appropriated to them, whom Christ in the vertue of his *Ascension*, continues to *give as gifts* to his people, himself *dwelling amongst* them; to the end that by this, as the most sure standing permanent means, *the Saints might be perfected, till we all* (even all the Saints in present and future ages) do come by this constant and daily Ordinance of his unto *the unity of the Faith and Knowledge
of the* [xv] *Son of God unto a perfect man, unto the measure of the* Eph. 4. 12.
stature of the fulness of Christ (which though growing on by parts
and piecemeal, will yet appear compleat, when *that great and general Assembly* shall be gathered, then when this world is ended, and these dispensations have had their fulness and period) and *so that from henceforth* (such a provision being
made for us) *we be no more children tossed to and fro, and carried* 14.
about with every wind of Doctrine.

And finally, this doth give a fresh and recent demonstration, that the *great Apostle* and *High-priest of our profession* is indeed *ascended* into
heaven, and continues there with power and care, *faithful as a son* Heb. 3. 6.
*over his own house, whose house are we, if we hold fast the confidence
and the rejoycing of the hope firm unto the end:* and shewes that he will, as he hath promised, be with his own Institutions to the end of the world.

It is true, that many sad miscarriages, divisions, breaches, fallings off from holy Ordinances of God, have along this time of tentation, (especially in the beginning of it) been found in some of our Churches; and no wonder, if what hath been said be fully considered: Many reasons might further be given hereof, that would be a sufficient Apology, without the help of a retortion upon other Churches (that promised themselves peace) how that more destroying ruptures have befallen them, and that in a wider sphere and compass; which though it should not justifie us, yet may serve to stop others mouthes.

Let *Rome* glory of the peace in, and *obedience* of her children, against the Reformed *Churches* for their divisions that [xvi] [oc]curred (especially in the first rearing of them) whilest we all know the causes of their dull and stupid peace to have been carnal interests, worldly correspondencies, and coalitions strengthened by gratifications of all sorts of men by that Religion, the principles of blinde Devotion, Traditional Faith, Ecclesiastical Tyranny, by which she keeps her children in bondage to this day. We are also certain, that the very same prejudice that from hence they would cast upon the Reformed (if they were just) do lye as fully against those pure Churches raised up by the Apostles themselves in those first times: for as *we have heard of their patience*, sufferings, consolations, and the transcending gifts poured out, and graces shining in them, *so we have heard complaints
of their divisions* too, of the *forsakings of their Assemblies*, as the Heb. 10. 22.
custom or *maner of SOME was* (which later were in that respect
felones de se, and needed no other *delivering up to Satan* as their punishment, then

what they executed upon themselves.) We read of the *shipwrack* also of *Faith* and a *good Conscience*, and *overthrowings of the faith of SOME*; and still but of *some*, not *all*, nor the *most*: which is one piece of an Apologie the Apostle again and again inserts to future ages, and through mercy we have the same to make.

And truly we take the confidence professedly to say, that these tentations common to the purest *Churches* of *Saints separated from the mixture of the world*, though they grieve us (for *who is offended, and we burn not?*) yet they do not at all stumble us, as to the truth of our way, had they been many more: We say it again, these stumble us no more (as to that point) then it doth offend us against the power of Religion it self, to have seen, and to see daily in *particular persons called out and separated from the world* [xvii] by an effectual work of conversion, that they for a *while do suffer* under disquietments, vexations, turmoils, unsettlements of spirit, that they are tossed with tempests and horrid tentations, such as they had not in their former estate, whilst they *walked according to the course of this world*: For *Peter* hath sufficiently instructed us whose business it is to raise such storms, even the *Devil's*; and also whose designe it is, that *after they have suffered a while*, thereby they shall be *setled*, *perfected*, *stablished*, that have so suffered, even *the God of all Grace*. And look what course of dispensation God holds to *Saints personally*, he doth the like to *bodies of Saints* in *Churches*, and the Devil the same for his part too: And that consolatory Maxim of the Apostle, *God shall tread down Satan under your feet shortly*, which *Paul* uttereth concerning the Church of *Rome*, shews how both *God* and *Satan* have this very hand therein; for he speaks that very thing in reference unto their divisions, as the coherence clearly manifests; and so you have both designs exprest at once.

Yea, we are not a little induced to think, that the *divisions*, breaches, *&c.* of those *primitive Churches* would not have been so frequent among the people themselves, and not the Elders onely, had not the freedom, liberties and rights of the Members (the Brethren, we mean) been stated and exercised in those Churches, the same which we maintain and contend for to be in ours.

Yea (which perhaps may seem more strange to many) had not those Churches been constituted of Members inlightned further then with notional and traditional knowledge, by a new and more powerful light of the *Holy Ghost*, wherein *they had been made partakers of the holy Ghost, and the heavenly gift, and their hearts had tasted the good Word of* [xviii] *God, and the Powers of the world to come*, and of such Members at lowest, there had not fallen out those kindes of divisions among them.

For experience hath shewn, that the most common sort of meer *Doctrinal Professors* (such as the most are now a days) whose highest elevation is but *freedom from moral scandal joyned* with *devotion* to Christ through meer education, such as in many *Turks* is found towards *Mahomet*, that these finding and feeling themselves not much concerned in the *active part* of *Religion*, so they may have the honor (especially upon a Reformation of a new Refinement) that themselves are approved Members, admitted to the Lords Supper, and their children to the Ordinance of Baptism; they *regard not other matters* (as *Gallio* did not) but do easily and readily give up themselves unto their Guides, being like dead fishes carried with the common stream; whereas those that have a further renewed light by a work of the holy Ghost, whether *saving* or *temporary*, are upon the quite contrary grounds apt to be busie about, and inquisitive into, what they are to receive and practise, or wherein their consciences are professedly concerned and involved: And thereupon they take the freedom to *examine* and *try the spirits*, *whether of God or no*: And from hence are more apt to dissatisfaction, and from thence to run into division, and many of such proving to be inlightned but with a *temporary*, not saving *Faith* (who have such a work of the Spirit upon them, and profession in them, as will and doth approve it self to the judgement of Saints, and ought to be so judged, until they be otherwise discovered) who at long run, prove hypocrites through indulgence unto lusts, and then out of their lusts persist [xix] to hold up these divisions unto breach of, or departings from Churches, and the Ordinances of God, and *God is even* with them for it, *they waxing worse and worse*, *deceiving and being deceived;* and even many of those that are sincere, through a mixture of darkness and erroneousness in their judgements, are for a season apt out of conscience *to be led away with the error of others*, *which lie in wait to deceive*.

Insomuch as the Apostle upon the example of those first times, foreseeing also the like events in following generations upon the like causes, hath been bold to set this down as a *ruled Case*, that likewise in other Churches so constituted and *de facto* empriviledged as that of the Church of *Corinth* was (which single Church, in the sacred Records about it, is the compleatest Mirror of Church-Constitution, Order and Government, and events thereupon ensuing, of any one Church whatever that we have story of) his Maxim is, *There must be also divisions* amongst you; he setly inserts an [*ALSO*][1] in the case, as that which had been in his own observation, and that which would be ἐπὶ τὸ πολὺ the fate of other Churches like thereunto, *so prophesieth he*: And he speaks this as peremtorily as he doth elsewhere in that other, *We must through many tribulations enter into the Kingdom of Heaven*: Yea, and that *all that will live godly in Christ Jesus*, *shall suffer persecution:* There is a [*MUST*] upon both alike, and we bless God, that we have run through both, and do say, and we say no more; *That as it was then*, *so is it now*, in both respects.

However, such hath been the powerful hand of Gods Providence in *these*, which have been the worst of our *Tryals*, That out of an approved experience and observation [xx] of the issue, we are able to adde that other part of the Apostles Prediction, That therefore *such rents must be*, *that they which are approved may be made manifest among you*; which holy issue God (as having aimed at it therein) doth frequently and certainly bring about in Churches, as he doth bring upon them that other fate of division. Let them therefore look unto it, that are the *Authors of such disturbances*, as the Apostle warneth, *Gal*. 5. 10. The *experiment is this*, That we have seen, and do daily see, that multitudes of holy and precious souls, and (in the holy Ghosts word) *approved Saints*, have been, and are the more rooted and grounded by means of these shakings, and do continue to cleave the faster to Christ, and the purity of his Ordinances, and value them the more by this cost God hath put them to for the enjoying of them, *who having been planted in the House of the Lord*, *have flourished in the Courts of our God*, in these evil times, to *shew that the Lord is upright*. And this experimented event from out of such divisions, hath more confirmed us, and is a lowder Apologie for us, then all that our opposites are able from our breaches to alleadge to prejudice us.

We will add a few words for *conclusion*, and give a more particular account of this our *DECLARATION*. In drawing up this *Confession of Faith*, we have had before us the *Articles of Religion*,[2] approved and passed by both Houses of *Parliament*, after advice had with an *Assembly of Divines*, called together by them for that purpose. To which Confes- June 20, 1648.

[1] [ ] in original.

[2] See *ante*, p. 350.

sion, for the substance of it, we fully assent, as do our Brethren of *New-England*,[1] and the Churches also of *Scotland*,[2] as each in their general Synods have testified.

[xxi] A few things we have added for obviating some erroneous opinions, that have been more broadly and boldly here of late maintained by the Asserters, then in former times; and made some other additions and alterations in *method*, here and there, and some clearer explanations, as we found occasion.

We have endeavored throughout, to hold to such Truths in this our Confession, as are more properly termed *matters of Faith*; and what is of *Church-order*, we dispose in certain Propositions by it self. To this course we are led by the Example of the Honorable *Houses of Parliament*, observing what was established, and what omitted by them in that *Confession* the Assembly presented to them. Who thought it not convenient to have matters of *Discipline* and *Church-Government* put into a *Confession of Faith*, especially such particulars thereof, as then were, and still are controverted and under dispute by men Orthodox and sound in Faith. The 30th *cap.* therefore of that Confession, as it was presented to them by the Assembly, which is of *Church-Censures*, their *Use*, *Kindes*, and in *whom placed*: As also *cap.* 31. of *Synods* and *Councels*, by *whom* to be *called*, of *what force* in their *decrees* and *determinations*. And the 4th *paragr.* of the 20th *cap.* which determines what *opinions* and practises *disturb the peace* of the Church, and how such disturbers ought to *be proceeded against* by the *Censures of the Church*, and punished by the *Civil Magistrate*. Also a great part of the 24th *cap. of Marriage* and *Divorce*. These were such doubtful assertions, and so unsutable to a Confession of Faith, as the *Honorable Houses* in their great Wisdom thought fit to lay them aside: There being nothing that tends more to heighten dissentings among Brethren, [xxii] then to determine and adopt the *matter* of their *difference*, under so high a title, as to be an *Article* of *our Faith*: So that there are two whole Chapters, and some Paragraphs in other Chapters in their Confession, that we have upon this account omitted; and the rather do we give this notice, because that Copy of the Parliaments, followed by us, is in few mens hands; the other as it came from the *Assembly*, being approved of in *Scotland*, was printed and hastened [i]nto the world before the *Parliament* had declared their Resolutions about it; which was not till *June* 20. 1648. and yet hath been, and continueth to be the Copy (ordinarily) onely sold, printed and reprinted for these *eleven* years.

Aug. 1647

After the 19th *cap. of the Law*, we have added a *cap. of the Gospel*, it being a Title that may not well be omitted in a Confession of Faith: In which Chapter, what is dispersed, and by intimation in the Assemblies Confession with some little addition, is here brought together, and more fully under one head.

That there are not Scriptures annexed as in some Confessions[3] (though in divers others it's otherwise) we give the same account as did the *Reverend Assembly* in the same case: which was this; *The Confession being large, and so framed, as to meet with the common errors, if the Scriptures should have been alleadged with any clearness, and by shewing where the strength of the proof lieth, it would have required a volume.*

Session 786.

We say further, it being our utmost end in this (as it is indeed of a *Confession*)

---

[1] See *ante*, p. 195. [2] *Ibid.*, p. 350.

[3] This absence of proof texts was remedied, as far as Connecticut was concerned, by the Saybrook Synod in 1708. Parliament compelled the Westminster Assembly to add them; see *ante*, p. 350.

humbly to give an account what we hold and assert in these matters; that others, especially the Churches of Christ may judge of us accordingly. [xxiii] This we aimed at, and not so much to instruct others, or convince gainsayers. These are the proper works of other institutions of Christ, and are to be done in the strength of express Scripture. *A Confession* is an Ordinance of another nature.

What we have laid down and asserted about *CHURCHES* and their *Government*, we humbly conceive to be the *Order* which Christ himself hath appointed to be observed, we have endeavored to follow Scripture-light; and those also that went before us according to that Rule, desirous of nearest uniformity with *reforming Churches*, as with our Brethren in *New-England*, so with others, that differ from them and us.

The Models and Platforms of this subject laid down by learned men, and practised by Churches, are various: We do not judge it *brotherly*, or *grateful*, to insist upon comparisons as some have done; but this experience teacheth, That the *variety*, and possibly the *disputes* and *emulatians* arising thence, have much strengthened, if not fixed, this unhapy perswasion in the mindes of some learned and good men, namely, *That there is no settled Order laid down in Scripture;* but it's left to the prudence of the Christian Magistrate, to compose or make choice of such a Form as is most sutable and consistent with their Civil Government. Where this opinion is entertained in the perswasion of Governors, there, Churches asserting their Power and Order to be *jure divino*, and the appointment of Jesus Christ, can have no better nor more honorable entertainment, then a Toleration or Permission.

Yet herein there is this remarkable advantage to all [xxiv] parties that differ, about what in Government is of Christs appointment; in that such *Magistrates* have a far greater latitude in conscience, to tolerate and permit the several forms of each so bound up in their perswasion, then *they* have to submit unto what the Magistrate shall impose: And thereupon the Magistrate exercising an indulgency and forbearance, with protection and encouragement to the people of God, so differing from him, and amongst themselves: Doth therein discharge as great a faithfulness to Christ, and love to his people, as can any way be supposed and expected from any Christian Magistrate, of what perswasion soever he is. And where this clemency from Governors is shewed to any sort of persons or Churches of Christ upon such a principle, it will in equity produce this just effect, That all that so differ from him, and amongst themselves, standing in equal and alike difference from the principle of such a Magistrate, he is equally free to give a like liberty to them, one as well as the other.

This faithfulness in our Governors we do with thankfulness to God acknowledge, and to their everlasting honor, which appeared much in the late Reformation. The *Hierarchie*, *Common-prayer-book*, and all other things grievous to Gods people, being removed, they made choice of an Assembly of learned men, to advise whɐ*t Government and Order is meet to be established in the room of these things; and because it was known there were different opinions (as always hath been among Godly men) about forms of Church-Government, there was by the *Ordinance* first sent forth to call an Assembly, not onely a choice made of persons of several perswasions to sit as *Members* there, but liberty given, to a *lesser number*, if [xxv] dissenting, to report their Judgements and Reasons, as well and as freely as the *major part*.

* *a* turned upside down.

Hereupon the Honorable House of Commons (an Indulgence we hope will never be forgotten) finding by papers received from them, that the Members of the Assembly were not like to compose differences amongst themselves, so as to joyn in the same Rule for Church-Government, did Order further as followeth: **That a Committee of Lords and Commons, &c. do take into consideration the differences of the Opinions in the Assembly of Divines in point of Church-Government, and to endeavor a union if it be possible; and in case that cannot be done, to endeavor the finding out some way, how far tender consciences, who cannot in all things submit to the same Rule which shall be established, may be born with according to the Word, and as may stand with the publique peace.**

By all which it is evident the Parliament purposed not to establish the Rule of Church-Government with such vigor, as might not permit and bear with a practise different from what they had established: In persons and Churches of different principles, if occasion were. And this Christian clemency and indulgence in our Governors, hath been the foundation of that *Freedom and Liberty*, in the managing of Church-affairs, which *our Brethren*, as well as *WE*, that differ from them, do now, and have many years enjoyed.

The Honorable Houses by several Ordinances of Parliament after much consultation, having settled Rules [xxvi] for Church-Government, and *such an Ecclesiastical Order* as they judged *would best joynt with the Laws and Government of the Kingdom*, did publish them, requiring the practise hereof throughout the Nation; and in particular, by the Ministers of the Province of *London*. But (upon the former reason, or the like charitable consideration) these *Rules* were not imposed by them under any *PENALTY* or rigorous inforcement, though freqnently urged thereunto by some.

Ordinance of March 14. 1645.

Our reverend Brethren of the Province of *London*, having considered of these Ordinances, and the Church-Government laid down in them, declared their opinions to be, *That there is not a compleat rule in those Ordinances;* also, *that there are many necessary things not yet established, and some things wherein their consciences are not so fully satisfied.* These Brethren in the same paper, have published also their joynt *Resolution to practise in all things according to the rule of the Word, and according to these Ordinances, so far as they conceive them correspond to it, and in so doing they trust they shall not grieve the spirit of the truly godly, nor give any just occasion to them that are contrary minded, to blame their proceedings.*

Considerations and Cautions from Sion Coll. June 19. 1646.

We humbly conceive (that *WE* being dissatisfied in these things as our Brethren) the like liberty was intended by the honorable Houses, and may be taken by us of the *Congregational way* (without blame or grief to the spirits of those *Brethren* at least) to resolve, or rather to continue in the same resolution and practise in these matters, which indeed were our practises in times of greatest opposition, and before this reformation was begun.

And as our Brethren, *the Ministers of London*, drew up and published their *opinions* and *apprehensions* about [xxvii] Church-Government into an intire System; so we now give the like publique account of our consciences, and the rules by which we have constantly practised hitherto; which we have here drawn up, and do present. Whereby it will appear how much, or how little we differ in these things from our Presbyterian Brethren.

And we trust there is no just cause why any man, either for our differing from the present settlement, it being out of conscience, and not out of *contempt*, or our differences one from another, being not *wilful*, should charge either of us with that odious reproach of *Schism*. And indeed, if not for our differing from the State-settlement, much less because we differ from our Brethren, our differences being *in some lesser things, and circumstances*, onely, as themselves acknowledge. And let it be further considered, that we have not broken from them or their Order by these differences (but rather they from us) and in that respect we less deserve their censure; our practise being no other then what it was in our breaking from Episcopacy, and long before Presbytery, or any such form as now they are in, was taken up by them; and we will not say how probable it is that the yoke of Episcopacy had been upon our neck to this day, if some such way (as formerly, and now is, and hath been termed *Schism*) had not with much suffering bin then practised & since continued in.

Jus divinum Minist. pub. by the Provost of London in the Preface.

For *Novelty*, wherewith we are likewise both charged by the enemies of both, it is true, in respect of the publique and open profession, either of Presbytery or Independency, this Nation hath been a stranger to each way, it's possible ever since it hath been Christian; though for our selves we are able to trace the footsteps of an Independent Congregational Way in the ancientest customs of [xxviii] the Churches, as also in the writings of our soundest Protestant Divines, and (that which we are much satisfied in) a full concurrence throughout in all the substantial parts of Church-Governments, with our Reverend Brethren the *old Puritan non-Conformists*, who being instant in prayer and much sufferings, prevailed with the Lord, and we reap with joy, what they sowed in tears. Our Brethren also that are for Presbyterial subordinations, profess what is of weight against *Novelty* for their way.

Puritanis. Ang. by Dr. Aims near 50 years since,[1] as the opinions of Whitehead, Gilbe, Fox, Dearing, Greenham, Cartwright, Venner, Fulk, Whitaker, Rainold, Perkins, &c.

And now therefore seeing the Lord, in whose hand is the heart of Princes, hath put into the hearts of our Governors to tolerate and permit (as they have done many years) persons of each perswasion, to enjoy their consciences, though neither come up to the *Rule established by Authority*: And that which is more, to give us both protection, and the same encouragement that the most devoted *Conformists* in those former superstitious times enjoyed, yea, and by a publique Law to establish this Liberty for time to come; and yet further, in the midst of our fears, to set over us a *Prince* that owns this Establishment, and cordially resolves to secure our churches in the enjoyment of these Liberties, if we abuse them not to the disturbance of the Civil Peace.

This should be a very great engagement upon the hearts of all, though of different perswasions, to endeavor our utmost, *joyntly* to promove the honor and prosperity of such a Government and Governors by whatsoever means, which in our Callings as Ministers of the Gospel, and as Churches of Jesus Christ the Prince of peace, we are any way able to; as also to be peaceably disposed one [xxix] towards another, and with mutual toleration to love as brethren, notwithstanding such differences, remembring, as it's very equal we should, the differences that are between *Presbyterians* and *Independents*, being differences between fellow-servants, and neither of them having authority given from God or man, to impose their opinions, one more then

[1] I. e., Bradshaw's *Puritanismus Anglicanus*, Frankfort, 1610; a collection of the opinions of leading Puritans, with a Preface by William Ames, the celebrated Puritan divine.

the other. That our Governors after so solemn an establishment, should thus bear with us both, in our greater differences from their Rule, and after this, for any of us *to take a fellow-servant by the throat*, upon the account of a lesser reckoning, and nothing due to *him* upon it: is to forget, at least not to exercise, that compassion and tenderness we have found, where we had less ground to challenge or expect it.

Our Prayer unto God is, That *whereto we have* already *attained*, *we* all *may walk by the same rule*, and that *wherein we are otherwise minded*, God would reveal it to us in his due time.

[xxx] Books sold by *John Allen* at the Sun Rising in *Pauls* Church-yard.

[list of 15 volumes].

A DECLARATION OF THE FAITH and ORDER Owned and practised in the CONGREGATIONAL CHURCHES IN ENGLAND.

CHAP. I.[1]

Of the holy Scripture.

ALthough the Light of Nature, and the Works of Creation and Providence, do so far manifest the Goodness, Wisdom and Power of God, as to leave men unexcusable; yet are they not sufficient to give that knowledge of God and of his Will, which is necessary unto salvation: Therefore it pleased the Lord at sundry times, and in divers maners to reveal himself, and to declare that his Will unto his Church; and afterwards for the better preserving and propagating of the truth, and for the more sure establishment and comfort of the Church against the corruption of the flesh, and the malice of Satan [2] and of the world, to commit the same wholly unto writing: which maketh the holy Scripture to be most necessary; those former ways of Gods revealing his Will unto his people, being now ceased.

II. Under the name of holy Scripture, or the Word of God written, are now contained all the Books of the Old and New Testament; which are these:

---

[1] In presenting the text of the Confession of Faith, I have printed such portions as were taken from the Westminster Confession in Roman; the parts added at the Savoy are in *black faced type*. I have also given in notes all parts *omitted* from the Westminster Confession, following the text printed by Dr. Schaff in his *Creeds of Christendom*, III: 600–673. The few changes from the Savoy made by the Massachusetts Synod of 1680 are also indicated, so that this text will serve as a representative of that Confession also. The Saybrook Confession is identical with that of 1680, save that it adds proof texts to each section.

Of the Old Testament.

Genesis, Exodus, Leviticus, Numbers, Deuteronomy, Joshua, Judges, Ruth, 1 Samuel, 2 Samuel, 1 Kings, 2 Kings, 1 Chronicles, 2 Chronicles, Ezra, Nehemiah, Esther, Job, Psalms, Proverbs, Ecclesiastes, The Song of Songs, Isaiah, Jeremiah, Lamentations, Ezekiel, Daniel, Hosea, Joel, Amos, Obadiah, Jonah, Micah, Nahum, Habakkuk, Zephaniah, Haggai, Zechariah, Malachi.

Of the New Testament.

Matthew,[1] Mark, Luke, John, The Acts of the Apostles, Pauls Epistle to the Romans, 1 Corinthians, 2 Corinthians, Galatians, Ephesians, Philippians, Colossians, 1 Thessalonians, 2 Thessalonians, 1 To Timothy, 2 To Timothy, To Titus, To Philemon, The Epistle to the Hebrews, The Epistle of James, The first and second Epistles of Peter, The first, second and third Epistles of John, the Epistle of Jude, The Revelation.

[3] All which are given by **the** inspiration of God to be the Rule of Faith and Life.

III. The Books commonly called Apocrypha, not being of Divine inspiration, are no part of the Canon of the Scripture; and therefore are of no authority in the Church of God, nor to be any otherwise approved or made use of, then other humane writings.

IV. The authority of the holy Scripture, for which it ought to be believed and obeyed, dependeth not upon the Testimony of any man or Church; but wholly upon God (who is Truth it self) the Author thereof; and therefore it is to be received, because it is the Word of God.

V. We may be moved and induced by the Testimony of the Church, to an high and reverent esteem of the holy Scripture. And the heavenliness of the Matter, the efficacy of the Doctrine, the majesty of the Style, the consent of all the parts, the scope of the whole, (which is, to give all glory to God) the full discovery it makes of the onely way of Mans Salvation, the many other incomparable excellencies, and the intire perfection thereof, are Auguments whereby it doth abundantly evidence it self to be the Word of God; Yet notwithstanding, our full perswasion and assurance of the infallible Truth and Divine Authority thereof, is from the inward work of the holy Spirit, bearing witness by and with the Word in our hearts.

[4] VI. The whole Counsel of God concerning all things necessary for his own Glory, mans Salvation, Faith and Life, is either expresly set down in Scripture, or by good and necessary con-

[1] West. prefaces: *The Gospels according to.*

sequence may be deduced from Scripture; unto which nothing at any time is to be added, whether by new Revelations of the Spirit, or Traditions of men. Nevertheless we acknowledge the inward illumination of the Spirit of God to be necessary for the saving understanding of such things as are revealed in the Word: And that there are some circumstances concerning the Worship of God and Government of the Church, common to humane actions and Societies, which are to be ordered by the Light of Nature and Christian prudence, according to the general Rules of the Word, which are always to be observed.

VII. All things in Scripture are not alike plain in themselves, nor alike clear unto all: yet those things which are necessary to be known, believed and observed for Salvation, are so clearly propounded and opened in some place of Scripture or other, that not onely the learned, but the unlearned, in a due use of the ordinary means, may attain unto a sufficient understanding of them.

VIII. The Old Testament in Hebrew (which was the Native Language of the people of God of old) and the New Testament in Greek (which at the time of[1] writing of it was most generally known to the Nations) being immediately inspired by God, and by his singular care and providence [5] kept pure in all Ages, are therefore Authentical; so as in all Controversies of Religion the Church is finally to appeal unto them. But because these Original Tongues are not known to all the people of God, who have right unto and interest in the Scriptures, and are commanded in the fear of God to read and search them; therefore they are to be translated into the vulgar language of every Nation unto which they come, that the Word of God dwelling plentifully in all, they may worship him in an acceptable maner, and through patience and comfort of the Scriptures may have hope.

IX. The infallible Rule of Interpretation of Scripture, is the Scripture it self ; And therefore when there is a question about the true and full sense of any Scripture (which is not manifold, but one) it must be searched and known by other places, that speak more clearly.

X. The Supreme Judge by which all controversies of Religion are to be determined, and all Decrees of Councels, Opinions of ancient Writers, Doctrines of men and private Spirits, are to be examined, and in whose Sentence we are to rest, can be no other, but the[2] **holy Scripture delivered by the Spirit; into which Scripture so delivered, our Faith is finally resolved.**

---

[1] West. adds: *the*.

[2] West. reads: *but the Holy Spirit speaking in the Scripture.*

[6]

CHAP. II.

Of God and of the holy Trinity.

THere is but one onely living and true God; who is infinite in Being and Perfection, a most pure Spirit, invisible, without body, parts, or passions, immutable, immense, eternal, incomprehensible, almighty, most wise, most holy, most free, most absolute, working all things according to the Counsel of his own immutable and most righteous Will, for his own Glory, most loving, gracious, merciful, long-suffering, abundant in goodness and truth, forgiving iniquity, transgression and sin, the rewarder of them that diligently seek him; and withal most just and terrible in his Judgements, hating all sin, and who will by no means clear the guilty.

II. God hath all Life, Glory, Goodness, Blessedness, in, and of himself; and is alone, in, and unto himself, All-insufficient, not[1] standing in need of any Creatures, which he hath made, nor deriving any glory from them, but onely manifesting his own glory in, by, unto, and upon them: He is the alone **Fountain**[2] of all Being, of whom, through whom, and to whom are all things; and hath most Soveraign dominion over them, to do by them, for them, or upon them, whatsoever himself pleaseth: In his sight all things are open and manifest, his Knowledge is infinite, infallible, and independent upon the creature, so as nothing is to him contingent or uncertain: He is most holy in all his Counsels, in all his Works, and in all his Commands. [7] To him is due from Angels and Men, and every other Creature, whatsoever Worship, Service or Obedience, **as Creatures, they owe unto the Creator, and whatever** he is **further** pleased to require of them.[3]

III. In the Unity of the God-head there be three Persons, of one Substance, Power and Eternity, God the Father, God the Son, and God the holy Ghost: The Father is of none, neither begotten, nor proceeding; The Son is eternally begotten of the Father; The holy Ghost eternally proceeding from the Father and the Son. **Which Doctrine of the Trinity is the foundation of all our Communion with God, and comfortable Dependence upon him.**[4]

CHAP. III.

Of Gods Eternal Decree.

GOd from all eternity did by the most wise and holy Counsel of his own Will, freely and unchangeably ordain whatsoever

[1] Saybrook reads *nor*. [2] West. reads: *foundation*. [3] Simple addition. [4] Ibid.

comes to pass: Yet so, as thereby neither is God the Author of sin, nor is violence offered to the will of the Creatures, nor is the liberty or contingency of second causes taken away, but rather established.

II. Although God knows whatsoever may or can come to pass upon all supposed Conditions, yet hath he not decreed any thing, because he foresaw it as future, or as that which would come to pass upon such Conditions.

[8] III. By the Decree of God for the manifestation of his Glory, some Men and Angels are predestinated unto everlasting Life, and others fore-ordained to everlasting Death.

IV. These Angels and Men thus predestinated, and fore-ordained, are particularly and unchangeably designed, and their number is so certain and definite, that it cannot be either increased or diminished.

V. Those of mankinde that are predestinated unto Life, God, before the foundation of the world was laid, according to his eternal and immutable purpose, and the secret counsel and good pleasure of his Will, hath chosen in Christ unto everlasting Glory, out of his meer free Grace and Love, without any fore-sight of Faith or good Works, or perseverance in either of them or any other thing in the Creature, as Conditions or Causes moving him thereunto, and all to the praise of his glorious Grace.

VI. As God hath appointed the Elect unto Glory, so hath he by the eternal and most free purpose of his Will fore-ordained all the means thereunto: Wherefore they who are elected, being faln in Adam, are redeemed by Christ, are effectually called unto Faith in Christ by his spirit working in due season, are justified, adopted, sanctified, and kept by his power, through Faith, unto salvation. Neither are any other redeemed by Christ, **or**[1] effectually [9] called, justified, adopted, sanctified and saved, but the Elect onely.

VII. The rest of mankinde God was pleased, according to the unsearchable Counsel of his own Will, whereby he extendeth or withholdeth mercy, as he pleaseth, for the glory of his soveraign power over his Creatures, to pass by and to ordain them to dishonor[2] and wrath for their sin, to the praise of his glorious Justice.

VIII. The Doctrine of this high mystery of Predestination is to be handled with special prudence and care, that men attending the will of God revealed in his Word, and yielding obedience

---

[1] Added to West.

[2] The reader will observe that this English work of the XVII. Century employs the so-called American spelling uniformly in such words as honor and the like.

thereunto, may from the certainty of their effectual Vocation, be assured of their eternal Election. So shall this Doctrine afford matter of praise, reverence and admiration of God, and of humility, diligence, and abundant consolation to all that sincerely obey the Gospel.

CHAP. IV.

Of Creation.

IT pleased God the Father, Son and holy Ghost, for the manifestation of the glory of his eternal Power, Wisdom and Goodness, in the beginning, to create or make **out**[1] of nothing the World, and all things therein, whether visible or invisible, in the space of six days, and all very good.

[10] II. After God had made all other creatures, he created Man, male and female, with reasonable and immortal Souls, endued with knowledge, righteousness and true holiness, after his own Image, having the Law of God written in their hearts, and power to fulfil it; and yet under a possibility of transgressing, being left to the liberty of their own Will, which was subject unto change. Besides this Law written in their hearts, they received a command not to eat of the Tree of the Knowledge of good and evil; which whiles they kept, they were happy in their communion with God, and had dominion over the Creatures.

CHAP. V.

Of Providence.

GOd the great Creator of all things, doth uphold, direct, dispose and govern all creatures, actions and things from the greatest even to[2] the least by his most wise and holy Providence, according **un**to[3] his infallible fore-knowledge, and the free and immutable counsel of his own Will, to the praise of the glory of his Wisdom, Power, Justice, Goodness and Mercy.

II. Although in relation to the fore-knowledge and decree of God, the first Cause, all things come to pass immutably and infallibly; yet by the same Providence he ordereth [11] them to fall out, according to the nature of second Causes, either necessarily, freely, or contingently.

III. God in his ordinary Providence maketh use of Means, yet is free to work without, above, and against them at his pleasure.

---

[1] Added to West. [2] 1680 reads *unto.* [3] West. and 1680 read *to.*

IV. The almighty Power, unsearchable Wisdom, and infinite Goodness of God, so far manifest themselves in his Providence, **in**[1] that **his determinate Counsel**[2] extendeth it self even to the first Fall, and all other sins of Angels and Men (and that not by a bare permission) **which also he most wisely and powerfully boundeth,** and otherwise order**eth** and govern**eth**[3] in a manifold Dispensation to his own **most**[4] holy ends; yet so, as the sinfulness thereof proceedeth onely from the Creature, and not from God, who being most holy and righteous, neither is, nor can be the author or approver of sin.

V. The most wise, righteous and gracious God doth oftentimes leave for a season his own children to manifold temptations, and the corruption of their own hearts, to chastise them for their former sins, or to discover unto them the hidden strength of corruption, and deceitfulness of their hearts, that they may be humbled; and to raise them to a more close and constant dependence for their support **upon**[5] himself, and to make them more watchful against all future occasions of sin, and for sundry other just and holy ends.

[12] VI. As for those wicked and ungodly men, whom God as a righteous Judge, for former sins, doth blinde and harden, from them he not onely withholdeth his grace, whereby they might have been inlightened in their understandings, and wrought upon in their hearts; but sometimes also withdraweth the gifts which they had, and exposeth them to such objects, as their corruption makes occasions of sin; and withal gives them over to their own lusts, the temptations of the world, and the power of Satan; whereby it comes to pass that they harden themselves, even under those means which God useth for the softning of others.[6]

VII. As the Providence of God doth in general reach to all Creatures, so after a most special maner it taketh care of his Church, and disposeth all things to the good thereof.

CHAP. VI.

Of the fall of Man, of Sin, and of the Punishment thereof.

God having made a Covenant of Works and Life, thereupon, with our first parents **and all their posterity in them, they** being seduced by the subtilty and temptation of

---

[1] West. omits *in*. [2] West. reads *it*.

[3] West. reads, *but such as hath joined with it a most wise and powerful bounding, and otherwise ordering and governing of them in a*, etc. [4] Added to West.

[5] West. reads *unto*. [6] The Saybrook reads *them*, a change of some importance.

Satan **did wilfully transgress the Law of their Creation, and break the Covenant** in eating the forbidden fruit.[1]

[13] II. By this sin they, **and we in them,**[2] fell from[3] original righteousness and communion with God, and so became dead in sin, and wholly defiled in all the faculties and parts of soul and body.

III. They being the Root, **and by God's appointment standing in the room and stead**[4] of all mankinde, the guilt of this sin was imputed, and[5] corrupted nature conveyed to all their posterity descending from them by ordinary generation.

IV. From this Original corruption, whereby we are utterly indisposed, disabled and made opposite to all good, and wholly enclined to all evil, do proceed all Actual transgressions.

V. This Corruption of nature during this life, doth remain in those that are regenerated; and although it be through Christ pardoned and mortified, yet both it self and all the motions thereof are truely and properly sin.

VI. Every sin, both original and actual, being a transgression of the righteous Law of God, and contrary thereunto, doth in its own nature bring guilt upon the sinner, whereby he is bound over to the wrath of God, and curse of the Law, and so made subject to death, with all miseries, spiritual, temporal and eternal.

[14]

CHAP. VII.

Of God's Covenant with Man.

THe distance between God and the Creature is so great, that although reasonable creatures do owe obedience unto him as their Creator, yet they could never have **attained the reward of life,**[6] but by some voluntary condecension on Gods part, which he hath been pleased to express by way of Covenant.

II. The first Covenant made with man, was a Covenant of Works, wherein life was promised to Adam, and in him to his posterity, upon condition of perfect and personal obedience.

III. Man by his fall having made himself uncapable of life

---

1 This paragraph in the Westminster reads: "Our first parents, being seduced by the subtilty and temptation of Satan, sinned in eating the forbidden fruit. This their sin God was pleased, according to his wise and holy counsel, to permit, having purposed to order it to his own glory."

2 A simple addition. Nothing is omitted from the West.

3 West. inserts *their*. 4 A simple addition. 5 West. inserts, *the same death in sin and.*

6 West. reads, *never have any fruition of him as their blessedness and reward but*, etc.

by that Covenant, the Lord was pleased to make a second, commonly called the Covenant of Grace; wherein he freely offereth unto sinners life and salvation by Jesus Christ, requiring of them faith in him that they may be saved, and promising to give unto all those that are ordained unto life, his holy Spirit, to make them willing and able to believe.

IV. This Covenant of Grace is frequently set forth in the Scripture by the name of a Testament, in reference to the death of Jesus Christ the Testator, and to the everlasting Inheritance, with all things belonging to it, therein bequeathed.

[15] V. **Although**[1] this Covenant **hath been** differently **and variously** administred **in respect of Ordinances and Institutions** in the time of the Law, and **since the coming of Christ in the flesh; yet for the substance and efficacy of it, to all its spiritual and saving ends, it is** one and the same; **upon the account of which** various dispensations, it is called the Old **and** New Testament.

CHAP. VIII.

Of Christ the Mediator.

IT pleased God, it his eternal purpose, to chuse and ordain the Lord Jesus his onely begotten Son, **according to a Covenant made between them both,**[2] to be the Mediator between God and Man; the Prophet, Priest, and King, the Head and Savior[3] of his Church, the Heir of all things, and Judge of the World; unto whom he did from all eternity give a people to be his seed, and to be by him in time redeemed, called, justified, sanctified, and glorified.

---

1 Here is a large variation from the West., possibly because a special chapter was to be added on the Gospel. The West. is as follows, in two sections:

"V. This covenant was differently administered in the time of the law, and in the time of the gospel: under the law it was administered by promises, prophecies, sacrifices, circumcision, the paschal lamb, and other types and ordinances, delivered to the people of the Jews, all fore-signifying Christ to come, which were for that time sufficient and efficacious, through the operation of the Spirit, to instruct and build up the elect in faith in the promised Messiah, by whom they had full remission of sins, and eternal salvation; and is called the Old Testament.

VI. Under the gospel, when Christ the substance was exhibited, the ordinances in which this covenant is dispensed are the preaching of the word and the administration of the sacraments of Baptism and the Lord's Supper; which, though fewer in number, and administered with more simplicity and less outward glory, yet in them it is held forth in more fullness, evidence, and spiritual efficacy, to all nations, both Jews and Gentiles; and is called the New Testament. There are not, therefore, two covenants of grace differing in substance, but one and the same under various dispensations."

2 Simple insertion, nothing omitted.

3 See *ante*, p. 371, note 2.

II. The Son of God, the second Person in the Trinity, being very and eternal God of one substance, and equal with the Father, did, when the fulness of time was come, take upon him Mans nature, with all the essential properties and common infirmities thereof, yet without sin, being conceived by the power of the holy Ghost, in the womb of the Virgin Mary of her substance: So that two whole per- [16] fect and distinct natures, the Godhead and the Manhood, were inseparably joyned together in one Person, without conversion, composition, or confusion; which Person is very God and very Man, yet one Christ, the onely Mediator between God and Man.

III. The Lord Jesus in his Humane nature, thus united to the Divine **in the Person of the Son,**[1] was sanctified and anointed with the holy Spirit above measure, having in him all the treasures of Wisdom and Knowledge, in whom it pleased the Father that all fulness should dwell, to the end that being holy, harmless, undefiled, and full of Grace and Truth, he might be throughly furnished to execute the Office of a Mediator and Surety; which Office he took not unto himself, but was thereunto called by his Father, who **also**[2] put all Power and Judgement into his hand, and gave him Commandment to execute the same.

IV. This office the Lord Jesus did most willingly undertake; which that he might discharge, he was made under the Law, and did perfectly fulfil it, **and underwent the punishment due to us, which we should have born and suffered, being made sin and a curse for us,**[3] endur**ing**[4] most grievous torments immediately from God in his soul, and most painful sufferings in his body, was crucified, and died, was buried, and remained under the power of death, yet saw no corruption, on the third day he arose from the dead with the same Body in which he suffered, with which also he ascended into Heaven, and there sitteth at the right hand of his Father, making intercession, and shall return to judge Men and Angels at the end of the world.

[17] V. The Lord Jesus by his perfect obedience and sacrifice of himself, which he through the eternal Spirit, once offered up unto God, hath fully satisfied the Justice of **God,**[5] and purchased not onely reconciliation, but an everlasting inheritance in the Kingdom of heaven, for all those whom the Father hath given unto him.

---

[1] Simple addition, no omission.
[2] Not in West.
[3] Simple addition to West.
[4] West. reads *endured.*
[5] West. reads *his Father.*

VI. Although the work of Redemption was not actually wrought by Christ, till after his Incarnation; yet the vertue, efficacy and benefits thereof were communicated to[1] the Elect in all ages, successively from the beginning of the world, in and by those Promises, Types and Sacrifices wherein he was revealed and signified to be the seed of the Woman, which should bruise the Serpents head, and the Lamb slain from the beginning of the world, being yesterday and to day the same, and for ever.

VII. Christ in the work of Mediation acteth according to both Natures, by each Nature doing that which is proper to[2] it self; yet by reason of the unity of the Person, that which is proper to one Nature, is sometimes in Scripture attributed to the Person denominated by the other Nature.

VIII. To all those for whom Christ hath purchased Redemption, he doth certainly and effectually apply and communicate the same, making intercession for them, and revealing unto them in and by the Word, the mysteries of salva- [18] tion, effectually perswading them by his Spirit to believe and obey, and governing their hearts by his Word and Spirit, overcoming all their enemies by his almighty Power and Wisdom, and in such maner and ways as are most consonant to his wonderful and unsearchable dispensation.

CHAP. IX.

Of Free-will.

GOd hath endued the Will of man with that natural liberty **and power of acting upon choice,**[3] that **it**[4] is neither forced, nor by any absolute necessity of Nature determined to **do**[5] good or evil.

II. Man in his state of Innocency had freedom and power to will and to do that which was[6] good and well pleasing to God; but yet mutably, so that he might fall from it.

III. Man by his fall into a state of sin, hath wholly lost all ability of will to any spiritual good accompanying salvation; so as a natural man being altogether averse from that good, and dead in sin, is not able by his own strength to convert himself, or to prepare himself thereunto.

IV. When God converts a sinner, and translates him into the state of grace, he freeth him from his natural bondage under sin, and by his grace alone inables him freely to will [19] and to do

[1] West. reads *unto*. [2] Saybrook reads *in*.
[3] Simple addition, nothing omitted from West. [4] *Ibid.* [5] *Ibid.*
[6] West. reads *is*.

that which is spiritually good; yet so, as that by reason of his remaining corruption, he doth not perfectly nor onely will that which is good, but doth also will that which is evil.

V. The will of man is made perfectly and immutably free to good alone in the state of Glory onely.

CHAP. X.

Of Effectual Calling.

ALl those whom God hath predestinated unto life, and those onely, he is pleased in his appointed and accepted time effectually to call by his Word and Spirit, out of that state of sin and death in which they are by nature, to grace and salvation by Jesus Christ, inlightning their mindes spiritually and savingly to understand the things of God, taking away their heart of stone, and giving unto them an heart of flesh, renewing their wills, and by his almighty power determining them to that which is good, and effectually drawing them to Jesus Christ; yet so, as they come most freely, being made willing by his grace.

II. This effectual Call is of Gods free and special grace alone, not from any thing at all foreseen in man, who is altogether passive therein, untill being quickned and renewed by the holy Spirit he is thereby enabled to answer this Call, and to embrace the grace offered and conveyed in it.

[20] III. Elect Infants dying in Infancy, are regenerated and saved by Christ,[1] who worketh when, and where, and how he pleaseth: so also are all other elect persons who are uncapable of being outwardly called by the Ministery of the Word.

IV. Others not elected, although they may be called by the Ministry of the Word, and may have some common operations of the Spirit, yet **not being effectually drawn by the Father, they neither do nor can**[2] come unto Christ, and therefore cannot be saved; much less can men not professing the Christian Religion, be saved in any other way whatsoever, be they never so diligent to frame their lives according to the Light of Nature, and the Law of that Religion they do profess: And to assert and maintain that they may, is very pernicious, and to be detested.

CHAP. XI.

Of Justification.

THose whom God effectually calleth, he also freely justifieth, not by infusing righteousness into them, but by pardoning

[1] West. adds, *through the Spirit.* [2] West. reads, *yet they never truly come unto Christ.*

their sins, and by accounting and accepting their person as righteous, not for anything wrought in them, or done by them, but for Christs sake alone; nor by imputing Faith it self, the act of believing, or any other Evangelical obedience to them, as their righteousness, but by imputing **Christs active obedience unto**[1] **the whole Law, and** [21] **passive obedience in his death for their whole and sole righteousness,**[2] they receiving and resting on him and his righteousness by Faith; which Faith they have not of themselves, it is the gift of God.

II. Faith thus receiving and resting on Christ, and his righteousness, is the alone instrument of justification; yet it is not alone in the person justified, but is ever accompanied with all other saving graces, and is no dead Faith, but worketh by Love.

III. Christ by his Obedience and Death did fully discharge the Debt of all those that are[3] justified, and did **by the sacrifice of himself, in the blood of his Cross, undergoing in their stead the penalty due unto them**[4] make a proper, real, and full satisfaction to **Gods**[5] Justice in their behalf: Yet in as much as he was given by the Father for them, and his Obedience and Satisfaction accepted in their stead, and both freely, not for any thing in them, their justification is onely of free grace, that both the exact justice and rich grace of God might be glorified in the justification of sinners.

IV. God did from all eternity decree to justifie all the Elect, and Christ did in the fulness of time dye for their sins, and rise again for their justification: Nevertheless, they are not justified **personally,**[6] until the holy Spirit doth in due time actually apply Christ unto them.

[22] V. God doth continue to forgive the sins of those that are justified; and although they can never fall from the state of justification, yet they may by their sins fall under Gods fatherly displeasure: and **in that condition they** have not **usually**[7] the light of his Countenance restored unto them, until they humble themselves, confess their sins, beg pardon, and renew their faith and repentance.

VI. The justification of Believers under the old Testament, was in all these respects one and the same with the justification of Believers under the new Testament.

---

[1] Saybrook reads *to*.

[2] West. reads, *but by imputing the obedience and satisfaction of Christ unto them, they receiving*, etc.

[3] West. adds, *thus*.

[4] A simple insertion, nothing is omitted from West.

[5] West. reads, *his Father's*.

[6] Not in West.

[7] West. reads, *and not have the light*, etc.

CHAP. XII.

Of Adoption.

ALl those that are **justified**, God vouchsafeth in[1] and for his onely Son Jesus Christ to make partakers of the grace of Adoption, by which they are taken into the number, and enjoy the liberties and priviledges of the Children of God, have his Name put upon them, receive the Spirit of Adoption, have access to the Throne of Grace with boldness, are enabled to cry Abba Father, are pitied, protected, provided for, and chastened by him as by a father, yet never cast off, but sealed to the day of Redemption, and inherit the promises as Heirs of everlasting Salvation.

[23]

CHAP. XIII.

Of Sanctification.

THey **that** are **united to Christ,** effectually called and regenerated, having a new heart and a new spirit created in them, through the vertue of Christs death and resurrection, are **also** further sanctified really and personally **through the same vertue,**[2] by his Word and Spirit dwelling in them; the dominion of the whole body of sin is destroyed, and the several lusts thereof are more and more weakned, and mortified, and they more and more quickned, and strengthned in all saving graces, to the practice of **all** true holiness, without which no man shall see the Lord.

II. This Sanctification is throughout in the whole man, yet imperfect in this life, there abideth[3] still some remnants of corruption in every part, whence ariseth a continual and irreconcileable war, the flesh lusting against the spirit, and the spirit against the flesh.

III. In which war, although the remaining corruption for a time may much prevail, yet through the continual supply of strength from the sanctifying Spirit of Christ, the regenerate part doth overcome, and so the Saints grow in grace, perfecting holiness in the fear of God.

---

1 Saybrook omits *in*.

2 This passage is somewhat altered from the Westminster, which reads, "They who are effectually called and regenerated, having a new heart and a new spirit created in them, are further sanctified, really and personally, through the virtue of Christ's death and resurrection, by his Word and Spirit," etc. The Confession of 1680, as usual, follows the Savoy, save in the first line: "*They that are effectually called*," etc., *i. e.*, almost a restoration of the Westminster reading.

3 1680 reads, *abide*.

[24] CHAP. XIV.

Of saving Faith.

THe grace of Faith, whereby the Elect are inabled to believe to the saving of their souls, is the work of the Spirit of Christ in their hearts, and is ordinarily wrought by the Ministery of the Word; by which also, and by the administration of the **Seals,** Prayer, **and other means,**[1] it is increased and strengthened.

II. By this Faith a Christian believeth to be true whatsoever is revealed in the Word, for the Authority of God himself speaking therein, and acteth differently upon that which each particular passage thereof containeth, yielding obedience to the commands, trembling at the threatnings, and embracing the promises of God for this life, and that which is to come. But the principal acts of saving Faith are, accepting, receiving, and resting upon Christ alone, for justification, sanctification, and eternal life, by vertue of the covenant of Grace.

III. This Faith, **although it be** different in degrees, **and may be** weak or strong, **yet it is in the least degree of it different in the kind or nature of it (as is all other saving grace) from the faith and common grace of temporary believers; and therefore, though it** may be many times assailed and weakened,[2] **yet it** gets the victory, growing up in many to the attainment of a full assurance through Christ, who is both the author and finisher of our Faith.

[25] CHAP. XV.

Of Repentance unto life **and salvation.**[3]

SUch of the Elect as are converted at riper years, having sometime lived in the state of nature, and therein served divers lusts and pleasures, God in their effectual calling giveth them Repentance unto life.

---

[1] This passage in the West. reads, *administration of the sacraments and prayer, it-is,* etc.

[2] Here the Savoy has considerable additional matter. The West. reads, "This faith is different in degrees, weak or strong; may be often and many ways assailed and weakened, but gets the victory;" etc.

[3] This chapter is wholly rewritten and rearranged. In the Westminster it reads,

"*Of Repentance Unto Life.*

Repentance unto life is an evangelical grace, the doctrine whereof is to be preached by every minister of the gospel, as well as that of faith in Christ.

II. By it a sinner, out of the sight and sense, not only of the danger, but also of the filthiness and odiousness of his sins, as contrary to the holy nature and righteous law of God, and upon the apprehension of his mercy in Christ to such as are penitent, so grieves for, and hates his sins, as

II. **Whereas there is none that doth good, and sinneth not, and the best of men may through the power and deceitfulness of their corruptions dwelling in them, with the prevalency of temptation, fall into great sins and provocations; God hath in the covenant of Grace mercifully provided, that Believers so sinning and falling, be renewed through repentance unto Salvation.**

III. **This saving Repentance is an Evangelical Grace,**[1] **whereby a person being by the holy Ghost made sensible of the manifold evils of his sin, doth by Faith in Christ humble himself for it with godly sorrow, detestation of it, and self-abhorrency, praying for pardon and strength of Grace, with a purpose, and endeavor by supplies of the Spirit, to walk before God unto all well-pleasing in all things.**

IV. **As Repentance is to be continued through the whole course of our lives, upon the account of the body of death, and the motions thereof; so** it is every mans duty to repent of his particular **known** sins particularly.[2]

[26] V. **Such is the provision which God hath made through Christ in the covenant of Grace, for the preservation of Believers unto salvation, that although** there is no sin so small, but it deserves damnation; yet there is no sin so great, that it **shall**[3] bring damnation **on them**[4] who truly repent;[5] **which makes the constant preaching of Repentance necessary.**

---

to turn from them all unto God, purposing and endeavoring to walk with him, in all the ways of his commandments.

III. Although repentance be not to be rested in as any satisfaction for sin, or any cause of the pardon thereof, which is the act of God's free grace in Christ; yet is it of such necessity to all sinners, that none may expect pardon without it.

IV. As there is no sin so small but it deserves damnation; so there is no sin so great, that it can bring damnation upon those who truly repent.

V. Men ought not to content themselves with a general repentance, but it is every man's duty to endeavour to repent of his particular sins, particularly.

VI. As every man is bound to make private confession of his sins to God, praying for the pardon thereof, upon which, and the forsaking of them, he shall find mercy: so he that scandalizeth his brother, or the Church of Christ, ought to be willing, by a private or public confession and sorrow for his sin, to declare his repentance to those that are offended; who are thereupon to be reconciled to him, and in love to receive him."

[1] Compare note above, section I.

[2] Compare note above, section V.

[3] West. reads *can.*

[4] Ibid., *upon those.*

[5] Compare note above, section IV.

CHAP. XVI.

Of good Works.

GOod works are onely such as God hath commanded in his holy Word, and not such as without the warrant thereof are devised by men out of blinde zeal, or upon any pretence of good intentions.[1]

II. These good Works done in obedience to Gods commandments, are the fruits and evidences of a true and lively Faith, and by them Believers manifest their thankfulness, strengthen their assurance, edifie their Brethren, adorn the profession of the Gospel, stop the mouthes of the adversaries, and glorifie God, whose workmanship they are, created in Christ Jesus thereunto, that having their fruit unto holiness, they may have the end eternal life.

[27] III. Their ability to do good works is not at all of themselves, but wholly from the Spirit of Christ: And that they may be enabled thereunto, besides the graces they have already received, there is required an actual influence of the same holy Spirit to work in them to will and to do, of his good pleasure; yet are they not hereupon to grow negligent, as if they were not bound to perform any duty, unless upon a special motion of the Spirit, but they ought to be diligent in stirring up the grace of God that is in them.

IV. They who in their obedience attain to the greatest height which is possible in this life, are so far from being able to supererogate, and to do more then God requires, as that they fall short of much, which in duty they are bound to do.

V. We cannot by our best works merit pardon of sin, or eternal life at the hand of God, by reason of the great disproportion that is between them, and the glory to come: and the infinite distance that is between us, and God, whom by them we can neither profit, nor satisfie for the debt of our former sins; but when we have done all we can, we have done but our duty, and are unprofitable servants: and because as they are good, they proceed from his Spirit, and as they are wrought by us, they are defiled and mixed with so much weakness and imperfection, that they cannot endure the severity of Gods judgement.[2]

[28] VI. Yet notwithstanding, the persons of Believers being accepted through Christ, their good works also are accepted in him, not as though they were in this life wholly unblameable

---

[1] West. reads, *intention.*

[2] Saybrook reads, *judgments.*

and unreproveable in Gods sight, but that he looking upon them in his son is pleased to accept and reward that which is sincere, although accompanied with many weaknesses and imperfections.

VII. Works done by unregenerate men, although for the matter of them they may be things which God commands, and of good use both to themselves and **to**[1] others: yet because they proceed not from a heart purified by Faith, nor are done in a right maner, according to the Word, nor to a right end, the glory of God; they are therefore sinful, and cannot please God, nor make a man meet to receive grace from God; and yet their neglect of them is more sinful, and displeasing unto God.

CHAP. XVII.

Of the Perseverance of the Saints.

THey whom God hath accepted in his beloved, effectually called and sanctified by his Spirit, can neither totally nor finally fall away from the state of grace, but shall certainly persevere therein to the end, and be eternally saved.

[29] II. This Perseverance of the Saints depends not upon their own free-will, but upon the immutability of the Decree of Election,[2] from the free and unchangeable love of God the Father, upon the efficacy of the merit and intercession of Jesus Christ, **and union with him, the oath of God,**[3] the abiding of **his**[4] Spirit, and of[5] the seed of God within them, and the nature of the Covenant of Grace, from all which ariseth also the certainty and infallibility thereof.

III. **And though**[6] they may through the temptation of Satan, and of the world, the prevalency of corruption remaining in them, and the neglect of the means of their preservation, fall into grievous sins, and for a time continue therein, whereby they incur Gods displeasure and grieve his holy Spirit, come to **have** their graces and comforts **impaired,**[7] have their hearts hardned, and their consciences wounded, hurt and scandalize others, and bring temporal judgements upon themselves; **yet they are and shall be kept by the power of God through faith unto salvation.**[8]

---

[1] Not in West.

[2] West. adds, *flowing.*

[3] A simple addition, nothing omitted from West.

[4] West. reads, *the.*

[5] 1680 omits *of.*

[6] Ibid., *Nevertheless.*

[7] West. reads, *come to be deprived of some measure of their graces and comforts.*

[8] An addition, West. ends with *themselves.*

CHAP. XVIII.

Of the Assurance of Grace and Salvation.

ALthough **temporary believers**[1] and other unregenerate men may vainly deceive themselves with false hopes, and carnal presumptions of being in the favor of God, and state[2] of salvation, which hope of theirs shall perish; yet [30] such as truely believe in the Lord Jesus, and love him in sincerity, endeavoring to walk in all good conscience before him, may in this life be certainly assured that they are in **the**[3] state of Grace, and may rejoyce in the hope of the glory of God, which hope shall never make them ashamed.

II. This[4] certainty is not a bare conjectural and probable perswasion, grounded upon a fallible hope, but an infallible assurance of faith, founded **on the blood and righteousness of Christ, revealed in the Gospel, and also upon** the inward evidence of those graces unto which promises are made, **and on** the **immediate witness** of the Spirit, **testifying our** Adoption, **and as a fruit thereof, leaving the heart more humble and holy.**

III. This infallible Assurance doth not so belong to the essence of Faith, but that a true believer may wait long, and conflict with many difficulties before he be partaker of it; yet being inabled by the Spirit to know the things which are freely given him of God, he may without extraordinary revelation in the right use of ordinary means attain thereunto: And therefore it is the duty of every one to give all diligence to make his[5] calling and election sure, that thereby his heart may be inlarged in peace and joy in the holy Ghost, in love and thankfulness to God, and in strength and chearfulness in the duties of obedience, the proper fruits of this assurance; so far is it from inclining men to looseness.

[31] IV. True believers may have the assurance of their salvation divers ways shaken, diminished and intermitted, as by negligence in preserving of it, by falling into some special sin, which woundeth the conscience, and grieveth the Spirit, by some

---

1 West. reads, *hypocrites*. 2 Ibid., *estate*. 3 Ibid., *a*.

4 This paragraph is rewritten. In the West. it reads, "This certainty is not a bare conjectural and probable persuasion, grounded upon a fallible hope; but an infallible assurance of faith, founded upon the divine truth of the promises of salvation, the inward evidence of those graces unto which these promises are made, the testimony of the Spirit of adoption witnessing with our spirits that we are the children of God: which Spirit is the earnest of our inheritance, whereby we are sealed to the day of redemption."

5 Saybrook reads *their*.

sudden or vehement temptation, by Gods withdrawing the light of his countenance,[1] suffering even such as fear him to walk in darkness, and to have no light; yet are they **neither**[2] utterly destitute of that seed of God, and life of Faith, that love of Christ and the Brethren, that sincerity of heart and conscience of duty, out of which by the operation of the Spirit this assurance may in due time be revived, and by the which in the mean time they are supported from utter despair.

CHAP. XIX.

Of the Law of God.

GOd gave to Adam a Law **of universal obedience written in his heart, and a particular precept of not eating the Fruit of the Tree of Knowledge of good and evil,**[3] as a Covenant of Works, by which he bound him and all his posterity to personal, entire, exact and perpetual obedience, promised life upon the fulfilling, and threatned death upon the breach of it, and indued him with power and ability to keep it.

II. This Law **so written in the heart,** continued to be a per-[32]fect Rule of righteousness after **the** fall **of man,**[4] and was delivered by God upon[5] mount Sinai in ten Commandments, and written in two Tables; the four first Commandments containing our duty towards God, and the other six our duty to man.

III. Beside this Law commonly called Moral, God was pleased to give to the people of Israel[6] Ceremonial Laws, containing several Typical Ordinances, partly of Worship,[7] prefiguring Christ, his Graces, Actions, Sufferings and Benefits, and partly holding forth divers Instructions of Moral Duties: All which Ceremonial Laws **being appointed onely to the time of Reformation, are by Jesus Christ the true Messiah and onely Law-giver, who was furnished with power from the Father for that end, abrogated and taken away.**[8]

IV. To them also[9] he gave sundry Judicial Laws, which expired together with the State of that people, not obliging any now

---

[1] West. adds *and.* [2] West. reads *never.*

[3] A simple addition, nothing is omitted from West.

[4] In the West. this reads, " This law, after his fall, continued to be a perfect rule of righteousness; and as such, was delivered by God," etc.

[5] 1680 and Saybrook read, *on.*

[6] West., 1680, and Saybrook add, *as a church under age.*

[7] Saybrook reads, *Worshiping.*

[8] West. reads, *All which ceremonial laws are now abrogated under the New Testament.*

[9] West. adds, *as a body politic.*

by vertue of that institution, their general equity **onely being still of moral use.**[1]

V. The Moral Law doth for ever binde all, as well justified persons as others, to the obedience thereof; and that not onely in regard of the matter contained in it, but also in respect of the Authority of God the Creator, who gave it: neither doth Christ in the Gospel any way dissolve, but much strengthen this obligation.

[33] VI. Although true Believers be not under the Law, as a Covenant of Works, to be thereby justified or condemned; yet it is of great use to them as well as to others, in that, as a rule of life, informing them of the Will of God, and their duty, it directs and bindes them to walk accordingly, discovering also the sinful pollutions of their nature, hearts and lives, so as examining themselves thereby, they may come to further conviction of humiliation for, and hatred against sin, together with a clearer sight of the need they have of Christ, and the perfection of his obedience. It is likewise of use to the regenerate, to restrain their corruptions, in that it forbids sin, and the threatnings of it serve to shew what even their sins deserve, and what afflictions in this life they may expect for them, although freed from the curse thereof threatned in the Law. The promises of it in like maner shew them Gods approbation of obedience, and what blessings they may expect upon the performance thereof, although not as due to them by the Law, as a Covenant of Works; so as a mans doing good, and refraining from evil, because the Law incourageth to the one, and deterreth from the other, is no evidence of his being under the Law, and not under Grace.

VII. Neither are the forementioned uses of the Law contrary to the grace of the Gospel, but do sweetly comply with it, the Spirit of Christ subduing and inabling the will of man to do that freely and chearfully, which the will of God revealed in the Law required[2] to be done.

[34] CHAP. XX.[3]

Of the Gospel, and of the extent of the Grace[4] thereof.

THe Covenant of Works being broken by sin, and made unprofitable unto life, God was pleased to give unto

[1] West. reads, *not obliging any other, now, further than the general equity thereof may require.*

[2] West. reads, *requireth.*

[3] This whole chapter is an addition of the Savoy to the Westminster.

[4] Saybrook reads, *Graces.*

the Elect the promise of Christ, the seed of the woman, as the means of calling them, and begetting in them Faith and Repentence: In this promise the Gospel, as to the substance of it, was revealed, and was therein effectual for the conversion and salvation of sinners.

II. **This promise of Christ, and salvation by him, is revealed onely in and by the Word of God; neither do the works of Creation or Providence, with the Light of Nature, make discovery of Christ, or of Grace by him, so much as in a general or obscure way; much less that men destitute of the revelation of him by the Promise or Gospel, should be enabled thereby to attain saving Faith or Repentance.**

III. **The revelation of the Gospel unto sinners, made in divers times, and by sundry parts, with the addition of Promises and Precepts for the obedience required therein, as to the Nations and persons to whom it is granted, is meerly of the Soveraign will and good pleasure of God, not being annexed by vertue of any promise to the due im-**[35] **provement of mens natural abilities, by vertue of common light received without it, which none ever did make or can so do: And therefore in all ages the Preaching of the Gospel hath been granted unto persons and nations, as to the extent or straitning of it, in great variety, according to the counsel of the will of God.**

IV. **Although the Gospel be the onely outward means of revealing Christ and saving Grace, and is as such abundantly sufficient thereunto; yet that men who are dead in trespasses, may be born again, quickned or regenerated, there is moreover necessary an effectual, irresistible work of the holy Ghost upon the whole soul, for the producing in them a new spiritual life, without which no other means are sufficient for their conversion unto God.**

CHAP. XXI.[1]

Of Christian Liberty, and Liberty of Conscience.

THe Liberty which Christ hath purchased for Believers under the Gospel, consists in their freedom from the guilt of sin, the condemning wrath of God, the **rigor and** curse of the[2] Law,

[1] This is chapter XX. in the Westminster, from this point onward the numbering of the chapters in the West. and Savoy is not identical.

[2] West. reads, *the curse of the moral law.*

and in their being delivered from this present evil world, bondage to Satan, and dominion of sin, from the evil of afflictions, the **fear and**[1] sting of death, the victory of the grave, and everlasting damnation; as also in their free access to God, and their yielding obedience unto him, not out of slavish fear, but a childe-like [36] love and willing minde: All which were common also to Believers under the Law, **for the substance of them;**[2] but under the New Testament the liberty of Christians is further inlarged in their freedom from the yoak of the Ceremonial Law, **the whole Legal administration of the Covenant of Grace,**[3] to which the Jewish Church was subjected, and in greater boldness of access to the throne of Grace, and in fuller communications of the free Spirit of God, then Believers under the Law did ordinarily partake of.

II. God alone is Lord of the Conscience, and hath left it free from the Doctrines and Commandments of men, which are in any thing contrary to his Word, **or not contained in it;**[4] so that to believe such Doctrines, or to obey such Commands out of conscience, is to betray true Liberty of Conscience; and the requiring of an implicit faith, and an absolute and blinde obedience, is to destroy Liberty of Conscience, and Reason also.

III. They who upon pretence of Christian Liberty do practise any sin, or cherish any lust, **as they do thereby pervert the main designe of the Grace of the Gospel to their own destruction; so they wholly**[5] destroy the end of Christian Liberty, which is, that being delivered out of the hands of our enemies, we might serve the Lord without fear, in holiness and righteousness before him all the days of our life.[6]

---

[1] Simple addition, nothing omitted from West.

[2] Ibid. [3] Ibid.

[4] West. reads, *or beside it in matters of faith or worship.*

[5] Ibid., *lust, do thereby destroy*, etc.

[6] The West. has this fourth paragraph which the Savoy, following the example of Parliament, omitted,

"IV. And because the power which God hath ordained, and the liberty which Christ hath purchased, are not intended by God to destroy, but mutually to uphold and preserve one another; they who, upon pretence of Christian liberty, shall oppose any lawful power, or the lawful exercise of it, whether it be civil or ecclesiastical, resist the ordinance of God. And for their publishing of such opinions, or maintaining of such practices, as are contrary to the light of nature, or to the known principles of Christianity, whether concerning faith, worship, or conversation; or to the power of godliness; or such erroneous opinions or practices, as, either in their own nature, or in the manner of publishing or maintaining them, are destructive to the external peace and order which Christ hath established in the church; they may lawfully be called to account, and proceeded against by the censures of the church, [and by the power of the Civil Magistrate]." The clause enclosed in brackets has been omitted by modern American Presbyterians.

[37]

CHAP. XXII.[1]

Of religious Worship, and the Sabbath-day.

THe light of Nature sheweth that there is a God, who hath Lordship and Soveraignty over all, is **just,**[2] good, and doth good unto all, and is therefore to be feared, loved, praised, called upon, trusted in, and served with all the heart, and all the soul, and with all the might: But the acceptable way of worshipping the true God is instituted by himself, and so limited **by**[3] his own revealed will, that he may not be worshipped according to the imaginations and devices of men, or the suggestions of Satan, under any visible representations, or any other way not prescribed in the holy Scripture.

II. Religious Worship is to be given to God the Father, Son, and holy Ghost, and to him alone; not to Angels, Saints, or any other Creatures;[4] and since the Fall, not without a Mediator, nor in the mediation of any other but of Christ alone.

III. Prayer with thanksgiving, being one special part of **natural**[5] worship, is by God required of all men; **but**[6] that it may be accepted, it is to be made in the name of the Son by the help of his Spirit, according to his will, with understanding, reverence, humility, fervency, faith, love, and perseverance; and **when with others**[7] in a known tongue.

[38] IV. Prayer is to be made for things lawful, and for all sorts of men living, or that shall live hereafter, but not for the dead, nor for those of whom it may be known that they have sinned the sin unto death.

V. The[8] reading of the Scriptures, Preaching, and hearing the word of God, singing of Psalms, as also the administration of **Baptism and the Lords Supper,** are all parts of religious Worship of God, **to be performed** in obedience unto God with understanding, faith, reverence, and godly fear: Solemn **Humiliations, with** Fastings and Thanksgiving upon **special** occasions,

---

[1] West. chapter XXI. [2] Simple addition, nothing omitted from West. [3] West reads, *to.*

[4] West. reads, *creature.* [5] West. reads, *religious.* [6] West. reads, *and.*

[7] West. reads, *and if vocal in a known tongue.*

[8] This section is re-written. The West. reads,

"V. The reading of the Scriptures with godly fear; the sound preaching; and conscionable hearing of the Word, in obedience unto God with understanding, faith, and reverence; singing of psalms with grace in the heart; as, also, the due administration and worthy receiving of the sacraments instituted by Christ; are all parts of the ordinary religious worship of God: besides religious oaths, vows, solemn fastings, and thanksgivings upon several * occasions: which are, in their several times and seasons, to be used in an holy and religious manner."

* The American Presbyterians have adopted the Savoy emendation, *special.*

are in their several times and seasons to be used in a holy and religious maner.

VI. Neither Prayer nor any other part of religious Worship, is now under the Gospel either tyed unto, or made more acceptable by any place, in which it is performed, or towards which it is directed; but God is to be worshipped every where in spirit and **in**[1] truth, as in private families daily, and in secret each one by himself. so more solemnly in the publique assemblies, which are not carelesly nor[2] wilfully to be neglected, or forsaken, when God by his Word or Providence calleth thereunto.

VII. As it is of the law of Nature, that in general a[3] proportion of time **by Gods appointment**[4] be set apart for the worship of God; so by[5] his Word in[6] a positive, moral, and per-
[39] petual commandment, binding all men in all ages, he hath particularly appointed one day in seaven for a Sabbath to be kept holy unto him, which from the beginning of the world to the resurrection of Christ, was the last day of the week, and from the resurrection of Christ was changed into the first day of the week, which in Scripture is called the Lords day, and is to be continued to the end of the World as the Christian Sabbath, **the observation of the last day of the week being abolished.**[7]

VIII. This Sabbath is then kept holy unto the Lord, when men after a due preparing of their hearts, and ordering[8] their common affairs beforehand, do not onely observe an holy rest all the day from their own works, words, and thoughts about their worldly imployments and recreations, but also are taken up the whole time in the publique and private exercises of his Worship, and in the duties of Necessity and Mercy.

CHAP. XXIII.[9]

Of lawful Oaths and Vows.

A Lawful Oath is a part of religious Worship, wherein[10] the person swearing **in truth, righteousness and judgement,**[11] solemnly calleth God to witness what he asserteth or promiseth,

---

[1] This addition of the Savoy is also accepted by American Presbyterians.

[2] West. reads, *or*.

[3] West. adds, *due*.

[4] A simple addition, nothing omitted from West.

[5] West. reads, *in*.

[6] Ibid., *by*.

[7] An addition, West. ends with *Sabbath*.

[8] West. inserts *of*.

[9] West. chapter XXII.

[10] West. reads *wherein*, *upon just occasion*, *the person*, etc.

[11] A simple addition, nothing omitted from West.

and to judge him according to the truth or falshood of what he sweareth.

[40] II. The name of God onely is that by which men ought to swear, and therein it is to be used with all holy fear and reverence: Therefore to swear vainly, or rashly, by that glorious or[1] dreadful name, or to swear at all by any other thing, is sinful and to be abhorred; yet as in matters of weight and moment an Oath is warranted by the Word of God under the new Testament, as well as under the Old; so a lawful Oath, being imposed by lawful authority in such matters, ought to be taken.

III. Whosoever taketh an Oath **warranted by the Word of God,**[2] ought duly to consider the weightiness of so solemn an act, and therein to avouch nothing but what he is fully perswaded is the truth: neither may any man binde himself by Oath to any thing, but what is good and just, and what he believeth so to be, and what he is able and resolved to perform. Yet it is a sin to refuse an Oath touching any thing that is good and just, being **lawfully**[3] imposed by Authority.

IV. An Oath is to be taken in the plain and common sense of the words, without equivocation or mental reservation: It cannot oblige to sin, but in any thing not sinful, being taken it bindes to performance, although to a mans own hurt; nor is it to be violated, although made to Hereticks or Infidels.

[41] V. A Vow, **which is not to be made to any Creature, but God alone,**[4] is of the like nature with a promissory Oath, and ought to be made with the like religious care, and to be performed with the like faithfulness.[5]

VI. Popish monastical Vows of perpetual single life, professed poverty, and regular obedience, are so far from being degrees of higher perfection, that they are superstitious and sinful snares, in which no Christian may intangle himself.

---

1 West. reads, *and*.

2 A simple addition to West.

3 West. reads, *being imposed by lawful authority*.

4 A simple addition, nothing omitted from West. The words are taken from West., section VI, see note below.

5 Between section V. and VI. the Savoy omits one whole section and part of a second from the Westminster. They read as follows,

"VI. It is not to be made to any creature, but to God alone: and that it may be accepted, it is to be made voluntarily, out of faith and conscience of duty, in way of thankfulness for mercy received, or for the obtaining of what we want, whereby we more strictly bind ourselves to necessary duties, or to other things, so far and so long as they may fitly conduce thereunto.

VII. No man may vow to do any thing forbidden in the Word of God, or what would hinder any duty therein commanded, or which is not in his own power, and for the performance whereof he hath no promise or ability from God. In which respects, popish monastical vows of perpetual single life, professed poverty, and regular obedience, are so far from being degrees of higher perfection, that they are superstitious and sinful snares, in which no Christian may entangle himself."

CHAP. XXIV.[1]

Of the Civil Magistrate.

GOd the supreme Lord and King of all the world, hath ordained civil Magistrates to be under him, over the people for his own glory and the publique good; and to this end hath armed them with the power of the sword, for the defence and incouragement of them that **do**[2] good, and for the punishment of evil doers.

II. It is lawful for Christians to accept and execute the Office of a Magistrate, when called thereunto: in the management[3] whereof, as they ought specially to maintain[4] Justice and Peace, according to the wholsome Laws of each Commonwealth; so for that end they may lawfully now [42] under the new Testament wage war upon just and necessary occasion.

III. **Although[5] the Magistrate is bound to incourage, promote, and protect the professor and profession of the Gospel, and to manage and order civil administrations in a due subserviency to the interest of Christ in the world, and to that end to take care that men of corrupt mindes and conversations do not licentiously publish and divulge Blasphemy and Errors in their own nature, subverting the faith, and inevitably destroying the souls of them that receive them: Yet in such differences about the Doctrines of the Gospel, or ways of the worship of God, as may befall men exercising a good conscience, manifesting it in their conversation, and holding the foundation, not disturbing others in their ways or worship that differ from them; there is no warrant for the Magistrate under the Gospel to abridge them of their liberty.**

---

[1] West. chapter XXIII.
[2] West. reads, *are*.
[3] Ibid., *managing*.
[4] West. adds, *piety*.

[5] This section has been more revised than any other in the Westminster confession, and is the only variation of moment between the Confessions of 1680 and of Saybrook, and the Savoy. The section omitted from the West. by the Savoy is as follows:

"III. The civil magistrate may not assume to himself the administration of the Word and Sacraments, or the power of the keys of the kingdom of heaven: yet he hath authority, and it is his duty to take order, that unity and peace be preserved in the Church, that the truth of God be kept pure and entire, that all blasphemies and heresies be suppressed, all corruptions and abuses in worship and discipline prevented or reformed, and all the ordinances of God duly settled, administered, and observed. For the better effecting whereof he hath power to call synods, to be present at them, and to provide that whatsoever is transacted in them be according to the mind of God."

The new section adopted at the Savoy did not however commend itself to the Massachusetts divines at Boston in 1680 or their followers at Saybrook in 1708. They rejected the greater part of the Savoy section and adopted in its stead the following, based in part on the IVth section of chapter XXI. (West. ch. XX.) rejected from the West. by the Savoy; see *ante*, p. 389, note 6.

"III. They who upon pretense of Christian liberty shall oppose any lawful power, or the

IV. It is the duty of people to pray for Magistrates, to honor their persons, to pay them Tribute and other dues, to obey their lawful commands, and to be subject to their Authority for conscience sake. Infidelity, or difference in Religion, doth not make void the Magistrates just and legal Authority, nor free the people from theiir[1] obedience to him: from which ecclesiastical persons are not exempted, much less hath the Pope any power or jurisdiction over them in their dominions, or over any of their people, and least of all to deprive them of their dominions or lives, if he shall judge them to be Hereticks, or upon any other pretence whatsoever.

[43]

CHAP. XXV.[2]

Of Marriage.[3]

MArriage is to be between one man and one woman: neither is it lawful for any man to have more then one wife, nor for any woman to have more then one husband at the same time.

II. Marriage was ordained for the mutual help of husband and wife, for the increase of mankinde with a legitimate issue, and of the Church with an holy seed, and for preventing of[4] uncleanness.

III. It is lawful for all sorts of people to marry, who are able

---

lawful exercises of it, resist the Ordinance of God, and for their publishing of such opinions, or maintaining of such practices as are contrary to the Light of Nature, or to the known Principles of Christianity, whether concerning faith, worship, or conversation, or to the power of godliness, or such erronious opinions or practices, as either in their own nature, or in the manner of publishing or maintaining them, are destructive to the external peace and order which Christ hath established in the Church, they may lawfully be called to account, and proceeded against by the censures of the Church, and by the power of the civil Magistrate; yet in such differences about the Doctrines of the Gospel, or wayes of the worship of God, as may befal men exercising a good conscience, manifesting it in their conversation, and holding the foundation, and duely observing the Rules of peace and order, there is no warrant for the Magistrate to abridge them of their liberty."

American Presbyterians have made a further revision, changing the West. Conf., in 1788, as follows,

"III. Civil magistrates may not assume to themselves the administration of the Word and Sacraments; or the power of the keys of the kingdom of heaven; or, in the least, interfere in matters of faith. Yet as nursing fathers, it is the duty of civil magistrates to protect the Church of our common Lord, without giving the preference to any denomination of Christians above the rest, in such a manner that all ecclesiastical persons whatever shall enjoy the full, free, and unquestioned liberty of discharging every part of their sacred functions, without violence or danger. And, as Jesus Christ hath appointed a regular government and discipline in his Church, no law of any commonwealth should interfere with, let, or hinder, the due exercise thereof, among the voluntary members of any denomination of Christians, according to their own profession and belief. It is the duty of civil magistrates to protect the person and good name of all their people, in such an effectual manner as that no person be suffered, either upon pretence of religion or infidelity, to offer any indignity, violence, abuse, or injury to any other person whatsoever: and to take order, that all religious and ecclesiastical assemblies be held without molestation or disturbance.

[1] Misprint.

[2] West., chapter XXIV.

[3] West. adds, *and Divorce.*

[4] Saybrook omits *of.*

with judgement to give their consent. Yet it is the duty of Christians to marry[1] in the Lord, and therefore such as profess the true Reformed religion, should not marry with Infidels, Papists, or other Idolaters: neither should such as are godly, be unequally yoaked by marrying with such as are[2] wicked in their life, or maintain damnable Heresie.[3]

IV. Marriage ought not to be within the degrees of consanguinity or affinity forbidden in the Word; nor can such incestuous Marriages ever be made lawful by any law of man, or consent of parties, so as those persons may live together as man and wife.[4]

[44]

CHAP. XXVI.[5]

Of the Church.

THe Catholique or Universal Church, which is invisible, consists of the whole number of the Elect, that have been, are, or shall be gathered into one under Christ, the Head thereof, and is[6] the Spouse, the Body, the fulness of him that filleth all[7] in all.

II. **The[8] whole body of men throughout the world, professing the faith of the Gospel and obedience unto God by Christ according unto it, not destroying their own pro-**

[1] West. adds, *only*. [2] West. adds, *notoriously*. [3] West. reads, *heresies*.

[4] At this point the Savoy, following the example of Parliament, makes a large omission from the Westminster. The latter reads as follows, from the point where the Savoy concludes: "The man may not marry any of his wife's kindred nearer in blood than he may of his own, nor the woman of her husband's kindred nearer in blood than of her own.

V. Adultery or fornication, committed after a contract, being detected before marriage, giveth just occasion to the innocent party to dissolve that contract. In the case of adultery after marriage, it is lawful for the innocent party to sue out a divorce, and after the divorce to marry another, as if the offending party were dead.

VI. Although the corruption of man be such as is apt to study arguments, unduly to put asunder those whom God hath joined together in marriage; yet nothing but adultery, or such wilful desertion as can no way be remedied by the Church or civil magistrate, is cause sufficient of dissolving the bond of marriage; wherein a public and orderly course of proceeding is to be observed; and the persons concerned in it, not left to their own wills and discretion in their own case."

[5] West., chapter XXV. [6] Saybrook omits *is*. [7] Ibid. adds *and*.

[8] The remaining sections of this chapter have been much changed in the Savoy. In the West. section II. reads:

"II. The visible Church, which is also catholic or universal under the gospel, (not confined to one nation as before under the law) consists of all those, throughout the world, that profess the true religion, and of their children; and is the kingdom of the Lord Jesus Christ, the house and family of God, out of which there is no ordinary possibility of salvation."

The III. and IV. sections of the West. are wholly omitted from the Savoy, they are:

"III. Unto this catholic visible Church, Christ hath given the ministry, oracles, and ordinances of God, for the gathering and perfecting of the saints, in this life, to the end of the world: and doth by his own presence and Spirit, according to his promise, make them effectual thereunto.

IV. This catholic Church hath been sometimes more, sometimes less, visible. And particular churches, which are members thereof, are more or less pure, according as the doctrine of the gospel is taught and embraced, ordinances administered, and public worship performed more or less purely in them."

fession by any Errors everting the foundation, or unholiness of conversation,[1] are, and may be called the visible Catholique Church of Christ, although as such it is not intrusted with the administration of any Ordinances, or have any officers to rule or govern in, or over the whole Body.[2]

III. The[3] purest Churches under heaven are subject both to mixture and error, and some have so degenerated as to become no Churches of Christ, but Synagogues of Satan: Nevertheless **Christ always hath had, and ever shall have a visible Kingdom in this world, to the end thereof, of such as believe in him, and make profession of his name.[4]**

IV. There[5] is no other Head of the Church but the Lord Jesus Christ; nor can the Pope of Rome in any sense be [45] Head thereof; but it is that Antichrist, that man of sin, and son of perdition, that exalteth himself in the Church against Christ, and all that is called God, **whom the Lord shall destroy with the brightness of his coming.[6]**

V. **As[7] the Lord in his care and love towards his Church, hath in his infinite wise providence exercised it with great variety in all ages, for the good of them that love him, and his own Glory: so according to his promise, we expect that in the later days, Antichrist being destroyed, the Jews called, and the adversaries of the Kingdom of his dear Son broken, the Churches of Christ being inlarged, and edified through a free and plentiful communication of light and grace, shall enjoy in this world a more quiet, peaceable and glorious condition then they have enjoyed.**

CHAP. XXVII.[8]

Of the Communion of Saints.

ALL Saints that are united to Jesus Christ their Head, by his Spirit and[9] Faith, **although they are not made thereby one person with him,[10]** have fellowship[11] in his Graces, Sufferings, Death, Resurrection and Glory: and being united to one another

---

[1] The Confessions of 1680 and Saybrook add, ***they and their children with them***,—doubtless influenced by the Half-Way Covenant.

[2] Ibid. read, "although as such it is not intrusted with any Officers to rule or govern over the whole body."

[3] This is section V. of the West.

[4] The West. closes thus: "Nevertheless, there shall be always a Church on earth to worship God according to his will."

[5] This is section VI. of the West.

[6] A simple addition, nothing omitted from West.

[7] This has no corresponding section in West.

[8] West. chapter XXVI.

[9] West. adds, *by*.

[10] A simple addition, nothing omitted from West.

[11] West. adds, *with him*.

in love, they have communion in each others gifts and graces, and are obliged to the performance of such duties, publique and private, as do conduce to their mutual good, both in the inward and outward Man.

[46] II. **All**[1] Saints are bound to maintain an holy fellowship and communion in the Worship of God, and in performing such other spiritual services as tend to their mutual edification; as also in relieving each other in outward things, according to their several abilities and necessities: which communion, **though especially to be exercised by them in the relations wherein they stand, whether in Families or Churches, yet**[2] as God offereth opportunity, is to be extended unto all those who in every place call upon the Name of the Lord Jesus.[3]

CHAP. XXVIII.[4]

Of the Sacraments.

SAcraments are holy Signs and Seals of the Covenant of Grace, immediately instituted by **Christ,**[5] to represent **him**[6] and his benefits, and to confirm our interest in him,[7] and solemnly to engage **us**[8] to the service of God in Christ, according to his Word.

II. There is in every Sacrament a spiritual relation, or sacramental union between the signe and the thing signified; whence it comes to pass that the names and[9] effects of the one are attributed to the other.

III. The grace which is exhibited in or by the Sacraments rightly used, is not conferred by any power in them, neither [47] doth the efficacy of a Sacrament depend upon the piety or intention of him that doth administer it, but upon the work of the Spirit, and the word of Institution, which contains together with a Precept authorizing the use thereof, a Promise of benefit to worthy receivers.

IV. There be onely two Sacraments ordained by Christ our Lord in the Gospel, that is to say, Baptism and the **Lords**[10] Supper;

---

1 West. reads, *Saints, by profession, are bound*, etc.

2 Simple addition, nothing omitted from West.

3 At this point the Savoy rejected the following section of the West.: "III. This communion which the saints have with Christ, doth not make them in anywise partakers of the substance of his Godhead, or to be equal with Christ in any respect: either of which to affirm is impious and blasphemous. Nor doth their communion one with another, as saints, take away or infringe the title or propriety which each man hath in his goods and possessions."

4 West. chapter XXVII. 5 West. reads, *God.* 6 Ibid., *Christ.*

7 West. adds, *as also to put a visible difference between those that belong unto the Church and the rest of the world.*

8 West. reads, *them.* 9 West. adds, *the.* 10 West. reads, *Supper of the Lord.*

neither of which may be dispensed by any but a Minister of the Word lawfully **called**.[1]

V. The Sacraments of the Old Testament, in regard of the spiritual things thereby signified and exhibited, were for substance the same with those of the New.

CHAP. XXIX.[2]

Of Baptism.

BAptism is a Sacrament of the New Testament, ordained by Jesus Christ[3] to be unto the party baptized[4] a signe and seal of the Covenant of Grace, of his ingraffing into Christ, of regeneration, of remission of sins, and of his giving up unto God through Jesus Christ to walk in newness of life; which **Ordinance**[5] is by Christs own appointment to be continued in his Church until the end of the world.

II. The outward Element to be used in this **Ordinance,**[6] is [48] Water, wherewith the party is to be baptized in the name of the Father, and of the Son, and of the holy Ghost, by a Minister of the Gospel lawfully called.[7]

III. Dipping of the person into the water is not necessary, but Baptism is rightly administred by pouring or sprinkling water upon the person.

IV. Not onely those that do actually profess faith in, and obedience unto Christ, but also the Infants of one or both believing parents are to be baptized, **and those onely.**[8]

V. Although it be a great sin to contemn or neglect this Ordinance, yet grace and salvation are not so inseparably annexed unto it, as that no person can be regenerated or saved without it; or that all that are baptized, are undoubtedly regenerated.

VI. The efficacy of Baptism is not tied to that moment of time wherein it is administred, yet notwithstanding, by the right use of this Ordinance, the grace promised is not onely offered, but really exhibited and conferred by the holy Ghost to such (whether of age or infants) as that grace belongeth unto, according to the counsel of Gods own Will in his appointed time.

VII. Baptism[9] is but once to be administred to any person.

---

1 West. reads, *ordained.* 2 West. chapter XXVIII.

3 West. adds, *not only for the solemn admission of the party baptized into the visible Church, but also to be*, etc.

4 West. reads, *unto him a sign.* 5 Ibid., *sacrament.* 6 Ibid.

7 West. adds, *thereunto*; and 1680 and Saybrook have the addition.

8 A simple addition, nothing omitted from West.

9 West. reads, *The sacrament of baptism.*

[49]

CHAP. XXX.[1]

Of the Lords Supper.

OUr Lord Jesus in the night wherein he was betrayed, instituted the Sacrament of his Body and Blood, called the Lords Supper, to be observed in his Churches[2] unto [3] the end of the world, for the perpetual remembrance, **and shewing forth**[4] of the Sacrifice of himself in his death, the sealing **of**[5] all benefits thereof unto true believers, their spiritual nourishment, and growth in him, their further ingagement in and to all duties which they owe unto him, and to be a bond and pledge of their communion with him, and with each other.[6]

II. In this Sacrament Christ is not offered up to his Father, nor any real Sacrifice made at all for remission of sin [7] of the quick or dead, but onely a **memorial**[8] of that one offering up of himself by himself upon the Cross once for all, and a spiritual Oblation of all possible praise unto God for the same; so that the Popish Sacrifice of the Mass (as they call it) is most abominable,[9] injurious to Christs **own**[10] onely Sacrifice, the alone propitiation for all the sins of the Elect.

III. The Lord Jesus hath in this Ordinance appointed his Ministers[11] to pray and bless the Elements of Bread and Wine, and thereby to set them apart from a common to an holy use, and to take and break the Bread, to take the Cup, and (they communicating also themselves) to give [50] both to the Communicants, but to none who are not then present in the Congregation.

IV. Private Masses, or receiving the Sacrament by a Priest, or any other alone, as likewise the denial of the Cup to the people, worshiping the Elements, the lifting them up, or carrying them about for adoration, and the reserving them for any pretended religious use, are contrary to the nature of this Sacrament, and to the Institution of Christ.

V. The outward Elements in this Sacrament duely set apart to the uses ordained by Christ, have such relation to him Crucified, as that truely, yet Sacramentally onely, they are sometimes called by the name of the things they represent, to wit, the Body and

---

1 West. chapter XXIX. 2 West. reads, *church.* 3 1680 reads, *to.*

4 A simple addition, nothing omitted from West. 5 Ibid.

6 West. adds, *as members of his mystical body.*

7 West. *sins,* 8 West. reads, *commemoration.* 9 Ibid., *abominably.* 10 West. reads, *one.*

11 West. adds, "appointed his ministers *to declare his word of institution to the people,* to pray" etc. This phrase, rejected in the Savoy, is restored in the confessions of 1680 and Saybrook, the latter however reading (possibly erroneously) *instruction* instead of *institution.*

Blood of Christ; albeit in substance and nature they still remain truly and onely Bread and Wine as they were before.

VI. That Doctrine which maintains a change of the substance of Bread and Wine into the substance of Christs Body and Blood (commonly called Transubstantiation) by consecration of a Priest, or by any other way, is repugnant not to Scripture alone, but even to common sense and reason, overthroweth the nature of the Sacrament, and hath been, and is the cause of manifold Superstitions, yea of gross Idolatries.

VII. Worthy Receivers outwardly partaking of the visible [51] Elements in this Sacrament, do then also inwardly by Faith, really and indeed, yet not carnally and corporally, but spiritually, receive and feed upon Christ crucified, and all benefits of his death; the Body and Blood of Christ being then not corporally or carnally in, with, or under the Bread **or**[1] Wine; yet as really, but spiritually present to the Faith of Believers in that Ordinance, as the Elements themselves are to their outward senses.

VIII. All[2] ignorant and ungodly persons, as they are unfit to enjoy communion with Christ, so are they unworthy of the Lords Table, and cannot without great sin against him, whilest they remain such, partake of these holy Mysteries, or be admitted thereunto; yea whosoever shall receive unworthily, are guilty of the Body and Blood of the Lord, eating and drinking **Judgement**[3] to themselves.

CHAP. XXXI.[5]

Of the state of Man[4] after Death, and of the Resurrection of the Dead.

THe Bodies of men after death return to dust, and see corruption, but their souls (which neither die nor sleep) having an immortal subsistence, immediately return to God who gave them, the souls of the righteous being then made perfect in holiness, are received into the highest Heavens, where they behold the face of

---

1 West. reads, *and*.

2 Though this section is in substantial agreement with the corresponding section in the West., it has been rewritten. The West. reads thus:

"VIII. Although ignorant and wicked men receive the outward elements in this sacrament, yet they receive not the thing signified thereby; but by their unworthy coming thereunto are guilty of the body and blood of the Lord, to their own damnation. Wherefore all ignorant and ungodly persons, as they are unfit to enjoy communion with him, so are they unworthy of the Lord's table, and cannot, without great sin against Christ, while they remain such, partake of these holy mysteries, or be admitted thereunto."

3 West. uses the word *damnation*.

4 West. reads, *men*, but the American revisers have adopted *man*.

5 This is chapter XXXII. in the West. Between the previous chapter and this occurs one of the most important omissions in the Savoy. Following the example set by Parliament, the Savoy,

God in light and glory, waiting for the full redemption of their bodies: And [52] the souls of the wicked are cast into Hell, where they remain in torment[1] and utter darkness, reserved to the Judgement of the great day: Besides these two places for[2] souls separated from their bodies, the Scripture acknowledgeth none.

II. At the last day such as are found alive shall not die, but be changed, and all the dead shall be raised up with the self-same

---

and its followers at Boston in 1680 and at Saybrook in 1708, reject two whole chapters of the Westminster, XXX. and XXXI. The omitted chapters are as follows:

"CHAPTER XXX.

Of Church Censures.

The Lord Jesus, as king and head of his Church, hath therein appointed a government in the hand of Church officers, distinct from the civil magistrate.

II. To these officers the keys of the kingdom of heaven are committed, by virtue whereof they have power respectively to retain and remit sins, to shut that kingdom against the impenitent, both by the Word and censures; and to open it unto penitent sinners, by the ministry of the gospel, and by absolution from censures, as occasion shall require.

III. Church censures are necessary for the reclaiming and gaining of offending brethren; for deterring of others from the like offences; for purging out of that leaven which might infect the whole lump; for vindicating the honour of Christ, and the holy profession of the gospel; and for preventing the wrath of God, which might justly fall upon the Church, if they should suffer his covenant, and the seals thereof, to be profaned by notorious and obstinate offenders.

IV. For the better attaining of these ends, the officers of the Church are to proceed by admonition, suspension from the Sacrament of the Lord's Supper for a season, and by excommunication from the Church, according to the nature of the crime, and demerit of the person.

CHAPTER XXXI.

Of Synods and Councils.

For the better government and further edification of the Church, there ought to be such assemblies as are commonly called synods or councils.

II. As magistrates may lawfully call a synod of ministers and other fit persons to consult and advise with about matters of religion; so, if magistrates be open enemies to the Church, the ministers of Christ, of themselves, by virtue of their office, or they, with other fit persons, upon delegation from their churches, may meet together in such assemblies.

III. It belongeth to synods and councils, ministerially, to determine controversies of faith, and cases of conscience; to set down rules and directions for the better ordering of the public worship of God, and government of his Church; to receive complaints in cases of maladministration, and authoritatively to determine the same: which decrees and determinations, if consonant to the Word of God, are to be received with reverence and submission, not only for their agreement with the Word, but also for the power whereby they are made, as being an ordinance of God, appointed thereunto in his Word.

IV. All synods or councils since the apostles' times, whether general or particular, may err, and many have erred; therefore they are not to be made the rule of faith or practice, but to be used as a help in both.

V. Synods and councils are to handle or conclude nothing, but that which is ecclesiastical: and are not to intermeddle with civil affairs which concern the commonwealth, unless by way of humble petition in cases extraordinary; or by way of advice for satisfaction of conscience, if they be thereunto required by the civil magistrate."

It is interesting to note that American Presbyterians have felt the need of revising chapter XXXI. of the Westminster Confession just given, and therefore, in 1788, added the following clauses to section I.: "And it belongeth to the overseers and other rulers of the particular churches, by virtue of their office, and the power which Christ hath given them for edification, and not for destruction, to appoint such assemblies; and to convene together in them, as often as they shall judge it expedient for the good of the Church."

At the same time they wholly rejected section II. of the same chapter.

[1] West. reads, *torments*. [2] 1680 reads *of*.

bodies, and none other, although with different qualities, which shall be united again to their souls for ever.

III. The bodies of the unjust shall by the Power of Christ be raised to dishonor; the bodies of the just by his Spirit unto honor, and be made conformable to his own glorious Body.

CHAP. XXXII.[1]

Of the last Judgement.

GOd hath appointed a day wherein he will judge the World in righteousness by Jesus Christ, to whom all Power and Judgement is given of the Father; in which day not onely the Apostate Angels shall be judged, but likewise all persons that have lived upon earth, shall appear before the Tribunal of Christ, to give an account of their thoughts, words and deeds, and to receive according to what they have done in the body, whether good or evil.

[53] II. The end of Gods appointing this day, is for the manifestation of the Glory of his Mercy in the eternal salvation of the Elect, and of his Justice in the damnation of the Reprobate, who are wicked and disobedient: for then shall the righteous go into everlasting Life, and receive that fulness of joy and **glory, with everlasting reward**[2] **in** the presence of the Lord; but the wicked who know not God, and obey not the Gospel of Jesus Christ, shall be cast into eternal torments, and be punished with everlasting destruction from the presence of the Lord, and from the glory of his Power.

III. As Christ would have us to be certainly perswaded that there shall be a[3] Judgement, both to deter all men from sin, and for the greater consolation of the godly in their adversity; so will he have that day unknown to men, that they may shake off all carnal security, and be always watchful, because they know not at what hour the Lord will come, and may be ever prepared to say, Come Lord Jesus, come quickly. Amen.

[Page 54 (unnumbered) is blank in the two earliest editions. In the third edition it contains an advertisement.]

---

[1] West. chapter XXXIII, and last.

[2] West. reads, *fullness of joy and refreshing which shall come from the presence*, etc.

[3] West. adds, *day of.*

[55]

Of the INSTITUTION of CHURCHES, And the ORDER Appointed in them by JESUS CHRIST.[1]

BY the appointment of the Father all Power for the Calling, Institution, Order, or Government of the Church, is invested in a Supreme and Soveraign maner in the Lord Jesus Christ, as King and Head thereof.

II. In the execution of this Power wherewith he is so entrusted, the Lord Jesus calleth out of the World unto Communion with himself, those that are given unto him by his Father, that they may walk before him in all the ways of Obedience, which he prescribeth to them in his Word.

[56] III. Those thus called (through the Ministery of the Word by his Spirit) he commandeth to walk together in particular Societies or Churches, for their mutual edification, and the due performance of that publique Worship, which he requireth of them in this world.

IV. To each of these Churches thus gathered, according unto his minde declared in his Word, he hath given all that Power and Authority, which is any way needfull for their carrying on that Order in Worship and Discipline, which he hath instituted for them to observe with Commands and Rules, for the due and right exerting and executing of that Power.

V. These particular Churches thus appointed by the Authority of Christ, and intrusted with power from him for the ends before expressed, are each of them as unto those ends, the seat of

[1] This Platform of Church Polity, the most original of the work at the Savoy, was never adopted by American Congregationalists, their principles being better set forth in the Cambridge Platform.

that Power which he is pleased to communicate to his Saints or Snbjects[1] in this world, so that as such they receive it immediately from himself.

VI. Besides these particular Churches, there is not instituted by Christ any Church more extensive or Catholique entrusted with power for the administration of his Ordinances, or the execution of any authority in his name.

[57] VII. A particular Church gathered and compleated according to the minde of Christ, consists of Officers and Members: The Lord Christ having given to his called ones (united according to his appointment in Church-order) Liberty and Power to choose Persons fitted by the holy Ghost for that purpose, to be over them, and to minister to them in the Lord.

VIII. The Members of these Churches are Saints by Calling, visibly manifesting and evidencing (in and by their profession and walking) their obedience unto that Call of Christ, who being further known to each other by their confession of the Faith wrought in them by the power of God, declared by themselves or otherwise manifested, do willingly consent to walk together according to the appointment of Christ, giving up themselves to the Lord, and to one another by the will of God in professed subjection to the Ordinances of the Gospel.

IX. The Officers appointed by Christ to be chosen and set apart by the Church so called, and gathered for the peculiar administration of Ordinances, and execution of Power or Duty which he intrusts them with, or calls them to, to be continued to the end of the world, are Pastors, Teachers, Elders, and Deacons.

X. Churches thus gathered and assembling for the Worship of God, are thereby visible and publique, and their As-[58]semblies (in what place soever they are, according as they have liberty or opportunity) are therefore Church or Publique Assemblies.

XI. The way appointed by Christ for the calling of any person, fitted and gifted by the holy Ghost, unto the Office of Pastor, Teacher or Elder in a Church, is, that he be chosen thereunto by the common suffrage of the Church it self, and solemnly set apart by Fasting and Prayer, with Imposition of Hands of the Eldership of that Church, if there be any before constituted therein: And of a Deacon, that he be chosen by the like suffrage, and set apart by Prayer, and the like Imposition of Hands.

XII. The Essence of this Call of a Pastor, Teacher or Elder unto Office, consists in the Election of the Church, together with

[1] Misprint.

his acceptation of it, and separation *by Fasting and Prayer*: And those who are so chosen, though not set apart by Imposition of Hands, are rightly constituted Ministers of Jesus Christ, in whose Name and Authority they exercise the Ministery to them so committed. The Calling of Deacons consisteth in the like Election and acceptation, with separation *by Prayer.*

XIII. Although it be incumbent on the Pastors and Teachers of the Churches to be instant in Preaching the Word, by way of Office; yet the work of Preaching the Word is not so peculiarly confined to them, but that others also gifted and fitted by the holy Ghost for it, and approved (being by [63][1] lawful ways and means in the Providence of God called thereunto) may publiquely, ordinarily and constantly perform it; so that they give themselves up thereunto.

XIV. However, they who are ingaged in the work of Publique Preaching, and enjoy the Publique Maintenance upon that account, are not thereby obliged to dispense the Seals to any other then such as (being Saints by Calling, and gathered according to the Order of the Gospel) they stand related to, as Pastors or Teachers; yet ought they not to neglect others living within their Parochial Bounds, but besides their constant publique Preaching to them, they ought to enquire after their profiting by the Word, instructing them in, and pressing upon them (whether young or old) the great Doctrines of the Gospel, even personally and particularly, so far as their strength and time will admit.

XV. Ordination alone without the Election or precedent consent of the Church, by those who formerly have been Ordained by vertue of that Power they have received by their Ordination, doth not constitute any person a Church-Officer, or communicate Office-power unto him.

XVI. A Church furnished with Officers (according to the minde of Christ) hath full power to administer all his Ordinances; and where there is want of any one or more Officers required, that Officer, or those which are in the Church, may administer all the Ordinances proper to their particular Duty and Offices; but where there are no teach-[60]ing Officers, none may administer the Seals, nor can the Church authorize any so to do.

XVII. In the carrying on of Church-administrations, no person ought to be added to the Church, but by the consent of the Church it self; that so love (without dissimulation) may be preserved between all the Members thereof.

---

[1] Misprint for [59].

XVIII. Whereas the Lord Jesus Christ hath appointed and instituted as a means of Edification, that those who walk not according to the Rules and Laws appointed by him (in respect of Faith and Life, so that just offence doth arise to the Church thereby) be censured in his Name and Authority: Every Church hath Power in it self to exercise and execute all those Censures appointed by him in the way and Order prescribed in the Gospel.

XIX. The Censures so appointed by Christ, are Admonition and Excommunication: and whereas some offences are or may be known onely to some, it is appointed by Christ, that those to whom they are so known, do first admonish the offender in private: in publique offences where any sin, before all; or in case of non-amendment upon private admonition, the offence being related to the Church, and the offender not manifesting his repentance, he is to be duely admonished in the Name of Christ by the whole Church, by the Ministery of the Elders of the Church; and if this Censure prevail not for his repentance, then he is to be cast out by Excommunication with the consent of the Church.

[61] XX. As all Believers are bound to joyn themselves to particular Churches, when and where they have opportunity so to do, so none are to be admitted unto the Priviledges of the Churches, who do not submit themselves to the Rule of Christ in the Censures for the Government of them.

XXI. This being the way prescribed by Christ in case of offence, no Church-members upon any offences taken by them, having performed their duty required of them in this matter, ought to disturb any Church-order, or absent themselves from the publique Assemblies, or the Administration of any Ordinances upon that pretence, but to wait upon Christ in the further proceeding of the Church.

XXII. The Power of Censures being seated by Christ in a particular Church, is to be exercised onely towards particular Members of each Church respectively as such; and there is no power given by him unto any Synods or Ecclesiastical Assemblies to Excommunicate, or by their publique Edicts to threaten Excommunication, or other Church-censures against Churches, Magistrates, or their people upon any account, no man being obnoxious to that Censure, but upon his personal miscarriage, as a Member of a particular Church.

XXIII. Although the Church is a Society of men, assembling [62] for the celebration of the Ordinances according to the appointment of Christ, yet every Society assembling for that end or purpose, upon the account of cohabitation within any civil Precincts and Bounds, is not thereby constituted a Church, seeing there may be wanting among them, what is essentially required thereunto; and therefore a Believer living with others in such a Precinct, may joyn himself with any Church for his edification.

XXIV. For the avoiding of Differences that may otherwise arise, for the greater Solemnity in the Celebration of the Ordinances of Christ, and the opening a way for the larger usefulness of the Gifts and Graces of the holy Ghost; Saints living in one City or Town, or within such distances as that they may conveniently assemble for divine Worship, ought rather to joyn in one Church for their mutual strengthning and edification, then to set up many distinct Societies.

XXV. As all Churches and all the Members of them are bound to pray continually for the good or prosperity of all the Churches of Christ in all places, and upon all occasions to further it; (Every one within the bounds of their Places and Callings, in the exercise of their Gifts and Graces) So the Churches themselves (when planted by the providence of God, so as they may have oppertunity and advantage for it) ought to hold communion amongst themselves for their peace, increase of love, and mutual edification.

[63] XXVI. In Cases of Difficulties or Differences, either in point of Doctrine or in Administrations, wherein either the Churches in general are concerned, or any one Church in their Peace, Union, and Edification, or any Member or Members of any Church are injured in, or by any proceeding in Censures, not agreeable to Truth and Order: it is according to the minde of Christ, that many Churches holding communion together, do by their Messengers meet in a Synod or Councel, to consider and give their advice in, or about that matter in difference, to be reported to all the Churches concerned; Howbeit these Synods so assembled are not entrusted with any Church-Power, properly so called, or with any Jurisdiction over the Churches themselves, to exercise any Censures, either over any Churches or Persons, or to impose their determinations on the Churches or Officers.

XXVII. Besides these occasional Synods or Councels, there are not instituted by Christ any stated Synods in a fixed Combination of Churches, or their Officers in lesser or greater Assemblies; nor are there any Synods appointed by Christ in a way of Subordination to one another.

XXVIII. Persons that are joyned in Church-fellowship, ought not lightly or without just cause to withdraw themselves from the communion of the Church whereunto they are so joyned: Nevertheless, where any person cannot continue in any Church without his sin, either for want of the Administration of any Ordinances instituted by Christ, or by his be-[64]ing deprived of his due Priviledges, or compelled to any thing in practice not warranted by the Word, or in case of Persecution, or upon the account of conveniency of habitation; he consulting with the Church, or the Officer or Officers thereof, may peaceably depart from the communion of the Church, wherewith he hath so walked, to joyn himself with some other Church, where he may enjoy the Ordinances in the purity of the same, for his edification and consolation.

XXIX. Such reforming Churches as consist of Persons sound in the Faith and of Conversation becoming the Gospel, ought not to refuse the communion of each other, so far as may consist with their own Principles respectively, though they walk not in all things according to the same Rules of Church-Order.

XXX. Churches gathered and walking according to the minde of Christ, judging other Churches (though less pure) to be true Churches, may receive unto occasional communion with them, such Members of those Churches as are credibly testified to be godly, and to live without offence.

FINIS.

XIII

THE "REFORMING SYNOD" OF 1679 AND 1680, AND ITS CONFESSION OF FAITH

EDITIONS AND REPRINTS

A. THE RESULT OF 1679

I. [Increase Mather] *The Necessity of Reformation With the Expedients thereunto, asserted. Boston; Printed by John Foster In the Year 1679.* 4° pp. vi, 15.[1]

II. Cotton Mather, *Magnalia*, London, 1702, ed. Hartford, 1853–5, II: 320–331 (without the Preface).

III. *The Results of Three Synods*, etc. Boston, 1725, pp. 94–118.

B. THE CONFESSION OF 1680

I. *A Confession of Faith Owned and consented unto by the Elders and Messengers of the Churches Assembled at Boston in New-England, May 12. 1680. Being the second Session of that Synod.* etc. Boston; Printed by John Foster 1680. 8° 5¼ x 3¼ inches, pp. vi, 65, with *Cambridge Platform.*

II. At Boston in 1699 in English and Indian, with *Cambridge Platform.*[2]

III. In the *Magnalia*, London, 1702, V: 5–19, ed. Hartford, 1853–5, II: 182–207.

IV. At Boston in 1725.[3]

V. At Boston in 1750.[4]

VI. At Boston in 1757, with *Cambridge Platform.*[5]

VII. In *The Original Constitution, Order and Faith of the New England Churches*, etc. Boston, 1812, with the *Cambridge Platform* (ed. 1808), and the *Propositions* of 1662.

VIII. In *The Cambridge and Saybrook Platforms of Church Discipline, with the Confession of Faith . . . adopted in 1680; and the Heads of Agreement . . . in 1690.* Boston: T. R. Marvin, 1829, pp. 69–113.

IX. In T. C. Upham, *Ratio Disciplinæ*, Portland, 1829, pp. 253–302.

X. In the *Manual* of the Old South Church, Boston, Mass., ed. Boston, 1841, pp. 13–66.[6]

---

1 Full title in reprint at the close of this chapter.

2 Catalogue of Collection of Mr. Brayton Ives, New York, 1891, No. 145; Prince Library, No. 24.23.

3 Brinley Sale Cat., No. 7492. 4 Prince, No. 14.60. 5 Brinley, No. 7493.

6 Given as the "Confession of Faith . . . of the Old South Church," but Mr. H. A. Hill, in his admirable History of that Church, has pointed out (I: 235, and II: 555) that it probably was never adopted by formal vote of the church. The consent of the minister to this confession at his settlement over the Old South was taken from the installation of Rev. Alexander Cumming in 1761 to that of Dr. J. M. Manning in 1857. At the settlement of Rev. G. A. Gordon, the present pastor, in 1884, it was omitted.

XI. In *Report*[1] *on Congregationalism, including a Manual of Church Discipline, together with the Cambridge Platform . . . and the Confession of Faith, adopted in 1680.* Boston, 1846, pp. 87–128.

XII. In the *Manual* of the Old South Church, Boston, Mass., ed. Boston, 1855.

XIII. In *The Cambridge Platform . . . and the Confession . . . 1680, to which is prefixed a Platform of Ecclesiastical Government, by Nath. Emmons.* Boston, 1855.

SOURCES

Records of . . . Massachusetts Bay, Boston, 1853–4, V: 215, 216, 244, 287.

Peter Thatcher, *MS. Diary* (some extracts are printed by Palfrey and Hill in the passages cited under *Literature* below).

LITERATURE

Hubbard, *General History of New England*,[2] ed. Boston, 1848, pp. 621–624. Cotton Mather, *Magnalia*, ed. Hartford, 1853–5, II: 179–181, 316–320, 331–338. Neal, *History of New England*,[3] London, 1720, II: 409–411. Cotton Mather, *Parentator. Memoirs of Remarkables in the Life and the Death of the Ever-Memorable Dr. Increase Mather*, Boston, 1724, pp. 81–87. Hutchinson, *History of the Colony of Massachusetts Bay*, ed. London, 1765, I: 324. Emerson, *Historical Sketch of the First Church in Boston*, Boston, 1812, pp. 127–129. Wisner, *History of the Old South Church in Boston*, Boston, 1830, pp. 15, 16. Palfrey, *History of New England*, III: 330–332. Lawrence, *Our Declaration of Faith and the Confession*, in *Cong. Quarterly*, VIII: 173–190 *passim* (Apl., 1866). Dexter, *Congregationalism, as seen in its Literature*, pp. 476–485. Doyle, *English in America; Puritan Colonies*, London, 1887, II: 272. H. A. Hill, *History of the Old South Church*, Boston, 1890, I: 231–235.

AS has been pointed out in enumerating the causes which led to the Half-Way Covenant, the passing away of the founders of New England brought forward a generation which, though in the main moral, had not that intensity of religious experience which characterized its predecessor. While it was true, as Cotton Mather affirmed in writing of this period, that[4]—

> "*New-England* was not become so degenerate a Country, but that there was yet Preserved in it, far more of Serious *Religion*, as well as of Blameless *Morality*, than was Proportionably to be seen in any Country upon the face of the Earth";

the declaration of Thomas Prince is also well founded, that[5]—

> "a little after 1660, there began to appear a *Decay:* And this increased to 1670, when it grew very visible and threatening, and was generally complained of and be-

[1] By a committee of which Dr. Leonard Woods was chairman.

[2] Hubbard was probably a member of the Synod, but his report is remarkably barren, and is largely made up from the Prefaces of the Results.

[3] Chiefly from Mather.

[4] *Parentator*, p. 82.

[5] *Christian History*, Boston, 1743, I: 94.

wailed bitterly by the Pious among them: And yet much more to 1680, when but few of the first Generation remained."

The number of additions to the full communion of the churches was small; while records of church discipline show that serious misconduct was by no means rare. Under such circumstances it is no wonder that the minds of faithful ministers were filled with concern.

The sense of alarm regarding the state of New England engendered by the decline of visible piety, was greatly intensified by a series of disastrous events which seemed to the men of that age divine judgments. The first fifty years of New England history were of unusual prosperity. With the exception of the short, sharp struggle with the Pequots in 1637, no war disturbed the borders of the land. During the Puritan ascendency in England the home government had been friendly, and even the restoration of the Stuarts had brought no serious political disaster. In spite of the "Navigation Acts,"[1] the trade of New England flourished and brought considerable wealth and increasing luxury to its ports. But this course of prosperity was rudely interrupted at the close of the third quarter of the seventeenth century. The Indians, who had been at peace with the white settlers for nearly forty years, and who had been well treated by the Puritans, broke out in warfare; and from June 20, 1675, to the death of Philip, August 12, 1676, threatened the existence of the colonies. This struggle, known from the chief Indian leader as Philip's war,[2] resulted in the elimination of the Indian problem from the category of questions vital to New England life; but at a terrible cost. Of the eighty or ninety towns to be found in Plymouth and Massachusetts colonies in 1675, ten or twelve were utterly destroyed,[3] while forty more were partially burned. Nor was the loss of property the most serious result of the contest. Between five and six

[1] These acts, the first of which was passed under the Commonwealth, Oct. 9, 1651, and which were strengthened in 1660, in their extreme form forbade the importation of goods into the colonies except in English vessels, and the export of their chief products except to English ports. They were long more honored in the breach than the observance.

[2] This war, which forms the political background of the Reforming Synod, is well described by Palfrey, *History of New England*, III: 132–230; and John Fiske, *Beginnings of New England*, pp. 199–241

[3] These figures are from Palfrey, III: 215.

hundred young and middle-aged men — a tenth of all of military age in the colonies — lost their lives; and to these victims must be added the scores of women and children who perished by the tomahawk or died amid the torments of the stake. An experience so ghastly and so universal might well seem to the ministry of that day a special outpouring of the wrath of God.

And, beyond the great disaster of the Indian war, the opening of the last quarter of the century was a period of losses unexampled in the history of the colonies. On November 27, 1676, the North Church in Boston and more than forty houses adjacent were burned.[1] Three years later, August 7–8, 1679, a yet more destructive conflagration swept away nearly all the business portion of the town.[2] Shipwreck also brought more than customary losses to the merchants of the colonies, while pestilences,[3] especially the dreaded small-pox, caused great mortality. And, as if to fill the cup of misfortune, the liberties of the colonies, especially of Massachusetts, were threatened[4] at this crisis of war and impoverishment, by the hostility of the Stuart government, which was making its hand heavy, and was to bring about, a little later, the tyranny of Dudley and Andros, itself the culmination of a series of acts of oppression, of which not the least exasperating to the ministry of New England were the efforts of English agents, begun with vigor in January, 1679, to introduce Episcopacy into the Puritan commonwealths.[5]

It was under these circumstances of disaster and, as was believed, of judgment, that Increase Mather,[6] the most prominent

---

1 See Increase Mather, *Returning unto God . . . a Sermon*, etc. Boston, 1680, Preface.

2 Peter Thacher's diary in Hill, *History of the Old South Church*, I: 230, 231; Hubbard says, *General History*, p. 649, "the burning of Boston . . . hath half ruined the whole Colony, as well as the town."

3 Increase Mather, *Returning unto God*, Preface.

4 See Palfrey, III: 273 *et seqq.*

5 Palfrey, III: 324.

6 Increase Mather is too familiar to need extended notice. Born June 21, 1639, youngest son of Richard Mather of Dorchester, he graduated at Harvard in 1656, and went the next year to England, where he was well received and given opportunities for preaching. Soon after the Restoration he returned to New England, and after preaching for the Second Church, Boston, from September, 1661, he was ordained its minister, May 27, 1664. From that time to his death he was a part of all that was done in New England. He became President of Harvard in June, 1685, and held the office till 1701; he took prominent part in defense of the colonial liberties, and served as agent for Massachusetts in England from 1688 to 1692, obtaining the new Massachusetts charter

minister of the second generation in New England, and pastor of the Second Church in Boston, aroused his brethren in the ministry to appeal to the Massachusetts General Court for the calling of a Synod.[1] The conception of such an assembly was one which might naturally have arisen in his mind, but the immediate suggestion may have come to Mather from a letter of Rev. Thomas Jollie, of Pendlton-nigh-Clitherow, in Lancashire, Eng., in which that Puritan divine recommended, under date of January 18, 1678, the summons of a Synod as the best means for securing the spiritual improvement of New England.[2] Whatever the influence of Jollie may have been, Mather succeeded in obtaining the signatures of eighteen of the more prominent of his ministerial brethren to his petition to the Court. First of the signers in the order in which the names were appended to the paper, was the venerable John Eliot of Roxbury, then came the name of Increase Mather, and next that of Samuel Torrey of Weymouth, Moses Fiske of Braintree followed, and then Josiah Flynt of Dorchester. The other signers, in their order, were Thomas Clark of Chelmsford, James Sherman of Sudbury, Joseph Whiting of Lynn, Samuel Cheever of Marblehead, Samuel Phillips of Rowley, Solomon Stoddard of Northampton, Samuel Whiting, Sen., of Lynn, Thomas Cobbett of Ipswich, Edward Bulkeley of Concord, John Sherman of Watertown, John Higginson of Salem, John Hale of Beverly, Samuel Whiting, Jr., of Billerica, and John Wilson of Medfield.

The document to which these autographs are appended is

---

from William and Mary. His later life was specially fruitful in writings for the press. He died Aug. 23, 1723. Increase Mather was essentially a conservative. As such his influence was directed toward the maintenance of that supremacy of the religious element in civil affairs which marked the founders of New England. As such he opposed changes in the practices of the churches, his ideal being, apparently, the state in which they were about the time of the Synod of 1662. His conservative attitude brought him much opposition, but no man in New England equaled him in influence in his lifetime. As a writer, his voluminousness is only exceeded, among the New England ministry, by his son, Cotton Mather. The sources of information regarding him are many, but they are best epitomized in Sibley, *Graduates of Harvard*, I: 410–470, where a list of biographical authorities will be found, together with as complete a catalogue of his writings as it is probably possible to make.

[1] "Upon a motion of Mr. *Mather* in Conjunction with others excited by him for it, the *General Court* called upon the Churches to send their Delegates for a *Synod*." Cotton Mather, *Parentator*, p. 84. Doubtless this petition was prepared at the annual Ministerial Convention, of which some account may be found in chapter XV of this volume.

[2] The letter is dated 18th of 11th m: 167$\frac{7}{8}$, and reads: "The advice I humbly offer for your awakning to duty in the reforming of your manifest evills and for preventing of threatning ruin is, that a Synod bee gathered to that purpose." 4 *Coll. Mass. Hist. Soc.*, VIII: 320.

apparently in the handwriting of Increase Mather;[1] and as its length is considerable and much of its matter is reproduced in substance in the Result of the Synod of 1679, a brief extract will suffice to indicate its quality. The petition first recounts with gratitude the inquiries into the evils of the times made by the General Court in October, 1675, in the stress of the Indian war, and the revisal and publication of laws undertaken by the Court with a view to the betterment of the country; but the signers feel constrained to be —

"humbly bold, in the fear of God, to declare unto the Honoured Court, as unto ye Representative of this people, as it followeth —

1. That according to our best discerning, those Reforming Laws (so called, wee fear, by many with slighting) have been, & are still likely to be ineffectual unto any part of the general work of Reformation proposed. . . . 2. That according to our best discerning, those Sins which are by Law entituled *provoking Evils*, and which give that wofull Title to those Reforming Laws, are in most, (especially most populous) places as general, as powerfull, as Incorrigible & Incurable, &, wee fear, more Judicial then they were before.[2] . . . 3. That according to our best descerning Gods anger is not yett turned away, but his hand is stretched out still. . . . Thus wee declare in the fear of God, not so much to inform (much less to reflect upon) yourselves, as to discharge our publick Trust, & to deliver our own Soules. And withal, that wee may from hence take occasion humbly to propose unto this Hon.ed Court.

j. Whether Civil Authority as it is vested in all persons of publick place & Trust, in every order more vigorously exerted, by a zealous prosecution of Laws against sin, to effect, would not give Life unto those Laws, & motion unto the work of Reformation. . . . 2. Forasmuch as wee cannot but acknowledge ourselves to be very defective in o^r^ place and work, Whether Churches & Elders ought not to bee moved, encouraged and assisted unto that which God calls for, & expects from them in the work of Reformation. . . . Wee find in Scripture that the Religious Reforming Magistrate did ever stirr up, and strengthen the churches & ministry unto the work of God in Apostatizing Times. . . . 3. Whether a Convention of the Churches by their Elders & messengers bee not extraordinarily necessary at this Time, as a most general means unto the attainment of these great ends proposed; & whether therefore God doth not now call the Churches thereunto. . . . Many things appear unto us, necessary in such an Assembly, which cannot bee orderly & effectually wrought otherwise — as

i. That there bee a more full enquiry made into the Causes & State of Gods Controversy with us. . . . 2. That these Churches, & this Ministry (which, respecting the persons of whom they are now Constituted are mostly other Churches, & another ministry) having never yett in this present Age, made any publick Confes-

---

[1] The petition has never been published. It may be found in the Massachusetts Archives, Vol. X: 197.

[2] Here follows a brief enumeration of most of those evils described in the Result of the Synod of 1679.

sion or profession of the faith & order of the Gospel, It may now seem very necessary for us so to do, at least by owning & asserting ye same faith and order of the Gospel in which these Churches were at first established, and of which o^r^ Fathers witnessed a good Confession in such an Assembly at Cambridge, in ye year 1648, and afterward left upon Record unto us in ye platform of Discipline, & other writings. And the rather wee Judge it necessary at this time, Because wee fear that these Churches are, & will be much endangered both by Ignorance & error, as also that both Churches & Elders may have a more right & full understanding one of another, that wee may bee the better prepared to hold fast our profession, & to stand fast together in an hour of Temptation, as also that wee may clear our selves of the suspicion & scandal of defection. 3. That the Churches may have opportunity for to labour (at least) to find out, and fix upon the right means and method of practice as to things which have been already clearly & firmly stated from the word of God, that so the Churches may Concurr, and assist one another therein, in a way of publick order, peace, union, & communion; more especially in that wherein wee are by practice to discharge ourselves faithfully in all duty unto the Children of the Covenant, which is a principal part of the neglect and defect of which wee are the more sadly sensible. . . . Unto all wee add, the consideration of the presence of Christ with, & ye blessing and success which hee hath given unto ye former Labours & Endeavours of the Churches in this way of his appointment.

Much Honored . . . wee have made this plain Address unto you, because wee have observed that all former Essayes unto Reformation have failed, & our hope thereof been frustrated; If therefore, there bee yett any hope in Israel concerning this matter, wee beleeve it will not bee attained untill Magistracy, Ministry, Churches & people rise up together, in their proper places & order, unto the work."

This petition was presented to the Massachusetts General Court at the session of May 28, 1679, and received immediate and favorable response. Possibly the undercurrent of criticism which flowed beneath the surface of the stream of the New England theocracy may have been more obvious to the legislators than the guarded words of the petitioners implied. Something more than a mere renewal of assent to the Cambridge Platform, a revisal of some of its sections, would have, apparently, found favor with the Legislature. But the main request of the petitioners was granted, and the Synod ordered in the following vote:[1]

"In ans^r^ to a motion made by some of the reuerend elders, that there might be a convening of the elders & messengers of the churches in forme of a synod, for the reuisall of the platforme of discipljne agreed vpon by the churches, 1647, and what else may appeare necessary for the preventing schishmes, hæresies, prophaness, & the establishment of the churches in one faith & order of the gospell, this Court doe approoue of the sajd motion, & order their assembling for the ends aforesajd on the second Wednesday in September[2] next, at Boston; and the secretary is required

[1] *Records . . . Mass. Bay*, V: 215, 216.

[2] Sept. 10.

seasonably to give notice hereof to the seuerall churches. It is further ordered, that the charges of this meeting shall be borne by the churches respectively.[1]

Quæstī 1.[2] What are the euills that haue provoked the Lord to bring his judgments on New England?

2 Quæst. What is to be donn that so those evills may be reformed."

In due course of time the colonial secretary, Edward Rawson, sent a certified copy of this vote to the ministers of the various churches under the Massachusetts jurisdiction, accompanied by a note curiously illustrative of the dependence of the churches on state authority. There was no longer, as in 1646,[3] a suggestion of unwillingness on the part of any of the legislators to command the churches. The note to the minister of the Old South Church, Boston, is as follows:[4]

"These fore the Rever'd Mr. Saml Willard, Teacher to the 3d Church in Boston To be communicated to the Church.

Rev'nd. Sir. These are only to inform yourself and church of the underwritten Generall Court's Answer and order, not doubting of your and their obedience and complyance therewith at the time, remayning

Your friend and servant

Boston 11th July 1679 Edw. Rawson Secty"

The order accompanying this note seems on the whole to have met with the favor of the churches, though it is interesting to observe that the First Church, Boston, which had been so reluctant to take part in the Cambridge Synod in 1646,[5] now gave but a grudging and guarded obedience to the call of the Court. Possibly the hesitation of this venerable body in this instance was due to a fear that the Synod would propose some unpalatable solution of its ten-years dispute with the seceding Old South, rather than to a zeal for the more abstract principles of churchly independence of civil control.[6] The majority of the churches felt no scruples, and a

[1] This was done. Peter Thacher, one of the messengers of the Old South, Boston, recorded in his diary: "6. Octo. 79. The deacons of our Church came and brought mee five pound for preaching and being a Messenger from the Church to the Synode," H. A. Hill, *Hist. Old South*, I: 234. The Dorchester church chose two messengers "& ye deacons weer desiered to take Care for their entertainment at Boston on ye Church acc^t." *Rec. First Ch., Dorchester*, p. 83.

[2] These questions, though thus recorded, seem no part of the vote of the Court. They are appended to the letter sent by Sec. Rawson to the Old South, as "Questions given in." Probably they were handed in to the legislature by the petitioners after the granting of the petition.

[3] See *ante*, p. 167. [4] H. A. Hill, *Hist. Old South*, I: 232. [5] See *ante*, pp. 171–174.

[6] This suggestion is made by Mr. Hill, *Hist. Old South*, I: 233. The First Church voted, Aug. 5, 1679, to be represented in the Synod, but added: "Tho wee doe not see light for the calling of a Synod att this time, yett there being one called: that what good theare is or may bee motioned may bee encouraged and evill prevented by our Testimony, wee are willing to send our Messengers

general fast was held throughout the colony to supplicate the divine blessing on the coming Assembly.[1]

The events of the first session of this Synod have been preserved in the graphic and contemporary record of Rev. Peter Thacher,[2] soon to be settled at Milton, Mass., but who, as a son of the lately deceased pastor of the Old South Church in Boston and a member of that body, represented that church as a delegate in the Synod.[3] His journal records:[4]

"10· Sept: 79· y^{s} day y^{e} Synod began $\frac{r}{m}$ Cobbet & $\frac{r}{m}$ Eliot[5] were Chouse Moderatours & w^{n} y^{y} had taken y^{e} names of y^{e} severall Chhs, w^{c} sent & y^{e} names of y^{s} y^{t}[6] y^{y} found several Churches had only sent Elders & not brethren with y^{m} where upon y^{e} Question was whether Elders of Chhs Ex Officio were not members & it was asserted y^{t} y^{e} matter of a Synod were Eld^{rs} & brethren[7] where upon it was agreed on y^{t} Letters in y^{e} Synods name Should be Sent to y^{e} Churches y^{t} had not done it[8] to request y^{t} y^{y} would doe it. In y^{e} afternoon y^{e} Plateforme of Church Discipline[9] was read & $\frac{r}{m}$ Shearman & $\frac{r}{m}$Oakes[10] being Chouse Moderators y^{e} Synod was adjurned till Eight a Clock y^{e} next morning.

11· Sept· 79· y^{e} Synod determined noe Vote should passe till y^{y} had answer from y^{e} Churches; where upon y^{e} first question about y^{e} provoking Evills was discoussd It was Lecture at first Chh Boston $\frac{r}{m}$ Russell preached it.[11] after Lecture y^{e} $govern^{r}$ came into y^{e} Synod.[12]

12· Sept· 79· y^{e} Second question was discussd what was y^{e} remidyes to remove gods $Judgem^{ts}$ & a Committee Chouse to Consider of y^{m} & what was said concerning y^{m} in y^{e} Synod & to bring y^{e} result unto y^{e} Synod. alsoe a fast to be y^{e} next twesday was

---

to it: Tho whatever is theire determined, wee looke upon and judge to bee no further binding to us than the light of Gods word is thereby cleared to our Consciences." *Ibid.*

[1] C. Mather, *Magnalia*, II: 318; *Parentator*, p. 84.

[2] His biography is given by Sibley, *Grad. of Harvard*, II: 370–379.

[3] Hill, *Old South Ch.*, I: 234.

[4] I owe this valuable record, now for the first time published in full, to the great kindness of Hon. Peter Thacher of Boston. Portions have been printed by Palfrey, *Hist. N. E.*, III: 330, 331; and Hill, *Old South Ch.*, I: 234.

[5] Rev. Messrs. Thomas Cobbett of Ipswich, now 71 years of age, and "Apostle" John Eliot of Roxbury, now 75. From the choice of other moderators speedily thereafter it would appear that this election was a tribute to age and distinction; the real burden of presiding over the discussion falling on younger shoulders.

[6] Perhaps we should interpret thus: *names of those that* [*represented the Churches,*] *they found*, etc.

[7] For further particulars regarding this important assertion of Congregational principles see Preface to the Result, pp. 424, 425 of this volume; *Magnalia*, ed. 1853–5, II: 318; Increase Mather, *Order of the Gospel*, p. 83.

[8] I. e., Churches that had not elected delegates.

[9] The Cambridge Platform.

[10] Rev. Messrs. John Sherman of Watertown, aged 66; and Urian Oakes of Cambridge, at this time acting president of Harvard College, aged 47.

[11] Rev. John Russell, once a minister at Wethersfield, Conn.; but since the founding of Hadley, Mass., in 1659, pastor of the church there.

[12] Simon Bradstreet.

appointed & $\frac{r}{m}$ Cobbet & $\frac{r}{m}$ Mather[1] where[2] to preach & whome y^e moderatours should call forth were to pray. $\frac{r}{m}$ Oakes, $\frac{r}{m}$ Russell, $\frac{r}{m}$ Mather, $\frac{r}{m}$ Torry,[3] $\frac{r}{m}$ Moody,[4] Capt. Richards Capt. fisher & Deacon Tilson where Chouse for y^e Committee.

Y^e Synod was adjourned till Twesday Eight a Clock was to be a fast.

16· Sept· 79· Y^{er} was a fast[5] in y^e Synod $\frac{r}{m}$ Higginson[6] began & prayed, y^n $\frac{r}{m}$ Cobbet preached Isa· 63· 7· $\frac{r}{m}$ Buckley[7] prayed. in y^e after=noon Old $\frac{r}{m}$ Eliot prayed $\frac{r}{m}$ Mather preached 99· ps· 6· y^n $\frac{r}{m}$ Cobbet went to prayer who was Exceedingly in larged y^{er} was much of god appeared in him. I desire to blesse god for y^s day my heart was much drawen forth y^s day & in family prayer afterward.

17· Sept· 79· in y^e morning y^e Synod considered of y^e returne made by y^e Chhs sent to[8] none of w^c refused to send only Newberry where upon y^y were received as members of y^e Synod. after y^s y^e Plateforme was read & approved for y^e substance by a Unanimous vote.[9] y^n y^e Committee's returne[10] was read over & some debate upon it.

18· Sept· 79· y^e Synod was upon y^e first question. Lecture first Chh $\frac{r}{m}$ Nat. Collins[11] preached [y^y are not humbled unto y^s day[12]][13] after Lecture y^e sins of oppression was in debate & soe $\frac{r}{m}$ Whellock[14] declared y^t y^{er} was a cry of injustice in y^t magistrates & ministers were not rated[15] w^c Occasioned a very warme discourse. $\frac{r}{m}$ stodder[16] charged y^e Deputy[17] with saying what was not true & y^e Deputy $Govern^r$[18] told him he deserved to be Laid by y^e heals &c.

---

[1] Increase Mather.

[2] Read *were*.

[3] Samuel Torrey of Weymouth.

[4] Joshua Moody of Portsmouth, N. H.

[5] See C. Mather, *Parentator*, p. 85.

[6] John Higginson of Salem.

[7] Edward Bulkeley of Concord.

[8] Insert a ;.

[9] The text of this vote approving the Cambridge Platform is given in the Preface to the Result, p. 425 of this volume. Cotton Mather, *Magnalia*, ed. 1853–5, II: 237–241, explains the changes in church practice which induced the Synod to introduce the phrase "for the substance of it."

[10] I. e., the Committee appointed Sept. 12, to consider evils and their remedies. The result was drawn up by Increase Mather, *Parentator*, p. 85; and was read to the Synod and discussed paragraph by paragraph, Preface to the Result, p. 425 of this volume.

[11] Probably Rev. Nathaniel Collins of Middletown, Conn., who, as a minister of another colony, must have been a visitor rather than a member of the Synod.

[12] Jer. xliv: 10.

[13] [ ] in original.

[14] This was "Rev." Ralph Wheelock, the "father of Medway." He had preached in England and in this country. He was one of the early settlers and a local magistrate at Dedham; and a founder of Medway. There he served as selectman, schoolmaster, and town representative to the General Court. He was now about 79 years old. That Thacher gives him the title of "Rev." shows the strength of usage even in the face of Puritan theory, for in his more than forty years of life in New England Wheelock was never pastor of a church. His opposition to the privileges of the real ministry is not therefore surprising. See Tilden, *Hist. Town of Medfield*, Boston, 1887, *passim*.

[15] I. e., taxed.

[16] Solomon Stoddard of Northampton.

[17] I. e., Wheelock, who had been "deputy" from Medway in the General Court.

[18] Thomas Danforth.

after we broke up ye deputy & severall others went home with Mr Stodder & ye Deputy asked forgivenesse of him & told him hee freely forgave him, but Mr Stodder was high.

19· Sept· 79· Ye Deputy owned his being in to great a heat & desired ye Lord to forgive &c: & Mr Stodder did something thô very little by a Deputy. Ys day yy discoursed ye remidyes & debated at ye End of Each Paragraph; yer was much debate about persons being admitted to full Communion & Mr Stodder ye Minister offered to dispute against it & brought one arguemt. Mr Mather was Respondent[1] Mr Oakes Moderatr but after some time ye rest of his arguemts. were deferred & at present It was Eased. ys Evening what was drawen up by ye comittee[2] & corrected by ye Synod in answer to both questions was Unanimously uoted. & an answer to ye Governrs two questions. alsoe a Committee was Chouse [Mr Oakes Mr Torry Mr all in,[3] Mr Willard,[4] Mr Mather, Capt. Richards[5] Mr Stodder Capt. Fisher[6]] to present what ye Synod hath done [after yy had prefaced it[7]] to ye Genll. Court in Octo· in order to have ye Chhs &c. & ye Ministers Mr Higginson & Mr Flint[8] being added were voted to draw up a Confession of faith against ye next Weensday before ye Generall Court of Election next, ye Committee was alsoe desired if ye Court approved of it to writte to ye Chhs of ye Vnited Colonyes & informe if yy pleased to send yer Elders & messengers it would be very gratefull.[9] after ys a psalme being Sung Mr Cobbet concluded with prayer."

The committee thus appointed presented the Result, known as the *Necessity of Reformation*, to the Court at its session October 15, 1679, on which occasion Increase Mather "Preached a very Potent Sermon, on the Danger of not being *Reformed by these Things*";[10] and the Court voted:[11]

"This Court, hauing pervsed the result of the late synod of Septemb, 1679, doe judge it meete to comend the same to the serious consideration of all the churches and people in this jurisdiction, hereby enjoyning and requiring all persons in their seuerall capacitjes concerned to a carefull and diligent reformation of all those provoking evills mentioned therein, according to the true intent thereof, that so the

---

[1] See Stoddard's own account of this discussion, p. 280 of this volume. The point is No. III. of the proposed remedies for the evils of the time (p. 433). Thacher has reversed the real position of Stoddard and Mather unless his "dispute against it" refers to the report of the Committee under discussion rather than to the phrase "persons being admitted to full communion." Stoddard was arguing in favor of his well known views.

[2] I. e., the Committee of Sept. 12.

[3] James Allen of the Boston First Church.

[4] Samuel Willard of the Boston Third, or Old South, Church.

[5] I suppose this is John Richards, a member of the Boston Second Church.

[6] Daniel Fisher, a member of the Dedham Church, prominent in colonial politics.

[7] The preface, as well as the result, was the work of Increase Mather, *Parentator*, p. 87.

[8] Josiah Flynt, Richard Mather's successor in the pastorate of the Dorchester Church.

[9] This suggestion came to nothing.

[10] *Parentator*, p. 85.

[11] *Records . . . Mass. Bay*, V: 244.

anger and displeasure of God, which hath binn many wayes manifested, maybe averted from this poore people, and his favour and blessing obteyned, as in former tjmes; and for this end hath ordered the same to be printed."

At the same time the Court appointed a committee "to consider our lawes already made, that may neede emendation, or may not so clearly be warranted from the word of God";[1] criticisms having been passed by the Synod.

There can be no doubt that the work of the Synod was beneficial. Churches were stirred up to renewed activity. Covenants were solemnly ratified. The young people were urged with some success, in many places, to undertake the Christian life.[2] But the political situation of the years after the Synod was such that any permanent good was difficult of accomplishment. The financial distress consequent upon Philip's war, the tyranny of Andros, the loss of the charter of Massachusetts, and quarrels with the French, made the closing years of the seventeenth century a period of gloom. The dissipations of military life and the engrossing problems of politics alike diminished men's interest in religion. The Synod was a palliative rather than a cure.

Though the Synod had made no revision of the Cambridge Platform, as the Court had thought possible, and though the conservative party, at least, rejoiced in the vote by which the Platform was ratified,[3] the Synod had appointed an able committee to draw up a Confession of Faith and report it to a second session of the body. That committee had no very arduous task. New England had no general Confession, but the Cambridge Synod had ratified the doctrinal parts of the Westminster Confession "for the substance thereof"; and the work of the Congregationalists at the

---

[1] *Ibid.*

[2] *Magnalia*, ed. 1853–5, II: 331–333. The Second Church in Boston, for example, renewed its covenant March 17, 1680; and the Third June 29. Sermons of peculiar solemnity delivered on those occasions by Increase Mather and Samuel Willard were printed. How the improvement of the Dorchester church was sought is told thus: "26 2 85 . . . ye same day ther was read ye Conclusion of ye Senod formerly agreed on as ye p'voking sines y^t^ we stood guilty off & to be Humbled for The 3 3 85 was read a pap from ye governor & Councell to excit ye Elders & minester to take Care of their flocks by goeing from hous to hous & see how ye people p'fitting by ye word & that instructing ye youth may goe forward at ye same time ye Elder p'posed y^t^ tow of ye tithing mens Squadrons at a time appointed should come together to some place for y^t^ end from 8 to 16 yeers of age to be Catechized & from 16 to 24 ye yong p'sons should come together to be discoursed with all ye maids by themselves & ye men by themselves." *Rec. First Ch. Dorchester*, p. 93.

[3] See preface to Result, p. 425 of this volume.

Savoy was well known. The two leading members of the committee, Mather and Oakes, had been in England while the Savoy Synod was in session and were well acquainted with its foremost men. It was natural, therefore, that the committee should recommend the adoption of the Savoy Confession, in practically unchanged form,[1] as the creed of the Massachusetts churches. Pursuant to its order on adjournment, the Synod met for its second session at Boston on May 12, 1680. In the absence of definite knowledge we may conjecture that the result was so far a foregone conclusion that the attendance was less than in September, 1679. Certainly Peter Thacher was not there, and we miss his guidance as to the events. Cotton Mather recorded in his *Parentator* :[2]

> "On *May*. 12. 1680. The *Synod* had a Second Session at *Boston*; When Our *Confession of Faith* was agreed upon. Though there were many Elder, and some Famous, Persons in that Venerable Assembly, yet Mr. *Mather*[3] was chosen their *Moderator*. He was then Ill, under the Approaches & Beginnings of a *Fever*; but so Intense was he on the *Business* to be done, that he forgot his *Illness*; and he kept them so close to their *Business*, that in *Two Days* they dispatch'd it: and he also Composed the *Præface* to the *Confession*."

That Preface declares that the Savoy Confession, slightly modified, "was twice publickly read, examined and approved of"[4] by the Synod; and that, as at Cambridge in 1648, desire to avoid any imputation of heresy from the Puritan party in England led the Synod to prefer the formulæ of well-known English assemblies to an expression of faith in its own language. The fact was that, however individual New England might be in church polity, no doctrinal peculiarities had been as yet developed on this side of the Atlantic. No doctrinal discussions of consequence had taken place. The New England churches still stood, as a body, with uncriticising loyalty on the basis of the Puritan theology of England as it had been in the first half of the seventeenth century.

The Confession, like the Result of the first session of the Synod, was duly reported to the Massachusetts General Court, and on June 11, 1680, that body voted as follows:[5]

---

1 The only alteration of any moment is in Chap. xxiv, sec. iii. See p. 393 of this volume.

2 Page 87. See also *Magnalia*, II: 180.

3 Increase Mather.

4 See p. 439 of this volume.

5 *Records* . . . *Mass. Bay*, V: 287.

"This Court, hauing taken into serious consideration the requests which hath been presented by seuerall of the reūnd elders, in the name of the late synod, doe approove thereof, and accordingly order the confession of faith agreed vpon at their second session, and the platforme of discipline, consented vnto by the synod at Cambridge, anno 1648, to be printed for the bennefit of these churches in present and after times."

Though heartily sympathizing with the statement of doctrine, the Court wisely refrained from commanding its use by the churches. Accepted as a fair expression of the belief of New England, it was reaffirmed and declared the faith of the colony of Connecticut at Saybrook in 1708. But it was never intended to be a substitute for the local creeds of individual churches. It was itself used as a local creed by at least two churches, the Old South of Boston[1] and the First Church of Cambridge,[2] and such use illustrates rather than disproves the freedom of the New England churches to formulate their faith each in its own way. That freedom enables a modern Congregationalist to view with pleasure the creed of 1680 as a noble testimony to the faith of our churches at that day, and a historic monument of which they have no reason to be ashamed; while he substitutes for its phraseology, if he chooses, what he may deem an expression of Scripture truth better adapted to the needs of the age in which he lives. He can admire the stately fabric of this seventeenth century Puritan creed as he admires the great cathedrals of the middle ages, without questioning at every turn how much of tinkering and repairing with modern, and it may be incongruous, architecture is desirable to fit it for present use.

---

1 See H. A. Hill, *Hist. Old South*, I: 234, 235; II: 555. See *ante*, p. 409.

2 See A. McKenzie, *Lectures on the History of the First Church in Cambridge*, Boston, 1873, p. 267.

THE SYNOD'S WORK

A. THE RESULT OF 1679

THE[1] NECESSITY | OF | REFORMATION | With the Expedients subservient | thereunto, asserted; | in Answer to two | *QUESTIONS* | I. *What are the Evils that have provoked the Lord to bring his Judg- | ments on New-England?* | II. *What is to be done that so those Evils may be Reformed?* | *Agreed upon by the* | *ELDERS* and *MESSENGERS* | *of the Churches assembled in the* | SYNOD | *At* Boston *in* New-England, | Sept. 10. 1679. | —— | *Mal.* 3. 7. Even from the dayes of your Fathers yee are gone away from mine Ordi- | nances, and have not kept them; Return unto me and I will return unto you, | saith the Lord of Host: but ye said, Wherein shall we return? | *Rev.* 2. 4, 5. Nevertheless I have somewhat against thee, because thou hast left thy | first love. Remember therefore from whence thou art fallen, and Repent, and doe thy first works; or else I will come unto thee quickly and will remove | thy Candlestick out of his place, except thou Repent. | —— | BOSTON; | Printed by *John Foster*. In the Year, 1679.

[ii blank]
[iii]

TO THE MUCH HONOURED
General Court
Of the *Massachusets Colony* now sitting at *Boston*
in *NEW-ENGLAND*

Right Worshipful, Worshipful, and much honoured in our Lord Jesus!

THe Wayes of God towards this his People, have in many respects been like unto his dealings with Israel of old: It was a great and high undertaking of our Fathers, when they ventured themselves and their little ones upon the rude waves of the vast Ocean, that so they might follow the Lord into this Land; a parallel instance not to be given, except that of our Father Abraham from Vr of the Chaldees, or that of his Seed from the land of Egypt; the Lord alone did lead them and there was no strange God with them. In the wilderness have we dwelt in safety alone, being made the subjects of most peculiar mercies and priviledges. The good will of him that dwelt in the bush hath been upon the head of those that were separated from their Brethren: and the Lord hath (by turning a Wilderness into a fruitful land) brought us into a wealthy place; he hath planted a Vine, having cast out the Heathen, prepared Room for it, and caused it to take deep rooting, and to

[1] On a fly-leaf, facing this title, is the approving vote of the Mass. Gen. Court of Oct. 15, 1679 (*ante*, p. 419), attested by Edward Rawson, Secretary.

fill the land, which hath sent out its boughs unto the Sea, and its branches to the River. If we ask of the dayes that are past, and look from the one side of heaven to the other, where can we find the like to this great thing which the Lord hath done? His planting these heavens, and laying the foundations of this earth, is (if any thing be) to be reckoned amongst the wonderful works of God which this age hath seen. If we look abroad over the face of the whole earth, where shall we see a place or people brought to such perfection and considerableness, in so short a time? Our adversaryes themselves being judges, it hath not been so with any of the outgoings of the Nations. We must then ascribe all these things, as unto the grace and abundant goodness of the Lord our God, so to his owning a religious design and interest; such was *New-Englands* in its primitive constitution. Our Fathers neither sought for, nor thought of great things for themselves, but did seek first the Kingdome of God, and his righteousness, and all these things were added to them. They came not into the wilderness to see a man cloathed in soft raiment. But that we have in too many respects, been forgetting the Errand upon which the Lord sent us hither; all the world is witness: [iv] And therefore we may not wonder that God hath changed the tenour of his Dispensations towards us, turning to doe us hurt, and consuming us after that he hath done us good. If we had continued to be as once we were, the Lord would have continued to doe for us, as once he did. This notwithstanding, we must not deny or disown what of God is remaining amongst us. There is cause to fear that the same evils for which the Lord is contending with us, are to be found in other Reformed Churches, and perhaps in an higher degree, then as yet with us; considering that these Churches doe still (through the grace of Christ) own both the faith and order of the Gospel, that was professed in the dayes of our Fathers: and there are a number of precious souls (a few names that have not defiled their garments with the sins of the times) we hope in every Congregation: only the present Generation in New-England, as to the body of it, in respect of the practice and power of Godliness, is far short of those whom God saw meet to improve in laying the foundations of his Temple here: and our iniquityes admit of sadder aggravations then can be said of others, because we sin against greater light, and means, and mercies then ever People (all circumstances considered) have done; and therefore the Lord is righteous in all the evil that hath befallen us. And it is high time for us to be earnest, as to an impartial *Scrutiny* concerning the causes of his holy displeasure against us, together with the proper Remedyes or Scripture expedients, for Reformation, that so the Lord, who hath said, Return unto me, and I will return unto you, may be at peace with us. Essayes respecting this matter have not been altogether wanting, but hitherto successless in a great degree. Wherefore, it hath pleased God so to dispose, as that your selves, who are the Honoured General Court of this Colony, have called upon all the Churches therein, to send their Elders and Messengers, that they might meet in form of a Synod, in order to a most serious enquiry, into the questions here propounded and answered. We cannot but hope this motion was of God, since (after the Prayers of his People have been solemnly and abundantly poured out before him that it might be so) evident Tokens of the Lords gracious presence in and with that Reverend Assembly, have been taken notice of; especially in that he was pleased so to enlighten the minds, and encline the hearts of his Servants, (the Messengers and Representatives of the Churches) as that there was an unanimity in their Votes and Determinations, and that not only with reference to the Answers unto those Questions, but other things then discussed and concluded on. There was at first some agitation about the matter of a *Regular*

Synod, by reason that some of the Churches (notwithstanding their Elders desiring them to send other Messengers also) sent their Elders alone. That which is expressed in the Platform of Discipline, concerning this particular, was assented unto, *viz.* that not only Elders, but other Messengers ought to be delegated by the Churches, and so to have their Suffrages in such Assemblyes. A Principle which doth agree with the Primitive Pattern, Act. 15. 23. And with the practice of the Churches in the ages next following the Apostles, as is evident from the writings of *Cyprian*, and others of the Ancients. And the interest of the People in such Conventions is strongly asserted and evinced by our *Juel*, *Whitaker*, *Parker*, and others against Papists and Prelates, who maintain that *Laicks* (as they call them) are not fit matter for a Synod. This Debate being issued, it was put to Vote, whether the Assembly did approve of *The Platform of Church Discipline*; & both Elders & Brethren did unanimously lift up their hands in the affirmative, not one appearing [v] when the Vote was propounded in the Negative, but it joyntly passed in these words,

"A Synod of the Churches in the Colony of the Massachusets, being called by "the honoured General Court to convene at Boston, the 10. of Sept. 1679. having "read and considered the Platform of Church Discipline, agreed upon by the Synod "assembled at Cambridge, Anno 1648. doe unanimously approve of the said Plat-"form, for the substance of it, desiring that the Churches may continue stedfast in "the order of the Gospel, according to what is therein declared from the Word of "God.["]

Now blessed be the God of our Fathers, that hath enclined our hearts to own that Cause and those Truths, which they did with so much industry and faithfulness gather from the Scriptures, and on the account whereof they were sometimes *Confessors*, and Sufferers, being *Exiles* in this Wilderness, where the Lord was pleased to shew them the Pattern of his House, and all the forms thereof; and we know not what Temptations (for there is an hour of Temptation coming upon all the world) we may yet meet with; wherefore, the obtaining of the Vote mentioned (had there been nothing else done) was well worth our coming together. But besides that, several dayes were spent, in discoursing upon the Questions herewith presented; when every Member of the *Synod* had full liberty to express himself: after which, some were chosen, to draw up what did appear to be the mind of the Assembly, and the mind of Christ, in whose name we came together, and considered of this matter. The Return made by those who had been appointed unto that Service, was read once and again, each Paragraph being duely and distinctly weighed in the ballance of the Sanctuary, and then, upon mature deliberation, the whole unanimously voted, as to the substance, end, and scope thereof. The things here insisted on, have (at least many of them) been oftentimes mentioned and inculcated by those whom the Lord hath set as Watchmen to the house of Israel, though alas! not with that success which their Souls have desired. It is not a small matter, nor ought it to seem little in our eyes, that the Churches have in this way confessed and declared the Truth, which coming from a *Synod* as their joint concurring Testimony, will carry more Authority with it, then if one man only, or many in their single capacityes, should speak the same things. And undoubtedly, the issue of this undertaking will be most signal, either as to mercy, or misery. If New-England remember whence she is fallen, and doe the first works, there is reason to hope that it shall be better with us then at our beginnings. But if this, after all other means in and by which the Lord hath been striving to reclaim us, shall be despised, or become ineffectual, we may dread what is like to follow. It is a solemn thought, that the Jewish Church had (as the Churches in New-England have this day) an opportunity to Reform (if they would) in Josiah's time, but because they had no heart unto it, the Lord quickly removed them out of his sight. What God out of his Soveraignty may doe for us, no man can say, but according to his wonted dispensations, we are a perishing People, if now we *Reform* not.

Now the Lord help you his Servants, under whose influence, and by whose encouragement, this Synod hath convened, to promote this matter, both by your Recommendation of these Conclusions unto the Churches, for their consideration and acceptance in the Lord, and otherwise according to your respective Relations and Capacities: and the Lord strengthen your hearts and hands therein; for much doth depend upon your Courage, Prudence, Zeal and Activity. We doe [vi] not read in the Scriptures, nor in History, of any notable general Reformation amongst a People, except the Magistrate did help forward the work. Haggai's and Zachary's Sermons, would never have built the Temple, if Zerubbabel and Shealtiel (godly Magistrates) had not improved their authority for that end. *Luther*, *Calvin*, *Zuingluis*, and other Reformers, would have laboured in vain, had not the Princes and Senators amongst whom they lived, promoted the interest of Reformation. Nor was it ever known, that the civil Authority in any place, did their utmost towards the suppression of growing Evils, but there was (at least wise for the present) some good effect thereof. These things are therefore commended to your most serious Consideration; It is (under God) by you that we enjoy great quietness. The good Lord continue the present Government, and Governours, under whose shadow (as sometimes the Remnant of Judah under Gedaliah) we have sat with great delight; and grant that every one (both Leaders and People) in their proper place and order, may up and be doing, and that the Lord our God may be with us, as he was with our Fathers.

Now be strong, O Zerubbabel, be strong, O Joshuah, and be strong all ye people of the land, saith the Lord, and work, for I am with you; according to the word that I covenanted with you, when ye came out of Egypt; so my Spirit remaineth amongst you; Fear ye not.

[1] QUEST. I.

VVHat are the Evils that have provoked the Lord to bring his Judgements on New-England?

Answ. That sometimes God hath had, and pleaded a Controversy with his People, is clear from the Scripture, Hos. 4. 1. and 12. 2. Mic 6. 1, 2. Where God doth plainly and fully propose, state and plead his Controversy, in all the parts and Causes of it, wherein he doth justifie himself, by the Declaration of his own infinite Mercy, Grace, Goodness, Justice, Righteousness, Truth and Faithfulness in all his proceedings with them; And judge his People, charging them with all those provoking Evils which had been the causes of that Controversy, and that with the most high, and heavy aggravation of their Sins, and exaggeration of the guilt and punishment, whence he should have been most just, in pleading out his Controversy with them, unto the utmost extremity of Justice and Judgement.

That God hath a Controversy with his New-England People is undeniable, the Lord having written his displeasure in dismal

Characters against us. Though Personal Afflictions doe oftentimes come only or chiefly for Probation, yet as to publick Judgements it is not wont to be so; especially when by a continued Series of Providence, the Lord doth appear and plead against his People. 2 Sam. 21. 1. As with us it hath been from year to year. Would the Lord have whetted his glitterring Sword, and his hand have taken hold on Judgement? Would he have sent such a mortal Contagion like a Beesom of Destruction in the midst of us? Would he have said, Sword! goe through the Land, and cut off man and Beast? [2] Or would he have kindled such devouring Fires, and made such fearfull Desolations in the Earth, if he had not been angry? It is not for nothing that the merciful God, who doth not willingly afflict nor grieve the Children of men, hath done all these things unto us; yea and sometimes with a Cloud hath covered himself, that our Prayer should not pass through. And although tis possible that the Lord may Contend with us partly on account of secret unobserved Sins, Josh. 7. 11, 12. 2 King. 17. 9. Psal. 90. 8. In which respect, a deep and most serious enquiry into the Causes of his Controversy ought to be attended. Nevertheless, it is sadly evident that there are visible, manifest Evils, which without doubt the Lord is provoked by. For,

I. There is a great and visible decay of the power of Godliness amongst many Professors in these Churches. It may be feared, that there is in too many spiritual and heart Apostacy from God, whence Communion with him in the wayes of his Worship, especially in Secret, is much neglected, and whereby men cease to know and fear, and love and trust in him; but take up their contentment and satisfaction in something else. This was the ground and bottom of the Lords Controversy with his People of old. Psal. 78. 8, 37. & 81. 11. Jer. 2. 5, 11, 13. And with his People under the New Testament also. Rev. 2. 4, 5.

II. The Pride that doth abound in New-England testifies against us. Hos. 5. 5. Ezek. 7. 10. Both spiritual Pride, Zeph. 3. 11. Whence two great Evils and Provocations have proceeded and prevailed amongst us.

1. A refusing to be subject to Order according to divine appointment, Numb. 16. 3. 1 Pet. 5. 5.

2. Contention. Prov. 13. 10. An evil that is most eminently against the solemn Charge of the Lord Jesus, Joh. 13. 34, 35. And that for which God hath by severe Judgements punished his People, both in former and latter Ages. This Malady hath been very general in the Country: we have therefore cause to fear that the Wolves which God in his holy Providence hath let loose upon us, have been sent to chastise his Sheep for their dividings and strayings one from another; and that the Warrs and Fightings, which have proceeded from the Lust of Pride in special, have been punished with the Sword, Jam. 4. 1. Job. 19. 29.

Yea, and Pride in respect to Apparel hath greatly abounded. [3] Servants, and the poorer sort of People are notoriously guilty in the matter, who (too generally) goe above their estates and degrees, thereby transgressing the Laws both of God and man, Math. 11. 8. Yea, it is a Sin that even the light of nature, and Laws of civil Nations have condemned. 1 Cor. 11, 14. Also, many, not of the meaner sort, have offended God by strange Apparel, not becoming serious Christians, especially in these dayes of affliction and misery, wherein the Lord calls upon men to put off their Ornaments, Exod. 33. 5. Jer 4. 30. A Sin which brings Wrath upon the greatest that shall be found guilty of it, Zeph. 1. 8. with Jer. 52. 13. Particularly, the Lord hath threatned to visit with Sword and Sickness, and with loathsome diseases for this very Sin. Isa 3. 16.

III. Inasmuch as it was in a more peculiar manner with respect to the second Commandment, that our Fathers did follow the Lord into this wilderness, whilst it was a land not sown, we may fear that the breaches of that Commandment are some part of the Lords Controversy with New-England. Church Fellowship, and other divine Institutions are greatly neglected. Many of the Rising Generation are not mindfull of that which their Baptism doth engage them unto, *viz.* to use utmost endeavours that they may be fit for, and so partake in, all the holy Ordinances of the Lord Jesus. Mat. 28. 20. There are too many that with profane Esau slight spiritual priviledges. Nor is there so much of Discipline, extended towards the Children of the Covenant, as we are generally agreed ought to be done. On the other hand, humane Inventions, and Will-worship have been set up even in Jerusalem. Men have set up their Thresholds by Gods Threshold, and their Posts by his Post. Quakers are false Worshippers: and such Anabaptists as have risen up amongst us, in opposition to the Churches of the Lord Jesus, receiving into their Society those that have been for scandal delivered unto Satan, yea, and improving those as Administrators of holy Things, who have been (as doth appear) *Justly* under Church Censures, do no better then set up an Altar against the Lords Altar. Wherefore it must needs be provoking to God, if these things be not duly and fully testified against, by every one in their several Capacityes respectively. Josh. 22. 19. 2 King. 23. 13. Ezek. 43. 8. Psal. 99. 8. Hos. 11. 6.

IIII. The Holy and glorious Name of God hath been polluted and profaned amongst us, More especially.

[4] 1. By Oathes, and Imprecations in ordinary Discourse; Yea, and it is too common a thing for men in a more solemn way to Swear unnecessary Oaths; whenas it is a breach of the third Commandment, so to use the blessed Name of God. And many (if not the most) of those that swear, consider not the Rule of an Oath. Jer. 4. 2. So that we may justly fear that because of swearing the Land mourns, Jer. 23. 10.

2. There is great profaness, in respect of irreverent behaviour in the solemn Worship of God. It is a frequent thing for men (though not necessitated thereunto by any infirmity) to sit in prayer time, and some with their heads almost covered, and to give way to their own sloth and sleepiness, when they should be serv-

ing God with attention and intention, under the solemn dispensation of his Ordinances. We read but of one man in the Scripture that slept at a Sermon, and that sin hath like to have cost him his life, Act. 20. 9.

V. There is much Sabbath-breaking; Since there are multitudes that do profanely absent themselves or theirs from the publick worship of God, on his Holy day, especially in the most populous places the Land; and many under pretence of differing apprehensions about the beginning of the Sabbath, do not keep a seventh part of Time Holy unto the Lord, as the fourth Commandment requireth, Walking abroad, and Travelling, (not meerly on the account of worshipping God in the solemn assemblyes of his people, or to attend works of necessity or mercy) being a common practice on the Sabbath day, which is contrary unto that Rest enjoyned by the Commandment. Yea, some that attend their particular servile callings and employments after the Sabbath is begun, or before it is ended. Worldly, unsuitable discourses are very common upon the Lords day, contrary to the Scripture which requireth that men should not on Holy Times find their own pleasure, nor speak their own words, Isai 58. 13. Many that do not take care so to dispatch their worldly businesses, that they may be free & fit for the dutyes of the Sabbath, and that do (if not wholly neglect) after a careless, heartless manner perform the dutyes that concern the sanctification of the Sabbath. This brings wrath, Fires and other Judgements upon a professing People, Neh. 3. 17, 18 Jer. 17. 27.

VI. As to what concerns Familyes and the Government thereof, [5] there is much amiss. There are many Familyes that doe not pray to God constantly morning and evening, and many more wherein the Scriptures are not daily read, that so the word of Christ might dwell richly with them. Some (and too many) Houses that are full of Ignorance and Profaness, and these not duely inspected; for which cause Wrath may come upon others round about them, as well as upon themselves. Josh. 22. 20. Jer. 5. 7. & 10. 25. And many Housholders who profess Religion, doe not cause all that are within their gates to become subject unto good order as ought to be. Ex. 20 10. Nay, children & Servants that are not kept in due subjection; their Masters, and Parents especially, being sinfully indulgent towards them. This is a sin which brings great Judgements, as we see in Eli's and David's Family. In this respect, Christians in this Land, have become too like unto the Indians, and then we need not wonder if the Lord hath afflicted us by them. Sometimes a Sin is discerned by the Instrument that Providence doth punish with. Most of the Evils that abound amongst us, proceed from defects as to Family Government.

VII. Inordinate Passions. Sinful Heats and Hatreds, and that amongst Church Members themselves, who abound with evil Surmisings, uncharitable and unrighteous Censures, Back-bitings, hearing and telling Tales, few that remember and duely observe the Rule, with an angry countenance to drive away the Talebearer: Reproachfull and reviling Expressions, sometimes to or of one another. Hence Law suits are frequent, Brother going to Law with Brother, and provoking and abusing one another in publick Courts of Judicature, to the Scandal of their holy Profession, Isa. 58. 4. 1 Cor 6 6, 7. And in managing the Discipline of Christ, some (and too many) are acted by their Passions & Prejudices more then by a spirit of Love & Faithfulness towards their Brothers Soul, which things are, as against the Law of Christ, so dreadfull violations of the Church Covenant, made in the presence of God.

VIII. There is much Intemperance. The heathenish and Idolatrous practice of Health-drinking is too frequent. That shamefull iniquity of sinfull Drinking is become too general a Provocation. Dayes of Training, and other publick Solemnityes, have been abused in this respect: And not only English but Indians have been debauched, by those that call themselves Christians, who have put their [6] bottles to them, and made them drunk also. This is a crying Sin, and the more aggravated in that the first Planters of this Colony did (as is in the Patent expressed) come into this Land with a design to Convert the Heathen unto Christ, but if instead of that, they be taught Wickedness, which before they were never guilty of, the Lord may well punish us by them. Moreover, the Sword, Sickness, Poverty, and almost all the Judgements which have been upon New-England, are mentioned in the Scripture as the woeful fruit of *That Sin.* Isa. 5. 11, 12. & 28. 1, 2. & 56. 9, 12. Prov. 23. 21, 29 30. & 21. 17. Hos. 7. 5. & 2. 8 9. There are more Temptations and occasions unto *That Sin*, publickly allowed of, then any necessity doth require; the proper end of Taverns, &c. being for the entertainment of Strangers, which if they were improved to that end only, a far less number would suffice: But it is a common practice for Town-dwellers, yea and Church-members, to frequent publick Houses, and there to misspend precious Time, unto the dishonour of the Gospel, and the scandalizing of others, who are by such examples induced to sin against God. In which respect, for Church-members to be unnecessarily in such Houses, is sinfull, scandalous, and provoking to God. 1 Cor. 8. 9 10. Rom. 14 21. Math. 17. 27. & 18. 7.

And there are other hainous breaches of the seventh Commandment. Temptations thereunto are become too common, viz. such as immodest Apparel, Prov. 7. 10 Laying out of hair, Borders, naked Necks and Arms, or, which is more abominable, naked Breasts, and mixed Dancings, light behaviour and expressions, sinful Company-keeping with light and vain persons, unlawfull Gaming, an abundance of Idleness, which brought ruinating Judgement upon Sodom, and much more upon Jerusalem. Ezek. 16. 49. and doth sorely threaten New-England, unless effectual Remedyes be throughly and timously applyed.

IX. There is much want of Truth amongst men. Promise-breaking is a common sin, for which New-England doth hear ill abroad in the world. And the Lord hath threatned for that transgression to give his People into the hands of their Enemies, and that their dead bodyes should be for meat unto the Fowls of heaven, and to the Beasts of the earth; which Judgements have been verified upon us, Jer. 34. 18, 20. And false Reports have been too common, yea, walking with slanders and Reproaches, and that sometimes against the most faithfull and eminent Servants of God. The Lord is not [7] wont to suffer such Iniquity to pass unpunished. Jer. 9. 4, 5. Numb. 16. 41.

X. Inordinate affection to the world. Idolatry is a God provoking, Judgement-procuring sin. And Covetousness is Idolatry. Eph. 5. 5. There hath been in many professors an insatiable desire after Land, and worldly Accommodations, yea, so as to forsake Churches and Ordinances, and to live like Heathen, only that so they might have Elbow-room enough in the world. Farms and merchandising have been preferred before the things of God. In this respect, the Interest of New-England seemeth to be changed. We differ from other out-goings of our Nation, in that it was not any worldly consideration that brought our Fathers into this wilderness, but Religion, even that so they might build a Sanctuary unto the Lords Name; Whenas now, Religion is made subservient unto worldly Interests. Such iniquity causeth War to be in the Gates, and Cityes to be burnt up. Judg. 8. 5. Math. 22. 5, 7. Wherefore, we cannot but solemnly bear witness against that practice of setling Plantations without any Ministry amongst them, which is to prefer the world before the Gospel. When Lot did forsake the Land of Canaan, and the Church which was in Abrahams Family, that so he might have better worldly Accommodations in Sodom, God fired him out of all, and he was constrained to leave his goodly pastures, which his heart (though otherwise a good man) was too much set upon. Moreover, that many are under the prevailing power of the sin of worldliness is evident,

1. From that oppression which the Land groaneth under. There are some Traders, who sell their goods at excessive Rates, Day-Labourers and Mechanicks are unreasonable in their demands; Yea, there have been those that have dealt deceitfully and oppressively towards the Heathen amongst whom we live, whereby they have been scandalized and prejudiced against the Name of Christ. The Scripture doth frequently threaten Judgments for the sin of oppression, and in special the oppressing Sword cometh as a just punishment for that evil. Ezek. 7. 11. and 22. 15. Prov. 28. 8. Isai. 5. 7.

2. It is also evident, that men are under the prevailing power of a worldly Spirit, by their strait-handedness, as to publick concernments. God by a continued series of providence, for many years one after another, hath been blasting the fruits of the Earth, in a great measure; and this year more abundantly; Now if we search the [8] Scriptures, we shall find, that when the Lord hath been provoked to destroy the fruits of the Earth, either by noxious Creatures, or by his own immediate hand in blastings or droughts, or excessive Rains, (all which judgments we have experience of) it hath been mostly for this sin of strait-handedness with reference

unto publick and pious concerns, Hag. 1. 9. Mal. 3. 8, 9, 11. As when peoples hearts and hands are enlarged upon these Accounts, God hath promised, (and is wont in his faithful providence to do accordingly) to bless with outward plenty and prosperity, Prov. 3. 9, 10. Mal. 3. 10 1 Cor. 9. 6, 8, 10. 2 Chron. 31. 10. So on the other hand, when men withold more then is meet, the Lord sends impoverishing judgments upon them, Prov. 11. 24.

XI. There hath been opposition unto the work of Reformation. Although the Lord hath been calling upon us, not only by the voice of his Servants, but by awfull judgments, that we should return unto him, who hath been smiting us; and notwithstanding all the good Laws that are established for the suppression of growing evils, yet men *will not* return every one from his evil way. There hath been great incorrigibleness under lesser judgments; Sin and sinners have many Advocates. They that have been zealous in bearing witness against the sins of the Times, have been reproached, and other wayes discouraged; which argueth an heart unwilling to Reform. Hence the Lords Controversy is not yet done, but his hand is stretched out still, Lev. 26. 23, 24. Isai. 12, 13.

XII. A publick Spirit is greatly wanting in the most of men. Few that are of Nehemiah's Spirit, Neh. 5. 15. All seek their own, not the things that are Jesus Christs; Serving themselves upon Christ, and his holy Ordinances. Matters appertaining to the Kingdome of God, are either not at all regarded, or not in the first place. Hence Schools of learning and other publick concerns are in a languishing state. Hence also are unreasonable complaints and murmurings because of publick charges, which is a great sin; and a private self-seeking Spirit, is one of those evils that renders the last Times perilous, 2 Tim. 3: 1.

XIII. There are sins against the Gospel, whereby the Lord hath been provoked. Christ is not prized and embraced in all his Offices and Ordinances as ought to be. Manna hath been loathed, the pleasant Land despised, Psal. 106. 24, Though the Gospel and Co-[9]venant of grace call upon men to repent, yet there are multitudes that refuse to Repent, when the Lord doth vouch safe them time and means. No sins provoke the Lord more then Impenitency & unbelief Jer. 8. 6. Zech. 7. 11, 12, 13. Heb. 3. 17, 18. Rev. 2. 21, 22. There is great unfruitfulness under the means of grace, and that brings the most desolating Judgements, Isai. 5. 4, 5. Math. 3. 10. and 21. 43.

Finally; there are several considerations, which seem to evidence, that the Evils mentioned are the matters of the Lords Controversy

1. In that (though not as to all) as to most of them they are sins which many are guilty of,

2. Sins which have been acknowledged before the Lord on dayes of Humiliation appointed by Authority, and yet not Reformed.

3. Many of them not punished (and some of them not punishable) by men, therefore the Lord himself doth punish for them.

QUEST. II.

VVHat is to be done that so these Evils may be Reformed.

Answ. I. It would tend much to promote the Interest of Reformation, if all that are in place above others, do as to themselves and Familyes, become every way exemplary. Moses being to Reform others began with what concerned himself and his. People are apt to follow the example of those that are above them. 2 Chron. 12. 1. Gal. 2. 14. If then, there be a divided heart, or any other of the Sins of the times, found in any degree among those (or any of them) that are Leaders, either as to Civil or Ecclesiastical Order, Reformation there would have a great and happy influence upon many.

II. Inasmuch as the present standing Generation (both as to Leaders and People) is for the greater part another Generation then [10] what was in New-England fourty years agoe, for us to declare our adherence unto the Faith and order of the Gospel, according to what is from the Scripture expressed in the Platform of Discipline, may be likewise a good means both to recover those that have erred from the Truth, and to prevent Apostacy for the Future.

III. It is requisite that persons be not admitted unto Communion in the Lords Supper without making a personal and publick profession of their Faith and Repentance, either orally, or in some other way, so as shall be to the just satisfaction of the Church; and that therefore both Elders and Churches be duely watchfull and circumspect in this matter. 1 Cor. 11. 28, 29. Act. 2. 41, 42. Ezek. 44. 7, 8, 9.

IIII. In order to Reformation, it is necessary that the Discipline of Christ in the power of it should be upheld in the Churches. It is evident from Christs Epistles to the Churches in the lesser Asia, that the evils and degeneracy then prevailing among Christians, proceeded chiefly from the neglect of Discipline. It is a known and true observation, that remissness in the exercise of Discipline, was attended with corruption of manners, and that did provoke the Lord to give men up to strong delusions in matters of Faith. Discipline is Christs Ordinance, both for the prevention of Apostacy in Churches and to recover them when collapsed. And these New English Churches, are under peculiar engagements to be faithfull unto Christ, and unto his Truth in this matter, by virtue of the Church Covenant, as also in that the management of Discipline according to the Scriptures, was the special design of our Fathers in coming into this wilderness. The degeneracy of the Rising Generation (so much complained of) is in a great measure to be attributed unto neglects of this nature. If all Church duty in these respects, were faithfully and diligently attended, not only towards Parents, but also towards the Children of the Church, according to the Rules of Christ, we may hope that the sunk and dying interest of Religion, will be revived, and a world of sin prevented for the future; and that Disputes respecting the Subject of Baptism, would be comfortably issued.

V. It is requisite that utmost endeavours should be used, in order unto a full supply of Officers in the Churches, according to Christs Institution. The defect of these Churches on this account is very lamentable, there being in most of the Churches only one Teaching Officer, for the burden of the whole Congregation to lye upon. The Lord Christ would not have instituted Pastors, Teachers, Ruling Elders (nor the Apostles have ordained Elders in every Church) Act. [11] 14. 23. Tit. 1. 5.) if he had not seen there was need of them for the good of his People; and therefore for men to think they can do well enough without them, is both to break the second Commandment, and to reflect upon the wisdome of Christ, as if he did appoint unnecessary Officers in his Church. Experience hath evinced, that personal instruction and Discipline, hath been an happy means to Reform degenerated Congregations; yea, and owned by the Lord for the conversion of many Souls: but where there are great Congregations, it is impossible for one man, besides his labours in publick, fully to attend these other things of great importance; and necessary to be done in order to an effectual Reformation of Familyes and Congregations.

VI. It is incumbent on the Magistrate, to take care that these Officers have due encouragement, and maintenance afforded to them. It is high injustice and oppression, yea, a Sin that cryes in the Lords ears for judgement, when wages is witheld from faithfull and diligent Labourers. Jam. 5. 4. And if it be so to those that labour about carnal things, much more as to those that labour day & night about the spiritual and eternal welfare of Souls, 1 Cor. 9. 11, 13, 14. And the Scripture is express that not only Members of Churches, but all that are taught in the word, are bound to communicate to him that Teacheth, and that in all good things. Gal. 6. 6. Luk. 10 7. 1 Tim. 5. 17, 18. If therefore People be unwilling to doe what justice and reason calls for, the Magistrate is to see them doe their duty in this matter. Wherefore, Magistrates, and that in Scriptures referring to the dayes of the New Testament, are said to be the Churches nursing Fathers. Isa. 49 23. For that it concerns them to take care that the Churches be fed with the bread and water of Life. The Magistrate is to be a keeper of both Tables, which as a Magistrate he cannot be, if he doe not promove the interest of Religion, by all those means which are of the Lords appointment. And we find in Scripture, that when the Lords Ministers have been forced to neglect the House of God, and goe every one into the field (as too much of that hath been amongst us) because the People did not allow them that maintenance which was necessary, the Magistrate did look upon himself as concerned to effect a Reformation. Neh. 13. 10.

VII. Due care and faithfulness with respect unto the establishment and execution of wholsome Laws, would very much promote the interest of Reformation. If there be no Laws established in the Common-wealth, but what there is Scripture warrant for, and those [12] Laws so worded, as that they may not become a snare unto any that are bound to animadvert upon the Violators of them, and that then they be impartially executed; Profaneness, Heresy, Schism, Disorders in Familyes, Towns, Churches would be happily prevented and Reformed. In special it is necessary, that those Laws for Reformation of provoking evils, enacted and emitted by the General Court in the day of our Calamity, should be duely considered, lest we become guilty of dissembling and dallying with the Almighty, and thereby Sin and Wrath be augmented upon us: in particular, those Laws which respect the Regulation of Houses for publick entertainment, that the number of such Houses doe not exceed what is necessary, nor any so entrusted but persons of known approved piety and Fidelity, and that Inhabitants be prohibited drinking in such Houses, and those that shall without License from Authority sell any sort of strong drink, be exemplarily punished. And if withal, inferiour Officers, Constables and Tithing men, be chosen constantly of the ablest and most prudent in the place, Authorized and Sworn to a faithful discharge of their respective Trusts, and duely encouraged in their just informations against any that shall transgress the Laws so established, we may hope that much of that prophaneness which doth threaten the ruine of the uprising Generation will be prevented.

VIII. Solemn and explicit Renewal of the Covenant is a Scripture Expedient for Reformation. We seldome read of any solemn Reformation but it was accomplished in this way, as the Scripture doth abundantly declare and testify. And as the Judgements which befel the Lords people of old are recorded for our Admonition, 1. Cor. 10. 11. So the Course which they did (according to God) observe in order to Reformation and averting those Judgements, is recorded for our imitation; And this was an Explicit Renovation of Covenant. And that the Lord doth call us to this work, these considerations seem to evince. 1. If Implicit Renewal of Covenant be an expedient for Reformation, and to divert impending wrath and Judgement, then much more an Explicit Renewal is so. But the first of these is Indubitable. In prayer, and more especially on dayes of solemn Humiliation before the Lord, there is an Implicit Renewal of Covenant, and yet the very dictates of natural Conscience put men upon such dutyes, when they are apprehensive of a day of wrath, approaching. If we may not Renew our Covenants with God, for fear lest men should not be true and faithful in doing what they promise, then we must not observe dayes of Fasting and Prayer; which none will say.

[13] 2. When the Church was overrun with Idolatry and Superstition, those whom the Lord raised up as Reformers, put them upon solemn Renewal of Covenant. So Asa, Jehojadah, Hezekiah, Josiah. By a parity of Reason, when Churches are overgrown with worldiness (which is spiritual Idolatry) and other corruptions, the same course may and should be observed in order to Reformation. Nay, 3. We find in Scripture, that when corruption in manners

(though not in Worship) hath prevailed in the Church, Renovation of Covenant hath been the expedient, whereby Reformation hath been attempted, and in some measure attained. The Jews have dreaded the sin of Idolatry ever since the Babylonian Captivity, Joh. 8. 41. But in Ezra's and Nehemiah's time, too much sensuality and Sabbath breaking, Oppression, Strait-handedness respecting the publick Worship of God (the very same sins that are found with us) were common, prevailing iniquityes. Therefore did those Reformers put them upon Renewing their Covenant, and solemnly to promise God that they would endeavour not to offend by those Evils as formerly, Ezra. 10. 3. Neh. 5. 12, 13. and 10. *per totum*, and 13. 15. 4. The things which are mentioned in the Scripture as grounds of Renewing Covenant, are applicable unto us, *e. g.* The averting of divine wrath is expressed as a sufficient Reason for attendance unto this duty. 2 Chron. 29. 10. Ezra 10 14. Again, being circumstanced with difficultyes and distresses is mentioned as the ground of Explicit Renovation of Covenant. Neh. 9. 38. Hence the Lords Servants, when so circumstanced, have been wont to make solemn vows (and that is an express Covenanting) Gen. 28. 20, 21. Judg. 11. 30. Numb. 21. 1, 2. Now that Clouds of wrath are hanging over these Churches, every one seeth; And that we are circumstanced with some distressing difficultyes is sufficiently known. This consideration alone, might be enough to put us upon more solemn engagements unto the Lord our God. 5. Men are hereby brought under a stronger obligation, unto better obedience. There is an Awe of God upon the Consciences of men when so obliged. As it is in respect of Oaths, they that have any Conscience in them, when under such Bonds, are afraid to violate them. Some that are but Legalists and Hypocrites, yet solemn Covenants with God, have such an Awe upon Conscience, as to enforce them unto an outward Reformation, and that doth divert temporal Judgements. And they that are sincere, will thereby be engaged unto a more close and holy walking before the Lord, and so become more eminently blessings unto the Societyes and places whereto they [14] do belong. 6. This is the way to prevent, (and therefore also to recover out of) Apostasy. In this respect, although there were no visible degeneracy amongst us, yet this Renovation of Covenant, might be of singular advantage. There was no publick Idolatry (nor other Transgression) allowed of in the dayes of Joshua. Judg. 2. 7. Josh. 23. 8. yet did Joshua perswade the children of Israel, to renew their Covenant; doubtless, that so he might thereby restrain them from future Idolatry and Apostasy. Josh. 24. 25. Lastly, The Churches which have lately and solemnly attended this Scripture expedient, for Reformation, have experienced the presence of God with them, signally owning them therein; How much more might a blessing be expected, should there be a general concurrence in this matter?

IX. In Renewing Covenant, it is needful that the sins of the Times should be engaged against, and Reformation thereof (in the name and by the help of Christ) promised before the Lord, Ezra 10. 3. Neh. 5. 12, 13. and Chap. 10.

X. It seems to be most conducive unto Edification and Reformation, that in Renewing Covenant, such things as are clear and indisputable be expressed, that so all the Churches may agree in Covenanting to promote the Interest of holiness, and close walking with God.

XI. As an expedient for Reformation, it is good that effectual care should be taken, respecting Schools of Learning. The interest of Religion and good Literature have been wont to rise and fall together. We read in the Scripture of Masters and Scholars, and of Schools and Colledges. 1 Chron. 25. 8. Mal. 2. 12. Act. 19. 9. and 22. 3. And the most eminent Reformers amongst the Lords People of old, thought it their concern to erect and uphold them. Was not Samuel (that great Reformer) President of the Colledge at Najoth, 1 Sam. 19. 18, 19. and is thought to be one of the first Founders of Colledges. Did not Elijah and Elisha, restore the Schools erected in the Land of Israel? And Josiah (another great Reformer) showed respect to the Colledge at Jerusalem. 2 King. 22. 14. Ecclesiastical Story informs, that great care was taken by the Apostles, and their immediate Successors, for the setling of Schools in all places, where the Gospel had been preached, that so the interest of Religion might be preserved, and the Truth propagated to succeeding Generations. It is mentioned as one of the greatest mercyes that ever God bestowed upon his People Israel, that he raised up of their Sons for Prophets, Amos 2. 11. which hath respect to their education in Schools [15] of Learning. And we have all cause to bless God that put it into the hearts of our Fathers to take care concerning this matter. For these Churches had been in a state most deplorable, if the Lord had not blessed the Colledge,[1] so as from thence to supply most of the Churches, as at this day. When New-England was poor, and we were but few in number Comparatively, there was a Spirit to encourage Learning and the Colledge was full of Students, whom God hath made blessings, not only in this, but in other Lands; but it is deeply to be lamented, that now, when we are become many, and more able then at the beginnings, that Society and other inferior Schools are in such a low and languishing State. Wherefore as we desire that Reformation and Religion should flourish, it concerns us to endeavour, that both the Colledge, and all other Schools of Learning in every place, be duely inspected and encouraged.

XII. Inasmuch as a thorough and heart Reformation is necessary, in order to obtaining peace with God, Jer. 3. 10. and all outward means will be ineffectual unto that end, except the Lord pour down his Spirit from on High, it doth therefore concern us to cry mightily unto God, both in ordinary and extraordinary manner, that he would be pleased to rain down Righteousness upon us, Isai. 32. 15. Hos. 10. 12. Ezek. 39. 29. Luk. 11. 13. Amen!

---

[1] Harvard.

FINIS.

B. THE CONFESSION OF 1680

A[1] | *CONFESSION* | OF | FAITH | *Owned and consented unto by the* | *Elders* and *Messengers* | of the Churches | Assembled at *Boston* in *New-England,* | *May* 12. 1680. | *Being the second Session of that* | SYNOD. | —— | —— | Eph. 4. 5. - - - *One Faith.* | Col. 2. 5. *Joying and beholding your Order, and the* | *stedfastness of your Faith in* Christ. | —— | BOSTON; | Printed by *John Foster.* 1680.

[ii blank]

[iii]

A Preface.

THE Lord Jesus Christ witnessed a good Confession, at the time when he said, To this end was I born, and for this cause came I into the World, that I should bear witness unto the Truth; *and he taketh notice of it, to the praise and high commendation of the Church in* Pergamus, *that they held fast his name, and had not denied his* Faith. *Nor are they worthy of the name of Christians, who though the Lord by his Providence call them publickly to own the Truth they have professed, shall nevertheless refuse to declare what they believe, as to those great and fundamental Principles in the Doctrine of Christ, the knowledge whereof is necessary unto Salvation. VVe find how ready the Apostle was to make* A Confession of his Faith; *though for that hopes sake he was accused, and put in chains. And the Martyrs of Jesus, who have laid down their lives in bearing witness to the truth, against the Infidelity, Idolatry, Heresy, Apostasie of the world, when Pagan, Arian, or overspread with Popish darkness*: *ha-*[iv]*ving their feet shod with the preparation of the Gospel of peace, were free and forward in their Testimony, confessing the Truth, yea sealing it with their blood.* With the heart man believeth unto Righteousness, and with the mouth Confession is made unto Salvation. *Rom.* 10. 10. *Nor is there a greater evidence of being in a state of salvation, then such a Confession, if made in times or places where men are exposed to utmost suffering upon that account.* 1 Joh. 4. 15. *And if Confession of Faith be, in some cases, of such importance and necessity, as hath been expressed*; *it must needs be in it self, a work pleasing in the sight of God, for his Servants to declare unto the world, what those Principles of Truth are, which they have received, and are* (*by the help of Christ*) *purposed to live and dye in the stedfast Profession of. Some of the Lords Worthyes have been of renown among his People in this respect*; *especially* Irenæus *and* Athanasius *of old, and of latter times* Beza, *all whose* (*not to mention others*) Confessions, *with the advantage which the Church of God hath received thereby, are famously known. And it must needs tend much to the honour of the dear and blessed name of the Lord Jesus, in case many Churches do joyn together in their Testimony. How signally the Lord hath owned the* Confession *of the four general* Synods *or* Councils *for the suppression of the Heresyes of those times, needs not to be said, since no man can be ignorant thereof, that hath made it his* [v] *concern to be acquainted with things of this nature. The Confession of the* Bohemians, *of the* Waldenses, *and of the Reformed Protestant Churches abroad* (*which also, to shew*

[1] On a fly-leaf, facing this title, is a copy of the approval of the Court (*ante*, p. 422), signed by its Secretary, Edward Rawson.

what Harmony in respect of Doctrine there is among all sincere Professors of the Truth, have been published in one Volume) all these have been of singular use, not only to those that lived in the Ages when these Declarations were emitted, but unto Posterity, yea unto this day.

There have been some who have reflected upon these New-English Churches *for our defect in this matter, as if our Principles were unknown; wheras it is well known, that as to matters of Doctrine we agree with other Reformed Churches: Nor was it that, but what concerns Worship and Discipline, that caused our Fathers to come into this wilderness, whiles it was a land not sown, that so they might have liberty to practice accordingly. And it is a ground of holy rejoycing before the Lord, that now there is no advantage left for those that may be disaffected towards us, to object any thing of that nature against us. For it hath pleased the only wise God so to dispose in his Providence, as that the Elders and Messengers of the Churches in the Colony of the* Massachusets *in* New-England, *did, by the Call and Encouragement of the honoured General Court, meet together* Sept. 10, 1679. *This Synod at their second Session, which was* May 12. 1680. *consulted and considered of a* [vi] *Confession of Faith. That which was consented unto by the Elders and Messengers of the* Congregational Churches *in* England, *who met at the* Savoy (*being for the most part, some small variations excepted, the same with that which was agreed upon first by the Assembly at* Westminster, *&* *was approved of by the Synod at* Cambridge *in* New-England, *Anno* 1648. *as also by a general* Assembly *in* Scotland) *was twice publickly read, examined and approved of: that little variation which we have made from the one, in compliance with the other may be seen by those who please to compare them. But we have (for the main) chosen to express our selves in the words of those Reverend Assemblyes, that so we might not only with one heart, but with one mouth glorifie God, and our Lord Jesus Christ.*

As to what concerns Church-Government, *we refer to the Platform of Discipline agreed upon by the Messengers of these Churches* Anno 1648. *& solemnly owned & confirmed by the late Synod.*

What hours of Temptation may overtake these Churches, is not for us to say. Only the Lord doth many times so order things, that when his People have made a good Confession, *they shall be put upon the trial one way or other, to see whether they have (or who among them hath not) been sincere in what they have done. The Lord grant that the loins of our minds may be so girt about with Truth, that we may be able to withstand in the evil day, and having done all, to stand.*

[1]

A CONFESSION OF FAITH.

[This Confession fills pages 1 to 65 of the little book, and is so nearly identical with the doctrinal part of that adopted at the Savoy Synod in 1658 that I have ventured to omit the text here, and to refer the reader to pages 367 to 402 of this volume, where the Savoy Confession may be found, and where the few variations of this Confession from its prototype are indicated in the notes.]

XIV

THE HEADS OF AGREEMENT OF 1691

Editions and Reprints

I. *Heads of Agreement Assented to by the United Ministers in and about London: Formerly called Presbyterian and Congregational, London, 1691.* 4° pp. [vi], 16.[1]

II. Cotton Mather, *Blessed Unions . . . a Discourse Which makes Divers Offers, for those Unions; Together with A Copy of those Articles, where-upon a most Happy Union, ha's been lately made between those two Eminent Partiès in England, which have now Changed the Names of Presbyterians, and Congregationals, for that of United Brethren*, Boston, 1692, 12° pp. x, 86, 12.

III. Cotton Mather, *Magnalia*, London, 1702, Book V: 59–61; ed. Hartford, 1853–5, II: 273–276.

IV. At New London in 1710, in connection with the Result of the Saybrook Synod, and in the subsequent editions of that Result.[2]

V. Neal, *History of New England*, London, 1720, II: 656–663.

VI. Bogue & Bennett, *History of Dissenters*, London, 1808–12; ed. 1833, I: 382–386.

VII. In *The Discipline Practised in the Churches of New England*, Whitchurch, Salop, England, 1823.

VIII. In *The Cambridge and Saybrook Platforms . . . with the Confession of . . . 1680; and the Heads of Agreement assented to by the Presbyterians and Congregationalists in England in 1690.* Boston, T. R. Marvin, 1829, pp. 125–132.

IX. T. C. Upham, *Ratio Disciplinæ*, Portland, 1829, pp. 303–311.

X. In *Congregational Order. The Ancient Platforms of the Congregational Churches of New England . . . Published by direction of the General Association of Connecticut*, Middletown, 1843, pp. 251–263.[3]

Sources

Matthew Mead, *Two Sticks made one, or the Excellence of Unity. Being a Sermon Preached by the Appointment of the Ministers of the Congregational and Presbyterian Perswasion, at their Happy Union. On the sixth day of April, 1691,*[4] London, 1691.

A Brief History of Presbytery and Independency, from their first original to this Time . . . With some remarks on the late Heads of Agreement,[5] etc., London, 1691.

---

[1] Full title in reprint at close of this chapter. [2] See next chapter.

[3] Dr. Dexter notes other editions of *Congregational Order*, as Hartford [1842] and 1845.

[4] Unfortunately about all the historical value of this sermon is in its title. The preacher gave abundant exhortation, but no facts.

[5] Anonymous, contains little of value.

Free Thoughts occasioned by the Heads of Agreement,[1] etc., London, 1691.

A History of the Union between the Presbyterian and Congregational Ministers in and about London, and the Causes of the Breach of it,[2] London, 2nd ed., 1698.

LITERATURE

Cotton Mather, *Blessed Unions*, etc.[3] C. Mather, *Magnalia*, London, 1702, ed. Hartford, 1853–5, II: 272. Neal, *History of New England*, London, 1720, II: 411. C. Mather, *Parentator. Memoirs of Remarkables in the Life and the Death of the Ever-Memorable Dr. Increase Mather*, Boston, 1724, pp. 147, 148. Bogue & Bennett, *History of Dissenters*, London, 1808–12; ed. 1833, I: 381. Bacon, *Discourse*, in *Cont. Eccles. History of Connecticut*, New Haven, 1861, pp. 35–37. Fletcher, *History of Independency*, London, 1862, IV: 266–268. J. Waddington, *Congregational History, 1567–1700*, London, 1874, pp. 675–677. Dexter, *Congregationalism, as seen in its Literature*, p. 489. Stoughton, *History of Religion in England*, London, 1881, V: 293–299.

THE Westminster Assembly and the later history of Parliament during the struggle with Charles I. showed clearly the radical difference in view between Presbyterians and Congregationalists. Alike in doctrine, in their hatred of prelacy, and in their conceptions of the proper forms of worship, and largely accordant in their views as to the nature of the ministry and its functions, their great point of divergence was in regard to the existence or non-existence of a national church. To such an institution the Presbyterians clung. In their estimation the local congregation was to be a part of a reformed church of England, responsible to a series of church courts which should knit together the whole. In the Congregational view, on the other hand, no such thing as a national church existed. There should be churches, each independent in its local concerns, each bound to its neighbors by links of fellowship and advice (though on this point English Congregationalism never arrived at any such clearness of conception as was attained in New England); but over these churches the Congregationalist would place no ecclesiastical body, self-constituted or representative of the churches as a whole, whose behests could bind the action of the smallest local congre-

[1] Anonymous, I have not seen this tract.

[2] An exceedingly well-informed account of the rupture of the Union, written by an anonymous Congregationalist.

[3] See No. II. under *Texts*. It contains little of value beyond a dedication to Matthew Mead, John Howe, and Increase Mather, as the authors of the Union.

gation. Here, then, was a radical and, as experience proved, irreconcilable difference of conception.

But though the great body of Presbyterians and Congregationalists walked in divided paths, there were not wanting a number of attempts at union under the Commonwealth. Such a union was effected, on principles which reflect credit on the Christian charity of the two parties, in the far northwestern counties of Cumberland and Westmoreland in 1656.[1] At about the same time similar associations came into being in Worcestershire, Devonshire, Essex, Dorset, Wiltshire, Hampshire, Yorkshire, and Lancashire.[2] But though these bodies had some partial success in fusing together the rival parties in these various districts of England, the populous region immediately about London saw no real union between them under the Commonwealth.

With the Restoration the whole situation was changed. The repressive acts of the government bore on Congregationalists and Presbyterians with impartial severity. The Act of Uniformity of 1662[3] drove some 2,000 Puritan ministers from their livings in the Church of England. The same year saw, for the first time since the Reformation, the prescription of episcopal ordination as a necessity for all who held benefices in the English Church. The Conventicle Act of 1664 rendered public worship, save in accordance with the rites of the Establishment, almost impossible;[4] while the Five Mile Act of 1665[5] made it very difficult for a Puritan minister to earn a living. Under such hardships the differences between Presbyterians and Congregationalists became less and

---

[1] *The Agreement of the Associated Ministers and Churches of the Counties of Cumberland, and VVestmerland* . . . London . . . 1656. Some extracts from this valuable tract, illustrative of the earlier union efforts between Congregationalists and Presbyterians, will be given at the close of this introduction.

[2] See the *Brief History of Presbytery and Independency*, London, 1691, p. 27; and Briggs, *American Presbyterianism*, New York, 1885, pp. 77, 78.

[3] Passed May 19, 1662, went into force August 24. There was an excuse for such an act in the removals made by the Parliament and Commonwealth; but the cost to the Church of England itself was appalling. Compare the remarks of J. R. Greene, *History of the English People*, III: 346, 347.

[4] May 7, 1664. This law forbade any religious meeting of more than five persons outside of one family, save in conformity with the Establishment, the penalty being transportation on conviction by a justice of the peace and without jury trial, on the third offense.

[5] Oct. 30, 1665. It forbade any non-conformist minister, who would not swear never to attempt any alteration in Church or State, to come within five miles of a corporate town or Parliament borough, or to teach school anywhere.

less. The national church, for which Presbyterians had longed, was evidently a dream impossible of realization. The persistent efforts of many of their leaders for some kind of a compromise which would give them a place in a more comprehensive Establishment were without result. It was evident that, hunted as they were, the most strenuous Presbyterians were in a position practically similar to that of the Congregationalists. They could maintain little more than isolated congregations, fortunate if able to secure advice and fellowship from other bodies similarly situated, but unable effectively to operate any elaborate system of church courts or ecclesiastical assemblies. So it came about that, under the pressure of persecution, the remnants of the two bodies drew closer together; and after the first relief from their burdens came in the Declaration of Indulgence of 1673, by which Charles II. wished to favor his Catholic friends and obtain some degree of popularity with the Non-conformists, the leaders of the Congregationalists and Presbyterians in the vicinity of London strove earnestly for a union. Renewed persecution in 1682 ended their attempts for the time.[1]

With the success of the Revolution of 1688, effected by the joint action of Churchmen and Non-conformists, and the consequent passage of the Toleration Act in 1689,[2] the right of Dissenters to exist and to worship was legally recognized, though under somewhat onerous conditions; but neither Congregationalists nor Presbyterians could look for any wide extended acceptance of their polities. All the circumstances of their situations counseled the union of bodies so similar in beliefs and practical administration. Much of that which had seemed important under the Commonwealth and which had divided the two parties, was now clearly a matter of theoretic desirability rather than practically attainable. Accordingly, not long after the passage of the Toleration Act

---

1 "Some Ministers several Years ago, [were stirred up] to attempt something towards the Healing of the Differences between the Brethren of the *Presbyterian* and *Congregational Persuasion*, in Matters of Discipline, but before they could bring their laudable Enterprize to any Ripeness, a stop was put to their Pious and Peaceable Undertaking, by the Persecution raised against them in the Year 1682." *Hist. of the Union between Presb. and Cong. Ministers*, etc. London, 1698, p. 1.

2 May 24, 1689.

representatives of the Presbyterian and Congregational ministers in the vicinity of London began to negotiate regarding an agreement.[1] The movement was throughout, it would appear, purely ministerial, and one in which the churches, as distinguished from their pastors, had no share.[2]

On the Congregational side the leading representative was Matthew Mead,[3] the pastor of a large church at Stepney, then a suburb of London. As a pronounced and earnest Non-conformist he had suffered persecution under Charles II. and James II., and, while in no sense a theologian or an orator of the first rank, was a worthy and honored representative of the Congregational body.

On the side of the Presbyterians the chief leader was John Howe,[4] famous for at least thirty-five years previous as the most eloquent of English preachers, and chaplain under Oliver and Richard Cromwell. Howe had been at that time a Congregationalist, but his kindly sympathy not only for Presbyterians but for the then proscribed clergymen of the abolished Establishment made him many friends among Episcopalians, and brought at the Restoration offers of profitable and distinguished preferment in the revived Church of England. But his conscience would not allow him to accept any of them, under the conditions of the repressive acts of the opening years of Charles II., and he was consequently the object of much persecution. On the first opportunity he had returned to London, and at the accession of William III. was looked upon as the foremost Dissenter in England. Howe's Non-conformity, though conscientious and self-sacrificing, was broad. He hoped with increasing earnestness, as time went on, that an adjustment might be reached by which he and like-minded men might be admitted to a place in a modified Established Church.[5] Nor did

---

1 "When *all true Englishmen* were freed from the dismal Fears of the return of *Popery* . . . the Endeavours for a nearer Coalition between the *Presbyterian* and *Congregational* Brethren were Reviv'd; Select Persons were Deputed by both sides to treat upon Terms of Union, and their Debates issued in the Heads of Agreement." *Hist. of the Union*, etc., p. 2.

2 Compare Bacon, *Discourse* in *Cont. Eccles. Hist. Conn.*, p. 36.

3 Died Oct. 16, 1699, aged 70. He had assisted Rev. William Greenhill, had been pastor at Great Brickhill, Bucks, till compelled to go to Holland on account of supposed connection with the "Rye-House Plot." On returning he became one of the leading preachers in the vicinity of London.

4 Among the many sources of information regarding Howe, I may distinguish the *Dict. of National Biography*, XXVIII: 85–88. He was now pastor of the Presbyterian church in Silver Street, London.

5 Compare Stoughton, *Hist. Religion in England*, V, 310, 311.

this hope seem wholly vain. Some of the more liberal of the prelates of the Church of England believed it feasible; one or two actually entered into correspondence with Howe regarding it. King William was known to be favorable to such an extension of the borders of the Established Church. Among the Dissenters these views of Howe found general sympathy in Presbyterian quarters, while the Congregationalists, disbelieving as they did in the desirability of a national church, almost unanimously rejected them. So it came about that, under his desire for an honorable union with the Church of England, Howe drifted from association with the Congregationalists, and, without apparently any radical change of view on the subject of church polity, was numbered with the Presbyterians.

The strongest influence, however, in the accomplishment of the Union seems to have been that of Increase Mather,[1] then serving as the agent of the Massachusetts Colony in England.

It seems not improbable that the first motion toward the Union came from the desires of the newly emancipated Puritans to perpetuate an educated ministry. At all events the first fruits of the new spirit of brotherliness appeared in the establishment, on July 1, 1690, by benevolent Puritans, of a Fund to aid feeble churches and to educate candidates for the pastoral office. For the furtherance of this enterprise the donors invited many of the ministers about London to advise with them, and they, accepting the call, appointed seven Presbyterian pastors, among them John Howe, and seven Congregational ministers, including Matthew Mead, as Trustees of the new General Fund.[2] The union in benevolence thus

---

[1] Compare C. Mather, *Blessed Unions*, (1692) p. [iii]; *Magnalia*, II: 272; *Parentator*, pp. 147, 148. The latter says: "There was an Happy UNION accomplished between those Two Religious Parties, which go under the Names of *Presbyterian* and *Congregational* . . . Dr. *Annestey* and Mr. *Vincent* and others, often Declared, That this *Union* would never have been Effected, if Mr. *Mather* had not been among them; and they often therefore Blessed GOD, for bringing him to *England*, and keeping him there. He had Thanks from the *Country*, as well as the *City* on that Account: And among the rest, a General Assembly of Ministers in *Devon*, sent up to *London* this Instrument.

'*Junij* 23. 1691. Agreed, That the Reverend Mr. *John Flavel*, Moderator of this Assembly send unto the Reverend Mr. *Matthew Mead*, Mr. *John How*, and Mr. *Increase Mather*, and give Them, and such Others as have been Eminently Instrumental in Promoting the *Union*, the Thanks of this Assembly, for the great Pains they have taken therein.'"

[2] Extracts from the documents and the names of the Trustees will be found in Briggs, *American Presbyterianism*, Appendix, pp. lvi-lix.

begun had doubtless a powerful effect in paving the way for fellowship in all church relationship.

Under the guidance of Mead, Howe, and Mather, the negotiations for full fellowship between the two parties made more rapid and favorable progress than at any earlier time in their history. Agreement was reached with substantial unanimity;[1] and, on April 6, 1691, the Union was formally declared at a joint meeting of the ministers of both parties settled in the vicinity of London, and celebrated by a sermon from Matthew Mead.[2] The movement thus begun at London spread rapidly to the country. Rev. John Flavel journeyed to Exeter with the express purpose of introducing the Union into Devonshire and Cornwall, and died just as he had accomplisned his task.[3] Similar associations were formed in Hampshire, Norfolk, Nottinghamshire, and the West Riding of Yorkshire.[4] For a time Presbyterian and Congregational ministers in England seemed really one body.

The document on which the Union was based, like similar compromises generally, minimizes as far as possible the distinguishing features of both systems. In a true sense it is open to the keen criticism of one of its contemporary Congregational opponents, that:[5]

"it was no more than a *Verbal Composition*, or a number of Articles *industriously* and *designedly* framed with great *Ambiguity*, that Persons retaining their different Sentiments about the same Things, might yet seem to Unite."

Part of this vagueness is doubtless due to the fact that the *Heads of Agreement* did not represent the theories of the signers regarding church government in their entirety. The agreement was not intended to be a complete treatise on ecclesiastical polity, but simply a treaty in accordance with which two bodies of men of somewhat divergent views might work together in harmony. But in so far as the document is positive, it leans in the direction of Congregationalism. It is, as Dr. Bacon affirmed, "in fact, though

1 "The *Congregational* Brethren who refused to come into the Union were but few, and are said to be no more then three." *Hist. of the Union*, etc., p. 5.

2 *Two Sticks made one*, etc. See *ante*, p. 440.

3 Palmer's abridgement of Calamy, *Nonconformist's Memorial*, London, 1775, I: 355.

4 Stoughton, *Hist. of Religion in England*, V: 294, 295.

5 *Hist. of the Union*, etc., p. 3.

not in name, a Congregational platform,"[1]— and one fairly accordant with the Cambridge Platform. That this was the case was natural. Of the three men most instrumental in its composition, two were Congregationalists, while the third, though at the time affiliated with the Presbyterians, was a Congregationalist by early training, and had joined his new associates more from approval of their general attitude toward possible union with the Church of England than from preference for the more permanent features of Presbyterianism. Then, too, the *Heads of Agreement* could not but recognize the existence of some divergence of views even in the Union, and the toleration of such divergence of necessity signified that some degree of liberty of judgment and action — that is to say, some measure of Congregational self-government — was allowed to the congregations whose ministers composed the association.[2] The *Heads of Agreement* contain no implication that church courts, synods, or general assemblies are desirable. It is indeed clearly affirmed that in cases affecting the welfare of the churches, advice is to be sought of the ministers of other churches. To be thoroughly Congregational, it should have included the brethren of other churches as well as their ministers. But the judgment thus invoked is no judicial sentence; it is no further binding than the results of a New England council.[3] Churches are defined, in a sense quite acceptable to Congregationalists, as "particular Societies of Visible Saints" (or as we should now say, professedly regenerate persons,) "who under Christ their Head, are statedly joined together for ordinary Communion with one another, in all the Ordinances of Christ."[4] And, furthermore, it is affirmed that these churches enjoy their right to the ordinances "upon their mutual declared consent and agreement *to walk together therein according to Gospel Rule*"[5]— an agreement which is a true covenant, though it may vary in "expliciteness." These churches have, severally, the "Right to chuse their own Officers" and to administer their own affairs;[6] and in such administration the consent at least

[1] *Contr. Eccles. Hist. Conn.*, p. 36.
[2] Compare *Ibid.*
[3] *Heads of Agreement*, § VI.
[4] *Ibid.*, § I: 2.
[5] *Ibid.*, § I: 4.
[6] *Ibid.*, § I: 6.

of the brethren is to be obtained.[1] No church is subordinate to any other and no "Officer, or Officers, shall exercise any *Power*, or have any *Superiority* over any other Church, or their Officers."[2] In calling a pastor churches are, ordinarily, to consult the neighboring ministers, and these ministers are, usually, to unite with the preaching officers of the church (in case such exist) in the candidate's ordination.[3] A wise provision declared that those who proposed to enter the Gospel ministry ought to be examined as to their "Gifts and fitness" by able pastors of churches.[4]

The leading features of the *Heads of Agreement* are thus essentially Congregational. They differ, indeed, on some points from the usages of the founders of New England, but save in their silence respecting the presence of representatives of the brethren in councils, they fairly set forth the practices of the third generation on New England soil; and, as such, partly justify the extravagant statement of Cotton Mather, that "'tis not possible . . . to give a truer description of our [New England] 'ecclesiastical constitution.'"[5] Even the uncertainty of the *Heads of Agreement* regarding the Ruling Eldership not unfairly represents the state of the New England mind at the close of the seventeenth century.

It is as a document of importance in New England church history, rather than in the story of English Congregationalism, that the *Heads of Agreement* have special value. Prepared, like the Savoy Confession, by Englishmen for English use (if we except the agency of Increase Mather), like that symbol, they have been chiefly employed in New England.

That they were so used was the natural result of the instrumentality of the one American, Increase Mather, who had a share in the formation of the Union. His son Cotton, on receipt of a copy, at once preached on them to his Boston congregation, and the two laudatory sermons which he then delivered, together with the text of the *Heads of Agreement*, were printed and circulated about New England in 1692.[6] When, ten years later, the greatest

---

[1] *Ibid.*, § I: 7; III: 3.
[2] *Ibid.*, § IV: 2.
[3] *Ibid.*, § II.
[4] *Ibid.*, § II: 7.
[5] *Magnalia*, II; 272.
[6] *Blessed Unions*, etc., Boston, 1692.

historical work that the first century of American Christianity produced, the *Magnalia*, was given to the world, the *Heads of Agreement* were given an honored place side by side with the New England symbols and declared to be the best possible exposition of existent Congregationalism. The Mathers seem to have been proud of their work and to have furthered the knowledge of it and esteem for it as far as possible. So it came about that when the Saybrook Synod met in 1708 to frame an ecclesiastical constitution for Connecticut, the *Heads of Agreement* were widely known in New England, and must have been thought by many to be the most modern and popular presentation of Congregationalism. They served well to set forth the principles which the Saybrook Synod wished to enunciate, and though incomplete without the addition of the fifteen Articles establishing Connecticut's peculiar consociational and associational system, the *Heads of Agreement* sweetened those Articles, softened their interpretation, and made them palatable to many who would otherwise have refused them. Approved with the rest of the Saybrook result by the General Court of the colony in October, 1708,[1] they continued a part of the legal basis of the Connecticut churches till 1784, when the Saybrook system was quietly omitted from the statutes.[2] But they remain as one of the factors which have shaped Connecticut Congregationalism.

The fate of this document in the land of its origin was curiously unlike that which characterized it in America. In England the *Heads of Agreement* proved ephemeral enough. Like the Savoy Confession they were soon forgotten; but for a different reason. The Union of which they were to be the foundation fell apart in the first strain of theologic controversy, and before the decade which saw their birth had closed Presbyterians and Congregationalists in the vicinity of London were as far apart as ever. The circumstances of this melancholy breach were closely connected with a doctrinal contest which convulsed all the Non-conformist bodies of England, and even involved some representatives

[1] *Conn. Records*, V., 87.

[2] Dr. L. Bacon, in *Contr. Eccles. Hist. Conn.*, p. 62.

of the Establishment.[1] Dr. Tobias Crisp had been an eminent clergyman under Charles I., and had long served as rector of Brinkworth, Wiltshire. His theory of imputation was so strenuous as to lead, so his opponents thought, to Antinomian results. He held, it would appear, that our Lord so took upon himself human sin as to become personally as sinful as man, and, on the other hand, all who believe so receive Christ's righteousness here as to become as holy as Christ. Crisp died in 1643, and the arguments which were to prove the bombshell in the united camp of Presbyterians and Congregationalists remained for nearly fifty years for the most part unpublished. But just about the time of the Union they were brought to light by Crisp's son, and printed with a note signed by several prominent Non-conformist ministers attesting the genuineness of the manuscript.[2] The views of Dr. Crisp were so extreme that the work was at once answered by Dr. Daniel Williams,[3] one of the chief Presbyterians of London, a preacher of power, a moderate Calvinist, and the founder of the great Non-conformist library, which is now one of the treasure-houses of the history of Puritanism. Imitating the example of the younger

[1] Some general facts of value regarding the Crispian dispute may be found in Stoughton, *History of Religion in England*, V: 296–300. Its connection with the Union between Presbyterians and Congregationalists is given in the anonymous *History of the Union . . . And The Causes of The Breach of it*, to which frequent reference has been made. While the immediate cause of the rupture of the Union was the Crispian dispute, there were evidences of friction from the first between Presbyterians and Congregationalists. Many leading Presbyterians at the time, and notably John Howe, hoped for some readjustment of the Establishment by which a portion at least of the Dissenters could be comprehended. The Congregationalists did not generally favor the idea. The author of the *Hist. of the Union* says (pp. 3–5): "They [Congregationalists] could not but observe how some of the Prime Promoters of this Union were such as in the time of Persecution had by their Compliance deserted the Cause of the *Non-conformists* [Howe had submitted to the Five Mile Act in 1665] . . . The Chief Leaders in the Union begin now to speak freely of this Business, and declare to this Purpose: *That it was the intendment of the Union to comprehend and include such as were for Sacramental Communion with the Church of* England. This is that which is disallowed generally by the *Congregational* Brethren. . . . They took Notice how some Aspiring Tempers of the *Presbyterian* Party begin to drive at *Jurisdiction* over other *Churches*. . . . They perceiv'd that there was a Design to discountenance the *Congregational* Churches up and down the Nation. They thought the Instances of *Sandwich* and *Marlborough* amounted to a Presumptive Evidence of this." On the other hand, the Presbyterians were offended that the Congregationalists held separate meetings "in Reference to things belonging to *Congregational Churches*, which were not proper and adviseable to be debated in Conjunction with the *Presbyterian Ministers*." (*Ibid.*, p. 6.)

[2] I have not seen this book, but I suppose it to be *Christ Made Sin*, London, 1691.

[3] In *Gospel Truth Stated and Vindicated*, London, 1692. This celebrated divine at his death, Jan. 16. 1716, left part of a considerable property to maintain his library for public use. This became the nucleus of the library once known, from its street location in London, as the "Red-Cross Library," but now removed to Grafton street and bearing the name of its founder.

Crisp, Williams procured the commendatory signatures of sixteen of the most prominent Presbyterian ministers of the day, a number which was increased on the publication of a second edition of his work to forty-nine, thus including more than half the Presbyterians in the Union.[1] The Congregationalists seem to have been no more pleased with the supposed Antinomianism of Dr. Crisp than the Presbyterians; but Dr. Williams was one of the Presbyterians who had seemed to them most filled, as the historian of the quarrel puts it, with "a *prejudiced Spirit* against the Government of the Congregational Churches, and the Order wherein they walk."[2] Anything from his pen must of course be suspicious, and as the Congregationalists read his reply to Crisp it appeared to them that Williams had fallen into errors no less serious than those he refuted, had voided the atonement of significance, and had attacked the fundamental doctrines of Protestantism generally. Thus it came about that, while a majority of the Presbyterians in the new Union supported Williams, a considerable number of Congregationalists opposed, and six of the latter joined in a "Paper of Exceptions"[3] which Rev. Isaac Chauncy[4] of London

---

[1] "The *Congregational Brethren* were offended at several Managements in the Union, but never Deserted it till *that* happened which forc'd them at last to leave it. *It was this*: Mr. *Daniel Williams* Published a Book against Dr. *Crisp*'s Opinions, and with the Confutation of the Doctor's Opinions, he did interweave several Notions of his own, which have been reckoned contrary to the Received and Approved Doctrine of the *Reformed Churches*. . . . This Book could not but give offence . . . yet it would have been pass'd by . . . if it had not been for the Attestation given to it by several *Presbyterian Ministers* of the Greatest Figure. . . . There were Sixteen concerned in the First Testimonial, and . . . in the Re-Printing of the Book the List of Names was increased from Sixteen to Forty Nine of the Union, which was by far the Majority of the *Presbyterian Party*, that were in it. It occasioned much grief of Heart to the *Congregational Brethren*." *Hist. of the Union*, etc., pp. 6, 7.

[2] *Hist. of the Union*, p. 3.

[3] They were Rev. Messrs. George Griffith, Thomas Cole, Nathanael Mather, Isaac Chauncy, Robert Trail, and Richard Taylor. The whole of the brief paper may be found in Chauncy's *Neomianism Unmask'd: or, the Ancient Gospel Pleaded, Against the Other, called a New Law or Gospel*, London, 1692–3, Part III, pp. 96, 97. The exceptions are wholly doctrinal, and are chiefly as follows: "2. Under a colour of opposing some old *Antinomian* Errors . . . he [Daniel Williams] falls in with them in their main Principle of vacating the Sanction of the moral Law. . . . 3. That to supply the room of the moral Law, vacated by him, he turns the Gospel into a new Law, in keeping of which we shall be justified for the sake of Christ's Righteousness, whereby he boldly strikes both at Law and Gospel, . . . making Qualifications and Acts of ours, a disposing, subordinate Righteousness, whereby we become capable of being justified by Christ's Righteousness. . . . 5. He teacheth, That the Righteousness of Christ is imputed only as to Effects, with a Purchase of a conditional Grant, *viz.* this Proposition, *He that believeth shall be saved* . . . Contrary to the Doctrine of Imputation and Redemption."

[4] Eldest son of Pres. Charles Chauncy of Harvard, born in 1632, graduated at Harvard in 1651 and went to England, where he resided till his death, Feb. 28, 1712. At this time he was min-

laid before the meeting of the United Ministers, October 17, 1692, and accompanied by a heated speech in which he gave "the Reasons why he look'd upon the Union to be broken, and Perverted from its right End, and therefore would be no longer a Member of it."[1] The Union as a whole was not as hot-headed as Mr. Chauncy; and as a means of re-establishing peace, appointed a non-partisan committee of five or six of their number who had never subscribed Williams's publication[2] to meet with "Five of the Noted Subscribers to it,"[3] and with the five protesting signers of the "Paper of Exceptions" who still remained members of the Union after Chauncy's withdrawal. But, as is frequent in such cases, "Many Meetings were held to little or no purpose,"[4] and negotiations dragged on till December, 1694, when "The *Objectors* were now Convinced, That they had Complain'd of Mr. *Williams*'s Errors, to Men who would give them no Reason to think they were *Impartial*, and from this time [the] *Congregational Brethren* grew weary of the Meeting of the Ministers at *Little St. Hellens*, [the meeting-place of the Union,] and did in a manner wholly withdraw from it."[5] At about the same time the Presbyterian and Congregational trustees of the General Fund fell apart into separate boards.[6] One more fruitless effort for adjustment was made in March, 1696;[7] but the breach in the London Union of Congregationalists and Presbyterians was irreparable. How far the country associations which had been formed on the basis of the *Heads of Agreement* were affected is difficult to say, but the object for which the *Heads of Agreement* were framed, viz.: the Union of Presbyterians and Congregationalists in and about London, had utterly failed.

ister of a church in London; and then, or a little later, divinity tutor in the Dissenter's Academy in London. An account of him and a list of his writings is given in Sibley, *Grad. of Harvard*, I: 302–307.

1 *Hist. of the Union*, pp. 7, 8.

2 *Ibid.*, p. 12. They were Rev. Messrs. Matthew Mead, Sam. Annestey, Edward Veale, John James, and Stephen Lobb. "Mr. [Matthew] Barker was also appointed to be one, but seldom met with them."

3 *Ibid.* Rev. Messrs. John Howe, Geo. Hammond, Vincent Alsop, Richard Mayo, and Sam. Slater.

4 *Ibid.*, p. 13.

5 *Ibid.*, p. 16.

6 See Briggs, *American Presbyterianism*, Appendix, p. lviii. The last joint meeting recorded was June 26, 1693; the first separate meeting of the Presbyterians was Feb. 5, 1695.

7 *Hist. of the Union*, etc., pp. 23–25.

UNION EFFORTS, 1656, 1691

A. Extracts from the Agreement of 1656

The | Agreement | of the | Associated Ministers & Churches | of the | Counties | of | Cumberland, | And | VVestmerland: | . . London 1656.

[3] . . . In order to the carrying on of this great work [of union], wee lay down and assent unto these general rules, as the Basis and Foundation which must support and bear up our following Agreement.

1 THat in the exercise of Discipline, it is not onely the most safe course, but also most conducing to brotherly union and satisfaction, That particular Churches carry on as much of their work with joynt and mutual assistance, as they can with conveniency and edification, and as little as may be in their actings, to stand distinctly by themselves, and apart from each other.

2. That in matters of *Church Discipline*, those things which belong onely *ad melius esse* † († Things not essential), ought to be laid aside, both in respect of publication and practice, rather then that the Churches peace should be hindered.

3. That where different principles lead to the same practice, wee may joyn together in that practice, reserving to each of us our own principles.

4. That when we can neither agree in principle, nor in practice, we are to bear with one another's differences, that are of a less and disputable nature, vvithout making them a ground of division amongt us.

[4] Yet notwithstanding,[1] we do not hereby binde up our selves from endeavouring to inform one another in those things wherein we differ, so that it be done with a spirit of love and meekness, and vvith resolutions to continue our brotherly amity and association, though in those particulars our differences should remain uncomposed.

Upon these grounds we agree as followeth.

[They then promise to preach faithfully, catechise, reprove prevalent sins, ask the consent of their people to a brief confession of faith and covenant (the two documents are given, and are similar to those used in New England), insist on "unblameable conversation" and acquaintance with the main doctrines of religion from all who come to the Supper, yet they]

[16] agree, not to press a declaration of the time and manner of the work of grace upon the people, as a necessary proof of their actual present right to the Lords Supper, nor to exclude persons meerly for want of that, yet will we accept it, if any will be pleased to offer it freely . . . [17] When a Minister is to be ordained

[1] Misprinted *wnotithstanding*.

unto a congregation, we agree, That godly and able mini-[18] sters of neighbor congregations, be called to be employed in the examination and trial of the fitness of the party to be set apart to that weighty Office, and in the act of Ordination.

Though we differ about the first subject of the power of the Keys,[1] yet forasmuch as we all agree, That the affairs of the Church are to be managed by the Officers thereof, therefore we conclude that the examination and determination of things in cases of admission and rejections, and other church acts, shall be permitted by the Officers; yet so that the people have notice of what they resolve and conclude upon, in matters of moment, that in case any thing be done against which the people may (upon probable grounds at least) object from the word of God, it may either be forborne, or their satisfaction endeavoured. . . .

[19] Albeit we differ as to the power of associated churches over particular congregations; yet, we agree that it is not only lawful and useful, but in many cases necessary, that several churches should hold communion and correspondency together; and to that end we resolve to associate our selves, & to keep frequent meetings for mutual advice and help, as occasion shall require.

VVe take our selves and our churches bound to follow whatsoever advice, direction or reproof, (being agreeable to the word) any of us shall receive from the Brethren in association with us. . .

[20] For the better carrying on of our intended association, we resolve to observe these following rules.

1. We judge it convenient to divide our selves into three associations, (*viz.*) at *Carlile*, at *Penrith*, and *Cockermouth*, and shall meet once a Moneth, or more or less, as occasion shall require, and the major part of the association shall think fit. . . .

2. At these meetings we shall hear and determine things of common concernment, endeavour to resolve doubts, compose differences, consider the justness & weight of the grounds and reasons of Ministers removals from any place, when such cases shall fall out, consult and advise about spe-[21] cial emmergencies that may happen to our Ministry or congregations in particular.

[They also agree that the three associations are "sometimes to meet all together."]

[1] *I. e.*, as to the seat of authority in church administration.

B. The Heads of Agreement, 1691

Heads of Agreement | Assented to by the | **United Ministers** | In and about London: | Formerly called | PRESBYTERIAN | and | CONGREGATIONAL. | —— | **Licensed and Entred according to Order.** | —— | *LONDON*: | Printed by *R. R.* for **Tho. Cockerill,** at the *Three Legs*, | and **John Dunton** at the *Raven*, in the | *Poultrey*. MDCXCI.

[ii blank]

[iii]

THE

Preface to the Reader.

ENdeavours *for an Agreement among Christians, will be grievous to none who desire the flourishing State of Christianity it self.*

The Success of these Attempts among us, must be ascribed to a Presence of God so signal, as not to be concealed; and seems a hopeful Pledg of further Blessings.

The favour of our Rulers in the present Established Liberty, we most thankfully acknowledg; and to Them we are studious to approve our selves in the whole of this Affair. Therefore we Declare against intermedling with the National *Church-Form: Imposing these Terms of Agreement on others, is disclaimed: All pretence to Coercive Power, is as unsuitable to our Principles, as to our Circumstances: Excommunication it self, in our respective Churches, being no other* [iv] *than a declaring such scandalous Members as are irreclaimable, to be incapable of Communion with us in things peculiar to Visible Believers: And in all, we expresly determine our purpose, to the maintaining of Harmony and Love among our selves, and preventing the inconveniences which humane weakness may expose to in our use of this Liberty.*

The general concurrence of Ministers and People in this City, and the great disposition thereto in other places, persuade us, this happy Work is undertaken in a season designed for such Divine influence, as will overcome all impediments to Peace, and convince of that Agreement which has been always among us in a good degree, tho neither to our selves nor others so evident, as hereby it is now acknowledged.

Need there any Arguments to recommend this Union? Is not this what we all have prayed for, and Providence by the directest indications hath been long calling and disposing us to? can either Zeal for God, or prudent [v] *regards to our selves remissly suggest it, seeing the Blessings thereof are so important, and when it's become in so many respects even absolutely necessary; especially as it may conduce to the preservation of the Protestant Religion, and the Kingdoms Weal; a subserviency whereto, shall always govern our United Abilities, with the same disposition to a concurence with all others who are duly concerned for those National Blessings.*

As these considerations render this Agreement desirable, so they equally urge a watchful care against all attempts of Satan to dissolve it, or frustrate the good effects thereof so manifestly destructive to his Kingdom. Therefore it's incumbent on us, to forbear condemning and disputing those different sentiments and practices we have expresly allowed for: To reduce all distinguishing Names, to that of United Brethren: *To admit no uncharitable jealousies, or censorious speeches; much less any debates whether Party seems most favour-*[vi]*ed by this Agreement. Such carnal regards are of small moment with us, who herein have used words less accurate, that neither side might in their various conceptions about lesser matters be contradicted, when in all substantials we are fully of one mind; and from this time hope more perfectly to rejoice in the Honour, Gifts, and Success of each other, as our* common *good.*

That we as United, *may contribute our utmost to the great concernments of our Redeemer, it's mutually resolved, we will assist each other with our Labours, and meet and consult, without the least shadow of separate or distinct Parties:*[1] *Whence we joyfully expect great Improvements in Light and Love, through the more abundant supplies of the Spirit; being well assured we herein serve that* Prince of Peace, of the increase of whose Government and Peace, there shall be no end.

This Agreement is already assented to by above Fourscore Ministers, and the Preface approved of.

(1)

HEADS of AGREEMENT
Assented to by the
United Ministers, &c.

The following Heads of AGREEMENT *have been Resolved upon, by the* UNITED *Ministers in and about* London, *formerly called* Presbyterian *and* Congregational; *not as a Measure for any* National

[1] In spite of this positive statement and the declaration below that the Preface was "approved of," the Congregationalists, at least, seem to have intended to preserve their separate identity even under the Union; a point on which, as they were much the smaller party, they were more sensitive than the Presbyterians. The author of the *History of the Union*, etc., says (p. 6): "The *Congregational Brethren* were troubled [by some actions of the Presbyterians], yet bearing with Patience what they could not redress, they kept their Station, and albeit they had some Meetings among themselves in Reference to things belonging to *Congregational Churches*, which were not proper and adviseable to be debated in Conjunction with the *Presbyterian Ministers*, yet they did not in the least judge themselves hereby to be guilty of making any Infractions upon the Union, because the *Congregational Brethren* do to this Day aver, That they never consented to the Preface that is set before the Heads of Agreement, as any part of the Articles of the Union."

Constitution, *but for the Preservation of Order in our Congregations, that cannot come up to the Common Rule by Law Established.*

I. *Of* CHURCHES *and* CHURCH-MEMBERS.

1. WE Acknowledge our *Lord Jesus Christ* to have One *Catholick Church*, or *Kingdom*, comprehending all that are united to Him, whether in *Heaven* or *Earth*. And do conceive the [2] whole multitude of *visible Believers*, and their Infant-Seed (commonly called the *Catholick Visible Church*) to belong to *Christ's Spiritual Kingdom* in this world: But for the notion of a *Catholick Visible Church* here, as it signifies its having been collected into any formed Society, under a Visible human[1] Head on Earth, whether *one* Person singly, or *many* collectively, We, with the rest of Protestants, unanimously disclaim it.[2]

2. We agree, That particular Societies of Visible Saints, who under Christ their Head, are statedly joined together for ordinary Communion with one another, in all the Ordinances of Christ, are *particular Churches*, and are to be owned by each other, as Instituted Churches of Christ, tho differing in *apprehensions* and *practice* in some lesser things.

3. That none shall be admitted as Members, in order to Communion in all [3] the special Ordinances of the Gospel, but such persons as are knowing and sound in the *fundamental Doctrines*[3] *of the Christian Religion*, without Scandal in their Lives; and to a Judgment regulated by the Word of God, are persons of visible Godliness[4] and Honesty; credibly professing cordial subjection to Jesus Christ.

4. A competent Number of such *visible Saints*, (as before described) do become the capable Subjects of stated Communion in all the *special Ordinances of Christ*, upon their mutual declared consent and agreement *to walk together therein according to Gospel Rule*. In which declaration, different degrees of *Expliciteness*, shall no way hinder such Churches from owning each other, as *Instituted Churches*.

5. Tho *Parochial Bounds* be not of *Divine Right*, yet for common Edification, the Members of a *particular Church* [4] ought (as much as conveniently may be) to live near one another.

6. That each *particular Church* hath Right to chuse[5] their own Officers; and being furnished with such as are *duly qualified* and

---

[1] Saybrook reads *common*.

[2] The Saybrook Synod added proof-texts to each paragraph of the *Heads of Agreement*, as well as to the *Confession* of 1680.

[3] Saybrook reads *Doctrine*. [4] Saybrook reads *Holiness*. [5] Saybrook reads *use*.

ordained according to the Gospel Rule, hath Authority from Christ for exercising Government, and of enjoying all the *Ordinances of Worship* within it self.

7. In the Administration of *Church Power*, it belongs to the *Pastors* and other *Elders* of every particular Church (if such there be)[1] to *Rule and Govern*: and to the Brotherhood to *Consent*, according to the *Rule of the Gospel.*

8. That all Professors as before described, are bound in duty, as they have opportunity, to join themselves as *fixed Members* of some particular Church; their thus joining, being part of their professed subjection to the *Gospel of Christ*, [5] and an instituted means of their Establishment and Edification; whereby they are under the *Pastoral Care*, and in case of *scandalous* or *offensive walking*, may be Authoritatively Admonished or Censured for their recovery, and[2] for vindication of the *Truth*, and the *Church* professing it.

9. That a *visible Professor* thus joined to a *particular Church*, ought to continue stedfastly with the said Church; and not forsake the Ministry and Ordinances there dispensed, without an orderly seeking a recommendation unto another Church. Which ought to be given, when the case of the person apparently requires it.

II. *Of the* MINISTRY.

1. WE agree, That the *Ministerial Office* is instituted by Jesus Christ, for the Gathering, Guiding, Edifying, and Governing of his *Church*; and to continue to the end of the world.

[6] 2. They who are called to this *Office*, ought to be endued with *competent Learning*, and *Ministerial Gifts*, as also with the Grace of God, sound in Judgment, not Novices in the Faith and Knowledg of the Gospel; without scandal, of holy Conversation, and such as *devote* themselves to the Work and Service thereof.

3. That ordinarily none shall be Ordained to the work of this Ministry, but such as are *called* and *chosen* thereunto by a particular Church.

4. That in so great and weighty a matter as the calling and chusing a *Pastor*, we judg it ordinarily requisite, That every such Church consult and advise with the *Pastors* of Neighbouring Congregations.

5. That after such *Advice* the Person consulted about, being chosen by the Brotherhood of that particular Church over [7]

[1] Saybrook omits ( ) signs.

[2] Saybrook omits *and.*

which he is to be set, and he accepting, be duly ordained, and set apart to his Office over them; wherein 'tis ordinarily requisite, That the *Pastors* of *Neighbouring Congregations* concur with the *Preaching-Elder*, or *Elders*, if such there be.

6. That whereas such *Ordination* is only intended for such as never before had been ordained to the *Ministerial Office*; If any judge, that in the case also of the removal of one formerly *Ordained*, to a new Station or *Pastoral Charge*, there ought to be a like Solemn recommending him and his Labours *to the Grace and Blessing of God*; no different Sentiments or Practice herein, shall be any occasion of *Contention* or *Breach of Communion* among us.

7. It is expedient, that they who enter on the work of *Preaching the Gospel*, be not only qualified for[1] Communion of Saints; but also that, except in *cases extraordinary*, they give proof of their *Gifts* and *fitness* [8] for the *said work*, unto the *Pastors* of Churches, of *known abilities* to discern and judge of their *qualifications*; That they may be sent forth with *Solemn Approbation* and *Prayer*; which we judge needful, that no doubt may remain concerning their being Called to[2] the work; and for preventing (as much as in us lieth) *Ignorant and rash Intruders.*

III. *Of* Censures.

1. As it cannot be avoided, but that in the *Purest Churches* on Earth, there will sometimes *Offences* and *Scandals* arise by reason of *Hypocrisie* and *prevailing corruption*; so Christ hath made it the Duty of every Church, to reform it self by *Spiritual Remedies*, appointed by him to be applied in all such cases; *viz. Admonition*, and *Excommunication.*

2. *Admonition*, being the rebuking of an *Offending Member* in order to convicti-[9]on, is in case of *private offences* to be performed according to the Rule in *Mat.* 18. *v.* 15, 16, 17. and in case of *Publick offences*, openly before the Church, as the *Honour of the Gospel*, and *nature of the Scandal* shall require: And if either of the *Admonitions* take place for the recovery of the *fallen Person*, all further proceedings in a way of *censure*, are thereon to cease, and *satisfaction* to be declared accordingly.

3. When all *due means* are used, according to the *Order of the Gospel*, for the restoring an *offending* and *scandalous Brother*; and he notwithstanding remains Impenitent, the Censure of *Excommunication* is to be proceeded unto; Wherein the *Pastor* and other

[1] Saybrook inserts *the*. [2] Saybrook reads *unto*.

Elders (if there be such) are to lead, and go before the *Church*; and the Brotherhood to give their consent, in a way of obedience unto Christ, and unto[1] the *Elders*, as over them in the Lord.

4. It may sometimes come to pass, [10] that a *Church-Member*, not otherwise Scandalous, may *sinfully withdraw*, and divide himself from the *Communion of the Church* to which he belongeth: In which case, when all *due means* for the reducing him, prove ineffectual, he having thereby cut himself off from *that Churches Communion*; the *Church* may justly esteem and declare it self discharged of any further inspection over him.

IV. *Of* Communion *of* Churches.

1. We Agree, that *Particular Churches* ought not to walk so distinct and separate from each other, as not to have care and tenderness towards one another. But their *Pastors* ought to have frequent meetings together, that by mutual Advice, Support, Encouragement, and Brotherly intercourse, they may strengthen the hearts and hands of each other in the *ways of the Lord.*

[11] 2. That none of *our* particular Churches shall be *subordinate* to one another; each being endued with *equality of Power* from Jesus Christ. And that none of the said particular Churches, their Officer, or Officers, shall exercise any *Power*, or have any *Superiority* over any other Church, or their Officers.

3. That known Members of particular Churches, constituted as aforesaid, may have occasional Communion with one another in the *Ordinances of the Gospel*, viz. the *Word*, *Prayer*, *Sacraments*, *Singing*[2] *Psalms*, dispensed according to the mind of Christ: Unless that Church, with which they desire Communion, hath any just exception against them.

4. That we ought not to admit any one to be a Member of our respective *Congregations*, that hath joined himself to another, without endeavours of mutual Satisfaction of the *Congregations*[3] concerned.

[12] 5. That *one Church* ought not to blame the Proceedings of *another*, until it hath heard what *that Church* charged, *its Elders*, or *Messengers*, can say in vindication of themselves from any charge of *irregular* or *injurious Proceedings.*

6. That we are most willing and ready to give an account of our *Church Proceedings* to each other, when desired; for preventing or removing any offences that may arise among us. Likewise we shall be ready to give the right hand of fellowship, and walk together according to the *Gospel Rules* of *Communion of Churches.*

---

[1] Saybrook reads *to.* [2] Saybrook inserts *of.* [3] Saybrook reads *Congregation.*

V. *Of* Deacons *and* Ruling Elders.

We agree, The Office of a *Deacon* is of Divine Appointment, and that it belongs to their Office to receive, lay out, and distribute the *Churches Stock* to its *proper uses*, by the direction of the *Pastor*, and Brethren if need be. And [13] whereas divers are of opinion, That there is also the Office of *Ruling Elders*, who labour not in *word and doctrine*; and others think otherwise; We agree, That *this difference* make no *breach* among us.

VI. *Of Occasional* Meetings[1] *of Ministers*, &c.

1. We agree, That in order to *concord*, and in any other *weighty* and *difficult* cases, it is needful, and according to the *mind of Christ*, that the Ministers of[2] several Churches be consulted and advised with about such matters.

2. That such Meetings may consist of *smaller* or *greater Numbers*, as the matter shall require.

3. That *particular Churches*, their respective *Elders*, and *Members*, ought to have a reverential regard to their judgment so given, and not dissent therefrom, without *apparent* grounds from the word of God.

[14]

VII. *Of our* Demeanour *towards the* Civil Magistrate.

1. We do reckon our selves obliged continually to pray for God's *Protection*, *Guidance*, and *Blessing* upon the *Rulers* set over us.

2. That we ought to yield unto them not only *subjection in the Lord*, but *support*, according to our station and abilities.

3. That if at any time it shall be their pleasure to call together any Number of us, or require any[3] *account* of our *Affairs*, and the state of our *Congregations*, we shall most readily express all *dutiful regard* to them herein.

VIII. *Of a* Confession *of* Faith.

As to what appertains to *soundness of Judgment* in *matters of Faith*, we esteem it sufficient, That a Church acknowledge the *Scriptures to be the word of God*, the *perfect and only Rule of Faith and* [15] *Practice*; and own either the Doctrinal part of those commonly called the *Articles* of the Church of *England*, or the *Con-*

---

[1] Saybrook reads *meeting*. [2] Saybrook inserts *the*. [3] Saybrook reads *an*.

fession, or *Catechisms*, *Shorter or Larger*, compiled by the *Assembly* at *Westminster*, or the *Confession* agreed on at the *Savoy*, to be agreeable to the said Rule.

IX. *Of our* Duty *and* Deportment *towards them that are not in Communion with us.*

1. We judge it our duty to bear a *Christian Respect* to all Christians, according to their several Ranks and Stations, that are not of our *Persuasion* or *Communion.*

2. As for such as may be ignorant of the Principles of the *Christian Religion*, or of *vicious conversation*, we shall in our respective Places, as they give us opportunity, endeavour to explain to them the *Doctrine of Life and Salvation*, and to our uttermost[1] persuade them to be reconciled to God.

[16] 3. That such who appear to have the *Essential Requisites* to *Church-Communion*, we shall willingly receive them in the Lord, not troubling them with Disputes about *lesser matters.*

As we Assent to the forementioned Heads of Agreement; *So we Unanimously Resolve, as the Lord shall enable us, to* Practice *according to them.*

FINIS.

[1] Saybrook reads *utmost.*

XV

THE PROPOSALS OF 1705, AND THE SAYBROOK PLATFORM OF 1708

A. Proposals of 1705

a. Full Text and Signatures

I. *Question and Proposals: What Further Steps are to be taken, that the Councils may have due Constitution and Efficacy*, etc. 12° [1705].[1]

II. In *Minutes of the Proceedings of the General Association of Massachusetts Proper* for 1814, pp. 5–9 (from a manuscript left by Cotton Mather); reprinted therefrom in the *Panoplist*, X: 322–324.

b. The Signatures Omitted

III. In Wise, *The Churches Quarrel Espoused*; *or, a Reply in Satyre, to certain Proposals made, in Answer to this Question: What further Steps*, etc., Boston, 1710; again in new editions of the same work in 1715, twice in 1772, and in 1860, all at Boston.

Literature

John Wise, *The Churches Quarrel Espoused* (as above), Boston, 1710, etc. Wise, *Vindication of the Government of New England Churches*, etc., Boston, 1717; again twice in 1772, and in 1860, all at Boston.[2] Cotton Mather, *Ratio Disciplinæ*, Boston, 1726, pp. 176–185. J. S. Clark, *Historical Sketch of the Cong. Churches in Mass.*, Boston, 1858, pp. 115–121. Clark, *Introductory Notice* to 1860 edition of Wise's works. M. C. Tyler, *History of American Literature*, New York, 1879, II: 105–110. Dexter, *Congregationalism, as seen*, etc., New York, 1880, pp. 491–502. H. A. Hill, *History of the Old South Church*, Boston, 1890, I: 331–334. A. P. Marvin, *Life and Times of Cotton Mather*, Boston. [1892], pp. 313, 314.

The Attempted Revival of the Proposals in 1814

Minutes of the Proceedings of the General Association of Massachusetts Proper, for 1814–16; reprinted also in the *Panoplist*, Boston, X: 316–328; XI: 357–379; XII: 369. Articles in *Panoplist*, XI: 507–518, 537–545; XII: 489–495. Theophilus [Samuel Spring], *Essay on the Discipline of Christ's House; containing Remarks on the "Plan of Ecclesiastical Order," which the General Association has presented for Publick Consideration*, Newburyport, 1816. [John Lowell], *Inquiry into the Right to change the Ecclesiastical Constitution of the Congregational Churches of Massachusetts*, Boston, 1816. Clark, *Historical Sketch of the Congregational Churches in Massachusetts*, pp. 252–254. Dexter, *Congregationalism, as seen*, etc., pp. 512, 513. H. A. Hill, *History of the Old South Church*, II: 381, 382.

---

[1] I have never seen this pamphlet; but it is clearly the original of the copy given by Wise.

[2] A re-statement of Congregational principles, called forth by the discussion aroused by the *Proposals*, rather than a direct reply to them.

B. The Saybrook Platform

Text and Editions

The Full Result. I. *a. A Confession of Faith, Owned and Consented to by the Elders and Messengers Of the Churches in the Colony of Connecticut, in New-England, Assembled by Delegation at Say-Brook September 9th.* 1708. New London, 1710. *b. The Heads of Agreement, Assented to by the United Ministers formerly called Presbyterian and Congregational. And also Articles for the Administration of Church Discipline Unanimously Agreed upon and consented to by the Elders and Messengers of the Churches in the Colony of Connecticut in New-England, Assembled by Delegation at Say-Brook, September 9th.* 1708. New London, 1710. 8° pp. ii, 116.

II. Same titles, New London, 1760.

III. Same titles, Bridgeport, 1810.

IV. Hartford, 1831.

V. Same titles, Hartford, 1838.

VI. In *Congregational Order*, Middletown, 1843, pp. 153–286.[1]

The Articles only. **1**. Trumbull, *History of Connecticut*, ed. Hartford, 1797, pp. 510–513, ed. New Haven, 1818, I: 483–486; **2**. *The Cambridge and Saybrook Platforms of Church Discipline, with the Confession of Faith of . . . 1680; and the Heads of Agreement . . . Illustrated with Historical Prefaces and notes*, Boston, 1829, pp. 115–123; **3**. Upham, *Ratio Disciplinæ*, Portland, 1829, pp. 311–316; **4**. Elliott, *The New England History*, New York, 1857, II: 119–124; **5**. Walker, *History of the First Church in Hartford*, Hartford, 1884, pp. 452–455.

Sources

1. *Records of the Colony of Connecticut*, V: (Hartford, 1870), pp. 51, 52, 87, 97, 98, 192, 193, 423, 449; XI: 333, 565, 566; **2**. Trumbull, *History of Connecticut*, ed. Hartford, 1797, pp. 508–514; ed. New Haven, 1818, I: 481–487.

The Varying County Interpretations

a. New Haven, Jonathan Todd, *A Faithful Narrative Of the Proceedings, of the First Society and Church in Wallingford, in their Calling, and Settling The Rev. Mr. James Dana*, etc. New Haven, 1759, pp. 33–37. Congregational Order, Middletown, 1843, pp. 284–286. *b*. Fairfield, Orcutt, *History of the Old Town of Stratford and the City of Bridgeport*, [New Haven], 1886, I: 312, 313. *150th Anniversary of the Fairfield County Consociation*, Bridgeport, 1886, pp. 32–34.

Literature

T. Clap, *Brief History and Vindication of the Doctrines Received and Established in the Churches of New England*, New Haven, 1755, *passim*. E. Stiles, *A Discourse on the Christian Union*, Boston, 1761, *passim*. [T. Fitch], *An Explanation of Say-Brook Platform*, Hartford, 1765. N. Hobart, *An Attempt to illustrate and Confirm The Ecclesiastical Constitution of the Consociated Churches . . . Occasioned by a late Explanation of the Saybrook Platform*, New Haven, 1765. T. Clap, *The Annals or History of Yale-College*, New Haven, 1766, pp. 12, 13. Trumbull, *History of Connecticut*, ed. Hartford, 1797, pp. 504–515, ed. New Haven, 1818, I: 478–488. T. Dwight, *Travels*, New Haven, 1822, IV: 423–435.

[1] Dr. Dexter gives other editions of 1842 and 1845.

L. Bacon, *Historical Discourses*, New Haven, 1839, pp. 189–192. D. D. Field, in *Congregational Order*, Middletown, 1843, pp. 11–72. L. Bacon, in *Contributions to Eccles. Hist. Conn.*, New Haven, 1861, pp. 31–62. Palfrey, *History of New England*, IV: 369–371. G. L. Walker, *History of the First Church*, Hartford, 1884, pp. 263–268. A. Johnston, *Connecticut*, Boston, 1887, pp. 230–235.

Part I

THE PROPOSALS OF 1705

THOUGH the Reforming Synod doubtless had some effect in bettering the religious condition of New England, the results were not what its promoters had hoped. The closing years of the seventeenth century were times of trial for New England; the loss of the Massachusetts charter, the tyranny of Andros, the vain efforts to secure a renewal of the ancient privileges of the leading colony, as well as the disastrous outcome of the two attempts to capture Quebec, and the demoralizing struggles with the Indians, together with the grim tragedy of the witchcraft delusion, all combined to make the political and commercial outlook of the colonies gloomy and to render a high degree of spiritual life difficult of maintenance in the churches. If the second generation on New England soil had shown a decided declension from the fervent zeal of the founders, the third generation was even less moved by the early ideals. The founders had borne part in a movement which had embraced a nation. They had been the leaders in an attempt to establish in a new England the principles of worship and church-government which were believed in and struggled for by a great party at home. For a time, the rulers of England had looked with favor on their enterprise and had sought counsel of their experience. But all this was changed. New England was no longer the vanguard of the great Puritan cause of the mother-land. That party in England had spent its force. New England had become of necessity provincial, when the triumph of Episcopacy in old England had made her cease to be a factor of consequence in the religious life of that land, for the bond between the home land and the new settlements across the sea had been religious far more than political or commercial. And in the struggles and disasters of the latter half of the seventeenth century the

New Englander had become narrower in thought and in sympathy than his father had been. If he had grown more tolerant toward variations in religion, it was the result of increasing religious indifferentism, itself the natural consequence of reaction from the high-wrought experiences of the first generation. It was with pathetic, almost exaggerated, consciousness of their own comparative feebleness that the ecclesiastical writers of the second and third generations looked back to the giants of the early days;[1] for the New England of 1700 was meaner, narrower, in every way less inspired with the sense of a mission to accomplish and an ideal to uphold, than the New England of 1650.

To the majority of the ministers of the time the outlook seemed full of peril. The recent political changes, and even more the passing away of the older generation, had greatly lessened the influence of the ministry on legislation and the conduct of government. The restiveness which had all along been more or less felt under the rule of the clerical element had gathered strength. In Boston foreign influence had established Episcopacy,[2] and though Episcopacy was distinctly an exotic on Massachusetts soil, there were an increasing number of persons throughout the churches who desired more or less modification of the prevalent strictness in regard to admissions and of the almost universal restriction of the choice of ministers to members in full communion. These two tendencies were brought most sharply into contrast at Boston, then, as now, the intellectual center of the commonwealth. The conservative party embraced most of the older and more prominent ministers of the colony. Its leader was unquestionably Increase Mather, teacher of the Second Church in Boston, and since 1685 president of Harvard, who, though far from universally popular, had been for thirty years the most influential minister in New England. With him may be reckoned, since they were one in

[1] See *e. g.* John Higginson and William Hubbard, *Testimony to the Order of the Gospel*, Boston, 1701. This is doubtless the fond recollection of two old men; but their tone of veneration is to be heard in many of the New Englanders of more youthful years at the close of the eighteenth century.

[2] On the origins of Episcopacy in Boston see Rev. Henry W. Foote, *Memorial Hist. of Boston*, I: 191–216. Efforts looking toward the establishment of Episcopal worship were made in 1679. In 1686 services were begun.

sympathy and aim, his son Cotton Mather,[1] from 1685 his colleague in the pastorate of the Boston Church. To the same party, also, belonged such ministers as James Allen of the Boston First Church, John Higginson and Nicholas Noyes of Salem, William Hubbard of Ipswich, Samuel Cheever of Marblehead, and Joseph Gerrish of Wenham. To these men the true method of bettering the religious state of New England seemed to lie in a return to the principles of the founders as illustrated in the Cambridge Platform; and such an enforcement of discipline within the local church and exercise of watch over the churches by councils representative of the whole fellowship of a colony or district as would prevent the incoming of looser fashions and preserve uniformity of discipline and procedure. All this implied an increase in ministerial and synodical authority,—an increase the more difficult to obtain at a time when the political and spiritual tide in Massachusetts ran strongly in the other direction.

The desires of this conservative party found chief expression in the two classes of meetings in which the ministers of that day gathered for conference, the Ministers' Convention and the District Associations. Though the general nature and the methods of each of these two classes of meetings in Massachusetts is clear, their origin is somewhat obscure. There is every reason to believe, however, that the Ministers' Convention can trace its source, in germ at least, to the beginning of the colony; while the local Associations, at least as continuously existing bodies, are of a much later date.[2]

It had been the custom from the earliest days of New England for the ministers to gather at the meetings of the General Court,[3] especially at the Court of Election in May. Their advice was

---

[1] By far the best picture of Cotton Mather is contained in Prof. Barrett Wendell's *Cotton Mather*, New York [1891].

[2] Valuable, though by no means exhaustive, articles on the history of these bodies are those by A. H. Quint in *Cong. Quart.*, II: 203–212; V: 293–304; and S. J. Spalding, *Ibid.*, VI: 161–175; also in *Cont. Eccles. Hist. Essex Co., Mass.*, pp. 8–56.

[3] Hints of such meetings are scattered through Winthrop's Journal, see *e. g.* I: 157, 363; II: 3, 76. The statement of Lechford is direct; *Plain Dealing*, Trumbull's reprint, p. 62. Whether the ministers met at first as an organized body is perhaps doubtful. The *Hist. Sketch of the Convention of the Cong. Ministers in Mass.*, Cambridge, 1821, p. 5, says that the "presumptive evidence" is "that there was no organized Convention before the year 1680."

frequently taken by that body while Massachusetts was administered in accordance with the first charter, and though by the close of the seventeenth century the ministry was no longer the political factor that it had been, these meetings were continued, and were occasions of considerable ceremony. Cotton Mather speaks of the custom in his *Magnalia* as existing "in each colony";[1] and in the *Ratio Disciplinæ* enters into quite a description of this annual Ministerial Convention, as it was early in the eighteenth century. He thus pictures the Assembly:[2]

"The Churches of *New-England* . . . have no *Provincial Synods* . . . The Thing among them that is the nearest thereunto, is a *General Convention* of Ministers, (which perhaps are not above half)[3] belonging to the *Province*, at the time of the *Anniversary Solemnity*, when the *General Assembly* of the Province meets, on the last *Wednesday* in the Month of *May*, to elect their *Counsellors* for the Year ensuing. *Then* the *Ministers*, chusing a *Moderator*, do propose Matters of public Importance, referring to the Interest of Religion in the Churches; and tho' they assume no *Decisive* Power, yet the Advice which they give to the People of GOD, has proved of great Use unto the Country.

There is now taken up the Custom, for (*Concio ad Clerum*,) a Sermon to be Preached unto the Convention of Ministers, on the day after the *Election*, by one of their Number, chosen to it by their *Votes*, at their Meeting in the preceeding Year.

At this *Convention*, Every Pastor that meets with singular Difficulties, has Opportunity to bring them under Consideration. But the Question most usually now considered, is of this Importance; *What may be further proposed, for the preserving and promoting of true PIETY in the Land*?

Excellent Things have been here Concerted and Concluded, for, *The Propagation of Religion*; and *Collections* produced for that Purpose in all the Churches.

And Motions have been hence made unto the *General Assembly* for such *Acts* and *Laws* as the *Morals* of the People have called for.

[[4] The *Governour* of the Province, and such Councellors as dwell in the City of *Boston*, together with the *Representatives* of the Town, & the Speaker of their *House*; are invited also to dine with the *Ministers*, at the Table, which the *Deacons* of the united Churches in *Boston* provide for them, the Day after the *Election* . . .]."

This Ministerial Convention, so well described by Cotton Mather, was far from being a Synod, but it discussed questions of great moment,[5] and its advice was much respected. It might be

---

[1] Ed., 1853–5, II: 271.

[2] Pp. 176, 177.

[3] *I. e.*, not more than half the ministers of the province were usually in attendance.

[4] The brackets are Mather's.

[5] *E. g.*, in 1697 the body protested against "tendencies which there are amongst us towards Deviations from the good Order wherein our Churches have . . . been happily established." In 1698 they decided, by a vote lacking but one of unanimity (Stoddard ?), that "the Church Covenant as Commonly practised in the Churches of New-England" is Scriptural. Increase Mather, *Order of the Gospel*, Boston, 1700, pp. 8, 9, 39.

made the instrument of a more centralized church government; or if not itself the head of a more consolidated ecclesiastical system, might recommend such a union to the churches.

Beside this Ministerial Convention, there were at the opening of the eighteenth century, five district Associations in Massachusetts,[1] all tracing their immediate origin to the Association meeting at Cambridge, which had been founded in October, 1690, and included most of the ministers in the vicinity of Boston. There had been Ministerial Meetings, similar to the later Associations, in the early days of the colony. Winthrop records, in November, 1633, that "The ministers in the bay and Sagus did meet, once a fortnight, at one of their houses by course, where some question of moment was debated;"[2] and that Skelton of Salem and Roger Williams "took some exception against it, as fearing it might grow in time to a presbytery,"—a fear which the governor did not share, for the ministers "were all clear in that point, that no church or person can have power over another church; neither did they in their meetings exercise any such jurisdiction." This little association doubtless included all of the few ministers then in Massachusetts who were able or willing to belong to it. Lechford, writing in 1641, found the same meeting and the same anti-Presbyterian fears;[3] and the *Body of Liberties*, adopted in December of that year, had expressly granted ministers "free libertie to meete monthly, quarterly, or otherwise, in convenient numbers and places;" but these meetings were to be "onely by way of brotherly conference and consultations."[4] The Ministers' Assembly which the Presbyterian ways of Rev. Messrs. Parker and Noyes called together at Cambridge in 1643 declared "that Consociation of churches, in way of more general meetings, yearly; and more privately, monthly, or quarterly; as *consultative Synods;* are very

[1] The signatures to the *Proposals* of 1705 show the existence of five Associations at that date. It illustrates the obscurity of the subject, however, that the careful article written by Dr. Quint 30 years ago knew nothing of the existence of two of the five and was unable to trace the third to a period earlier than nearly 20 years subsequent to 1705.

[2] Winthrop, ed. 1853, I: 139. Sagus is Lynn.

[3] *Plain Dealing*, Trumbull's reprint, p. 37. Dr. Trumbull has illustrated the passage, as usual, with notes of great value.

[4] *Ibid.*, notes p. 38; 3 *Coll. Mass. Hist. Soc.*, VIII: 234, 235.

comfortable, and necessary for the peace and good of the churches."[1]

But, for reasons not now very easy to discover, unless it be for fear of Presbyterian tendencies, these early meetings seem to have fallen into complete disuse. Rev. Thomas Shepard of Charlestown, in his election sermon of 1672,[2] declared that he remembered such gatherings in his childhood, and there were "hundreds yet living" who could "remember the ministers meetings in the several towns by course, at Cambridge, Boston, Charlestown, Roxbury, &c." And the much later satire of John Wise, *The Churches Quarrel Espoused*, confirms the testimony of Shepard that they were disused by the close of the third quarter of the seventeenth century. "About Thirty years ago, more or less," he says (writing about 1710), "there was no appearance of the Associa ions of Pastors in these Colonies, and in some Parts and Places, there is none yet."[3]

The permanent reëstablishment of Ministers' Associations came about through English example. On September 7, 1655, such a body had been formed at Bodmin, in Cornwall.[4] Its meetings were not probably of long continuance; by the summer of 1659, the journal had closed. But the book of its Records passed into the possession of one of its members, Rev. Charles Morton; and Morton came to New England in 1686, and became speedily the pastor at Charlestown. A man of much influence in the colony, it is probable that it was his endeavors which resulted in the organization of the first permanent district Association in Massachusetts, on October 13, 1690. This body embraced most of the ministers in the vicinity of Boston, and was often called by that name,[5] though its meetings, at least during the early part of its history, were "at the College in Cambridge, on a Monday at

---

[1] *Ibid.*, Hanbury, *Memorials*, II: 343.

[2] *Eye Salve, or a Watchword from our Lord Jesus Christ unto His Churches*, p. 29; quoted by Quint, *Cong. Quart.*, II: 204.

[3] Second ed., 1715, p. 79.

[4] The record book of this body, containing a list of the members of the Bodmin Association, and also the members and doings of the Cambridge, Mass., Association from 1690 to 1704, is in the possession of the Mass. Hist. Society. It is described and the names of members given by A. H. Quint, *Cong. Quarterly*, II: 204–207.

[5] It is so called in the signatures to the *Proposals*, of 1705. Its meeting place was eventually Boston, but its records from 1704 to 1753 are lost. See *Cong. Quart.*, V: 294.

nine or ten of the clock in the morning, once in six weeks, or oftener."[1] Its pledge of union and its rules were based on those of the Bodmin body. The example thus set was followed by the organization of similar bodies, in Essex County, about Weymouth, about Sherborne, and in Bristol County, during the last decade of the seventeenth and first three or four years of the eighteenth centuries.[2]

These organizations felt their purpose to be deliberative, as well as social. That at Cambridge had for its aim:[3]

"1. To debate any matter referring to ourselves.

2. To hear and consider any cases that shall be proposed unto us, from churches or private persons.

3. To answer any letters directed unto us, from any other associations or persons.

4. To discourse of any question proposed at the former meeting."

Under these rules the body set itself, led, it may well be believed, by the Mathers, to a general overhauling and strengthening of Congregational usage.[4] The most conspicuous of these attempts to put a stricter interpretation on current Congregationalism are perhaps the following:[5]

"Synods, duly composed of messengers chosen by them whom they are to represent, and proceeding with a due regard unto the will of God in his word, are to be

---

[1] Its rules are given in full in the *Magnalia*, ed. 1853–5, II: 271, 272.

[2] Indications of the existence of another association, in Essex Co. (Salem it is called in the signatures of 1705), may be found in the records of the Cambridge body as early as Nov., 1691. *Cong. Quart.*, II: 208. When the next association further north than Salem, that at Bradford, was organized in 1719, its formula of union was the same as that of Bodmin and Cambridge. As the Bradford association probably sprang from that at Salem, it indicates a common origin for all. The Cambridge records as early as 1692 imply the existence of at least three associations. Dr. Quint conjectured that the third was Plymouth. But Plymouth does not appear in the list of signers of 1705, where we find instead, Weymouth, Sherborne, and Bristol.

[3] *Magnalia*, II: 272, Rule vi.

[4] Cotton Mather gives the texts of a long series of conclusions of this body, the Matherine origin of most of which seems evident from their style, *Magnalia*, II: 239–269. An enumeration of the main subjects treated shows the scope of the discussions: 1. Right of a minister to officiate in a church not his own; 2. Ruling elders; 3. Powers of councils; 4. Powers of ministers in their churches; 5. Visitation of the sick in epidemics; 6. When a minister may leave his people; 7. Marriage with the sister of a deceased wife: 8. Discipline of the baptized children of the church; 9. Just divorce; 10. Ordination; 11. Who choses a minister; 12. Resignation of Ministry; 13. Inquiries by pastors into scandals; 14. Secrets confided to ministers; 15. Duty toward withdrawers from communion; 16. Usury; 17. Special days of religious observance; 18. Eating blood and things strangled; 19. Use of ceremonies in God's worship; 20. Cards, dice, etc.; 21. Respect due to public places of worship; 22. Drinking of healths; 23. Instrumental music in the worship of God; 24. Administration of baptism by the unordained; 25. Marriage of Cousin-Germans; 26. Relation of church-discipline to civil conviction. Other topics may be found in the MS. records.

[5] Both *Magnalia*, II: 248. It is hardly needful to point out that by "synod" is signified what is now known as a "council."

reverenced, as *determining* the mind of the Holy Spirit concerning things necessary to be 'received and practised,' in order to the edification of the churches therein represented."

"Synods being of apostolic example, recommend[1] as a necessary ordinance, it is but reasonable that their judgment be acknowledged as *decisive*, the affairs for which they are ordained; and to deny them the power of such a judgment, is to render a necessary ordinance 'of none effect.'"

In these votes we see evidently the conservative feeling that individual churches and ministers should be repressed and limited by the decisive power of councils in their possible departures from the general opinion of their associates. It was this feeling which found its sharpest expression in Massachusetts history in the Proposals of 1705.

But there were not wanting those, especially among the younger ministry, and even in the Cambridge Association itself, to whom a return to the ideals of early New England was distasteful, and who looked upon the proposed strengthening of the ecclesiastical machinery as a menace to liberty of thought and action. The leaders of this party were four youngerly men of position; two of them being John Leverett[2] and William Brattle,[3] graduates of Harvard in 1680, who had become tutors in the College in 1685, the year which saw the beginning of Increase Mather's presidency, and who had taken practical charge of the college during Mather's long absence in England as agent for the colony. Leverett was destined to be Mather's second successor at the head of the college, holding that office from 1707 to his death in 1724; while Brattle, in 1696, became pastor of the Cambridge church. With these two men were associated Thomas Brattle,[4] brother of the Cambridge pastor, and from 1693 to 1713 treasurer of Harvard; and Ebenezer Pemberton,[5] a graduate of Harvard in 1691 and a tutor in that institution, who, from August 28, 1700, to his death, in February, 1717, was colleague pastor of the Third, or Old South Church, in Boston. Occupying a position between the Mathers and the innovators, and not without sympathy for the latter, was Samuel Wil-

---

1 Recommended?

2 For his biography, see Sibley, *Graduates of Harvard*, III: 180–198. 3 *Ibid.*, pp. 200–207.

4 *Ibid.*, II: 489–498. Thomas Brattle graduated in 1676.

5 See H. A. Hill, *History of the Old South Church*, I., *passim.*

lard,[1] a man considerably older than either of the four just enumerated, the teacher of the Old South Church in Boston from 1678 to 1707, the vice-president of Harvard from 1699 to 1707, and from the practical deposition of Increase Mather in 1701 in fact, though not in name, the president of the college.

The alterations sought by these men were not numerous, and to the modern student of their stories do not seem startling. Yet they are very significant as a step further away from the older New England Congregationalism and from the restraining hand of a stronger ecclesiastical government, just at the time when the Mathers and their friends were trying to restore something of the waning power of the clergy in political affairs and to revive the discipline of the churches. The work of the innovators was in two principal directions, the founding of a new church, sympathetic with their beliefs, in Boston; and the exclusion of the Mathers from the control of Harvard. Probably the personal element of opposition to these eminent conservatives was as prominent a motive in the controversy as any.

The changes desired by the innovators centered about the mode of admission to full communion. The older New England custom, still almost universally prevalent, required, at least in the case of those who were not baptized children of the church, a public relation of religious experience. In most churches such declarations, either oral or written, were expected from all. This requirement was felt by many to be a burden, especially as the prevailing type of piety was not ardent or emotional. The South Church in Boston had gone so far in 1678 as to allow those who so wished to present their "relations" to the ministers rather than to the church.[2] Then, too, the feeling had been growing in some quarters that all, or at least all baptized male adults, who contributed to the minister's support should have a voice in his selection, and the choice should not be confined, as was the usage, to members in full communion.[3] A third change desired by some, and notably,

[1] *Ibid.;* and Sibley, *Grad. of Harvard*, II: 13–36.

[2] Hill, *Hist. Old South*, I: 229.

[3] The rule was not without exceptions. In 1672 the non-communicants at Salem had shared in the choice of a minister, and at Dedham in 1685. Robbins, *Hist. Second Ch.*, Boston, 1852, pp. 41, 42: Palfrey, *Hist. N. E.*, IV: 190.

it is probable, by Thomas Brattle, on whom Episcopal forms had made an impression,[1] was what would now be called an "enrichment" of the service. The early Puritans, in their revulsion from all set forms, had disused the Lord's prayer, and usually read the Scriptures in public worship only to expound them verse by verse.[2] Reading without comment was "dumb reading,"[3] and was thought to savor of the prayer-book. The innovators desired that some portion of the Scripture, chosen by the minister, should be read at every service, and they saw advantages in the devotional reading of passages without explanation and in the repetition of the Lord's prayer. A fourth alteration desired was an extension of the right to baptism, so that not only children of those in the covenant of the churches, but any children presented by any professing Christian who would stand sponsor for their religious training should receive the ordinance.[4]

These were the looser positions held by the innovators, though not at first, it would appear, in an aggressively controversial manner; but to the Mathers and the rest of the conservative party

[1] See Sibley, *Graduates of Harvard*, II: 491.

[2] While the use of the Lord's prayer was not wholly disapproved by the conservatives of the age of which we treat, the rarity of their employment of it may be judged by a story told by Increase Mather, *Order of the Gospel*, Boston, 1700, p. 118: "Mr. *Jeremiah Burroughs* . . . [a Congregational member of the Westminster Assembly, died 1646] once when he preached his *Expository Lectures* was prevented from coming to the Assembly exactly at the Hour appointed. If he should at that time have inlarged in Prayer as he usually did, the Auditors would have been detained longer then they expected. Nor was he willing to begin his Exposition without any Prayer at all, he therefore began it with only Praying in the words of *the Lords Prayer*. This report I believe; for my most Dear and Honoured Friend Dr. *William Bates*, late Pastor of a Church in *Hackney* near *London* . . . assured that he was then present and an *Ear Witness* of what I have now related."

As regards reading the Scriptures, see Cotton Mather, *Ratio Disciplinæ*, pp. 63–68. By the time he wrote the practice had become not uncommon; yet in June, 1765, the General Association of Connecticut felt constrained to call on the local Associations of the Colony to promote the "making the Public reading of the Sacred Scriptures a part of the Public worship in our churches"; and as late as 1810, the Litchfield South Consociation passed votes favoring the practice. See Walker, *Hist. First Church in Hartford*, p. 224.

[3] I. Mather, *Order of the Gospel*, p. 47.

[4] This practice, not unlike that of god-parents of the English Church, became widely prevalent in the eighteenth century. Numerous illustrations might be cited from the Records of the First Church, Hartford. There the first entry is of Sept. 4, 1709. But the ground of the concession seems to have been usually servitude or pupilage in the family of those who stood sponsors. Thus, "Aug. 23, 1730. Deacon Sheldon offered three negroe children born in his house to Baptisme & in publick engaged to take care they should be brought up in the christian faith. They were named George: Cuffy: & Susanna"; or, "Sept. 8. 1717. Elisabeth Vibert, servant to Aaron Cooke, who publickly engaged to bring her up in the Christian faith." But sometimes the relationship is not so apparent, *e. g.*, "Octob. 9. 1715. Joseph, a child offered to baptism by Homer Howard, he publickly engaging to bring it up in the Christian faith."

they seemed to call for vigorous opposition. Nor were the Mathers wrong in their estimate of the danger to the old order of things which these novelties threatened. Accordingly, when Cotton Mather published his *Life of . . . Jonathan Mitchel*[1] in 1697, Increase Mather took occasion in a prefatory "Epistle Dedicatory," addressed "To the Church at Cambridge in New-England, and to the Students of the Colledge there," to set forth Mitchell's view of the necessity of "relations" preparatory to admission to church-membership, and to make pointed exhortations to the church, the tutors, and the students to be true to Mitchell's theories, in a way that must have seemed dictatorial, and was doubtless exasperating, to the innovators.

The "Epistle Dedicatory" was dated May 7, 1697, and in August of the same year the Mathers took occasion to attack another of the projects dear to the Brattles and their friends. Doubtless at the suggestion of its pastors, the Second Boston Church sent a letter of admonition to the Church in Charlestown, "for betraying the liberties of the churches, in their late putting into the hands of the whole inhabitants the choice of a minister."[2]

These two actions, showing clearly the spirit of the conservative party and the determination of the Mathers to enforce their views, seem to have inclined the innovators to take decided action. There were now three Congregational churches in Boston; two, the First and Second, strongly conservative, and the other more divided in feeling, but possessing prominent conservatives like Lieut.-Gov. Stoughton, Waitstill Winthrop, and Judge Sewall among its membership. None would therefore represent the innovators' views, and they determined to found a fourth[3] church.

The movement to this end seems to have taken shape late in

---

[1] Cotton Mather reprinted the whole tract, with the preface, in the *Magnalia*, ed. 1853–5, II: 66–113.

[2] Robbins, *History of the Second Church in Boston*, p. 42.

[3] For the founding of Brattle Church, see Lothrop, *History of the Church in Brattle Street*, Boston, 1851; Quincy, *History of Harvard University*, ed. Boston, 1860, I: 127–144, 486, 487, 502; Robbins, *History of the Second Church in Boston*, pp. 40–44; Palfrey, *Hist. N. E.*, IV: 189–191; A. McKenzie in *Memorial History of Boston*, II: 204–211; Sibley, *Graduates of Harvard*, biographies of the Brattle and Leverett; Brooks Adams, *Emancipation of Massachusetts*, Boston, 1887, pp. 237–254; H. A. Hill, *Hist. Old South Church*, I: 308–313. Wendell, *Cotton Mather*, *passim*.

1697; and in January, 1698, Thomas Brattle transferred to a body of associates, of which he was a leader, the site for the new meeting-house on what was then called Brattle's Close.[1] Here a plain, unpainted building was at once erected.[2] The thoughts of the associates turned toward Benjamin Colman as their future minister. This able and remarkable man had graduated at Harvard in 1692, and had therefore been under the instruction of Leverett and William Brattle. He was, moreover, the intimate friend of Ebenezer Pemberton and shared his innovating sentiments. Colman was in England at the time the erection of the new meeting-house was begun; and thither urgent letters were sent to him in May, 1699, by Leverett, William Brattle, Simon Bradstreet,[3] and Pemberton, reïnforcing a formal call signed by Thomas Brattle and four others, in the name of the associates.[4] The call was accepted, and as his reception by the three existing Boston churches was not likely to be favorable, by advice of his Boston friends, Colman procured ordination at the hands of the London Presbytery, August 4, 1699. On November first, Colman was in Boston, a full-fledged minister according to Presbyterian ideas, but no clergyman in the view of stricter Congregationalists; and on November 17th, the associates put forth a *Manifesto*,[5] declaring their firm adherence to the doctrinal standards of the churches, as set forth in the Westminster Confession, and their desire for fellowship with other churches; but asserting all the principles which we have seen cherished by the innovators, except that regarding the use of the Lord's prayer.[6] The publication of this declaration was followed, on December 12th,

---

1 Sibley, *Grad. of Harvard*, II: 491, 492.

2 Described in *Memorial Hist. Boston*, II: 207.

3 Bradstreet was minister at Charlestown, the man whose election as colleague with Morton by the votes of the whole community had called out the protests of the Boston Second Church.

4 An illustration of the prominence to be given by the church which was soon to be organized to the element which had heretofore been debarred from a share in church government may be seen in the fact that Thomas Brattle was only a half-way member of the Third Church when he thus acts as chairman of this body which thus calls a minister. The call is in Lothrop, *Hist. Brattle Ch.*, pp. 45-47.

5 The Church was hence long nicknamed the "Manifesto Church." The text may be found in Lothrop, *Hist. Brattle St. Ch.*, pp. 20-26; and a good abstract in the *Memorial Hist., Boston*, II: 208. Its authorship is uncertain, but has been usually attributed to Colman.

6 Though the use of the Lord's prayer is not mentioned in the "Manifesto," tradition asserts that it was used from the beginning in the services of Brattle Church. Lothrop, *Hist. Brattle Church*, p. 51.

by the organization of a church of fourteen members, without aid of council or countenance from other churches.

All this was thoroughly at variance with the older New England theory and practice; to the Mathers it seemed the dawning of a "day of temptation begun upon the town and land," brought about by "a company of headstrong men in the town, the chief of whom are full of malignity to the holy ways of our churches," who "have published, under the title of a *Manifesto*, certain articles that utterly subvert our churches."[1] When, therefore, the new church, in accordance with a vote passed on the day of its organization, made overtures looking toward fellowship with the other Boston churches, Increase Mather and James Allen, representing the Second and First churches, replied, under date of December 28th, that they could not join in the proposed fast unless the innovators would give "the satisfaction which the law of Christ requires for your [their] disorderly proceedings."[2] Two days later the eminent conservative ministers of Salem, John Higginson and Nicholas Noyes, addressed an earnest letter of reproof to the new church.[3] But the pastor of the Third Boston Church, Samuel Willard, and some of the members of his church, even conservative laymen like Stoughton and Sewall, strove for peace. A partial reconciliation was effected, so that on January 31, 1700, all the Boston Congregational ministers united with Mr. Colman and his congregation in the religious exercises appropriate to a fast, and thus gave them the desired recognition.[4]

But though both the Mathers took part in this fraternal service, the victorious innovators were a sore grievance to them; and therefore in March,[5] 1700, Increase Mather published what is one of the most interesting, but at the same time controversial, tracts

[1] C. Mather's Journal, in Quincy, *History of Harvard University*, ed. Boston, 1860, I: 486, 487; Brooks Adams, *Emancipation of Mass.*, pp. 245–247.

[2] Adams, *Ibid.*, pp. 247, 248; Lothrop, *Hist. Brattle St. Church*, pp. 55, 56.

[3] Lothrop, *Ibid.*, pp. 28–37.

[4] Sewall gives some account of the negotiations and the services of the fast. *5 Coll. Mass. Hist. Soc.*, VI: 2, 3. For Cotton Mather's statement see Quincy, *Hist. Harvard*, I: 487.

[5] Preface dated "1 m, 1700." The *Memorial Hist. of Boston*, II: 209, interprets this as Jan., but C. Mather's Journal shows that the printing of an "antidote," doubtless the *Order*, was just suspended at the finishing of the first sheet when the reconciliation was effected in January. Quincy, *Ibid.*

of Congregational history, his *Order of the Gospel.*[1] This little work, while it called no man by name, distinctly attacked the whole recent movement and its leaders.

"If," said Mather, "we Espouse such principles as these, Namely, *That Churches are not to Enquire into the Regeneration of those whom they admit vnto their Communion. That Admission to Sacraments is to be left wholly to the prudence and Conscience of the Minister. That Explicit Covenanting with God and with the Church is needless. That Persons not Qualified for Communion in special Ordinances shall Elect Pastors of Churches. That all Professed Christians have right to Baptism. That Brethren are to have no voice in Ecclesiastical Councils. That the Essence of a Ministers call is not in the Election of the People, but in the Ceremony of Imposing hands. That Persons may be Established in the Pastoral Office without the Approbation of Neighbouring Churches or Elders*; We then give away *the whole Congregational cause* at once, and a great part of the *Presbyterian Discipline* also."[2]

The various proposed innovations were opposed in detail; and the recent action by which the Brattle Church had organized and provided itself with a minister without the advice of neighboring churches was severely condemned in principle. Mather found Colman's foreign ordination particularly abhorrent. "To say," he remarked, "that a *Wandring Levite* who has no Flock is a Pastor, is as good sense as to say, that he that has no Children is a Father."[3] Nor did Mather's innovating subordinates at the College escape censure; he exhorted: "Let the Churches Pray for the *Colledge* particularly, that God may ever Bless that Society with faithful *Tutors* that will be true to Christs Interest and theirs, and not Hanker after new and loose wayes."[4]

To this little book an anonymous reply was issued in the same year, entitled *Gospel Order Revived*, and conjecturally the joint product of Rev. Messrs. Benjamin Colman, Simon Bradstreet, and John Woodbridge,[5] perhaps also of William Brattle.[6] The answer was personal and not very reverential; it distinctly charged Increase Mather with showing one spirit in London and another in

[1] Printed at Boston and reprinted the same year in London.

[2] *Order of the Gospel*, p. 8. Some of these views were those already entertained by Rev. Solomon Stoddard of Northampton, Mass., which were to be given to the world the same year in his *Doctrine of Instituted Churches;* a work probably called out by the *Order*.

[3] *Ibid.*, p. 102.

[4] *Ibid.*, pp. 11, 12.

[5] So Sibley, *Grad. of Harvard*, I: 455. It has sometimes been attributed to Stoddard, but with no certainty, and also credited to Solomon Southwick, see *Nation*, LV: 415.

[6] Adams, *Emancipation of Mass.*, p. 250.

Boston, and it laughed at some of his criticisms of uncommenting reading as if they were a valuation of Mather's own comments above the word of God. Yet the expression which perhaps most stirred the Mathers was in the advertisement prefaced to the work, which declared that "the Press in *Boston* is so much under the aw of the Reverend Author, whom we answer, and his Friends, that we could not obtain of the Printer there to print the following Sheets."[1] The extent to which this allegation was true caused not a little discussion;[2] and the work was answered, in 1701, by a pretty personal pamphlet, not improbably written by Cotton Mather, and certainly prefaced by his father.[3] But though Increase Mather denounced the writer of *Gospel Order Revived*, whom he supposed to be Colman, as "of a very unsanctified temper and spirit," and affirmed that Thomas Brattle had done as "a moral heathen would not have done," the Brattle Church grew and flourished. The conservative party were the defeated party; and it is not to be wondered that those who loved the New England of the fathers felt alarmed at the outlook.

Their alarm was the greater because the conservative party in Boston had employed other means to check the growth of the innovating movement beside the publication of pamphlets. On May 30, 1700, about three months after the issue of Increase Mather's *Order of the Gospel*, the Ministerial Convention brought together its annual assemblage of the pastors of the province at Boston.[4] And, under Mather's lead,[5] they passed the following vote, designed to prevent the establishment of a second Brattle Church:[6]

"To prevent the great mischief to the Evangelical Interests, that may arise from the unadvised proceedings of People to gather Churches in the Neighbourhood,

---

[1] Leaf before title. The work was printed in New York, though no place is given on the title.

[2] See Thomas, *Hist. Printing in America*, II: 346; Palfrey, *Hist. N. E.*, IV: 191. The statement seems only partially true.

[3] *A Collection of Some of the Many Offensive Matters, Contained in a Pamphlet, entituled, The Order of the Gospel Revived*, Boston, 1701.

[4] Our knowledge of this meeting of the Convention and its vote is due to Increase Mather, *Disquisition Concerning Ecclesiastical Councils*, Boston, 1716, p. 38; [Reprinted in *Cong. Quarterly*, XII: 365, 366.]

[5] Mather says, *Ibid.*, "This was the Vote which passed at the mentioned *Convention*. When also he that writes these Lines, was desired to *Address the Churches* accordingly. What has hitherto retarded, I need not mention."

[6] See note 4 above.

it is provided, that the Result of the Synod, in 1662, relating to the Consociation of Churches [1] may be Republished, with an Address to the Churches, Intimating our desires (and so far as we are Concerned our purposes) to see that Advice carefully attended, and the irregular Proceedings of any People hereafter contrary to that Advice, not Encouraged."

It needed something more than the republication of the hasty votes of bygone Synods to stay the tendencies of the time.

Of course matters could not stop here. Increase Mather was president of Harvard College, but that institution had, as we have seen, come largely under the control of the innovators. The college was in a precarious state.[2] Left without a charter by the revocation of the charter of the colony under which the corporation had been created, vain attempts were made to procure new incorporation in 1692, 1696, 1697, 1699, and 1700; attempts in which the Mathers tried to maintain the interests of the conservative party, but which all came to naught through causes ultimately traceable to the determination of the English government that nothing should be done unfavorable to Episcopacy. But Increase Mather, though president, refused to reside at Cambridge. His ministry over the largest congregation in Boston was a point of vantage which he would not lightly resign. His services to the colony and to the college were of the highest value,[3] but the fact of his non-residence caused annoyance. In February, 1693, the lower House of the General Court had passed a vote that the "President shall be Resident at ye Colledge." [4] In June, 1695, this vote was repeated,[5] and in December, 1698, the request was enforced by the offer of a considerable increase in salary.[6] In July, 1700, the Court in more positive language than before insisted that Mather should go to Cambridge, and so peremptory was the demand that for a few weeks the president resided at the college.[7] But he

[1] See *ante*, pp. 337–339. Mather republished it on pp. 40–47, of his *Disquisition*.

[2] The relations of the Mathers to the college is very unsympathetically told by Quincy in his valuable *History of Harvard College*, ed. 1860, I: 57–126. This is still the fullest treatment of the subject. See also Robbins, *Hist. Second Ch., Boston*, pp. 44–64; Palfrey, *Hist. N. E.*, IV: 192–196; Sibley, *Grad. of Harvard*, I: 423–430; Brooks Adams, *Emancipation of Mass.*, pp. 261–285; H. A. Hill, *Hist. Old South Church*, I: 319–323; Wendell, *Cotton Mather*, *passim*.

[3] Even Quincy admits this. Compare the discriminating remarks of Robbins, *Hist. Second Church*, pp. 44–47, 52–54.

[4] Sibley, *Grad. of Harvard*, I: 425.

[5] *Ibid.*, 425, 426.

[6] *Ibid.*, 426.

[7] *Ibid.*, 427.

longed for Boston, his health at Cambridge was not good, and by October 17, 1700, he was once more away from the college. And now Mather's many opponents whom politics, the prominence of his son in the witchcraft trials,[1] and especially the late Brattle Church quarrel, had stirred up against him, saw the opportunity to remove his influence either from Boston or Cambridge. Mather was alarmed, and in April, May, and June, 1701, actually resided at Cambridge. But again his homesickness for Boston overcame him, and the danger of resigning his church for a precarious post at the head of an unchartered college, harrassed as he was by constant attacks, impressed him; and, therefore, on June 30, 1701, he wrote to Lieut. Governor Stoughton a letter for presentation to the General Court in which he announced his return to Boston, and expressed his "desire that the General Court would as soon as may be, think of another Præsident for the Colledge."[2] This letter he followed up by a personal meeting with the legislature on August 1st, at which he declared his willingness to resume charge of the college on the old basis of non-residence.[3] The president had underrated the strength of the opposition. He felt with reason that his claims to the gratitude of the colony were considerable and he apparently believed that he could induce the legislature to abandon the obnoxious requirement rather than dispense with his services. That body, however, took a different view. It summoned Vice-President Samuel Willard of the Third Boston Church to take charge of the college and to reside at Cambridge.[4] But Willard felt the same unwillingness to leave his church that Mather had experienced. He delayed the decision of the question. And, therefore, on September 5, 1701, Mather's friends renewed the proposition that the presidency should once more be offered to him. The lower House passed the resolution;[5] its membership was largely from the country, and was at once conservative religiously,

---

[1] Calef's *More Wonders of the Invisible World*, London, 1700, reached Boston just at this juncture, Nov., 1700. Calef had been aided in its composition by the Brattles and it undoubtedly hurt the Mathers at a critical moment. Compare Wendell, *Cotton Mather*, p. 150.

[2] Letter in Quincy, *Hist. Harvard Univ.*, I: 501, 502; see also Sibley, I: 428.

[3] Sibley, *Ibid.*

[4] *Ibid.*

[5] Quincy, *Hist. Harvard Univ.*, I: 115, 116; where quotations are given from Court Records.

and not so ambitious politically as to have felt slighted, as did some of the upper House, at the appointments made by the English government on Mather's suggestion when the new charter had been granted in 1691. But the Council or upper House, composed largely of residents in Boston and its vicinity, to some extent sympathetic with the religious movement of the Brattles and even more filled with political grudges against Increase Mather, which his domineering disposition had done much to foster and little to heal, sent a committee to Willard to ascertain on what terms he would take the administration of the college. He replied that he was willing to visit Cambridge "once or twice every Week . . . And Performe the Service used to be done by former Presidents."[1] This put him on exactly the same footing as Mather; but how fully the feeling of the upper House had turned against the old president is shown in the action of that body after hearing the report of its committee. On September 6th, it negatived the proposition of the lower House that the presidency be offered to Mather, and took Willard on his own terms.[2] In this latter action the lower House concurred. A show of consistency was maintained in that Willard continued to wear the title of vice-president, while the presidency remained nominally vacant; but the defeat of the Mathers was none the less obvious, and their defeat was that of the whole conservative party. It left a feeling of bitterness as long as Increase and Cotton Mather lived,[3] for the struggle had been a serious and honest attempt to preserve the college from what they deemed essential spiritual harm, as well as a contest into

---

[1] Sibley, I: 429.

[2] *Ibid.*, I: 429; II: 22; Quincy, *Hist. Harvard Univ.*, I: 115, 116; Hill, *Old South Church*, I: 322, 323.

[3] See Sewall's diary, 5 *Mass. Hist. Coll.*, VI: 43-45; C. Mather, *Parentator*, p. 173. On the death of Vice-President Willard in 1707, the Mathers hoped that one or the other of them would be elected, but the office fell to their old opponent, John Leverett, "He had eight votes, Dr. Increase Mather three, Mr. Cotton Mather, one, and Mr. Brattle of Cambridge, one." (Sewall, *Ibid.*, 196). Leverett died in 1724, the year after the death of Increase Mather, and Cotton Mather again hoped for election, and hoped for it too quite as much that he might advance the conservative cause as for personal aggrandizement. But he was disappointed. The choice fell on Rev. Joseph Sewall, on Rev. Benjamin Colman, who both declined; and, finally, on Rev. Benjamin Wadsworth, who accepted. The second of these choices was exasperating enough to Mather, and he exclaimed in his diary, "The corporation of our Miserable Colledge do again . . . treat me with their accustomed Judgment and Malignity." (See for this and other quotations, Wendell, *Cotton Mather*, pp. 292-4.) But as far as any control of the college by the Mathers was concerned the action of 1701 was final.

which more selfish motives entered; and the defeat seemed not only a great personal slight but the ruin of the cause which the father and son believed to be that of the Gospel.

Conscious thus of failure in resisting the tide of innovation in the town of Boston and in the college, the conservative party would not give up the struggle without further effort to buttress the ancient Congregational system. They felt that the churches and ministers might be banded together for mutual assistance in a more effective way than they had been. And such is often the curious effect of the lapse of a little time, or the attainment of a fixed position in a community, in modifying ecclesiastical struggles, that we find some men once prominent among the Brattle Church innovators now supporting associational movements which had for their design the prevention of similar organizations in the future. Indeed there is abundant evidence that Benjamin Colman himself was not long in ranging himself among the more conservative forces in the Massachusetts colony.[1]

The steps which led to this consociational movement are obscure, but as far as the writer can ascertain the initiation was in the Minister's Convention of June 1, 1704. That body issued the following circular letter to the churches:[2]

"*Boston*, 1. d. IV. m. 1704.

To Serve the Great Intentions of Religion, which is lamentably decaying in the Country: It is proposed,

I. That the *Pastors* of the Churches do *personally Discourse* with the *Young People* in their Flocks, and with all possible Prudence and Goodness endeavour to win their Consent unto the *Covenant of Grace*, in all the Glorious Articles of it.

II. That unto this Purpose, the *Pastors* do take up that Laborious, but engaging Practice, of making their *Personal Visits* unto all the Families that belong unto their Congregations.

III. That the *Pastors* in this Way of Proceeding, bring on their People as far as they can, publickly, and solemnly to Recognize the *Covenant* of GOD, and come into such a Degree of the *Church-State*, as they shall be willing to take their Station in: But not to leave off, till they shall be qualified for, and perswaded to, Communion with the Church in *all* special Ordinances.

---

[1] See his signature to the following document. By 1735 he was of the opinion, that "The *Consociation of Churches* is the very Soul and Life of the Congregational Scheme . . . without which we must be *Independent*, and with which all the Good of *Presbyterianism* is attainable." Dexter, *Cong. as seen*, p. 512.

[2] Text in C. Mather, *Ratio Disciplinæ*, pp. 178, 179; and, with the signatures, in *Panoplist*, X: 320, 321.

IV. That for such as have submitted unto the *Government* of CHRIST in any of His Churches, no *Pastors* of any other Churches, any way go to shelter them under their Wing, from the *Discipline* of those, from whom they have not been fairly recommended.

V. That they who have not actually Recognized their Subjection to the *Discipline* of CHRIST in His Church, yet should, either upon their *obstinate Refusal* of such a Subjection, or their falling into other *Scandals*, be faithfully treated with proper *Admonitions*: About the Method and Manner of managing which *Admonitions*, the *Pastors* with their several Churches, will be left unto the Exercise of their own Discretion.

VI. It is desired and intended, if the Lord please, That at the *General Convention* of the Ministers, there may be given in by each of the *Pastors* present, An Account of their *Progress* and *Success* in that holy Undertaking, which has been proposed: That so, the Lord may have the *Glory of His Grace*, and the *Condition of Religion* may be better known and served among us.

VII. As a Subserviency to those Good and Great Intentions, it is proposed, That the *Associations* of the Ministers in the several Parts of [the] Country may be strengthened; And the several *Associations* may by *Letters* hold more free Communications with one another.[1]

Voted and unanimously consented unto.

Present,

Samuel Willard, *Moderator*.	John Fox,[11]
Ebenezer Pemberton,	Rowland Cotton,[12]
Benjamin Colman,	Jonathan Pierpont,[13]
John Hancock,[2]	Jonathan Sparhawk,[14]
Thomas Blowe,—?[3]	Joseph Belcher,[15]
Cotton Mather,	John Clark,[16]
Grindal Rawson,[4]	Benjamin Wadsworth,[17]
Nehemiah Walter,[5]	Joseph Gerrish,[18]
Thomas Barnard,[6]	Peter Thatcher,[19]
James Allen,[7]	James Sherman,[20]
Samuel Torrey,[8]	Jonathan Russel,[21]
Moses Fiske,[9]	Thomas Bridge,[22]
Joseph Green,[10]	John Danforth."[23]

This earnest and practical vote was reinforced by a circular letter sent out by the Cambridge Association in November, 1704, — that body serving not only as the agent by whom the resolutions of the Minister's Convention were presented to the churches, but

[1] Here ends the copy in the *Ratio Disciplinæ*.
[2] Lexington. [3] *I. e.*, Thomas Blowers of Beverly. [4] Mendon.
[5] Roxbury. [6] Andover. [7] Boston First Church. [8] Weymouth.
[9] Braintree. [10] Salem Village, now Danvers. [11] Woburn.
[12] Sandwich. [13] Reading. [14] Bristol. The name should be John.
[15] Dedham. [16] Exeter, N. H. [17] Boston First Church.
[18] Wenham. [19] Milton. [20] Sudbury. [21] Barnstable.
[22] Without charge, soon to be settled as one of the ministers of the Boston First Church.
[23] Dorchester.

adding exhortations even more favorable to a strengthening of ecclesiastical government:[1]

"Cambridge November 6. 1704

Dear Brethren,

The Ministers w° sometimes meet at Cambridge have thought it proper to entertain you wth certain proposalls agreed awhile ago, by a much greater convention of Ministers at Boston.

The copy of ye proposalls here inclosed will sufficiently give you to understand ye intentions of them. And we have all possible reason to believe your good affections for such intentions. . . .

But that the Pastours of our Churches may more comfortably enjoy ye assistance of one another, w^c^ doubtless y^y^ all find more than a little needfull for y^m^ under ye difficulty w^c^ in their ministry y^y^ often meet withall, you are very sensible how usefull their well-formed associations may be unto y^m^. The most early times of New-England propounded and practised y^m^.

Our Churches did betimes feel ye benefit of y^m^: and it is to be hoped, y^t^ where such associations have been already formed, y^y^ will be lively maintained, & preserved, & faithfully carried on. And where y^y^ are not yet formed, ye Lord will stir up his servants to consider w^t^ to do, y^t^ y^y^ may not incur ye inconveniencies of him y^t^ is alone.

But there is one thing more, w^c^ has been greatly desired, & never yet so fully attained. It is, That ye severall associations of Ministers may uphold some communion & correspondence wth one another, & y^t^ y^y^ would freely cōmunicate unto each other by letters, w^t^ever y^y^ may apprehend a watchful regard unto ye great interests of Religion among us may call to be considered.

It is with a speciall respect unto ye design y^t^ ye ministers of ye Association sometimes meeting at Cambridge, do now make ye essay; & having laid these things before you, do heartily recomend you & all your studies to serve him, unto ye blessing of ye Lord.

They do it by ye hand of
Syrs yo^rs^
Sam^ll^ Willard, moder^tr^.

To ye Reverend
to be cōmunicated."

The next step in the movement is obscure, owing to the loss of the records of the Cambridge-Boston Association and the Minister's Convention at this point. When the veil is once more lifted it is nearly a year later, Sept. 11, 1705, when nine delegates, representing the five Associations of Boston, Weymouth, Salem, Sherborne, and Bristol, met at Boston,[2] and two days later, agreed upon the

[1] From the manuscript records of the Cambridge Association.

[2] The Dorchester church records note: "Sept. 11. 1705. A meeting of ye Delegates of ye Associations at Boston." p. 127.

Proposals of 1705.[1] Exactly how this committee was appointed is not stated, but that it was no chance coming together is shown by its declaration that it met "according to former agreement." If conjecture may be allowed a place, it seems probable that the resolutions of the Ministers' Convention of 1704, and the commendatory letter by which they were accompanied, awakened a response which seemed to warrant further action. This action may well have taken the form of a vote at the Ministers' Convention of May, 1705,[2] favoring a further extension of associational powers, and naming a place and time at which representatives of the Associations should come together and draw up the desired scheme.

However this may have been, the fact is certain that on September 13, 1705, the following *Proposals* were approved by a committee representing, for aught that we know to the contrary, all the Associations then existing in Massachusetts.

THE PROPOSALS OF 1705

Question and Proposals.

Question.

WHat[3] *further Steps are to be taken, that the*[4] *Councils may have*[5] *due Constitution and Efficacy in supporting, preserving and well ordering the Interest*[6] *of the Churches in the Country?*

---

[1] The date and place and signatures are given in the copy of the Proposals printed in the *Panoplist*, X: 323. In the copy prefixed by John Wise to his *Churches Quarrel Espoused* the names are intentionally suppressed, and the phrase "Delegates of the Associations reads ' Association," implying that the committee represented one association instead of five. The Dorchester records give the following: "Sept. 13. . . . The Same Day, The Delegates or Representatives of the ministers of yᵉ Associations in yᵉ Province — yᵗ came to Boston, agreed Sundry Things about Stated Councills, to be cōmunicated to yᵉ Churches (& Pastors)." p. 127.

[2] I know little regarding the events of this meeeting. The date was May 31st; and Sewall speaks of dining with the ministers, in company with the governor and other magistrates, at Mr. Willard's house (5 *Coll. Mass. Hist. Soc.*, VI: 132). But I think we can go a little farther. The "Question" which the "Proposals" answer was clearly not propounded by the Committee that drafted the Proposals. By what body was it so probably submitted to them as by the Ministers' Convention? This origin of the "Question" in the Convention of 1705 seems doubly probable in view of the prompt ratification of the "Proposals" which answered it by the Convention of 1706.

[3] I follow the text given by Wise, *Churches Quarrel*, ed. 1715 (the earliest accessible to me), pp. 1–4, as more nearly representing that actually laid before the *churches* than the text in the *Panoplist*.

[4] Panoplist omits *the*. [5] Ibid. inserts *their*. [6] Ibid. *interests*.

1st Part, It was Proposed,

1st, That the Ministers of the Country form themselves into Associations, that may meet at proper times to Consider such things as may properly lie[1] before them, Relating to their own faithfulness towards[2] each other, and the common Interest[3] of the Churches; and that each of those[4] Associations have a Moderator for a certain time, who shall continue till another be Chosen, who may call them together upon Emergencies.

In these Associations,

2dly.[5] That Questions and Cases of importance, either provided by themselves, or by others presented unto them, should be upon due deliberation Answered.

3dly, That Advice be taken by the Associated Pastors from time to time, e're they Proceed to any action[6] in their Particular Churches, which[7] be likely to produce any imbroilments. That the Associated Pastors do Carefully and Lovingly treat each other with that watchfulness which may be of Universal Advantage; and that if any Minister be accused to the Association whereto he belongs, of Scandal or Heresie, the matter shall be there[8] examined, and if the Associated Ministers find just accusation[9] for it, they shall direct to[10] the Calling of a Council, by whom such an Offendor is to be proceeded against.

4thly, That the Candidates of the Ministry undergo a due Tryal by some one or other of the Associations, concerning their Qualifications for the Evangelical Ministry; and that no particular Pastor or Congregation Imploy any one in Occasional Preaching, who has not been Recommended by a Testimonial under the Hands of some Association.[11]

5thly, That they should together be consulted by Bereaved Churches, to Recommend to them such Persons as may be fit to be imployed amongst[12] them for present Supply, from whom they may in due time proceed to chuse a Pastor.

6thly, That hereunto may be referred the Direction of Proceeding[13] in any of their particular Churches, about the Convening of Councils that shall be thought necessary, for the Welfare of the Churches.

---

[1] Ibid. *lay.* [2] Ibid. *toward.* [3] Ibid. *interests.* [4] Ibid. *these.* [5] Ibid. inserts, *It is expected.* [6] Ibid. *actions.* [7] Ibid. inserts, *may.* [8] Ibid. *thus.* [9] Ibid. *occasion.* [10] Ibid. omits *to.*

[11] This most important section, embodying the principles of ministerial licensure which have since prevailed in New England, was probably drawn in substance from the *Heads of Agreement*, II: 7 (See p. 459, *ante*). Heretofore each church had "licensed" whom it would — the action of a local church in voting to hear any man being his warrant to preach. The importance of the change here proposed is attested by its permanence.

[12] Panoplist, *among.* [13] Ibid. *proceedings.*

7thly, That the several Associations in the Country, maintain a due Correspondence with one another, that so the state of Religion may be better known and secured[1] in all the Churches, and particularly it is thought necessary to the well-being of these Churches, that all the Associations of[2] the Country meet together by their Respective Delegates once in a year.[3]

8thly, And *finally*, That Ministers Disposed[4] to Associate, endeavour in the most efficacious manner they can, to Prevail with such Ministers as unreasonably neglect such Meetings with their Brethren in their proper Associations, that they would not expose themselves to the Inconveniencies that such Neglects cannot but be attended withal.

Second Part, It is Proposed,

1st. That these Associated Pastors, with a proper Number of Delegates from their several Churches, be formed into a standing or stated Council, which shall Consult, Advise and Determine all Affairs that shall be proper matter for the Consideration of an Ecclesiastical Council within their respective Limits, except always, the Cases are such as the Associated Pastors[5] judge more convenient to fall under the Cognizance of some other Council.

2dly, That to this end these Associated Pastors, with their Respective Churches, shall Consociate and Combine according to what has been by the Synods of these Churches recommended, that they act as Consociated Churches in all holy Watchfulness and Helpfulness towards each other; and that each Church choose and depute one or more to Attend their Pastor,[6] as Members of the Council in their Stated Sessions, or occasionally, as Emergencies shall call for.

3dly, That these Messengers from the several Consociated Churches shall be chosen once a year at the least.

4thly, It is propounded, as that which from our beginning has been Recommended, that the Churches thus Consociated for these purposes, have a stated time to meet in their Council, and once in a year seems little enough, that they may Inquire into the Condition of the Churches, and Advise such things as may be for the[7] Advantage of our holy Religion. But the more particular time is best left to the Determination of each respective Association.

5thly, That the Associations[8] shall Direct when there is Occasion for this Council to Convene, on any Emergency, and shall

---

1 Ibid. *served.* 2 Ibid. *in.*

3 Ibid. adds, *to concert matters of common concern to all the churches.*

4 Ibid. adds *thus.* 5 Ibid. adds *may.* 6 Ibid. *Pastors.* 7 Ibid. adds *common.*

8 Ibid. *Association.*

direct whether the whole, or only a certain Number of these Consociated Pastors and Churches shall Convene on such Occasions.

6thly, It appears agreeable to the present Condition of our Churches, and from our beginnings acknowledged, That no Act of [1] the Councils are to be reckoned [2] as Concluded and decisive, for which there has not been the Concurrence of the Major part of the Pastors therein concerned.

7thly, The Determinations of the Councils thus Provided, for the necessities of the Churches, are to be looked upon as final and decisive, except agrieved Churches and Pastors,[3] have weighty Reasons to the contrary, in which Cases there should be Provision for a further hearing; and it seems proper that the Council Convened on this occasion, should consist of such Pastors [4] as may be more for number than the former, and [5] they should be such, as shall be directed to, and convened for this purpose by the Ministers of an [6] Association, near to that whereto these of the former Council belonged, unto which the agrieved should according apply themselves, and in this way expect a final Issue.

8thly, If a particular Church will not be Reclaimed by Council from such gross Disorders as plainly hurt the common Interest [7] of *Christianity*, and are not meer tolerable differences in Opinion, but are plain Sins against the Command & Kingdom of our Lord Jesus Christ, the Council is to declare that Church no longer fit for Communion with the Churches of the Faithful; and the Churches represented in the Council, are to Approve, Confirm and Ratifie the Sentence, and with-draw from the Communion of the Church that would not be healed: Nevertheless, if any Members of the disorderly Church, do not justifie their Disorders, but suitably testifie against them, these are still to be received to the wonted Communion by [8] the Churches; and if after [9] due waiting, the Church be not recovered, they may upon [*Advice*][10] be actually taken in as Members of some other Church in the Vicinity.

These Proposals were [11] Assented to by the Delegates of the Association,[12] meet according to former Agreement, at *B.*——[13] *September* 13*th.* 1705. To be Commended to the several Associated Ministers [14] in the several parts of the Country, to be duly Considered, that so, what may be judged for the Service of our Great Lord, and his Holy Churches, may be further Proceeded in."

---

[1] Ibid. *Acts in.* [2] Ibid. *received.* [3] Ibid. *or persons.*

[4] Ibid. adds *and Churches*, a more probable reading.

[5] Ibid. adds *that.* [6] Ibid. *any.* [7] Ibid. *interests.* [8] Ibid. *of.* [9] Ibid. adds *all.*

[10] Ibid. reads (*upon fit advice*), evidently a better reading. [11] Ibid. *are.*

[12] Ibid. *Associations*, a better reading. [13] Ibid. *Boston.*

[14] Ibid. *Associations and Ministers*, a better reading.

[Thus far both texts agree; but here the *Mather-Panoplist* text adds the signatures and endorsement as follows.]

"Samuel Willard, *Mod.*
Cotton Mather,
Ebenezer Pemberton.[1] } *Boston.*[2]
Samuel Torry,[3]
John Danforth,[4] } *Weymouth.*
Samuel Cheever,[5]
Joseph Gerrish,[6] } *Salem.*
Grindal Rawson,[7] *Sherburne.*
Samuel Danforth[8] for Bristol *Association.*

Further approved and confirmed, and a resolution to pursue, with the Divine assistance, in all suitable methods, the intention of the said proposals:—By a General Convention of the Ministers at *Boston*; 30*d.* 3*m.*[9] 1706.

Attested by
SAMUEL WILLARD, *Mod.*"

[Instead of the signatures and endorsement, the Wise text ends thus.]

"*At an Association-Meeting, the fore-going Proposals were Read and Assented to*, &c. Present,[10]
Nov. 5. 1705."

There is nothing necessarily inconsistent between the two. It is evident that the resolutions were approved by the committee of the five Associations on September 13, 1705. What Wise used would appear to be a circular letter to the churches; and, from its concluding clause, a circular sent out with the added endorsement of an Association. Unfortunately Wise's refusal to give the names of the members present makes it impossible to say which the Association was, but in view of the importance of the Cambridge-Boston body, and its agency in 1704 in sending and recommending the action of the Ministers' Convention of that year to the churches, it can hardly be doubted that that was the body which

1 Pemberton was now associated with Willard in the ministry of the Third Boston Church.
2 *I. e.*, in the name of the Boston Association, identical with the Cambridge body.
3 Weymouth. 4 Dorchester. 5 Marblehead. 6 Wenham.
7 Mendon. 8 Taunton. 9 May 30.
10 Wise declares, "where the Place was, or the Persons who were present in this Randezvouze, shall never be told by me, unless it be Extorted by the Rack." *Churches Quarrel*, ed. 1715, p. 115.

approved the resolutions on November 5.[1] The formal approval by the Ministers' Convention followed on May 30, 1706.

Doubtless the influence of the Mathers had much to do with these proceedings, though their hand does not conspicuously appear.[2] But in view of the agency of five Associations in their composition, and the approval of the *Proposals* by the body representative of all the Massachusetts ministers, it is hardly just to affirm with Prof. Tyler that "the document was understood to have been the work of the two Mathers, backed by a coterie of clerical admirers,"[3] nor have Drs. J. S. Clark[4] or H. M. Dexter[5] spoken with their accustomed accuracy in representing the *Proposals* as the device of Cambridge-Boston Association alone. They represented a wide-spread feeling in favor of stricter church government, a feeling which such liberal sympathizers as Ebenezer Pemberton and Benjamin Colman shared. So far from being the work of a faction, it would be hard to show what elements of then existent Boston Congregationalism were unrepresented in their production.

If, then, a large portion of the ministers of Massachusetts desired the establishment of stricter church government, why did these propositions fail to produce greater results? The first portion, relating to the formation of ministerial associations, was largely put in practice; the second part, with its recommendation of standing councils, remained a dead letter. Probably the reasons have been as well stated by Cotton Mather as by any one. Speaking of the first part, he says:[6]

"These *Proposals* have not yet been in all regards *universally* complied withal. Nevertheless, the Country is full of *Associations*, formed by the *Pastors* in their several Vicinities, for the Prosecution of *Evangelical Purposes*."

---

[1] Little weight can be laid on the point, but it is interesting to note that Nov. 5, 1705, was a Monday, the regular meeting day of the Cambridge Association.

[2] It has doubtless been observed that the name of Increase Mather is seen in none of the lists of signers, as far as known.

[3] *Hist. of American Literature*, II: 106. Prof. Tyler falls into the further error of saying that it was issued without any signature attached.

[4] *Sketch of the Cong. Churches in Mass.*, p. 115.

[5] *Congregationalism, as seen in its Literature*, 491–494. Dr. Dexter's treatment of the whole matter is unsatisfactory, and chronologically reversed, in that he discusses the Saybrook Platform before the Proposals. References a few pages on show that he was acquainted with the *Panoplist* text, but he could not have had it in mind while writing this passage; nor does he seem to have noticed the signatures or the approval by Convention.

[6] *Ratio*, p. 181.

And after outlining the scheme of standing councils, he adds:[1]

> "Such *Proposals* as these found in one of the *New-English* Colonies[2] a more general Reception (and even a Countenance from the Civil Government) than in the Rest. In the other,[3] there were some very considerable Persons among the *Ministers*, as well as of the *Brethren*, who thought the *Liberties* of *particular Churches* to be in danger of being too much *limited* and *infringed* in them. And in a Deference to these Good Men, the *Proposals* were never prosecuted, beyond the Bounds of *meer Proposals*. . . . There was indeed a Satyr, Printed against these *written Proposals*, and against the Servants of GOD that made them. Nevertheless, those *Followers of the Lamb*, remembring the Maxim of, *Not Answering*, used the Conduct which the University of *Helmstadt* lately prescribed under some Abuses put upon them; *Visum est non alio Remedio quam generoso Silentio et pio Contemptu, utendum nobis esse.*"

Mather's reference is of course to the brilliant attack on these *Proposals* put forth in 1710 by Rev. John Wise of what is now Essex, Mass., but was then known as Chebacco parish in Ipswich, under the title of *The Churches Quarrel Espoused*, etc.; and which Wise followed in 1717 by a powerful exposition of what he believed to be the system set forth in the Cambridge Platform, the *Vindication of the Government of New England Churches.* The vigor and cogency of these tracts has been justly praised.[4] They are certainly the most able exposition of the democratic principles which modern Congregationalism has come to claim as its own that the eighteenth century produced. Yet, without abating the respect due to Wise for his work, or minimizing the influence which his books exercised on political thought when republished on the eve of the revolutionary war, it may justly be questioned whether their effect in bringing to naught the *Proposals* in Massachusetts has not been rated higher than it should.[5] Wise's satire was not published till four years after the ratification of the *Proposals* by the Massachusetts Convention, and not till two years after Connecticut had inaugurated a similar system. Some influence other than the *Churches Quarrel Espoused* must have hindered, or the scheme would have come into practice long before that tract was given to the world. Mather clearly indicates another reason than the work

---

[1] *Ibid.*, pp. 184, 185. [2] Connecticut. [3] Massachusetts.

[4] See Clark, *Hist. Sketch Cong. Chs. in Mass.*, pp. 115–121; Tyler, *Hist. American Literature*, II: 104–116; Dexter, *Cong. as seen*, pp. 493–502.

[5] *E. g.*, by the writers cited in the previous note.

of Wise. The *Proposals* in Massachusetts were opposed by "some very considerable Persons," both lay and clerical; and, what is even more important, they were not supported by the legislature, as the similar propositions were in Connecticut. Here, then, was the real point of break-down. As will be shown, the Saybrook Articles met with plentiful opposition, but they had the power of the General Court behind them, and were therefore put into practice. In Massachusetts, on the other hand, the civil authorities stood aloof, and without legislative support it was impossible to introduce the stricter system in either colony. Nothing could have been more diverse than the legislative situation in the two colonies. Probably the General Court of Connecticut was never in a state more favorable to the enactment of an ecclesiastical constitution than in 1708. It was still under its semi-independent charter, able to choose its own upper House and governor. That governor was a minister, Gurdon Saltonstall, warmly attached to the church system of the colony, popular alike with his ministerial associates and with the legislature, and a believer in the desirability of a stricter organization of the churches. The Connecticut Court had long been accustomed to interfere in the affairs of the churches; such interference was not unpopular with as representative men as the trustees of Yale College.[1]

The situation of the Massachusetts General Court was far different. That body had received an entirely new constitution in 1692, and one that practically ended the old-time clerical influence. The lower House was still chosen by the people; but the upper House, though nominated by the General Court, was subject to the veto power of the governor, a veto freely exercised;[2] and the governor was of royal appointment, with authority to reject all bills distasteful to him. The governor at this time was the notorious Joseph Dudley, no friend to the Congregational churches of Massachusetts, whose religious position may be judged by a letter to the Lords of Trade in England, of July, 1704, in which he com-

[1] See their proposition of 1703 requesting the ministers to unite in an appeal to the General Court to approve a confession of faith, in the next section of this chapter (p. 498).

[2] In 1703 Dudley rejected 5 nominations, in 1704, 2, and in 1706, 2. Palfrey, IV: 253, 254, 291, 299.

plains that the Court used its right of nomination to the upper House "to affront every loyal and good man that loves the Church of England and dependence on her Majesty's government";[1] and who, while not wholly cutting loose from the Roxbury Congregational church of which he was a member, worshiped much in the Boston Episcopal chapel, and signed a petition to the archbishop of Canterbury, in 1703, in which he and his associates are styled "the members of the Church at Boston."[2] The upper House, too, which in Connecticut we shall see readily passed the Saybrook bill, was not likely in Massachusetts to be so compliant with the wishes of the ministers. Its membership was largely from Boston and the immediate vicinity, and there was already growing up in the commercial and governmental center of Massachusetts a class more influenced by trade and crown appointments than desire to maintain the discipline of the churches of the colony or the old spirit of political independence. The *Proposals* of 1705 could not, in any reasonable probability, have passed the Massachusetts legislature; and failing of legislative support there was enough opposition both in that colony and Connecticut to prevent the establishment of any similar system. That the ecclesiastical development of Massachusetts and Connecticut in the last century ran in divergent paths was due, in no small degree, to the differing character of their respective governors and General Courts.

The *Proposals*, which thus came to naught as far as Massachusetts was concerned, had a posthumous fame for a brief period at the beginning of the Unitarian controversy more than a hundred years later. Though printed as late as 1772,[3] they had been forgotten; and when discovered in manuscript by Prof. William Jenks and communicated to the *General Association of Massachusetts Proper*[4] at its meeting at Dorchester in June, 1814,[5] they were thought by some to be exactly suited to the distracted state of the

[1] *Ibid.*, p. 292. [2] *Ibid.*, pp. 297, 298. [3] In Wise's works, see *ante*, p. 463.
[4] *I. e.*, exclusive of Maine. It is the present "General Association."
[5] For the literature of this discussion, see *ante*, p. 463.

churches then existing, and were accordingly referred to a committee for further report. That report was made at the Association's meeting at Royalston in June, 1815, by Rev. Dr. Jedidiah Morse of Charlestown, and after giving such facts regarding the *Proposals* as were accessible to the committee, declared that the propositions were "in various respects such, that in their [the committee's] opinion congregational ministers cannot consistently recommend or approve them."[1] The committee then proposed a plan of its own for stricter church government, which after lying over a year, was given a timid vote of approval that amounted practically to a burial. All efforts to strengthen the ecclesiastical government of Massachusetts had failed.

PART II
THE SAYBROOK PLATFORM OF 1708

While the events just considered were in progress in Massachusetts, a similar movement, to some extent induced by the proceedings in the older colony, was in progress in Connecticut. The Half-Way controversy had resulted in 1669 in the toleration of some divergence in ecclesiastical usage "vntill better light in an orderly way doth appeare";[2] but the same differences of opinion which had been shown in the questions propounded by the General Court in 1666[3] continued, and the low state of religion which marked the closing years of the seventeenth century led to much discipline and not a little quarrel in the churches.[4] The feeling was widespread throughout the colony, and the adjacent parts of Massachusetts,[5] that some strengthening of church-government was desirable, for the same reasons that it was sought in the vicinity of Boston.

The movement which led to the Saybrook Synod in Connecticut ran parallel to and was in considerable degree conducted by

[1] *Panoplist*, XI: 360. [2] See *ante*, p. 277.
[3] *Conn. Records*, II: 54, 55; and *ante*, p. 274.
[4] Compare Trumbull, *Connecticut*, ed. 1818, I: 480.
[5] See Stoddard's views, for instance, *Instituted Churches*, p. 28.

men who were engaged in founding Yale College, and these men were in turn affiliated in some measure with those in eastern Massachusetts who were seeking a stricter church government. The connection between the founding of Yale College and the party about Boston who were opposed to the liberalizing of Harvard and the rejection of the influence of the Mathers has been pressed too far by President Quincy,[1] and it has been clearly shown that the desire of the ministers of Connecticut, long cherished especially in the coast towns of the old New Haven colony, that they might have "a nearer and less expensive seat of learning,"[2] amply accounts for the establishment of the Connecticut college. It had its birth independently of Boston ecclesiastical quarrels. But while thus moved by Connecticut rather than Massachusetts interests, the men who founded Yale College in 1701 were in active sympathy with the conservative party in Boston. Evidence of this cordiality of feeling is ample. The earliest document in the archives of the college is a beautifully written "Scheme for a College" endorsed in Cotton Mather's handwriting,[3] and though its proposals were not adopted, it manifests that active interest which Cotton Mather always felt in the institution, and which led him, in 1718, to secure the benefactions from Elihu Yale which carried the college through its severest struggles and led to the bestowal upon it, at Mather's suggestion, of the name "Yale."[4] A second fact shows that this interest was not one-sided. On August 7, 1701, "the first fixed date"[5] in the history of Yale Col-

---

[1] Quincy, *History of Harvard University*, ed. 1840, I: 197–200, says: "The projectors of it [Yale] were aware of the advantage which would result to their seminary, should it be made satisfactory to the predominant religious party in Massachusetts. . . . They took their measures accordingly." But Kingsley, in his review of Quincy's work (*Biblical Repository*, July, Oct., 1841, Jan., 1842), has made it plain that the impulse did not go out from Massachusetts. It may be queried, however, whether in his zeal to answer Quincy, Kingsley did not minimize the real sympathy which existed between the conservatives at Boston and the founders in Connecticut. See also Woolsey, *Hist. Discourse . . . before . . . Yale College . . . 150 years after the founding*, New Haven, 1850, with a very valuable appendix of documents; Prof. F. B. Dexter, *Founding of Yale College*, *Papers of New Haven Hist. Soc.*, III: 1–31; Prof. S. E. Baldwin, *Eccles. Constitution of Yale College*, *Ibid.*, III: 405–410.

[2] Prof. Dexter, as cited, p. 3. See also Woolsey, *Discourse*, p. 7.

[3] Certainly older than Sept., 1701. See Prof. Dexter, as cited, p. 4. The document is professedly anonymous. Text in Woolsey, *Discourse*, pp. 83–86. It was addressed to Rev. Messrs. Noyes, Buckingham, and Pierpont.

[4] Letters in Quincy, *Hist. Harvard Univ.*, I: 524–527.

[5] Prof. Dexter, as cited, p. 5. The letter is lost.

lege, the ministers most concerned in its founding, Israel Chauncy of Stratford, Thomas Buckingham of Saybrook, Abraham Pierson of Killingworth, James Pierpont of New Haven, and Gurdon Saltonstall of New London, wrote to Isaac Addington, secretary of Massachusetts colony, and to his friend, Judge Samuel Sewall, both men of strong conservative sympathies in religion, asking for the draft of a charter for the proposed college. To this request Addington and Sewall responded, furnishing the desired paper, and accompanying it by a letter dated October 6, 1701, in which they say:[1]

"We should be very glad to hear of flourishing schools and a College at Connecticut, and it would be some relief to us against the sorrow we have conceived for the decay of them in this [Massachusetts] province."

The draft of the charter was indeed seriously modified by its recipients, and the clauses by which Addington and Sewall would have secured orthodoxy by the prescription of certain text-books were stricken out in the charter granted to the college by the Connecticut General Court;[2] but these communications show to whom in Massachusetts the founders of Yale turned for sympathy. Nor is this all. In the period between the application for a form of a charter and its receipt, Increase Mather wrote, by reason of the request of an unnamed Connecticut minister, setting forth some suggestions for the organization of the college, and declaring that he had also written on the same subject to Rev. Thomas Buckingham of Saybrook.[3] These letters are sufficient to show the degree of cordiality and ready communication existing between the leading Connecticut ministers and the conservative party about Boston.

Yale College having been organized with four of the five ministers who wrote to Addington and Sewall as its trustees,[4] and with them Rev. Messrs. James Noyes of Stonington, Samuel Mather of

---

[1] Letter in Woolsey, *Discourse*, pp. 91, 92; their draft, *Ibid.*, pp. 92–94.

[2] The Charter of Yale College is dated "Octr 9: 1701," the day of the assembly of the General Court. It was probably enacted the 16th. See Prof. Dexter, *Biog. Sketches of the Graduates of Yale*, pp. 2–5, where the full text is given. Addington and Sewall had proposed that the Westminster Confession and Ames's *Medulla Theologiæ*, should be required studies. The founders seem to have had no objection to their use, but preferred to put the prescription in the by-laws rather than the charter. See Laws of 1726 (probably much older) in Prof. Dexter's *Biog. Sketches*, p. 349.

[3] Letter dated "Boston, Sept. 15, 1701," in Woolsey, *Discourse*, pp. 86, 87.

[4] Gurdon Saltonstall, then of New London, was not included.

Windsor, Samuel Andrew of Milford, Timothy Woodbridge of Hartford, Noadiah Russell of Middletown, and Joseph Webb of Fairfield, its trustee meetings became altogether the most representative ecclesiastical gatherings in the colony. The assembled ministers soon discussed other matters than college business. As a result, at their meeting at Guilford in 1703 they sent forth the following circular letter, to sound the churches as to the desirability of a united confession of faith, the first step, as far as can be ascertained, toward the Saybrook Synod.

"Att a meeting of Sundry Elders
held at Guilford mar: 17. 170$\frac{2}{3}$.

It being an hopefull expedient for securing y^{e} truths of our Religion, both to our people, & their & our Posterity, & that w^{e} may wth y^{e} divine Blessing tend to our preservation from heresie, & Apostasie, w^{r}in we have y^{e} Godly examples of our Christian Brethren in other parts, & Provinces; y^{r}fore we cañot but earnestly desire & intreat, y^{t} our Brethren in ye Ministry of ye Gospel wthin this Colony would as we have done well peruse ye assemblies Confession of Faith, as also y^{t} made by ye Synod held at Boston *may 12. 1680* & manifest in convenient season y^{r} concurrence wth us in addressing our Religious Government, as soon as we may be prepared, y^{t} they would please to recommend to our people & y^{r} posterity ye following Confession of Faith, *viz*, y^{t} agreed upon by y^{e} Rever^{d}. assembly at Westminster, as it is comprised in & Represented by y^{e} Confession made by y^{e} Synod in Boston May 12. 1680. & printed by y^{t} Governm^{t}. & we request you^{d} signifye y^{r} minds to y^{e} Rev^{d}. M^{r}. Buckingham in Say=Brook, Mr Woodbridge in Hartford, Mr Davenport in Stratford, & m^{r}. Andrew, or Pierpont in Milford or N=Haven, yt so from you we may understand how far y^{r} is a generall concurrence in y^{e} p'mises.[1]

Abrah: Pierson
Tho: Buckingham
T: Woodbridge
James Pierp[on]t
Noadiah Russel
Saml Russel[2]
Tho: Ruggles."[3]

What response this appeal elicited cannot be affirmed with definiteness. But it shows clearly the drift of thought among the leading ministers of Connecticut, though the absence of record

[1] From the manuscript in the archives of Yale University. Clap, *Annals . . . of Yale College*, New Haven, 1766, p. 12, represented this as a proposition for a general synod of all Connecticut churches, and Trumbull (*Connecticut*, I: 478), who follows him, copies his declaration that there were county meetings in consequence, which prepared the way immediately for the Saybrook synod by adopting the Westminster confession and drawing up rules for church discipline; but both are unwarranted inferences from the paper here given.

[2] Of Branford, Conn., elected trustee of Yale in 1701 after the granting of the charter.

[3] The minister at Guilford at whose house the meeting was held. He was not a trustee.

makes it impossible to say what steps were next taken. It is not till five years later that we again find light. Meanwhile the attempts of the ecclesiastical leaders of Massachusetts to establish standing councils had borne fruit in 1705 and 1706, and cannot have been unfamiliar to their friends in Connecticut.[1] The thought of the ministers of Connecticut turned toward something more than the approval of a confession of faith, they would now couple with it the establishment of a system of stricter government like that attempted in Massachusetts. And, in December, 1707, an event well-nigh without a parallel in American history occurred; a leading minister of the colony, Gurdon Saltonstall of New London, was called directly from the pulpit to the governor's chair,—a post which he continued to fill till his death in 1724. Saltonstall had experienced in his own pastorate the evils of a church quarrel,[2] and on his election to the governorship it would appear that the movement for stricter government went more rapidly forward.[3] Sometime between May 13 and 22, 1708, the following bill was introduced into and passed the upper House, of which the governor was then a member. In its original form it called, apparently, only for assemblages of ministers;[4] but somewhere in its passage, either in the upper House, or more probably among the representatives of the towns who passed it on May 24th,[5] the statute was amended so as to summon the brethren of the churches as well as their pastors, and thus render the bodies for which it called truly synods:[6]

"This Assembly, from their own observation and from the complaint of many others, being made sensible of the defects of the discipline of the churches of this government, arising from the want of a more explicite asserting the rules given for that end in the holy scriptures, from which would arise a firm establishment amongst ourselves, a good and regular issue in cases subject to ecclesiastical discipline, glory to Christ our head, and edification to his members, hath seen fit to ordein and require, and it is by authoritie of the same ordeined and required, that the ministers

---

1 No further proof is needed than that the Saybrook Articles are taken to some extent verbally from the Proposals of 1705.

2 Caulkins, *Hist. of New London*, 1852, p. 377.

3 Stiles, *Discourse on the Christian Union*, Boston, 1761, p. 69, is doubtless correct in the statement that the endorsement of the Connecticut legislature to the proposition for the Saybrook synod was procured "very much through the influences of the honorable Gurdon Saltonstall, Esq.; Governor of the colony."

4 Bacon, *Discourse* in *Cont. Eccles. Hist. Conn.*, p. 33, shows that the clause calling for the messengers of the churches was interlined in the original bill at some time during its passage.

5 *Ibid.*, p. 32.

6 *Conn. Records*, V: 51.

of the churches in the several counties of this government shall meet together at their respective countie towns, with such messengers as the churches to which they belong shall see cause to send with them[1] on the last Monday in June next,[2] there to consider and agree upon those methods and rules for the management of ecclesiastical discipline which by them shall be judged agreeable and comformable to the word of God, and shall at the same meeting appoint two or more of their number to be their delegates, who shall all meet together at Saybrook, at the next Commencement to be held there, when they shall compare the results of the ministers of the several counties,[3] and out of and from them to draw a form of ecclesiastical discipline which by two or more persons delegated by them shall be offered to this Court at their sessions at Newhaven in October next, to be considered of and confirmed by them, and that the expence of the above mentioned meetings be defrayed out of the publick treasury of this Colonie."

Pursuant to this order, the representatives of the churches of each county met, though no records of their doings have survived.[4] By these councils, ministers and delegates were chosen to be present at the anniversary of the infant college, and naturally convenience, together with the prominence of the men involved, brought it about that eight of the twelve ministers thus selected to represent the Connecticut churches were trustees of the college.[5] The ministerial element was in the decided predominance. The messengers from New London County to the Saybrook Synod were two, while Hartford and Fairfield Counties sent one each, and New Haven was represented by no laymen. Doubtless other brethren were appointed who did not appear at the meeting. But there is no reason to hold that the body which gathered at Saybrook Sept. 9, 1708, was not fairly able to voice the sentiments of the Connecticut churches as a whole.[6]

Of the course of discussion we know nothing; but its results are evident. The Synod recommended that the Savoy Confession,

---

1 See p. 499, note 4.

2 June 28, 1708.

3 This clause also suggests that the invitation of representatives of the brethren was an afterthought.

4 The Preface to the *Articles* says, " These several Councils having met and drawn up some Rules of Church Government did by their Delegates meet and Constitute one General Assembly," etc., ed. 1710, p. 96. The meeting at New London was ordered to choose a minister for Lebanon, and that at Fairfield one for Stratford, by the paternal legislature. *Conn. Records*, V: 54.

5 Compare Dr. G. L. Walker, *Hist. First Ch. Hartford*, p. 265.

6 Dr. Bacon, *Cont. Eccles. Hist. Conn.*, pp. 38, 39, is inclined to dispute this, but without very adequate ground.

as adopted by the Massachusetts Synod of 1680,[1] should be the doctrinal basis of the Connecticut churches. This action was simply the carrying out of the suggestion which many of the same ministers had already made in 1703.[2] To formulate rules for church government was not so easy, however; and here the result, though unanimous, must be regarded as a partial compromise.[3] The Synod adopted the *Heads of Agreement*,[4] which had been widely circulated in New England and lauded by the Mathers as the best exposition of Congregationalism. This constitution formed the more liberal side of the Saybrook result, the side appealed to in later times by those who wished to minimize its strictness.[5] But to affirm them alone would not have given the stricter government which the legislature desired. The Synod, therefore, compared the various drafts prepared by the county councils,[6] and adopted that presented by the New Haven delegates, though with modifications suggested by the more Presbyterianly inclined representatives of Hartford.[7] The result was the fifteen *Articles for the Administration of Church Discipline*. To all the documents, Confession, Heads of Agreement, and Articles, the Synod appended proof texts. Fortunately a very early copy of its minutes has been preserved and is as follows:[8]

---

[1] See *ante*, pp. 367–402. [2] See *ante*, p. 498.

[3] Noah Hobart of Fairfield wrote, *Attempt to Illustrate . . . The Eccles. Constitution of the Consociated Chs. . . . of Conn.*, New Haven, 1765, p. 8: "a man must be a perfect Stranger to the Principles and Temper of that Time, who is capable of supposing that either of these Parts of our Constitution [the Heads of Agreement and Articles], taken singly or without its Connection with the other, would have been unanimously agreed upon and consented to by that body of men."

[4] See *ante*, pp. 456–462.

[5] *E. g.* [Thomas Fitch] *An Explanation of Say-Brook Platform*, Hartford, 1765, pp. 3, 4: "If there be any expressions of one of those parts of the constitution, which seem to be inconsistent with some expressions in the other, in that case, the articles of discipline are to be so explained and understood, as to comport and agree with the heads of agreement, and not *vice versa*."

[6] Preface to ed. 1710, p. 96.

[7] Rev. Chauncey Whittelsey of New Haven wrote of Rev. (and later Pres.) Ezra Stiles, Mch. 4, 1761, "Mr. Noyes [pastor at New Haven 1716–1761] has told me that he understood, that the Draught of New-Haven County, (which was chiefly made by Mr. Pierpont [pastor at New Haven 1684–1714]) was mainly preferred; but some Clauses put into it, in Conformity to Mr. Woodbridge of Hartford and some others, who were inclined to the Presbyteryan Side." MS. Coll. of Yale University. See also Stiles, *Christian Union*, p. 70.

[8] MS. Records of Hartford North Association. This, or a similar, copy was followed by Trumbull, *Connecticut*, I: 482–486.

THE SAYBROOK MEETING AND ARTICLES

"At a Meeting of the Delegates from the Councills of the Several Countys of Connecticutt Colony In N: England In America at Saybrook Sep. 9th 1708.

Present

From the Councill of Hartf^{d} County

The Reu^{d} { Timothy Woodbridge[1]
Noadiah Russell[2]
Stephen Mix[3] }

Messeng^{r} Jno Haynes Esqr[4]

From the Councill of Fairfeild County

The Rev^{d} { Charles Chauncey[5]
Jno Davenport[6] }

Messen^{r} Deacon Sam^{ll} Hoit[7]

From the Council of N: London County:

The Rev^{d} { James Noyes[8]
Thos Buckingham[9]
Moses Noyes[10]
Jno Woodward[11] }

Messen^{rs} { Robert Chapman[12]
Deacon Wm Parker[13] }

Present

From the Councill of New Haven County:

The Rev^{d} { Sam^{ll} Andrew[14]
James Pierpont[15]
Sam^{ll} Russell[16] }

The Rev^{d} { James Noyes & Thos Buckingham } Being Chosen Moderators.

The Rev^{d} { Stephen Mix and Jno Woodward } Being Chosen Scribes.

In complyance wth an ord^{r} of the Gen^{ll} Assembly May 13 1708 After Humble Addresses to the Throne of Grace for the Divine presence assistance and Blessing upon us, having our Eyes upon the word of God and the Constitution of our Chhs for the advancment of Gods Glory and the further order and edification of our Chhs,

We agree that the Confession of faith owned & Consented unto by the Elders and Messengers of the Chhs assembled at Boston In New England May 12 1680 being the Second Session of that Synod be Recom̅ended to the Honble the Gen^{ll} Assembly of this Colony at the next Session for their Publick testimony thereto as the faith of the Chhs of this Colony.

Wee agree also that the Heads of Agreement assented to by

1 Hartford First Church, trustee of Yale.
2 Middletown, trustee.
3 Wethersfield.
4 Of Hartford.
5 Stratfield, now Bridgeport.
6 Stamford.
7 Of Stamford.
8 Stonington, trustee.
9 Saybrook, trustee.
10 Lyme, trustee.
11 Norwich.
12 Of Saybrook.
13 Also of Saybrook.
14 Milford, trustee.
15 New Haven, trustee.
16 Branford, trustee.

the vnited Ministers formerly Called Presbyterian & Congregationall be observed by the Chhs thrôout this Colony.

And for the Better Regulation of the Administration of Chh. Discipline In Relation to all Cases Ecclesiasticall both In Particular Chhs and In Councills to the full Determining and Executing of the Rules in all such Cases

It is agreed

Impr. That the Elder or Eldrs of a particular Chh wth the Consent of the Brethren of the Same have power and ought to exercise Chh Discipline according to the Rule of Gods word in Relation to all Scandals that fall out wthin the same. And it may be meet in all Cases of Difficulty for the Respective Pastrs of Particular Chhs to take advice of the Eldrs of the Chhs In the Neighbourhood before they proceed to Censure in such Cases.[1]

2. That the Chhs wch are Neighbouring each to other shall consociate for the mutuall affording to each other such assistance as may be requisite upon all occasions ecclesiasticall:[2] And that the particular Pastrs & Chhs within the Respective Countys in this Government shall be one Consociation (or more if they judge meet) for the end aforesd.

3. That all Cases of Scandall that fall out wthin the Circuit of any of the aforesd Consociations shall be bro't to a council of the Eldrs and also Messengrs of the Chhs wthin the sd Circuit, i: e. ye Chhs of one Consociation if they see cause to send Messengrs when their [there] shall be need of a Council for the Determination of them.

4. That according to the com̄on practice of our Chhs nothing shall be Deemed an act or judgment of any Council which hath not the Majr part of the Eldrs present concurring and such a number of the Messengrs present as make the Majority of the Council: provided that if any Chh shall not see Cause to send any Messengr to the Council or the persons chosen by them shall not attend; neither of these shall be any obstruction to the proceedings of the Council or Invalidate any of their acts [3]

---

[1] Compare *Proposal* of 1705, Pt. 1, sec. 3, *ante*, p. 487.

[2] The compilers of *Congregational Order* (1843, p. 268) thus explain the scope of this phrase: "usage includes Ordinations, Installations, and dismissions of Pastors; examinations of candidates for ordination or installation, in respect to their soundness in the faith and their qualifications for the work of the ministry; occasions in which advice is regularly asked by the churches or individual members; the hearing of appeals from the decisions of a consociated church; hearing and determining cases of discipline or difficulty submitted to the consociation previous to trial; trial of pastors accused of scandal or heresy on complaint or call of the association; and in general, — deliberations and advice concerning matters of common interest to the churches."

[3] Compare *Proposals* of 1705, pt. 2, sec. 6 *Congregational Order* observes: "In respect to this article there is a diversity of usage. Most of the consociations have for many years voted by a joint ballot [*i. e.*, elders and messengers together], and a majority of the whole forms the decision."

5. That when any case is orderly bro't before any Council of the Chhs it shall there be heard and Determined which (vnless utterly removed from thence) shall be a finall Issue,[1] and all parties therein Concerned shall sit down & be Determined theirby; And the Councill so hearing and Giving the Result or finall Issue in the s^d Case as afores^d shall see their Determinations or judgment duly Executed and attended in such way or manner as shall in their judgm^t be most suitable & agreeable to the word of God.

6. That if any Past^r and Chh doth obstinately refuse a due attendance and Conformity to the Determination of the Council that has Cognizance of the Case & Determines it as above, after due patience used they shall be Reputed guilty of Scandalous Contempt & dealt wth as the Rule of Gods word In such Case doth provide, & the Sentence of Non-Comunion shall be Declared ag^t such Past^r & Chh, and the Chhs are to approve of the s^d Sentence by w^thdrawing from the Comunion of the Past^r & Chh which so refuseth to be healed.[2]

7. That in Case any Difficultys shall arise in any of the Chhs in this Colony which cannot be Issued w^thout Considerable Disquiet, that Chh in wch they arise or that Minist^r or member aggreived with them shall apply themselves to ye Council of the Consociated Chhs of the Circuit to which the s^d Chh belongs, who if they see Cause shall thereon convene hear and determine such Cases of Difficulty unless the matter brôt before y^m shall be judged so great in the nature of it, or so doubtfull in the Isue or of such Generall Concern that ye s^d Council shall judge best that it be refered to a fuller Council consisting of the Chhs of the other Consociation within the same County (or of the next adjoyning Consociation of another County if their be not two Consociations in the County where the difficulty ariseth) who together with themselves shall hear judge, determine and finally Issue such Case according to the word of God.[3]

8. That a particular Chh in wch any difficulty doth arise may if they see cause call a Council of the Consociated Chhs of the Circuit to which the s^d Chh belongs before y^y proceed to Sentence y^rin, but their [there] is not the same Liberty to an offending brother to call the s^d Council before the Chh to wch he belongs proceed to excomunication in the s^d Case unless wth the Consent of the Chh.

9. That all the Chhs of the Respective Consociations shall

[1] Compare *Proposals*, pt. 2, sec. 7, *ante*, p. 489.

[2] Compare *Proposals*, pt. 2, sec. 8. *Ibid.*

[3] Compare *Proposals*, pt. 2, sec. 7. *Ibid.*

Choose if they see cause one or Two members of each Chh to represent them in the Councils of the s^d Chhs as occasion may call for them, who shall stand in that capacity till new be Chosen for the same service unless any Chh shall Incline to Choose their messeng^rs anew upon the Convening of such Councils.[1]

10. That the Minist^r or Minist^rs of the County Towns, and where their are no minist^rs in such Town the Two next Minist^rs to the s^d Town shall as soon as Conveniently may be appoint a time & place for the meeting of the Elders and Messeng^rs of the Chhs in the s^d County In order to y^r forming themselves into one or more Consociations and notify the s^d Time & place to the Eld^rs and Chhs of that County, who shall attend at the same, the Eld^rs In their own persons and ye Chhs by their Messeng^rs if they see cause to send them, which Elders and Messeng^rs so assembled In Councells as allso any other Councill hereby allowed off [of] shall have power to adjourn y^mselves as need shall be for the space of one year after the Begining or first Session of the s^d Councill and no longer, and that Minist^r who was chosen at the last Session of any Councill to be moderat^r shall with the advice & consent of Two more Eld^rs (or In case of the Moderat^rs death any Two Eld^rs of the same Consociation) call another Councill w^thin the Circuit w^n they shall judge their is need thereof, and all Councills may prescribe Rules as Occasion may require & whatsoever they shall judge needfull within their Circuit for the well performing and orderly Managing the severall acts to be attended by them, or Matters that come under their cognizance.[2]

11. That if any person or persons orderly Complained off [of] to a Councill or that are witnesses to such Complaints have [having] regular Notification to appear shall refuse or neglect so to do in the Place and at the time specifyed in the warning given, except y^y or he give some Satisfying reason thereof to the s^d Councill, they shall be judged guilty of Scandalous contempt.[3]

12. That the teaching Eld^rs of Each County shall be one Association (or more if they see cause) which Association or Associations shall assemble twice a year at Least at such time and place as they shall appoint to Consult the Dutys of their office & the Com̄on Interest of the Chhs, who shall consider & resolve Questions & Cases of Importance which shall be offered by any amoung

---

[1] Compare *Proposals*, pt. 2, sec. 2; *ante*, p. 488. *Congregational Order*, p. 276, remarks: "the general usage is to appoint delegates for a single council only."

[2] Contrast this method of calling with that of the *Proposals*, pt. 2, sec. 5; *ante*, p. 488.

[3] This article has of course no counterpart in the less elaborately worked out *Proposals*.

y^m^selves or others,[1] who shall have power of examining & Recom̄ending the Candidates of the Ministry to the work thereof.[2]

13. That the s^d^ Associated Eld^rs^ shall take notice of any amoung y^m^selves that may be accused of Scandall or Heresy unto or Cognizable by them, examine the matters & if they find just occasion shall direct to the calling of the councill where such offend^rs^ shall be duly proceeded against.[3]

14. That the Associated Past^rs^ shall also be consulted by Bereaved Chhs belonging to their Association & recom̄end to such Chhs such persons as may be fit to be called & settled in the Work of the Gospell Ministry amoung them,[4] and if such bereaved Chhs shall not seasonably call & settle a minist^r^ amoung them the s^d^ associated Past^rs^ shall Lay the State of such bereaved Chh before the Gen^ll^ Assembly[5] of this Colony that they may take such order concerning them as shall be found necessary for y^r^ peace & edification.

15. That it be recom̄ended as expedient that all the Associations of this Colony do meet in the Gen^ll^ Association by their respective Delegates one or more out of each Association once a year,[6] the first meeting to be at Hartford at the time of the Gen^ll^ Election next ensuing the Date hereof[7] and so annually in all the Countys successively at such Time and Place as y^y^ the s^d^ Delegates shall in their Annuall Meetings appoint.

The above written Draught voted and agree by ye Councill above as Attest { Stephen Mix / J^no^ Woodward } Scribes"

This report, so important for the ecclesiastical history of Connecticut, was immediately laid before the General Court at its

[1] Compare *Proposals*, pt. 1, sec. 1 and 2; *ante*, p. 487.

[2] Compare *Proposals*, pt. 1, sec. 4. The still existing system of ministerial licensure, recommended in the *Heads of Agreement* (*ante*, p. 458–9) was thus established in Mass. and Conn.

[3] Taken to a large extent verbally from the *Proposals*, pt. 1, sec. 3, *ante*, p. 487. The Conn. General Association in 1822 put an explanatory interpretation on this article, of which this is the chief clause: "the 13th article is decisive, that it is the duty of an Association to receive an accusation against a pastor belonging to it, and to make provision for his trial before the Consociation; and your committee are convinced, that the Platform does not warrant a Consociation to receive an accusation against a pastor, unless it come through the hands of the Association, of which he is a member." Upham, *Ratio Disciplinæ*, p. 316. *Congregational Order*, p. 281, remarks: "Happily for the reputation and usefulness of the ministry in Connecticut, precedents for settling this inquiry are rare."

[4] Taken with some modification of expression from the *Proposals*, pt. 1, sec. 5; *ante*, 487.

[5] *I. e.*, the Conn. legislature. The contemporary records are full of instances of legislative interference in parish affairs. *Congregational Order*, p. 282, observes: "until the last thirty years, [before 1843] the churches . . . were accustomed to consult the associated pastors and to employ candidates recommended by them."

[6] To a large extent verbally from the *Proposals*, pt. 1, sec. 7, *ante*, p. 488.

[7] May 12, 1709. This was the first General Association to come into being and the body has ever since been maintained.

October session at New Haven and approved by the following vote, enacting it into the law of the colony:[1]

"The Reverend Ministers delegates from the elders and messengers of the churches in this government, met at Saybrook, September 9th, 1708, having presented to this Assembly a Confession of Faith, Heads of Agreement, and Regulations in the Administration of Church Discipline, as unanimously agreed and consented to by the elders and messengers of all the churches in this government: This Assembly do declare their great approbation of such a happy agreement, and do ordain that all the churches within this government that are or shall be thus united in doctrine, worship, and discipline, be, and for the future shall be owned and acknowledged established by law Provided always, that nothing herein shall be intended and construed to hinder or prevent any society or church that is or shall be allowed by the laws of this government, who soberly differ or dissent from the united churches hereby established, from exercising worship and discipline in their own way, according to their consciences."[2]

The Court followed this act of approval at its next session, May, 1709, by an order[3] that the first meeting of the General Association, then in session at Hartford should "revise and prepare for the press" the various symbols adopted at Saybrook, and that they should forthwith be printed. As a result, the little volume was issued in 1710 from the press which Gov. Saltonstall had caused to be established at New London, and has the distinction of being the first book published in Connecticut. The edition of 2,000, paid for by the Colony, was distributed in 1714, by the order of the Government.[4] Once more, in 1760, it was put forth at colonial charges in an edition of the same size and placed in each town in the colony.[5]

The system thus inaugurated was received with varying approval by the churches. Even in the Synod itself, though the vote was unanimous, the views of the members as to the extent of the new constitution were divided.[6] But the chief opportunity for expression of opinion was in the meetings of the pastors and churches of the respective counties called in the spring of 1709 to put the new system into practice by the establishment of associa-

---

[1] *Conn. Records*, V: 87.

[2] This clause was the further ratification of a toleration act, based on the English toleration act of 1689, which the Conn. legislature had passed in May, 1708, at the same session which issued the call for the Saybrook Synod. This act granted freedom of worship to dissenters on the same terms as in England,—requiring the payment of their taxes for the support of the established order. *Conn. Records*, V: 50.

[3] *Ibid.*, V 97, 98.

[4] The votes and orders are in *Conn. Records*, V: 192, 423, 449.

[5] See *Conn. Rec.*, XI: 333, 565. I give the date of the second edition, the votes are of 1759 and 61. The copies were ordered "distributed to the several towns in this Colony according to their publick lists."

[6] Compare *ante*, p. 501; Trumbull, *Conn.*, I: 487.

tions and consociations. The churches of Hartford County were the first to act. On February 1 and 2, 1709, the representatives of eleven of the fourteen or fifteen churches then in the county,—ten ministers and twelve laymen,—met at Hartford and organized two Consociations; and the same ministers formed themselves, on February 2d, into two Associations, coextensive with the Consociations. According to the vote of this county council:[1]

> "The Chhs of Hartford [3],[2] Windsor [2] Farmington & Symsbury shall be of one Consociation and the Chhs of Weathersfield, Middletown Waterbury[3] Glassenbury Haddam, Windham and Colchester shall be of the other Consociation in the County of Hartford."

The scribe of this council, Stephen Mix, had been scribe also of the Saybrook Synod, and two of the three other Saybrook delegates were present; and the new ecclesiastical system seems to have met with general approval, at least no amendment or modification is suggested in the minutes.

No other county than Hartford formed more than one Consociation at this time. In New London County, later the scene of much opposition by individual churches to the Saybrook system, a Consociation was formed on March 2, 1709, by a council of five ministers and eight laymen, from seven churches.[4] Here apparently, as in Hartford County, the result of the Synod was accepted without modification. But both in Hartford and New London Counties there were individual churches really, if not openly, out of sympathy with the new system. At East Windsor the church never approved of it, though for a time silent under it, and the result was a quarrel which embittered the later pastorate of Timothy Edwards.[5] At Norwich, where John Woodward, one of the scribes of the Synod, was pastor, the introduction of the system was the cause of a bitter dispute which eventually cost Woodward his pulpit and led his church wholly to renounce the Saybrook Platform.[6]

---

1 From the MS. records of the Hartford North Association.

2 East Hartford had not been set off as a separate town.

3 Simsbury, Middletown, and Waterbury were the churches unrepresented in this council. Hartford County had then a much larger territorial extent than at present.

4 Quoted from the records of New London Association in *Cong. Order*, pp. 41, 42.

5 See Stiles, *Ancient Windsor*, pp. 240–246.

6 See Caulkins, *History of Norwich*, pp. 284–288.

If Hartford and New London Counties, as a whole, accepted the Saybrook system as it came from the Synod, New Haven found it too strict and Fairfield esteemed it too liberal. The latter acted in a council at Stratfield, now Bridgeport, on March 16 and 17, 1709.

"Sigillum[1]
Consociationis
Fairfieldensis

At a Consociation or meeting of the Elders and Messengers of the County of Fairfield at Stratfield March 16, $170\frac{8}{9}$.

The Revd. Mr. John Davenport[2] chosen Moderator

Present from ye
Chh of Fairfield
The Revd Mr. Joseph Webb
Messengers
Deacon John Thomson
Mr. Samuel Cobbet.

From ye Chh of Stratford.
Messengers
Joseph Curtiss Esqr.
Mr. Samuel Sherman.

From ye Chh of Stratfield.
The Revd. Mr. Charles Chauncey
Messenger.
Lieut. James Bennet.

From ye Chh of Stamford.
The Revd. Mr. Jno. Davenport.
Messengers.
Deacon Samll Hoit[2]
Mr. Jos. Bishop

From ye Chh of Danbury.
The Revd. Mr. Seth Shove.
Messengers.
Lieut. James Beebee
Mr. James Benedict.

From ye Chh of Norwalk.
The Revd Mr. Stephen Buckingham.
Messenger
Deacon Zerubbabel Hoit.

From ye Chh of Woodbury.
The Revd. Mr. Anthony Stoddard.
Messengers.
Deacon John Sherman
Deacon Matthew Mitchell

The Revd. Mr. Charles Chauncey Scribe.[2] After Solemn Seeking of God for divine guidance, direction and blessings the Council convened.

The Acts of ye Council at Saybrook, September 9, 1708 were read the first time as also the general Assembly's approbation and sanction thereof, October 1708.

Voted in Council to adjourn till 8 of ye clock in ye morning.

The Consociation being met according to adjournment, after prayer made it was agreed

Imps. That all the Chhs. in ye County of Fairfield be one Consociation.

2. That ye Pastors met in our Consociation have power with ye Consent of the Messengers of our Chhs. chosen and attending, Authoritatively Judicially and Decisively to determine ecclesiastically affairs brôt to their Cognizance according to the Word of God and that our Pastors with the concurrence and consent of the Messengers of our Chhes to be chosen and that shall attend upon all future occasions, have like Authoritative, Judicial and Decisive power of Determination of affairs ecclesiasticall, and that in further and fuller meetings of two Consociations together compliant with ye conclusions of ye sd Councill at Saybrook, there is the like Authoritative, Judiciall and Decisive power of Determination of Ecclesiastical affairs according to ye word of God.

3. That by Elder or Elders of a particular Chh in said Saybrook conclusions mentioned in Paragraph ye first is understood only in ye teaching Elder or teaching Elders.[3]

---

[1] The original of this document is preserved in the records of the Stratfield church (First Church in Bridgeport), and is printed in Orcutt, *Hist. of the Old Town of Stratford and the City of Bridgeport*, [New Haven], 1886, I: 312, 313; and *The 150th Anniversary of the Fairfield County Consociations*, Bridgeport, 1886, pp. 32-34.

[2] The entire Fairfield County delegation at Saybrook.

[3] *I. e.*, ministers only.

4. That in ye 6th Paragraph of sd conclusions we do not hold ourselves obliged in our practice to use ye phrase of ye sentence of Non Communion but in ye stead thereof to use ye phrase of ye sentence of Excommunication which may in our judgment be formally applied in ye Cases expressed in said Paragraph.

The Councill adjourned till half an hour past two oclock in ye afternoon.

5. That to ye orderly begining of a case before a Councill of our Chhes. ye aggrieved member shall make application unto ye moderator of the Councill or Consociation for ye time being or in case of ye moderator's death to ye free[1] Senr Pastor of ye Consociation who upon his desire shall receive attested copies of ye Chhs proceedings with ye aggrieved member from their minister and ye sd. Moderator with the two free senr. Pastors of ye Circuit or in ye Case premised of ye death of ye Moderator ye sd 2 senr. pastors of ye circuit being satisfied there is sufficient cause shall warn ye convening of the Consociation.

6. That a Copy of a Warning to appear before ye Councill the time and place being notified being read in the hearing or left in ye house of the ordinary abode of a scandalous member or witness concerning the case depending before two members of the designation of the Scribe[2] for ye time being and signed by the sd Scribe be adjudged a regular notification.

7. That a copy of a Warning to appear before ye Pastor or Chh. ye place and time notified being read in ye hearing or left in the ordinary abode of an offending member or witness needfull in the case before two members appointed by the pastor and signed by him shall be a fair notification ye neglect whereof unless upon sufficient reason shall be reputed a scandalous contempt in our respective Chhes.

8. That all persons that are known to be Baptized shall in ye places where they dwell be subject to ye Censures of admonition and excommunication in case of scandall committed and obstinately persisted in.

9. That the Moderator and Scribe now chosen be accounted to stand in ye same respective capacities for ye time being untill a new regular choice be made, and so for the future.

10. That ye Judgment of y^e Consociation or Councill be executed by any Pastor appointed thereto by y^e Councill when y^e Pastor that hath already dealt in y^e case hath not a freedome of conscience to execute y^e same.

The above Acts and Conclusions of the present Consociation unanimously Voted March 17, 170$\frac{8}{9}$.

Signed Charles Chauncey, Scribe.

The above and foregoing is a true Copy of the Originall Compared.

pr. Samuel Cooke.[3]

This was an interpretation not far removed from Presbyterianism. The strong judicial flavor of the Saybrook Articles was increased till the Fairfield interpretation made the Consociation fully a church court.[4] The sentence of non-communion was not

---

[1] *I. e.*, not concerned in the dispute.

[2] As I take it, a comma should be inserted after "depending"; and the meaning is that this reading or leaving the notification is to be in the presence of two witnesses named by the scribe issuing the summons. So in the next section.

[3] Chauncey's successor in the Stratfield pastorate, 1715–1747.

[4] Article 2 of Fairfield Interpretation. It is interesting to note that in 1846 the Fairfield West Consociation, a direct representative of the body with which we have to do, voted, "As concerns the relations of Consociation to consociated churches, and its power over them, it disclaims, and

severe enough to be the penalty of a delinquent church,—the churches of Fairfield would change that to the un-Congregational extreme of excommunication, as if they had full right to cast an erring church out of the fold of Christ.[1] At the same time the method of calling the Consociation, notifying the accused and witnesses, and executing judgments rendered, was far more minutely laid down than in the Saybrook Platform and given a more judicial tone.[2]

But while Fairfield County thus emphasized, by the unanimous vote of the representatives of its churches, the stricter interpretation of the meaning of the work at Saybrook, the churches of New Haven County moved in the other direction. The churches of that county were the last to act, delaying their ratification till April 13, 1709. The story of their meeting was told in 1759 by Rev. Jonathan Todd, in a controversial pamphlet,[3] and is as follows:

"The Rev'd Mr. *Pierpont* the Minister of *New-Haven*, accordingly,[4] appointed a Meeting of the Elders and Messengers of the *County* of *New-Haven* at *Branford*, the 13th of *April*, 1709, for that Purpose;[5] and notified the Time and Place, to the Elders and Churches of the County. Most of the Elders and Churches by their Messengers, attended, tho' with particular Instructions (as I was informed by One, who was very active in bringing about such a Consociation of the Churches) to take Care to secure their congregational Privileges. When they came together, many of the Messengers of the Churches, had some Doubts, whether their congregational Liberties were sufficiently guarded, in some of the Articles. The Rev'd Mr. *Andrew* and Mr. *Pierpont* interpreted these Articles to their Satisfaction: They insisted that the Sense of those Articles, or Clauses of Articles, that they were in greatest Doubt about, should be written and fixed, to prevent a different interpretation hereafter. This was agreed to, (as I was informed, by One who was acquainted with the Doings of the Council at *Say-Brook*, and of this at *Branford*) and then the Council came into the following Resolve and Covenant, viz.

---

always has disclaimed, all legislative power. . . . In cases of difficulty and discipline submitted to Consociations by the churches, it simply gives advise." *150th Anniversary of the Consociations* [*of*] *Fairfield*, p. 21. This certainly implies a good deal of modification of view, and a good deal of forgetting of history also, in the lapse of 137 years.

[1] *Ibid.*, Art. 4. [2] *Ibid.*, Arts. 5, 6, 7, 10.

[3] *A Faithful Narrative, of Proceedings of the First Society and Church in Wallingford in their calling and settling the Rev. J. Dana.* New Haven, 1759, pp. 34-37. It is perhaps needless to observe that the writer favored a loose construction of the Articles. He was pastor at East Guilford, now Madison, 1733-91. He could easily have enjoyed the personal acquaintance of several of the New Haven County ministers active in 1709. Part of this document is printed in *Cong. Order*, pp. 284-286.

[4] *I. e.*, in accordance with Article X. of the Saybrook Platform, of which Todd has just been speaking.

[5] *I. e.*, organizing a consociation.

'At a Council of the Elders and Messengers of the Churches of *New-Haven, Milford, Branford, Derby* and *East-Guilford*,[1] in the County of *New-Haven*, convened at *Branford, April* 13, 1709, After Invocation on the LORD, for his gracious Presence and Conduct, the Rev'd *Samuel Andrew* and *James Pierpont*, were chosen Moderators.

The Rev'd *S. Andrew*[2]
J. Pierpont,[3]
S. Russel[4]
J. Moss,[5]
J. Hart[6] } Elders Present.

Messengers present.

J. Punderson
A. Bradly, } From *New-Haven* Church,
D. Buckingham
S. Eels } From *Milford* Church,
J. Rose
P. Tyler } From *Branford* Church,
J. Nichols, from *Derby* Church,
N. Bradly, from *East-Guilford* Church.

"*Ordered, and voted, that a Record be made of all Votes and Determinations that shall be made by this Council.*

"Whereas Communion of Saints, is an appointed and sanctified Means of Christian Edification; and Communion of Churches, a principal Means for the Preservation of Peace, Order, Establishment, and Consolation of the Churches; considering also, (notwithstanding the wise and pious Care of our Rev'd Fathers, the Founders of these Churches, to assert the Duty of such Communion, by giving the Right Hand of Fellowship to said Churches) that thro' the Corruption of the Times, the too great Slackness, and Inadvertency of our own Hearts; our several Churches have of late been over remiss, in making due Use of said Means: *Therefore humbling ourselves before* GOD *for, and begging his Forgiveness thro'* JESUS CHRIST, *for past Omissions*; *We now, whose Names are here specified, for ourselves, and in Behalf of the several Churches from whence we are come, according to the Method agreed on by the Council of all the Churches*[7] *in this Colony, met at* Say-Brook, Sept. 9. 1708, *do (until we shall otherwise agree) form ourselves into one Consociation*; *and thro' the strength of* CHRIST (*without whom we can do nothing*) *promise for the Future, we will better mutually watch over each other, and be ready at all Times, according to the* Rule of GOD's Word, *to be helpful to each other, in the Service and Work of the Kingdom of our* LORD JESUS CHRIST, *as we may have Opportunity for the same, and be called thereunto, according to the said Method and Rule, agreed on at said Council at* Say-Brook.

"Some Members desiring the Council's Sense of *several Articles* in the written[8] Method of managing Discipline, as it was agreed on by the Council at *Say-Brook. Sept.* 9. 1708.

---

[1] The New Haven County churches not represented were Guilford and Wallingford. There is reason to believe that the Wallingford pastor, at least, was detained by bodily infirmity.

[2] Samuel Andrew of Milford, member of Saybrook Synod.

[3] James Pierpont of New Haven, also at Saybrook.

[4] Samuel Russell of Branford, the third member of the delegation at Saybrook.

[5] Joseph Moss of Derby.

[6] John Hart of East Guilford, now Madison.

[7] Dr. Bacon deemed the representation of the General Court, that the Saybrook Synod spoke the voice of the Connecticut churches as a whole, very cool and audacious.— *Cont. Eccles. Hist. Conn.*, p. 38. But this New Haven County council evidently looked upon the Saybrook body as universally representative.

[8] This was literally true,— the Saybrook platform was not *printed* till 1710.

'Voted as follows,

'1. As to the first *Art.*[1] we conclude, *If the Majority of the Brethren don't consent, the Elders can't proceed to act: If the Elders can't consent, the Fraternity can't proceed; in which Case, it is proper to seek Council.*

'2. The second *Art.* we understand to be *an Explanation, or revival of the Duty engaged by our Churches, when they give the right Hand of Fellowship.*

'3. By *all Cases of Scandal* in Art. third, we suppose *such Cases as need a Council for their Determination.*

'4. A major Part of the Elders we suppose necessary: *As in a particular Church, the Brethren can't act without the Elders, so in a Council, the Messengers may not make an act of Council, without the Elders, or the major Part of them.*

'5. *Shall see their Determination,* &c. *i. e.* shall by themselves, or some of their Number, deputed thereunto, *observe whether the Council of GOD, sought in this Way, may be complied with or refused.*

'6. *Contempt of Council,* sought of GOD, or offer'd in a Way of GOD, must be scandalous, or a just Offence, and to be dealt in: And that Clause, viz, *The Churches are to approve of said Sentence,* &c. We understand as the Platform expresseth it, viz. *The Churches being informed of the Council's Judgment, and the Churches approving said Sentence, then the* Non-Communion *to be declared.*[2] *Without Approbation of Churches, There can't be a* Non-Communion *of said Churches.*

'7. The 7th Article *provides* only *for joining two Councils, in weighty, difficult and dangerous Cases.*

'8. *Churches may call a Council before they proceed to censure, but* without their Allowance, *no* PARTICULAR *Person shall have a Council before Excommunication.*

'9. That as no Members of a Council can remain such, for longer than one Year; *so the Council* [Churches?] *may choose new Messengers for every Council, if they see Cause.*

'10. The 10th Article *directs to the calling the first Council, and adjourning the same, not beyond a Year, and how a further Council may* afterwards *be called.*

'11. The 11th Artic. *shews how Persons concern'd may be obliged to attend with their Cases and Evidence, on a Council.*

'12. The 12th Artic. *is the Revival of our former Ministers' Meetings, for the Ends and good Services formerly aim'd at; wherein our People did rejoice for a Season, and hope yet will.*

'13. The 13th Art. *shews, how a* Minister *offending, may be proceeded against, 'til by the Council of that Consociation, he be reclaim'd, or* removed from his Office.

A true Copy of the Acts of Council,

Test. *Joseph Moss,* Scribe.

A true Copy, from the Record of the Association of *New-Haven County,*

examined by *Thomas Ruggles,*[3]

Keeper of the Association's Book of Records."

With these modifications, the Saybrook system went into general operation throughout the Colony. It had the hearty support

---

[1] To see the full minimizing force of these resolutions they should be compared, article by article, with the Saybrook Platform, *ante*, pp. 503–506.

[2] Compare Cambridge Platform, ch. XV, sec. 2, par. 3; *ante*, pp. 230–231. Contrast also with Fairfield interpretation, sec. 4. *ante*, p. 510.

[3] This was doubtless Thomas Ruggles, Jr., pastor at Guilford when Todd published this document.

of the colonial government and of the majority of the ministry. Its chief trial came when the "Great Awakening" of 1740–41 produced radical diversities of view as to methods of Christian evangelization in many of the churches. In the separations[1] and divisions which followed, especially in Eastern Connecticut, the system operated in favor of the conservatives. In general, it produced a feeling of sympathy with the Presbyterianism of the Middle Colonies, rather than with the more independent Congregationalism of Massachusetts, which led to many coöperant efforts in endeavors to resist Episcopacy and evangelize the newer settlements to the westward during the latter part of the eighteenth century and the beginning of our own.[2] This feeling of kinship to Presbyterianism rather than to pure Congregationalism had frequent and curious illustration. As late as Feb. 5, 1799, the Hartford North Association united in the following astounding declaration:[3]

"This Association gives information to all whom it may concern, that the Constitution of the Churches in the State of Connecticut, founded on the common usage, and the confession of faith, heads of agreement, and articles of church discipline, adopted at the earliest period of the Settlement of this State,[4] is not Congregational, but contains the essentials of the church of Scotland, or Presbyterian Church in America, particularly as it gives a decisive power to Ecclesiastical Councils; and a Consociation consisting of Ministers and Messengers or a lay representation from the churches is possessed of substantially the same authority as a Presbytery. The judgements, decisions and censures in our Churches and in the Presbyterian are mutually deemed valid. The Churches, therefore, of Connecticut at large and in our districts in particular, are not now and never were from the earliest period of our settlement, Congregational Churches, according to the ideas and forms of Church order contained in the book of discipline called the Cambridge Platform; there are, however, Scattered over the State, perhaps ten or twelve Churches which are properly called Congregational,[5] agreeable to the rules of Church discipline in the book above mentioned. Sometimes indeed the associated churches of Connecticut are loosely and vaguely, tho improperly, termed Congregational."

But even before the adoption of this declaration the Saybrook

---

[1] The Separatists are treated in the *New Englander*, XI: 195; in *Cont. Eccles. Hist. Conn.*, pp. 253–9; and, best of all, by Miss Larned, *Hist. Windham County, Conn.*, Worcester, 1874, I: 393–485.

[2] Some instances will be given in the next chapter.

[3] Records;—also quoted in G. L. Walker, *Hist. First Ch., Hartford*, pp. 358, 359. It was agreed upon by fifteen ministers of the County.

[4] This affirmation, and several which follow, are the more remarkable perversions of history in view of the publication at Hartford, two years before this declaration, of the first volume of Trumbull's *Connecticut*.

[5] *I. e.*, churches which rejected the Saybrook system.

system had ceased to have the special sanction of the law. The revision of the statutes which followed the Revolution, in 1784, silently repealed the legal authority of the Saybrook establishment by omitting all reference to it; though it still required all inhabitants of a parish, who were not declared supporters of some other form of worship, to contribute to the maintenance of the Congregational ministry. In the political upheaval of 1818, when the present constitution of Connecticut was adopted, this remaining shred of the old ecclesiastical establishment was swept away, and all special privileges denied to the Congregational body. Since that time all religious associations in Connecticut have been purely voluntary.

But the consociational system in Connecticut long survived its legal disestablishment. Always subject to a variety of constructions of greater or less strictness, it yet had such a hold upon the churches that as late as 1841 all but 15 of the 246 churches then existing in Connecticut were consociated.[1] Yet consociationism had for years been relaxing the closeness of its hold, and during the two decades from 1850 to 1870 the process of disintegration went rapidly on. The purging out of the leaven of Presbyterianism through the reviving sense of the integrity and sufficiency of Congregationalism under the teachings of eminent men, of whom Dr. Bacon of New Haven may serve as an example, had much to do with this result. Much, too, was due to the influence of widespread doctrinal discussions, and much also to the multiplication of new churches in the rapidly growing towns. The freer union of "Conferences"[2] has taken the place of the old Consociations in almost every portion of Connecticut. Yet Consociations still survive. There are still bodies known as the Consociations of Fairfield East, and West, Litchfield South, and New Haven East, and they still report a membership of 71 out of 306 churches of the Congregational order in the state;[3] but in practical administration these unions now

[1] *Congregational Order*, p. 52.

[2] In Connecticut a "Conference" is in no sense a council and has no judicial powers whatever. It is a body for friendly discussion, for mutual assistance in Christian work, and it chooses representatives to state and national conferences and councils. It does not pass upon ministerial fitness or settle church quarrels.

[3] *Minutes of Conn. General Conference*, 1892.

differ little from Conferences. As a system of strong ecclesiastical government the structure erected by the Saybrook Synod is now a thing of the past. Great diversity of view as to the usefulness of some of its provisions still obtains. But there can be no question that it has essentially modified the Congregationalism of America from what it would have been without the example of Connecticut. Connecticut set the pattern for those annual meetings of the churches of each state which have become a feature of our polity; nor is it too much to affirm that the example of mutual helpfulness given by the Consociations of Connecticut, though not followed elsewhere to the extent of establishing standing councils, has been chiefly instrumental in forming the Conferences in which the churches of counties and other local divisions are almost everywhere affiliated. The familiar local ministerial Association was not indeed original to Connecticut. It took deep root in Massachusetts soil. But in the popularization of that institution, and in making it, as it still is in large sections of our land, the agent in ministerial licensure, the influence of Connecticut has been decisive. The results of the Saybrook system are not the property of one colony alone but of all our American Congregational heritage.[1]

---

[1] Compare the judicious remarks of Dr. Bacon, *Cont. Eccles. Hist. Conn.*, pp. 68–70.

THE SAYBROOK RESULT

A | CONFESSION | OF | FAITH | *Owned and Consented to by the* | Elders and Messengers | Of the CHURCHES | In the Colony of *CONNECTICUT* in | NEW-ENGLAND, | Assembled by Delegation at *Say-Brook* | *September 9th.* 1708. | —— | Eph. 4 5. *One Faith.* | Col. 2. 5. *Joying and beholding your* | *Order and the steadfastness of your* | *Faith in Christ.* | —— | New-London in N. E. | Printed by Thomas Short, | 1710.

[ii blank]
[1]

A Preface.

AMong the Memorable Providences relating to our *English Nation* in the last *Century*, must be acknowledged the setling of *English Colonies* in the *American* parts of the World; Among all which this hath been Peculiar unto and to the distinguishing Glory of that Tract called *New-England*, that the Colonies there were Originally formed, not for the advantage of *Trade and a Worldly Interest*: But upon the most noble Foundation, even of *Religion, and the Liberty of their Consciences*, with respect unto the Ordinances of the Gospel Administred in the Purity and Power of them; an happiness then not to be enjoyed in their Native Soil.

We joyfully Congratulate the Religious Liberty of our Brethren in the late Auspicious Reign of K. William, and Q. Mary, of Blessed Memory, & in the present Glorious Reign, and from the bottom of our Hearts bless the Lord whose Prerogative it is to reserve the Times and Seasons in his own hand, who also hath Inspired the Pious Mind of Her most Sacred Majesty,[1] whose Reign we constantly [2] and unfeignedly Pray, may be long and Glorious, with Royal Resolutions, Inviolably to maintain the Toleration.

Deus enim - - hæc Otia fecit.

Undoubtedly if the same had been the Liberty of those Times, our Fathers would have been far from Exchanging a most pleasant Land (*dulce solum patriæ*) for a vast and howling Wilderness; Since for the enjoyment of so desirable Liberty a considerable number of Learned, Worthy and Pious Persons were by a Divine Impulse and Extraordinary concurrence of Dispositions engaged to adventure their Lives Families and Estates upon the vast Ocean,[2] *following the Lord into a Wilderness, a Land then not sown:* Wherein Innumerable difficulties staring them in the Face were outbid by Heroick Resolution, Magnanimity & confidence in the Lord alone. [3]*Our Fathers trusted in the Lord and were delivered, they trusted in him and were not confounded.* It was *their* care *to be with the Lord*, and their indulgence,[4] That *the Lord was with them*, to a Wonder preserving supporting protecting and animating them; dispatching and destroying the *Pagan Natives* by extraordinary Sickness and Mortality, that there might [5]*be room for his People to serve the Lord our God in.*

---

[1] Queen Anne.
[2] Jer. 2. 2.
[3] Psal. 22. 4, 5.
[4] 2 Chron. 15. 2.
[5] Psal. 80. 8, 9.

It was the Glory of our Fa-[3]thers, that they heartily professed the only Rule of their Religion from the very first to be the Holy Scripture, according whereunto, so far as they were perswaded upon diligent Inquiry, Solicitous search, and faithful Prayer conformed was their Faith, their Worship together with the whole Administration of the House of Christ, and their manners, allowance being given to humane Failures and Imperfections.

That which they were most Solicitous about, and wherein their Liberty had been restrained, respected the Worship of God and the Government of the Church of Christ according to his own appointment, their Faith and Profession of Religion being the same, which was generally received in all the Reformed Churches of Europe, and in Substance the Assemblies Confession, as shall be shown anon.

It cannot be denied, that the Usage of the Christian Church whose Faith wholly rested upon the word of God respecting Confessions of Faith is very Ancient and that which is universally acknowledged to be most so, and of Universal acceptance and consent is commonly called the Apostles Creed, a Symbol sign or Badge of the Christian Religion, called the Apostles, not because they composed it, for then it must have been received into the Canon of the Holy Bible, but because the mat-[4]ter of it agreeth with the Doctrine & is taken out of the Writings of the Apostles. Consequent hereunto, as the necessity of the Church for the Correcting Condemning & Suppressing of *Heresy* & *Error* required, have been emitted Ancient and Famous Confessions of Faith composed and agreed upon by Oecumenical Councils, *e. g.* Of *Nice* against *Arrius*, of *Constantinople* against *Macedonius*, of *Ephesu* against *Nestorius*, of *Chalcedon* against *Eutyches*. And when the Light of Reformation broke forth to the dispersing of Popish darkness, the Reformed Nations agreed upon Confessions of Faith, famous in the World and of especial service to theirs and standing Ages. And among those of latter times Published in our Nation most worthy of Repute and Acceptance we take to be the Confession of Faith, *Composed by the Reverend Assembly of Divines Convened at Westminster*, with that of the *Savoy*, in the substance and in expressions for the most part the same: the former[1] professedly assented & attested to, by the Fathers of our Country by Unanimous Vote of the Synod of Elders and Messengers of the Churches met at *Cambridge* the last of the 6*th. Month* 1648. The latter owned and consented to by the Elders and Messengers of the Churches Assembled at *Boston. May* 12*th.* 1680. The same we doubt not to profess to have been the constant Faith of the [5] Churches in this Colony from the first Foundation of them. And that it may appear to the Christian World, that our Churches do not maintain differing Opinions in the Doctrine of Religion, nor are desirous for any reason to conceal the Faith we are perswaded of: The Elders and Messengers of the Churches in this *Colony of Connecticut in New England*, by vertue of the Appointment and Encouragement of the Honourable the General Assembly, Convened by Delegation at *Say Brook, Sept* 9*th.* 1708. Unanimously agreed, that the Confession of Faith owned and Consented unto by the Elders and Messengers of the Churches Assembled at *Boston* in *New-England May* 12*th.* 1680. *Being the second Session of that Synod*, be Recommended to the Honourable the General Assembly of this Colony at their next Session, for their Publick Testimony thereto, as the Faith of the Churches of this Colony, which Confession together with the Heads of Union and Articles for the Administration of Church Government herewith emitted were Presented unto and approved and established by the said General Assembly at *New-Haven* on the 14*th.* of *October* 1708.

---

[1] See the Preface to the Platform of Church Discipline, *ante*, p. 195.

This Confession of Faith we offer as our firm Perswasion well and fully grounded upon the Holy Scripture, and Commend the same unto all and particularly to the people of our Colony to be examined accepted and constantly maintained. We do not assume to our-[6]selves, that any thing be taken upon trust from us, but commend to our people these following Counsels.

I. *That You be immoveably and unchangeably agreed in the only sufficient, and invariable Rule of Religion, which is the Holy Scripture the fixed Canon,*[1] *uncapable of addition or diminution.* You ought to account nothing ancient, that will not stand by this Rule,[2] nor any thing new that will. Do not hold your selves bound to Unscriptural Rites in Religion, wherein Custom it self doth many times misguid. Believe it to be the honour of Religion to resign and captivate our Wisdom and Faith to Divine Revelation.[3]

II. *That You be determined by this Rule in the whole of Religion. That Your Faith be right and Divine, the Word of God must be the foundation of it, and the Authority of the Word the reason of it.*[4] You may believe the most Important Articles of Faith, with no more than an Humane Faith; And this is evermore the cause, when the Principle Faith is resolved into, is any other than the holy Scripture. For an Orthodox Christian to resolve his Faith, into Education Instruction and the perswasion of others is not an higher reason, than a *Papist, Mahometan*, or *Pagan* can produce for his Religion.

[7] Pay also unto God the Worship, that will bear the Tryal of and receive Establishment by this Rule. Have always in Readiness a Divine Warrant for all the Worship you Perform to God. Believe that Worship is accepted and that only, which is directed unto, and Commanded, and hath the promise of a Blessing from the Word of God. Believe that Worship not Divinely Commanded *is in vain*,[5] nor will answer the Necessities and Expectations of a Christian, and is a Worshipping, you know not what.[6] Believe in all Divine Worship, it is not enough that this or that Act of Worship is not forbidden in the Word of God; If it be not Commanded, and you perform it, You may fear, You will be found Guilty and exposed to Divine Displeasure.[7] *Nadab and Abihu* paid dear for Offering in Divine Worship that which the Lord Commanded them not. It is an honour done unto Christ, when you account that only Decent Orderly and Convenient in his House, which depends upon the Institution and appointment of himself, who is the only Head and Law-giver of his Church.

III. That you be well grounded in the firm Truths of Religion. We have willingly taken pains to add the Holy Scriptures, whereon every point of Faith contained in this Confessi-[8]on doth depend, and is born up by, and commend the same to your diligent perusal, that You be established in the truth and your Faith rest upon its proper Basis, the Word of God.[8] Follow the Example of the Noble *Bereans*, Search the Scriptures, Grow in Grace and the knowledge of Christ, be not Children in Understanding, but Men. Labour for a sound confirmed Knowledge of these Points in the Evidence of them. See that they be deeply rooted in your Minds and Hearts, that so You be not an easie prey to such as lie in wait to deceive.[9] For the want hereof to be condoled is the Unhappiness of many ever learning and never coming to the knowledge of, the Truth.[10]

---

[1] Isa. 8. 20. Rev. 21. 18, 19.
[2] Jer. 6. 16. Mat. 19. 8. Jer. 44. 17.
[3] Mat. 11: 27. 1 Joh. 5. 9.
[4] Luk. 10. 26.
[5] Mat. 15. 9.
[6] Joh. 4. 22. Jer. 7. 22.
[7] Leu. 10. 1, 2.
[8] Acts 17. 10, 11. Joh. 5. 39. 2 Pet. 3. 18. 1 Cor. 14. 20.
[9] Eph. 4. 13, 14.
[10] 2 Tim. 3. 7.

IV. *That having applyed the Rule of Holy Scripture to all the Articles of this Confession, and found the same upon Tryal the Unchangable and Eternal truths of God:*[1] You *remember and hold* them *fact* [*fast*], *Contend earnestly for* them as *the Faith once delivered to the Saints.* Value them as Your great Charter, the Instrument of Your Salvation, the Evidence of your not failing of the Grace of God, and receiving a Crown that fadeth not away.[2] Maintain them, and every of them all your dayes with undanted Resolution against all opposition, whatever the event be, and the same transmit safe and pure [9] to Posterity: Having bought the Truth, on no hand sell it. Believe[3] *the Truth will make you free: Faithful is he that hath promised: So shall none take away your Crown.*

Finally, *Do not think it enough that your Faith and Order be according to the Word of God, but live accordingly.*[4] It is not enough to believe well, You run your selves into the greatest hazzard unless you be careful to live well, and that this be,[5] All your Life and Conversation must be agreeable to the Rule of Gods Word This is the Rule of a Christian Conversation and Practical Reformation [6] Rest not in *the form of Godliness, denying the power of it.* Stir up an holy Zeal, *Strengthen the things that remain that are ready to die,* Be not carried away with the Corruptions Temptations and evil Examples of the Times, but be *blameless & without Rebuke, the Sons of God in a froward Generation.* [7] *They shall walk with me in white, for they are worthy.*

Remember ye our Brethren in this Colony; That we are a part of that Body, [8] for which the Providence of God hath wrought Wonders and are obliged by and Accountable for all the Mercies dispensed from the beginning of our Fathers settling this Country until now. *There he spake with us,*[9] That the practical piety [10] and serious Religion of our progenitors is exemplary and for our Imitation,[10] and will reflect confounding shame on us, if we prove Degenerate. The Lord grant that the noble design of our Fathers in coming to this Land, may not be forgotten by us, nor by our Children after us, even the Interest of Religion, which we can never Exchange for a Temporal Interest without the Fowlest Degeneracy and most Inexcusable Defection.[11] To Conclude the Solemn Rebukes of Providence from time to time in a series of Judgments, and in particular, *the General drought in the Summer past, together with the grievous Disapointment of our Military Undertaking, the Distresses Sickness and Mortality of our Camp cannot successfully be Improved but by a self humbling Consideration of our Ways and a thorough Repentance of all that is amiss:*[12] So will the God of our Fathers be our God, and he will be a Wall of Fire round about us and the Glory in the midst of us in this present and all succeeding Generations. AMEN.

[Pp. 11–90 contains the Confession of Faith, identical with that adopted at Boston in 1680, and slightly modified from the Savoy Declaration of 1658. The full text and variations will be found *ante*, pp. 367–402 of this work. The Saybrook divines added proof texts to each article.]

---

[1] Rev. 3. 3. Jude 3. [2] 1 Cor. 15. 18. 1 Cor. 16. 13. Psal. 78. 5.
[3] Jon. 23. 23. Joh, 8 32 Heb. 10 13. Rev. 3. 11. [4] Tit 2. 11, 12.
[5] Gal. 6. 16, Mic. 6. 8. [6] 2 Tim 3 15. Rev. 3 19. Rev. 3 2. Phil. 2. 15.
[7] Rev. 3. 4. [8] Hos. xii. 2, 3. [9] Hosea xii 4. [10] 2 Tim. 1. 5. Job 8. 8.
[11] 2. 17. Jer. 2. 21. [12] Isa. 26. 9. Gen. 43. 23. Zach. 2. 5.

[p. 91] THE | Heads of Agreement, | Assented to by the United Ministers, | formerly called *PRESBYTERIAN* | and *CONGREGATIONAL.* | And also | Articles | **For the Administration** | OF | CHURCH DISCIPLINE | Unanimously | Agreed upon and consented to by the | ELDERS and MESSENGERS of | the Churches in the Colony of | *CONNECTICUT* in New-England | Assembled by Delegation at *Say-Brook* | *September 9th.* 1708. | —— | Phil. 3. 5. *Let us therefore, as many as be per- | fect, be thus minded; and if in any thing ye | be otherwise minded, God shall reveal even | this unto you.* | Eph. 4 3. *Endeavouring to keep the Unity of | the Spirit in the bond of Peace.* | —— | *New London* Printed by *Thomas Short*, 1710

[92 blank]
[93]

The PREFACE.

THere is no Constitution on Earth hath ever been established on such sure foundations, nor so fully provided for its subsistance as the Church of God. *It being built on the Prophets and Apostles, Jesus Christ himself being the chief Corner Stone.* Hence therefore it hath from its holy hill, beheld the Ruines of the greatest States and most flourishing Empires, having continued in safety, free from the fatal Accidences of Time, and triumphed not only over the Rage of men, but also the repeated Insults of the gates of Hell. And tho' it hath been often straitned as to its extent, and lessened as to its number, yet hath remained firm on its own Basis: yea, when most reduced, it hath forever made good that Motto, *Depressa Resurgo*; and so it shall continue to the end of the World: But to the shame of its Offenders, the Church hath suffered most from the Wounds, which she hath received in the house of her Friends, from those Wolves, that have come to Her in Sheeps Cloathing. Damnable Errors and Heresies have arisen from within her, whereby she hath sometimes been cast into horrible shades of Darkness, as Rev. 9. 2 *When the bottomless pit was opened, the smoke ascending darkned the Sun and Air.* Yet [94] when thus grievously Blackned, a Comeliness remained still. Otherwhiles She is seen bleeding with the Wounds of *Schism and Contention*, Offensive and hurtful to Her Sacred Head and Members for the Undivided head rejoyceth in an Undivided Body *His undefiled is but one* Cant. 6. 9. As She becomes divided, She becomes defiled: And hereby also the mutual Offices of the respective Members of this Undefiled one are Interrupted to the prejudice of the Whole. Whence follow great disorders, as when the Eye will not see for the Hand nor the Head take care of the Feet, nor our Union to Christ be acknowledged a sufficient bond to establish a relation between *Members in particular* 1 *Cor.* 12. 27. Gods Providence forever bears the upper hand in these Events, who suffers the corrupt Minds of Men to run into Errors and Divisions, *that the approved may be made manifest* 1 *Cor* 11. 19 Such ill minded Persons being threatned with a Wo, that are the Authors or Promoters of such Offences. *The Atheist endeavours to overthrow the whole Constitution of Religion: The Deist to take away all that part of it, that promiseth sinners any safety from the Wrath to come, and retain no more than what is enough to condemn him, and to take away all excuse for his disobedience Rom.* 1. 20. The Church of Christ hath also been a great sufferer from the Immoralities and disorderly walking of those that are related to Her, whose *Leaven hath sometimes hazarded the whole lump* 1 *Cor* 5. 6. Whose un-[95]seemly Practises have given advantage to Enemies to speak evil of the Ways of God, and to question the Truth of our holy Religion & the sincerity of the Professors thereof. These must be acknowledged to be *Spots and Blemishes* 2. *Pet.* 2. 13. The Wisdom of our Law giver King and Judge, who alone hath the Original soveraignty of giving being to, and laying the Foundations of the Church, and whose only is the Legislative power therein, hath given such ample Rights & Priviledges to the Church and such Excellent Rules for its Government, as are Inviting to Strangers, *like a City set on a Hill, Mat.* 5. 14. And hath lodged the Executive power in approved hands, that those who love the Church may be in peace, and Her Enemies may find Her *Terrible as an Army with Banners,* and that She might yield seasonable edification to those that walk Regularly within Her limits, and be able to Discharge Her self of Impenitent and Incorrigible Offenders Many of the forementioned mischiefs have to our sorrow afflicted the Churches within this Government, and by degrees we have fallen under much decay. Whereupon our *difficulties* have been of a long time trouble some, for the healing of our Wounds, a more Explicate asserting the Rules of Government sufficiently provided in the Holy Word hath been thought highly expedient Wherefore,

The Honourable, the General Assembly of this Colony out of a Tender regard to the [96] welfare of the Churches within the limits of their Government, were pleased to appoint the several Elders of each County with Messengers from their Churches to meet in Council, in which they should endeavour to agree in some General Rules Conformable to the Word of God for a method of Discipline to be practised in our Churches These several Councils having met & drawn up some Rules of Church Government did by their Delegates meet and Constitute one General Assembly of the Churches of this Colony at *Say Brook, Sept.* 9*th.* 1708. Who after a full Consent and Agreement unto the Confession of Faith Assented unto by the Synod of *Boston*; Did being Studious of keeping *the Unity of the Spirit in the Bond of peace, Eph* 4. 2. Agree that the Heads of Agreement Assented to by the United Brethren formerly called *Presbyterian and Congregational,* in *England,* be observed by the Churches throughout this Colony, which are herewith Published, and after Consideration of the several draughts of the County Councils, did with a Christian Condescention, and Fraternal Amicableness Unanimously Agree to the Articles for the Administration of Church Discipline now offered to Publick View, all which being presented, were allowed of and Established by the General Assembly of this Colony, as by their Acts appears for the better satisfaction of our People, we have undertaken a task, acceptable we trust unto many, [97] tho' it escape not the Exceptions of some, in subjoyning Scriptures for Confirmation of the Heads of Agreement, which we have not seen added thereunto. The aforesaid Articles consist in Two Heads, *The one holding forth the power of particular Churches in the Management of Discipline confirmed by Scriptures annexed.*

The other, *serves to preserve promote or recover the Peace and Edification of the Churches by the Means of a Consociation of the Elders, and Churches or of an Association of Elders*: Both which we are agreed have Countenance from the Scriptures and the Propositions in Answer to the Second Question given by the Synod met at *Boston* 1662[1] In both which having respect to the Divine Precepts of Fraternal

[1] See *ante*, pp. 337–339.

Union, and that Principle universally acknowledged, *Quod tangit omnes debet tractari abomnibus*. The Scriptures are added for the Illustration of the substance of the abovementioned Articles, yet with an Apprehension, that there may be alterations made and further Condescentions Agreed upon, which shall afterwards appear necessary for the Order and Edification of our Churches.

As we have laboured in this affair to approve our selves unto God, so we are cheerful with humble Prayer for his Blessing to recommend the Heads of Agreement with the subsequent Articles unto the acceptance and [98] observation of our People, hoping till it please the Lord to send forth further light and truth in these more Controversal Matters, this Method may be a blessed means of our better Unanimity & success in our Lords Work for the Gathering and Edifying of the Body of Christ, for which we bespeak the concuring Prayers of all that fear the LORD.

[Pp. 99–116 contain the "Heads of Agreement" (full text *ante*, pp. 456–462); and the "Articles" (*ante*, pp. 503–506). To each section of both these documents the Saybrook divines added proof texts.]

XVI

THE PLAN OF UNION, 1801

Editions and Reprints[1]

I. *Minutes of the General Assembly of the Presbyterian Church*, etc., *1789 to 1820.* Philadelphia, [1847,] pp. 224, 225 (1801).

II. *Proceedings of the General Association of Connecticut*, 1801, pp. 4, 5.

III. *Connecticut Evangelical Magazine*, II: 116.

IV. Zebulon Crocker, *Catastrophe of the Presbyterian Church, in 1837, including a full view of the recent Theological Controversies in New England*, New Haven, 1838, pp. 11–14.

V. William S. Kennedy, *The Plan of Union: or a History of the Presbyterian and Congregational Churches of the Western Reserve; with Biographical Sketches of the early Missionaries*, Hudson, Ohio, 1856, pp. 150, 151.

VI. *Congregational Quarterly*, V: 133, 134.

Literature

Minutes of Presbyterian General Assembly, and the *Proceedings of the General Association of Connecticut*, for 1800, 1801, 1835, 1837, etc. Zebulon Crocker, as above cited. *Proceedings of the General Convention of Cong. Ministers and Delegates . . . at Albany . . . October, 1852*, New York, 1852. *New Englander*, XI: 72–92. *The Plan of Union of 1801*, etc., *and Reasons why it should be abandoned*, etc., New York, 1852. W. S. Kennedy, as above cited. James H. Dill, John D. Pierce, Henry Cowles, John C. Hart, articles on Congregationalism in New York, Ohio, and Michigan, *Congregational Quarterly*, I: 151–158; II: 190–197; V: 132–142, 248–254. E. H. Gillett, *History of the Presbyterian Church*, Philadelphia, [1864,] *passim*. C. Cutler, *History of Western Reserve College*, Cleveland, 1876. Fairchild, *Oberlin: the Colony and the College*, 1883. Punchard, *History of Congregationalism*, V. *passim*. A. H. Ross, *Union Efforts between Congregationalists and Presbyterians: Results and Lessons*, Port Huron, 1889. *Papers of the Ohio Society of Church History*, Vol. I.

THE eighteenth century was not favorable for Congregational creed-making. The failure of the movement for stricter church government in Massachusetts and its success in Connecticut put the two leading colonies of New England on somewhat divergent paths. The loss of ministerial influence over the civil authorities of the larger colony had been real for a gen-

[1] Neither the editions nor the literature can claim to be exhaustive. For some of the references I am indebted to Prof. F. H. Foster of Pacific Seminary.

eration, but was clearly manifest when the Massachusetts government failed to call a synod in 1725;[1] and this tendency to separate the interests of church and state increased throughout New England all through the century. It was no longer possible to call a general assembly of the churches of New England as a whole, or of a province, in the old way, by government authority. And if the way of the founders of New England was no longer feasible, the modern method of voluntary union was not yet possible. The whole political tendency of the century was toward the emphasis of local independence, and the growth of the democratic element in church and state was essentially decentralizing. This inclination away from external bonds of union was increased by the sharp division of sentiment which manifested itself in many parts of New England between the supporters of the revival measures of the leaders of the "Great Awakening" of 1740–41, and those who looked upon religious excitement as perilous. That remarkable movement led to the rise of a new school of theology,—that of Edwards and his pupils,—and as a consequence theologic differences first become a factor of division among the churches. All these tendencies, coupled with the low state of religion which marked most of the century, made any general synods or councils, such as the seventeenth century had seen, impossible; and produced a general indifference to what would now be called "denominational interests" as distinguished from the concerns of the local church.

Meanwhile in Connecticut the working of the Saybrook system was such as to increase the sympathy of the churches for the Presbyterians of the Middle Provinces and diminish their intimacy of relationship with their brethren of Massachusetts. A widespread fear of establishment of Episcopacy in the colonies led, just before the revolutionary war, to the establishment of an annual joint convention of representatives of the Synod of New

[1] The petition to the General Court, signed by Cotton Mather in the name of the Ministers' Convention, is in Hutchinson, *Hist. Mass.*, ed. 1767, II: 322, 323. The upper House approved, but the lower House put off consideration of the question, the Boston Episcopalians appealed to England, and the English government disapproved. See also Palfrey, IV: 454–456.

York and Philadelphia and the Associations of Connecticut.[1] This body met from 1766 to 1775, and corresponded with Dissenters in England, collected the ecclesiastical legislation of the colonies, tried to ascertain the religious preferences of their inhabitants, and sought the union of the non-prelatical churches in opposition to encroachment.

The effect of these joint meetings and of the ecclesiastical constitution of Connecticut was seen in the declaration of unity in all essentials with Presbyterianism adopted by the Hartford North Association in 1799,[2] and is curiously illustrated by a vote of no less representative a body than the Connecticut General Association, in 1805, appointing a committee to "publish a new and elegant edition of the ecclesiastical constitution of the Presbyterian Church in Connecticut,"[3] meaning thereby the Saybrook Platform. Under such circumstances it is no wonder that, in the eyes of many, the differences between Congregationalism and Presbyterianism seemed peculiarities of geographical location rather than fundamental distinctions in polity.

It was when the Presbyterians of the Middle States and the Congregationalists of Connecticut felt themselves so much one, that a home-missionary problem of hitherto unknown importance arose, affecting both bodies, and seeming to make coöperation doubly desirable. Even before the revolutionary struggle the sons of Connecticut had begun to emigrate to what is now Vermont and central New York. That contest interrupted the exodus, but after the war was over the outpouring began again in increased volume. By the close of the last century, emigration from Connecticut was extensive, and at the dawn of the present century was pouring into the region of northern Ohio, which Con-

[1] The Minutes of this Convention were published in 1843 by Rev. David D. Field, under the auspices of the Conn. General Association, *Minutes of the Convention of Delegates from the Synod of N. Y. and Phila., and from the Associations of Conn.*, etc. Hartford. The proposition came from the Presbyterian body, to the General Association of Conn. It was heartily accepted and a "Plan of Union" drawn up wherein those to be united in Convention are described as "Pastors of the Congregational, Consociated, and Presbyterian Churches in North America." All jurisdiction over the churches is disclaimed. It was also decided to ask the ministers of Mass., New Hampshire, and Rhode Island to send delegates; but the ministers of those provinces, though maintaining correspondence with the Convention, preferred not to be represented in its deliberations. *Ibid.*, pp. 5, 6, 10, 11, 18.

[2] *Ante*, p. 514.

[3] *Minutes Conn. Gen. Assoc.*, 1805, p. 5.

necticut had reserved in settlement of its claims to western territory.[1] In Vermont the immigration was of almost pure New England origin, and here New England religious institutions soon took root; but in New York and Ohio the settlers from Connecticut encountered other new-comers from Pennsylvania and colonies even further southward, who had been trained in Presbyterianism.

The Connecticut churches were early awake to their obligations to their sons and daughters of the dispersion. At its meeting in Mansfield in June, 1774, the Connecticut General Association voted: [2]

"This association taking into Consideration the State of ye Settlements now forming in the Wilderness to the Westward & North-westward of us, who are mostly destitute of a preached Gospel, many of which are of our Brethren Emigrants from this Colony, think it advisable that an attempt should be made to send missionaries among them, and for obtaining a Support for such Missionaries would recommend it to the several Ministers in this Colony to promote a Subscription among their people for this purpose."

This appeal met with encouraging response and two pastors[3] were directed to be sent out on a tour of "5 or 6 months" in 1775. The revolutionary war prevented the carrying out of the plan as proposed.[4] But a considerable sum was collected,[5] and in 1780 the Association asked two pastors to act as missionaries in Vermont.[6] In 1788 and 1791 the subject was further discussed, and in 1792 a missionary was appointed and legislative permission sought for the raising of funds.[7] The next year eight missionaries were named, all settled pastors, who were to go on tours of four months each and receive as compensation four and a half dollars weekly and an allowance of four dollars a week to supply their vacant pulpits.[8] The same number, but for the most part new men, were sent out in 1794.[9] The movement was now fully launched. And now in 1798, after having sounded the local Associations of the State on the subject through a committee appointed in 1797,[10]

---

[1] The story of the settlement of Northern Ohio is well told in Hinsdale, *Old Northwest*, New York, 1888. A clearer picture of the conditions of life in these settlements in 1800 is the autobiographic sketch of Rev. Joseph Badger, the first Congregational missionary to the Reserve, in *Am. Quarterly Register*, XIII: 317–328 (Feb., 1841). The *Diary of Thomas Robbins, D.D.*, Boston, 1886, also is valuable as illustrating early missionary life.

[2] *Records of the General Association*, 1738–1799, Hartford, 1888, p. 76. See also *Cont. Eccles. Hist. Conn.*, pp. 163, 164.

[3] *Records*, pp. 79, 80. [4] *Ibid.*, pp. 85, 86. [5] *Ibid.*, p. 100.

[6] *Ibid.*, p. 107. [7] *Ibid.*, pp. 125, 141, 142. [8] *Ibid.*, p. 148. [9] *Ibid.*, p. 154. [10] *Ibid.*, p. 173.

the General Association of Connecticut organized itself as a Missionary Society, the first Congregational missionary society in America, having as its object, "to christianize the Heathen in North America, and to support and promote Christian Knowledge in the new settlements within the United States."[1] In 1800 the *Connecticut Evangelical Magazine* was established, designed to spread a knowledge of missions, as well as to be a medium of discussion and a repository of Christian biography, and its profits, which were considerable,[2] were turned over to the "Missionary Society of Connecticut." In 1802 that society was chartered by the State. The good example of Connecticut led to the formation of a missionary association in Massachusetts in 1799.[3]

Meanwhile the relations between the Congregationalists of Connecticut and the Presbyterian General Assembly were becoming very friendly. In 1790 the General Association voted that a further degree of union with the Presbyterians was desirable, and a committee of correspondence was appointed to secure this result.[4] The General Assembly was more than willing;[5] in 1791 a joint committee representing it and the Connecticut Association met at New Haven and provided for united representation.[6] The doings of these commissioners were approved by the Association and the Assembly in 1792; and three representatives of the Connecticut churches were sent to the General Assembly.[7] The next year three Presbyterian delegates took their seats in the General Association, and on the request of the Presbyterians in 1794 it was agreed by both sides that the representatives of each body should have full right to vote in the meetings of the other.[8] And not only did they exercise this privilege, but plans for Presbyterian denominational growth, like the establishment of a seminary in Kentucky,[9] were referred to, and approved by, the Connecticut

[1] The Constitution may be found *Ibid.*, pp. 177–180. See also *Conn. Evang. Mag.*, I: 13.

[2] The profits of the first year were reported at $1,759.60. *Ibid.*, II: 80.

[3] See *Evang. Mag.*, I: 352–356.

[4] *Records of the Gen. Association*, 1738–1799, p. 133.

[5] See *Minutes of the Gen. Assembly*, 1791, pp. 29, 33.

[6] The minutes of the meeting of this joint committee are given in the *Rec. of the Gen. Association*, pp. 189–191. They agreed that representatives should not vote.

[7] *Association Records*, p. 142. *Minutes of the Gen. Assembly*, pp. 52, 64.

[8] *Association Rec.*, p. 154; *Gen. Assembly*, p. 80.

[9] *Association Rec.*, p. 160.

Association. From this degree of coöperation to union in missionary enterprise was but a step. Presbyterian and Congregational missionaries were working in the same fields and were in constant contact. Accordingly, in 1800, the question of a permanent adjustment of the relations of the two polities on missionary ground was raised in the Connecticut General Association.[1] There is every reason to believe that the originator of the discussion was the younger Jonathan Edwards, long the pastor of the Second Church in New Haven, but now president of Union College and a delegate from the General Assembly to the Connecticut body.[2] His residence in a section of the state of New York then rapidly filling with settlers had familiarized him with the questions involved, while his relations to both denominations were such as to give him little preference for the polity of either. The Association considered the matter favorably and appointed Edwards on a committee, associating with him Rev. Dr. Nathan Williams of Tolland, Rev. Nathan Strong of Hartford,[3] and Rev. Jonathan Freeman,[4] a Presbyterian delegate like Edwards representing the General Assembly, giving them instructions "to prepare a report on that subject." This they did, and the next day [5]—

"The following report of the Committee on the friendly intercourse of Missionaries was read, considered, and approved.

"The Rev[d] Mess[rs] John Smalley,[6] Levi Hart,[7] and Samuel Blatchford [8] are hereby appointed a Committee of this General Association, to confer with a committee to be appointed by the General Assembly of the Presbyterian Church, if they see fit to appoint such Committee, to consider the measures proper to be adopted both by this Association and said Assembly, to prevent alienation, to promote harmony and to establish, as far as possible, an uniform system of Church government, between those habitants of the new Settlements, who are attached to the Presbyterian form of church Government, and those who are attached to the congregational form: and to make report to this Association. Any two of the said committee are hereby empowered to act.

---

[1] *MS. Records of 1800*, p. 18. The meeting was at Norfolk.

[2] Jonathan Edwards was born at Northampton, Mass., in 1745; graduated at Princeton in 1765; pastor at New Haven, 1769–1795, pastor at Colebrook, Conn., 1796–1799; president of Union College, Schenectady, N. Y., to his death in Aug. 1, 1801. In gifts and experiences he was curiously like his father. Edwards's name heads the list in the record, but Williams seems to have been chairman of the committee.

[3] Williams and Strong were trustees of the Conn. Miss. Society.

[4] Of the Presbytery of Hudson, churches of Hopewell and Deer Park.

[5] MS. *Records of General Association*, 1800. See also *Minutes of General Assembly*, p. 212.

[6] New Britain.

[7] Griswold.

[8] Bridgeport. These three were the regular delegates to the next meeting of the General Assembly.

"Resolved that a copy of the foregoing paragraph be transmitted to the said Gen. Assembly, and that they be respectfully requested by the Moderator of this G. Association to concurr in the measure now proposed."

At the same time the Association requested the trustees of the Connecticut Missionary Society to direct their missionaries to promote friendly intercourse with the Presbyterians in their fields.

Having thus the support of the Connecticut churches, the proposition for agreement came before the General Assembly in May, 1801. That body was favorably inclined and voted as follows:[1]

"The Rev. Drs. Edwards,[2] McKnight,[3] and Woodhull,[4] the Rev. Mr. Blatchford,[5] and Mr. Hutton,[6] were appointed a committee, to consider and digest a plan of government for the churches in the new settlements agreeably to the proposal of the General Association of Connecticut, and report the same as soon as convenient."

Two days later[7] their report was "taken up and considered, and after mature deliberation on the same, approved" by the General Assembly. This report, the celebrated *Plan of Union*, reads thus:[8]

PLAN OF UNION.

"Regulations adopted by the General Assembly of the Presbyterian Church in America, and by the General Association of the State of Connecticut, (provided said Association agree to them,) with a view to prevent alienation, and to promote union and harmony in those new settlements which are composed of inhabitants from these bodies.

1. It is strictly enjoined on all their missionaries to the new settlements, to endeavour, by all proper means, to promote mutual forbearance, and a spirit of accommodation between those inhabitants of the new settlements who hold the Presbyterian, and those who hold the Congregational form of church government.

2. If in the new settlements any church of the Congregational order shall settle a minister of the Presbyterian order, that church may, if they choose, still conduct their discipline according to Congregational principles, settling their difficulties among themselves, or by a council mutually agreed upon for that purpose. But

---

1 *Gen. Assembly*, Minutes of 1801, pp. 212, 221.

2 Jonathan Edwards, whom we have before met in Connecticut.

3 Of New York city.

4 Of Freehold, N. J.

5 Delegate from Conn. Gen. Association.

6 A layman, a ruling elder of the Albany Presbytery and an associate of Edwards.

7 They reported the day after appointment but the business was laid over. *Gen. Assembly Minutes*, p. 222.

8 Text from *Ibid.*, pp. 224, 225.

if any difficulty shall exist between the minister and the church, or any member of it, it shall be referred to the Presbytery to which the minister shall belong, provided both parties agree to it; if not, to a council consisting of an equal number of Presbyterians and Congregationalists, agreed upon by both parties.

3. If a Presbyterian church shall settle a minister of Congregational principles, that church may still conduct their discipline according to Presbyterian principles, excepting that if a difficulty arise between him and his church, or any member of it, the cause shall be tried by the Association to which the said minister shall belong, provided both parties agree to it; otherwise by a council, one-half Congregationalists and the other Presbyterians, mutually agreed upon by the parties.

4. If any congregation consist partly of those who hold the Congregational form of discipline, and partly of those who hold the Presbyterian form, we recommend to both parties that this be no obstruction to their uniting in one church and settling a minister; and that in this case the church choose a standing committee from the communicants of said church, whose business it shall be to call to account every member of the church who shall conduct himself inconsistently with the laws of Christianity, and to give judgment on such conduct. That if the person condemned by their judgment be a Presbyterian, he shall have liberty to appeal to the Presbytery; if he be a Congregationalist, he shall have liberty to appeal to the body of the male communicants of the church. In the former case, the determination of the Presbytery shall be final, unless the church shall consent to a farther appeal to the Synod, or to the General Assembly; and in the latter case, if the party condemned shall wish for a trial by a mutual council, the cause shall be referred to such a council. And provided the said standing committee of any church shall depute one of themselves to attend the Presbytery, he may have the same right to sit and act in the Presbytery as a ruling elder of the Presbyterian church.

On motion,

Resolved, That an attested copy of the above plan be made by the Stated Clerk, and put into the hands of the delegates from this Assembly to the General Association, to be by them laid before that body, for their consideration; and that if it should be approved by them, it go into immediate operation."

The *Plan of Union*, thus approved by the Presbyterian legislative body, was duly laid before the Connecticut General Association at its meeting in Litchfield, June 16, 1801, by the three Presbyterian delegates, Rev. Dr. John McKnight, of the committee which prepared it, Rev. Archibald Alexander,[1] and Rev. John B. Linn,[2] and promptly ratified without alteration.[3]

This agreement was entered into with perfect good faith and with entire cordiality on both sides. It was intended to affect only the missionary churches on the frontier of civilization, and the framers seem to have had little thought that those churches would ever grow to be a great factor in American Christian life, and that what was well enough as an expedient in raw communities would have a different aspect when these wilderness plantations grew populous.

The *Plan of Union* was probably as fair an arrangement as could have been devised. If some of its features were non-Congregational, like the "standing committee" court of discipline in a mixed church, others were non-Presbyterian, as, for instance, the granting of the rights of a ruling elder in a Presbytery to a church delegate. It provided that when church and pastor were in disagreement the case should be tried according to the system which the minister represented, if both parties agreed thereto; if not, then by a mutual council equally drawn from the adherents to either polity. To churches and church members the rights of their respective systems were reserved.

But in actual practice the *Plan* produced Presbyterian churches in a large proportion of the instances in which it was applied to pure Congregational material. Estimates are of course somewhat conjectural, but a contemporary observer of the early workings of the *Plan* judged that by 1828 it had added "more than six hundred" to the Presbyterian churches in New York and Pennsylvania, and the states and territories lying west of them;[4] and a careful student of recent date has affirmed that "the Plan of Union transformed over two thousand churches, which were in origin

---

[1] Afterward the distinguished professor at Princeton, at this time of Virginia.

[2] Pastor First Presb. Ch., Philadelphia.

[3] *Minutes of Gen. Association*, 1801, p. 5.

[4] Z. Crocker, *Catastrophe of the Presbyterian Ch.*, p. 44.

and usages Congregational, into Presbyterian churches."[1] As a speaker at the Albany Convention of 1852 declared, "they have milked our Congregational cows, but have made nothing but Presbyterian butter and cheese."[2] But it would be unjust to blame the Presbyterians for this state of affairs. The fault was chiefly Congregational. The feeling was widespread in New England that Congregationalism could not thrive in new communities, that a "stronger government" was desirable for frontier towns.[3] Connecticut consociationism had fostered distrust in regard to the Congregationalism of the rest of New England, and a large proportion of the emigrants were from Connecticut. Men of Congregational training were prepared to look upon Presbyterianism as possessed of much that was attractive. On the other hand, if the denominational consciousness of Congregationalism was weak that of Presbyterianism was awake and considerably assertive.[4]

But two circumstances in particular worked to bring about the superior success of Presbyterianism, especially in Ohio, and to a considerable extent elsewhere. The first was that Congregational ministers largely became members of Presbyteries. That this was the fact was due in part to Congregational apathy, in part to geographical considerations. The *Plan of Union* had contemplated the founding of Associations as well as Presbyteries on missionary soil.[5] But the Presbyteries of Pennsylvania were friendly and close at hand. That of Beaver spread its protection over the whole of the Western Reserve when the settlements began, ministers were few, and of those few a large proportion were Presbyterians in the pay of the Connecticut Society, the scantiness of the salaries rendering it harder to get men from New England than from Pennsylvania. Fellowship seemed worth more than form, and it was natural that ministers of Congregational views should prefer to join an existing Presbytery rather than organize a feeble Association. When numbers increased an effort was made to organize

---

[1] The late Rev. Dr. A. H. Ross, *Union Efforts between Cong. and Presb.: Results and Lessons.* Port Huron, 1889, p. 7.

[2] Rev. Edward A. Lawrence, then of Marblehead, *Proceedings of the Gen. Convention held at Albany*, etc., p. 71.

[3] Dr. Heman Humphrey of Pittsfield, at Albany Convention. Speech, *Ibid.*, p. 70.

[4] Compare speech of Rev. Asa Turner of Denmark, Iowa, at Albany Convention, *Ibid.*, pp. 71–73; see also *Cong. Quart.*, V: 137.

[5] *Plan of Union*, sec. 3.

Associations in 1812–14, but it was defeated by the vigorous resistance of one or two determined Presbyterians and the good-natured lukewarmness of Congregationalists.[1] It was not till 1834 that a "Congregational Union" was founded in the Western Reserve, and not till 1836 that an Association was organized, and something of this experience was that of most of the territories in which the *Plan of Union* was put in operation. Now it was but natural that what ministers thought good for themselves they thought good for the churches. They joined the Presbyteries, their churches naturally followed in many instances, for to remain Congregational was to lack fellowship.

Closely connected with this cause for Presbyterian ascendency was a second. A church once joined to a Presbytery could not readily relinquish the connection. As Dr. Ross has expressed it:[2]

"the Plan provided no way for the withdrawal of a Congregational church from a Presbytery. . . . On Congregational principles a church may by majority vote carry itself and its property into a willing Presbytery; but on Presbyterian principles no church can withdraw from an unwilling Presbytery by majority vote."

Add to these two considerations the fact that western Congregationalism, when it dared to show an independent spirit, was viewed by many in New England, especially after the rise of Oberlin with its Arminianly inclined type of theology, as infected with doctrinal novelties from which churches more under Presbyterian control were supposedly exempt,[3] and it is no wonder that for years the Congregationalists of New England beheld the steady swelling of the ranks of Presbyterianism through their westward migrating sons and daughters.

But though the *Plan of Union* thus added to the number of Presbyterian churches, it by no means satisfied all Presbyterians. The decade of 1830 to 1840 was one of much theologic discussion

---

1 The Presbyterian champion was Rev. Thomas Barr; see on this matter Cowles, *Ohio Congregational*, *Cong. Quart.*, V: 137–139; Hart, *Cong. in Ohio*, *Ibid.*, V: 248–253; Punchard, *Congregationalism*, V: 198–216.

2 *Union Efforts between Cong. and Presb.: Results and Lessons*, p. 3. Other reasons for dissatisfaction with the workings of the *Plan of Union* are given by Dr. Ross and by Prof. Cowles (*Cong. Quart.*, V: 134–136). Its results in Western New York are described by Rev. J. C. Dill, *Cong. Quart.*, I: 151–158; in Michigan by J. D. Pierce, *Ibid.*, II: 190–197. See also Punchard, V: *passim.*

3 This unjust suspicion of the western churches was wide-spread. Compare *New Englander*, XI: 75–78; *Cong. Quart.*, II: 196; and especially the debates and resolutions of the Albany Convention of 1852, when it was a prime subject of discussion, *Proceedings*, pp. 13, 14, 53–63.

in New England and the Presbyterian field. The stricter Presbyterians had long looked upon many of the representatives of New England "new divinity" as of questionable orthodoxy, and this feeling had been intensified when the teachings of Prof. Nathaniel W. Taylor at New Haven began to cause serious division in Connecticut Congregationalism and led to the founding, in 1834, of a conservative theological seminary at East Windsor, Conn. The points in dispute related chiefly to the nature and purpose of sin, and the extent of human inability to turn to God; and discussion in New England between the supporters and opponents of "New Haven theology" waxed exceedingly bitter.[1]

While these disputes excited New England, similar doctrinal questions agitated the Presbyterian church, and New England discussions were transplanted to that part of the Presbyterian body which had been largely drawn from New England, — the portion formed under the *Plan of Union.* To the more conservative Presbyterians, Rev. Drs. Lyman Beecher of Cincinnati and Albert Barnes of Philadelphia, seemed heretical; while the churches of New York and Ohio largely looked upon them as champions. The trials of these distinguished men on charges of doctrinal unsoundness increased the bitterness between the "Old School" and "New School" factions;[2] and, to the heated thought of the conservatives, New England seemed the source of false doctrine and the churches formed under the *Plan of Union* peculiarly exposed to error owing to their lack of a full Presbyterian constitution. The "Old School" party, desirous of cutting loose from what they believed a dangerous connection with Congregationalists, exalted denominational enterprises and discountenanced the further use of union channels of missionary agency, like the American Board of Foreign Missions and the American Home Missionary Society; the "New School" favored these common societies. Feeling grew;

[1] An excellent summary of Dr. Taylor's views is that given by Prof. Fisher, *Schaff-Herzog Cyclopædia*, III: 2306. A good idea of the spirit in which the discussion was carried on may be gained from Zebulon Crocker, *Catastrophe of the Presb. Ch. in 1837, including a full view of the recent Theological Controversies in New England*, New Haven, 1838. Crocker gives an extended bibliography of the Taylor-Tyler controversy.

[2] For these trials and the general story of the abolition of the *Plan of Union* and the division of the Presbyterian Church, see Gillett, *Hist. of the Presbyterian Church*, Philadelphia [1864], II: 443-552.

in 1834 a memorial, drawn up by conservatives in the vicinity of Cincinnati, denounced the *Plan of Union* to the General Assembly and charged the Synods formed in accordance with its provisions with dangerous laxness in their administration and with the toleration of false doctrine.[1] The Assembly, however, did not hear the prayer of the memorialists. But the conservatives persisted, and called a convention of "Old School" sympathizers to meet at Pittsburg in the spring of 1835.[2] It was largely attended[3] and denounced the *Plan of Union* once more. In the Assembly of 1835, which followed this convention, the "Old School" party was in the majority, and favored a discontinuance of the *Plan of Union*, going so far as to vote:[4]

"that our brethren of the General Association of Connecticut, be, and they hereby are, respectfully requested to consent that said Plan shall be, from and after the next meeting of that Association, declared to be annulled."

Curiously, this vote was never presented to the Connecticut body.

But in 1836 the "Old School" sympathizers were unable to control the Assembly, and their attempt to condemn Albert Barnes and the "New School" teaching failed.[5] Of course nothing adverse to the *Plan of Union* was done. Alarmed at their defeat, the "Old School" party now once more gathered a preliminary convention, in the spring of 1837, at Philadelphia; this body addressed a memorial to the Assembly about to be convened, repeating the charges of doctrinal unsoundness, insisting on the abrogation of the *Plan of Union*, and demanding that every Presbytery not fully Presbyterian in its organization be cut off from the church.[6] And when the Assembly met on May 18, 1837, it was found that, as in the body of 1835, the majority was on the "Old School" side. Having the upper hand once more the conservatives now pushed their cause. The memorial of the convention of 1837 was promptly taken up,[7] and on May 22d, the following report was adopted:[8]

[1] *Ibid.*, 463–485.
[2] *Ibid.*, 488–491.
[3] "41 Presbyteries and 13 minorities of Presbyteries were represented." *Ibid.*, 490.
[4] *Ibid.*, 491. Crocker, *Catastrophe*, p. 36.
[5] *Gen. Assem. Minutes*, of 1836, pp. 268–271.
[6] Gillett, *Hist. Presb. Ch.*, II: 497–499.
[7] Minutes of 1837, p. 418.
[8] *Ibid.*, pp. 419, 420.

"In regard to the relation existing between the Presbyterian and Congregational Churches, the committee recommend the adoption of the following resolutions:

"1. That between these two branches of the American Church, there ought, in the judgment of this Assembly, to be maintained sentiments of mutual respect and esteem, and for that purpose no reasonable efforts should be omitted to preserve a perfectly good understanding between these branches of the Church of Christ.

"2. That it is expedient to continue the plan of friendly intercourse, between this Church and the Congregational Churches of New England, as it now exists."

So far all was plain sailing; the real meaning of the report was in the third resolution, and on that heated debate ensued. It was not till the next afternoon that the test came; by a vote of 129 to 123 it was ordered that the question be put,[1] and by 143 votes to 110 it was declared:[2]

"3. But as the 'Plan of Union' adopted for the new settlements, in 1801, was originally an unconstitutional act on the part of that Assembly—these important standing rules having never been submitted to the Presbyteries—and as they were totally destitute of authority as proceeding from the General Association of Connecticut, which is invested with no power to legislate in such cases, and especially to enact laws to regulate churches not within her limits; and as much confusion and irregularity have arisen from this unnatural and unconstitutional system of union, therefore, it is resolved, that the Act of the Assembly of 1801, entitled a 'Plan of Union,' be, and the same is hereby abrogated."

The "Old School" party having thus begun, its other projects were soon brought to vote. The Synod of the Western Reserve was declared no part of the Presbyterian Church, since formed under the *Plan of Union*.[3] For the same alleged reasons the Synods of Utica, Geneva, and Genesee were next excluded; the operations of the American Home Missionary Society, and the American Education Society were declared "exceedingly injurious to the peace and purity of the Presbyterian Church;" a list of doctrinal errors was condemned; and the Philadelphia Presbytery, to which Albert Barnes belonged, ordered dissolved. Of course there could be but one outcome. The Presbyterian Church was rent in sunder; and the next year, 1838, saw two bodies, each claiming to be the General Assembly. Of these, the "Old School" body held to the acts of 1837, while the "New School" still maintained the *Plan of Union* and coöperated in missionary enterprise with the Congregationalists.

The action of the Assembly came to the ears of the Connecti-

---

[1] *Ibid.*, p. 421.

[2] *Ibid.*

[3] The facts in this paragraph may be found in the Minutes of 1837, *passim*.

cut General Association at its meeting in New Milford in June, 1837, though for the first time in years no Presbyterian delegates were present. But no very positive action was taken. A committee was appointed to consider the matter, but its report was referred to the next Association meeting, "not intending by this postponement to imply consent to the abrogation of the Plan of Union."[1] But the trustees of the Connecticut Missionary Society presented a report to the Association which was really pusillanimous:[2]

"The 'Plan of Union' between the General Association of Connecticut, and the General Assembly of the Presbyterian Church,—under which so much good has been accomplished, and so many churches constituted by the Missionaries of our Society, was dissolved at the late meeting of the General Assembly. The Synod of the Western Reserve has also been declared not to be a portion of the Presbyterian Church. What course the Synod will take, in consequence of this measure, the Directors are not informed; but as their exclusion was chiefly owing to their want of a complete Presbyterian organization, and not to error in doctrine, we may still congratulate the Society that its labors in this section of our country have not been in vain; and it may continue its benefactions to these churches, as constituting an interesting part of the body of Christ."

The next General Association, that of 1838, voted "that with respect to the Plan of Union, all action of this Body be for the present suspended."[3] And so the matter rested.

But while these events were in progress, Congregationalism was at last beginning to wake up to a degree of denominational self-recognition. Men began to feel that it had an independent mission outside of New England. Its western churches were demonstrating their right to be. Signs of this quickening sense of its own value appeared in the organization of State Associations on what had been fields of missionary effort under the *Plan of Union*. Such an organization was effected in New York in 1834, the Western Reserve followed in 1836, then came Iowa in 1840, Michigan in 1842, Illinois in 1844, all of Ohio in 1852, and Indiana in 1858. Western Congregationalism felt that it deserved recognition rather than distrust, and the spirit of the denomination at last began to stir in the long apathetic frame. On October 5, 1852, there gathered at Albany, New York, the first meeting of a synodical character, representative of Congregationalism as a whole, which had assembled since the Cambridge body of 1646–8.

[1] *Proceedings of Gen. Association*, 1837, pp. 5, 9. [2] *Ibid.*, p. 13. [3] *Ibid.*, 1838, p. 8.

This "Convention,"[1] as it styled itself, came together on the call of the General Association of New York, which had invited all Congregational churches in the United States to send pastors and delegates. The response had been hearty, and the body numbered four hundred and sixty-three, from seventeen States, and including in its membership the leaders of the denomination. Its business, as announced by its Business Committee, of which Rev. Dr. Leonard Bacon of New Haven was chairman, was to discuss:[2]

"1. The construction and practical operation of the 'Plan of Union between Presbyterians and Congregationalists,' agreed upon by the General Assembly of the Presbyterian Church, and the General Association of Connecticut, in 1801.

2. The building of Church Edifices at the West.

3. The system and operations of the American Home Missionary Society.

4. The intercourse between the Congregationalists of New England and those of other States.

5. The local work and responsibility of a Congregational Church.

6. The bringing forward of Candidates for the Ministry.

7. The re-publication of the Works of our standard Theological writers."

The first item, that relating to the *Plan of Union*, was referred to a committee of ten, "two from New England, and one from each of the other States represented,"[3] and after a full debate,[4] the following report was unanimously adopted:[5]

"*Whereas*, the Plan of Union formed in 1801, by the General Assembly of the Presbyterian Church and the General Association of Connecticut, is understood to have been repudiated by the said Assembly before the schism in that body of 1838, though this year acknowledged as still in force by the General Assembly which met last at Washington, D. C.;[6] and

Whereas, many of our Presbyterian brethren, though adhering to this Plan in some of its provisions, do not, it is believed, maintain it in its integrity; especially in virtually requiring Congregational Ministers settled over Presbyterian Churches, and Congregational Churches having Presbyterian Ministers, to be connected with Presbyteries; and

Whereas, whatever mutual advantage has formerly resulted from this Plan to the two denominations, and whatever might yet result from it if acted upon impartially, its operation is now unfavorable to the spread and permanence of the Congregational polity, and even to the real harmony of these Christian communities:—

---

[1] For the doings of this body see *Proceedings of the General Convention of Cong. Ministers and Delegates in the United States, held at Albany, N. Y., on the 5th, 6th. 7th, and 8th of Oct., 1852.* New York, 1852. Compare also *New Englander*, XI: 72–92; and Dexter, *Cong. as seen*, p. 515.

[2] *Proceedings*, etc., pp. 11, 13.

[3] *Ibid.*, pp. 12, 14. Oregon and the District of Columbia, probably as not concerned, were not represented on the committee.

[4] A full report of the debate is given *Ibid.*, pp. 69–76.

[5] *Ibid.*, pp. 19, 20.

[6] I. e., the "New School" Assembly.

Resolved, 1st. That in the judgment of this Convention it is not deemed expedient that new Congregational Churches, or Churches heretofore independent, become connected with Presbyteries.

2d. That in the evident disuse of the said Plan, according to its original design, we deem it important, and for the purposes of union sufficient, that Congregationalists and Presbyterians exercise toward each other that spirit of love which the Gospel requires, and which their common faith is fitted to cherish; that they accord to each other the right of pre-occupancy, where but one Church can be maintained; and that, in the formation of such a Church, its ecclesiastical character and relations be determined by a majority of its members.

3d. That in respect to those Congregational Churches which are now connected with Presbyteries, — either on the above-mentioned Plan, or on those of 1808 and 1813,[1] between Congregational and Presbyterian bodies in the State of New York,— while we would not have them violently sever their existing relations, we counsel them to maintain vigilantly the Congregational privileges which have been guaranteed them by the Plans above mentioned, and to see to it that while they remain connected with Presbyteries, the true intent of those original arrangements be impartially carried out."

The Convention also passed resolutions discountenancing charges of doctrinal unsoundness and disorder in practice vaguely made against the western churches, and urging a more intimate acquaintance between east and west.[2] Its great work of practical value in denominational extension was its call for $50,000 (which proved $61,891 when the response had been made to the appeal[3]) for the erection of church-edifices in Ohio, Michigan, Wisconsin, Iowa, Illinois, Missouri, Indiana, and Minnesota.[4] From the meeting of the Albany Convention there has been growing sympathy between all branches of Congregationalism, east and west, and a growing self-respect and confidence in its own right to be.

The *Plan of Union* was now no more. Only the "New School" body regarded it as of any value, and they were pretty much convinced of its uselessness. As denominational consciousness grew on either side, churches formed under it sought their own affinities. It had proved itself essentially a failure. Formed by good men, with the best of intentions, it did not and could not secure the harmony between the two systems that was desired. It was sure to lead to misunderstandings. The churches planted under its

1 Some hints regarding these local modifications of the *Plan of Union* may be found in Gillett, *Hist. Presb. Ch.*, II: 107, 112–114; and Punchard, V: 56–59.

2 *Proceedings*, etc., pp. 13, 14.

3 *Reports of the Sec. and Treas. of the Central Com. appointed by the Albany Cong. Convention for disbursing the Fifty Thousand Dollar Building Fund*, New York, 1856, p. 6.

4 *Proceedings*, etc., pp. 16–18, 22–24.

rules were in an anomalous position, neither Congregational nor Presbyterian. On the whole it must be said, that efficient as the *Plan of Union* seemed at the time of its formation in gathering together the feeble benevolences of the churches and in giving the Gospel message to remote settlements, it would have been better had it never been made.

XVII

THE ENGLISH DECLARATION OF 1833

EDITIONS AND REPRINTS

I. *Minutes of the Congregational Union of England and Wales* for 1833, pp. 23–28. The *Declaration* was issued in a large edition separately as a tract by the Union, and since 1858 has been annually published in the English *Congregational Year-Book.*

II. In Schaff, *Creeds of Christendom*, New York, 1877, III: 730–734.

III. In Waddington, *Congregational History*, IV (1800–1850): 653–656.

SOURCES

Documents Connected with the Formation and Early Proceedings of the Congregational Union of England and Wales, Reprinted [London], 1839.

Congregational Magazine, London, 1831, 2, 3, *passim.*

LITERATURE

Schaff, *Creeds of Christendom*, I: 833–835. Dexter, *Cong. as seen*, etc., pp. 674, 675. Stoughton, *Religion in England from 1800 to 1850*, London, 1884, II: 102–112.

THE attempted union of the Presbyterians and Congregationalists of England into a single body, after the Toleration Act of 1689 had freed Non-conformists from their worst legal disabilities, has been described in an earlier chapter, and the failure of this association has been pointed out.[1] The immediate effect of the release of the Non-conformists from active persecution was not the growth which might have been expected. The old Puritan flame had burned low, the closing years of the seventeenth and the beginning of the eighteenth centuries were seasons of spiritual deadness in England as well as America, and a cold intellectuality in the pulpit took the place, to a large degree, of the Puritan earnestness. From 1717 onward, discussions regarding the Trinity rent the Presbyterian churches, which constituted the most numerous of the Dissenting bodies at the beginning of the eighteenth century, and so swept the churches of that order away

[1] *Ante*, pp. 441–452.

from their ancient faith that by the year 1750 they were prevailingly Arian, and by 1800 Unitarian.[1] These errors scarcely touched the Congregational body; and, as a consequence, as the last century wore on, Congregationalism increased and Presbyterianism decreased until the former became the more influential in English religious life.[2] But, in spite of such conspicuous lights in its ministry as Isaac Watts and Philip Doddridge, the Congregational denomination did not really flourish; associational meetings were largely neglected,[3] congregations dwindled, and other evidences of decline were apparent, until the great Wesleyan revival awoke new life in all Non-conformist circles. None of the older bodies of Dissenters felt and profited by that movement more than the Congregationalists, and to the evangelical impulse thus received the modern growth of English Congregationalism is largely due.

This new life brought with it desire for extension and for further fellowship in religious work. As a consequence, Associations were revived where they had fallen into decay, new ones were formed,[4] and the last few years of the eighteenth century saw the beginnings of a missionary activity at home and abroad which continued in increasing power into the present century. The denomination grew in consciousness of its real unity. By 1806 the London Board, which had administered Congregational funds since the breach of the old Union based on the *Heads of Agreement*,[5] proposed a General Union of the churches of our order in England, but the time was not yet quite ready.[6] In Scotland matters moved more rapidly, probably because the Congregational

---

[1] Arianism was popularized in England by William Whiston (1667–1752) Prof. at Cambridge. Traces of Arian sentiments may be found in Milton, Locke, and earlier writers. Whiston's most influential book, *Primitive Christianity Revived*, was published in 1711. These views were embraced by Joseph Hallet and James Pierce, Presbyterian ministers at Exeter, as early as 1717, and though strenuously opposed, widely permeated the Presbyterian body. See Bogue & Bennett, *Hist. of Dissenters*, ed. London, 1833, II: 165–197; and Stoughton, *Religion in England from 1800 to 1850*, London, 1884, I: 205–229.

[2] Stoughton, *Religion in Eng. under Q. Anne and the Georges*, London, 1878, II: 247.

[3] Compare Bogue & Bennett, *Ibid.*, II: 282.

[4] *Ibid.*, II: 565. By 1808 the authors were able to say that there was "scarcely a county" in southern England in which Associations were not vigorously at work. Stoughton states that the first of the modern Cong. Associations of ministers and churches was that formed in Devonshire in 1785; and the second in Kent in 1792; *Religion in England under Q. Anne and the Georges*, II: 272. Probably some had never died out.

[5] *Ante*, p. 452.

[6] Stoughton, *Religion in Eng.*, *1800–1850*, II: 104.

churches were much fewer in number; and a meeting at Edinburgh, in November, 1812, resolved on a Union for that country,—the first annual meeting of the organization being held on May 6, 1813.[1]

But, as the third decade of the present century drew to a close, the political and ecclesiastical condition of England made a consolidation of denominational interests seem increasingly desirable. The industrial changes, the agitation which resulted in the abolition of Test and Corporation Acts in 1828 and in Catholic emancipation in 1829, and the movement for the revision of the constitution which produced the Reform Bill of 1832, all profoundly stirred English society. The Congregationalists, in common with other Dissenters, were now no longer subject to galling political disabilities, their position was materially improved and they might well look for rapid growth; but these changes had aroused the conservative spirit of the Church of England also, and Congregationalists might expect increased opposition.

It was under these circumstances that a two-fold movement was begun looking toward the strengthening of denominational fellowship. The first of these efforts resulted, largely through the instrumentality of Rev. John Blackburn of Pentonville, and of Mr. Joshua Wilson of London, in securing the lease of a building in Blomfield Street, Finsbury Circus, London, as denominational headquarters from 1830 onward.[2] The second effort brought about the Union. That Union was advocated by Mr. Blackburn through the *Congregational Magazine*,[3] and was also independently urged by the Dorset Association through correspondence with other County Associations, begun in 1829.[4] As a result of this agitation, a Provisional Committee of twelve laymen and twelve ministers interested in the plan met at London June 7, 1830;[5] and by direction of this Committee a letter was sent out on January 24, 1831,[6] to

[1] The Union was suggested by a deacon of the church at Musselburg, William Tait, in Sept., 1812; the idea was taken up by the Association at Dalkeith, and a general meeting to favor the project held at Edinburgh, Nov. 4, 1812, in Thistle St. Chapel. See Waddington, *Cong. Hist.*, IV: 233, 234.

[2] Waddington, *Ibid.*, IV: 351-353; Stoughton, *Religion in Eng., 1800-1850*, II: 102-104.

[3] Waddington, *Ibid.*, IV: 348-362. [4] *Ibid.* [5] *Ibid.*, 359.

[6] Proceedings and letter in *Doc. Connected with the Formation . . . of the Cong. Union*, Reprint, pp. 5-7.

all County Associations asking them to send delegates to a general meeting at London in the following May.

In accordance with this invitation such an assembly came together on May 10 and 13, with an attendance of 82 ministers and 19 laymen. Here it was found that of the various Associations of England which had responded twenty favored the Union, while two hesitated.[1] Under these encouraging circumstances the meeting proceeded to form a constitution for the proposed body, expressing its advisory and non-judicial character; and to appoint a committee to complete the organization. By this committee the matter was once more presented to the churches, — this time in definite form, — and, in accordance with a vote of the convention of 1831, a new meeting was held at London on May 8 and 11, 1832. It now appeared that twenty-six Associations of the thirty-four in England had approved the plan, while eight hesitated or failed to take action.[2] The meeting therefore, May 8, 1832, voted that "the Union be now formed";[3] and it has continued in increasing usefulness to this day.

It was at the same session at which this Union was organized that[4]—

> "the Rev. J. A. James[5] then introduced a paper, containing a Declaration of the principles of faith and order of the Congregational Body, drawn up by an individual at the request of several brethren in town and country."

The "individual" here referred to was Mr. James's neighbor, Rev. George Redford of Worcester,[6] to whose pen the Declaration was due. The meeting listened to it with attention; but, believing any discussion of it to be premature before it had been laid before the churches, it voted unanimously, on May 11, to ask the approval of the Associations both as to the expediency and the

---

[1] *Ibid.*, p. 9. [2] *Minutes of 1832*, Reprint, p. 15. [3] *Ibid.*, p. 18. [4] *Ibid.*, p. 20.

[5] Of Birmingham.

[6] Rev. George Redford was born in London Sept. 27, 1785. He studied at Hoxton and Glasgow, was settled at Uxbridge for 14 years, and became prominent in denominational circles as one of the editors of the *Cong. Magazine*. From 1826 onward, till ill-health compelled his retirement, he was settled at Worcester. He died May 20, 1860. He received the degree of LL.D. from Glasgow, and that of D.D. from Amherst (Mass.). See *Cong. Year-Book, 1861*, London, 1861, pp. 230–233. Regarding the authorship of the Declaration that sketch says that a few emendations were made by Mr. James, "but substantially, and almost verbally, it was Dr. Redford's own composition."

form of the proposed Declaration.[1] In accordance with this vote it was transmitted to the churches, accompanied by a letter signed by the secretary of the Union, Joseph Turnbull, under date of June 4, 1832,—a letter which so well sets forth the purpose of the Declaration that a quotation is interesting.[2]

> "It was felt that such a document was but little required for our own information, and must necessarily be an imperfect statement of the sentiments held by us. . . . Still it was concluded that, for the information of others, not of our denomination, it was essentially requisite, at the present time. . . . It was stated by several brethren, that they were persuaded a very large proportion of our countrymen take us to be either SOCINIANS or METHODISTS. . . . Had not the Declaration of our fathers, at a meeting in the Savoy in the year 1658,[3] become scarce, and almost obsolete, it might have been referred to . . . but, considering that Declaration, though most orthodox, as too wordy and too much extended for our purpose, we were glad to receive the summary before us, as much more compendious, and more appropriate to the present need."

Evidently the churches thought well of the document thus submitted to them, at least for the use specified in this letter, for their representatives, in the meeting of the Union on May 7, 1833, expressed their satisfaction at the reception with which it had met and voted that it be referred to a committee[4] for some slight verbal revision,[5] and then[6]

> "accepted as the Declaration of the Congregational Body, with the distinct understanding, that it is not intended as a test or creed for subscription."

On the further report of the revision committee, May 10, 1833, the Declaration was unanimously approved.[7] It was at once issued as a tract, and the Union was informed in 1834 that nearly 20,000 copies had already been circulated.[8]

The Declaration is a sweet-spirited statement of which the English churches have no cause to be ashamed. In doctrine it is Calvinistic and distinctly Evangelical. Its departures from the earlier creeds of Puritanism are not essential. In regard to church polity it asserts a *jure divino* Congregationalism with much positiveness. Dr. Stoughton, writing in 1884, affirmed it as his opinion

---

[1] *Minutes of 1832*, Reprint, pp. 20, 21.
[2] *Ibid.*, pp. 29, 30.
[3] *Ante*, pp. 367–408.
[4] *Minutes of 1833*, p. 22.
[5] The text of the original draft may be found in *Minutes of 1832*, pp. 23–28. It differs very slightly from the form finally adopted.
[6] *Minutes of 1833*, p. 22.
[7] *Ibid.*, p. 28.
[8] *Minutes of 1834*, p. 4.

that "no member of the denomination who has reached an advanced age can deny that these articles set forth the current belief of fifty years ago."[1] He also stated that "the declaration created little discussion."[2] But when asked, about 1876, by Prof. Schaff, to express the present attitude of Congregationalists in England toward the Declaration, Dr. Stoughton inclined to the opinion that, partly on grounds of doctrine, but even more because such statements are now deemed unwise interferences with Christian liberty, the Declaration if newly presented would not now be adopted by the Union.[3] No man was better able to form a judgment on this point than Dr. Stoughton. But whether he was right or wrong, the Declaration is still given an honored place in each issue of the *Year-Book* of the Congregational Union of England and Wales.

[1] *Religion in Eng., 1800–1850*, II: 109. [2] *Ibid.*, 110.
[3] Schaff, *Creeds of Christendom*, I: 833–835.

THE ENGLISH DECLARATION.

"The[1] CONGREGATIONAL CHURCHES in England and Wales, frequently called Independents, hold the following Doctrines, as of Divine authority, and as the foundation of christian faith and practice.

They are also formed and governed according to the principles hereinafter stated.

PRELIMINARY NOTES.

1. It is not designed, in the following summary, to do more than to state the leading doctrines of faith and order maintained by Congregational Churches in general.

2. It is not proposed to offer any *proofs*, *reasons*, or *argu*-[24]*ments*, in support of the doctrines herein stated, but simply to *declare* what the denomination believes to be taught by the pen of inspiration.

3. It is not intended to present a *scholastic* or *critical* confession of faith, but merely such a statement as any intelligent member of the body might offer, as containing its leading principles.

4. It is not intended that the following statement should be put forth with any authority, or as a standard to which assent should be required.

5. Disallowing the utility of Creeds and Articles of religion as a bond of union, and protesting against subscription to any human formularies, as a term of communion, Congregationalists are yet willing to declare, for general information, what is commonly believed among them; reserving to every one the most perfect liberty of conscience.

6. Upon some minor points of doctrine and practice, they, differing among themselves, allow to each other the right to form an unbiassed judgment of the word of God.

7. They wish it to be observed, that, notwithstanding their jealousy of subscription to Creeds and Articles, and their disapproval of the imposition of any human standard, whether of faith or discipline, they are far more agreed in their doctrines and practices than any church which enjoins subscription, and enforces a human standard of orthodoxy; and they believe that there is no minister and no church among them that would deny the substance of any one of the following doctrines of religion; though each might prefer to state his sentiments in his own way.

PRINCIPLES OF RELIGION.

I. The Scriptures of the Old Testament, as received by the Jews, and the books of the New Testament, as received by the

[1] From the *Reprint* of *Minutes* of 1833, pp. 23–28.

Primitive Christians from the Evangelists and Apostles, Congregational Churches believe to be divinely inspired, and of supreme authority. These writings, in the languages in which they were originally composed, are to be consulted, by the aids of sound criticism, as a final appeal in all controversies; but the common version they consider to be adequate to the ordinary purposes of Christian instruction and edification.

II. They believe in one God, essentially wise, holy, just, and good; eternal, infinite, and immutable, in all natural and moral perfections; the Creator, Supporter, and Governor of all beings, and of all things.

III. They believe that God is revealed in the Scriptures, as the Father, the Son, and the Holy Spirit, and that to each are [25] attributed the same divine properties and perfections. The doctrine of the Divine existence, as above stated, they cordially believe without attempting fully to explain.

IV. They believe that man was created after the divine image, sinless, and in his kind perfect.

V. They believe that the first man disobeyed the divine command, fell from his state of innocence and purity, and involved all his posterity in the consequences of that fall.

VI. They believe that therefore all mankind are born in sin, and that a fatal inclination to moral evil, utterly incurable by human means, is inherent in every descendant of Adam.

VII. They believe that God having, before the foundation of the world, designed to redeem fallen man, made disclosures of his mercy, which were the grounds of faith and hope from the earliest ages.

VIII. They believe that God revealed more fully to Abraham the covenant of his grace; and, having promised that from his descendants should arise the Deliverer and Redeemer of mankind, set that Patriarch and his posterity apart, as a race specially favored and separated to his service; a peculiar church, formed and carefully preserved, under the divine sanction and government, until the birth of the promised Messiah.

IX. They believe that, in the fulness of the time, the Son of God was manifested in the flesh, being born of the Virgin Mary, but conceived by the power of the Holy Spirit; and that our Lord Jesus Christ was both the Son of man and the Son of God, partaking fully and truly of human nature, though without sin, equal with the Father, and "the express image of his person."

X. They believe that Jesus Christ, the Son of God, revealed, either personally in his own ministry, or by the Holy Spirit in the ministry of his apostles, the whole mind of God for our salvation; and that by his obedience to the divine law while he lived, and by his sufferings unto death, he meritoriously "obtained eternal redemption for us;" having thereby vindicated and illustrated divine justice, "magnified the law," and "brought in everlasting righteousness."

XI. They believe that, after his death and resurrection, he ascended up into heaven, where, as the Mediator, he "ever liveth" to rule over all, and to "make intercession for them that come unto God by him."

XII. They believe that the Holy Spirit is given in consequence of Christ's mediation, to quicken and renew the hearts of men; and that his influence is indispensably necessary to bring a sinner to true repentance, to produce saving faith, to regenerate the heart, and to perfect our sanctification.

XIII. They believe that we are justified through faith in Christ; as "the Lord our righteousness," and not "by the works of the Law."

[26] XIV. They believe that all who will be saved were the objects of God's eternal and electing love, and were given by an act of divine sovereignty to the Son of God; which in no way interferes with the system of means, nor with the grounds of human responsibility, being wholly unrevealed as to its objects, and therefore incapable of becoming a rule of human duty.

XV. They believe that the Scriptures teach the final perseverance of all true believers to a state of eternal blessedness; which they are appointed to obtain through constant faith in Christ, and uniform obedience to his commands.

XVI. They believe that a holy life will be the necessary effect of a true faith, and that good works are the certain fruits of a vital union to Christ.

XVII. They believe that the sanctification of true Christians, or their growth in the graces of the Spirit, and meetness for heaven, is gradually carried on through the whole period, during which it pleases God to continue them in the present life; and that, at death, their souls, perfectly freed from all remains of evil, are immediately received into the presence of Christ.

XVIII. They believe in the perpetual obligation of Baptism, and the Lord's Supper: the former to be administered to all converts to Christianity and their children, by the application of water to the subject, "in the name of the Father and of the Son and of the Holy Ghost;" and the latter to be celebrated by Christian churches as a token of faith in the Saviour, and of brotherly love.

XIX. They believe that Christ will finally come to judge the whole human race according to their works; that the bodies of the dead will be raised again; and that as the Supreme Judge, he will divide the righteous from the wicked, will receive the righteous into "life everlasting," but send away the wicked into "everlasting punishment."

XX. They believe that Jesus Christ directed his followers to live together in christian fellowship, and to maintain the communion of saints; and that, for this purpose, they are jointly to observe all divine ordinances, and maintain that church-order and discipline which is either expressly enjoined by inspired institution, or sanctioned by the undoubted example of the apostles and of apostolic churches.

PRINCIPLES OF CHURCH-ORDER AND DISCIPLINE.

I. The Congregational Churches hold it to be the will of Christ that true believers should voluntarily assemble together to observe religious ordinances, to promote mutual edification and holiness, to perpetuate and propagate the gospel in the world, [27] and to advance the glory and worship of God, through Jesus Christ; and that each Society of believers, having these objects in view in its formation, is properly a christian church.

II. They believe that the New Testament contains, either in the form of express statute, or in the example and practice of apostles and apostolic churches, all the articles of faith necessary to be believed, and all the principles of order and discipline requisite for constituting and governing christian societies; and that human traditions, fathers and councils, canons and creeds, possess no authority over the faith and practice of Christians.

III. They acknowledge Christ as the only Head of the church, and the officers of each church, under him, as ordained to administer his laws impartially to all; and their only appeal, in all questions touching their religious faith and practice, is to the Sacred Scriptures.

IV. They believe that the New Testament authorizes every christian church to elect its own officers, to manage all its own affairs, and to stand independent of, and irresponsible to, all authority, saving that only of the supreme and divine Head of the church, the Lord Jesus Christ.

V. They believe that the only officers placed by the apostles over individual churches, are the bishops or pastors, and the deacons; the number of these being dependent upon the numbers of the church; and that to these, as the officers of the church, is committed respectively the administration of its spiritual and temporal concerns; — subject, however, to the approbation of the church.

VI. They believe that no persons should be received as members of christian churches, but such as make a credible profession of Christianity, are living according to its precepts, and attest a willingness to be subject to its discipline; and that none should be excluded from the fellowship of the church, but such as deny the faith of Christ, violate his laws, or refuse to submit themselves to the discipline which the word of God enforces.

VII. The power of admission into any christian Church, and rejection from it, they believe to be vested in the church itself, and to be exercised only through the medium of its own officers.

VIII. They believe that christian churches should statedly meet for the celebration of public worship, for the observance of the Lord's Supper, and for the sanctification of the first day of the week.

IX. They believe that the power of a christian church is purely spiritual, and should in no way be corrupted by union with temporal or civil power.

X. They believe that it is the duty of christian churches to hold communion with each other, to entertain an enlarged affection for each other, as members of the same body, and to co-ope- [28] rate for the promotion of the christian cause; but that no church, nor union of churches, has any right or power to interfere with the faith or discipline of any other church, further than to separate from such as, in faith or practice, depart from the gospel of Christ.

XI. They believe that it is the privilege and duty of every church to call forth such of its members as may appear to be qualified, by the Holy Spirit, to sustain the office of the ministry: and that christian churches unitedly ought to consider the maintenance of the christian ministry, in an adequate degree of learning, as one of its especial cares; that the cause of the gospel may be both honourably sustained, and constantly promoted.

XII. They believe that church officers, whether bishops or deacons, should be chosen by the free voice of the church, but that their dedication to the duties of their office should take place with special prayer, and by solemn designation, to which most of the churches add the imposition of hands by those already in office.

XIII. They believe that the fellowship of every christian church should be so liberal as to admit to communion in the Lord's Supper, all whose faith and godliness are, on the whole, undoubted, though conscienciously differing in points of minor importance; and that this outward sign of fraternity in Christ should be co-extensive with the fraternity itself, though without involving any compliances which conscience would deem to be sinful."

XVIII

THE "BURIAL HILL" DECLARATION OF FAITH; AND THE STATEMENT OF PRINCIPLES OF POLITY, 1865

EDITIONS[1] AND REPRINTS

A. THE DECLARATION

I. *Debates and Proceedings of the National Council of Congregational Churches, Held at Boston, Mass., June 14–24, 1865*, Boston, 1866, pp. 401–403. [Not wholly accurate.]

II. *Congregational Quarterly*, X: 377, 378 [accurate].

III. *Ecclesiastical Polity. The Government and Communion Practised by the Congregational Churches in the United States*, Boston, 1872 [1879], pp. 77–80.

IV. Schaff, *Creeds of Christendom*, New York, 1877, III: 734–736.

V. *Congregationalist*, June 1, 1893.

B. THE PRINCIPLES

I. *Debates and Proceedings*, etc., pp. 463, 464.

II. Dexter, *Congregationalism . . . as seen in its Literature*, p. 517.

LITERATURE

The *Debates and Proceedings*, above cited, give the reports and discussions leading to the Declaration and Statement in full.

THE Albany Convention of 1852 clearly manifested the real unity of Congregationalism, east and west, and the abandonment of the *Plan of Union* gave impetus to the growing consciousness of the denomination. As a consequence, a stronger desire began to be felt for some outward manifestation of Congregational brotherhood. This dawning sense of the continental mission of Congregationalism was strengthened by the war of the rebellion,—a crisis in which national spirit in all its forms was aroused and in which the Congregational churches, unlike the Presbyterians, found themselves substantially united in support of the triumphant cause. Accordingly, when the failure of the rebellion became probable, and it was evident to far-sighted observers that the South and Southwest would be unbarred to Congregationalism as never before, and that a new epoch in national history

[1] Owing to the accessible character of the literature, I have given only the most important. The religious, and to some extent the secular, newspapers of the period contain references.

had opened,[1] movements began having for their aim the gathering of a representative Convention wherein the churches might deliberate as to the best methods of improving the opportunities of the hour.

The motion looking toward the Council began with the "Convention of the Congregational Churches of the Northwest." This organization, representative of the churches of Michigan, Illinois, Indiana, Wisconsin, Iowa, Missouri, and Minnesota, and having for its main purpose the choice of trustees of Chicago Theological Seminary, was induced by Rev. Dr. T. M. Post of St. Louis, to vote, at its meeting at Chicago, April 27, 1864, in view of the results of the war:[2]

> "That the crisis demands general consultation, coöperation, and concert among our churches, and to these ends, requires extensive correspondence among our ecclesiastical associations, or the assembling of a National Congregational Convention."

This proposal was presented to the Illinois General Association at its meeting at Quincy, May 27, 1864, and was received with hearty approval.[3] The Association voted to overture the other Congregational state bodies to unite in promoting a "National Convention," and recommended that the body meet at Springfield, Mass., or Albany, N. Y., on Sept. 6, 1864; and that its membership be, like that of the Albany Convention of 1852, the pastor and a delegate from every Congregational church that should choose to send. The proposition thus addressed to the Congregationalists of the country was favorably received, and during the summer and autumn of 1864[4] the plan of a National Convention was ratified by the state organizations of Indiana, Michigan, Iowa, Ohio, Rhode Island, Maine, Connecticut, Vermont, Massachusetts, New York, and Minnesota, in the order named. New Hampshire disapproved, though at least one prominent local association of that state favored the proposal. Each of the approving state conventions empowered a committee to join in perfecting arrangements for the National Convention, and on Nov. 16, 1864, at the invitation of the trustees of the American Congregational Union,[5] the various

---

[1] See *Debates and Proceedings of the National Council . . . 1865*, p. 1.
[2] The full vote is given *Ibid.*, pp. 1, 2. See also *Minutes of Convention*, etc., p. 16.
[3] *Ibid.*, p. 2. [4] *Ibid.*, p. 3. [5] *Ibid.*

committees met in the Broadway Tabernacle Church, New York, and organized a preliminary conference.

By this conference the proposed assembly was styled a "National Council,"[1] and its membership was determined to be representatives, both clerical and lay, chosen by the churches gathered in their local conferences or associations, in the proportion of two for each ten churches, or major fraction thereof, joined in such local body. Boston was proposed as the place of meeting, and the date of assembly fixed for the second Wednesday in June, 1865.[2] A variety of topics for discussion by the National Council were also determined upon by the preliminary conference, of which those of most concern here are the fifth and sixth,[3] "the expediency of issuing a statement of Congregational church polity," and "the expediency of setting forth a declaration of the Christian faith, as held in common by the Congregational churches." The conference appointed a committee to report to the Council on each of these topics; that charged with the question of polity being composed of Rev. Dr. Leonard Bacon,[4] Rev. A. H. Quint,[5] and Rev. Dr. H. M. Storrs;[6] and that having to do with the declaration of faith embracing Rev. Dr. J. P. Thompson,[7] Rev. Prof. G. P. Fisher,[8] and Rev. Prof. E. A. Lawrence.[9] The preliminary conference then issued a call[10] to the churches to elect representatives to the proposed Council, and adjourned, having done all that could be expected in preparing the way for the great denominational assembly.[11]

Pursuant to this summons, the National Council gathered in the Old South Meeting-house, Boston, on June 14, 1865, with a membership[12] of five hundred and two delegates, sixteen representatives of Congregational bodies in foreign lands, and fourteen persons whose connection with the Council was honorary. The

---

[1] *Ibid.*, p. 8. [2] *Ibid.*, June 14. [3] *Ibid.*, p. 7. [4] Of New Haven, Conn.

[5] Then of New Bedford, Mass. [6] Then of Cincinnati, O.

[7] New York city. [8] Yale Divinity School.

[9] Theological Institute of Conn., then at East Windsor Hill, Conn., now Hartford Theological Seminary. [10] In full, *Ibid.*, pp. 12–16.

[11] The call was signed by representatives of State bodies in every case except that of New Hampshire, a committee of the Hopkinton Association signed as representing part of the N. H. Churches. [12] The names are given in full, *Ibid.*, pp. 19–25.

permanent moderator of the body was Gov. William A. Buckingham of Connecticut, assisted by Rev. Dr. J. P. Thompson and Hon. C. G. Hammond;[1] and its scribes were Rev. H. M. Dexter,[2] Dea. Samuel Holmes,[3] and Rev. Messrs. Philo R. Hurd,[4] M. K. Whittlesey,[5] and E. P. Marvin.[6] So far its officers were similar to those of the Synods of the seventeenth century, but a power in directing the discussions appeared in the National Council unknown to the earlier bodies, in name at least, though its equivalent was doubtless to be found in them also,—the "Business Committee." This influential committee, chosen by the Council, consisted of Rev. A. H. Quint, Rev. Drs. Samuel Wolcott,[7] and Benjamin Labaree,[8] and Deacons Philo Carpenter[9] and S. F. Drury.[10] This committee was charged with preparing "a docket for the use of the moderator," and save "by special vote of the Council, no business" was to be "introduced which has not . . . passed through the hands of the committee."[11] Its guidance was felt throughout the session.

It was on the third day of the session, June 16, that the committee on the Declaration of Faith made, through its chairman, a report, of which these are the essential portions:[12]

"The committee appointed by the preliminary conference to prepare a Declaration of Faith, to be submitted to the Council, respectfully report:—

That, in the light of the discussions of that conference upon the expediency of such a Declaration, and also of the general principles of our polity, they could not regard it as their function to prepare a Confession of Faith to be imposed by act of this, or of any other body, upon the churches of the Congregational order. 'It was the glory of our fathers, that they heartily professed the only rule of their religion, from the very first, to be the Holy Scriptures;'[13] and particular churches have always exercised their liberty in 'confessions drawn up in their own forms'[14] . . . Whatever the diversities of metaphysical theology apparent in these various confessions, they yet, with singular unanimity, identify the faith of the Congregational churches with the body of Christian doctrine known as Calvinistic; and hence such Confessions as that of the Westminster divines, and that of the Savoy Synod, have been accredited among these churches as general symbols of faith.

---

1 Chicago. 2 Then of Boston. 3 New York city.
4 Romeo, Mich. 5 Ottawa, Ill. 6 Medford, Mass.
7 Cleveland, O. 8 Middlebury, Vt. 9 Chicago. 10 Olivet, Mich.

11 "Rules of Order" of the Council, *Debates and Proceedings*, p. 57.

12 In full, *Ibid.*, pp. 95–98. It would appear to have been prepared largely by Prof. Lawrence, *Ibid.*, p. 347.

13 Preface of Saybrook Platform, *ante*, p. 518.

14 *Magnalia*, ed. 1853–5, II: 181.

It has not appeared to the committee expedient to recommend that this Council should disturb this 'variety in unity'—as Cotton Mather happily describes it—by an attempted uniformity of statement in a Confession formulating each doctrine in more recent terms of metaphysical theology. It seemed better to characterize, in a comprehensive way, the doctrines held in common by our churches, than thus to individualize each in a theological formula. . . .

With these views, as the result of prolonged and careful deliberation, the committee unanimously recommend that the Council should declare, by reference to historical and venerable symbols, the faith as it has been maintained among the Congregational churches from the beginning; and also that it should set forth a testimony on behalf of these churches, for the Word of Truth now assailed by multiform and dangerous errors; and, for this end, they respectfully submit the following

RECITAL AND DECLARATION.

When the churches of New England assembled in a general synod at Cambridge, in 1648, they declared their assent, "for the substance thereof," to the Westminster Confession of Faith. When, again, these churches convened in a general synod[1] at Boston, in 1680, they declared their approval (with slight verbal alterations) of the doctrinal symbol adopted by a synod of the Congregational churches in England, at London, in 1658, and known as the "Savoy Confession," which in doctrine is almost identical with that of the Westminster Assembly. And yet again, when the churches in Connecticut met in council at Saybrook, in 1708, they 'owned and consented to' the Savoy Confession as adopted at Boston, and offered this as a public symbol of their faith.

Thus, from the beginning of their history, the Congregational churches in the United States have been allied in doctrine with the Reformed churches of Europe, and especially of Great Britain. The eighth article of the "Heads of Agreement," established by the Congregational and Presbyterian ministers in England in 1692,[2] and adopted at Saybrook in 1708, defines this position in these words:[3] 'As to what appertains to soundness of judgment in matters of faith, we esteem it sufficient that a church acknowledge the Scriptures to be the Word of God, the perfect and only rule of faith and practice, and own either the doctrinal parts of those commonly called the Articles of the Church of England, or the Confession or Catechisms, shorter or larger, compiled by the Assembly at Westminster, or the Confession agreed on at the Savoy, to be agreeable to the said rule.'

And now, when after the lapse of two centuries, these churches are again convened in a General Council at their primitive and historical home, it is enough for the first of those ends enumerated by the synod at Cambridge,—to wit, 'the maintenance of the faith entire, within itself,'—that this Council, referring to those ancient symbols as embodying, for substance of doctrine, the constant faith of the churches here represented, declares its adherence to the same, as being 'well and fully grounded upon the Holy Scriptures,'[4] which is 'the only sufficient and invariable rule of religion.'[5]

But having in view, also, the second end of a public confession enumerated by the Cambridge Synod,—to wit, 'the holding forth of unity and harmony both amongst and with other churches,'[6]—we desire to promote a closer fellowship of all

---

[1] The reader need hardly be reminded that the Synod of 1680 was not general, but a local Massachusetts body.

[2] Should be 1691.

[3] See *ante*, pp. 461, 462.

[4] Saybrook Preface, *ante*, p. 519.

[5] *Ibid.*

[6] *Ante*, p. 194.

Christian denominations in the faith and work of the gospel, especially against popular and destructive forms of unbelief, which assail the foundations of all religion, both natural and revealed; which know no God but nature; no Depravity but physical malformation, immaturity of powers, or some incident of outward condition; no Providence but the working of material causes and of statistical laws; no Revelation but that of consciousness; no Redemption but the elimination of evil by a natural sequence of suffering; no Regeneration but the natural evolution of a higher type of existence; no Retribution but the necessary consequences of physical and psychological laws.

As a testimony, in common with all Christian believers, against these and kindred errors, we deem it important to make a more specific declaration of the following truths:—

There is one personal God, who created all things; who controls the physical universe, the laws whereof he has established; and who, holding all events within his knowledge, rules over men by his wise and good providence and by his perfect moral law.

God, whose being, perfections, and government are partially made known to us through the testimony of his works and of conscience, has made a further revelation of himself in the Scriptures of the Old and New Testaments,—a revelation attested at the first by supernatural signs, and confirmed through all ages since by its moral effects upon the individual soul, and upon human society; a revelation authoritative and final. In this revelation, God has declared himself to be the Father, the Son, and the Holy Ghost; and he has manifested his love for the world through the incarnation of the Eternal Word for man's redemption, in the sinless life, the expiatory sufferings and death, and the resurrection of Jesus Christ, our Lord and Saviour, and also in the mission of the Holy Ghost, the Comforter, for the regeneration and sanctification of the souls of men.

The Scriptures, confirming the testimony of conscience and of history, declare that mankind are universally sinners, and are under the righteous condemnation of the law of God; that from this state there is no deliverance, save through 'repentance toward God, and faith in the Lord Jesus Christ;' and that there is a day appointed in which God will raise the dead, and will judge the world, and in which the issues of his moral government over men shall be made manifest in the awards of eternal life and eternal death, according to the deeds done in the body.

Joseph P. Thompson,
Edward A. Lawrence,
George P. Fisher."

This report, after a little discussion as to whether the issuance of a Declaration of Faith was contemplated by the bodies whose overtures originated the call of the Council, was referred to a special committee, consisting of Rev. John O. Fiske,[1] Prof. D. J. Noyes,[2] Rev. Drs. Nahum Gale,[3] Joseph Eldridge,[4] and Leonard Swain,[5] Dr. A. G. Bristol,[6] Rev. J. C. Hart,[7] Dea. S. S. Barnard,[8] and Rev. G. S. F. Savage,[9] "with instructions to consider the pro-

[1] Bath, Me. [2] Dartmouth Coll. [3] Lee, Mass. [4] Norfolk, Conn. [5] Providence, R. I. [6] Rochester, N. Y. [7] Kent, O. [8] Detroit, Mich. [9] Chicago.

priety of submitting to the Council a declaration of the common faith of our churches, and if thought advisable, to report such declaration."[1] To the committee thus charged, Profs. Samuel Harris,[2] E. A. Park,[3] E. A. Lawrence,[4] Noah Porter,[5] J. H. Fairchild,[6] and Joseph Haven,[7] were a little later added, doubtless with a desire thus to have the wisdom of as large a number of technically trained theologians as possible.

This new committee, on June 21, made a somewhat longer report than that of its predecessor,[8] employing in part the same language, but making considerably more elaborate statements in regard to several doctrines, especially that of the church, and introducing the following affirmation as its third paragraph :[9]

> "In conformity therefore, with the usage of previous councils, we, the elders and messengers of the Congregational churches in the United States, do now profess our adherence to the above-named Westminster and Savoy Confessions for 'substance of doctrine.' We thus declare our acceptance of the system of truths which is commonly known among us as Calvinism, and which is distinguished from other systems by so exalting the sovereignty of God as to 'establish' rather than take away the 'liberty' or free-agency of man, and by so exhibiting the entire character of God as to show most clearly 'the exceeding sinfulness of sin.'"

On the reading of this report by the chairman of the committee, Rev. John O. Fiske, its adoption was moved by Rev. Dr. Samuel Wolcott;[10] whereupon Rev. Uriah Balkam,[11] a clerical neighbor of the chairman, at once proposed to amend by substituting the report of the previous committee. A sharply contested debate now ensued,[12] having to do at first with the relative merits of the two reports, but resolving itself speedily into the approval or disapproval of the paragraph quoted from the report of the second committee declaring the faith of Congregationalists to be Calvinism.

The first to speak was Rev. Dr. Thompson, chairman of the first committee, who now urged the adoption of the report of its successor. Rev. Dr. Wolcott followed in similar strain. Mr.

---

[1] *Debates and Proceedings*, pp. 100, 134.
[2] Bangor Sem. [3] Andover Sem. [4] East Windsor Hill, now Hartford Sem. [5] Yale.
[6] Oberlin. [7] Chicago Sem. [8] In full, *Debates and Proceedings*, pp. 344-347.
[9] Paragraphs 1 and 2 are identical with the corresponding portions of the previous report.
[10] Cleveland, O. [11] Lewiston, Me. [12] In full, *Ibid.*, pp. 347-357.

Balkam of course supported his amendment; but Rev. Dr. Bacon[1] and Profs. Porter and Lawrence argued in favor of the second report. At this point Mr. Balkam, seeing that the sentiment of the council favored the declaration prepared by the second committee, withdrew his amendment. But no sooner had he done so than the debate was brought to a focus by a new amendment, offered by Rev. Dr. Joshua Leavitt,[2] proposing "to strike out from the third paragraph the words 'which is commonly known among us as Calvinism,' etc." The mover declared himself a Calvinist, but was confident that the use of any party name was liable to cause much misunderstanding as to the real position of the denomination. His opposition to the paragraph was supported by Rev. Drs. W. W. Patton,[3] and S. W. S. Dutton,[4] while Rev. Dr. J. M. Sturtevant[5] desired the preparation of a modern confession of faith, in language of the present, and without reference to previous formulas. On the other hand, Prof. Park deprecated the amendment, and affirmed:[6]

> "We are Calvinists, mainly, essentially, in all the essentials of our faith: and the man who, having pursued a three years' course of study,—having studied the Bible in the original languages,—is not a Calvinist, is not a respectable man. . . . I should be utterly and perfectly ashamed to have this amendment pass."

The views of Prof. Park were evidently those of a majority of the Council, and the amendment was declared rejected without a count of votes. Fruitless motions were now made by those opposed to the disputed section to lay the report upon the table, to adjourn, and to postpone further consideration till the next session; but finally the growing lateness of the hour led to an adjournment before a vote was reached. It so happened that, in accordance with a plan settled upon four days before, the Council agreed to meet the next morning not in Boston, but on Burial Hill in Plymouth, to which historic spot it was drawn by memories of the Congregationalists of that Scrooby-Leyden company whose ashes have rested there since the fatal winter of their first landing on American shores. A reunion on so memorable a spot, under circumstances

---

[1] New Haven, Conn.
[2] New York city.
[3] Chicago.
[4] New Haven, Conn.
[5] Jacksonville, Ill.
[6] *Ibid.*, p. 357.

so provocative of generous sentiment, seemed to some of the cooler leaders of the Council an opportunity to secure the united declaration of faith which the previous day's session had failed to bring. It was clear that, if pushed to a vote, the report of the second committee with its Calvinistic paragraph would command the suffrages of a large proportion of the Council; it was plain also that its adoption would displease many, who without being exclusively or even generally Arminian in their sentiments deprecated any party shibboleth. And, therefore, a few prominent members, of whom Rev. A. H. Quint, chairman of the Business Committee, was leader, determined to present to the Council, at its session on Burial Hill, a new Declaration, embodying the main points of the former reports, but avoiding the objectionable phrases. Such a draft was prepared, and so great was the pressure of business during the hours between the adjournment and the meeting at Plymouth, that the last sentences of the proposed formula were written by Mr. Quint, with a hat as his tablet, on the train as it rolled Plymouth-ward. Arrived on Burial Hill, the Council assembled in regular form, on the morning of June 22d; and Mr. Quint, in the name of its Business Committee, presented what has since been known as the "Burial Hill Declaration."[1] At the conclusion of its reading, Rev. Dr. Bacon moved its adoption, and its reference, together with the report of the second committee which had caused the debate of the day before, to a new committee for perfection. Rev. George Allen[2] raised his voice in protest against the document as "sectarian." Dea. Charles Stoddard[3] supported the views of Dr. Bacon, and Prof. Porter came to the aid of the same cause, though deprecating the presentation of a symbol under circumstances making debate almost impossible, and conditioning his approval on the insertion of a paragraph from the report of the second committee asserting the adaptability of Congregationalism to promote church unity and discountenancing ecclesiastical subdivision in small communities. The addition was promptly accepted

[1] I do not give the form read on Burial Hill here because it differs but slightly from the Declaration as finally adopted, and which will be found a little later. The full text is in *Debates and Proceedings*, pp. 361–363.

[2] Worcester, Mass.

[3] Boston, Mass.

by Mr. Quint, who now urged that only the paper presented on Burial Hill be approved by the Council, and that the committee of revision be empowered to do no more than make merely verbal alterations, not affecting the sense. These conditions were accepted by Dr. Bacon, and on a vote the declaration was adopted with but two dissenting voices.

The Declaration thus accepted at Plymouth was submitted for revision to a committee appointed the next day, after the return of the Council to Boston, and composed of Prof. William A. Stearns,[1] Rev. Dr. W. W. Patton,[2] and Rev. Julius A. Reed;[3] but their action had been expressly limited, and their changes were few and unimportant.[4] After a few hours' deliberation the revisers reported the completed form to the Council, and the Declaration was adopted by a rising vote, without opposition,—June 23, 1865. In its final foım it is as follows:[5]

BURIAL HILL DECLARATION.

"*Standing by the rock where the Pilgrims set foot upon these shores, upon the spot where they worshipped God, and among the graves of the early generations, we, Elders and Messengers of the Congregational churches of the United States in National Council assembled,—like them acknowledging no rule of faith but the word of God,—do now declare*[6] *our adherence to the faith and order of the apostolic and primitive churches*[7] *held by our fathers, and substantially as*[8] *embodied in the confessions and platforms which our Synods of 1648 and 1680 set forth or reaffirmed. We declare that the experience of the nearly two and a half centuries which have elapsed since the memorable day when our sires founded here a Christian Commonwealth, with all the development of new forms of error since their times, has only deepened our confidence in the faith and polity of these fathers.* We bless God[9] for the inheritance of these doctrines.[10] We invoke the help of

---

1 Amherst College. 2 Chicago. 3 Davenport, Iowa.

4 In full, *Debates and Proceedings*, p. 421. They will be indicated in the notes to the Declaration.

5 From *Cong. Quart.*, X: 377. That which is taken from the report of the second committee is here printed in Roman, the Burial Hill additions in *Italics*. The "Calvinistic" clause is of course omitted. Considerable rearrangement in order was made in the portions taken from the report.

6 Before revision, "reiterate."

7 *Ibid.* inserts "as."

8 *Ibid.*, reads "as substantially."

9 *Ibid.*, "the God of our Fathers."

10 *Ibid.* adds, "which have been transmitted to us, their children."

the Divine Redeemer, that, through the presence of the promised Comforter, He will enable us to transmit them in purity to our children.

In the times that are before us as a nation, times at once of duty and of danger, we rest all our hope in the gospel of the Son of God. It was the grand peculiarity of our Puritan Fathers, that they held this gospel, not merely as the ground of their personal salvation, but as declaring the worth of man by the incarnation and sacrifice of the Son of God; and therefore applied its principles to elevate society, to regulate education, to civilize humanity, to purify law, to reform the Church and the State, and[1] to assert and defend liberty; in short, to mould and redeem, by its all-transforming energy, everything that belongs to man in his individual and social relations.

It was the faith of our fathers that gave us this free land in which we dwell. It is by this faith only that we can transmit to our children a free and happy, because a Christian, commonwealth.

We[2] hold it to be a distinctive excellence of our Congregational system, that it exalts that which is more, above that which is less, important, and by the simplicity of its organization, facilitates, in communities where the population is limited, the union of all true believers in one Christian church; and that the division of such communities into several weak and jealous societies, holding the same common faith, is a sin against the unity of the body of Christ, and at once the shame and the scandal of Christendom.

We rejoice that, through the influence of our free system of apostolic order, we can hold fellowship with all who acknowledge Christ; and act efficiently in the work of restoring unity to the divided Church, and of bringing back harmony and peace among all 'who love our Lord Jesus Christ in sincerity.'

Thus[3] *recognizing the unity of the Church of Christ in all the world, and knowing that we are but one branch of Christ's people, while adhering to our own peculiar faith and order, we extend to all believers the hand of Christian fellowship, upon the basis of those great fundamental truths in which all Christians should*[4] *agree. With them* we confess our faith in God, the Father, the Son, and the Holy Ghost, the only living and true God; in Jesus Christ, the incarnate Word, who is exalted to be our Redeemer and King; and in the Holy Comforter, who is present in the Church to regenerate and sanctify the soul.

---

[1] *Ibid.* omits "and."

[2] This is the paragraph inserted on Burial Hill at the request of Prof. Porter.

[3] Before revision, "But." [4] *Ibid.*, "may."

With the whole Church, we confess the common sinfulness and ruin of our race, and acknowledge that it is only through the work accomplished by the life and expiatory death of Christ that believers in him[1] are justified before God,[2] receive the remission of sins, and through the presence and grace of the Holy Comforter[3] are delivered from the power of sin, and[4] perfected in holiness.

We believe also in the[5] organized and visible Church, in the ministry of the Word, in the sacraments of Baptism and the Lord's Supper, in the resurrection of the body, and in the final judgment, the issues of which are eternal life and everlasting punishment.

We receive these truths on the testimony of God, given[6] through prophets and apostles, and in the life, the miracles, the death, the resurrection, of his Son, our Divine Redeemer,—a testimony preserved for the Church in the Scriptures of the Old and New Testaments, which were composed by holy men as they were moved by the Holy Ghost.

Affirming now our belief that those who thus hold 'one faith, one Lord, one baptism,' together constitute the one Catholic Church, the several households of which, though called by different names, are the one body of Christ; and that these members of his body are sacredly bound to keep 'the unity of the spirit in the bond of peace,' *we declare that we will coöperate with all who hold these truths. With them we will* carry the gospel into every part of this land, *and with them we will go into all the world, and 'preach the gospel to every creature.'* May He to whom 'all power is given in heaven and earth' fulfil the promise which is all our hope: 'Lo, I am with you alway, even to the end of the world.' AMEN."

Thus came into being the only Declaration of Faith which a body representative of American Congregationalism as a whole had approved since 1648,—a distinction which it still retains.[7] As compared with the Puritan symbols of two centuries before, it shows great advance in simplicity and catholicity. If it has little of their strength and definiteness, it has little of their narrowness and omniscience. It distinctly recognizes the Congregational

[1] *Ibid.*, "that *we* are."

[2] *Ibid.* adds, "and."

[3] *Ibid.* reads, "Comforter alone that we hope to be delivered."

[4] *Ibid.* adds, "to be."

[5] *Ibid.*, "an."

[6] *Ibid.* adds, "originally."

[7] The "Oberlin Declaration," which forms the subject of the next chapter, is hardly sufficiently creed-like to rob this Declaration of this distinction.

body as but one of the Christian household. It has the merit of reasonable brevity. But it is also marked by the flavor of time and place, and by a certain exuberance of expression, natural perhaps to the sentiments of the hour, but hardly consonant with the judicial precision usually looked for in a statement of intellectual conviction. The historic feeling which prompted the recognition of the *Platform* of 1648 and the *Confession of 1680* as standards of Congregationalism was true; but the general phraseology of the Declaration leaves the question of the relation to present Congregational belief of the statements of those symbols regarding particular doctrines little clearer than before. The reaffirmation may mean much or little. The doctrines that the Declaration specifically enumerates form but an outline, and are presented in the most general language. In a statement of broad principles, rather than specific beliefs, issued on a historic occasion as a memorial rather than as a formula for permanent local use, these characteristics are not necessarily demerits; but they have operated to prevent the adoption of the Burial Hill Declaration as the creed of individual churches, and have made it to be comparatively little known and little used.

While these debates regarding the Confession of Faith had been in progress, a very similar discussion had taken place in the Council with reference to Church Polity. It will be remembered that the preliminary conference had appointed Rev. Dr. Bacon, Rev. A. H. Quint, and Rev. Dr. H. M. Storrs a committee[1] to report to the Council on "the expediency of issuing a statement of Congregational church polity." Of that committee, Dr. Storrs was unable to fulfil his appointment; but the chairman prepared, with the concurrence of his remaining colleague, an elaborate and very extensive platform of church polity,[2] modeled in size, language, and arrangement on the Cambridge Platform, but intended to present the actual, contemporary usages of the denomination. To this was appended a briefer epitome of Congregational

[1] See *ante*, 555.

[2] In full, *Debates and Proceedings*, pp. 102–133.

principles, not unadapted for use in church manuals. This report was presented to the Council on June 16, and fills twenty-seven large pages of rather fine print. As in the case of the report of the first committee on the Declaration, the Council immediately referred the document to a new special committee, embracing Rev. J. P. Gulliver,[1] Prof. Samuel Harris,[2] Rev. Nelson Bishop,[3] Prof. E. A. Park, Rev. J. G. Davis,[4] Rev. Dr. Joshua Leavitt,[5] Prof. S. C. Bartlett,[6] Rev. Messrs. Jesse Guernsey[7] and Charles C. Salter,[8] Judge Lester Taylor,[9] Rev. Messrs. James S. Hoyt[10] and J. D. Liggett;[11] to whom the Council afterwards added Rev. E. F. Burr.[12] This large body deliberated till June 23, and did not present its conclusions till after the adoption of the Declaration. Then it was found that the opinions were not unanimous. The chairman and ten others of the committee joined in a paper[13] in which they expressed general approval of the report, but held that it was impossible for the Council to perfect it in the brief session yet remaining; and that even were it possible so to perfect the platform and epitome, false impressions of imposition by synodical power might arise were they issued by the authority of the Council. The majority therefore recommended that the Council approve the statement of polity in a general way, but refer it to a special committee of twenty-five to be revised in a number of specified particulars, and such other ways, not inconsistent with its fundamental principles, as should seem best; and that it should be issued by the committee of revision over the signatures of its members. Such were the suggestions of the majority; but one member, Rev. Dr. Leavitt, presented a minority statement,[14] in which he recommended that the platform and epitome of polity be published without approval as an interesting addition to our denominational literature; and that instead of setting forth a minute and technical treatise on church government, the Council simply declare a few principles of church polity of the most general

[1] Norwich, Conn. [2] Bangor, Me. [3] Windsor, Vt.
[4] Amherst, N. H. [5] New York city. [6] Chicago.
[7] Dubuque, Iowa. [8] Minneapolis, Minn. [9] Claridon, O.
[10] Port Huron, Mich. [11] Leavenworth, Kan. [12] Lyme, Conn.
[13] *Debates and Proceedings*, pp. 427–430. [14] *Ibid.*, pp. 430–437.

character, avoiding all denominational coloring, and declaring willingness to unite with all churches owned of Christ.[1]

These two conflicting recommendations naturally led to debate.[2] Rev. Mr. Gulliver supported his position, and Rev. Dr. Leavitt his. Rev. Dr. Zachary Eddy[3] moved the adoption of the suggestions of the majority. Rev. Mr. Quint defended the original report from some of the criticisms of both wings of the second committee and opposed the appointment of a revising body of unwieldy numbers. Prof. Bartlett replied and defended the views of the majority of the second committee. Prof. Park followed in the same strain. Dr. Bacon then began an elaborate historical argument, setting forth with much power the desirability of a statement of polity, an argument interrupted by the arrival of the hour of adjournment but resumed at the next morning session. At that session Rev. Mr. Gulliver moved as an amendment that the original committee be added to the revisers, and Rev. Dr. Edward Beecher[4] supported the appointment of the proposed revision committee and expounded at length his views of the proper content of a work on Congregational polity. Prof. Lawrence heartily approved of Mr. Gulliver's amendment. At this point Rev. Dr. Joseph Eldridge,[5] moved by some expressions of Mr. Gulliver, the chairman of the second committee, in the current issue of the New York *Independent* derogatory of Connecticut consociationism, entered on a personal reply and a eulogy of that system. This was somewhat irrelevant to the purpose of the debate, and Prof. Park now proposed, as an amendment to Mr. Gulliver's amendment, the following resolution, which forms the only statement of Congregational polity adopted by the Council:[6]

STATEMENT OF CONGREGATIONAL PRINCIPLES.

"*Resolved*, That this Council recognizes as distinctive of the Congregational polity—

First, The principle that the local or Congregational church derives its power and authority directly from Christ, and is not

[1] His principles are *Ibid.*, pp. 436, 437. As far as any character can be ascribed to their very general statements they seem pure Independency.

[2] *Ibid.*, pp. 437–464.

[3] Northampton, Mass.

[4] Galesburg, Ill.

[5] Norfolk, Conn.

[6] *Debates and Proceedings*, pp. 463, 464.

subject to any ecclesiastical government exterior or superior to itself.

Second, That every local or Congregational church is bound to observe the duties of mutual respect and charity which are included in the communion of churches one with another; and that every church which refuses to give an account of its proceedings, when kindly and orderly desired to do so by neighboring churches, violates the law of Christ.

Third, That the ministry of the gospel by members of the churches who have been duly called and set apart to that work implies in itself no power of government, and that ministers of the gospel not elected to office in any church are not a hierarchy, nor are they invested with any official power in or over the churches."

This admirable epitome of the principles of modern Congregationalism was unanimously approved, and the report of the majority of the second committee, as amended by Mr. Gulliver, was duly adopted. Between such an affirmation of the most general facts of Congregationalism and the seventeenth century platforms a comparison is difficult; but one difference is clear. The positions of the first and second articles are unchanged, the latter half of the third would have met the approval of the fathers at Cambridge, but a Mather or a Cotton would have looked with astonishment on the statement that the duly established ministry implies "no power of government." Yet in this the Statement reflects the position of present Congregationalism, that in matters of government the minister is at most but the moderator of the deliberations of the membership. The development of Congregationalism has carried its polity to its logical outcome in pure democracy, and this fact here finds definite expression.

The Council fulfilled its vote and appointed the revision committee, to consider the platform and epitome of Dr. Bacon and Mr. Quint, as follows:[1] Rev. Dr. Bacon, Rev. Mr. Quint, Rev. Dr. H. M. Storrs, Prof. Park, Prof. Harris, Prof. Bartlett, Prof. Fisher, Prof. Fairchild,[2] Rev. J. P. Gulliver, Rev. Dr. Benjamin

[1] *Ibid.*, p. 486.

[2] Oberlin.

Labaree, Pres. Mark Hopkins,[1] Rev. William Barrows,[2] Rev. Dr. J. M. Sturtevant, Rev. Dr. T. M. Post,[3] Rev. Dr. Edward Beecher, Rev. Dr. William Salter,[4] Rev. J. S. Hoyt, Rev. David Burt,[5] Rev. Dr. J. P. Thompson, Hon. Woodbury Davis,[6] Hon. Henry Stockbridge,[7] Hon. J. H. Brockway,[8] Rev. N. A. Hyde,[9] Rev. Dr. Leonard Swain, Rev. Richard Cordley,[10] Asahel Finch, Esq.,[11] Warren Currier, Esq.,[12] and, by special vote, Rev. Dr. Rufus Anderson.[13] This committee did its work with much care, thoroughly digesting the forms presented to the Council, and published its result in 1872, with the approving signatures of its twenty-six surviving members.[14] It is a valuable statement, the product of much thought, and deserving of great respect. But owing perhaps to the willingness of our churches to be a law unto themselves, and the distaste of the present age for minute prescriptions and elaborate definitions, this document, sometimes known as the "Boston Platform," has never been widely known and has latterly been well-nigh forgotten. It has hardly merited this fate, but the days of elaborate platforms, like that of Cambridge, are as fully past as those of lengthy confessions.

---

1 Williams Coll. 2 Reading, Mass. 3 St. Louis, Mo. 4 Burlington, Ia.
5 Winona, Minn. 6 Portland, Me. 7 Baltimore, Md.
8 Ellington, Conn. 9 Indianapolis, Ind. 10 Lawrence, Kan.
11 Milwaukee, Wis. 12 St. Louis, Mo. 13 Sec. A. B. C. F. M.

14 *Ecclesiastical Polity, The Government and Communion Practised by the Congregational Churches in the United States of America, Which were Represented by Elders and Messengers in a National Council at Boston, A. D. 1865*, Boston, 1872, 2d ed. 1879.

XIX

THE CONSTITUTION OF THE NATIONAL COUNCIL AND "OBERLIN DECLARATION", 1871

TEXT

Minutes of the National Council of the Congregational Churches of the United States of America, at the First Session, Held in Oberlin, Ohio, November 15–21, 1871, pp. 29–32, 63–67; in the Minutes of subsequent sessions of the Council; in *Ecclesiastical Polity, The Government and Communion Practised by the Congregational Churches*, etc., Boston, 1872 [1879], pp. 81–86 [without the "Declaration on the Unity of the Church"].

THE success of the Council of 1865 in fostering a spirit of unity and a sense of a common mission among Congregationalists was conspicuous. While the body was without legislative authority, as becomes a Congregational synod, the representative character of its membership and the moderation and wisdom of its actions, only a small part of which have been had in review, gave it a wide influence. It was felt that so potent a possible factor in denominational life should not be occasional, but permanent and regularly recurring. While a few ministers, and some of them of eminent fame in the denomination, feared a possible loss of independence to the churches, the majority were ready to welcome an established Council. These views found expression in a manner well described in the note introductory to the *Minutes* of the Oberlin Council:[1]

"On the approach of the two hundred and fiftieth anniversary of the landing of the Pilgrims, the Church of the Pilgrimage, at Plymouth, Mass., invited the churches to meet by delegates at New York, to consider the appropriateness of particular action in celebrating this fifth jubilee. Such a meeting was held March 2, 1870; and it appointed a general committee for its purposes, consisting of Hon. Edward S. Tobey, Rev. William W. Patton, D.D., Rev. Henry M. Dexter, D.D., Samuel Holmes, A. S. Barnes, Rev. Ray Palmer, D.D., and Rev. Alonzo H. Quint, D.D.; of which the first named was chairman, Rev. Dr. Dexter, secretary, and Mr. Holmes, treasurer.

[1] Pp. 7, 8.

Among the acts of this committee was the calling of a *Pilgrim Memorial Convention*, which met at Chicago, Ill., April 27, 1870, open to delegates from all the churches in the United States.

Of that convention, B. W. Tompkins, of Connecticut, was *Moderator;* Hon. E. D. Holton, of Wisconsin, Rev. Samuel Wolcott, D.D., of Ohio, and Rev. George F. Magoun, of Iowa, *Vice-Moderators;* Rev. Henry C. Abernethy, of Illinois, Rev. Philo R. Hurd, D.D., of Michigan, and Rev. L. Smith Hobart, of New York, *Secretaries;* and Rev. William W. Patton, D.D., of Illinois, Dr. Samuel Holmes, of New York, Hon. C. J. Walker, of Michigan, James L. Kearnie, of Missouri, and Rev. Rowland B. Howard, of Illinois, *Business Committee.*

Among the resolutions adopted by that large convention were the following:

Resolved, That this Pilgrim Memorial Convention recommend to the Congregational State Conferences and Associations, and to other local bodies, to unite in measures for instituting on the principle of fellowship, excluding ecclesiastical authority, a permanent National Conference.

The General Conference of Ohio was the first to propose definite action. That Conference appointed a committee (Rev. A. Hastings Ross[1] being made chairman) to correspond with the other State organizations and propose a convention to mature the plan. The several State organizations approved of the proposed National organization, and appointed committees. The General Association of New York proposed that a meeting of these committees be held in Boston, December 21, 1870, and its committee (Rev. L. Smith Hobart,[2] chairman), issued circulars to that effect. The Committee of the General Association of Massachusetts adopted the proposal, and issued invitations accordingly."

Thus the steps leading to the permanent National Council were similar to those which had brought about the Council of 1865. In accordance with this invitation, committees representing the state organizations of Maine, New Hampshire, Massachusetts, Rhode Island, Connecticut, New York, New Jersey, Ohio, Michigan, Minnesota, and Wisconsin, met in Boston at the time suggested,[3] and formed a convention with Rev. Dr. E. B. Webb[4] as moderator, Hon. A. C. Barstow[5] as assistant moderator, Pres. William E. Merriman[6] as scribe, and Hon. H. S. McCall[7] as assistant scribe. This body unanimously—

"*Resolved,* That it is expedient, and appears clearly to be the voice of the churches, that a National Council of the Congregational Churches of the United States be organized";

and invited the churches to meet by delegates appointed in pro-

[1] Then of Springfield, O. [2] New York city.

[3] For their doings in full, see *Minutes* of Oberlin Council, pp. 9–12.

[4] Boston. [5] Providence, R. I. [6] Ripon, Wis. [7] New York.

portion substantially like the representation in the Council of 1865, at such time and place as a preliminary committee appointed by the convention should designate. It also suggested the outline of a constitution to be presented to the Council that was to be, and entrusted its preparation, as well as the call of the Council, to the following persons,—Rev. Dr. A. H. Quint,[1] Pres. W. E. Merriman, Prof. S. C. Bartlett,[2] Dea. Samuel Holmes,[3] Maj. Gen. O. O. Howard,[4] Rev. Dr. W. I. Buddington,[5] and Hon. A. C. Barstow.[6]

Pursuant to the call of this preliminary committee, the desired Council met at Oberlin, Ohio, November 15, 1871, with an attendance of 276 delegates from twenty-five states and territories, and fourteen honorary and corresponding members. After effecting a temporary organization, with Hon. Erastus D. Holton[7] as moderator, and Dea. Samuel Holmes as scribe, the Council received the report on the proposed constitution and considered it, paragraph by paragraph, at five sessions. The section relating to faith[8] was referred to a special committee,—Prof. S. C. Bartlett, Hon. Elisha Carpenter,[9] Hon. C. J. Walker,[10] Rev. Drs. I. E. Dwinell[11] and D. T. Fiske[12]; and various slight modifications of the document were suggested and adopted. A debate and two ballots resulted in the choice of "Council" as the designation of the body. But no serious alterations were made in the draft, and on Nov. 17, the following agreement was unanimously adopted:

"THE CONSTITUTION.

The Congregational churches of the United States, by elders and messengers assembled, do now associate themselves in National Council:

To express and foster their substantial unity in doctrine, polity, and work; and

To consult upon the common interests of all the churches, their duties in the work of evangelization, the united development of their resources, and their relations to all parts of the kingdom of Christ.

---

1 New Bedford, Mass. 2 Chicago Sem. 3 Montclair, N. J. and New York city. 4 Washington, D. C. 5 Brooklyn, N. Y. 6 Providence, R. I. 7 Milwaukee, Wis. 8 Paragraph 4. 9 Hartford, Conn. 10 Detroit, Mich. 11 Sacramento, Cal. 12 Newburyport, Mass.

They agree in belief that the Holy Scriptures are the sufficient and only infallible rule of religious faith and practice; their interpretation thereof being in substantial accordance with the great doctrines of the Christian faith, commonly called evangelical, held in our churches from the early times, and sufficiently set forth by former General Councils.[1]

They agree in the belief that the right of government resides in local churches, or congregations of believers, who are responsible directly to the Lord Jesus Christ, the One Head of the church universal and of all particular churches; but that all churches, being in communion one with another as parts of Christ's catholic church, have mutual duties subsisting in the obligations of fellowship.

The churches, therefore, while establishing this National Council for the furtherance of the common interests and work of all the churches, do maintain the Scriptural and inalienable right of each church to self-government and administration; and this National Council shall never exercise legislative or judicial authority, nor consent to act as a council of reference.

And for the convenience of orderly consultation, they establish the following Rules:—

I. *Sessions.*—The churches will meet in National Council every third year. They shall also be convened in special session whenever any five of the general State organizations shall so request.

II. *Representation.*—The churches shall be represented, at each session, by delegates, either ministers or laymen, appointed in number and manner as follows:—

1. The churches, assembled in their local organizations, appoint one delegate for every ten churches in their respective organizations, and one for a fraction of ten greater than one-half, it being understood that whenever the churches of any State are directly united in a general organization, they may, at their option, appoint the delegates in such body, instead of in local organizations, but in the above ratio of churches so united.

2. In addition to the above, the churches united in State organization appoint by such body one delegate, and one for each ten thousand communicants in their fellowship, and one for a major fraction thereof:—

3. It being recommended that the number of delegates be, in all cases, divided between ministers and laymen, as nearly equally as is practicable.

[1] This clause, from the word "practice" onward, was substituted for a direct reference to the Burial Hill Declaration by the special committee, to whom this paragraph was referred.

4. Such Congregational general societies for Christian work, and the faculties of such theological seminaries, as may be recognized by this Council, may be represented by one delegate each, such representatives having the right of discussion only.

III. *Officers.*— 1. At the beginning of every stated or special session, there shall be chosen by ballot, from those present as members, a moderator, and one or more assistant moderators, to preside over its deliberations.

2. At each triennial session, there shall be chosen by ballot a secretary, a registrar, and a treasurer, to serve from the close of such session to the close of the next triennial session.

3. The secretary shall receive communications for the Council, conduct correspondence, and collect such facts, and superintend such publications, as may from time to time be ordered.

4. The registrar shall make and preserve the records of the proceedings of the Council; and for his aid, one or more assistants shall be chosen at each session, to serve during such session.

5. The treasurer shall do the work ordinarily belonging to such office.

6. At each triennial session, there shall be chosen a provisional committee, who shall make needful arrangements for the next triennial session, and for any session called during the interval.

7. Committees shall be appointed, and in such manner, as may from time to time be ordered.

8. Any member of a church in fellowship may be chosen to the office of secretary, registrar, or treasurer; and such officers as are not delegates shall have all the privileges of members, except that of voting.

IV. *By-Laws.*[1]— The Council may make and alter By-laws at any triennial session.

V. *Amendments.*— This constitution shall not be altered or amended, except at a triennial session, and by a two-thirds vote, notice thereof having been given at a previous triennial session, or the proposed alteration having been requested by some general State organization of churches, and published with the notification of the session."

The work on the constitution was completed on the afternoon of November 17. On the evening before, the Council had listened to a paper by Rev. Dr. William I. Buddington[2] on the Unity of the

[1] I omit the by-laws as of temporary importance. [2] Brooklyn, N. Y.

Church. That paper was referred, on the morning after its presentation, to a committee composed of Rev. Dr. Leonard Bacon, Rev. Dr. Truman M. Post,[1] and Charles B. Lines, Esq.;[2] and on November 18 these brethren reported, and the Council adopted, a declaration which the Council "ordered to be put on record in close proximity to the constitution,"[3] and which has ever since been regarded as part of the basis of the body. It runs thus:[4]

"DECLARATION ON THE UNITY OF THE CHURCH.

The members of the National Council, representing the Congregational churches of the United States, avail themselves of this opportunity to renew their previous declarations of faith in the unity of the church of God.

While affirming the liberty of our churches, as taught in the New Testament, and inherited by us from our fathers, and from martyrs and confessors of foregoing ages, we adhere to this liberty all the more as affording the ground and hope of a more visible unity in time to come. We desire and purpose to coöperate with all the churches of our Lord Jesus Christ.

In the expression of the same catholic sentiments solemnly avowed by the Council of 1865, on the Burial Hill at Plymouth, we wish, at this new epoch of our history, to remove, so far as in us lies, all causes of suspicion and alienation, and to promote the growing unity of council and of effort among the followers of Christ. To us, as to our brethren, 'There is one body and one spirit, even as we are called in one hope of our calling.'

As little as did our fathers in their days, do we in ours, make a pretension to be the only churches of Christ. We find ourselves consulting and acting together under the distinctive name of Congregationalists, because, in the present condition of our common Christianity, we have felt ourselves called to ascertain and do our own appropriate part of the work of Christ's church among men.

We especially desire, in prosecuting the common work of evangelizing our own land and the world, to observe the common and sacred law, that in the wide field of the world's evangelization, we do our work in friendly coöperation with all those who love and serve our common Lord.

---

[1] St. Louis, Mo.

[2] Waubaunsee, Kan.

[3] *Minutes* of Oberlin Council, p. 36.

[4] *Ibid.*, pp. 31, 32, 65, 66.

We believe in 'the holy catholic church.' It is our prayer and endeavor, that the unity of the church may be more and more apparent, and that the prayer of our Lord for his disciples may be speedily and completely answered, and all be one; that by consequence of this Christian unity in love, the world may believe in Christ as sent of the Father to save the world."

The National Council, thus established, has more than vindicated its right to be. Though subject to protest during its early years from the churches of New Jersey[1] and New York[2] as a possible menace to Congregational independence, it has always had the support of a vast majority of the Congregational body, and has already substantially outlived criticism. It has unified the statistics of the denomination, it has relieved friction between the benevolent societies of our body, it has been largely instrumental in making some of them truly representative of the churches, and will doubtless eventually bring all into directly responsible connection, and above all it has fostered the spirit of denominational unity and fellowship, which the Congregationalism of the first half of this century so largely lacked, and which is essential to all permanent growth.

Its statements of faith, adopted at Oberlin, are valuable as illustrating the catholicity of spirit which has accompanied this growth of denominational consciousness. In matters of doctrine the constitution is more important for what it does not affirm than for that which it declares. Though nowhere expressly stated, the understanding at Oberlin at its adoption, and the interpretation since usually put upon it, is that it holds out the olive branch of denominational fellowship to brethren of Arminian sympathies, and is but a further illustration of that desire not to limit Congregational brotherhood to those who hold exclusively the system known as "Calvinism," which was already manifest in the Council of 1865.

[1] The General Association of this state protested in 1877 and 1880 against the continuance of the National Council as a regularly recurrent body, meeting to give advice in denominational matters. *Minutes* of Council of 1877, pp. 19, 22, 37, 38; of 1880, pp. 15, 16, 26, 27, 186-191.

[2] The General Association requested in 1880 that the Council refrain from expressing opinions by votes, and the Hudson River Association asked the same year that the functions of the Council be more clearly defined. See references in previous note.

XX

THE "COMMISSION" CREED OF 1883

TEXT

The Congregationalist for March 6, 1884, and other contemporary religious papers; Huntington, *Outlines of Congregational History*, Boston, 1885, pp. 189–194; Boardman, *Congregationalism*, Chicago [1889], pp. 62, 63.

LITERATURE

The *Minutes* of the National Council of 1880; Religious newspapers contemporary with its publication.

THE doctrinal expressions put forth by the Councils of 1865 and 1871 were the first united confessions which American Congregationalism had produced for more than two hundred years. But they were far from universally satisfactory. Their language was too general, and they were not adapted to form the creed-expressions of local churches, newly founded or desiring to modify their creeds. It was, moreover, a question in many minds how far the allusions of the Burial Hill Confession to the symbols of 1648 and 1680 implied that those venerable documents were authoritative standards of modern Congregationalism. On a strict construction of that Declaration it certainly appeared that the Council at Plymouth reaffirmed the doctrinal statements of those ancient formulæ with substantial fullness; but it might well be that this reference to the productions of these seventeenth century synods was, as Dr. Bacon styled it, merely a "rhetorical discourse."[1] So strongly was the desire felt for a simple declaration, in modern language, that the Oberlin Council of 1871 put on record its judgment that there had[2]—

"come up, from all quarters, earnest calls for some brief manual of doctrine and polity for use in the families and Sunday-schools of our churches";

and, hearing that a manual was in "preparation by the Congregational Publishing Society," the assembly at Oberlin appointed a

[1] *Independent*, Oct. 14, 1880.

[2] *Minutes* of National Council, 1871, p. 41.

committee of five to whom it could be submitted for approval.[1] The publication of the so-called "Boston Platform," in 1872, by the committee appointed by the Council of 1865, made the committee of the Council of 1871 feel discharged of any further duty in the matter.[2] But the lack of such an outline of doctrine was increasingly felt, and led, in 1879, to the appointment by the Congregational Association of Ohio of a committee, of which Rev. James Brand[3] was chairman, to consider what might be done to supply the want. At its suggestion the Ohio Association, at its meeting in Wellington in May, 1880, adopted an elaborate memorial, addressed to the National Council, setting forth the deficiencies of the previous declarations, and the inexpediency of reaffirming the seventeenth century creeds, and asking the Council to take into consideration, in such way as should seem best to it, the desirability of a "formula that shall not be mainly a reaffirmation of former confessions, but that shall state in precise terms in our living tongue the doctrines which we hold to-day."[4] This memorial was seconded by similar appeals from the General Conference of Minnesota,[5] and the Central South Conference of Tennessee;[6] and the three memorials were duly laid before the National Council on November 11, 1880, at its session in St. Louis, Mo.[7] There they were reinforced by an able and convincing historical and argumentative paper by Prof. Hiram Mead.[8] The Council referred this paper and the memorials to a committee consisting of Rev. Dr. A. L. Chapin,[9] Rev. C. D. Barrows,[10] Rev. Dr. S. R. Dennen,[11] Rev. Dr. N. A. Hyde,[12] Rev. F. P. Woodbury,[13] Dea. D. C. Bell,[14] and J. E. Sargent, Esq.[15] This committee sympathized with the memorialists, and at its recommendation,[16] the Council, on Nov. 15, adopted the following resolutions:[17]

"*Resolved*, (1) That the paper on creeds[18] be printed, and receive the thoughtful consideration of the churches.

---

[1] *Ibid.*, p. 46. [2] *Minutes* of 1874, p. 32.
[3] Oberlin, O. See *Minutes* of 1880, p. 133. [4] In full, *Ibid.*, pp. 133–138.
[5] *Ibid.*, pp. 139, 140. [6] *Ibid.*, pp. 138, 139. [7] *Ibid.*, p. 13.
[8] *Ibid.*, pp. 144–173. Of the Theo. Sem., Oberlin, O. [9] Beloit, Wis.
[10] Lowell, Mass. [11] New Haven, Conn. [12] Indianapolis, Ind.
[13] Rockford, Ill. [14] Minneapolis, Minn. [15] Concord, N. H.
[16] Its report in full, *Ibid.*, pp. 198, 199. [17] *Ibid.*, pp. 24, 25.
[18] Prof. Mead's.

Resolved, (2) That a committee of seven be appointed, who shall, as soon as practicable after the adjournment of the Council, select from among the members of our churches, in different parts of our land, twenty-five men of piety and ability, well versed in the truths of the Bible, and representing different shades of thought among us, who may be willing to confer and act together as a commission to prepare, in the form of a creed or catechism, or both, a simple, clear, and comprehensive exposition of the truths of the glorious gospel of the blessed God, for the instruction and edification of our churches.

Resolved, (3) That the committee of seven take pains to secure the willing co-operation of the men selected; that the commission be left, without specific instructions from this body, to adopt their own methods of proceeding, and to take time as they may find necessary to perfect their work; and that the result of their labors, when complete, be reported — not to this Council, but to the churches and to the world through the public press — to carry such weight of authority as the character of the commission and the intrinsic merit of their exposition of truth may command."

In accordance with this vote, the Council appointed the same committee to whose recommendation the resolutions were due to select the twenty-five commissioners;[1] and, as a result of their choice, the following ministers and teachers, designed to be widely representative of Congregationalism, geographically and theologically, were selected to prepare the desired creed,[2] — Pres. Julius H. Seelye,[3] Prof. Charles M. Mead,[4] Rev. Dr. Henry M. Dexter,[5] Rev. Dr. Edmund K. Alden,[6] Rev. Dr. Alexander McKenzie,[7] Rev. Dr. James G. Johnson,[8] Prof. George P. Fisher,[9] Rev. Dr. George Leon Walker,[10] Prof. William S. Karr,[11] Prof. George T. Ladd,[12] Rev. Dr. Samuel P. Leeds,[13] Rev. Dr. David B. Coe,[14] Rev. Dr. William M. Taylor,[15] Rev. Dr. Lyman Abbott,[16] Rev. Dr. Augustus F. Beard,[17] Pres. William W. Patton,[18] Pres. James H. Fairchild,[19] Pres. Israel W. Andrews,[20] Rev. Dr. Zachary Eddy,[21] Prof. James T. Hyde,[22] Rev. Dr. Edward P. Goodwin,[23] Rev. Dr. Alden B. Robbins,[24] Rev. Dr. Constans L. Goodell,[25] Rev. Dr. Richard Cordley,[26] and Prof. George Mooar.[27]

After much deliberation and correspondence, and much labor in sub-committees and as a whole, the Commission, on Dec. 19, 1883, put forth its creed, as follows:[28]

[1] *Ibid.*, p. 24.
[2] *Minutes* of 1883, p. 23.
[3] Pres. Amherst College.
[4] Andover Sem.
[5] Editor *Congregationalist*.
[6] Sec'y A. B. C. F. M.
[7] Cambridge, Mass.
[8] Rutland, Vt.
[9] Yale Sem.
[10] Hartford, Conn.
[11] Hartford Theo. Sem.
[12] Bowdoin Coll., Me., then Yale.
[13] Hanover, N. H.
[14] Sec. A. H. M. S.
[15] New York city.
[16] Editor *Christian Union*.
[17] Syracuse, N. Y.
[18] Pres. Howard Univ.
[19] Pres. Oberlin Coll.
[20] Marietta Coll., O.
[21] Detroit, Mich.
[22] Chicago Sem.
[23] Chicago, Ill.
[24] Muscatine, Ia.
[25] St. Louis, Mo.
[26] Emporia, Kan.
[27] Pacific Sem.
[28] From copy sent to members of the committee for signature.

"STATEMENT OF DOCTRINE:

I. We believe in one God, the Father Almighty, Maker of heaven and earth, and of all things visible and invisible;

And in Jesus Christ, His only Son, our Lord, who is of one substance with the Father; by whom all things were made;

And in the Holy Spirit, the Lord and Giver of life, who is sent from the Father and Son, and who together with the Father and Son is worshiped and glorified.

II. We believe that the providence of God, by which he executes his eternal purposes in the government of the world, is in and over all events; yet so that the freedom and responsibility of man are not impaired, and sin is the act of the creature alone.

III. We believe that man was made in the image of God, that he might know, love, and obey God, and enjoy him forever; that our first parents by disobedience fell under the righteous condemnation of God; and that all men are so alienated from God that there is no salvation from the guilt and power of sin except through God's redeeming grace.

IV. We believe that God would have all men return to him; that to this end he has made himself known, not only through the works of nature, the course of his providence, and the consciences of men, but also through supernatural revelations made especially to a chosen people, and above all, when the fullness of time was come, through Jesus Christ his Son.

V. We believe that the Scriptures of the Old and New Testaments are the records of God's revelation of himself in the work of redemption; that they were written by men under the special guidance of the Holy Spirit; that they are able to make wise unto salvation; and that they constitute the authoritative standard by which religious teaching and human conduct are to be regulated and judged.

VI. We believe that the love of God to sinful men has found its highest expression in the redemptive work of his Son; who became man, uniting his divine nature with our human nature in one person; who was tempted like other men, yet without sin; who by his humiliation, his holy obedience, his sufferings, his death on the cross, and his resurrection, became a perfect Redeemer; whose sacrifice of himself for the sins of the world declares the righteousness of God, and is the sole and sufficient ground of forgiveness and of reconciliation with him.

VII. We believe that Jesus Christ, after he had risen from the dead, ascended into heaven, where, as the one mediator between God and man, he carries forward his work of saving men; that he sends the Holy Spirit to convict them of sin, and to lead them to repentance and faith; and that those who through renewing grace turn to righteousness, and trust in Jesus Christ as their Redeemer, receive for his sake the forgiveness of their sins, and are made the children of God.

VIII. We believe that those who are thus regenerated and justified, grow in sanctified character through fellowship with Christ, the indwelling of the Holy Spirit, and obedience to the truth; that a holy life is the fruit and evidence of saving faith; and that the believer's hope of continuance in such a life is in the preserving grace of God.

IX. We believe that Jesus Christ came to establish among men the kingdom of God, the reign of truth and love, righteousness and peace; that to Jesus Christ, the Head of his kingdom, Christians are directly responsible in faith and conduct; and that to him all have immediate access without mediatorial or priestly intervention.

X. We believe that the Church of Christ, invisible and spiritual, comprises all true believers, whose duty it is to associate themselves in churches, for the maintenance of worship, for the promotion of spiritual growth and fellowship, and for the conversion of men; that these churches, under the guidance of the Holy Scriptures and in fellowship with one another, may determine — each for itself — their organization, statements of belief, and forms of worship, may appoint and set apart their own ministers, and should co-operate in the work which Christ has committed to them for the furtherance of the gospel throughout the world.

XI. We believe in the observance of the Lord's Day, as a day of holy rest and worship; in the ministry of the word; and in the two sacraments, which Christ has appointed for his church: Baptism, to be administered to believers and their children, as a sign of cleansing from sin, of union to Christ, and of the impartation of the Holy Spirit; and the Lord's Supper, as a symbol of his atoning death, a seal of its efficacy, and a means whereby he confirms and strengthens the spiritual union and communion of believers with himself.

XII. We believe in the ultimate prevalence of the kingdom of Christ over all the earth; in the glorious appearing of the great God and our Saviour Jesus Christ; in the resurrection of the dead;

and in a final judgment, the issues of which are everlasting punishment and everlasting life."[1]

To this creed were appended the signatures of twenty-two of the twenty-five commissioners. Three of the twenty-five, Rev. Dr. E. K. Alden, Prof. W. S. Karr, and Rev. Dr. E. P. Goodwin, declined to sign the document, the two former as failing adequately to represent their views in various particulars, and the latter assigning as his reason inability to be present at the meetings of the commission. But probably the creed was agreed upon with as great a degree of unanimity as any statement of faith in modern language, and of a definite character, would be in the present age by an equal number of representatives of any of the Protestant communions of America. It has had, and still has, its critics; but its reception has justified the appointment of the commission, and it is increasingly referred to as a standard of doctrine by ministerial and missionary candidates. The free system of Congregationalism allows every church to formulate its own creed; but this confession is coming more and more to be employed as a local statement of faith, especially by newly formed churches. Its merits are obvious. It is simple, clear, and modern. It represents a fair consensus of the actual present faith of the Congregational churches. Though imposed by no authority, and accepted only in so far as it is its own commendation, it gives the Congregational body what no other considerable denomination of Christians in America possesses,—a widely recognized creed, written in the language and expressing the thought of living men. As such it is vindicating its usefulness more and more.

The long story of the development of Congregational platforms and confessions has thus been passed in review. It is a history of strength and of weakness, of apprehensions of divine

[1] A form for admission of members to the church was prepared, somewhat hastily, by the Commission. It has never given general satisfaction, and the National Council of 1889 appointed a committee to revise it. *Minutes*, pp. 33, 43. Their report has not yet been made.

truth and of occasional mistake. The history of the intermingling forces of the human and the divine in the unfolding of the Kingdom of God on earth must ever be so. But the story has been told to little purpose if two essential features of Congregational life have not appeared,—those of unity and growth. The fathers of the sixteenth and seventeenth centuries, applying the Reformation principle of the authority of the Word of God to polity as well as to doctrine, sketched out the essential features of a Congregational church as they believed it to be divinely appointed. In common with their Puritan brethren they formulated the doctrinal system of the Gospel as they read it in the same divine record. On the basis of their two-fold work Congregationalism still stands. The essential features of the church as it appeared to them are the distinctive characteristics of a Congregational church to-day. The great truths which they maintained constitute, in their broad outline, the doctrinal basis of modern Congregationalism.

But the Congregational body of to-day is no mere residuum of sixteenth century discussions. If the main lines of its doctrine and polity were then laid down, it has made progress along them all. The fathers recognized the right of the brethren to a share in church-government, though they limited this right by the large prerogatives of ministerial office; modern Congregationalism has seen the wisdom of their trust and has removed their barriers, so that now its system is a pure democracy. The fathers believed that the churches should have upon them the restraining hand of the civil magistrate; modern Congregationalism has learned that in brotherly admonition rather than in legal coercion the truer remedy for churchly evils is to be found. To the civil government the fathers looked for the call of a general assembly of the churches; modern Congregationalism has found that in voluntary association is to be obtained the benefits that they sought, without the dangers of their method. And it has also discovered that a far greater range of Christian activities than the fathers dreamed of, in home and foreign missions, in the training of Christian ministers, in charitable work for the needy in body and spirit, can be carried on by the associated effort of Congregational churches, without forfeiting the self-government of the local congregation which the fathers justly prized.

So, too, in doctrine. The fathers stood on the common basis of Puritanic Calvinism; modern Congregationalism is simpler, less scholastic in its faith, more catholic in its sympathies. If it is less confident than were the fathers that it understands all the secrets of the divine counsel, it is more conscious of its duties toward a suffering and sinning world. The Gospel it presents is essentially the same that the fathers set forth as the basis of their faith, but it holds that Gospel to be intended for all men and to be wide enough in its provisions of redemption for the needs of the whole human race.

As has been the past, so, under the good hand of God, we may expect the future to be. Congregationalism can no more rest in its present status than in that of the Cambridge Platform. It will preserve its historic continuity, its roots will run back deep into the past, but it will, we may believe, deepen in knowledge and broaden in sympathy till it comes to the full measure of the pattern in accordance with which the Master designed his church on earth to be fashioned.

APPENDIX

INTRODUCTION TO THE 1960 EDITION

DOUGLAS HORTON

Since 1925, when *The Creeds and Platforms of Congregationalism* went out of print, there has been a mounting demand for its republication among those interested in maintaining the literary milestones of Protestant history. This year, which marks the one hundredth anniversary of the author's birth, seems an appropriate one in which to give to the world a reprint of the book. This is therefore at once a contribution to contemporary scholarship and a monument to a great scholar, Williston Walker.

The reprint reproduces Dr. Walker's own edition without change by jot or tittle. It contains not only the text of documents of primary value, mirroring the originals with incredible accuracy, but also the author's careful narrative, illuminating each document in its historical setting and connecting them all with each other.

It is of particular interest to note which of the creeds and platforms from which choice might have been made were actually selected for publication by this historian. Of the two general methods according to which they might have been chosen, Dr. Walker uses chiefly that of the history of ideas. The connecting thread upon which the documents are strung is the idea of Congregationalism. All those included illustrate this idea, and not one is included which does not. The other possible method of selection would have put the emphasis not on a concept but on the development of Congregationalism as a particular social group. The documents regarded as important, being associated with the ongoing group, would for the most part have also been ideologically connected, since this group, like any other, has tended to maintain a continuity of thought; but that there is none the less a difference between the two methods is shown in Dr. Walker's choice of materials for his very early chapters.

His first sentence — "Modern Congregationalism is a legitimate outcome of a consistent application to church polity of the principles of the Reformation" — marks Congregationalism as a principle or set of principles. On this basis Robert Browne "must be accounted the father of modern Congregationalism," since he was the first to enunciate those principles systematically. Those for which he stood and the philosophy of church life into which they ramified through the generations are abundantly set forth in all the chapters of the book. This method derives from a high idealism: the group is conceived as taking shape around the idea: a Congregationalist is one who accepts the tenets of Congregationalism. Always legitimate, this method was the natural one to follow in the Congregationalism of the later nineteenth century.

In the interval between Dr. Walker's time and now, however, a sea change has come over the thinking of American Congregationalism, paralleling a like change in Protestantism in general. During this time sociology has flowered into an accepted science. Groups, large and small, now have a standing in the thought of historians of society such as they have never had before, being regarded as basic quantities to which ideas are related as coefficients. Most important of all, Congregationalists, together with many other Protestants, have in this interval rediscovered the church. The *koinonia* has come into its own.

Modern American Congregationalists are likely to hold that true *koinonia* occurs when the local church has the same authority as the communion as a whole, in such wise that the two, in deep mutual respect, maintain continual dialogue with one another. This definition counts that denomination in which the whole dominates the local church as over-authoritative and that in which the local church takes precedence over the whole as anarchic. This they believe was taken for granted by the fathers of the seventeenth century. The Apologeticall Narration (which one could wish had been included among Dr. Walker's texts, so significant a platform it became for British Congregationalism) breathes the spirit of the *koinonia*. The five ranking Congregationalists of the Westminster Assembly repudiated the idea of sheer independency in local churches: to them it was

> "the most to be abhorred maxime . . . that a . . . particular society of men professing the name of Christ . . . should . . . arrogate unto themselves an exemption from giving account"

to "their neighbour churches." Contemporary Congregationalism in New England produced the Cambridge Platform of, by, and for the fellowship.

In the middle and late eighteen hundreds, however, with their Emersonian stress on individualism, the fact of the total communion, while remaining a matter of weight, had become secondary to many Congregationalists. The local churches came first, the communion second: the former indeed were conceived as creating the latter.

Congregational leaders today are disturbed by this conception. To them local churches do not create the communion any more than the communion creates the local churches. It is obvious that local churches do organize the denomination and its agencies of fellowship and that the denomination and its agencies do in like manner establish local churches, but this is the action of secondary causes, which would not take place if Christ had not entered history. It is Christ who gives the Church power, feeding strength to the local church through the whole company of churches and to the whole company through the local church. He is immediately present alike to each church and to the whole. The situation is a dialectical one (to use an adjective which has also achieved new meaning since Dr. Walker's day); the whole is not itself except as it is made up of free and autonomous parts with direct access to Christ, but the parts are not themselves except as they belong to the whole which is also informed by Christ. In this view a Congregationalist is a member of the group which enjoys Christ in these relationships. This is the essence of contemporary Congregationalism.

There is ground for believing that the need for giving an unshadowed place to the *koinonia* was felt more strongly by Dr. Walker than by the rank and file of his fellow churchmen in his day, but he did not feel it so dominantly as to be willing to let the thought of Congregationalism as a body of people in history eclipse the thought of Congregationalism as the polity to which they devoted themselves. Had he lived today, with today's powerful accent on the church as church, he might have shifted his emphasis, and in that case he would probably not have put the very early documents in his collection in the same category as the rest, for though these are most relevant illustrations of the idea of Congregationalism, they had little or no effect upon the formation, nor were they themselves expressions, of the Congregational people except, if at all, in a most indirect way.

All the chapters in the book except the first four treat documents which informed and affected the life of the ongoing Congregational community as we know it today. The "Commission" Creed of 1883 (to begin at the end of the register), the Constitution of the

National Council, and the Oberlin Declaration of 1871, though the last two of these were accepted only by the National Council, and the first only by a commission, are of this character. So are all the other instruments that one encounters as he works back through chapter five. Some of them, like the Creed and Covenant of the Salem Church, were highly local, but the Salem Church was in good and regular standing with the entire communion, being a free unit within a connection which included all the churches of the Bay, and so its symbols become a possession and concern of the entirety.

In regard to the second, third, and fourth chapters, however, which contain and comment upon the documents of the London-Amsterdam congregation — "A True Description out of the Word of God of the Visible Church" (1589), written by Henry Barrowe and John Greenwood, "A True Confession" (1596) and "The Points of Difference" (1603), probably from the pen of Henry Ainsworth and Francis Johnson — the question for the historian of the Congregational communion is whether that congregation is really and directly related to this communion. That the London-Amsterdam Church held to a Congregational idea, that it belonged to Congregationalism's "pre-history" in an ideal sense, does not admit of doubt — but can actual ecclesiastical links be found between it and modern Congregationalism? The ecclesiastical genealogist has no difficulty tracing back American Congregationalism to the churches of the Plymouth, Massachusetts Bay, Connecticut, and New Haven colonies, but what were their antecedents? Is the London-Amsterdam Church the ancestor of these four? It is patently not the ancestor of the latter three, though a little something might be said for relating it to Plymouth.

The Leyden-Plymouth Church was not an offshoot of the one at Amsterdam; it was never united with it except for *ad hoc* conversations; but there was mutual recognition between them of a sort. They at least did not condemn each other as antichristian; yet the difference in spirit between them is detectable even to this day. That of the Amsterdam congregation was the attitude of out-and-out Separatism, which regarded the Church of England as so thoroughly infected with the virus of popery and "will-worship" in general as to be no longer a true church. In 1624 this congregation refused to accept the letter of transfer (as we should put it) of Sabine Staresmore from that part of the Leyden-Plymouth Church which had remained at Leyden. The character of the Leyden-Plymouth group, on the other hand, had become more tolerant with the passing years. By 1617 they were willing to acknowledge that the fruits and effects of the doctrine taught even in the Church of England were "to the begetting of saving fayth in thousands in the land (conformistes and reformistes)." They were quite ready to accept the general view of the non-Separatist Puritans who entered New England in the other three colonies. (Here it might be noted that one of the very few conjectures of Dr. Walker that subsequent investigation has corrected is his hypothesis that Plymouth converted the Bay to its way of thinking. That the opposite is truer to the fact is proved by the well-documented research of Champlin Burrage, Perry Miller, and others.) Given the divergence of temper between the London-Amsterdam congregation and that which settled in Plymouth, it is possible only with extremest difficulty to consider the former a participant in the same *koinonia* that united the churches of New England. Nor was this church any closer to the Congregationalism of the England of the Dissenting Brethren.

Even farther removed from the fellowship which is Congregationalism were the churches founded by Robert Browne, the author of the "Booke which Sheweth the Life and Manners of All True Christians" (1582), with which chapter one deals. Nothing is known of his congregation in Norwich after 1603, and by that same year his congregation in Middelburg had apparently disappeared. This was before the Scrooby-Leyden-Plymouth Church was gathered. Nor was there any link of comity between Browne's churches and the London-Amsterdam group, which was careful to indicate in its publications that its members were "*falsely* called Brownists," "commonly (but *unjustly*) called Brownists." Robert Browne is now known to have been a man of brilliant thought who lived in a time and situation comparable to those which have had to be faced in our day by people whose government is in the hands of a tyrannical party. He apparently did what a man with a purpose contrary to the purposes of his rulers has always done under such conditions — the best he could. He resisted, outwardly and actively while it was possible, inwardly and passively when compelled to obey. There is no occasion to think that he was broken in mind when he made his capitulation to his enemy the bishop, who could address him in the name of the British government. In another generation he might have been able to make a different decision, but the easiest way to understand the one he actually came to is to regard it as his conception of the best strategy at that juncture. But this by no means relates his congregations and the literature he published to the living body of Congregationalism in history. Truly he was the father of modern Congregationalism in the idea, and truly he was not the father of the Congregational fellowship.

It is to be hoped that some historian of today, inspired by Dr. Walker's work, will gather and annotate a companion collection of creeds and platforms illustrating the developing idea of Congregationalism before 1582, which would serve as an introduction to this volume. Documents showing the Congregational strain running through the Christian church from its beginnings would be of paramount value to students. How useful it would be to have within the covers of a single book, for example, the basic instruments of some of the more congregational monastic orders of the Middle Ages; the written procedures of selected town and country parishes of Great Britain previous to the Reformation (especially those particular parishes exempt from the jurisdiction of a bishop), where British-American Congregationalism had its centuries of gestation; the constitution of at least one of the independent non-English-speaking churches in England like that of John a Lasco; the official papers making a parish its own patron through the purchase of the advowson (before Archbishop Laud outlawed the practice); and pertinent documents associated with the Reformation on the Continent, such as the Hessian Church Constitution of 1526 and some of the Anabaptist pronouncements more recently brought to light.

Another companion volume of Congregational creeds and platforms would assemble those that have come out since 1893, when Dr. Walker's classic was originally published. The editor of such a collection would be hard put to it to know how to include all the appropriate material. The amendments which in 1913 altered the constitution of the National Council in this country in an epoch-making way, the corresponding improvements which have been made in the constitution of the Congregational Union of England and Wales and in those of other unions throughout the world, the Constitution of the General Council of Congregational *Christian* Churches of 1931, with all the changes made in it since then, the British Congregational-Presbyterian concordat, and now the Basis of Union between the Congregational Christian Churches and the Evangelical and Reformed Church and the Constitution of the United Church of Christ, not to mention the constitutions of other united churches in which Congregationalism forms a part — all these would cry for space. Pages would be needed for the text, with commentary, of the Statement of Faith adopted at Kansas City and the corresponding statement of the United Church of Christ, which breaks new ground in the making of creeds, being in the form of an outpouring of gratitude to God for his mighty acts. Since *The Creeds and Platforms* was first published the International Congregational Council has risen into vigorous being, and it has its own constitution, its own statement of Essential Congregationalism. It may almost be said that the last seventy-five years have seen as many significant official utterances of Congregationalism as did the combined previous three centuries.

A third companion volume which no one in his day or ours would have been better equipped to write than Dr. Walker himself would contain the state papers having to do with the critical moments of Congregational history. This has already been done for the Puritan revolution in England, but for American Congregationalism an abbreviated codex of New English ecclesiastical laws would be even more important to church historians for the simple reason that for the first two hundred years of the history of Massachusetts and Connecticut the state in completely Erastian fashion did duty as the denominational framework for the churches: it provided a unifying bond between them. The Puritans brought with them not merely a church: they brought a civilization — one which called for both a state and a church interlaced in such a way that declarations of a town meeting or a general court often became platforms for ecclesiastical procedure. No inter-colony or inter-state, and remarkably few intra-colony or intra-state synods were called in American Congregationalism between 1648 and 1852 because none or few were needed, since the colonial and, later, the state legislative assemblies were available for the discussion of all relationships among the churches. Meetings of ministers and, in the early nineteenth century, of voluntary associations, such as those which launched the American Board of Commissioners for Foreign Missions, provided forums for the fellowship, but the bedrock legislation as to the founding, maintenance, and ministry of the churches was in the hands of the state in Connecticut until 1818 and in Massachusetts until 1834. It is not strange that the overwhelming number of congregations under the Plan of Union in the early part of the nineteenth century became Presbyterian: the wonder is that more of them did not, for when a Congregationalist crossed the western border of Massachusetts or Connecticut into New York State, he left behind him the primary symbol and organ of connection in Congregationalism. The line between the days of the state church and those of the state-free church in New England is much more of a watershed than many have recognized it to be: all New English ecclesiastical thinking before that time was against one background, as all since then has been against another, and all appeals today to precedent in that yesterday have to be corrected accordingly. This is the fundamental reason, for instance, why regularly meeting synods with authority over themselves are as good Congregationalism today as they were bad Congregationalism in the days of the theocracy. For those earlier times scholars need before them the civil religious laws of the land — the creeds and ecclesiastical platforms of the state, as it were — in order to understand the life of the churches.

Dr. Walker's book itself, however, could not be added to without impairing its present usefulness. This is therefore a reprint and not a new edition. It is a book so well written that time has only enhanced its standing. The historian Champlin Burrage says of it, "It is one of the three or four best and most scholarly books relating to Congregational history yet published. It is unpartizan in tone, independent in thought, and replete with minute knowledge." With this judgment the whole fraternity of church historians has concurred.

And speaking of that fraternity, though I must and do personally accept responsibility for what I have said in this introduction, I am most grateful to the historians of the seminaries associated with the Congregational Christian Council of Theological Schools who have consented to read my manuscript and suggest improvements.

Douglas Horton

CONSTITUTION INCLUDING THE KANSAS CITY STATEMENT OF FAITH (1913)

Despite the moves toward greater centralization that were made in the national meetings of 1865 and 1871, the Congregational churches continued in relatively loose association at the turn of the century. The basic structure created at Oberlin in 1871 remained intact: a National Council, meeting triennially, served in a purely advisory and informational capacity for the churches, regional groups, and benevolent societies across the country.

But several recent developments made it increasingly evident that the denomination needed a national structure with real, and not merely advisory, authority. First, the uneven development of state conferences and associations suggested the usefulness of a central clearing house for these organizations, both to strengthen them and to facilitate their communication. In 1907, an attempt to forge a union with the Methodist Protestant Church and the United Brethren Churches was aborted, its failure attributed by some to the National Council's limited, advisory status. Not least important, seven domestic and four overseas agencies and societies were functioning wholly independently, their missions and fund-raising activities overlapping and competing.

As a consequence, two special committees were authorized at the council meeting of 1907 to examine several recommendations about the future of the denomination. A Committee of Fifteen, reporting in Boston three years later, reached no firm conclusions; but a Committee on Polity addressed the issues more decisively, submitting several far-reaching resolutions. These affirmed the strengthening of state conferences and associations; formally enlarged the moderator's function to include service between national meetings; and reshaped the office of secretary into one of active leadership, management, and promotion. Even more important, the Committee on Polity recommended that another group be appointed to consider further the questions "on which the Council is in doubt." Thus was the Commission of Nineteen appointed—a body of major significance in the history of modern Congregationalism—with directions to submit to the next council a proposal for a new administrative plan for the churches. The commission's formal mandate was threefold: to create a new constitution and bylaws for the denomination; to clarify the role of the secretary, who was henceforth to serve as administrator *ad interim* for the council; and to propose a plan for coordinating and consolidating the various benevolent societies.

The Commission of Nineteen was composed of some of the most active lay and clerical members of the denomination. Rev. William Eleazar Barton served as secretary and Frank Knight Sanders as chair; their fellow members were Henry Mahan Beardsley, Rev. Nehemiah Boynton, Rev. Raymond Calkins, Samuel Billings Capen, Edward Dwight Eaton, Rev. Oliver Huckel, Rev. Henry Hopkins Kelsey, Frank Kimball, Rev. Charles Smith Mills, William Webster Mills, Charles Sumner Nash, Rev. Rockwell Harmon Potter, Henry Albert Stimson, Williston Walker, Lucien Calvin Warner, Arthur Holbrook Wellman, and John Meek Whitehead. Three subcommittees were appointed: one, headed by Secretary William Barton, an authority on ecclesiastical law, dealt with the constitution and bylaws; a second, headed by Charles Sumner Nash, president of Pacific Theological Seminary (now Pacific School of Religion), worked on defining the role of the secretary; and a third, led by Williston Walker, then professor of ecclesiastical history at Yale, dealt with the relation of the benevolent societies to the National Council.

The commission began its work immediately, meeting five times between 1910 and 1913 and engaging in extensive correspondence with the local churches, regional bodies, and benevolent societies. In the prefatory statement to its report at the National Council in Kansas City, Missouri, in October 1913, the chair and secretary of the group sounded a hopeful note: the test votes leading to the final adoption of the report, they said, were "notable alike for what they manifested of individual loyalty to conscience and a wonderful and vital unity that binds us together as a denomination."

[1]Arvel M. Steece, "The Commission of Nineteen." *Bulletin* of the Congregational Library 40, No. 1 (Fall 1988): 13–16.

That sense of unity, in a real way, pointed toward a new era for Congregationalism as a corporate body, as a *church*, not only as a loose aggregate of church*es*. The new constitution and bylaws, now proposed after an extensive informal referendum, provided for biennial (rather than triennial) sessions of the National Council and a membership that would serve for two successive councils instead of only one. The moderator was defined as having a representative function between meetings of the councils, but (in deference to the traditional insistence on the right of private judgment) his actions and statements were to be devoid of formal authority "except as inhere in the reason of them." An Executive Committee was created to transact the business of the council *ad interim* and to plan council meetings. The Commission of Nineteen recommended that a "Committee on Missions" be chosen by the National Council, with supervisory authority over the societies. The council was to become the majority of the voting membership of the societies, with a minority of members-at-large to be chosen by the societies themselves. Finally, the role of the secretary was clarified and enlarged: in addition to the standard functions of the office, the secretary was now given administrative authority and the right to represent the National Council in ecumenical endeavors and in relation to the several societies.

Prefacing the constitution and bylaws was a statement of faith—understood, like the two statements that had preceded it in 1865 and 1883—as a "testimony, not a test" of that which Congregationalists generally believed. The Kansas City Statement, as it came to be called, comprised the three sections on faith, polity, and the wider fellowship that preceded the body of the constitution. Far briefer than earlier formulations, it differed from them in content in two important respects. First, the new statement represented a decisive move away from anything like explicitly Calvinist theology. Adopted, though not without debate, without allusion to the sinfulness of humankind, Christ's atoning work, the existence of a system of eternal rewards and punishments, or the sacraments, the statement was a clear break with the past. Generally orthodox in tone, it avoided specific doctrinal references that might antagonize a fellowship that by 1913 had become theologically widely diversified. Second, the statement reflected the hopeful—some would say naive—progressivism of its time. Written before World War I and the Depression had undercut the optimistic dreams of a generation, the statement used consciously transformational language to suggest humanity's partnership with God in promoting peace, justice, knowledge, and "brotherhood."

Like the declarations that preceded it, the Kansas City Statement affirmed the autonomy of the local church, but it expressed support for fellowship and cooperation "in matters of common concern." And in a strongly worded affirmation of ecumenical commitment—a harbinger, perhaps, of future developments—the framers expressed their intent to "unite . . . in hearty cooperation" with all branches of the Church catholic in answer to Jesus' prayer "that they all may be one."

CONSTITUTION AND BY-LAWS OF 1913*

CONSTITUTION.

The Congregational Churches of the United States, by delegates in National Council assembled, reserving all the rights and cherished memories belonging to this organization under its former constitution, and declaring the steadfast allegiance of the churches composing the Council to the faith which our fathers confessed, which from age to age has found its expression in the historic creeds of the Church universal and of this communion, and affirming our loyalty to the basic principles of our representative democracy, hereby set forth the things most surely believed among us concerning faith, polity, and fellowship:

FAITH.

We believe in God the Father, infinite in wisdom, goodness, and love; and in Jesus Christ, his Son, our Lord and Saviour, who for us and our salvation lived and died and rose again and liveth evermore; and in the Holy Spirit, who taketh of the things of Christ and revealeth them to us, renewing, comforting, and inspiring the souls of men. We are united in striving to know the will of God as taught in the Holy Scriptures, and in our purpose to walk in the ways of the Lord, made known or to be made known to us. We hold it to be the mission of the Church of Christ to proclaim the gospel to all mankind, exalting the worship of the one true God, and laboring for the progress of knowledge, the promotion of justice, the reign of peace, and the realization of human brotherhood. Depending, as did our fathers, upon the continued guidance of the Holy Spirit to lead us into all truth, we work and pray for the transformation of the world into the kingdom of God; and we look with faith for the triumph of righteousness and the life everlasting.

*The Constitution and By-Laws are here reprinted as they originally appeared. Later, the so-called Kansas City Statement of Faith was often reprinted as a single unit without the subheadings of faith, polity, and the wider fellowship.

POLITY.

We believe in the freedom and responsibility of the individual soul, and the right of private judgment. We hold to the autonomy of the local church and its independence of all ecclesiastical control. We cherish the fellowship of the churches, united in district, state, and national bodies, for counsel and coöperation in matters of common concern.

THE WIDER FELLOWSHIP.

While affirming the liberty of our churches, and the validity of our minsitry, we hold to the unity and catholicity of the Church of Christ, and will unite with all its branches in hearty coöperation; and will earnestly seek, so far as in us lies, that the prayer of our Lord for his disciples may be answered, that they all may be one.

United in support of these principles, the Congregational Churches in National Council assembled agree in the adoption of the following Constitution:

ARTICLE I. — NAME.

The name of this body is the National Council of the Congregational Churches of the United Statse.

ARTICLE II. — PURPOSE.

The purpose of the National Council is to foster and express the substantial unity of the Congregational churches in faith, polity, and work; to consult upon and devise measures and maintain agencies for the promotion of their common interests; to coöperate with any corporation or body under control of or affiliated with the Congregational churches, or any of them; and to do and to promote the work of the Congregational churches of the United States in their national, international, and interdenominational relations.

ARTICLE III. — MEMBERS.

1. *Delegates.* *(a)* The churches in each District Association shall be represented by one delegate. Each association having more than ten churches shall be entitled to elect one additional delegate for each additional ten churches or major fraction thereof. The churches in each State Conference shall be represented by one delegate. Each conference having churches whose aggregate membership is more than ten thousand shall be entitled to elect one additional delegate for each additional ten thousand members or major fraction thereof. States having associations but no conference, or vice versa, shall be entitled to their full representation.

(b) Delegates shall be divided, as nearly equally as practicable, between ministers and laymen.

(c) The Secretary and the Treasurer shall be members *ex officiis*, of the Council.

(d) Any delegate who shall remove from the bounds of the conference or association by which he has been elected to the Council shall be deemed by the fact of that removal to have resigned his membership in the Council, and the Conference or Association may proceed to fill the unexpired term by election.

2. *Honorary Members.* Former moderators and assistant moderators of the Council, ministers serving the churches entertaining the Council, persons selected as preachers or to prepare papers, or to serve upon committees or commissions chosen by the Council, missionaries present who are in the service of the American Board of Commissioners for Foreign Missions and have been not less than seven years in that service, together with one delegate each from such theological seminaries and colleges as are recognized by the Council, may be enrolled as honorary members and shall be entitled to all privileges of members in the meeting of the Council except those of voting and initiation of business.

3. *Corresponding Members.* The Council shall not increase its own voting membership, but members of other denominations, present by invitation or representing their denominations, representatives of Congregational bodies in other lands, and other pesons present who represent important interests, or have rendered distinguished services,

may, by vote, be made corresponding members, and entitled to the courtesy of the floor.

4. *Vacancies and Alternates.* Each state or district organization may provide in its own way for filling vacancies in its delegation. In the absence of any special rule on the part of such state or district body, the Council will recognize the right of the delegates present to fill vacancies in their own delegation.

An alternate or substitute enrolled as a member of the Council and certified to the societies for membership therein shall be thereafter deemed a member instead of the primary delegate for the term for which that delegate was elected.

5. *Terms of Membership.* At its stated meeting in 1915, the National Council will divide all delegates, unless they shall have been so divided by the bodies electing them, into two classes, to serve respectively for two and four years. Thereafter the term of delegates shall be four years.

The term of a member shall begin at the opening of the next stated meeting of the Council after his election, and shall expire with the opening of the second stated meeting of the Council thereafter. He shall be a member of any intervening special meeting of the Council.

ARTICLE IV. — MEETINGS.

1. *Stated Meetings.* The churches shall meet in National Council once in two years, the time and place of meeting to be announced at least six months previous to the meeting.

2. *Special Meetings.* The National Council shall convene in special meeting whenever any seven of the general state organizations so request.

3. *Quorum.* Delegates present from a majority of the states entitled to representation in the Council shall constitute a quorum.

ARTICLE V. — BY-LAWS.

The Council may make and alter By-Laws at any stated meeting by a two-thirds vote of members present and voting; provided, that no new By-Law shall be enacted and no By-Law altered or repealed on the day on which the change is proposed.

Article VI. — Amendments.

This Constitution shall not be altered or amended, except at a stated meeting, and by a two-thirds vote of those present and voting, notice thereof having been given at a previous stated meeting, or the proposed alteration having been requested by some general state organization of churches entitled to representation in the Council, and published with the notification of the meeting.

BY-LAWS.

I. — The Call of a Meeting of the Council.

1. The call for any meeting shall be issued by the Executive Committee and signed by their chairman and by the Secretary of the Council. It shall contain a list of topics proposed for consideration at the meeting. The Secretary shall seasonably furnish blank credentials and other needful papers to the scribes of the several district and state organizations of the churches entitled to representation in the Council.

2. The meetings shall ordinarily be held in the latter part of October.

II. — The Formation of the Roll.

Immediately after the call to order the Secretary shall collect the credentials of delegates present, and these persons shall be *prima facie* the voting membership for purposes of immediate organization. Contested delegations shall not delay the permanent organization, but shall be referred to the Committee on Credentials, all contested delegations refraining from voting until their contest is settled.

III. — The Moderator.

1. At each stated meeting of the Council there shall be chosen from among the members of the Council, a Moderator and a first and

a second Assistant Moderator, who shall hold office for two years and until their successors are elected and qualified.

2. The Moderator immediately after his election shall take the chair, and after prayer shall at once proceed to complete the organization of the Council.

3. The representative function of the Moderator shall be that of visiting and addressing churches and associations upon their invitations, and of representing the Council and the Congregational churches in the wider relations of Christian fellowship, so far as he may be able and disposed. It is understood that all his acts and utterances shall be devoid of authority and that for them shall be claimed and to them given only such weight and force as inhere in the reason of them.

4. The Moderator shall preside at the opening of the stated meeting of the Council following that at which he is elected, and may deliver an address on a subject of his own selection.

IV. — The Secretary.

The Secretary shall keep the records and conduct the correspondence of the Council and of the Executive Committee. He shall edit the Year-Book and other publications, and shall send out notices of all meetings of the Council and of its Executive Committee. He shall aid the committees and commissions of the Council and shall be secretary of the Commission on Missions. He shall be available for advice and help in matters of polity and constructive organization, and render to the churches such services as shall be appropriate to his office. He may, like the Moderator, represent the Council and the churches in interdenominational relations. For his aid one or more assistants shall be chosen at each meeting of the Council to serve during such meeting.

V. — The Treasurer.

The Treasurer shall receive and hold all income contributed or raised to meet the expenses of the Council, shall disburse the same on the orders of the Executive Committee, and shall give bond in such sum as the Executive Committee shall from time to time determine.

VI. — Term of Office.

The term of office of the Secretary, Treasurer, and of any other officer not otherwise provided for shall begin at the close of the meeting at which they are chosen, and continue until the close of the next stated meeting, and until their successors are elected and qualified.

VII. — Committees.

As soon as practicable after taking the chair, the Moderator shall cause to be read to the Council the names proposed by the Nominating Committee for a Business Committee and a Committee on Credentials. These names shall be chosen so as to secure representation to different parts of the country, and the names shall be published in the denominational papers at least one month before the meeting of the Council, and printed with the call of the meeting. The Council may approve these nominations or change them in whole or in part.

1. *The Committee on Credentials.* The Committee on Credentials shall prepare and report as early as practicable a roll of members. Of this committee the Secretary shall be a member.

2. *The Business Committee.* The Business Committee shall consist of not less than nine members. It shall prepare a docket for the use of the Council, and subject to its approval. All business to be proposed to the Council shall first be presented to this committee, but the Council may at its pleasure consider any item of business for which such provision has been refused by the committee.

3. *The Nominating Committee.* The Nominating Committee shall consist of nine members, to be elected by the Council on the nomination of the Moderator, and shall serve from the close of one stated meeting till the close of the following stated meeting of the Council. Five members shall be so chosen for four years, and four for two years, and thereafter members shall be chosen for four years. This comittee shall nominate to the Council all officers, committees, and commissions for which the Council does not otherwise provide. But the Council may, at its pleasure, choose committees, commissions, or officers by nomination from the floor or otherwise as it shall from time to time determine.

4. *The Executive Committee.* The Executive Committee shall consist of the Moderator, the Secretary, and nine other persons, and shall be so chosen that the terms of the elected members shall ultimately be six years, the term of three members expiring at each stated meeting of the Council.

5. *Other Committees.* (*a*) Other committees may be appointed from time to time, and in such manner as the Council shall determine, to make report during the meeting at which they are appointed.

(*b*) On such committees any member of the Council, voting or honorary, is eligible for service.

(*c*) All such committees terminate their existence with the meeting at which they are appointed.

(*d*) No question or report will be referred to a committee except by vote of the Council.

(*e*) Committees shall consist of five persons unless otherwise stated.

(*f*) Unless otherwise ordered, the first named member of a committee shall be chairman.

VIII. — The Executive Committee.

1. The Executive Committee shall transact such business as the Council shall from time to time direct, and in the intervals between meetings of the Council shall represent the Council in all matters not belonging to the corporation and not otherwise provided for. They shall have authority to contract for all necessary expenditures and to appoint one or more of their number who shall approve and sign all bills for payment; shall consult the interests of the Council and act for it in intervals between meetings in all matters of business and finance, subject to the approval of the Council; and shall make a full report of all their doings, the consideration of which shall be first in order of business after organization.

2. They may fill any vacancy occurring in their own number or in any commission, committee, or office in the intervals of meeting, the persons so appointed to serve until the next meeting of the Council.

3. They shall appoint any committee or commission ordered by the Council, but not otherwise appointed; and committees or commis-

sions so appointed shall be entered in the minutes as by action of the Council.

4. They shall select the place, and shall specify in the call the place and precise time at which each meeting of the Council shall begin.

5. They shall provide a suitable form of voucher for the expenditures of the Council, and shall secure a proper auditing of its accounts.

6. They shall prepare a definite program for the Council, choosing a preacher and selecting topics for discussion and persons to prepare and present papers thereon.

7. They shall assign a distinct time, not to be changed except by special vote of the Council, for

(*a*) The papers appointed to be read before the Council.

(*b*) The commissions appointed by one Council to report at the next, which may present the topics referred to them for discussion or action.

(*c*) The benevolent societies and theological seminaries.

All other business shall be set for other specified hours, and shall not displace the regular order, except by special vote of the Council.

IX. — Commissions.

1. Special committees appointed to act *ad interim,* other than the Executive Committee and Nominating Committee, shall be designated as commissions.

2. Commissions are expected to report at the next meeting following their appointment, and no commission other than the Commission on Missions shall continue beyond the next stated meeting of the Council except by special vote of the Council.

3. No commission shall incur expense except as authorized by the Council, or its Executive Committee.

4. Any member in good standing of a Congregational church is eligible for service on any commission, or *ad interim* committee.

5. Commissions shall choose their own chairmen, but the first named member shall call the first meeting and act as temporary chairman during the organization of the commission.

X. — Congregational National Societies.

With the consent of our National Missionary Societies, whose approval is a necessary preliminary, the following shall define the relation of these societies to the National Council:

The foreign missionary work of the Congregational churches of the United States shall be carried on under the auspices of the American Board of Comissioners for Foreign Missions and the coöperating Woman's Boards of Missions; and the home missionary work of these churches, for the present under the auspices of the Congregational Home Missionary Society, the American Missionary Association, the Congregational Education Society, the Congregational Church Building Society, the Congregational Sunday-School and Publishing Society, and the Congregational Board of Ministerial Relief, hereinafter called the Home Societies, and the Woman's Home Missionary Federation.

1. *The American Board of Commissioners for Foreign Missions.* This Board and the coöperating Woman's Boards shall be the agency of the Congregational churches for the extension of Christ's kingdom abroad.

a. Membership. The voting membership of the American Board shall consist, in addition to the present life members, of two classes of persons.

(*1*) One class shall be composed of the members of the National Council, who shall be deemed nominated as corporate members of the American Board by their election and certification as members of the said National Council, said nominations to be ratified and the persons so named elected by the American Board. Their terms as corporate members of the American Board shall end, in each case, when they cease to be members of the National Council.

(2) There may also be chosen by the American Board one hundred and fifty corporate members-at-large. The said one hundred and fifty corporate members-at-large shall be chosen in three equal sections, and so chosen that the term of each section shall be ultimately six years, one section being chosen every second year at the meeting in connection with the meeting of the National Council. No new voting members, other than herein provided, shall be created.

b. Officers and Committees. The officers and committees of the

American Board shall be such as the Board itself may from time to time determine.

c. Meetings. Regular meetings of the American Board shall be held annually. That falling in the same year in which the National Council holds its meeting shall be held in connection with the meeting of said Council. Meetings in other years shall be held at such time and place as the Board may determine. Important business, especially such as involves extensive modifications of policy, shall, so far as possible, be reserved for consideration in those meetings held in connection with the meeting of the National Council.

d. Reports. It shall be the duty of the American Board to make a full and accurate report of its condition and work to the National Council at each stated meeting of that body.

2. *The Home Societies.* These societies, with the Woman's Home Missionary Federation, shall be the agencies of the Congregational churches for the extension of Christ's kingdom in the United States.

a. Membership. The voting membership of the several home societies shall consist, in addition to such existing life members and other members of the society in question as may be regarded as legally necessary, of two classes of persons.

(*1*) One class shall be composed of the members of the National Council so long as they remain members of said Council.

(2) There may also be chosen corporate members-at-large by the said societies, in the following numbers, viz.: by the Congregational Home Missionary Society, ninety; by the American Missionary Association, sixty; by the Congregational Church Building Society, thirty; by the Congregational Education Society, eighteen; by the Congregational Sunday-School and Publishing Society, eighteen; and by the Congregational Board of Ministerial Relief, nine. The said corporate members-at-large shall be chosen by each of the said societies in three equal sections and so chosen that the term of each section shall be ultimately six years, one section being chosen every second year at the meeting held in connection with the meeting of the National Council. In this selection one fifth of the said corporate members-at-large may be chosen from the organizations for the support of Congregational activities affiliated in the Woman's Home Missionary Federation. No

new voting members, other than herein provided, shall be created by any society.

b. Officers and Committees. The officers and committees of the several home societies shall be such as the societies themselves may from time to time determine.

c. Meetings. Regular meetings of the Home Societies shall be held annually. Those falling in the same year in which the National Council holds its meeting shall be held in connection with the meeting of said Council. Meetings in other years shall be held at such times and places as the societies themselves may determine. Important business, especially such as involves extensive modifications of policy, shall, so far as possible, be reserved for consideration in those meetings held in connection with the meeting of the National Council.

d. Reports. It shall be the duty of each of the Home Societies to make a full and accurate report of its condition and work to the National Council at each stated meeting of that body.

XI. — The Commission on Missions.

1. On nomination by the standing Committee on Nominations, the National Council shall elect fourteen persons, and on nomination by the several national societies, home and foreign, shall also elect one person from each society, and on similar nomination one each from the whole body of Woman's Boards of Foreign Missions and from the Woman's Home Missionary Federation; who, together with the Secretary of the National Council *ex officio*, shall constitute a Commission on Missions.

2. *Members.* The members of the Commission on Missions shall be divided as nearly as possible into two equal sections in such manner that the term of each section shall be ultimately four years and the term of one section shall expire at each biennial meeting of the Council. In these choices due consideration shall be given to convenience of meeting, as well as to the geographical representation of the churches. No member except the Secretary of the National Council, whether nominated by the Standing Committee on Nominations of the National

Council or by the societies, who has served on said Commission for two full successive terms of four years each, shall be eligible for reëlection until after two years shall have passed. Unpaid officers of any of the missionary societies of the churches shall be eligible to this Commission, but no paid officer or employee of a missionary society shall be eligible. The Commission shall choose its own chairman, and have power to fill any vacancy in its own number until the next stated meeting of the Council.

3. *Duties.* While the Commission on Missions shall not be charged with the details of the administration of the several missionary societies, it shall be its duty to consider the work of the home and foreign societies above named, to prevent duplication of missionary activities, to effect all possible economies in administration, and to seek to correlate the work of the several societies so as to secure the maximum of efficiency with the minimum of expense. It shall have the right to examine the annual budgets of the several societies and have access to their books and records. It may freely give its advice to the said societies regarding problems involved in their work, and it shall make recommendations to the several societies when, in its judgment, their work can be made more efficient or economical. It shall make report of its action to the National Council at each stated meeting of that body, and present to said Council such recommendations as it may deem wise for the furtherance of the efficiency and economical administration of the several societies. In view of the evident conviction of a large portion of the churches that the multiplicity of the Congregational Home Societies is not consistent with the greatest economy and efficiency, the Commission on Missions shall examine present conditions and shall recommend to the National Council such simplification or consolidation as shall seem expedient.

4. *Expenses.* The members of the Commission on Missions shall serve without salary. The necessary expenses of the Commission shall be paid from the treasury of the National Council, and said Council may limit the amount of expense which may be incurred in any year. All bills for payment shall be certified by the chairman of the Commission.

XII. — The Corporation for the National Council.

1. The corporate members of the corporation shall consist of fifteen persons, elected by the Council at stated meetings, and of the Moderator and Secretary associated *ex officiis* with them.

2. The terms for which corporate members are elected shall be six years.

3. The corporate members elected at the meeting of 1910 are divided into two classes of eight and seven respectively. The successors of the class of eight shall be chosen at the meeting of 1913 and of the class of seven at the meeting of 1915. Those so elected shall hold office until their successors are duly elected.

4. The corporation shall have a treasurer. He shall administer his office as the by-laws of the corporation may provide.

5. The corporation shall receive and hold all property, real and personal, of the Council, and all property, real and personal, which may be conveyed to it in trust, or otherwise, for the benefit of Congregational churches or of any Congregational church; and acting for the Council between the meetings of the Council in all business matters not otherwise delegated or reserved, shall do such acts and discharge such trusts as properly belong to such a corporation and are in conformity to the constitution, rules, and instructions of the Council.

6. The corporation may adopt for its government and the management of its affairs standing by-laws and rules not inconsistent with its charter nor with the constitution, by-laws, and rules of the Council.

7. The corporation shall make such reports to the Council as the Council may require.

XIII. — Devotional and Other Services.

1. In the sessions of the National Council, half an hour every morning shall be given to devotional services, and the daily sessions shall be opened with prayer and closed with prayer or singing. The evening sessions shall ordinarily be given to meetings of a specially religious rather than of a business character.

2. The Council will seek to promote in its sessions a distinctly

spiritual uplift, and to this end will arrange programs for the presentation of messages for the general public attending such gatherings. But the first concern of the Council shall be the transaction of the business of the denomination so far as that shall be intrusted to it by the churches; and the Council will meet in separate or executive session during the delivery of addresses whenever the necessity of the business of the Council may appear to require it.

XIV. — Time Limitation.

No person shall occupy more than half of an hour in reading any paper or report, and no speaker upon any motion or resolution, or upon any paper read, shall occupy more than ten minutes, without the unanimous consent of the Council.

In ease of discussion approaching the time limit set for it, the Moderator may announce the limitation of speeches to less than ten minutes, subject to the approval of the Council.

XV. — The Printing of Reports.

Such reports from commissions and statements from societies or theological seminaries as may be furnished to the Secretary seasonably in advance of the meeting may be printed at the discretion of the Executive Committee, and sent to the members elect, together with the program prepared. Not more than ten minutes shall be given to the presentation of any such report.

XVI. — The Publication of Statistics.

The Council will continue to make an annual compilation of statistics of the churches, and a list of such ministers as are reported by the several state organizations. The Secretary is directed to present at each stated meeting comprehensive and comparative summaries for the two years preceding.

XVII. — Fellowship with Other Bodies.

The Council, as occasion may arise, will hold communication with the general Congregational bodies of other lands, and with the general ecclesiastical organizations of other churches of evangelical faith in our own land, by delegates appointed by the Council or by the Executive Committee.

INTERPRETATIONS.

The following resolutions were adopted by the Council for the guidance of such committees as may be affected:

1. Membership in the Council shall entitle one to voting membership in the several benevolent societies only when the certificate of election as delegate is approved by the Committee on Credentials of the National Council.

2. In the absence of a delegate from the first stated meeting of the Council after his election, the properly accredited substitute, being duly enrolled and present, succeeds the primary delegate for the entire unexpired term.

3. If any delegate cannot be present at the first meeting of the Council after his election, he may send his certificate of election to the Committee on Credentials, and if his place is not filled by a substitute, properly enrolled, the primary delegate shall be enrolled as a member *in absentia,* such enrollment being equivalent to attendance as evidence of membership.

4. The substitute for the primary delegate shall have the same privilege of presenting his credentials *in absentia,* accorded to the delegate; and if said primary delegate shall not be enrolled, and the credentials are approved, the name of the substitute shall be inserted in the roll as having qualified as a member of the Council.

"*Resolved,* That in interpreting the provisions of Article II, Section 1, Subsection *a*, of the Constitution, adopted October 25, 1913, with regard to states having associations, but no conference, or vice versa, the following rules shall prevail:

"If a state conference contains no district association, its churches shall nevertheless be entitled to representation as if they all constituted a single district association.

"If a state has no conference, but has one or more district associations which belong to no conference, all such associations in that state shall be entitled to representation as if they together constituted a state conference."

INDEX